STRUCTURED COBOL: A PRAGMATIC APPROACH

ROBERT T. GRAUER

University of Miami

MARSHAL A. CRAWFORD

Programming Consultant

PRENTICE-HALL, INC., Englewood Cliffs, New Jersey 07632

Library of Congress Cataloging in Publication Data

GRAUER, ROBERT T (date)
    Structured COBOL: A Pragmatic Approach

    (Prentice-Hall software series)
    Previous ed. (c1978) published under title:
COBOL.
    Includes bibliographical references and index.
    1. COBOL (Computer program language)
2. Structured programming. I. Crawford,
Marshal A., 1943– II. Title. III. Series.
QA76.73.C25G7 1981   001.64'24   80–22283
ISBN 0–13–854455–7

To our families

Prentice-Hall Software Series
Brian W. Kernighan, advisor

Editorial/production supervision by Kathryn Gollin Marshak
Interior design by Nancy Milnamow
Cover design by Alon Jaedicker
Manufacturing buyer: Joyce Levatino

Printed in the United States of America

10 9 8 7 6 5 4 3 2 1

Prentice-Hall International, Inc., *London*
Prentice-Hall of Australia Pty. Limited, *Sydney*
Prentice-Hall of Canada, Ltd., *Toronto*
Prentice-Hall of India Private Limited, *New Delhi*
Prentice-Hall of Japan, Inc., *Tokyo*
Prentice-Hall of Southeast Asia Pte. Ltd., *Singapore*
Whitehall Books Limited, *Wellington, New Zealand*

CONTENTS

Preface   xi

Section I   **INTRODUCTION TO DATA PROCESSING**   1

Chapter 1   INTRODUCTION _____ 3

Overview, *3*   Pseudocode, *8*
Punched Card Input, *3*   Flowcharts, *9*
Printed Output, *5*   A First Look at COBOL, *12*
Structure of a Computer, *5*   Summary, *13*
Machine Versus Higher-Level Languages, *5*   Review Exercises, *15*
The First Problem, *8*   Problems, *15*

Chapter 2   THE PROGRAMMING PROCESS: COBOL OVERVIEW _____ 19

Overview, *19*   Putting It Together, *29*
A Problem-Solving Procedure, *19*   Summary, *29*
Elements of COBOL, *20*   Review Exercises, *30*
The COBOL Coding Form, *23*   Problems, *30*
Keypunching, *23*   Projects, *31*
Submitting a Program to the Computer, *27*
  OS JCL   DOS JCL

Chapter 3   THE PROCEDURE DIVISION _____ 35

Overview, *35*
COBOL Notation, *35*
Arithmetic Verbs, *36*
  ADD   SUBTRACT   MULTIPLY
    DIVIDE   COMPUTE
READ, *41*
WRITE, *41*
OPEN, *42*
CLOSE, *42*

MOVE, *42*
PERFORM, *44*
1F, *45*
  Significance of the Period
STOP, *46*
Summary, *46*
Review Exercises, *47*
Problems, *48*

Chapter 4   THE OTHER DIVISIONS _____ 51

Overview, *52*
Identification Division, *52*
Environment Division, *53*
Data Division, *53*
Picture Clause, *54*
  Level Numbers
File Section, *55*

Working-Storage Section, *56*
  VALUE CLAUSE   Assumed Decimal
  Point   Editing Numeric Data
Writing a Complete Program, *59*
Summary, *65*
Review Exercises, *66*
Problems, *67*
Projects, *69*

Chapter 5   DEBUGGING, I _____ 71

Overview, *71*
Errors in Compilation, *71*
A Second Example, *76*
Errors in Execution, *76*
Error Detection: The Structured Walk-
  through, *82*

Summary, *83*
Review Exercises, *86*
Problems, *86*

Chapter 6   PROGRAMMING STYLE, I _____ 92

Overview, *92*
Coding Standards, *92*
  Data Division   Procedure Division
  Both Divisions
Structured Programming, *95*
  Implementation in COBOL   Selection
  Structure   Iteration Structure

An Improved Tuition Billing Program, *99*
Summary, *102*
Review Exercises, *102*
Problems, *103*

Chapter 7   MORE ABOUT THE PROCEDURE DIVISION _____ 107

Overview, *107*
The IF Statement, *107*
   Class Tests   Relational Tests   Sign
   Test   Condition Name Tests   Compound
   Test   Implied Conditions   Nested IF's
PERFORM, *113*
INSPECT, *115*
Duplicate Data Names, *116*
   Qualification   CORRESPONDING Option

DISPLAY, *118*
ACCEPT, *119*
READ INTO, *120*
WRITE FROM, *120*
ROUNDED and SIZE ERROR Options, *121*
Summary and a Complete Example, *124*
Review Exercises, *126*
Problems, *127*
Projects, *131*

Chapter 8   THE DATA DIVISION _____ 134

Overview, *134*
Editing, *134*
Signed Numbers, *135*
Condition Names, *136*
Multiple Records, *137*
COPY Clause, *137*
A Complete Example, *138*
Tables, *141*
   OCCURS Clause   Processing a Table   Rules for
   Subscripts   Suggestions   REDEFINES
   Clause   Table Lookups

Subprograms and the Linkage Section, *146*
Summary, *153*
Review Exercises, *153*
Problems, *154*
Projects, *155*

Chapter 9   TABLES _____ 158

Overview, *158*
Subscripting Versus Indexing, *158*
Binary Search, *159*
Direct Access to Table Entries, *161*
COBOL Formats, *162*
   OCCURS Clause   SET Verb   USAGE
   Clause   SEARCH Verb
Two-Dimension Tables, *164*
Table Lookups: A Complete Example,
   165

Two-Dimension Tables: A Complete
   Example, *168*
Three-Dimension Tables, *171*
PERFORM VARYING, *172*
Three-Dimension Tables: A Complete
   Example, *173*
Summary, *177*
Review Exercises, *178*
Problems, *178*
Projects, *179*

Chapter 10   SORTING _____ 182

Overview, *182*
Vocabulary, *182*
COBOL Implementation, *183*
SORT Verb: INPUT PROCEDURE/
    OUTPUT PROCEDURE, *191*
SORT Verb: USING/GIVING, *191*

INPUT PROCEDURE/OUTPUT
    PROCEDURE Versus USING/
    GIVING, *192*
Summary, *192*
Review Exercises, *192*
Problems, *193*
Projects, *194*

Chapter 11   PROGRAMMING STYLE, II _____ 196

Overview, *196*
Debugging, *196*
Maintainability, *197*
Error Processing, *198*
Generality, *199*
Efficiency, *200*
More on Structured Programming, *201*
    Case Structure (GO TO DEPENDING)
A Rationale for Structured Programming, *202*
Top Down Versus Bottom Up Programming,
    203

Stepwise Refinement, *204*
Pseudocode, *206*
Control Breaks: A Completed Program, *206*
Top Down Development, *206*
    Hierarchy Charts   Top Down Testing   Merging
    Files: A Completed Program
Summary, *217*
Review Exercises, *217*
Problems, *217*
Projects, *218*

Section IV   THE ROLE OF BAL IN DEEPER UNDERSTANDING   223

Chapter 12   NECESSARY BACKGROUND _____ 225

Overview, *225*
Number Systems, *225*
    Binary   Decimal to Binary   Binary
    Addition   Hexadecimal   Decimal to
    Hexadecimal   Hexadecimal Addition
    Binary to Hexadecimal Conversion
Internal Data Representation, *229*
    Packed Numbers   Binary Numbers   Two's
    Complement Notation   The COBOL USAGE
    Clause and Data Formats

Base/Displacement Addressing, *233*
Instruction Formats, *234*
Summary, *236*
Review Exercises, *236*
Problems, *237*

Chapter 13   DEBUGGING, II _____ 238

Overview, *238*
The Memory Dump, *238*
Dump Reading: Example 1 (Failure to
    Initialize a Counter), *240*
Dump Reading: Example 2 (Bad Input Data),
    247

The STATE and FLOW Options, *249*
MVS Implications, *250*
Extension to DOS, *251*
Summary, *251*
Problems, *252*

Chapter 14   INSIGHT INTO THE COBOL COMPILER _____ 255

Overview, 255
Conversion Instructions, 256
Instructions That Move Data, 257
Add Instructions, 258
COBOL From the Viewpoint of BAL, 259
   Data Division Map   Literal Pool and Register
   Assignment   Procedure Division Map
COBOL Add Instructions With Similar Data
   Types, 261

COBOL Add Instructions With Dissimilar
   Data Types, 264
Addition of Similar Data Types With an
   Unsigned Operand, 265
Adding Operands That Are Not Aligned, 266
Summary, 267
Review Exercises, 269
Problems, 269

Section V   FILE PROCESSING   273

Chapter 15   MAGNETIC TAPE: CONCEPTS AND COBOL IMPLICATIONS _____ 273

Overview, 273
Tape Characteristics and Capacity, 273
Timing Considerations, 276
Identifying Files on Tape, 277
COBOL Requirements, 277
   Environment Division   Data
   Division   Procedure Division
Record Formats, 281

File Maintenance, 281
Backup, 283
Case Study, 283
Summary, 287
Review Exercises, 289
Problems, 289
Projects, 290

Chapter 16   MAGNETIC DISK: CONCEPTS AND COBOL IMPLICATIONS _____ 293

Overview, 293
Magnetic Disk: Physical Characteristics, 293
   Capacity   Timing   File Organization
Sequential Processing, 298
Indexed Organization (IBM/ISAM
   Implementation)
   COBOL Implications   Creation of an ISAM
   File   Random (Direct) Access of an ISAM
   File   ISAM/VSAM Coding Differences

Additional COBOL Elements (VSAM and
   the ANS 74 Standard), 307
Summary, 309
Review Exercises, 309
Problems, 310
Projects, 310

Chapter 17   DOS JCL _____ 311

Overview, 311
DOS Components, 311
A Basic Job Stream, 312
   JOB Statement   OPTION Statement   EXEC
   Statement   / (Slash Asterisk) Statement*
   /& (Slash Ampersand) Statement
Device Assignments, 315
   ASSGN Statement   PAUSE Statement
Processing Tape Files, 318
   LBLTYP Statement   TLBL Statement

Processing Disk Files, 321
   DLBL Statement   EXTENT Statement
Sequential Processing, 323
Nonsequential Processing, 324
Summary, 326
Review Exercises, 327
Problems, 327

Chapter 18   OS JCL _____ **329**

Overview, *329*
Classification of OS Systems, *329*
The Compile, Link, and Go Process, *330*
Basic Job Stream, *330*
   System Output and the Procedure Concept
JOB Statement, *335*
EXEC Statement, *335*
DD Statement, *337*
   Additional DD Statements
Processing Tape Files, *338*
   DISP (DISPosition) Parameter   UNIT Parameter   VOL (VOLume) Parameter   LABEL Parameter   DSN(DSName or Data Set Name) Parameter

Processing Files on Direct-Access Devices, *342*
   SPACE Parameter   UNIT Parameter   Generation Data Groups   DCB Parameter
Using the COBOL Sort
Subprograms
Summary
Review Exercises
Problems

APPENDIXES   **355**

Appendix A   Report Writer _____ **357**

Overview, *357*
Vocabulary, *357*
An Example: A Double Control Break
   Program, *358*

Data Division Requirements, *358*
Procedure Division Requirements, *363*
Summary, *364*
Review Exercises, *365*

Appendix B   COBOL RESERVED WORDS _____ **366**

Appendix C   IBM OS/VS COBOL REFERENCE FORMAT SUMMARY _____ **370**

Appendix D   ASSEMBLER FORMATS _____ **380**

Index _____ **383**

PREFACE

We are indebted to the many instructors who have adopted our earlier work, *COBOL: A Pragmatic Approach,* and thereby inspired this new book. We further acknowledge the numerous reviews and thoughtful comments that became the basis for this new approach.

The change of greatest importance is that *every* illustrative program is structured. This contrasts with the earlier approach of beginning with an unstructured program in an effort to get students on the machine as quickly as possible. We still espouse the early "hands on" philosophy, but no longer introduce unstructured programs only to later reeducate the reader. This comes from our own as well as the (now) widespread acceptance of structured programming; in short, do it right from the beginning.

In addition, we are happy to report the following changes and/or additions that have been incorporated into *Structured COBOL: A Pragmatic Approach.*

1. Greater attention to pseudocode and hierarchy chart with decreased emphasis on the traditional flowchart.
2 Inclusion of material on top down testing, stepwise refinement, and the structured walkthrough.
3. Strict adherence to the ANS 74 standard. (While some IBM extensions and/or deviations are included, these discussions *explicitly* state any deviation from the standard.)
4. Revision of most of the original COBOL illustrations to reflect our own increased awareness and attention to programming style.
5. Inclusion of over 20 additional programming projects (at the end of the appropriate chapters) for classroom assignment.
6. Inclusion of an appendix on Report Writer, as this once ignored facility appears to be on an upswing.
7. Expansion of Chapter 18 (OS JCL) to include material on SORT, subprograms, and MVS. Updating of Chapter 17 (DOS JCL) to include material on DOS/VS.
8. Expansion of Chapter 13 (ABEND debugging) to include the STATE and FLOW options.
9. Expansion of the discussion on indexed files to include COBOL coding differences between VSAM and ISAM implementation. The former adheres to the ANS 74 standard; the latter does not.

Why another book on COBOL? In recent years, universities have been criticized for failing to provide computer science and business graduates who are sufficiently versed in commercial data processing. This statement is partially justified for two reasons:

1. Most COBOL courses provide only "textbook" coverage and are sorely lacking in practical, i.e., commercial emphasis. Such subjects as JCL, file processing, debugging, structured programming, documentation, standards, and testing are glossed over or missed entirely.
2. College curricula traditionally treat COBOL and BAL in separate courses and do not provide an adequate link between the two. Although the COBOL programmer can and does exist without knowledge of Assembler, even a superficial understanding promotes superior capability to write efficient COBOL and is invaluable in debugging.

The primary objective of this book is to bridge the gap between traditional university curricula and the needs of industry. We address ourselves directly to the preceding statements and attempt to produce the well-rounded individual who can perform immediately and effectively in a third or fourth-generation environment.

The scope of the book is extensive, ranging from an introduction to data processing, to maintaining sequential and nonsequential files. A student may use this book without any previous exposure to data processing. Students with limited knowledge of COBOL can also use it since complete coverage will require two semesters. The text is modular in design so that Sections III, IV, and V may be covered in any order after Sections I and II are completed (see the accompanying diagram).

Modular Organization

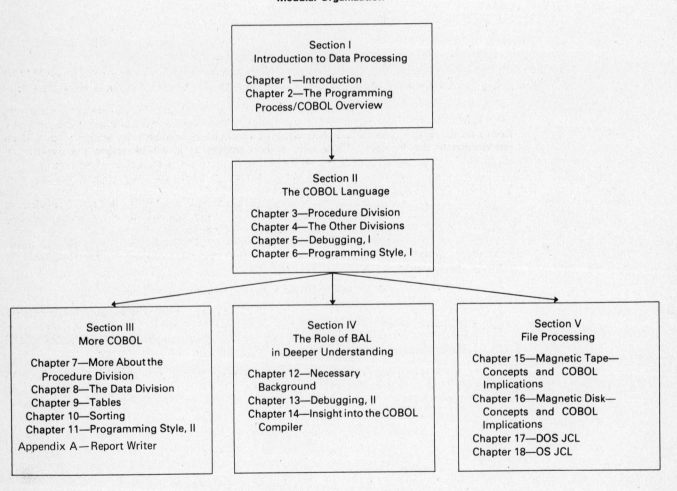

Section I
Introduction to Data Processing

Chapter 1—Introduction
Chapter 2—The Programming
Process/COBOL Overview

Section II
The COBOL Language

Chapter 3—Procedure Division
Chapter 4—The Other Divisions
Chapter 5—Debugging, I
Chapter 6—Programming Style, I

Section III
More COBOL

Chapter 7—More About the
Procedure Division
Chapter 8—The Data Division
Chapter 9—Tables
Chapter 10—Sorting
Chapter 11—Programming Style, II
Appendix A—Report Writer

Section IV
The Role of BAL
in Deeper Understanding

Chapter 12—Necessary
Background
Chapter 13—Debugging, II
Chapter 14—Insight into the COBOL
Compiler

Section V
File Processing

Chapter 15—Magnetic Tape—
Concepts and COBOL
Implications
Chapter 16—Magnetic Disk—
Concepts and COBOL
Implications
Chapter 17—DOS JCL
Chapter 18—OS JCL

In addition to the material on standard COBOL, there are two chapters devoted to debugging, two to JCL, two to programming style, two to file processing, and two on the role of BAL in better understanding COBOL. Although the JCL and BAL chapters pertain directly to IBM systems, ANS 74 COBOL is emphasized, so that the majority of the text relates to non-IBM installations as well. Inclusion of the IBM material, however, should enable the book to be used as a "programmer's guide" in that it contains a wealth of information that is not usually found in one place.

The authors wish to thank Karl Karlstrom of Prentice-Hall for making possible our entry into the world of publishing, Steve Cline, our editor, and Kathryn Marshak, our production editor. We thank our principal reviewers, Dr. Thomas DeLutis of Ohio State University, Dr. Jan L. Mize of Georgia State University, for their help and continued encouragement. Steve Shatz and Art Cooper are to be commended for their thoroughness in proofreading the galleys. We appreciate Ed Ramsey's help with some of the COBOL listings. We thank our many colleagues for their fine suggestions; these include Ken Anderson, Peter Baday, Jeff Borow, Les Davidson, Don Dejewski, Giselle Goldschmidt, Sam Ryan, Sue and Steve Wain, and anyone else whom we inadvertently omitted. Finally, we thank our typists, Francie Makoske and Deborah Miller, whose ability to interpret our scratches on yellow pads never ceased to amaze.

ROBERT T. GRAUER
MARSHAL A. CRAWFORD

Section   I

INTRODUCTION TO DATA PROCESSING

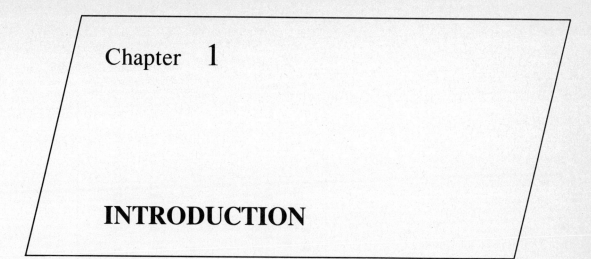

Chapter 1

INTRODUCTION

OVERVIEW

This book is about computer programming. In particular it is about COBOL, a widely used commercial programming language. Programming involves the translation of a precise means of problem solution into a form the computer can understand. Programming is necessary because, despite reports to the contrary, computers cannot think for themselves. Instead they do *exactly* what they have been instructed to do, and these instructions take the form of a computer program. The advantage of the computer stems from its speed and accuracy. It does not do anything that a human being could not if he or she were given sufficient time.

All computer applications consist of three phases: input, processing, and output. Information enters the computer, it is processed (i.e., calculations are performed), and the results are communicated to the user. Input can come from punched cards, magnetic tape or disk, computer terminals, or any of a variety of other devices. Processing encompasses the logic to solve a problem, but in actuality all a computer does is add, subtract, multiply, divide, or compare. All logic stems from these basic operations, and the power of the computer comes from its ability to alter a sequence of operations based on the results of a comparison. Output can take several forms. It may consist of the ubiquitous 11 × 14⅞ computer listing or printout, or it may be payroll checks, computer letters, mailing labels, magnetic tape, punched cards, etc.

We shall begin our study of computer programming by describing punched card input and printed output in some detail. We shall consider the structure of a computer and contrast machine- and problem-oriented languages. We shall pose a simple problem and develop the logic and COBOL program to solve it. The rapid entrance into COBOL is somewhat different from the approach followed by most textbooks, but we believe in learning by doing. There is nothing very mysterious about COBOL programming, so let's get started.

PUNCHED CARD INPUT

The punched card (Figure 1.1) has been around a long time. Its development was motivated by the U.S. Constitution (that is not a typographical error). Our Constitution requires that a federal census be taken every ten years. As the country expanded, processing of census data consumed increasing amounts of time (three years for the 1880 census), and the government needed a faster way of tabulating data. Herman Hollerith introduced the 80-column card in the late 1880s, and it has been with us ever since. (Mechanical devices, which were not computers, were available in

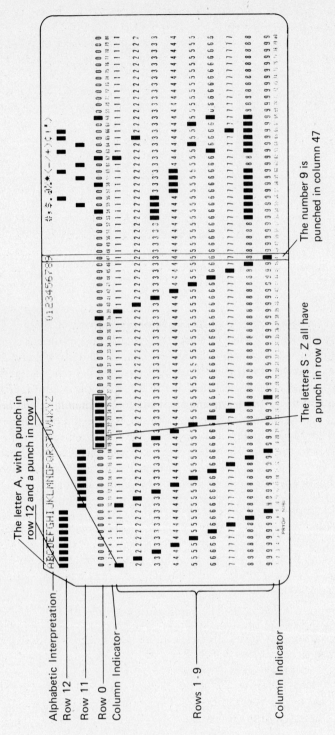

Alphabetic Interpretation

Row 12

Row 11

Row 0

Column Indicator

The letter A, with a punch in row 12 and a punch in row 1

Rows 1 - 9

The letters S - Z all have a punch in row 0

Column Indicator

The number 9 is punched in column 47

FIGURE 1.1 *The 80-Column Card*

the nineteenth century to process these cards.) Another interesting sidelight is the size of the punched card; it has the dimensions of the dollar bill of 1880.

The punched card has 80 vertical columns, each of which consists of 12 rows and contains a single character. Each character has its own unique combination of row punches. The letter A, for example, has a punch in row 12 and row 1 (see Figure 1.1). The letter B has a punch in row 12 and row 2. In Figure 1.1, A and B appear in columns 1 and 2, respectively. The upper three rows of the card (rows 12, 11, and 0) are known as zones, and the other rows as digits. Every letter has two punches: one zone and one digit. The letters A through I all have the same zone, i.e., row 12. The letters J through R all have a punch in row 11 and S through Z in row 0. The numbers 0 through 9 contain a single punch in the appropriate row. The bottom edge of the card indicates the column. The column indicator, in conjunction with the alphabetic information at the very top, indicates what is punched where; e.g., column 47 contains the number nine.

As a test of your understanding, what character is punched in column 26 of Figure 1.1? (Answer: Z.) What punches are required for the letter X? (Answer: row 0 and row 7.) In what column does X appear? (Answer: column 24.)

The computer is colorblind, and hence it does not matter if information is punched on red, white, or blue cards. Some installations, however, require that the first or last card in a deck be a specified color. This is to delineate one deck from another and is totally for human convenience. The very top edge of the card in Figure 1.1 interprets the information on the card. Again this is for human convenience only. The card reader senses the holes that are punched and does not refer to the interpreted information. Indeed, the latter need not be present at all.

PRINTED OUTPUT

The most widely used medium for computer output is the $11 \times 14\frac{7}{8}$ printout (alias listing, readout, etc.). Just as a computer must be told which card columns contain incoming data, it must also be told where to print its output. The $11 \times 14\frac{7}{8}$ form typically contains 132 print positions per line and 66 lines per page. Figure 1.2 contains a print layout form commonly used by programmers to plan their output. As can be seen from Figure 1.2, "THIS IS A PRINT LAYOUT FORM" is to appear on the tenth line from the top, beginning in column 15 and extending to column 41.

It makes no difference to the computer if printing is on wide or narrow paper, single- or multiple-part forms, mailing labels, payroll checks, etc. The machine is only interested in knowing what information is to appear and where. This is accomplished via instructions in a program.

STRUCTURE OF A COMPUTER

A computer can be thought of as a collection of electronic devices that (1) accept data, (2) perform calculations, and (3) produce results. A functional representation is shown in Figure 1.3.

We have already spoken about input and output. Main storage, i.e., the computer's memory, stores instructions and data while they are being processed. The size of a computer is measured by the capacity of its memory. Large modern machines have memory capacities of several million characters.

The central processing unit (CPU) is the "brain" of the computer. It consists of an arithmetic and logical unit (ALU) and a control unit. The ALU actually executes instructions; i.e., it adds, subtracts, multiplies, divides, and compares. The control unit monitors the transfer of data between main storage, input/output (I/O) devices, and the ALU. It decides which instruction will be executed next and is the "boss" of the computer.

Speed of execution is another way in which computers are measured. The ALU of a modern machine can execute millions of instructions per second. The time to execute a single instruction is expressed in microseconds (millionths of a second) or nanoseconds (billionths of a second).

MACHINE VERSUS HIGHER-LEVEL LANGUAGES

Each computer has its own unique machine language tied to specific locations in its memory. Human beings, however, think in terms of problems and use quantities with mnemonic significance,

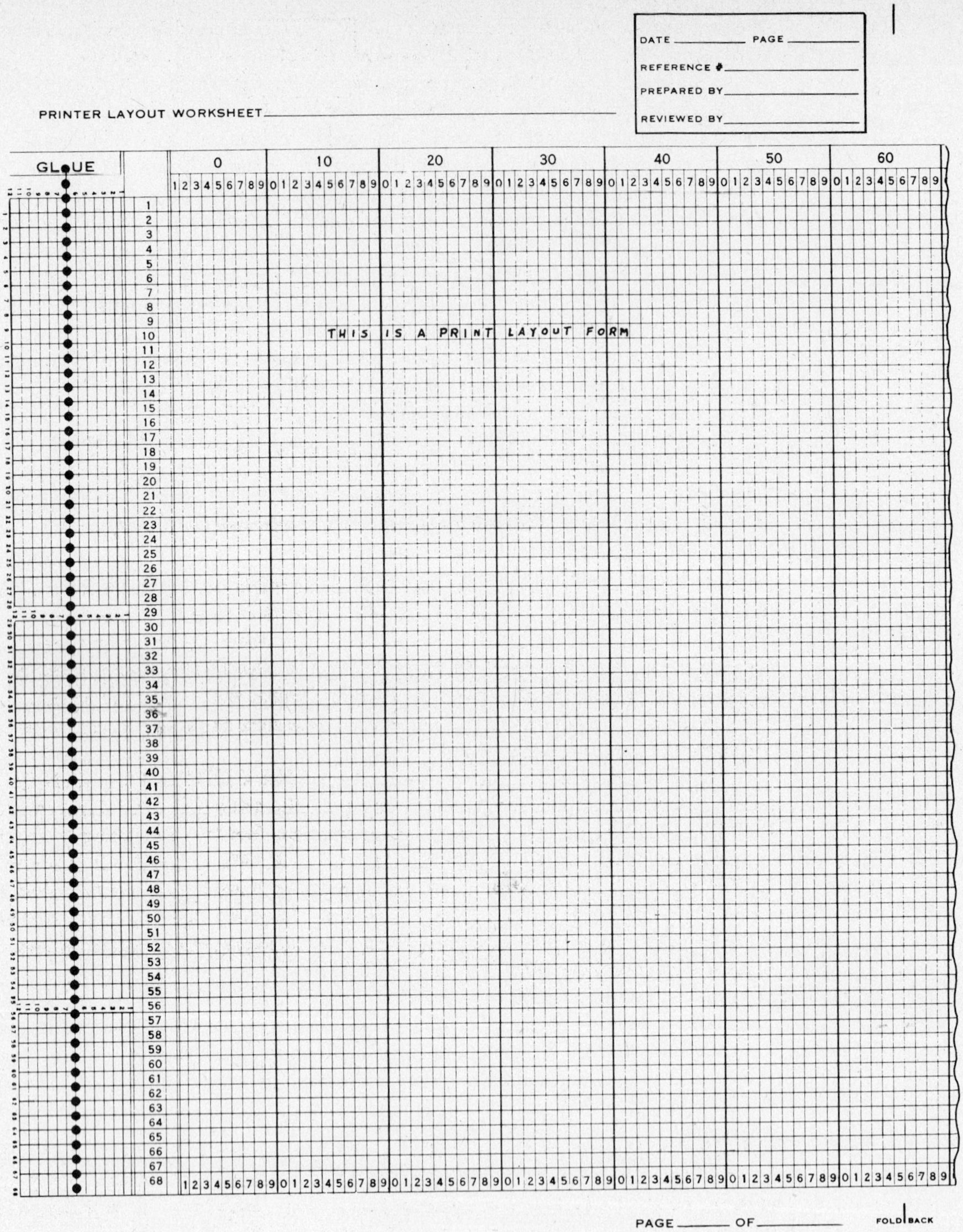

PRINTER LAYOUT WORKSHEET _____

THIS IS A PRINT LAYOUT FORM

PAGE _____ OF _____   FOLD BACK

FIGURE 1.2 *Print Layout Form*

e.g., HOURS, RATE, PAY, etc. We might say that a person thinks in a problem-oriented or higher-level language, while in actuality the computer functions in a machine-oriented or lower-level language. The two are related through a *compiler,* which is a computer program that translates a problem language into a machine language. COBOL is an example of a problem-oriented language for business systems. The COBOL compiler is itself a machine language program written in the language of the machine on which it is executed.

The wide availability of COBOL compilers provides tremendous flexibility for individual pro-

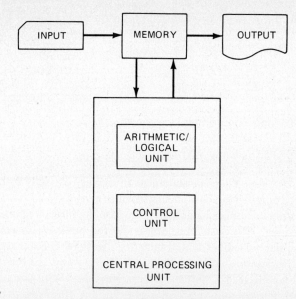

FIGURE 1.3 *Functional Representation of a Computer*

grams. A COBOL program written for an IBM computer can also execute on a Univac, Honeywell, NCR, or any other machine that has a COBOL compiler. In each instance the input to the compiler is the same, i.e., a COBOL program (in actuality there are slight variations from compiler to compiler). The output from the compiler is different. An IBM compiler produces an IBM machine language program, a Univac compiler produces Univac machine language, etc. However, this does not concern the COBOL programmer. All that one need know, and indeed care about, is COBOL; the compiler does the rest.

Consider a simple COBOL statement, MULTIPLY HOURS BY RATE GIVING PAY. This takes HOURS, multiplies it by RATE, and puts the result into PAY. The values of HOURS and RATE are unchanged as a result of this instruction. For this instruction to execute, the compiler has to assign locations in its memory to HOURS, RATE, and PAY. It will multiply HOURS by RATE in a work area (known as an accumulator or register) and put the result into PAY.

Assume that the compiler decides to store HOURS, RATE, and PAY in locations 1000, 2000, and 3000, respectively. It then generates a sequence of three machine instructions to accomplish the intended multiplication:

```
LOAD      1000
MULTIPLY  2000
STORE     3000
```

The first instruction, LOAD 1000, brings the contents of location 1000 (HOURS) into the accumulator. The next instruction multiplies the contents of the accumulator by the contents of location 2000 (RATE). The result remains in the accumulator. Finally, the STORE instruction puts the contents of the accumulator into location 3000 (PAY). (Note that these instructions are typical of compilers in general and vary from computer to computer.) Table 1.1 illustrates what happens as a result of these three machine instructions. It assumes values of 40 and 5 for HOURS and RATE, respectively. It shows the contents of locations 1000, 2000, 3000, and the accumulator before and after each of the three machine language instructions are executed. Prior to the LOAD instruction the contents of both locations 3000 and the accumulator are immaterial. After the LOAD has been executed, the contents of location 1000 have been brought into the accumulator. After the MULTIPLY, the contents of the accumulator are 200, and after the STORE the contents of location 3000 are also 200. Note that the initial contents of locations 1000 and 2000 are unchanged throughout.

TABLE 1.1 Machine Instructions to Multiply HOURS by RATE

| | Memory contents | | | | | | | |
| | Before | | | | After | | | |
Instruction	1000 (HOURS)	2000 (RATE)	3000 (PAY)	ACCUM	1000 (HOURS)	2000 (RATE)	3000 (PAY)	ACCUM
LOAD 1000	40	5	?	?	40	5	?	40
MULTIPLY 2000	40	5	?	40	40	5	?	200
STORE 3000	40	5	?	200	40	5	200	200

A single COBOL statement invariably expands to one or more machine language statements after compilation. This phenomenon is known as *instruction explosion* and is a distinguishing characteristic of compiler languages. Compare the three machine language statements to the single COBOL statement. Obviously, the latter is shorter, but it is also easier to write, since the COBOL programmer need not remember which memory locations contain the data. In the early days of the computer age, there were no compilers, and all programs were written in machine language. Then someone had a remarkably simple yet powerful idea: Why not let the computer remember where data are kept? The compiler concept was born, and things have never been the same since.

THE FIRST PROBLEM

We are ready for our first problem statement. Input is a set of student cards, one card per student. Each card contains the student's name (columns 1 to 25), number of completed credits (columns 26 to 28), and major (columns 29 to 43). Figure 1.4 contains the card of John Doe, an engineering major, who has completed 30 credits.

The registrar has asked for a list of engineering students who have completed at least 110 credits. We are to develop a COBOL program that can process a file of student records in the format of Figure 1.4. To accomplish this, our program must incorporate the logic shown in Figure 1.5.

PSEUDOCODE

Figure 1.5 illustrates a technique known as *pseudocode* or *structured English* as a means of expressing program logic. Our program is to begin with an initialization or housekeeping function, i.e., something

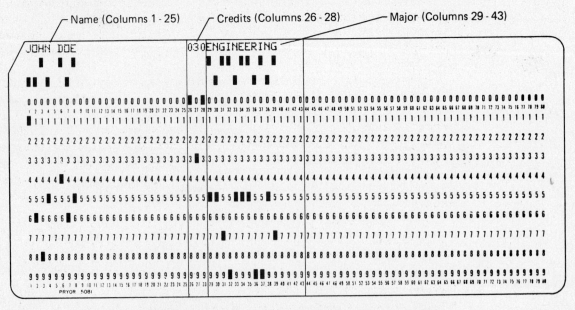

FIGURE 1.4 *Data Card for the Engineering Senior Problem*

SECTION I: INTRODUCTION TO DATA PROCESSING

Initialization — (or Housekeeping) — e.g. read first record or write a report heading

<pre>
┌ DO while there are data cards

 ┌ IF this student is an engineering major and has at least 110 credits
 │   write his name on registrar's list

 │ ELSE

 └   Do nothing more with this student

 │ Read next record

└ ENDDO
</pre>

Termination — e.g. print total number of students and stop

FIGURE 1.5 *Pseudocode for the Engineering Senior Problem*

done once at the start of processing, e.g., reading the *first* record or writing a heading at the beginning of a report. Next, there is a series of instructions which is executed repeatedly, i.e., once for each incoming record. These consist of determining if the record just read is an engineering major with the requisite number of credits. If both conditions are met, the name will be written on the registrar's list; if either condition is not met, nothing further is done with the particular record. The next record is read and the loop is repeated. When *all* the records have been read, the iteration sequence is finished, and a termination routine is entered. This in turn may print a total and/or simply stop processing.

Pseudocode is a relatively recent technique that uses instructions similar to those of a computer language to describe program logic. It is *not,* however, bound by precise syntactical rules as are formal programming languages such as COBOL. Nor is it bound by any rules for indentation, which is done strictly at the discretion of the person using it. The purpose of pseudocode is simply to convey program logic in a straightforward and easy-to-follow manner. A more traditional method for accomplishing the same thing is a flowchart.

FLOWCHARTS

A flowchart is a pictorial representation of the logic inherent in a program. In effect, one takes a problem statement and constructs a logical blueprint that is subsequently incorporated into the COBOL program. A set of standard flowchart symbols has been adopted by the American National Standards Institute and is shown in Figure 1.6. A flowchart to determine the engineering students with at least 110 credits is shown in Figure 1.7. This flowchart expresses the same logic as the pseudocode of Figure 1.5, albeit in different form.

The authors hope that the logic inherent in Figure 1.7 proves easily understandable, but include Table 1.2 to provide additional insight. There is, however, one complication, i.e., the presence of two read blocks (blocks 3 and 10) and the *end-of-file* test in block 5. The necessity for these blocks is mandated by the nature of the COBOL read instruction. The function of a read is to obtain a record, but there will always be a point when a read is attempted and no record is found; i.e., all the records have already been read. Since one does not know in advance how many records a file contains, the read instruction must also signal the end-of-file condition. Thus, if a file contains *two* records, it is actually read *three* times (once for each record, and once to indicate that all records have been read).

With this in mind, consider Figure 1.7 and assume there are only two records in the file, A and B. Record A is read by block 3. The end of file has not been reached, so blocks 7 through 9 are executed for record A. Record B is read in block 10. Again, the end of file has not been reached, so blocks 7 through 9 are executed for record B. When block 10 is executed a second time, the end of file is reached. Hence, the next execution of block 5 falls through to STOP. In summary, three reads have been executed, two records were processed, and the third read registered the end of file.

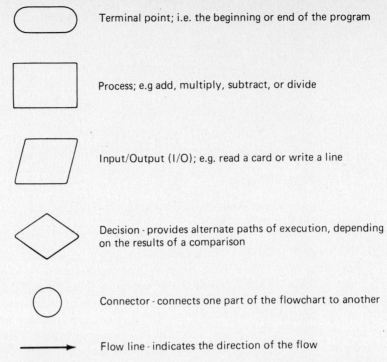

Terminal point; i.e. the beginning or end of the program

Process; e.g add, multiply, subtract, or divide

Input/Output (I/O); e.g. read a card or write a line

Decision - provides alternate paths of execution, depending on the results of a comparison

Connector - connects one part of the flowchart to another

Flow line - indicates the direction of the flow

FIGURE 1.6 *American National Standards Institute Flowchart Symbols*

To better understand how a flowchart and subsequent program function, we shall concoct some test data for the problem statement and run it through the flowchart. Assume data cards have been prepared for four students as follows:

Student Name	Credits	Major
John Adams	90	Political science
Adam Smith	120	Economics
Orville Wright	115	Engineering
Francis Key	80	Music

The flowchart begins execution with the start and housekeeping blocks. The third block reads the first data card, John Adams. The end of file has not been reached, so block 5 directs flow to block 7, the test for engineering majors with at least 110 credits. John Adams "fails" the test; hence control passes through the connector in block 9 to the read of block 10. The data for Adam Smith are now stored in the computer's memory. Control flows through the connector of block 4 to the end-of-file test in block 5. Adam Smith fails the test of block 7, causing flow to pass directly to the connector in block 9. So far, the data for two students, Adams and Smith, have been completely processed, but neither has passed the qualification test.

Control flows from the connector of block 9 to the read in block 10, whereupon Orville Wright is read into memory. Since Wright is an engineering major with 110 credits, his name is written in block 8.

Francis Key is next read into memory in block 10. Control flows through the connector in block 4 to the end-of-file test in block 5. (Note that, while Key is the last record, the end-of-file condition has *not* yet been detected.) Key fails the qualification test, whereupon control flows to the read in block 10. This time the end of file is detected so that, when control again reaches the end-of-file test in block 5, processing will be directed to the stop statement in block 6.

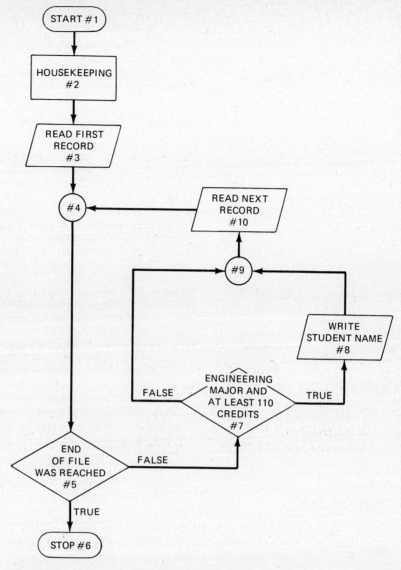

FIGURE 1.7 *Flowchart to Select Engineering Majors with 110 Credits or More*

It is useful to summarize this discussion by tabulating the number of times each block in Figure 1.7 is executed:

Block Number		Times Executed	Explanation
1	Start	1	At beginning of program
2	Housekeeping	1	At beginning of program
3	Initial read	1	At beginning of program to read first record, i.e., Adams
4	Connector	5	Entered five times (marks the beginning of the repetition or loop structure)
5	End-of-file test	5	Once for each of four records; once to sense end-of-file condition
6	Stop	1	Executed once at program's end
7	Qualification test	4	Once for each student

8	Write	1	Executed for Wright only, since no one else passed test of block 7
9	Connector	4	Entered four times (marks the end of the selection structure)
10	Read	4	Reads every record *but* the first, and senses end of file

TABLE 1.2 Block-by-Block Explanation of Flowchart in Figure 1.7

Block Number	Symbol	Explanation
1	Terminal	Every flowchart contains a START block indicating where the program begins.
2	Processing	As a rule, most programs require some initial processing, the nature of which is not always apparent in the problem statement. A good practice is to include a HOUSEKEEPING block at the beginning of a flowchart.
3	I/O	Reads the first record only. Note that if the file is empty, execution of block 5 will cause the program to "fall through" without entering blocks 7–10 inclusive.
4	Connector	Serves as an entry point into a loop for processing records.
5	Decision	Tests whether the end-of-file condition has been reached. If so, control goes to block 6; if not, control goes to block 7.
6	Terminal	Signals the end of processing.
7	Decision	Tests whether the student currently being processed is an engineering major with at least 110 credits. If so, control passes to block 8, then block 9. If not, control passes directly to block 9.
8	I/O	Writes information on any student reaching this point.
9	Connector	Terminates the selection structure.
10	I/O	Reads the next record, after which the connector in block 4 is reentered, and the end-of-file condition is tested in block 5. Note that when the end-of-file is sensed in block 10, control passes to blocks 4, 5, and 6, consecutively.

A FIRST LOOK AT COBOL

We shall now proceed to COBOL. Figure 1.8 is a COBOL program written for the flowchart in Figure 1.7. The syntactical rules for COBOL are extremely precise, and we certainly *do not* expect you to remember them after a brief exposure to Figure 1.8. We do believe, however, that immediate exposure to a real program is extremely beneficial in terms of stripping the mystical aura that too often surrounds programming. Further, we believe Figure 1.8 will become easier to understand after some brief explanation.

 Figure 1.8 is made clearer when we realize that every COBOL program consists of four divisions, which must be in a specified order:

Identification division	This division contains the program and author's name. It can also contain other identifying information such as date written or installation name.
Environment division	This division mentions the computer on which the program is to be compiled and executed (usually one and the same). It also specifies the I/O devices to be used by the program.
Data division	This division describes the data. In card and print files, for example, it specifies the incoming card columns and outgoing print positions, respectively.
Procedure division	This division contains the program logic, i.e., the instructions the computer is to execute in solving the problem.

A line-by-line description of Figure 1.8 is given in Figure 1.9. We would hope the reader has a general understanding of the data and procedure divisions for Figure 1.8. If not, we expect

```
00001          IDENTIFICATION DIVISION.
00002          PROGRAM-ID.     FIRSTTRY.
00003          AUTHOR.         CRAWFORD.
00004          ENVIRONMENT DIVISION.
00005          CONFIGURATION SECTION.
00006          SOURCE-COMPUTER. IBM-370.
00007          OBJECT-COMPUTER. IBM-370.
00008          INPUT-OUTPUT SECTION.
00009          FILE-CONTROL.
00010              SELECT CARD-FILE ASSIGN TO UT-S-SYSIN.
00011              SELECT PRINT-FILE ASSIGN TO UT-S-SYSOUT.
00012          DATA DIVISION.
00013          FILE SECTION.
00014          FD  CARD-FILE
00015              LABEL RECORDS ARE OMITTED
00016              RECORD CONTAINS 80 CHARACTERS
00017              DATA RECORD IS CARD-IN.
00018          01  CARD-IN.
00019              05   CARD-NAME          PICTURE IS A(25).
00020              05   CARD-CREDITS       PICTURE IS 9(3).
00021              05   CARD-MAJOR         PICTURE IS A(15).
00022              05   FILLER             PICTURE IS X(37).
00023          FD  PRINT-FILE
00024              LABEL RECORDS ARE OMITTED
00025              RECORD CONTAINS 133 CHARACTERS
00026              DATA RECORD IS PRINT-LINE.
00027          01  PRINT-LINE.
00028              05   FILLER             PICTURE IS X(8).
00029              05   PRINT-NAME         PICTURE IS X(25).
00030              05   FILLER             PICTURE IS X(100).
00031          WORKING-STORAGE SECTION.
00032          77 DATA-REMAINS-SWITCH      PICTURE IS X(2)   VALUE SPACES.
00033          PROCEDURE DIVISION.
00034          MAINLINE.
00035              OPEN INPUT CARD-FILE, OUTPUT PRINT-FILE.
00036              READ CARD-FILE,
00037                  AT END MOVE 'NO' TO DATA-REMAINS-SWITCH.
00038              PERFORM PROCESS-CARDS
00039                  UNTIL DATA-REMAINS-SWITCH = 'NO'.
00040              CLOSE CARD-FILE, PRINT-FILE.
00041              STOP RUN.
00042
00043          PROCESS-CARDS.
00044              IF CARD-CREDITS NOT < 110 AND CARD-MAJOR = 'ENGINEERING'
00045                  MOVE SPACES TO PRINT-LINE
00046                  MOVE CARD-NAME TO PRINT-NAME
00047                  WRITE PRINT-LINE.
00048              READ CARD-FILE,
00049                  AT END MOVE 'NO' TO DATA-REMAINS-SWITCH.
```

FIGURE 1.8 *The First COBOL Program*

to answer many of your questions in Chapter 2. Further, we believe that when you actually run your own programs in Chapter 2, everything will crystallize.

Assume the student cards for Adams, Smith, Wright, and Key were input to the COBOL program of Figure 1.8. Output would consist of a single line of output for Orville Wright. Can you examine the data division and determine in which print positions his name would appear? (Answer: positions 9 to 33.)

Obviously, it doesn't pay to go through the effort described herein for a mere four students. The advantages of the computer are realized only when large amounts of data are processed.

SUMMARY

This chapter is intended as an introduction to COBOL programming and the text that follows. In reality, we have presented a substantial amount of material in terms of the fundamental concepts that were developed. We trust the true significance of this information will be better appreciated as you progress through the text. In the meantime, a recap should prove helpful:

1. Every computer application consists of input, processing, and output.
2. Input and output must be precisely specified as to content and location.

3. The computer cannot think for itself but must be told precisely what to do. This is done through a series of instructions known as a program.
4. The computer does not do anything that a human being could not do if given sufficient time. The advantages of a computer stem from its speed and accuracy.
5. Human beings think in terms of problem-oriented languages, while the computer functions in machine language. Compilation relates the two.
6. The flowchart and/or pseudocode are representations of the logic embodied in a computer program.

00001	Header for IDENTIFICATION DIVISION.
00002	Names the program as FIRSTTRY.
00003	Identifies the author.
00004	Header for ENVIRONMENT DIVISION.
00005	Beginning of CONFIGURATION SECTION.
00006	Identifies IBM-370 as the SOURCE-COMPUTER.
00007	Identifies IBM-370 as the OBJECT-COMPUTER.
00008	Beginning of INPUT-OUTPUT SECTION, which identifies I/O devices.
00009	Beginning of FILE-CONTROL paragraph, which connects file names to I/O devices.
00010	States that CARD-FILE is to come from system device SYSIN.
00011	States that PRINT-FILE is to come from system device SYSOUT.
00012	Header for DATA DIVISION.
00013	Beginning of FILE SECTION.
00014–00017	FD (File Description) for CARD-FILE, which was specified in the ENVIRONMENT DIVISION in line 00010.
00018–00022	Specification of which columns contain which data, as per program definition. Notice that only the first 43 columns contain data but that the last 37 columns contain FILLER.
00023–00026	FD (File Description) for PRINT-FILE, which was specified in the ENVIRONMENT DIVISION in line 00011.
00027–00030	Description of a line of output; PRINT-NAME is to appear in print positions 9–33.
00031	Identifies the WORKING-STORAGE SECTION.
00032	Defines a data-name, DATA-REMAINS-SWITCH, which will indicate the end of file has been reached.
00033	Header for PROCEDURE DIVISION.
00034	Signals the beginning of the first paragraph in the Procedure Division.
00035	The OPEN statement makes the files CARD-FILE and PRINT-FILE available for processing.
00036–00037	This statement reads the first record in the file. The AT END clause in line 37 is part of the READ statement. It causes NO to be moved to DATA-REMAINS-SWITCH when the end of file is reached. The value of this switch controls the action of the subsequent PERFORM verb.
00038–00039	The PERFORM verb signals a transfer of control to the first statement in the designated routine, PROCESS-CARDS, a paragraph that consists of lines 43 to 49 inclusive. Thus the PERFORM statement of lines 38 and 39 causes execution of lines 43 to 49. The UNTIL condition is tested *prior* to executing the paragraph, which is continually re-executed until the condition is met, i.e., until DATA-REMAINS-SWITCH is set to NO, when the end of file condition is sensed in the READ statement(s). When this happens, the perform ends and control passes to line 40, the statement after the perform.
00040	Open files must be closed prior to terminating execution.
00041	STOP RUN terminates execution.
00042	A blank line to visually set off the next paragraph.
00043	PROCESS-CARDS is a paragraph name and signals the beginning of a new paragraph. (Notice how lines 44 to 49 are indented under the paragraph name of line 43.)
00044–00047	These lines collectively form a *single* IF statement, which is terminated by the period in line 47. If both conditions of line 44 are met, then lines 45 to 47 are collectively executed. If, however, one or both conditions are not met, then lines 45 to 47 are bypassed.
00048–00049	Regardless of whether lines 45 to 47 are executed, lines 48 and 49 are always executed to read the next record, and eventually sense the end of file to terminate the perform.

FIGURE 1.9 *Line-by-Line Description of COBOL Program*

REVIEW EXERCISES

TRUE FALSE

☐ ☐ **1.** A compiler translates a machine-oriented language into a problem-oriented language.

☐ ☐ **2.** A compiler translates a higher-level language into a lower-level language.

☐ ☐ **3.** A compiler is a computer program.

☐ ☐ **4.** The COBOL compiler for a Univac computer is identical to the COBOL compiler for an IBM computer.

☐ ☐ **5.** The "instruction explosion" stems from the fact that a single machine language statement generates several COBOL statements.

☐ ☐ **6.** A microsecond is one-billionth of a second.

☐ ☐ **7.** It is realistic to expect the CPU of a large, modern computer to execute 60 million instructions per minute.

☐ ☐ **8.** It is realistic to expect the memory of a large, modern computer to contain a million characters or more.

☐ ☐ **9.** A single program, written in machine language, can run on a variety of computers.

☐ ☐ **10.** A COBOL program can run on a variety of computers.

☐ ☐ **11.** There are four divisions in a COBOL program.

☐ ☐ **12.** The divisions of a COBOL program may appear in any order.

☐ ☐ **13.** Data description appears in the identification division.

☐ ☐ **14.** Computers can "think" for themselves.

☐ ☐ **15.** The 80-column punched card is more than 50 years old.

☐ ☐ **16.** A COBOL program must be punched on red, white, or blue cards.

☐ ☐ **17.** The control unit is part of the ALU.

☐ ☐ **18.** The ALU decides which instruction will be executed next.

☐ ☐ **19.** No statement in a computer program may be executed more than once.

☐ ☐ **20.** A rectangle is the standard flowchart symbol for a decision block.

☐ ☐ **21.** Computer output must be directed onto $11 \times 14\frac{7}{8}$ sheets.

☐ ☐ **22.** A LOAD instruction changes the contents of an accumulator (see Table 1.1).

☐ ☐ **23.** A STORE instruction changes the contents of an accumulator (see Table 1.1).

☐ ☐ **24.** A MULTIPLY instruction changes the contents of both an accumulator and a storage location (see Table 1.1).

☐ ☐ **25.** Pseudocode serves the same function as a flowchart.

☐ ☐ **26.** Pseudocode must be written according to precise syntactical rules.

PROBLEMS

1. Given the following sequence of machine language instructions,

```
LOAD      500
MULTIPLY  600
STORE     700
```

complete the following table of memory contents:

| | Memory contents | | | | | | | |
| | Before | | | | After | | | |
Instruction	500	600	700	ACC	500	600	700	ACC
LOAD 500	10	20	?	?	?	?	?	?
MULTIPLY 600	?	?	?	?	?	?	?	?
STORE 700	?	?	?	?	?	?	?	?

2. Assume that our hypothetical computer also has a machine language ADD instruction in addition to the LOAD, MULTIPLY, and STORE instructions described in the text. Specifically, "ADD X" will add the contents of location X to the contents of the accumulator and leave the sum in the accumulator. Show the series of machine language instructions that would probably be generated for the COBOL instruction "ADD A, B, C GIVING D." Assume A, B, C, and D are in locations 100, 200, 300, and 400, respectively.

3. Given the flowchart of Figure 1.7 and the following student data,

Student Name	Credits	Major
Merriweather Lewis	115	Travel
John Kennedy	115	Political science
Alex Bell	90	Engineering
George Sand	85	Literature
John Roebling	115	Engineering

how many times, and for which students, will blocks 1 to 10 be executed?

4. Given the COBOL program of Figure 1.8, indicate what changes would have to be made if
   (a) We wanted MUSIC students rather than ENGINEERING students?
   (b) We wanted students with 60 or fewer credits?
   (c) The student major was contained in columns 60 to 74 of the incoming card?
   (d) We wanted engineering students *or* students with 110 credits or more?
   Note: Treat parts (a), (b), (c), and (d) independently.

5. Which division in a COBOL program contains:
   (a) The CONFIGURATION SECTION?
   (b) The FILE SECTION?
   (c) Statements to open and close files?
   (d) The description of incoming data?
   (e) The description of outgoing data?
   (f) The author's name?
   (g) The program's name?
   (h) Statements to read information?
   (i) Statements to write information?
   Note: Use Figure 1.8 as a guide, and indicate specific line numbers where the information is found.

6. Your programming supervisor has drawn a flowchart for you to code. He left the flowchart on his dining room table at home and unfortunately his three-year-old son, Benjy, cut it up into pieces with a pair of scissors. Your supervisor collected the pieces (shown below) and has asked you to rearrange them properly into a correct flowchart; do so. The flowchart is to read a file of cards with each card containing three *unequal* numbers A, B, and C. Write out the *greater* of the two sums (A + B) and (B + C) for each card *only* if A is less than 50.

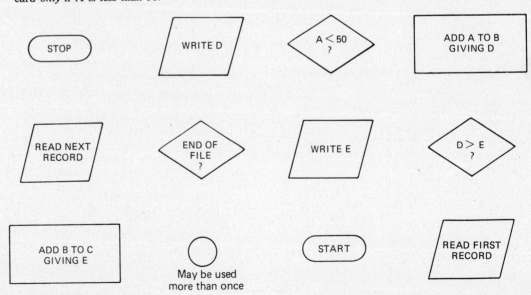

7. Figure 1.10 contains a COBOL program to process a file of employee records and print the names of programmers under 30. Use Figure 1.8 as a guide and restore the missing information so that the program will run as intended.

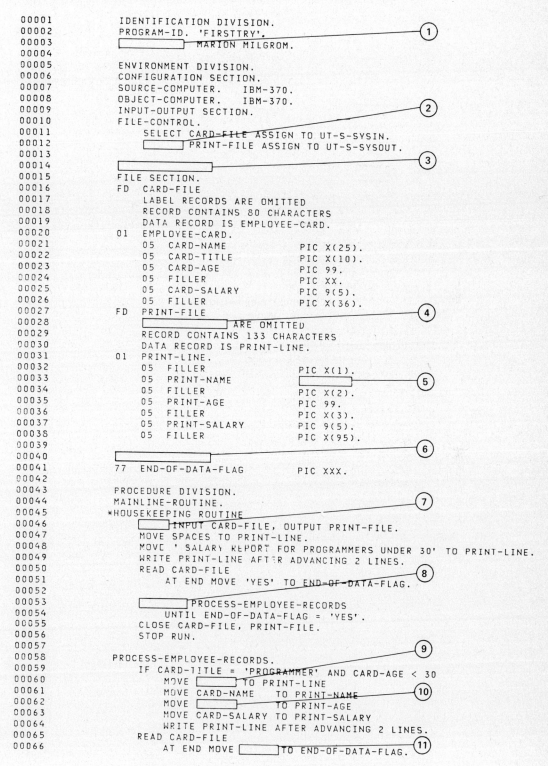

```
00001          IDENTIFICATION DIVISION.
00002          PROGRAM-ID.  'FIRSTTRY'.                              ①
00003          ⬚——— MARION MILGROM.
00004
00005          ENVIRONMENT DIVISION.
00006          CONFIGURATION SECTION.
00007          SOURCE-COMPUTER.  IBM-370.
00008          OBJECT-COMPUTER.  IBM-370.
00009          INPUT-OUTPUT SECTION.                                 ②
00010          FILE-CONTROL.
00011              SELECT CARD=FILE ASSIGN TO UT-S-SYSIN.
00012              ⬚ PRINT-FILE ASSIGN TO UT-S-SYSOUT.
00013                                                                ③
00014          ⬚
00015          FILE SECTION.
00016          FD  CARD-FILE
00017              LABEL RECORDS ARE OMITTED
00018              RECORD CONTAINS 80 CHARACTERS
00019              DATA RECORD IS EMPLOYEE-CARD.
00020          01  EMPLOYEE-CARD.
00021              05  CARD-NAME        PIC X(25).
00022              05  CARD-TITLE       PIC X(10).
00023              05  CARD-AGE         PIC 99.
00024              05  FILLER           PIC XX.
00025              05  CARD-SALARY      PIC 9(5).
00026              05  FILLER           PIC X(36).
00027          FD  PRINT-FILE                                        ④
00028              ⬚ ARE OMITTED
00029              RECORD CONTAINS 133 CHARACTERS
00030              DATA RECORD IS PRINT-LINE.
00031          01  PRINT-LINE.
00032              05  FILLER           PIC X(1).
00033              05  PRINT-NAME       ⬚                           ⑤
00034              05  FILLER           PIC X(2).
00035              05  PRINT-AGE        PIC 99.
00036              05  FILLER           PIC X(3).
00037              05  PRINT-SALARY     PIC 9(5).
00038              05  FILLER           PIC X(95).
00039                                                                ⑥
00040          ⬚
00041          77  END-OF-DATA-FLAG     PIC XXX.
00042
00043          PROCEDURE DIVISION.
00044          MAINLINE-ROUTINE.                                     ⑦
00045          *HOUSEKEEPING ROUTINE
00046              ⬚ INPUT CARD-FILE, OUTPUT PRINT-FILE.
00047              MOVE SPACES TO PRINT-LINE.
00048              MOVE ' SALARY REPORT FOR PROGRAMMERS UNDER 30' TO PRINT-LINE.
00049              WRITE PRINT-LINE AFTER ADVANCING 2 LINES.
00050              READ CARD-FILE                                    ⑧
00051                  AT END MOVE 'YES' TO END=OF-DATA-FLAG.
00052
00053              ⬚ PROCESS-EMPLOYEE-RECORDS
00054                  UNTIL END-OF-DATA-FLAG = 'YES'.
00055              CLOSE CARD-FILE, PRINT-FILE.
00056              STOP RUN.
00057                                                                ⑨
00058          PROCESS-EMPLOYEE-RECORDS.
00059              IF CARD-TITLE = 'PROGRAMMER' AND CARD-AGE < 30
00060                  MOVE ⬚ TO PRINT-LINE
00061                  MOVE CARD-NAME TO PRINT-NAME                  ⑩
00062                  MOVE ⬚ TO PRINT-AGE
00063                  MOVE CARD-SALARY TO PRINT-SALARY
00064                  WRITE PRINT-LINE AFTER ADVANCING 2 LINES.
00065              READ CARD-FILE
00066                  AT END MOVE ⬚ TO END-OF-DATA-FLAG.           ⑪
```

FIGURE 1.10 *COBOL Program with Missing Elements*

8. World Wide Sales, Inc., wishes to promote one of its employees to head the South American Division. The selected employee must speak Spanish, be 40 or younger, and hold a college degree. The programming manager has prepared the necessary flowchart (see figure below), but unfortunately Benjy and his scissors got to it first (see Problem 6). Your job is to put the flowchart together. Note well that there may be more than one employee who qualifies for the position. Accordingly, the flowchart includes the necessary logic to count and print the number of qualified employees and to print the name of every such employee.

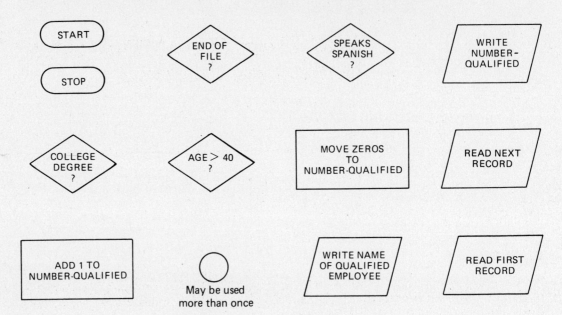

Chapter 2

THE PROGRAMMING PROCESS: COBOL OVERVIEW

OVERVIEW

One objective of this book is to teach you COBOL programming. A broader objective is to teach you how to solve problems using the computer. To this end, we shall present a generally accepted problem-solving procedure consisting of six steps:

1. Problem statement and analysis
2. Flowcharting and/or pseudocode
3. Coding
4. Program testing: phase 1 (compilation)
5. Program testing: phase 2 (execution)
6. Documentation

You probably have a broad appreciation for this procedure from Chapter 1. In this chapter we shall first expand the procedure in general fashion and then cover specifics to enable you to run your own program. We shall discuss the elements of COBOL, the COBOL coding form, keypunching, and finally submission to the computer.

At the end of Chapter 1 we presented a COBOL program that prints a listing of engineering majors who had completed at least 110 credits. At the conclusion of this chapter we shall ask you to keypunch the program of Chapter 1 and to submit it to your computer center. "Seeing is believing" is especially pertinent to data processing. We are very confident that after you have seen computer output from your own program, many of your questions will answer themselves. In other words, we would not be surprised if you were a bit confused after reading Chapter 1. *However, the sooner you get down to running a program, the sooner things will resolve themselves.* You could read this book until all hours of the night but to no avail unless you interact heavily with the computer.

A PROBLEM-SOLVING PROCEDURE

The first step is to obtain a clear statement of the problem containing a complete description of the input and desired output. The problem statement should also contain processing specifications. It is not enough to say calculate quality point average (QPA). Rather the method for calculating QPA must be given as well.

Once the input, output, and processing specifications have been enumerated, a flowchart is drawn, and/or pseudocode is developed. Either technique summarizes the logic to be used in solving the problem. Careful attention to this step simplifes subsequent coding.

Coding is the translation of a flowchart or pseudocode into COBOL. Coding must be done within well-defined COBOL rules and coding conventions. In subsequent sections in this chapter we shall discuss the elements of COBOL and the COBOL coding form.

After the program is coded, it is keypunched and submitted to the computer. The first thing the machine has to do is translate the COBOL program into machine language. Initial attempts at compilation are apt to contain several errors, which may be due to misspellings, missing periods, misplaced parentheses, etc. Corrections are made, and the program is recompiled. Only after the compilation has been successfully completed can we proceed to the next step. Compilation errors are thoroughly discussed in Chapter 5.

After compilation, we begin program execution, where we are apt to encounter logical errors. In this step the computer does exactly what we instructed it to do, but we may have done so incorrectly. For example, assume the word OR replaced the word AND in line 44 of Figure 1.8, the engineering senior problem. The program would then select *either* engineering majors *or* seniors. Either way, it would function differently from the original, logically correct version. The program would still compile perfectly in that the COBOL syntax was correct. It would not, however, execute as intended. Corrections are made, the program is recompiled, and testing continues.

Documentation requires explicit explanation of a program's input, logic, and output. A program is well documented if a programmer, other than the original author, can step in and easily handle any desired modifications. Documentation can consist of flowcharts, pseudocode, or a host of other techniques beyond the scope of this book. It is particularly important in a commercial environment.

Figure 2.1 is a flowchart of the problem-solving procedure. Note the presence of two decision blocks, which indicate the iterative nature of the entire process. Very few, if any, programs compile correctly on the first shot—hence the need to recode or rekeypunch specific statements. Similarly, very few programs execute properly on the first test and thus the need to reflowchart, recode, recompile, etc. Figure 2.1 also contains two dotted boxes for keypunching and preparation of job control language (JCL). These are definite steps to the beginner but not significant enough to merit explicit mention in the previous discussion.

We now return to the engineering senior problem of Chapter 1. In the introductory chapter we skipped over some of the blocks in Figure 2.1 and ended with a working COBOL program. Our purpose there was to provide a rapid introduction to COBOL to give the reader an immediate feeling of what programming is all about. Now we shall retrace our steps; in particular we shall discuss the elements of COBOL, the COBOL coding form, keypunching, and submission to the computer.

ELEMENTS OF COBOL

COBOL consists of six language elements: reserved words, programmer-supplied names, literals, symbols, level numbers, and pictures. Every COBOL statement contains at least one reserved word that gives the entire statement its meaning. Reserved words have special significance to the compiler and are used in a rigidly prescribed manner. They must be spelled correctly, or the compiler will not be able to recognize them. The list of reserved words varies from compiler to compiler, and a comprehensive list is given in Appendix B. The beginner is urged to refer frequently to this appendix for two reasons: (1) to ensure the proper spelling of reserved words used in his program, and (2) to avoid the inadvertent use of reserved words as programmer-supplied data names.

The programmer supplies his own names for paragraph, data, and file names. A paragraph name is a tag to which the program refers, e.g., PROCESS-CARDS or MAINLINE in Figure 1.8. File names are specified in several places throughout a COBOL program, but their initial appearance is in the environment division, e.g., CARD-FILE and PRINT-FILE in Figure 1.8. Data names are the elements on which instructions operate, e.g., CARD-NAME, CARD-CREDITS, and CARD-MAJOR in Figure 1.8. A programmer chooses his own names within the following rules:

1. A programmer-supplied name can contain the letters A to Z, the digits 0 to 9, and the hyphen (-). No other characters are permitted, not even blanks.
2. Data names must contain at least one letter. Paragraph and section names may be all numeric.
3. A programmer-supplied name cannot begin or end with a hyphen.
4. Reserved words may not be used as programmer-supplied names.
5. Programmer-supplied names must be 30 characters or less.

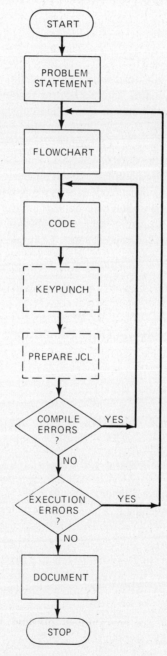

FIGURE 2.1 *The Programming Process*

The following examples should clarify the rules associated with programmer-supplied names:

Programmer-Supplied Name	Explanation
SUM	Invalid—reserved word
SUM-OF-X	Valid
SUM OF X	Invalid—contains blanks
SUM-OF-X-	Invalid—ends with a hyphen
SUM-OF-ALL-THE-XS	Valid
SUM-OF-ALL-THE-XS-IN-ENTIRE-PROGRAM	Invalid—more than 30 characters
GROSS-PAY-IN-$	Invalid—contains a character other than a letter, number, or hyphen
12345	Valid as a paragraph name but invalid as a data name

A 🔲literal🔲 is an exact value or constant. It may be *numeric,* i.e., a number, or *nonnumeric,* i.e., enclosed in quotes. Literals appear throughout a program and are frequently used to compare the value of a data name to a specified constant. Consider line 44 of Figure 1.8:

IF CARD-CREDITS NOT < 110 AND CARD-MAJOR = 'ENGINEERING'

In the first portion CARD-CREDITS is compared to 110, a numeric literal. The second part contains a nonnumeric literal, ENGINEERING. Nonnumeric literals are contained in quotes and may be up to 120 characters in length. Anything, including blanks, numbers, or reserved words, may appear in the quotes and be part of the literal. Numeric literals can be up to 18 digits and may begin with a leading (leftmost) plus or minus sign. The latter may contain a decimal point but cannot end on a decimal point. Examples are shown:

Literal	Explanation
123.4	Valid numeric literal
'123.4'	Valid nonnumeric literal
+123	Valid numeric literal
'IDENTIFICATION DIVISION'	Valid nonnumeric literal
123.	Invalid numeric literal—cannot end on a decimal point
123—	Invalid numeric literal—the minus sign must be in the leftmost position

🔲Symbols🔲 are of three types, punctuation, arithmetic, and relational, and are contained in Table 2.1.

TABLE 2.1 COBOL Symbols

Category	Symbol	Meaning
Punctuation	.	Denotes end of COBOL entry
	,	Delineates clauses
	;	Delineates clauses
	" " or ' '	Sets off nonnumeric literals
	( )	Encloses subscripts or expressions
Arithmetic	+	Addition
	−	Subtraction
	*	Multiplication
	/	Division
	**	Exponentiation
Relational	=	Equal to
	>	Greater than
	<	Less than

The use of relational and arithmetic symbols is described in detail later in the text, beginning in Chapter 3. Commas and semicolons are used to improve the legibility of a program, and their omission (or inclusion) does not constitute an error. Periods, on the other hand, should be used after a sentence, and their omission could cause difficulty. Thus, there are two rules with respect to punctuation symbols. The first is an absolute requirement; i.e., violation will cause compiler errors. The second is strongly recommended; i.e., violation will *not* cause compiler errors but could cause execution errors.

1. A space must follow and cannot precede a comma, semicolon, and period. (Thus a space is a valid and necessary symbol.)
2. All entries should be terminated by a period.

Consider these examples:

1. OPEN INPUT CARD-FILE, OUTPUT PRINT-FILE.
2. OPEN INPUT CARD-FILE OUTPUT PRINT-FILE.
3. OPEN INPUT CARD-FILE, OUTPUT PRINT-FILE
4. OPEN INPUT CARD-FILE , OUTPUT PRINT-FILE.
5. OPEN INPUT CARD-FILE,OUTPUT PRINT-FILE.

Examples 1 and 2 are perfect. Example 3 is missing a period; although that is not an error, it does violate our second guideline. In example 4, the comma is preceded by a space. Example 5 is missing a space after the comma.

Level numbers and pictures are discussed more fully in Chapter 4 under the data division. Level numbers describe the relationship of items in a record. For example, under CARD-FILE in Figure 1.8 there was a single 01-level entry and several 05 entries. In general, the higher (numerically) the level number, the less significant the entry; i.e., 05 is less important than 01. Entries with higher numeric values are said to belong to the levels above them. Thus, in Figure 1.8 the several 05-level entries belong to their respective 01-level entries.

Pictures describe the nature of incoming or outgoing data. A picture of 9's means the entry is numeric, a picture of A's implies the entry is alphabetic, and a picture of X's says the entry can contain both alphabetic and numeric data. Note, however, that alphabetic pictures are seldom used; i.e., even names can contain apostrophes or hyphens, which are alphanumeric rather than alphabetic in nature.

THE COBOL CODING FORM

The COBOL compiler is very particular about the information it receives; i.e., certain areas of the punched card are reserved for specific elements of COBOL. For example, division and section headers are required to begin between columns 8 and 11, whereas most other statements may begin in or past column 12. Further, there are additional rules for continuation (what happens if a sentence doesn't fit on one card), comments, optional sequencing of source statements in columns 1 to 6, and program identification in columns 73 to 80. Rules of the coding sheet are summarized in Table 2.2 and illustrated in Figure 2.2. The latter shows completed forms for the engineering senior problem of Chapter 1.

KEYPUNCHING

Professional programmers generally have their programs keypunched by someone else. Students do not have this luxury, and, for this reason, we have included a brief section on keypunching. Figure 2.3 shows an IBM 029 keypunch, and Figure 2.4 shows the keyboard layout. As you can see, a keypunch bears a strong resemblance to a typewriter, and its operating instructions are summarized on page 24. They may appear complicated now, but after you have punched a few cards by yourself, this material will become second nature.

TABLE 2.2 Rules for the COBOL Coding Form

Columns	Explanation and Use
1–6	Optional sequence numbers: If this field is coded, the compiler performs a sequence check on incoming COBOL statements by flagging any statements out of order. Most commercial installations encourage the use of this option. For students, however, we do not advocate its use if you are keypunching your own programs.
7	Used to indicate comments and for continuation of nonnumeric literals: A comment may appear anywhere in a COBOL program and is indicated by an * in column 7. Comments appear on the source listing but are otherwise ignored by the compiler. We encourage their use to facilitate program documentation. Column 7 is also used to indicate continuation of nonnumeric literals, and this is more fully explained in Chapter 4.
8–11	Known as the "A margin": Division headers, section headers, paragraph names, FD's, and 01's all begin in the A margin. Division and section headers are followed immediately by a period, and the rest of the line is blank. Paragraph names are also followed by a period but may contain additional information on the line.
12–72	Known as the "B margin": All remaining entries begin in or past column 12. COBOL permits considerable flexibility here, but individual installations have their own requirements. We, for example, begin PICTURE clauses in the same column, e.g. column 48, for better legibility. (We shall discuss this further in Chapter 6.)
73–80	Program identification: a second optional field, which is ignored by the compiler. Different installations have different standards. However, we suggest you omit these columns if keypunching your own programs.

OPERATING INSTRUCTIONS FOR THE 029 KEYPUNCH:

1. Turn the power switch on.
2. Place sufficient blank cards in the feed hopper. Cards must be placed with the 9 edge down.
3. Set all toggle switches to the off (down) position with the exception of two PRINT switches. Push the drum switch to the right.
4. Press the FEED key, causing a card from the feed hopper to drop.
5. Press the REG key, causing the card to register in the punch station.
6. Punch to your heart's content, keeping the following in mind:
   a. The space bar skips a space; i.e., it leaves a column blank.
   b. Most keys contain two characters (Figure 2.4). The lower character is punched by just hitting the appropriate key. The upper character is punched by holding the numeric shift and hitting the key simultaneously.
   c. The column indicator shows the next column to be punched.
7. When you have finished punching, hit the REL (release) key to move the completed card from the punch area.
8. Hit the FEED key to bring in another blank card and return to step 5.

Some hints at speeding up:

1. Use of the AUTO FEED switch: If this switch is turned on (up position), hitting the REL key also causes a new card to feed. In effect, step 8 is eliminated from the above procedure.
2. Use of the DUP (duplicate) key: Very often one may punch 30 or 40 columns correctly and then make an error. Unlike a typewriter, where one can merely backspace and retype the correction, the entire card must be done over. The most expeditious procedure is to
   a. Place the incorrect card in the read station.
   b. FEED a blank card into the punch station and hit REG.
   c. Depress the DUP key until you reach the column containing the error (this will copy the information from the incorrect card to the blank card).
   d. Punch corrected information as normal. If possible, use the DUP key after the correction.
   e. Verify that the new card is correct.
   f. Throw away, immediately, the incorrect card.

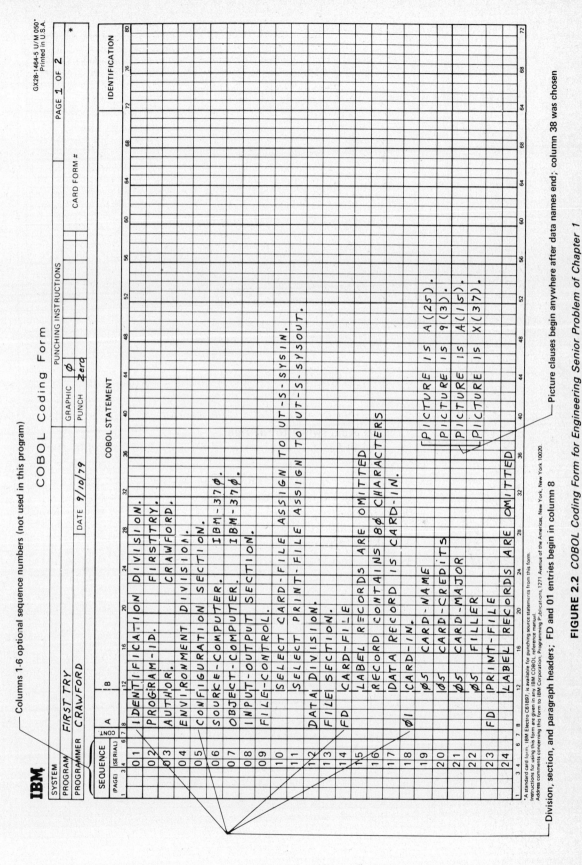

FIGURE 2.2 *COBOL Coding Form for Engineering Senior Problem of Chapter 1*

Columns 1-6 optional sequence numbers (not used in this program)

IBM

COBOL Coding Form

SYSTEM	
PROGRAM *FIRST TRY*	
PROGRAMMER *CRAWFORD*	DATE *9/10/79*

PUNCHING INSTRUCTIONS

| GRAPHIC | Ø | | |
| PUNCH | *Zero* | CARD FORM # | |

PAGE *1* OF *2*

GX28-1464-5 U/M 050*
Printed in U.S.A.

*

SEQUENCE		CONT.	A	B	COBOL STATEMENT	IDENTIFICATION
(PAGE)	(SERIAL)					
0 1			IDENTIFICATION DIVISION.	
0 2			PROGRAM-ID. FIRSTTRY.	
0 3			AUTHOR. CRAWFORD.	
0 4			ENVIRONMENT DIVISION.	
0 5			CONFIGURATION SECTION.	
0 6			SOURCE-COMPUTER. IBM-37Ø.	
0 7			OBJECT-COMPUTER. IBM-37Ø.	
0 8			INPUT-OUTPUT SECTION.	
0 9			FILE-CONTROL.	
1 0			SELECT CARD-FILE ASSIGN TO UT-S-SYSIN.	
1 1			SELECT PRINT-FILE ASSIGN TO UT-S-SYSOUT.	
1 2			DATA DIVISION.	
1 3			FILE SECTION.	
1 4			FD CARD-FILE	
1 5			LABEL RECORDS ARE OMITTED	
1 6			RECORD CONTAINS 8Ø CHARACTERS	
1 7			DATA RECORD IS CARD-IN.	
1 8		Ø1	CARD-IN.	
1 9			Ø5 CARD-NAME [PICTURE IS A(25).	
2 0			Ø5 CARD-CREDITS PICTURE IS 9(3).	
2 1			Ø5 CARD-MAJOR PICTURE IS A(15).	
2 2			Ø5 FILLER [PICTURE IS X(37).	
2 3			FD PRINT-FILE	
2 4			LABEL RECORDS ARE OMITTED	

Picture clauses begin anywhere after data names end; column 38 was chosen

Division, section, and paragraph headers; FD and 01 entries begin in column 8

*A standard card form, IBM Electro C61897, is available for punching source statements from this form.
Instructions for using this form are given in any IBM COBOL reference manual.
Address comments concerning this form to IBM Corporation, Programming Publications, 1271 Avenue of the Americas, New York, New York 10020.

CHAPTER 2: THE PROGRAMMING PROCESS: COBOL OVERVIEW

25

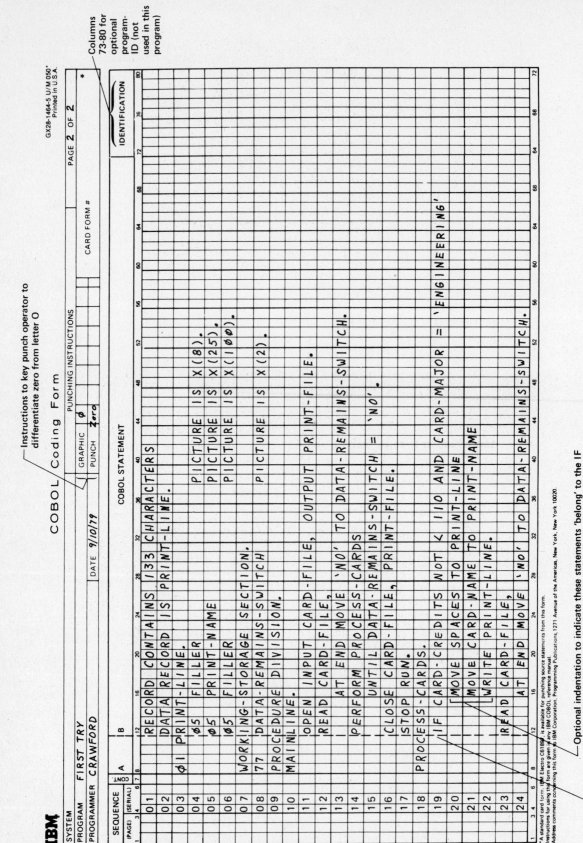

FIGURE 2.2 (continued)

Instructions to key punch operator to differentiate zero from letter O

Columns 73-80 for optional program-ID (not used in this program)

Optional indentation to indicate these statements 'belong' to the IF

Procedure Division statements begin in or past column 12

COBOL/Coding Form

GX28-1464-5 U/M 050*
Printed in U.S.A.

PAGE **2** OF **2**

SEQUENCE		A	B	COBOL STATEMENT
01			RECORD CONTAINS 133 CHARACTERS.
02			DATA RECORD IS PRINT-LINE.
03		Ø1	PRINT-LINE.
04			Ø5 FILLER PICTURE IS X(8).
05			Ø5 PRINT-NAME PICTURE IS X(25).
06			Ø5 FILLER PICTURE IS X(100).
07			WORKING-STORAGE SECTION.
08		77	DATA-REMAINS-SWITCH PICTURE IS X(2).
09			PROCEDURE DIVISION.
10			MAINLINE.
11			OPEN INPUT CARD-FILE, OUTPUT PRINT-FILE.
12			READ CARD-FILE,
13			AT END MOVE 'NO' TO DATA-REMAINS-SWITCH.
14			PERFORM PROCESS-CARDS
15			UNTIL DATA-REMAINS-SWITCH = 'NO'.
16			CLOSE CARD-FILE, PRINT-FILE.
17			STOP RUN.
18			PROCESS-CARDS.
19			IF CARD-CREDITS NOT < 110 AND CARD-MAJOR = 'ENGINEERING'
20			MOVE SPACES TO PRINT-LINE
21			MOVE CARD-NAME TO PRINT-NAME
22			WRITE PRINT-LINE.
23			READ CARD-FILE,
24			AT END MOVE 'NO' TO DATA-REMAINS-SWITCH.

SYSTEM
PROGRAM FIRST TRY
PROGRAMMER CRAWFORD   DATE 9/10/79

PUNCHING INSTRUCTIONS
GRAPHIC Ø
PUNCH zero
CARD FORM #

IDENTIFICATION

*A standard card form, IBM Electro 081897 is available for punching source statements from this form.
Instructions for using this form are given in any IBM COBOL reference manual.
Address comments concerning this form to IBM Corporation, Programming Publications, 1271 Avenue of the Americas, New York, New York 10020.

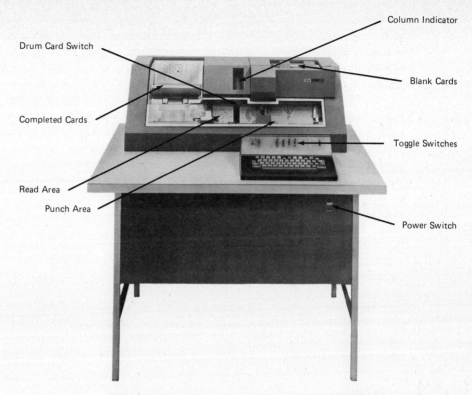

FIGURE 2.3 *IBM 029 Keypunch (Courtesy of IBM.)*

3. Organization: We cannot overemphasize the need for preparation prior to the keypunch room. In our college, students are usually waiting for a machine, and it is difficult, and indeed unfair to those waiting, to take time to think under those circumstances. It is imperative that you be well organized and know precisely what you intend to punch *before* sitting down at the machine.

FIGURE 2.4 *Keyboard for IBM 029 Keypunch (Courtesy of IBM.)*

SUBMITTING A PROGRAM TO THE COMPUTER

Modern computers are highly sophisticated devices capable of executing many different kinds of programs. Accordingly, a computer must be told precisely what program to execute, where the program is coming from, and where to obtain the data. These tasks are accomplished through the operating system and JCL (job control language). An operating system consists of a series of programs, which include the COBOL compiler, that enables the computer to function. The operating system is supplied by the computer manufacturer because it is far too complex to be developed by individual installations. Job control language is the method of communication with the operating system.

In Chapters 17 and 18 we shall study in detail JCL for DOS and OS, the two most widely used operating systems. For the present, however, we shall cover only the minimum JCL that must accompany a COBOL program when it is submitted to the computer. Your instructor may want to embellish this material, or perhaps your computer center has a handout to make the information clearer. If not, much of what we say in this section must be "taken on faith" until you cover the JCL chapters.

OS JCL

A set of JCL statements is known collectively as a job stream. Figure 2.5 contains the job stream necessary to run a COBOL program under OS, but undoubtedly there will be minor variations at your installation. The JOB statement always starts a new job stream. The name of the job, GRAUER in Figure 2.5, can be no more than eight characters and immediately follows the //. The EXEC card invokes a procedure known as COBUCLG, which calls the COBOL compiler. The next statement, //COB.SYSIN DD *, indicates that the COBOL deck follows immediately. The first /* signals the end of the COBOL deck. //GO.SYSIN DD * tells the computer that data follow next, and the second /* indicates the end of the data. The // signals the end of the job stream.

DOS JCL

In Chapter 1 we learned that a COBOL program is first translated into machine language (compilation) and that the machine language program is subsequently executed. In reality, there is an additional step known as linkage editing. The linkage editor is part of the operating system. It takes the output of the COBOL compiler and combines it with other routines in the operating

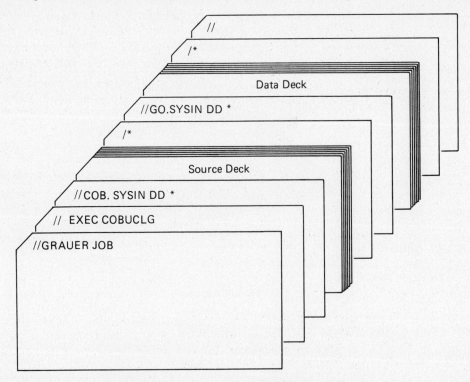

FIGURE 2.5 *OS JCL for the First COBOL Program*

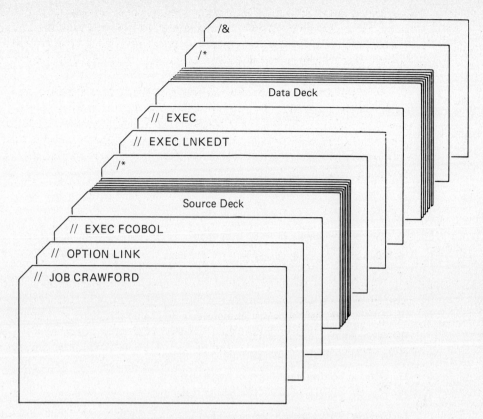

FIGURE 2.6 *DOS JCL for the First COBOL Program*

system to enable the subsequent execution. Figure 2.6 illustrates the DOS JCL necessary and draws attention to the linkage editor.

The JOB statement signals the start of a new job stream. The job name, CRAWFORD in Figure 2.6, must be eight characters or less. The OPTION statement allows the linkage editor to be called if compilation is successful. // EXEC FCOBOL invokes the COBOL compiler and is followed immediately by the COBOL source deck. The first /∗ signals the end of the COBOL program. // EXEC LNKEDT calls the linkage editor, and // EXEC executes the generated machine language program. The // EXEC statement is followed immediately by the data. The second /∗ indicates the end of the data, and the /& signals the end of the job stream.

PUTTING IT TOGETHER

"One learns by doing." This time-worn axiom is especially true for programming. We have covered a lot of material since you first began reading Chapter 1. Now it is time to put everything together and actually run your first program. Keypunch the coding from Figure 2.2. Prepare the appropriate JCL. Make up your own test data and submit the job.

We believe, in fact we are very sure, that after you receive your first computer printout everything will fall into place.

SUMMARY

The programming process was presented. It consisted of six steps: analysis, flowcharting or pseudo-code, coding, compilation, execution, and documentation. Errors in compilation and execution are to be expected in the first several attempts; hence the procedure assumes an iterative nature.

The COBOL language consists of six elements: reserved words, programmer-supplied names, literals, symbols, level numbers, and pictures. Rules for the COBOL coding form were covered, and keypunching was discussed briefly.

Finally, the procedure for submitting jobs to the computer was presented. All computers function through an operating system, which is a set of programs supplied by the manufacturer. Job control language (JCL) is the means of communication with the operating system. Elementary JCL to compile and execute COBOL programs under both DOS and OS was supplied.

REVIEW EXERCISES

TRUE   FALSE

☐   ☐   **1.** Nonnumeric literals may not contain numbers.

☐   ☐   **2.** Numeric literals may not contain letters.

☐   ☐   **3.** A data name cannot contain any characters other than letters or numbers.

☐   ☐   **4.** Columns 1 to 6 are never used on the coding sheet.

☐   ☐   **5.** The use of columns 73 to 80 is optional.

☐   ☐   **6.** File names typically appear in three divisions.

☐   ☐   **7.** Column 8 is used as a continuation column.

☐   ☐   **8.** The rules for forming paragraph names and data names are exactly the same.

☐   ☐   **9.** A data name cannot consist of more than 30 characters.

☐   ☐   **10.** A nonnumeric literal cannot contain more than 30 characters.

☐   ☐   **11.** A numeric literal can contain up to 18 digits.

☐   ☐   **12.** Division headers must begin in the A margin.

☐   ☐   **13.** Division headers must begin in column 8.

☐   ☐   **14.** Section headers must begin in column 12.

☐   ☐   **15.** Paragraph names must begin in column 8.

☐   ☐   **16.** Picture clauses can appear in column 12 or after.

☐   ☐   **17.** If a program compiles correctly, then it must execute correctly.

☐   ☐   **18.** Reserved words may appear in a nonnumeric literal.

☐   ☐   **19.** Reserved words may be used as data names.

☐   ☐   **20.** JCL is used to communicate with the operating system.

PROBLEMS

1. Indicate whether the entries below are valid as data names. If any entry is invalid, state the reason.
(a) NUMBER-OF-TIMES
(b) CODE
(c) 12345
(d) ONE TWO THREE
(e) IDENTIFICATION-DIVISION
(f) IDENTIFICATION
(g) HOURS-
(h) GROSS-PAY
(i) GROSS-PAY-IN-$

2. Classify the entries below as being valid or invalid literals. For each valid entry, indicate if it is numeric or nonnumeric; for each invalid entry, indicate the reason it is invalid.
(a) 567
(b) 567.
(c) −567
(d) +567
(e) +567.
(f) '567.'
(g) 'FIVE SIX SEVEN'
(h) '−567'
(i) 567−

(j) 567+

(k) '567+'

3. Indicate whether the following entries are acceptable according to the COBOL rules for punctuation. Correct any invalid entries.

(a) CLOSE CARD-FILE,PRINT-FILE.

(b) CLOSE CARD-FILE PRINT-FILE.

(c) CLOSE CARD-FILE, PRINT-FILE

(d) CLOSE CARD-FILE , PRINT-FILE.

(e) CLOSE CARD-FILE, PRINT-FILE.

4. (a) Which division(s) does not contain paragraph names?

(b) Which division(s) contain the SELECT statement(s)?

(c) Which division(s) contains level numbers?

(d) Which division(s) contain data names?

(e) Which division(s) contain reserved words?

(f) Which division(s) contain picture clauses?

(g) Which division(s) does not contain file names?

5. Modify the COBOL program of Figure 2.2 to accommodate *all* the following:

(a) Major is moved to columns 50 to 64 of the data card.

(b) Print the names of *all* students, regardless of major, who have completed 110 credits or more.

(c) Print the major in print positions 40 to 54 in addition to the student's name.

Code and then keypunch the necessary changes. Rerun the program.

6. Restudy the section on keypunching in this chapter. Go to a keypunch machine (IBM 029) and (by trial and error if necessary) keypunch either the JCL in Figure 2.5 or the JCL in Figure 2.6. Learn to use the DUP key and duplicate the first card (JOB card) four times. Save the JCL for later assignments.

PROJECTS

1. Develop a flowchart (or pseudocode) and a corresponding COBOL program for the EAST-WEST telephone company (serving 400 residents on an unknown island in the mid-Pacific). The object of the program is to process a customer file and indicate the payment due from each resident. (Residents come into the telephone office and pay their bill in person.) If column 42 of an incoming record contains an X, it means the customer is retired and pays only $2.00. All others pay $5.00. Incoming records are in the following format:

Field	Columns	Picture
LAST-NAME	1–15	X(15)
FIRST-NAME	16–30	X(15)
POST-OFFICE-BOX	31–34	9(4)
TELEPHONE-NUMBER	36–40	9(5)
RETIRED-INDICATOR	42	X

The printed output should contain all five fields from the input record in columns 2 to 16, 18 to 32, 41 to 44, 56 to 60, and 65, respectively. In addition, it should print the amount due in columns 70 to 74. Use the following test data:

MERKLE	RICHARD	0135 00025
OBRIEN	ROBERT	0625 00321
MERKLE	OLIVE	0330 00250 X
BLAKELY	BRIAN	0279 00639
KESSEL	SILVIA	0217 00433
SLY	CAREY	0934 00372
KARVAZY	KAREN	0666 00218 X
CRAWFORD	STACY	0555 00319 X
CRAWFORD	AMY	0567 00417

2. Develop pseudocode (or a flowchart) and a corresponding COBOL program for the Inter-City Piano Company. The program is to process a file of customers and produce a list of people eligible for a discount on buying a piano. Individuals with more than 15 lessons that have not already purchased a piano are

eligible and should appear on the output. Individuals with 15 or fewer lessons or individuals who have already purchased a piano are not eligible. The format of the input records is as follows:

Field	Columns	Picture
LAST-NAME	1–15	X(15)
FIRST-NAME	16–25	X(10)
ADDRESS	26–50	X(25)
CITY	51–75	X(25)
NUMBER-OF-LESSONS	76–78	9(3)
PURCHASE-INDICATOR	80	X

Note: Y means already purchased.
N means not purchased.

The output print positions are 2 to 16, 18 to 27, 29 to 53, 55 to 79, 81 to 83, and 86 for the six incoming fields. No additional data need appear in the output, but remember *only* those customers eligible for a discount are to appear. Use the following test data:

CRAWFORD	SHERRY	15004 GOOD MEADOW CT.	GAITHERSBURG	011 N
KARVAZY	KAREN	P. O. BOX 1013	GAITHERSBURG	017 Y
MORSE	KENNETH	11800 SILENT VALLEY LN.	GAITHERSBURG	014 N
PLUMETREE	MICHELE	14717 PEBBLE HILL RD.	GAITHERSBURG	027 N
SLY	MATTHEW	15001 GOOD MEADOW CT.	GAITHERSBURG	019 N
POWERS	NANCY	525 ORCHARD WAY	SILVER SPRINGS	024 Y
BLAKELY	KRISTEN	15005 ORCHARD WAY	SILVER SPRINGS	008 Y
BROWN	JENNIFER	11 HEATHER DRIVE	COLORADO SPRINGS	021 N
TARTLETON	KIMBERLY	BOX 395	NORTH LAPLATA	004 N

3. Develop a flowchart (or pseudocode) and a COBOL program that will

(a) Read a file of employee cards.
(b) Print the name, salary, age, and location of every employee who
   (i) Earns between $20,000 and $30,000,
   (ii) Works in New York or Chicago,
   (iii) Is 35 years or younger.

The data for each employee are punched according to the following format:

Field	Columns	Picture
NAME	6–20	X(15)
SALARY	25–29	9(5)
LOCATION	40–50	X(11)
AGE	51–52	9(2)

Use any appropriate print positions for your output. Run your program with appropriate test data, and be careful to develop sufficient data to test your program adequately. As an extra, print a suitable heading line at the beginning of the report. In addition, count the number of qualified employees, and print that number at the end of the report.

Section II

THE COBOL LANGUAGE

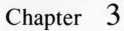

Chapter 3

THE PROCEDURE DIVISION

OVERVIEW

The procedure division is the portion of a COBOL program that contains the logic; it is the part of the program that "actually does something." In this chapter we shall cover several of the basic COBOL verbs. We shall begin with those which do arithmetic: ADD, SUBTRACT, MULTIPLY, DIVIDE, and COMPUTE. We shall look at the READ, WRITE, OPEN, and CLOSE verbs for use in I/O (input/output) operations. We shall study the MOVE verb, which transfers data from one area of memory to another. We shall learn about the IF statement, which enables choice, and the PERFORM verb to implement a loop. Finally we shall cover the STOP RUN to terminate program execution.

All the above verbs have a variety of options. For the most part, we shall use only the more elementary formats and defer additional coverage to later chapters.

COBOL NOTATION

COBOL is an "English-like" language. As such, it has inherent flexibility in the way a particular entry may be expressed; i.e., there are a number of different, but equally acceptable, ways to say the same thing. Accordingly, a standard notation is used to express permissible COBOL formats as follows:

1. COBOL reserved words appear in uppercase (capital) letters.
2. Reserved words that are required are underlined; optional reserved words are not underlined.
3. Lowercase words denote programmer-supplied information.
4. Brackets ([ ]) indicate optional information.
5. Braces ({ }) indicate that one of the enclosed items must be chosen.
6. Three periods (. . .) mean that the last syntactical unit can be repeated an arbitrary number of times.

This notation is clarified by example: consider the condition portion in the IF statement:

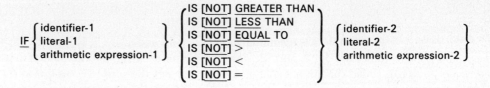

The format for the IF statement has IF underlined and in uppercase letters; thus IF is a required reserved word. The first set of braces means that either a literal, identifier, or arithmetic expression must appear; all are in lowercase letters, indicating they are programmer supplied. The next set of braces forces a choice among one of three relationships: greater than, less than, or equal to. In each case, IS appears in capital letters but is not underlined; hence its use is optional. Brackets denote NOT as an optional entry. THAN is an optional reserved word, which may be added to improve legibility. Finally, a choice must be made between literal-2, identifier-2, or arithmetic expression-2.

Additional flexibility is supplied in that $>$, $<$, and $=$ may be substituted for GREATER THAN, LESS THAN, and EQUAL, respectively. Returning to the engineering senior problem of Chapter 1, in which CARD-MAJOR is compared to engineering, all the following are acceptable:

```
IF CARD-MAJOR IS EQUAL TO 'ENGINEERING' . . .
IF CARD-MAJOR EQUAL 'ENGINEERING' . . .
IF 'ENGINEERING' IS EQUAL TO CARD-MAJOR . . .
IF CARD-MAJOR = 'ENGINEERING' . . .
```

ARITHMETIC VERBS

In this section we shall use the notation to study the COBOL verbs for arithmetic: ADD, SUBTRACT, MULTIPLY, DIVIDE, and COMPUTE. (The ROUNDED and SIZE ERROR options for these verbs are discussed in Chapter 7.) The true beginner may be well advised to skip the material on ADD, SUBTRACT, MULTIPLY, and DIVIDE, and concentrate instead on the COMPUTE statement.

✱ ADD

The ADD verb has two basic formats:

$$\underline{ADD} \begin{Bmatrix} \text{identifier-1} \\ \text{literal-1} \end{Bmatrix} \begin{bmatrix} \text{identifier-2} \\ \text{literal-2} \end{bmatrix} \ldots \underline{TO} \text{ identifier-m [identifier-n]} \ldots$$

and

$$\underline{ADD} \begin{Bmatrix} \text{identifier-1} \\ \text{literal-1} \end{Bmatrix} \begin{Bmatrix} \text{identifier-2} \\ \text{literal-2} \end{Bmatrix} \begin{bmatrix} \text{identifier-3} \\ \text{literal-3} \end{bmatrix} \ldots \underline{GIVING} \text{ identifier-m [identifier-n]} \ldots$$

Note that one or several identifiers (literals) may precede identifier-m. Regardless of which format is chosen, i.e., GIVING or TO, only the value of identifier-m (and beyond) is changed. In the "TO" option, the values of identifier-1, identifier-2, etc., are added to the initial contents of identifier-m. In the "GIVING" option, the sum does not include the initial value of identifier-m. Simply stated, the "TO" option includes the initial value of identifier-m in the final sum, while the "GIVING" option ignores the initial value. Examples 3.1 and 3.2 illustrate both formats.

Example 3.1

ADD A B TO C.

Before execution:	A	5	B	10	C	20
After execution:	A	5	B	10	C	35

In Example 3.1, the initial values of A, B, and C are 5, 10, and 20, respectively. After execution the values are 5, 10, and 35. The instruction took the initial value of A (5), added the value of B (10), added the initial value of C (20), and put the sum (35) back into C.

Example 3.2

ADD A B GIVING C.

Before execution: A `5`   B `10`   C `20`

After execution: A `5`   B `10`   C `15`

In Example 3.2, the initial value of A (5) is added to the initial value of B (10), and the sum (15) replaces the initial value of C.

Table 3.1 contains additional examples of the ADD instruction. In each instance, the instruction is assumed to operate on the initial values of A, B, and C, (5, 10, and 30, respectively). Note that the last example changes the values of both B and C.

TABLE 3.1 The ADD Instruction

Data name	A	B	C
Value *before* execution	5	10	30
Value *after* execution of			
ADD A TO C.	5	10	35
ADD A B TO C.	5	10	45
ADD A 18 B GIVING C.	5	10	33
ADD A 18 B TO C.	5	10	63
ADD 1 TO B, C.	5	11	31

✳ SUBTRACT

The SUBTRACT verb also has two formats:

SUBTRACT $\begin{Bmatrix} \text{identifier-1} \\ \text{literal-1} \end{Bmatrix}$ $\begin{bmatrix} \text{identifier-2} \\ \text{literal-2} \end{bmatrix}$ . . . FROM identifier-m [identifier-n] . . .

SUBTRACT $\begin{Bmatrix} \text{identifier-1} \\ \text{literal-1} \end{Bmatrix}$ $\begin{bmatrix} \text{identifier-2} \\ \text{literal-2} \end{bmatrix}$ . . . FROM $\begin{Bmatrix} \text{identifier-m} \\ \text{literal-m} \end{Bmatrix}$ GIVING identifier-n [identifier-o] . . .

In the first format, the initial value of identifier-m is replaced by the result of the subtraction. In the second format, the initial value of either identifier-m or literal-m is unchanged as the result is stored in identifier-n (and beyond).

Example 3.3

SUBTRACT A FROM B.

Before execution: A `5`   B `15`

After execution: A `5`   B `10`

In Example 3.3, the SUBTRACT verb causes the value of A (5) to be subtracted from the initial value of B (15) and the result (10) to be stored in B. Only the value of B was changed.

Example 3.4

SUBTRACT A FROM B GIVING C.

Before execution: A `5`   B `15`   C `100`

After execution: A $\boxed{5}$ B $\boxed{15}$ C $\boxed{10}$

In the "FROM . . . GIVING" format of Example 3.4, the value of A (5) is subtracted from the value of B (15), and the result (10) is placed in C. The values of A and B are unchanged, and the initial value of C (100) is replaced by 10. Table 3.2 contains additional examples. In each example, the instruction is assumed to operate on the initial contents of A, B, and C.

TABLE 3.2 The SUBTRACT Instruction

Data name	A	B	C	D
Value *before* execution	5	10	30	100
Value *after* execution of				
SUBTRACT A FROM C.	5	10	25	100
SUBTRACT A B FROM C.	5	10	15	100
SUBTRACT A B FROM C GIVING D.	5	10	30	15
SUBTRACT 10 FROM C, D.	5	10	20	90

MULTIPLY

The MULTIPLY verb has two formats:

MULTIPLY $\begin{Bmatrix} \text{identifier-1} \\ \text{literal-1} \end{Bmatrix}$ BY identifier-2 [identifier-3] . . .

MULTIPLY $\begin{Bmatrix} \text{identifier-1} \\ \text{literal-1} \end{Bmatrix}$ BY $\begin{Bmatrix} \text{identifier-2} \\ \text{literal-2} \end{Bmatrix}$ GIVING identifier-3 [identifier-4] . . .

If GIVING is used, then the result of the multiplication is stored in identifier-3 (and beyond). IF GIVING is omitted, then the result is stored in identifier-2 (and beyond).

Example 3.5

MULTIPLY A BY B.

Before execution: A $\boxed{10}$ B $\boxed{20}$

After execution: A $\boxed{10}$ B $\boxed{200}$

Example 3.6

MULTIPLY A BY B GIVING C.

Before execution: A $\boxed{10}$ B $\boxed{20}$ C $\boxed{345}$

After execution: A $\boxed{10}$ B $\boxed{20}$ C $\boxed{200}$

Table 3.3 contains additional examples of the MULTIPLY verb.

TABLE 3.3 The MULTIPLY Instruction

Data name	A	B	C
Value *before* execution	5	10	30
Value *after* execution of			
MULTIPLY B BY A GIVING C.	5	10	50
MULTIPLY A BY B GIVING C.	5	10	50
MULTIPLY A BY B.	5	50	30
MULTIPLY B BY A.	50	10	30
MULTIPLY A BY 3 GIVING B, C.	5	15	15

✳ DIVIDE

The DIVIDE verb has three formats:

$$\text{DIVIDE} \begin{Bmatrix} \text{identifier-1} \\ \text{literal-1} \end{Bmatrix} \underline{\text{INTO}} \text{ identifier-2 [identifier-3]} \ldots$$

$$\text{DIVIDE} \begin{Bmatrix} \text{identifier-1} \\ \text{literal-1} \end{Bmatrix} \begin{Bmatrix} \underline{\text{INTO}} \\ \underline{\text{BY}} \end{Bmatrix} \begin{Bmatrix} \text{identifier-2} \\ \text{literal-2} \end{Bmatrix} \underline{\text{GIVING}} \text{ identifier-3 [identifier-4]} \ldots$$

$$\text{DIVIDE} \begin{Bmatrix} \text{identifier-1} \\ \text{literal-1} \end{Bmatrix} \begin{Bmatrix} \underline{\text{INTO}} \\ \underline{\text{BY}} \end{Bmatrix} \begin{Bmatrix} \text{identifier-2} \\ \text{literal-2} \end{Bmatrix} \underline{\text{GIVING}} \text{ identifier-3 } \underline{\text{REMAINDER}} \text{ identifier-4}$$

In the first format the quotient replaces the initial value of identifier-2. If more than one identifier follows the word INTO, then identifier-1 is divided into each of them in turn, with the quotient replacing each identifier's original contents. In the second format, the quotient replaces the initial value of identifier-3. The third format retains the remainder in a separate field. Consider Examples 3.7 and 3.8.

Example 3.7

DIVIDE A INTO B.

Before execution: A | 10 | B | 50 |

After execution: A | 10 | B | 5 |

Example 3.8

DIVIDE A INTO B GIVING C REMAINDER D.

Before execution: A | 10 | B | 51 | C | 13 | D | 17 |

After execution: A | 10 | B | 51 | C | 5 | D | 1 |

In Example 3.7, the initial value of B (50) is divided by the value of A (10), and the quotient (5) replaces the initial value of B. In Example 3.8, which uses the "GIVING" option, the quotient goes into C, the remainder in D, and the values of A and B are unaffected.

Table 3.4 contains additional examples of the DIVIDE verb.

TABLE 3.4 The DIVIDE Instruction

Data name	A	B	C
Value *before* execution	5	10	30
Value *after* execution of			
DIVIDE 2 INTO B.	5	5	30
DIVIDE 2 INTO B GIVING C.	5	10	5
DIVIDE B BY 5 GIVING A.	2	10	30
DIVIDE A INTO B, C.	5	2	6
DIVIDE A INTO B GIVING C.	5	10	2
DIVIDE 3 INTO A GIVING B REMAINDER C.	5	1	2

✳ COMPUTE

Any operation that can be done in an ADD, SUBTRACT, MULTIPLY, or DIVIDE statement may also be done using the COMPUTE instruction. In addition, the COMPUTE statement can combine different arithmetic operations in the same statement. For example, consider the following algebraic statement: X = 2(A + B)/C. A and B are first added together, the sum is multiplied by 2, and the product is divided by C. The single algebraic statement requires three COBOL arithmetic statements as shown. (Note that the true value of X is not obtained until after the last statement is executed.)

ADD A B GIVING X.
MULTIPLY 2 BY X.
DIVIDE C INTO X.

The above statements can be combined into a single COMPUTE with obvious benefits:

COMPUTE X = 2 * (A + B) / C.

The general format of the COMPUTE statement is

COMPUTE identifier-1 = arithmetic-expression

Expressions are formed according to the following rules:

1. The symbols +, −, *, /, and ** denote addition, subtraction, multiplication, division, and exponentiation, respectively.
2. An expression consists of data names, literals, arithmetic symbols, and parentheses. Spaces must precede and follow arithmetic symbols.
3. Parentheses are used to clarify and in some cases alter the sequence of operations within a COMPUTE. Anything contained within the parentheses must also be a valid expression. The left parenthesis is preceded by a space, and the right parenthesis is followed by a space.

The COMPUTE statement calculates the value on the right side of the equal sign and stores it in the data name to the left of the equal sign. Expressions are evaluated as follows:

1. Anything contained in parentheses is evaluated first as a separate expression.
2. Within the expression, exponentiation is done first, then multiplication or division, then addition or subtraction.
3. If rule 2 results in a tie, e.g., both addition and subtraction are present, then evaluation proceeds from left to right.

Table 3.5 contains examples to illustrate the formation and evaluation of expressions in a COMPUTE statement.

TABLE 3.5 The COMPUTE Instruction

Data name	A	B	C	Comments
Value *before* execution	2	3	10	Initial values
Value *after* execution of				
COMPUTE C = A + B.	2	3	5	Simple addition
COMPUTE C = A + B * 2.	2	3	8	Multiplication done *before* addition
COMPUTE C = (A + B) * 2.	2	3	10	Parentheses evaluated first
COMPUTE C = A ** B.	2	3	8	Algebraically, $c = a^b$
COMPUTE C = B ** A.	2	3	9	Algebraically, $c = b^a$

Table 3.6 should further clarify evaluation of the COBOL COMPUTE. This table contains several algebraic expressions and the corresponding COMPUTE statements to accomplish the intended logic. Note that parentheses are often required in the COMPUTE that are not present in the algebraic counterpart. Parentheses may also be optionally used to clarify the intent of a COMPUTE statement; however, their use in Table 3.6 is mandatory in all instances.

TABLE 3.6 The COMPUTE Instruction Continued

Algebraic expression	COBOL COMPUTE
$x = a + b$	COMPUTE X = A + B.
$x = \dfrac{a + b}{2}$	COMPUTE X = (A + B) / 2.
$x = \dfrac{(a + b)c}{2}$	COMPUTE X = (A + B) * C / 2.
$x = \dfrac{a + b}{2c}$	COMPUTE X = (A + B) / (2 * C).
$x = \sqrt{a}$	COMPUTE X = A ** .5.
$x = \dfrac{a^2 + b^2}{c^2}$	COMPUTE X = (A ** 2 + B ** 2) / C ** 2.

✳ READ

An abbreviated format of the READ verb is

<u>READ</u> file-name AT <u>END</u> statement

As an example, consider lines 36 and 37 of the engineering senior problem in Figure 1.8.

```
READ CARD-FILE,
    AT END MOVE 'NO' TO DATA-REMAINS-SWITCH.
```

This statement causes a record (e.g., a card) to be read into main storage. If, however, the end-of-file condition has been reached, i.e., there are no more cards, then control passes to the statement(s) following the AT END clause. In this case, 'NO' will be moved to DATA-REMAINS-SWITCH when the end of file is sensed.

Look carefully at Figure 1.8. The file name (CARD-FILE) in the READ statement appears in four other lines in the COBOL program. It is in a SELECT statement in the environment division (line 10), in an FD in the data division (line 14), and in an OPEN and CLOSE in the procedure division (lines 35 and 40).

✳ WRITE

An abbreviated format of the WRITE verb is

$$\underline{\text{WRITE}} \text{ record-name} \left[\left\{ \begin{matrix} \text{AFTER} \\ \hline \text{BEFORE} \end{matrix} \right\} \text{ADVANCING} \left\{ \begin{matrix} \text{integer LINES} \\ \text{PAGE} \end{matrix} \right\} \right]$$

The WRITE statement transfers data from main storage to an output device. The ADVANCING option controls line spacing on a printer; if omitted, single spacing occurs. If AFTER ADVANCING 3 LINES is used, the printer triple spaces (i.e., skips two lines and writes on the third). Logically enough, the BEFORE option causes the line to be written first, after which the specified number of lines are skipped. Specification of PAGE, in lieu of LINES, will cause output to begin on top of a new page.

Note that the WRITE statement contains a *record* name, whereas the READ statement contains a *file* name. The record name in the WRITE will appear as an 01 entry in the file section of the data division. The file in which it is contained will appear in SELECT, FD, OPEN, and CLOSE statements.

OPEN

Every file in a COBOL program must be "opened" before it can be accessed. The OPEN verb causes the operating system to initiate action to make a file available for processing. For example, it can ensure that the proper reel of tape has been mounted.

The format of the OPEN is

$$\text{OPEN} \begin{Bmatrix} \underline{\text{INPUT}} \\ \underline{\text{I-O}} \\ \underline{\text{OUTPUT}} \end{Bmatrix} \text{file-name-1 [,file-name-2 . . .]}$$

Notice that one must specify the type of file in an OPEN statement. INPUT is used for a file that can be read only (e.g., a card file). OUTPUT is used for a file that can be written only (e.g., a print file). An I-O file can be both read or written, and such files are not discussed until Chapter 16.

Line 35 of the engineering senior problem contains an OPEN in which two files are opened in the same statement.

OPEN INPUT CARD-FILE, OUTPUT PRINT-FILE.

An alternative way to accomplish the same thing is to use two OPEN statements:

OPEN INPUT CARD-FILE.
OPEN OUTPUT PRINT-FILE.

CLOSE

All files must be closed before processing terminates. The format of the CLOSE is simply

<u>CLOSE</u> file-name-1 [,file-name-2] . . .

Notice that several files may be closed in the same statement. Further, the type of file, i.e., INPUT, OUTPUT, or I-O, is not specified. Statement 40 in the engineering senior problem provides an example:

CLOSE CARD-FILE PRINT-FILE.

MOVE

The MOVE statement accomplishes data transfer, i.e., the movement of data from one storage location to another. The format is

$$\underline{\text{MOVE}} \begin{Bmatrix} \text{identifier-1} \\ \text{literal} \end{Bmatrix} \underline{\text{TO}} \text{ identifier-2 \ \ [identifier-3] . . .}$$

Consider the following three examples:

MOVE 80 TO PRICE-PER-CREDIT.
MOVE 'ABC UNIVERSITY' TO SCHOOL-NAME.
MOVE CARD-NAME TO PRINT-NAME.

The first example moves a numeric literal, 80, to the data name PRICE-PER-CREDIT. The second moves a nonnumeric literal, ABC UNIVERSITY, to SCHOOL-NAME. The third example is taken from line 46 of the engineering senior problem and transfers data from an input to an output area for subsequent printing.

The figurative constants, ZEROS and SPACES, are frequently used in a MOVE as shown:

```
MOVE SPACES TO PRINT-LINE.
MOVE ZEROS TO TOTAL-NUMBER.
```

The first statement moves spaces (i.e., blanks) to the data name PRINT-LINE. The second statement moves numeric zeros to TOTAL-NUMBER.

One final point: As can be seen from the MOVE format, a given quantity may be moved to several data names in the same statement. For example,

```
MOVE 10 TO FIELD-A FIELD-B FIELD-C.
```

is equivalent to

```
MOVE 10 TO FIELD-A.
MOVE 10 TO FIELD-B.
MOVE 10 TO FIELD-C.
```

The results of a MOVE depend on the picture of the receiving field; i.e., whenever the receiving field has a picture different from that of the sending field, a conversion must take place. Further, certain moves are not permitted. Table 3.7 summarizes the rules of the MOVE. (It is not necessary that the reader commit Table 3.7, or the discussion that follows, to memory. Instead be aware that certain restrictions exist and know where to turn when questions arise later. Numeric edited fields are discussed in Chapters 4 and 8.)

TABLE 3.7 Rules of the MOVE Statement

| Source field | Receiving field | | | | |
	Group	Alphabetic	Alpha-numeric	Numeric	Numeric edited
Group	Valid	Valid	Valid	Valid	Valid
Alphabetic	Valid	Valid	Valid	Invalid	Invalid
Alphanumeric	Valid	Valid	Valid	Invalid	Invalid
Numeric	Valid	Invalid	Integers only	Valid	Valid
Numeric edited	Valid	Invalid	Valid	Invalid	Invalid

Inspection of Table 3.7 shows that an alphabetic field cannot be moved to a numeric field and vice versa. However, even Table 3.7 does not tell the whole story; e.g., what happens if a field with a picture of X(3) is moved to a picture of X(5) or vice versa? Two additional statements clarify the action of the move:

1. Data moved from an alphanumeric area to an alphanumeric area are moved one character at a time from left to right. If the receiving field is bigger than the sending field, it is padded on the right with blanks; if the receiving field is smaller than the sending field, the rightmost characters are truncated.
2. A numeric field moved to a numeric field is always aligned according to the decimal point. If the receiving field is larger than the sending field, high-order zeros are added. If the receiving field is smaller than the sending field, the high-order positions are truncated.

Statements 1 and 2 are illustrated in Table 3.8.

One final point: The preceding discussion pertains to elementary items only. *If the receiving field is a group item, the move takes place as though the receiving field were an alphanumeric item, with padding or truncation on the right as necessary.*

TABLE 3.8 Illustration of the MOVE Statement

Source field		Receiving field	
Picture	Contents	Picture	Contents
X(5)	A B C D E	X(5)	A B C D E
X(5)	A B C D E	X(4)	A B C D
X(5)	A B C D E	X(6)	A B C D E _
9(5)	1 2 3 4 5	9(5)	1 2 3 4 5
9(5)	1 2 3 4 5	9(4)	2 3 4 5
9(5)	1 2 3 4 5	9(6)	0 1 2 3 4 5

✳PERFORM

The PERFORM statement is one of the most powerful in COBOL. It enables transfer of control to and from a procedure (e.g., a paragraph) elsewhere in the program. The significance of this capability is that a complex program can be divided into a series of clear and straightforward routines. The mainline portion of the program consists essentially of a series of PERFORM statements. This style of programming is known as *top-down* development and has the immediate benefit of easy legibility. (See Chapters 6 and 11 on structured programming.)

The PERFORM statement has multiple forms and is so important that it is discussed in several other places (see Chapters 6 through 9).

Consider now the simplest form and the following code:

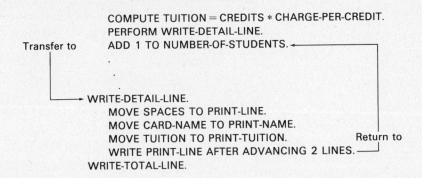

```
         COMPUTE TUITION = CREDITS * CHARGE-PER-CREDIT.
         PERFORM WRITE-DETAIL-LINE.
Transfer to   ADD 1 TO NUMBER-OF-STUDENTS.
         .
         .
     WRITE-DETAIL-LINE.
         MOVE SPACES TO PRINT-LINE.
         MOVE CARD-NAME TO PRINT-NAME.
         MOVE TUITION TO PRINT-TUITION.        Return to
         WRITE PRINT-LINE AFTER ADVANCING 2 LINES.
     WRITE-TOTAL-LINE.
         .
         .
```

The statement PERFORM WRITE-DETAIL-LINE transfers control to the first statement in the paragraph WRITE-DETAIL-LINE. When every statement in WRITE-DETAIL-LINE has been executed (i.e., when the next paragraph name is encountered), control returns to the statement immediately after the PERFORM, i.e., to the ADD statement.

If the UNTIL clause is specified, the condition in the UNTIL clause is tested *prior* to any transfer of control. The performed paragraph is executed until the condition is met; i.e., if the condition is not satisfied, transfer takes place as described in the preceding paragraphs. When the condition is satisfied, control passes to the statement following the PERFORM.

Iteration is accomplished by using the UNTIL clause, specifying a condition, and modifying that condition during execution of the performed paragraph. Consider:

```
MOVE 'NO' TO END-OF-FILE-SWITCH.
PERFORM READ-A-CARD
      UNTIL END-OF-FILE-SWITCH = 'YES'.



READ-A-CARD.



READ CARD-FILE, AT END MOVE 'YES' TO END-OF-FILE-SWITCH.
```

The paragraph READ-A-CARD will be performed until END-OF-FILE-SWITCH equals 'YES', i.e., until there are no more data cards. When the end of file is reached, the END-OF-FILE-SWITCH is set to YES. This causes the next test of the UNTIL condition to be met and prevents the READ-A-CARD paragraph from further execution.

IF

The IF statement is one of the more powerful in COBOL. For the present, our concern is only a few of the available options, and we shall defer additional discussion to Chapters 6 and 7. The format of the IF statement is

IF condition statement-1 [ELSE statement-2]

The condition in the IF statement involves the comparison of two quantities. The syntax of the condition was presented under COBOL formats at the beginning of this chapter.

The IF statement may be used with or without the ELSE option. The action of the IF is best described with the aid of Figures 3.1 and 3.2.

In Figure 3.1 a condition is tested. If the condition is true, then statement-1 is executed, after which execution continues with statement-3. If the condition is false, execution bypasses statement-1 and continues immediately with statement-3.

A condition is also tested in Figure 3.2. If true, then statement-1 is executed followed by statement-3. If the condition is false, then statement-2 is executed, followed by statement-3.

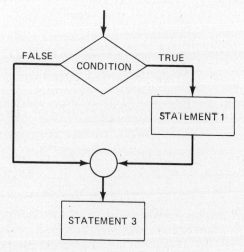

FIGURE 3.1 *IF Statement without the ELSE Option*

Significance of the Period

It is important to emphasize that a period terminates the action in the IF statement. Consider lines 44 to 47 from the engineering senior problem:

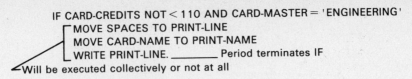

IF CARD-CREDITS NOT < 110 AND CARD-MASTER = 'ENGINEERING'
┌ MOVE SPACES TO PRINT-LINE
│ MOVE CARD-NAME TO PRINT-NAME
└ WRITE PRINT-LINE. _____ Period terminates IF
Will be executed collectively or not at all

If the condition is met, then *every* statement between the condition and the period will be executed. Hence, when an engineering senior is processed, two MOVE statements and one WRITE are executed. If the condition is *not* met, then all three statements, i.e., two MOVES and a WRITE, are bypassed. (Note that indentation in an IF statement is strictly for legibility and not a COBOL requirement. We like to indent detail lines four spaces under their associated IF.)

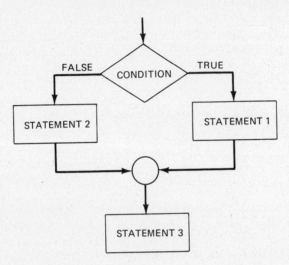

FIGURE 3.2 *IF Statement with the ELSE Option*

STOP

Every program must have at least one STOP statement; the format is

$$STOP \begin{Bmatrix} literal \\ RUN \end{Bmatrix}$$

When STOP RUN is encountered, execution of the COBOL program terminates, and control passes back to the operating system. The literal option can be used to print a message to the operator, but its use is not encouraged.

It is important to realize that STOP RUN is usually *not* the last physical statement in the procedure division. Further, there may be more than one of these statements in a given program, but this is not recommended. STOP RUN means the programmer wants the job to cease execution because the program has come to a logical end.

SUMMARY

Several procedure division verbs were introduced as shown:

Arithmetic:

    ADD
    SUBTRACT
    MULTIPLY
    DIVIDE
    COMPUTE

Input/output:

READ
WRITE
OPEN
CLOSE

Selection:

IF

Iteration:

PERFORM

Data transfer:

MOVE

Program termination:

STOP RUN

In the next chapter we shall study the other divisions in a COBOL program.

REVIEW EXERCISES

TRUE   FALSE

☐   ☐   **1.** One ADD instruction can change the value of more than one data name.

☐   ☐   **2.** Both GIVING and TO may be present in the same ADD instruction.

☐   ☐   **3.** A valid ADD instruction may contain neither GIVING nor TO.

☐   ☐   **4.** Both FROM and GIVING may appear in the same SUBTRACT instruction.

☐   ☐   **5.** The use of GIVING is optional in the MULTIPLY verb.

☐   ☐   **6.** The reserved word INTO must appear in a DIVIDE statement.

☐   ☐   **7.** In the DIVIDE statement, the dividend is always identifier-1.

☐   ☐   **8.** Multiplication and division can be performed in the same MULTIPLY statement.

☐   ☐   **9.** Multiplication and addition can be performed in the same COMPUTE statement.

☐   ☐   **10.** In a COMPUTE statement, with no parentheses, multiplication is always done before subtraction.

☐   ☐   **11.** In a COMPUTE statement, with no parentheses, multiplication is always done before division.

☐   ☐   **12.** Parentheses are sometimes required in a COMPUTE statement.

☐   ☐   **13.** The COMPUTE statement changes the value of only one data name.

☐   ☐   **14.** The IF statement must always contain the ELSE option.

☐   ☐   **15.** The PERFORM statement transfers control to a paragraph elsewhere in the program, and returns control to the statement immediately following when the paragraph has completed execution.

☐   ☐   **16.** A program may contain more than one STOP RUN statement.

☐   ☐   **17.** STOP RUN must be the last statement in the procedure division.

☐   ☐   **18.** The ADVANCING option is mandatory in the WRITE statement.

☐   ☐   **19.** The READ statement contains a record name.

☐   ☐   **20.** The WRITE statement contains a record name.

☐   ☐   **21.** The OPEN and CLOSE statements are optional.

☐   ☐   **22.** The period has little effect in an IF statement.

□ □ **23.** An IF statement can cause the execution of several other statements.

□ □ **24.** If the ELSE clause is satisfied in an IF statement, it can cause execution of several statements.

PROBLEMS

1. Some of the following arithmetic statements are invalid. Identify those which are invalid, and state why they are unacceptable to the COBOL compiler.
(a) ADD A B C.
(b) SUBTRACT 10 FROM A, B.
(c) SUBTRACT A FROM 10.
(d) ADD A TO B GIVING C.
(e) SUBTRACT A FROM B GIVING C.
(f) MULTIPLY A BY 10.
(g) MULTIPLY 10 BY A.
(h) MULTIPLY A BY 10 GIVING B, C.
(i) DIVIDE A BY B.
(j) DIVIDE A INTO B.
(k) DIVIDE A INTO B GIVING C.
(l) DIVIDE B BY A GIVING C.
(m) COMPUTE X = A + B.
(n) COMPUTE X = 2(A + B).
(o) COMPUTE V = 20 / A − C.

2. Complete the table. In each instance, refer to the *initial* values of A, B, C, and D.

Data name	A	B	C	D
Value *before* execution	4	8	12	1
Value *after* execution of				
ADD 1 TO D, B.				
ADD A B C GIVING D.				
ADD A B C TO D.				
SUBTRACT A B FROM C.				
SUBTRACT A B FROM C GIVING D.				
MULTIPLY A BY B, C.				
MULTIPLY B BY A.				
DIVIDE A INTO C.				
DIVIDE C BY A.				
DIVIDE C BY B GIVING D REMAINDER A.				
COMPUTE D = A + B / 2 * D.				
COMPUTE D = (A + B) / (2 * D).				
COMPUTE D = A + B / (2 * D).				
COMPUTE D = (A + B) / 2 * D.				
COMPUTE D = A + (B / 2) * D.				

3. Complete the table for valid statements only. In each instance, refer to the *initial* value of A, B, C, and D. If a MOVE statement is invalid, indicate it as such and state the reason why.

Date Name	A	B	C	D
Value *before* execution	5	6	7	8
Value *after* execution of				
MOVE C TO SPACE.				
MOVE ZERO TO A, B, C.				
MOVE D TO B.				
MOVE SPACE TO A, B.				
MOVE 'X' TO A.				
MOVE A TO 'X'.				

4. Develop procedure division code to calculate weekly withholding taxes as follows:

16% on first $200.
18% on amounts between $200 and $240.
20% on anything over $240.

Thus if John Jones earned $300, his withholding tax would be

16% of $200	$= .16 \times 200 =$	32.00
+18% on amount between $200 and $240	$= .18 \times 40 \ =$	7.20
+20% on amount over $240	$= .20 \times 60 \ =$	12.00
	TOTAL $=$	$51.20

Assume that GROSS-PAY is already calculated. Further assume that the proper data division entries have been established to handle decimal points (more on this in Chapter 4).

5. Some of the following statements are invalid. Indicate those which are, and state why they are invalid. (Assume FILE-ONE and FILE-TWO are file names, and RECORD-ONE is a record name.)
   (a) OPEN INPUT RECORD-ONE.
   (b) OPEN INPUT FILE-ONE OUTPUT FILE-TWO.
   (c) OPEN INPUT FILE-ONE.
   (d) CLOSE OUTPUT FILE-ONE.
   (e) READ FILE-ONE.
   (f) READ FILE-ONE AT END PERFORM END-OF-JOB-ROUTINE.
   (g) READ RECORD-ONE AT END PERFORM END-OF-JOB-ROUTINE.
   (h) WRITE RECORD-ONE.
   (i) WRITE RECORD-ONE AFTER ADVANCING TWO LINES.
   (j) WRITE RECORD-ONE BEFORE ADVANCING TWO LINES.
   (k) CLOSE FILE-ONE FILE-TWO.
   (l) WRITE FILE-ONE.
   (m) WRITE RECORD-ONE AFTER ADVANCING PAGE.

6. Write COBOL COMPUTE statements to accomplish the intended logic:
   (a) $x = a + b + c$

   (b) $x = \dfrac{a + bc}{2}$

   (c) $x = a^2 + b^2 + c^2$

   (d) $x = \dfrac{a + b}{2} - c$

   (e) $x = a + b$

   (f) $x = \sqrt{\dfrac{a + b}{2c}}$

   (g) $x = \sqrt{\dfrac{a^2 + b^2}{c^2 - d^2}} + 2e$

7. Write procedure division code for the following:

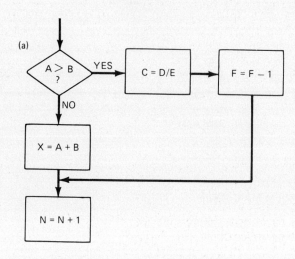
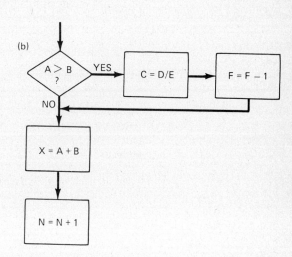

8. Given the following procedure division:

```
PROCEDURE DIVISION.
FIRST-PARAGRAPH.
    MOVE ZEROS TO FIELD-A FIELD-B.
    PERFORM SECOND-PARAGRAPH.
    PERFORM THIRD-PARAGRAPH.
    PERFORM SECOND-PARAGRAPH.
    STOP RUN.
SECOND-PARAGRAPH.
    ADD 10 TO FIELD-A.
    ADD 20 TO FIELD-B.
THIRD-PARAGRAPH.
    MULTIPLY FIELD-A BY FIELD-B GIVING FIELD-C.
    DIVIDE FIELD-A INTO FIELD-B GIVING FIELD-D.
```

(a) What are the final values for FIELD-A, FIELD-B, FIELD-C, and FIELD-D?

(b) How many times is each paragraph executed?

9. Complete the following table, showing the contents of the receiving field. If a particular move is invalid, indicate it as such (assume elementary moves only).

	Sending field		Receiving field	
	Picture	*Contents*	*Picture*	*Contents*
(a)	A(4)	H O P E	X(4)	
(b)	A(4)	H O P E	9(4)	
(c)	A(4)	H O P E	A(3)	
(d)	A(4)	H O P E	X(5)	
(e)	9(4)	6 7 8 9	A(4)	
(f)	9(4)	6 7 8 9	9(3)	
(g)	9(4)	6 7 8 9	9(5)	
(h)	999V9	6 7 8 9	9(4)	
(i)	999V9	6 7 8 9	9(4)V9	
(j)	999V9	6 7 8 9	9(3)V99	
(k)	999V9	6 7 8 9	99V99	

Note: The V in questions (h), (i), (j), and (k) indicates an assumed decimal point (see Chapter 4).

10. Consider the following two sets of COBOL code, which differ only in their indentation and the presence of an extra period in the second example. Discuss the differences in resulting action caused by the presence of the extra period. Use flowcharts to illustrate your answer.

EXAMPLE 1

```
IF UNION-MEMBER = 'YES'
    PERFORM MAIL-UNION
ELSE                              No Period
    ADD 1 TO NON-MEMBER-TOTAL
    PERFORM MAIL-COMPANY.
```

EXAMPLE 2

```
          IF UNION-MEMBER = 'YES'
             PERFORM MAIL-UNION
          ELSE                              ┌── Extra Period
             ADD 1 TO NON-MEMBER-TOTAL.◄
          PERFORM MAIL-COMPANY.
```

11. Supply Procedure Division Statements as indicated:
   (a) Code two equivalent statements, an ADD and a COMPUTE, to add 1 to the counter NUMBER-QUALIFIED-EMPLOYEES.
   (b) Code a COBOL statement to add the contents of five fields, MONDAY-SALES, TUESDAY-SALES, WEDNESDAY-SALES, THURSDAY-SALES, and FRIDAY-SALES, storing the result in WEEKLY-SALES.
   (c) Code a COBOL statement to subtract the fields FED-TAX, STATE-TAX, FICA, and VOLUNTARY-DEDUCTIONS, from GROSS-PAY, and put the result in NET-PAY.
   (d) Code a single COBOL statement to calculate NET-AMOUNT-DUE, which is equal to the GROSS-SALE minus a 2% discount.
   (e) Recode part (d), using *two* statements (a MULTIPLY and a SUBTRACT).
   (f) Code a COBOL statement to compute GROSS-PAY, which is equal to HOURS-WORKED times HOURLY-RATE.
   (g) Code a *single* COBOL statement to compute GROSS-PAY, which is equal to REG-HOURS-WORKED times HOURLY-RATE plus OVERTIME-HOURS times HOURLY-RATE times 1.5.
   (h) Code a COBOL statement to determine AVERAGE-SALARY by dividing TOTAL-SALARY by NUMBER-OF-EMPLOYEES.
   (i) Code a COBOL COMPUTE equivalent to the algebraic statement:

$$x = \frac{(a+b)c}{de}$$

   (j) Code a COBOL COMPUTE equivalent to the algebraic statement:

$$x = \frac{-b + \sqrt{b^2 - 4ac}}{2a}$$

   Note that raising a number to the .5 power is equivalent to calculating its square root.

Chapter 4

THE OTHER DIVISIONS

OVERVIEW

Chapter 1 began with a rapid introduction to COBOL. We learned that there are four divisions in a COBOL program and that they must come in a specified order: IDENTIFICATION, ENVIRONMENT, DATA, and PROCEDURE. In the previous chapter we studied the procedure division, which contains the logic of a COBOL program. Now we shall look at the other divisions in order to write a complete COBOL program.

The emphasis in this chapter is on the data division. We shall begin with level numbers and picture clauses. Next we shall look at the file and working-storage sections. Finally, we shall learn how to edit data and "dress-up" printed reports.

The chapter ends with the development of a complete program for tuition billing. It is a substantial problem and will require you to use everything covered so far. However, at the conclusion of this chapter you will be well on your way toward writing meaningful programs.

IDENTIFICATION DIVISION

The identification division is the first of the four divisions in a COBOL program. Its function is to provide identifying information about the program, such as author, date written, security, etc. The division consists of a division header and up to six paragraphs, as follows:

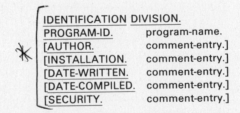

```
IDENTIFICATION DIVISION.
PROGRAM-ID.        program-name.
[AUTHOR.           comment-entry.]
[INSTALLATION.     comment-entry.]
[DATE-WRITTEN.     comment-entry.]
[DATE-COMPILED.    comment-entry.]
[SECURITY.         comment-entry.]
```

Only the division header and PROGRAM-ID paragraph are required. The remaining paragraphs are optional and contain documentation about the program. The DATE-COMPILED paragraph is worthy of special mention. If it is used, the compiler will automatically insert the current date during program compilation. A completed identification division is shown below:

```
IDENTIFICATION DIVISION.
PROGRAM-ID.      TUITION.
```

52

```
AUTHOR.         GRAUER AND CRAWFORD.
INSTALLATION.   GRAUER AND CRAWFORD SCHOOL OF DATA PROCESSING.
DATE-WRITTEN.   SEPTEMBER 1, 1981.
DATE-COMPILED.  The compiler will supply the date of compilation.
SECURITY.       TOP SECRET—INSTRUCTORS ONLY.
```

Coding for the identification division follows the general rules described in Chapter 2. The division header and paragraph names begin in columns 8 to 11 (A margin). All other entries begin in or past column 12 (B margin).

ENVIRONMENT DIVISION

Initially, we consider two functions of the environment division:

1. It identifies the computer to be used for compiling and executing the program (usually one and the same). This is done in the configuration section.
2. It relates the files used in the program to I/O devices. This is done in the input-output section.

The nature of these functions makes the environment division heavily dependent on the computer on which one is working. Thus the environment division for a COBOL program on a Univac system is significantly different from that of a program for an IBM configuration. You should consult either your instructor or computer center for the proper entries at your installation.

The configuration section has the format

```
CONFIGURATION SECTION.
SOURCE-COMPUTER.  computer-name.
OBJECT-COMPUTER.  computer-name.
```

The section header and paragraph names begin in the A margin. The computer name entries begin in or past column 12.

The input-output section relates the files known to the COBOL program to the files known to the operating system. A *file* is a collection of *records* of similar purpose. In the engineering senior problem of Chapter 1, each data card is a record, and the set of data cards is known collectively as a file. Similarly, each printed line of output is a record, and the set of print lines is a file.

Each file in a COBOL program has its own SELECT statement and ASSIGN clause, which appear in the file-control paragraph of the input-output section of the environment division. The format of the ASSIGN clause varies from compiler to compiler. The coding below is taken from lines 8 to 11 in the engineering senior problem and is for an **IBM OS** system:

```
INPUT-OUTPUT SECTION.
FILE-CONTROL.
     SELECT CARD-FILE ASSIGN TO UT-S-SYSIN.
     SELECT PRINT-FILE ASSIGN TO UT-S-SYSOUT.
```

As before, section headers and paragraph names begin in the A margin (columns 8 to 11). SELECT statements begin in or past column 12.

The dependence of the environment division on the individual computer installation bears repeating. You should consult either your instructor or computer center for the proper statements to use in your program.

DATA DIVISION

The data division describes all data fields used in the program. The number of characters in each data item are specified and also classified as to type, e.g., numeric or alphabetic. Finally, the relationship among data is described. The description of data is accomplished through the picture clause and level numbers.

PICTURE Clause

All data names are described according to size and class. Size specifies the number of characters in a field. Class denotes the type of field. For the present we shall restrict type to alphabetic, numeric, or alphanumeric, denoted by A, 9, or X, respectively. The size of a field is indicated by the number of times the A, 9, or X is repeated. Thus a data name with a picture of AAAA or A(4) is a four-position alphabetic field. In similar fashion, 999 and X(5) denote a three-position numeric field and a five-position alphanumeric field, respectively.

Level Numbers

Data items in COBOL are classified as either elementary or group items. A *group* item is one that can be further divided, whereas an *elementary* item cannot be further divided. As an example, consider Figure 4.1, depicting a student exam card.

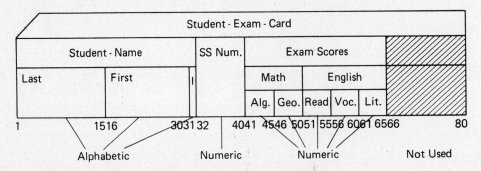

FIGURE 4.1 *Student Exam Card*

In Figure 4.1, student-name is considered a group item since it is divided into three fields: last-name, first-name, and initial. Last-name, first-name, and middle-initial are elementary items since they are not further divided. Social-security-number is an elementary item. Exam-scores is a group item, as are math and English. Algebra, geometry, reading, etc., are elementary items.

Level numbers are used to describe the hierarchy between group and elementary items; in effect, they show which elementary items comprise a group item. Level numbers can assume values of 01 to 49 inclusive, 66, 77, and 88. (Levels 66 and 88 have special meanings; 88-level entries are mentioned in Chapters 7 and 8; 66-level entries are not covered. 77-Level entries appear in the working-storage section of the data division and are discussed later in this chapter.) Level numbers and picture clauses are best described by example. Consider the data division statements of Figure 4.2, which correspond to the student exam card of Figure 4.1.

```
01   STUDENT-EXAM-CARD.
     05   STUDENT-NAME.
          10   LAST-NAME          PICTURE IS X(15).
          10   FIRST-NAME         PICTURE IS X(15).
          10   MID-INITIAL        PICTURE IS A.
     05   SOC-SEC-NUM             PICTURE IS 9(9).
     05   EXAM-SCORES.
          10   MATH.
               15   ALGEBRA       PICTURE IS 99999.
               15   GEOMETRY      PICTURE IS 9(5).
          10   ENGLISH.
               15   READING       PICTURE IS 99999.
               15   VOCABULARY    PICTURE IS 99999.
               15   LITERATURE    PICTURE IS 99999.
     05   FILLER                  PICTURE IS X(15).
```

FIGURE 4.2 *Data Division Code for Level Numbers and Picture Clauses*

The data division code of Figure 4.2 is in accordance with basic rules pertaining to level numbers:

1. 01 is used to denote the record as a whole.
2. 02–49 are used for subfields in the record.
3. Only elementary items have picture clauses.

Level numbers need not be consecutive as long as elementary items have a numerically higher level number than the group item to which they belong.

In Figure 4.2 STUDENT-EXAM-CARD has a level number of 01. STUDENT-NAME is a subfield of STUDENT-EXAM-CARD, and hence it has a higher level number (05). LAST-NAME, FIRST-NAME, and MID-INITIAL are subfields of STUDENT-NAME, and all have the level number 10. SOC-SEC-NUM and EXAM-SCORES are also subfields of STUDENT-EXAM-CARD and have the same level number as STUDENT-NAME. EXAM-SCORES in turn is subdivided into two group items, MATH and ENGLISH, which in turn are further subdivided into elementary items.

Each elementary item *must* have a picture clause to describe the data it contains. LAST-NAME has "PICTURE IS X(15)," denoting a 15-position alphanumeric field. (Names often have nonalphabetic characters, e.g., O'Brien, and hence should be classified alphanumeric rather than alphabetic.) There is no picture entry for STUDENT-NAME since that is a group item. The parentheses in a picture entry denote repetition; thus the entries of 9(5) and 99999 for ALGEBRA and GEOMETRY both depict 5-position numeric fields. Finally, note the FILLER entry with "PICTURE IS X(15)." FILLER denotes a field with no useful information, i.e., data that are not referenced in this program. X(15) denotes 15 positions of alphanumeric data. Since the student-exam-card of Figure 4.1 is presumed to contain 80 columns, all 80 columns must be accounted for. The last field (EXAM-SCORES, ENGLISH, or LITERATURE) ends in column 65; hence the need for an entry to account for the last 15 columns.

Considerable flexibility is permitted with level numbers and picture clauses. Any level numbers from 02 to 49 are permitted in describing subfields as long as the basic rules are followed. Thus 04, 08, and 12 could be used in lieu of 05, 10, and 15. Next the picture clause itself can assume any one of four forms: PICTURE IS, PICTURE, PIC IS, or PIC. Finally, parentheses may be used to signal repetition of a picture type; i.e., A(3) is equivalent to AAA. Figure 4.3 is an alternative way of coding Figure 4.2 with emphasis on the above flexibility.

FILE SECTION

The file section is typically the first section in the data division. It describes every file mentioned in a SELECT statement in the environment division. (If, however, there are no input-output files, then there is no need for the file section.)

```
01   STUDENT-EXAM-CARD.
     04   STUDENT-NAME.
          08   LAST-NAME        PIC X(15).
          08   FIRST-NAME       PIC X(15).
          08   MID-INITIAL      PIC A.
     04   SOC-SEC-NUM           PIC 9(9).
     04   EXAM SCORES.
          08   MATH.
               12   ALGEBRA     PIC 9(5).
               12   GEOMETRY    PIC 99999.
          08   ENGLISH.
               12   READING     PIC 9(5).
               12   VOCABULARY  PIC 99999.
               12   LITERATURE  PIC 99999.
     04   FILLER                PIC X(15).
```

FIGURE 4.3 *Data Division Code for Level Numbers and Picture Clauses: II*

The file section contains both file description (FD) and record description entries (i.e., level number and picture clause). We have already discussed the latter. An abbreviated format for the file description (FD) entry is as follows:

```
FD    file-name
      LABEL {RECORDS ARE} {OMITTED }
            {RECORD  IS }  {STANDARD}
      [RECORD CONTAINS integer-1 CHARACTERS]
      [DATA RECORD IS data-name-1]
```

FD itself appears in the A margin, followed by the file name beginning in column 12. The FD may contain several clauses, three of which are shown. Only the last clause has a period. The LABEL RECORDS clause is the only required entry, but it is accepted practice to code the others as well.

The FD provides information about the physical characteristics of a file. The RECORD CONTAINS clause specifies the number of characters per record (this entry should equal the sum of the picture clauses in the record description). The LABEL RECORDS clause has special meaning for tape and disk files (Chapters 15 and 16). For card and print files, however, we use the following entry: LABEL RECORDS ARE OMITTED. Finally, the DATA RECORD clause specifies the name of the 01 entry for that file. A completed FD for the file of student-exam-cards of Figure 4.1 is coded in Figure 4.4.

```
FD    STUDENT-FILE
      LABEL RECORDS ARE OMITTED
      RECORD CONTAINS 80 CHARACTERS
      DATA RECORD IS STUDENT-EXAM-CARD.
```

FIGURE 4.4 *FD for the file of Student-Exam-Cards*

In Figure 4.4 STUDENT-FILE is the *file* name that would appear in a SELECT statement for the file (see environment division in this chapter). STUDENT-EXAM-CARD is the *record* name, i.e., the 01 entry in Figure 4.2 or 4.3.

WORKING-STORAGE SECTION

The working-storage section is used for storing intermediate results and/or constants needed by the program. In effect, it defines data used by the program that are not read during program execution.

Working-storage typically contains two types of entries. The first is for independent, elementary items, i.e., those data names that have no hierarchical relationship to one another. These entries are assigned level number 77 and precede all other entries in working storage. Group items, beginning with level 01, are the second type of entry appearing in working storage. Group items follow 77-level entries and use level numbers as discussed earlier.

An example of a working-storage section appears in Figure 4.5.

A recent trend, however, is to do away with 77-level entries in favor of grouping similar entries under the same 01 entry in working-storage; see discussion in Chapter 6.

```
WORKING-STORAGE SECTION.
77    TOTAL-STUDENTS      PIC 9(3)      VALUE ZEROS.
77    PRICE-PER-CREDIT    PIC 99        VALUE 80.
01    HEADING-LINE.
      05   FILLER         PIC X(5)      VALUE SPACES.
      05   FILLER         PIC X(12)     VALUE 'STUDENT NAME'.
      05   FILLER         PIC X(5)      VALUE SPACES.
      05   FILLER         PIC X(5)      VALUE 'MAJOR'.
      05   FILLER         PIC X(106)    VALUE SPACES.
```

FIGURE 4.5 *An Example of the Working-Storage Section*

VALUE Clause

Figure 4.5 introduces the VALUE clause, which has the general form

<u>VALUE</u> IS literal

Literals are of three types: numeric (e.g., 80), nonnumeric (e.g., 'MAJOR'), and figurative constant (e.g., ZERO). Numeric and nonnumeric literals were discussed in Chapter 2 as a basic COBOL element. Figurative constants are COBOL reserved words with preassigned values. COBOL contains six of these constants, but only ZERO (equivalent forms are ZEROS and ZEROES) and SPACE (also SPACES) are discussed here.

The value clause associated with a particular data name must be consistent with the corresponding picture clause. It is *incorrect* to use a nonnumeric literal with a numeric picture or a numeric literal with a nonnumeric picture. Consider

```
(correct)     05   FIELD-A   PIC 9   VALUE 2.
(incorrect)   05   FIELD-B   PIC X   VALUE 2.
(incorrect)   05   FIELD-C   PIC 9   VALUE '2'.
(correct)     05   FIELD-D   PIC X   VALUE '2'.
```

Only the entries for FIELD-A and FIELD-D are correct. FIELD-B has a nonnumeric picture but a numeric value. FIELD-C has a numeric picture but a nonnumeric value (remember, anything enclosed in quotes is a nonnumeric literal).

Assumed Decimal Point

Incoming numeric data are not allowed to contain actual decimal points. On first reading, that statement may be somewhat hard to take, so let's repeat it in different words. If incoming decimal data are contained on cards, no decimal points will be punched on the cards. Undoubtedly this should "bother" you. How, for example, does one read a field containing dollars and cents? The answer is an assumed decimal point.

Consider the COBOL entry

```
05   HOURLY-RATE   PICTURE IS 9V99.
```

✳ Everything is familiar except the "V" embedded in the picture clause. The "V" means an *implied* decimal point; i.e., HOURLY-RATE is a three-digit (there are three 9's) numeric field, with two of the digits coming after the decimal point.

To check your understanding, assume that 9876543210 is punched in columns 1 to 10 of an incoming data card and that the following data division entries apply:

```
01   INCOMING-DATA-CARD.
     05   FIELD-A     PIC 9V99.
     05   FIELD-B     PIC 99V9.
     05   FIELD-C     PIC 9.
     05   FIELD-D     PIC V999.
     05   FILLER      PIC X(70).
```

The values of FIELD-A, FIELD-B, FIELD-C, and FIELD-D are 9.87, 65.4, 3, and .210, respectively. FIELD-A is contained in the first three columns with two digits after the decimal point. FIELD-B is contained in the next three columns, i.e., in columns 4, 5, and 6, with one digit after the decimal point. FIELD-C is contained in column 7 with no decimal places. Finally, FIELD-D is contained in columns 8, 9, and 10, with three decimal places. The last 70 columns do not contain data, as indicated by the FILLER entry.

Editing Numeric Data

Incoming numeric fields typically do not contain anything other than digits. On the other hand, it is highly desirable to have dollar signs, commas, decimal points, etc., appear in printed reports.

The problem is resolved by the use of editing symbols. Consider the two entries for FIELD-A and FIELD-A-EDITED:

```
05   FIELD-A          PIC 9V99.
05   FIELD-A-EDITED   PIC 9.99.
```

FIELD-A is a three-digit numeric field, with two digits after the decimal point. FIELD-A-EDITED is a four-position edit field containing an actual decimal point. In a COBOL program all calculations would be done using FIELD-A. Then, just prior to printing, FIELD-A is moved to FIELD-A-EDITED, and the latter field is printed. For example,

Before MOVE:

FIELD-A `7 8 3`   FIELD-A-EDITED `? . ? ?`

After execution of MOVE FIELD-A TO FIELD-A-EDITED:

FIELD-A `7 8 3`   FIELD-A-EDITED `7 . 8 3`

Notice that the decimal point actually takes a position in FIELD-A-EDITED. However, it does not occupy a position in FIELD-A, as it (the decimal point) is only implied.

There are many editing symbols in COBOL, and complete discussion is deferred to Chapter 8. For the present, we shall discuss the $, comma, and decimal point.

The appearance of a single $ causes a dollar sign to print in the indicated position.

```
05   FIELD-B          PIC 9(3)V99.
05   FIELD-B-EDITED   PIC $9(3).99.
```

Before MOVE:

FIELD-B `6 5 4 3 2`   FIELD-B-EDITED `$ ? ? ? . ? ?`

After execution of MOVE FIELD-B TO FIELD-B-EDITED:

FIELD-B `6 5 4 3 2`   FIELD-B-EDITED `$ 6 5 4 . 3 2`

Notice that the dollar sign and decimal point both take up a position in FIELD-B-EDITED.

It is also possible to obtain a "floating" dollar sign by using multiple dollar signs in the edited field. In this instance a single $ prints immediately to the left of the leftmost significant digit. Thus,

```
05   FIELD-C          PIC 9(3)V99.
05   FIELD-C-EDITED   PIC $$$$.99.
```

Before MOVE:

FIELD-C `0 0 1 2 3`   FIELD-C-EDITED `$ $ $ $ . ? ?`

After execution of MOVE FIELD-C TO FIELD-C-EDITED:

FIELD-C `0 0 1 2 3`   FIELD-C-EDITED `    $ 1 . 2 3`

SECTION II: THE COBOL LANGUAGE

A single dollar sign prints immediately before the leftmost digit in the field. FIELD-C-EDITED is a seven-position field, but the first two positions hold blanks.

The presence of a comma as an editing symbol causes a comma to print if it is preceded by a significant digit. If, however, a comma is preceded only by zeros, then it is suppressed. Consider

```
05   FIELD-D            PIC 9(4).
05   FIELD-D-EDITED     PIC $$,$$9.
```

Before Move:

FIELD-D | 8 | 7 | 6 | 5 | FIELD-D-EDITED | $ | $ | , | $ | $ | ? |

After execution of MOVE FIELD-D TO FIELD-D-EDITED:

FIELD-D | 8 | 7 | 6 | 5 | FIELD-D-EDITED | $ | 8 | , | 7 | 6 | 5 |

The comma prints in the indicated position. Suppose, however, that the contents of FIELD-D were 0087, instead of 8765. Now FIELD-D-EDITED would be

Before Move:

FIELD-D | 0 | 0 | 8 | 7 | FIELD-D-EDITED | $ | $ | , | $ | $ | ? |

After execution of MOVE FIELD-D TO FIELD-D-EDITED:

FIELD-D | 0 | 0 | 8 | 7 | FIELD-D-EDITED | | | | $ | 8 | 7 |

Notice that the dollar sign floats and that the comma is suppressed. Note also that all numeric moves are accomplished so that decimal alignment is maintained with truncation or addition of insignificant zeros. Information on editing is summarized in Table 4.1.

TABLE 4.1 Use of Editing Symbols

Source field		Receiving field	
PICTURE	CONTENTS	PICTURE	CONTENTS
9(4)	0678	9(4)	0678
9(4)	0678	$9(4)	$0678
9(4)	0678	$$$$$	$678
9(4)V99	123456	9(4).99	1234.56
9(4)V99	123456	$9(4).99	$1234.56
9(4)V99	123456	$9,999.99	$1,234.56
9(4)	0008	$,$$$	$8
9(4)V9	12345	9(4)	1234
9(4)V9	12345	9(4).99	1234.50

WRITING A COMPLETE PROGRAM

Our text began with the presentation of a complete COBOL program in Chapter 1 (the engineering senior program). Our objective at that time was to remove the aura surrounding computer programming and to give the reader an immediate feel for COBOL. Since that time, we have come a long way. In Chapter 2 we learned the elements of COBOL, the rules of the coding sheet, and the procedure for problem solving. In Chapter 3 we studied the basic verbs of the procedure division. In this chapter we learned about the other divisions. Now we are ready to put this material together and solve a detailed problem about student billing.

Specifications for the student billing problem are as follows:

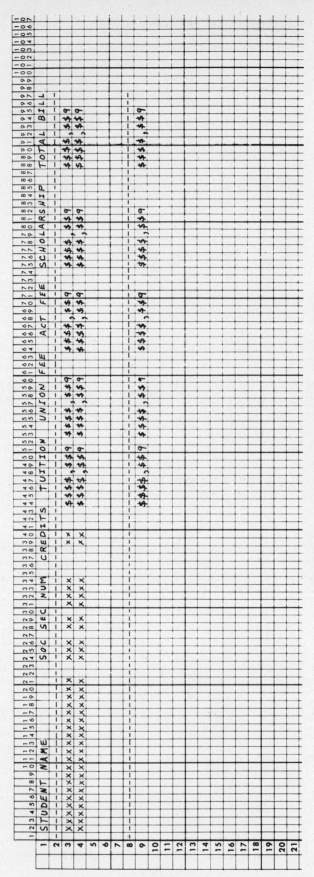

FIGURE 4.6 *Required Output for Tuition Billing Problem*

SECTION II: THE COBOL LANGUAGE

INPUT: A record has been prepared for every student in XYZ University with information as follows:

Field	Card Columns	Picture
Student name	1–20	A(20)
Social security no.	21–29	9(9)
Credits	30–31	99
Union member	32	A
Scholarship	33–36	9(4)

PROCESSING: Student bills are to be calculated for every student as follows:

Tuition	$80 per credit
Union fee	$25 for members, $0 for nonmembers (members have a "Y" in column 32)
Activity fee	$25: 6 credits or less
	$50: 7 to 12 credits
	$75: more than 12 credits
Scholarship	Amount, if any, is punched in columns 33 to 36
Student bill	Tuition + union fee + activity fee − scholarship

In addition, university-wide totals for each of these fields are required.

OUTPUT: Printed output is to be in accordance with Figure 4.6. Note the presence of literal information in the heading line and the dashed line after the heading line and before the total line. Also notice the use of edited data fields. A page heading routine is *not* required; i.e., the heading line is required to appear only once before the first student record (see Problem 7).

The logical requirements of the tuition billing problem are shown in Figure 4.7. Figure 4.7a contains a flowchart and Figure 4.7b depicts pseudocode. Realize that both the flowchart and pseudocode express the same thing, i.e., the logic required to solve a problem.

The traditional flowchart is becoming less popular owing to the increased use of pseudocode. One reason for this can be seen by comparing Figures 4.7a and b. The logic in the iteration structure of Figure 4.7a flows from the *bottom up*, which obscures the logic flow of the overall flowchart. Pseudocode, however, flows from the *top down*, a more natural way of program development.

Regardless of which technique you choose, neither the blocks in a flowchart nor the statements in pseudocode will correspond one to one with statements in a procedure division. This is as it should be. A flowchart and/or pseudocode is intended only as a guide in writing a program. Either depicts the logic in that program, but at a higher level of aggregation. Indeed, if we insisted on one-to-one correspondence, we would in effect be writing the program twice.

Figure 4.8 contains the COBOL program for the tuition billing problem. It encompasses all the material covered to date and indeed is somewhat formidable the first time you see it. We suggest you take it in pieces and review those sections of the text as you need them. Some highlights:

1. The identification division: COBOL lines 1 to 3.
2. The environment division: COBOL lines 5 to 12. The two SELECT statements are applicable to our installation and may not be appropriate at yours.
3. The FD's for CARD-FILE and PRINT-FILE: COBOL lines 16 to 19 and 27 to 30.
4. The description for the incoming data: COBOL lines 20 to 26. Notice how this matches the problem description and the presence of the FILLER entry.
5. The use of edit symbols in a detail line: COBOL lines 31 to 48. The symbol "B" causes blanks to be inserted in the social security number (line 35). This is discussed further in Chapter 8.
6. 77-Level entries in working-storage: COBOL lines 51 to 60. Notice how all quantities are initialized. (A later version of this program, Figure 6.4, will eliminate the 77-level entries in favor of grouping related items under a common 01.)

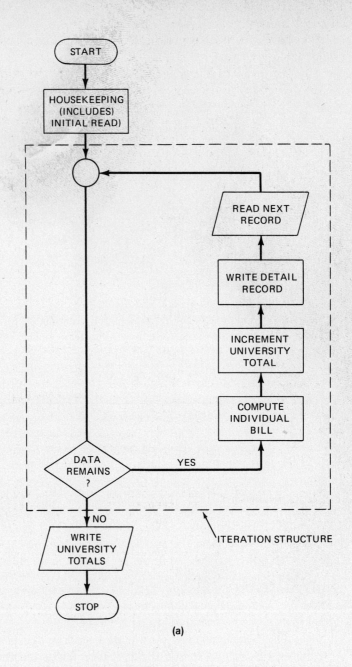

(a)

Read student-file at end indicate no more data
Write heading line(s)
┌ Do while data remains
│   Compute individual bill
│   Increment university totals
│   Write detail record
│   Read student file at end indicate no more data
└ END DO
Write university totals
Close files
Stop run

(b)

FIGURE 4.7 *Logical Requirements for the Tuition Billing Problem:* (a) *Flowchart for Tuition Billing Problem* (b) *Pseudocode for Tuition Billing Problem*

7. Two 01 entries in working-storage: COBOL lines 61 to 82. This is done to establish a heading line.
8. The initial read statement in the MAINLINE paragraph of the procedure division.
9. The PERFORM statement of lines 92 and 93, which will continually execute the paragraph PROCESS-A-CARD (lines 98 to 128) as long as there are data. Note well that the *last* statement of the performed routine is a READ, which sets a switch to turn off the perform when the end of file is reached.
10. Incrementing university totals: COBOL lines 109 to 113.
11. Writing a detail line for each student: COBOL lines 116 to 125.
12. The use of comments, denoted by an asterisk in column 7: COBOL lines 108 and 115.

The COBOL program of Figure 4.8 was tested, and sample output appears in Figure 4.9.

```
00001          IDENTIFICATION DIVISION.
00002          PROGRAM-ID.    'TUITION'.
00003          AUTHOR.        THE BURSAR.
00004
00005          ENVIRONMENT DIVISION.
00006          CONFIGURATION SECTION.
00007          SOURCE-COMPUTER.  IBM-370.
00008          OBJECT-COMPUTER.  IBM-370.
00009          INPUT-OUTPUT SECTION.
00010          FILE-CONTROL.
00011              SELECT CARD-FILE ASSIGN TO UT-S-SYSIN.
00012              SELECT PRINT-FILE ASSIGN TO UT-S-SYSOUT.
00013                                          SELECT and FD for CARD-FILE
00014          DATA DIVISION.
00015          FILE SECTION.
00016          FD  CARD-FILE
00017          LABEL RECORDS ARE OMITTED
00018          RECORD CONTAINS 80 CHARACTERS
00019          DATA RECORD IS STUDENT-CARD.
00020          01  STUDENT-CARD.
00021              05  STUDENT-NAME        PICTURE IS A(20).
00022   Description 05  SOC-SEC-NO         PICTURE IS 9(9).
00023   of incoming 05  CREDITS            PICTURE IS 9(2).
00024   record      05  UNION-MEMBER       PICTURE IS A.
00025              05  SCHOLARSHIP        PICTURE IS 9(4).
00026              05  FILLER             PICTURE IS X(44).
00027          FD  PRINT-FILE
00028          LABEL RECORDS ARE OMITTED
00029          RECORD CONTAINS 133 CHARACTERS
00030          DATA RECORD IS PRINT-LINE.
00031          01  PRINT-LINE.
00032              05  FILLER             PICTURE IS X.
00033              05  PRINT-STUDENT-NAME PICTURE IS A(20).
00034              05  FILLER             PICTURE IS X(2).
00035              05  PRINT-SOC-SEC-NO   PICTURE IS 999B99B9999.
00036   Definition 05  FILLER             PICTURE IS X(4).
00037   of detail  05  PRINT-CREDITS      PICTURE IS 99.
00038   line       05  FILLER             PICTURE IS X(3).
00039              05  PRINT-TUITION      PICTURE IS $$$$,$$9.
00040              05  FILLER             PICTURE IS X.
00041              05  PRINT-UNION-FEE    PICTURE IS $$$$,$$9.
00042              05  FILLER             PICTURE IS X(3).
00043              05  PRINT-ACTIVITY-FEE PICTURE IS $$$$,$$9.
00044              05  FILLER             PICTURE IS X(3).
00045              05  PRINT-SCHOLARSHIP  PICTURE IS $$$$,$$9.
00046              05  FILLER             PICTURE IS X(5).
00047              05  PRINT-IND-BILL     PICTURE IS $$$$,$$9.
00048              05  FILLER             PICTURE IS X(38).
00049                                                Initialization of
00050          WORKING-STORAGE SECTION.             77 level entries
00051          77  DATA-REMAINS-SWITCH    PICTURE IS X(2)  VALUE SPACES.
00052          77  TUITION                PICTURE IS 9(4)  VALUE ZEROS.
00053          77  ACTIVITY-FEE           PICTURE IS 9(2)  VALUE ZEROS.
00054          77  UNION-FEE              PICTURE IS 9(2)  VALUE ZEROS.
00055          77  INDIVIDUAL-BILL        PICTURE IS 9(6)  VALUE ZEROS.
```

FIGURE 4.8 *Student Billing Problem*

```
00056     77  TOTAL-TUITION               PICTURE IS 9(6)  VALUE ZEROS.
00057     77  TOTAL-SCHOLARSHIP           PICTURE IS 9(6)  VALUE ZEROS.
00058     77  TOTAL-ACTIVITY-FEE          PICTURE IS 9(6)  VALUE ZEROS.
00059     77  TOTAL-UNION-FEE             PICTURE IS 9(6)  VALUE ZEROS.
00060     77  TOTAL-IND-BILL              PICTURE IS 9(6)  VALUE ZEROS.
00061     01  DASHED-LINE.
00062         05  FILLER              PICTURE IS X      VALUE SPACES.
00063         05  FILLER              PICTURE IS X(97)  VALUE ALL '-'.
00064         05  FILLER              PICTURE IS X(35)  VALUE SPACES.
00065     01  HEADER-LINE.
00066         05  FILLER          PICTURE IS X.
00067         05  HDG-NAME        PICTURE IS X(12)  VALUE 'STUDENT NAME'.
00068         05  FILLER          PICTURE IS X(10)  VALUE SPACES.
00069         05  HDG-SOC-SEC     PICTURE IS X(11)  VALUE 'SOC SEC NUM'.
00070         05  FILLER          PICTURE IS X(2)   VALUE SPACES.
00071         05  HDG-CREDITS     PICTURE IS X(7)   VALUE 'CREDITS'.
00072         05  FILLER          PICTURE IS X(2)   VALUE SPACES.
00073         05  HDG-TUITION     PICTURE IS X(7)   VALUE 'TUITION'.
00074         05  FILLER          PICTURE IS X(2)   VALUE SPACES.
00075         05  HDG-UNION-FEE   PICTURE IS X(9)   VALUE 'UNION FEE'.
00076         05  FILLER          PICTURE IS X(2)   VALUE SPACES.
00077         05  HDG-ACTIVITY    PICTURE IS X(7)   VALUE 'ACT FEE'.
00078         05  FILLER          PICTURE IS X(2)   VALUE SPACES.
00079         05  HDG-SCHOLAR     PICTURE IS X(11)  VALUE 'SCHOLARSHIP'.
00080         05  FILLER          PICTURE IS X(2)   VALUE SPACES.
00081         05  HDG-TOTAL-BILL  PICTURE IS X(10)  VALUE 'TOTAL BILL'.
00082         05  FILLER          PICTURE IS X(36)  VALUE SPACES.
00083     PROCEDURE DIVISION.
00084     MAINLINE.
00085         OPEN INPUT CARD-FILE, OUTPUT PRINT-FILE.
00086         MOVE HEADER-LINE TO PRINT-LINE.
00087         WRITE PRINT-LINE AFTER ADVANCING PAGE.
00088         MOVE DASHED-LINE TO PRINT-LINE.
00089         WRITE PRINT-LINE AFTER ADVANCING 1 LINE.
00090         READ CARD-FILE
00091             AT END MOVE 'NO' TO DATA-REMAINS-SWITCH.
00092         PERFORM PROCESS-A-CARD
00093             UNTIL DATA-REMAINS-SWITCH = 'NO'.
00094         PERFORM WRITE-UNIVERSITY-TOTALS.
00095         CLOSE CARD-FILE, PRINT-FILE.
00096         STOP RUN.
00097
00098     PROCESS-A-CARD.
00099         COMPUTE TUITION = 80 * CREDITS.
00100         MOVE ZERO TO UNION-FEE.
00101         IF UNION-MEMBER = 'Y' MOVE 25 TO UNION-FEE.
00102         MOVE 25 TO ACTIVITY-FEE.
00103         IF CREDITS > 6 MOVE 50 TO ACTIVITY-FEE.
00104         IF CREDITS > 12 MOVE 75 TO ACTIVITY-FEE.
00105         COMPUTE INDIVIDUAL-BILL = TUITION + UNION-FEE + ACTIVITY-FEE
00106             - SCHOLARSHIP.
00107
00108     *** INCREMENT UNIVERSITY TOTALS
00109         ADD TUITION TO TOTAL-TUITION.
00110         ADD UNION-FEE TO TOTAL-UNION-FEE.
00111         ADD ACTIVITY-FEE TO TOTAL-ACTIVITY-FEE.
00112         ADD INDIVIDUAL-BILL TO TOTAL-IND-BILL.
00113         ADD SCHOLARSHIP TO TOTAL-SCHOLARSHIP.
00114
00115     *** WRITE DETAIL LINE
00116         MOVE SPACES TO PRINT-LINE.
00117         MOVE STUDENT-NAME TO PRINT-STUDENT-NAME.
00118         MOVE SOC-SEC-NO TO PRINT-SOC-SEC-NO.
00119         MOVE CREDITS TO PRINT-CREDITS.
00120         MOVE TUITION TO PRINT-TUITION.
00121         MOVE UNION-FEE TO PRINT-UNION-FEE.
00122         MOVE ACTIVITY-FEE TO PRINT-ACTIVITY-FEE.
00123         MOVE SCHOLARSHIP TO PRINT-SCHOLARSHIP.
00124         MOVE INDIVIDUAL-BILL TO PRINT-IND-BILL.
00125         WRITE PRINT-LINE AFTER ADVANCING 1 LINE.
00126
00127         READ CARD-FILE
00128             AT END MOVE 'NO' TO DATA-REMAINS-SWITCH.
00129
```

Use of figurative constant

Definition of heading line

Writing the heading line

Initial read

Calculation of ACTIVITY-FEE (can be replaced by a nested IF - See Chapter 6)

Building a detail line

READ statement goes at end of performed routine

FIGURE 4.8 *(continued)*

```
00130              WRITE-UNIVERSITY-TOTALS.
00131                  MOVE DASHED-LINE TO PRINT-LINE.
00132                  WRITE PRINT-LINE AFTER ADVANCING 1 LINE.
00133                  MOVE SPACES TO PRINT-LINE.
00134                  MOVE TOTAL-TUITION TO PRINT-TUITION.
00135                  MOVE TOTAL-UNION-FEE TO PRINT-UNION-FEE.
00136                  MOVE TOTAL-ACTIVITY-FEE TO PRINT-ACTIVITY-FEE.
00137                  MOVE TOTAL-SCHOLARSHIP TO PRINT-SCHOLARSHIP.
00138                  MOVE TOTAL-IND-BILL TO PRINT-IND-BILL.
00139                  WRITE PRINT-LINE AFTER ADVANCING 2 LINES.
```

FIGURE 4.8 *(continued)*

STUDENT NAME	SOC SEC NUM	CREDITS	TUITION	UNION FEE	ACT FEE	SCHOLARSHIP	TOTAL BILL
JOHN SMITH	123 45 6789	15	$1,200	$25	$75	$0	$1,300
HENRY JAMES	987 65 4321	15	$1,200	$0	$75	$500	$775
SUSAN BAKER	111 22 3333	09	$720	$0	$50	$500	$270
JOHN PART-TIMER	456 21 3546	03	$240	$25	$25	$0	$290
PEGGY JONES	456 45 6456	15	$1,200	$25	$75	$0	$1,300
H. HEAVY-WORKER	789 52 1234	18	$1,440	$0	$75	$0	$1,515
BENJAMINE LEE	876 87 6876	18	$1,440	$0	$75	$0	$1,515
			$7,440		$450	$1,000	$6,965

FIGURE 4.9 *Sample Output of Tuition Billing Problem*

SUMMARY

We certainly have covered a lot of material since we began. No doubt your head is swimming with vaguely familiar terms: A-margin, division-header, paragraph-name, etc. Our objective is for you to write meaningful COBOL programs, not to have you memorize what must appear to be an endless list of rules. You must eventually remember certain things, but we have found the best approach is to pattern your first few COBOL programs after existing examples. To that end, we have spent considerable time developing the engineering senior and tuition billing problems. Everything you need to know to get started is contained in those listings (Figures 1.8 and 4.8) if only you will take the time to look. As a further aid, see Figure 4.10, which contains a skeleton outline of a COBOL program and some helpful hints.

Finally, we shall present a list of guidelines for writing COBOL programs:

1. The four divisions must appear in specified order: identification, environment, data, and procedure. Division headers begin in column 8 and always appear on a line by themselves.
2. The environment and data divisions contain sections with fixed names. The identification division does not contain any sections. (The procedure division may contain programmer-defined sections; however, this is usually not done in beginning programs.)
3. The data division is the only division without paragraph names. In the identification and environment divisions the paragraph names are fixed. In the procedure division, they are determined by the programmer. Paragraph names begin in column 8.
4. Any entry not required to begin in column 8 may begin in or past column 12.
5. The COBOL program executes instructions sequentially as they appear in the procedure division, unless a transfer of control statement, for example PERFORM, is encountered.
6. Every file must be opened and closed. A file name will appear in at least four statements: SELECT, FD, OPEN, and CLOSE. In addition, the READ statement will contain the file name of an input file, whereas the WRITE statement contains the record name of an output file.
7. Every program must contain at least one STOP RUN statement.

One final word: *Programming is learned by doing.* You can read forever, but reading alone will not teach you COBOL. You *must write* programs for this material to have real meaning. The true learning experience comes when you pick up your own listings in the machine room.

```
IDENTIFICATION DIVISION.
PROGRAM-ID.    8-Character name.
AUTHOR.        Your name.
ENVIRONMENT DIVISION.
CONFIGURATION SECTION.
SOURCE-COMPUTER.    Computer name.
OBJECT-COMPUTER.    Computer name.
INPUT-OUTPUT SECTION.
FILE-CONTROL.
      SELECT CARD-FILE ASSIGN TO . . . . . . .
      SELECT PRINT-FILE ASSIGN TO . . . . . .
DATA DIVISION.
FILE SECTION.
FD   CARD-FILE
      LABEL RECORDS ARE OMITTED
      RECORD CONTAINS 80 CHARACTERS          ⎤ Typical FD for a card file.
      DATA RECORD IS STUDENT-CARD.           ⎦
01   STUDENT-CARD.
     05 etc.
FD   PRINT-FILE
      LABEL RECORDS ARE OMITTED
      RECORD CONTAINS 133 CHARACTERS         ⎤ Typical FD for a print file.
      DATA RECORD IS PRINT-LINE.             ⎦
01   PRINT-LINE.
     05 etc.
WORKING-STORAGE SECTION.
77  . . . . . . .
77  EOF-SWITCH    PIC XXX VALUE'NO'.    ] Controls performed routine
01  entries (if any)
PROCEDURE DIVISION.
MAINLINE.
      OPEN INPUT CARD-FILE OUTPUT PRINT-FILE.   ⎤ Housekeeping consists
      READ CARD-FILE                             | of opening files and
          AT END MOVE 'YES' TO EOF-SWITCH.       ⎦ the initial read.
      PERFORM PROCESS-RECORDS                    ⎤ COBOL implementation of
          UNTIL EOF-SWITCH = 'YES'.              ⎦ iteration structure.
      CLOSE CARD-FILE, PRINT-FILE.               ⎤ Termination includes closing
      STOP RUN.                                  ⎦ files and stop run.
PROCESS-RECORDS.
      .
      .
      .
      your logic here
      .
      .
      READ CARD-FILE                             ⎤ Last line of performed
          AT END MOVE 'YES' TO EOF-SWITCH.       ⎦ routine is a read.
```

FIGURE 4.10 *Skeleton Outline of a COBOL Program*

REVIEW EXERCISES

TRUE   FALSE

☐   ☐   **1.** The identification division may contain up to six paragraphs.

☐   ☐   **2.** The PROGRAM-ID paragraph is the only required paragraph in the identification division.

☐   ☐   **3.** A flowchart and pseudocode are equivalent ways of saying the same thing.

☐   ☐   **4.** A COBOL program that runs successfully on a UNIVAC system would also run successfully on an IBM system with no modification whatsoever.

☐   ☐   **5.** Level numbers may go from 1 to 77 inclusive.

☐   ☐   **6.** An 01-level entry cannot have a picture clause.

☐	☐	**7.** All elementary items have a picture clause.
☐	☐	**8.** 77-Level entries may appear anywhere in the data division.
☐	☐	**9.** 01-Level entries may appear in both the file and working-storage sections of the data division.
☐	☐	**10.** A data name at the 10 level will always be an elementary item.
☐	☐	**11.** A data name at the 05 level may or may not have a picture clause.
☐	☐	**12.** PICTURE, PICTURE IS, PIC, and PIC IS are *all* acceptable forms of the picture clause.
☐	☐	**13.** "PICTURE IS 9(3)" and "PICTURE IS 999" are equivalent entries.
☐	☐	**14.** The file section is required in every COBOL program.
☐	☐	**15.** The working-storage section is required in every COBOL program.
☐	☐	**16.** Blocks in a flowchart should correspond one to one with statements in the procedure division.

PROBLEMS

1. Consider the accompanying time card. Show an appropriate record description for this information in COBOL; use any picture clauses that you think appropriate.

TIME-CARD								
NAME			NUMBER	DATE			HOURS
FIRST	MIDDLE	LAST		MO	DA	YR	

2. In which division(s) do we find
(a) PROGRAM-ID paragraph?
(b) FILE-CONTROL paragraph?
(c) CONFIGURATION SECTION?
(d) WORKING-STORAGE SECTION?
(e) FILE SECTION?
(f) FD's?
(g) AUTHOR paragraph?
(h) DATE-COMPILED paragraph?
(i) INPUT-OUTPUT SECTION?
(j) File names?
(k) Level numbers?
(l) Paragraph names?
(m) STOP RUN statements?
(n) SELECT statements?
(o) VALUE clauses?
(p) PICTURE clauses?

3. Given the following record layout for incoming data cards:

```
01  EMPLOYEE-CARD.
    05  SOC-SEC-NUMBER          PICTURE IS 9(9).
    05  EMPLOYEE-NAME.
        10  LAST-NAME           PICTURE IS A(12).
        10  FIRST-NAME          PICTURE IS A(10).
        10  MIDDLE-INIT         PICTURE IS A.
    05  FILLER                  PICTURE IS X.
    05  BIRTH-DATE.
        10  BIRTH-MONTH         PICTURE IS 99.
        10  BIRTH-DAY           PICTURE IS 99.
        10  BIRTH-YEAR          PICTURE IS 99.
    05  FILLER                  PICTURE IS X(3).
    05  EMPLOYEE-ADDRESS.
        10  NUMBER-AND-STREET.
            15  HOUSE-NUMBER    PICTURE IS X(6).
```

```
                15   STREET-NAME          PICTURE IS X(10).
            10   CITY-STATE-ZIP.
                15   CITY                 PICTURE IS X(10).
                15   STATE                PICTURE IS X(4).
                15   ZIP                  PICTURE IS 9(5).
        05   FILLER                       PICTURE IS X(3).
```

(a) List all groups items.
(b) List all elementary items.
(c) State the columns in which the following fields are found:

    1. SOC-SEC-NUMBER
    2. EMPLOYEE-NAME
    3. LAST-NAME
    4. FIRST-NAME
    5. MIDDLE-INIT
    6. BIRTH-DATE
    7. BIRTH-MONTH
    8. BIRTH-DAY
    9. BIRTH-YEAR
   10. EMPLOYEE-ADDRESS
   11. NUMBER-AND-STREET
   12. HOUSE-NUMBER
   13. STREET-NAME
   14. CITY-STATE-ZIP
   15. CITY
   16. STATE
   17. ZIP

4. Given the following record layout (assume that FIELD-I is the last entry under FIELD-A),


```
            01   FIELD-A
                05   FIELD-B
                    10   FIELD-C
                    10   FIELD-D
                05   FIELD-E
                05   FIELD-F
                    10   FIELD-G
                    10   FIELD-H
                    10   FIELD-I
```

answer true or false:
(a) FIELD-C is an elementary item.
(b) FIELD-E is an elementary item.
(c) FIELD-E should have a picture.
(d) FIELD-F should have a picture.
(e) FIELD-B must be larger than FIELD-C.
(f) FIELD-C must be larger than FIELD-D.
(g) FIELD-C must be larger than FIELD-H.
(h) FIELD-B and FIELD-D end in the same column.
(i) FIELD-A and FIELD-I end in the same column.
(j) FIELD-E could be larger than FIELD-F.
(k) FIELD-D could be larger than FIELD-E.
(l) FIELD-F and FIELD-G start in the same column.

5. Show the value of the edited result for each of the following entries:

Sending field		Receiving field	
PICTURE	CONTENTS	PICTURE	CONTENTS
(a) 9(6)	123456	9(6)	
(b) 9(6)	123456	9(8)	
(c) 9(6)	123456	9(6).99	
(d) 9(4)V99	123456	9(6)	
(c) 9(4)V99	123456	9(4)	
(f) 9(4)V99	123456	$$$$$9.99	
(g) 9(4)V99	123456	$$$,$$9.99	
(h) 9(6)	123456	$$$$,$$9.99	

6. Modify the tuition billing problem to account for *all* the following:
   (a) The grade point average (GPA) is in columns 33 to 36 of each data card as a 9V999 number. The scholarship amount is no longer contained in the input record, but is calculated as per the description in part (b).
   (b) The scholarship award is a function of grade point average rather than a flat amount as follows:

GPA	Scholarship
>3.500	20% reduction in tuition
3.001–3.500	15% reduction in tuition
2.500–3.000	10% reduction in tuition
<2.500	No scholarship

   (c) Calculate and print the total number of credits taken by all students.
   (d) Calculate and print the *average* GPA (weigh the GPA of each student equally).

7. Modify the tuition billing problem to accommodate a page heading routine as follows: A maximum of 50 students is to appear on each page, and the heading line and row of dashes are to appear on top of every page. Thus, if there were 178 records, heading lines would appear (before the 1st, 51st, 101st, and 151st students). There will still be only one total line.

PROJECTS

1. Write a program to itemize expenses for a building contractor. Each expenditure appears on a separate data card according to the following format:

Columns	Field	Picture
1–8	DATE-OF-EXPENDITURE	X(8)
10	AUTHORIZATION-CODE	X
12–13	ITEM-TYPE	XX
15–39	ITEM-DESCRIPTION	X(25)
41–45	NUMBER-ORDERED	9(5)
47–55	UNIT-COST	9(7)V99

Print a heading line at the beginning of the report. Print a detail line for each incoming record that includes all incoming fields, as well as a calculated field equal to the NUMBER-ORDERED times the UNIT-COST. Accumulate a running total for cost, and print a total line at the end of processing. Use the following test data.

06/03/80	4	HD	ROOFING NAILS 15 LBS	00006	000000392
07/04/80	2	JL	GRAVEL-TRUCK LOAD	00042	000014000
06/05/80	4	AA	BATHROOM SINK–TYPE A	00094	000008000
06/20/80	2	JL	INDOOR LUMBER $2 \times 3 \times 10$	02200	000000550
06/20/80	2	JL	CEMENT 50 LB BAGS	00320	000001570
07/15/80	3	FN	TRUSSES	00015	000012345
09/15/80	3	RF	ROOF TILES	04000	000000250

2. Write a program to print all shipments of furniture from a manufacturer to three different warehouses. One card is made up and punched every time a shipment is made. The card has the following format:

Columns	Field	Picture
1–6	DATE-OF-SHIPMENT	X(6)
7–13	ANTICIPATED-REVENUE	9(7)
14–15	TYPE-OF-SHIPMENT	XX
16	WAREHOUSE	X
23–52	PERSON-WHO-AUTHORIZED	X(30)

Design and print an appropriate heading line(s). Print a detail line for each incoming record. Keep a total of the anticipated-revenue for each warehouse (A, B, or C) and at the end of the run print three total lines, one for each warehouse. Sample test data are provided.

0212810030000ALC	RUSS FALLOWES
0214810070000NRC	RUSS FALLOWES
0219810002500NNB	DALE MANDRONA
0221810044000ALC	RAY DELODI
0228810010700RLA	PAUL ARON
0302810000200NCC	ART COOPER
0302810004600NNB	DALE MANDRONA
0309810004800NRB	DALE MANDRONA
0309810092000RLA	RAY DELODI

3. Write a COBOL program to calculate the gross pay for the XYZ Widget Company. A single data card has been prepared for every employee according to the format

Columns	Field	Picture
1–25	NAME	X(25)
26–30	HOURS-WORKED	999V99
31–35	HOURLY-RATE	9(3)V99

Gross pay is to be computed as follows:

1. Straight time for the first 40 hours.
2. Time and a half for the next 8 hours (i.e., hours 41 to 48).
3. Double time for anything over 48 hours.

Federal withholding tax is to be calculated for each employee as per the specifications in Problem 4, Chapter 3. Compute also the net pay for each employee, which is simply gross pay minus federal withholding. Design and print heading, detail, and total lines to include employee name, hours worked, hourly rate, gross pay, federal tax, and net pay. Finally, develop your own data to *adequately* test the program.

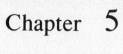

Chapter 5

DEBUGGING, I

OVERVIEW

Very few computer programs run successfully on the first attempt. Indeed the programmer is realistically expected to make errors, and an important "test" of a good programmer is not whether he or she makes mistakes but how quickly they are detected and corrected. Since this process is such an integral part of programming, two entire chapters are devoted to debugging. In the present chapter we shall consider errors in compilation and errors in execution in which the program goes to a normal end of job. In a later chapter we shall consider errors resulting in an "ABEND," or abnormal end-of-job, condition.

Compilation errors occur in the translation of COBOL to machine language and result because the programmer has violated a rule of the COBOL grammar, e.g., a missing period, a misspelled word, or an entry in a wrong column. Execution errors result after the program has been successfully translated to machine language and are generally of two types:

1. The computer was able to execute the entire program, but the calculated results are different from that which the programmer expected or intended.
2. The computer is unable to execute a particular instruction and comes to an abnormal end of job, e.g., division by zero or addition of nonnumeric data.

Execution errors of the first type may be caused by an incorrect translation of a proper flowchart or pseudocode to the programming language, or by a correct translation of an incorrect flowchart. In either case, there is an error in logic that is generating incorrect output.[1]

Execution errors of the second type are deferred to Chapter 13. At that point we shall introduce the memory print or core dump as an important debugging tool. For the present, however, we shall restrict our discussion to compilation errors and execution errors of the first type.

ERRORS IN COMPILATION

There are four types of IBM COBOL compiler error messages or diagnostics; they are listed in order of increasing severity:

W   Warning diagnostic: calls attention to what may cause a potential problem. A program can

---

[1] A more complete treatment of this topic, in the form of 15 COBOL listings with logic errors, can be found in Section 3 of R. Grauer, *A COBOL Book of Practice and Reference,* Prentice-Hall Inc., Englewood Cliffs, N.J., 1981.

compile and execute with several W-level diagnostics present; however, ignoring these messages could lead to errors in execution.

C Conditional diagnostic: requires the compiler to make an assumption in order to complete the compilation. Execution is typically suppressed, and if not, usually inaccurate.

E Error diagnostic: a severe error in that the compiler cannot make corrections and therefore cannot generate object instructions. Execution will not take place. Any statement flagged as an E-level error is ignored and treated as if it were not present in the program.

D Disaster diagnostic: an error of such severity that the compiler does not know what to do and cannot continue. D-Level diagnostics are extremely rare, and one practically has to submit a FORTRAN program to the COBOL compiler to cause a D-level message.

The COBOL compiler tends to rub salt in a wound in the sense that an error in one statement can cause error messages in other statements that appear correct. For example, should you have an E-level error in a SELECT statement, the compiler will flag the error, ignore the SELECT statement, and then flag any other statement which references that file even though those other statements are otherwise correct. (See Figure 5.2).

Often simple mistakes such as omitting a card or misspelling a reserved word can lead to a long and sometimes confusing set of error messages. The only consolation is that compiler errors can disappear as quickly as they occurred. Correction of the misspelled word or insertion of the missing card will often eliminate several errors at once.

Proficiency in debugging comes from experience; the more programs you write, the better you become. To give you a truer feel as to what to expect in your own programs, we have taken the tuition billing problem from Chapter 4 and deliberately changed several of the statements to cause compilation errors.

Consider the two pages of COBOL code and the one page of diagnostics in Figure 5.1. The COBOL compiler first lists the source program and then summarizes the compiler errors that have occurred. Each message references a card (i.e., statement) number, an IBM message number, and contains a brief explanation of the error. Some of the error causes will be immediately obvious; others may require you to seek help. As you progress through this book and gain practical experience you will become increasingly self-sufficient.

Let us examine the errors:

Card 11   W   LABEL RECORDS CLAUSE MISSING . . .
Card 11 is the SELECT statement for CARD-FILE. The diagnostic, however, refers to the FD for this field in cards 16 to 18 and, sure enough, the LABEL RECORDS CLAUSE has been omitted. Since this is a W-level diagnostic, the compiler indicates what action it is taking; in this case it will extract the necessary information from the DD card, a JCL statement.
Correction: Insert a card LABEL RECORDS ARE OMITTED between lines 16 and 17.

Card 12   C   RECORD SIZE IN RECORD-CONTAINS CLAUSE DISAGREES WITH COM-PUTED RECORD SIZE . . .
Card 12 points to the SELECT statement for PRINT-FILE, and as before the error is actually in the FD for this file. Card 28 states there are 133 characters in a record, but the actual computed record size from lines 31 to 47 is 131; hence the message.
Correction: Increase the number of print positions by two, from 131 to 133, by expanding a picture clause; e.g., FILLER in line 47.

Card 58   E   'UNION' INVALID IN DATA DESCRIPTION . . .
Note the occurrence of TOTAL UNION FEE in line 58; the -'s between the parts of the name are missing. In COBOL a data name is followed by a blank, and the compiler does not know how to handle what it thinks are three data names in a row (TOTAL, UNION, and FEE) in line 58.
Correction: Insert -'s to read TOTAL-UNION-FEE.

Card 68   W   END OF SENTENCE SHOULD PRECEDE 05 . . .

Any level number must follow a completed statement, but the period ending line 67 has been removed. In this instance, the compiler assumes that the period is present, so no harm is done, but it is poor programming to permit such W-level diagnostics to remain. Moreover, there are situations in which a missing period can be very damaging.

Correction: Insert a period at the end of card 67.

Card 83   E   'START' SHOULD NOT BEGIN A-MARGIN.

A subtle error and one that typically sends the beginner for help. START is intended as a paragraph name, and paragraph names must begin in the A-MARGIN, so what's the problem? START, however, is a reserved word in COBOL (see Appendix B), and its usage is severely restricted; it may not be used as a paragraph name.

Correction: Choose another paragraph name, e.g., START-THE-PROGRAM.

Card 83   E   SYNTAX REQUIRES QISAM-FILE WITH NOMINAL KEY . . .

A most perplexing error and an example of how one mistake can cause several other diagnostics to appear. This error stems from the previous error concerning the word START.

Correction: No action required other than the previous correction.

Card 89   E   CRD-FILE NOT DEFINED. STATEMENT DISCARDED.

Perhaps your initial reaction is that the compiler made a mistake. CARD-FILE is defined with a SELECT statement in line 11 and an FD beginning in line 16. Take another look. Lines 11 and 16 define CARD-FILE, not CRD-FILE. You know they are the same, but the compiler does not.

Correction: Change to CARD-FILE in statement 89.

Card 98   W   ASTERISK NOT PRECEDED BY A SPACE. ASSUME SPACE.

An easy error to fix; remember all arithmetic operators, +, −, *, /, and **, must be preceded and followed by a blank.

Correction: Insert a space before the *.

Card 98   E   CREDITS NOT UNIQUE . . .
102
103
118

A message of "not unique" means that there is more than one data item with the same name. In this case we find CREDITS is defined in line 22 and again in line 36 (it should be PRINT-CREDITS as in Chapter 4), and the compiler does not know which is which.

Correction: Restore uniqueness to the data name, e.g., PRINT-CREDITS in line 36 or use qualification. (See Chapter 7.)

Card 108   W   SUPERFLUOUS TO FOUND IN ADD STATEMENT. IGNORED.

Check the syntax of the COBOL ADD verb in Chapter 3 and observe that the TO option is not permitted with the GIVING option.

Correction: Eliminate TO in line 108.

Card 109   E   TOTAL-UNION-FEE NOT DEFINED . . .
134

Another example of how one error can cause several others. In line 58 the -'s were omitted in the definition of TOTAL-UNION-FEE; thus insofar as the compiler is concerned this data name (i.e., TOTAL-UNION-FEE) does not exist.

Correction: This diagnostic will disappear with the correction to line 58.

Card 111   E   DNM-2-412 MAY NOT BE USED AS AN ARITHMETIC OPERAND IN ADD STATEMENT . . .

This error becomes easy to understand once we guess that DNM-2-412 refers to TOTAL-IND-BILL in line 111. (In Chapter 13, we shall introduce the data division map, which relates compiler names, e.g., DNM-2-412, to programmer-defined data names.) Observe that in the definition of TOTAL-IND-BILL in line 59 a picture of X(6) was specified; this is not a numeric picture that is required in arithmetic operations; hence the error.

Correction: Change X(6) to 9(6) in line 59.

```
00001          IDENTIFICATION DIVISION.
00002          PROGRAM-ID.  'TUITION'.
00003          AUTHOR.      THE BURSAR.
00004
00005          ENVIRONMENT DIVISION.
00006          CONFIGURATION SECTION.
00007          SOURCE-COMPUTER.  IBM-370.
00008          OBJECT-COMPUTER.  IBM-370.
00009          INPUT-OUTPUT SECTION.                  ┌─ LABEL RECORDS clause missing in this FD
00010          FILE-CONTROL.
00011              SELECT │CARD-FILE│ ASSIGN TO UT-S-SYSIN.
00012              SELECT │PRINT-FILE│ ASSIGN TO UT-S-SYSOUT.
00013                                             ┌─ PICTURE clauses do not sum to 133 in this FD
00014          DATA DIVISION.
00015          FILE SECTION.
00016          FD  CARD-FILE
00017              RECORD CONTAINS 80 CHARACTERS
00018              DATA RECORD IS STUDENT-CARD.
00019          01  STUDENT-CARD.
00020              05  STUDENT-NAME          PICTURE IS A(20).
00021              05  SOC-SEC-NO            PICTURE IS 9(9).
00022              05  CREDITS               PICTURE IS 9(2).
00023              05  UNION-MEMBER          PICTURE IS A.
00024              05  SCHOLARSHIP           PICTURE IS 9(4).
00025              05  FILLER                PICTURE IS X(44).
00026          FD  PRINT-FILE
00027              LABEL RECORDS ARE OMITTED
00028              RECORD CONTAINS 133 CHARACTERS
00029              DATA RECORD IS PRINT-LINE.
00030          01  PRINT-LINE.
00031              05  FILLER                PICTURE IS X.
00032              05  PRINT-STUDENT-NAME    PICTURE IS A(20).
00033              05  FILLER                PICTURE IS X(2).
00034              05  PRINT-SOC-SEC-NO      PICTURE IS 999B99B9999.
00035              05  FILLER                PICTURE IS X(4).
00036  Missing PRINT─ 05       │CREDITS│     PICTURE IS 99.
00037              05  FILLER                PICTURE IS X(3).
00038              05  PRINT-TUITION         PICTURE IS $$$$,$$9.
00039              05  FILLER                PICTURE IS X.
00040              05  PRINT-UNION-FEE       PICTURE IS $$$$,$$9.
00041              05  FILLER                PICTURE IS X(3).
00042              05  PRINT-ACTIVITY-FEE    PICTURE IS   $$,$$9.
00043              05  FILLER                PICTURE IS X(3).
00044              05  PRINT-SCHOLARSHIP     PICTURE IS $$$$,$$9.
00045              05  FILLER                PICTURE IS X(5).
00046              05  PRINT-IND-BILL        PICTURE IS $$$$,$$9.
00047              05  FILLER                PICTURE IS X(38).
00048
00049          WORKING-STORAGE SECTION.
00050          77  DATA-REMAINS-SWITCH       PICTURE IS X(2)  VALUE SPACES.
00051          77  TUITION                   PICTURE IS 9(4)  VALUE ZEROS.
00052          77  ACTIVITY-FEE              PICTURE IS 9(2)  VALUE ZEROS.
00053          77  UNION-FEE                 PICTURE IS 9(2)  VALUE ZEROS.
00054          77  INDIVIDUAL-BILL           PICTURE IS 9(6)  VALUE ZEROS.
00055          77  TOTAL-TUITION             PICTURE IS 9(6)  VALUE ZEROS.
00056          77  TOTAL-SCHOLARSHIP         PICTURE IS 9(6)  VALUE ZEROS.
00057          77  TOTAL-ACTIVITY-FEE        PICTURE IS 9(6)  VALUE ZEROS.
00058          77  │TOTAL UNION FEE│         PICTURE IS 9(6)  VALUE ZEROS.
00059          77  TOTAL-IND-BILL            PICTURE IS 9(6)  VALUE ZEROS.
00060          01  DASHED-LINE.      Missing hyphens
00061              05  FILLER        PICTURE IS X      VALUE SPACES.
00062              05  FILLER        PICTURE IS X(97)  VALUE ALL '-'.
00063              05  FILLER        PICTURE IS X(35)  VALUE SPACES.
00064          01  HEADER-LINE.
00065              05  FILLER        PICTURE IS X.                   Missing period
00066              05  HDG-NAME      PICTURE IS X(12)  VALUE 'STUDENT NAME'.
00067              05  FILLER        PICTURE IS X(10)  │VALUE SPACES│
00068              05  HDG-SOC-SEC   PICTURE IS X(11)  VALUE 'SOC SEC NUM'.
00069              05  FILLER        PICTURE IS X(2)   VALUE SPACES.
00070              05  HDG-CREDITS   PICTURE IS X(7)   VALUE 'CREDITS'.
00071              05  FILLER        PICTURE IS X(2)   VALUE SPACES.
00072              05  HDG-TUITION   PICTURE IS X(7)   VALUE 'TUITION'.
00073              05  FILLER        PICTURE IS X(2)   VALUE SPACES.
00074              05  HDG-UNION-FEE PICTURE IS X(9)   VALUE 'UNION FEE'.
00075              05  FILLER        PICTURE IS X(2)   VALUE SPACES.
```

FIGURE 5.1 *COBOL Listing with Diagnostics*

```
00076                 05   HDG-ACTIVITY         PICTURE IS X(7)    VALUE 'ACT FEE'.
00077                 05   FILLER               PICTURE IS X(2)    VALUE SPACES.
00078                 05   HDG-SCHOLAR          PICTURE IS X(11)   VALUE 'SCHOLARSHIP'.
00079                 05   FILLER               PICTURE IS X(2)    VALUE SPACES.
00080                 05   HDG-TOTAL-BILL       PICTURE IS X(10)   VALUE 'TOTAL BILL'.
00081                 05   FILLER               PICTURE IS X(36)   VALUE SPACES.
00082            PROCEDURE DIVISION.
00083            START.───────────── Reserved word used as paragraph name
00084                 OPEN INPUT CARD-FILE, OUTPUT PRINT-FILE.
00085                 MOVE HEADER-LINE TO PRINT-LINE.
00086                 WRITE PRINT-LINE AFTER ADVANCING PAGE.
00087                 MOVE DASHED-LINE TO PRINT-LINE.
00088                 WRITE PRINT-LINE AFTER ADVANCING 1 LINE.
00089                 READ CRD-FILE ───── Misspelled file name, should be CARD-FILE
00090                     AT END MOVE 'NO' TO DATA-REMAINS-SWITCH.
00091                 PERFORM PROCESS-A-CARD
00092                     UNTIL DATA-REMAINS-SWITCH = 'NO'.
00093                 PERFORM WRITE-UNIVERSITY-TOTALS.
00094                 CLOSE CARD-FILE, PRINT-FILE.
00095                 STOP RUN.
                                               Missing space before *
00096
00097            PROCESS-A-CARD.                            Multiple definition in lines 22 and 36
00098                 COMPUTE TUITION = 80* CREDITS.
00099                 MOVE ZERO TO UNION-FEE.
00100                 IF UNION-MEMBER = 'Y' MOVE 25 TO UNION-FEE.
00101                 MOVE 25 TO ACTIVITY-FEE.
00102                 IF CREDITS > 6 MOVE 50 TO ACTIVITY-FEE.
00103                 IF CREDITS > 12 MOVE 75 TO ACTIVITY-FEE.
00104                 COMPUTE INDIVIDUAL-BILL = TUITION + UNION-FEE + ACTIVITY-FEE
00105                     - SCHOLARSHIP.
                                          TO does not belong
00106
00107            *** INCREMENT UNIVERSITY TOTALS
00108                 ADD TUITION TO TOTAL-TUITION GIVING TOTAL-TUITION.
00109                 ADD UNION-FEE TO TOTAL-UNION-FEE.
00110                 ADD ACTIVITY-FEE TO TOTAL-ACTIVITY-FEE.
00111                 ADD INDIVIDUAL-BILL TO TOTAL-IND-BILL.
00112                 ADD SCHOLARSHIP TO TOTAL-SCHOLARSHIP.
00113
                                          PICTURE X(6) incorrectly used in definition in line 59
00114            *** WRITE DETAIL LINE
00115                 MOVE SPACES TO PRINT-LINE.
00116                 MOVE STUDENT-NAME TO PRINT-STUDENT-NAME.
00117                 MOVE SOC-SEC-NO TO PRINT-SOC-SEC-NO.
00118                 MOVE CREDITS TO PRINT-CREDITS.
00119                 MOVE TUITION TO PRINT-TUITION.───── Multiple definition in lines 22 and 36
00120                 MOVE UNION-FEE TO PRINT-UNION-FEE.
00121                 MOVE ACTIVITY-FEE TO PRINT-ACTIVITY-FEE.
00122                 MOVE SCHOLARSHIP TO PRINT-SCHOLARSHIP.
00123                 MOVE INDIVIDUAL-BILL TO PRINT-IND-BILL.
00124                 WRITE PRINT-FILE AFTER ADVANCING 1 LINE.
00125                                     ───── Should be PRINT-LINE
00126                 READ CARD-FILE
00127                     AT END MOVE 'NO' TO DATA-REMAINS-SWITCH.
00128
00129            WRITE-UNIVERSITY-TOTALS.   Put hyphens in WS definition in line 58
00130                 MOVE DASHED-LINE TO PRINT-LINE.
00131                 WRITE PRINT-LINE AFTER ADVANCING 1 LINE.
00132                 MOVE SPACES TO PRINT-LINE.
00133                 MOVE TOTAL-TUITION TO PRINT-TUITION.
00134                 MOVE TOTAL-UNION-FEE TO PRINT-UNION-FEE.
00135                 MOVE TOTAL-ACTIVITY-FEE TO PRINT-ACTIVITY-FEE.
00136                 MOVE TOTAL-SCHOLARSHIP TO PRINT-SCHOLARSHIP.
00137                 MOVE TOTAL-IND-BILL TO PRINT-IND-BILL.
00138                 WRITE PRINT-LINE AFTER ADVANCING 2 LINES.
```

FIGURE 5.1 (continued)

```
11   IKF2133I-W   LABEL RECORDS CLAUSE MISSING. DD CARD OPTION WILL BE TAKEN.
12   IKF2146I-C   RECORD SIZE IN RECORD-CONTAINS CLAUSE DISAGREES WITH COMPUTED RECORD SIZE. 00131
                  ASSUMED.
58   IKF1037I-E   UNION INVALID IN DATA DESCRIPTION. SKIPPING TO NEXT CLAUSE.
68   IKF1043I-W   END OF SENTENCE SHOULD PRECEDE 05 . ASSUMED PRESENT.
83   IKF1087I-W   ' START ' SHOULD NOT BEGIN A-MARGIN.
83   IKF4050I-E   SYNTAX REQUIRES QISAM-FILE WITH NOMINAL KEY . FOUND END-OF-SENT . STATEMENT
                  DISCARDED.
```

Diagnostics for Figure 5.1

CHAPTER 5: DEBUGGING, I   75

```
89     IKF3001I-E     CRD-FILE NOT DEFINED. STATEMENT DISCARDED.
98     IKF1007I-W     ASTERISK NOT PRECEDED BY A SPACE. ASSUME SPACE.
98     IKF3002I-E     CREDITS NOT UNIQUE. DISCARDED.
102    IKF3002I-E     CREDITS NOT UNIQUE. TEST DISCARDED.
103    IKF3002I-E     CREDITS NOT UNIQUE. TEST DISCARDED.
108    IKF4008I-W     SUPERFLUOUS TO FOUND IN ADD STATEMENT. IGNORED.
109    IKF3001I-E     TOTAL-UNION-FEE NOT DEFINED. SUBSTITUTING TALLY .
111    IKF4019I-E     DNM=2-412  (AN) MAY NOT BE USED AS ARITHMETIC OPERAND IN ADD STATEMENT.
                      ARBITRARILY SUBSTITUTING TALLY .
118    IKF3002I-E     CREDITS NOT UNIQUE. DISCARDED.
118    IKF3001I-E     PRINT-CREDITS NOT DEFINED.
124    IKF4050I-E     SYNTAX REQUIRES RECORD-NAME . FOUND DNM=1-244 . STATEMENT DISCARDED.
134    IKF3001I-E     TOTAL-UNION-FEE NOT DEFINED. DISCARDED.
```

Diagnostics for Figure 5.1 *(continued)*

Card 118   E   PRINT-CREDITS NOT DEFINED.
This diagnostic pertains to the nonunique message from lines 98, 102, 103, and 108.
Correction: If we eliminate that diagnostic by distinguishing between CREDITS and PRINT-CREDITS, then this message will also disappear.

Card 124   E   SYNTAX REQUIRES RECORD-NAME . . .
Statement 124 is WRITE PRINT-FILE. . . . The problem here is that PRINT-FILE is a file name, not a record name. Remember, in COBOL, read a file name but write a record name.
Correction: Statement 124 should read WRITE PRINT-LINE. . . .

A SECOND EXAMPLE

Let us return to the tuition billing program of Chapter 4 and make one very slight change. Statement 12 will now read "SERECT PRINT-FILE . . ." instead of "SELECT PRINT-FILE. . . ." Consider the COBOL listing and associated diagnostics of Figure 5.2; the latter are as follows:

Card 12   E   INVALID WORD SERECT . . .
This is to be expected; the compiler does not recognize the word SERECT.
Correction: Substitute SELECT for SERECT.

Card 30   E   FILE-NAME NOT DEFINED IN A SELECT . . .
While there is nothing wrong with the COBOL FD in lines 27 to 30, the SELECT statement for these lines had been previously flagged by an E-level error and consequently discarded. Thus it appears to the compiler as though there is no SELECT statement for PRINT-FILE.
Correction: None required beyond fixing card 12.

Card 85   E   . . . NOT DEFINED. DISCARDED.
86   What do these 25 errors have in common? Each one contains a data name initially
ETC.   defined in the FD for PRINT-FILE. However, since the SELECT statement was in error and subsequently discarded, the FD is also ignored, and all these data names are effectively undefined, a definite case of the COBOL compiler "rubbing it in."
Correction: None required beyond fixing card 12.

The point of this example is that a seemingly simple error in one statement can lead to a large number of errors in other related statements that disappear when the initial error is corrected. However, don't expect all errors you don't understand to just go away. There is always a logical explanation for everything a computer does, and sometimes it may take quite a while to find it.

ERRORS IN EXECUTION

After a program has been successfully compiled, it proceeds to execute and therein lie the strength and weakness of the computer. The primary attractiveness of the machine is its ability to perform

SECTION II: THE COBOL LANGUAGE

```
00001          IDENTIFICATION DIVISION.
00002          PROGRAM-ID.  'TUITION'.
00003          AUTHOR.      THE BURSAR.
00004
00005          ENVIRONMENT DIVISION.
00006          CONFIGURATION SECTION.
00007          SOURCE-COMPUTER.  IBM-370.
00008          OBJECT-COMPUTER.  IBM-370.
00009          INPUT-OUTPUT SECTION.
00010          FILE-CONTROL.
00011              SELECT CARD-FILE ASSIGN TO UT-S-SYSIN.
00012              SERECT PRINT-FILE ASSIGN TO UT-S-SYSOUT.
00013                   └─ Misspelling - causes all all errors
00014          DATA DIVISION.
00015          FILE SECTION.
00016          FD  CARD-FILE
00017              LABEL RECORDS ARE OMITTED
00018              RECORD CONTAINS 80 CHARACTERS
00019              DATA RECORD IS STUDENT-CARD.
00020          01  STUDENT-CARD.
00021              05  STUDENT-NAME          PICTURE IS A(20).
00022              05  SOC-SEC-NO            PICTURE IS 9(9).
00023              05  CREDITS               PICTURE IS 9(2).
00024              05  UNION-MEMBER          PICTURE IS A.
00025              05  SCHOLARSHIP           PICTURE IS 9(4).
00026              05  FILLER                PICTURE IS X(44).
00027          FD  PRINT-FILE
00028              LABEL RECORDS ARE OMITTED
00029              RECORD CONTAINS 133 CHARACTERS
00030              DATA RECORD IS PRINT-LINE.
00031          01  PRINT-LINE.
00032              05  FILLER                PICTURE IS X.
00033              05  PRINT-STUDENT-NAME    PICTURE IS A(20).
00034              05  FILLER                PICTURE IS X(2).
00035              05  PRINT-SOC-SEC-NO      PICTURE IS 999B99B9999.
00036              05  FILLER                PICTURE IS X(4).
00037              05  PRINT-CREDITS         PICTURE IS 99.
00038              05  FILLER                PICTURE IS X(3).
00039              05  PRINT-TUITION         PICTURE IS $$$$,$$9.
00040              05  FILLER                PICTURE IS X.
00041              05  PRINT-UNION-FEE       PICTURE IS $$$$,$$9.
00042              05  FILLER                PICTURE IS X(3).
00043              05  PRINT-ACTIVITY-FEE    PICTURE IS $$$$,$$9.
00044              05  FILLER                PICTURE IS X(3).
00045              05  PRINT-SCHOLARSHIP     PICTURE IS $$$$,$$9.
00046              05  FILLER                PICTURE IS X(5).
00047              05  PRINT-IND-BILL        PICTURE IS $$$$,$$9.
00048              05  FILLER                PICTURE IS X(38).
00049
00050          WORKING-STORAGE SECTION.
00051          77  DATA-REMAINS-SWITCH       PICTURE IS X(2)   VALUE SPACES.
00052          77  TUITION                   PICTURE IS 9(4)   VALUE ZEROS.
00053          77  ACTIVITY-FEE              PICTURE IS 9(2)   VALUE ZEROS.
00054          77  UNION-FEE                 PICTURE IS 9(2)   VALUE ZEROS.
00055          77  INDIVIDUAL-BILL           PICTURE IS 9(6)   VALUE ZEROS.
00056          77  TOTAL-TUITION             PICTURE IS 9(6)   VALUE ZEROS.
00057          77  TOTAL-SCHOLARSHIP         PICTURE IS 9(6)   VALUE ZEROS.
00058          77  TOTAL-ACTIVITY-FEE        PICTURE IS 9(6)   VALUE ZEROS.
00059          77  TOTAL-UNION-FEE           PICTURE IS 9(6)   VALUE ZEROS.
00060          77  TOTAL-IND-BILL            PICTURE IS 9(6)   VALUE ZEROS.
00061          01  DASHED-LINE.
00062              05  FILLER        PICTURE IS X         VALUE SPACES.
00063              05  FILLER        PICTURE IS X(97)     VALUE ALL '-'.
00064              05  FILLER        PICTURE IS X(35)     VALUE SPACES.
00065          01  HEADER-LINE.
00066              05  FILLER        PICTURE IS X.
00067              05  HDG-NAME      PICTURE IS X(12)     VALUE 'STUDENT NAME'.
00068              05  FILLER        PICTURE IS X(10)     VALUE SPACES.
00069              05  HDG-SOC-SEC   PICTURE IS X(11)     VALUE 'SOC SEC NUM'.
00070              05  FILLER        PICTURE IS X(2)      VALUE SPACES.
00071              05  HDG-CREDITS   PICTURE IS X(7)      VALUE 'CREDITS'.
00072              05  FILLER        PICTURE IS X(2)      VALUE SPACES.
00073              05  HDG-TUITION   PICTURE IS X(7)      VALUE 'TUITION'.
00074              05  FILLER        PICTURE IS X(2)      VALUE SPACES.
00075              05  HDG-UNION-FEE PICTURE IS X(9)      VALUE 'UNION FEE'.
```

FIGURE 5.2 *COBOL Listing with Invalid SELECT Statement*

```
00076          05  FILLER           PICTURE IS X(2)    VALUE SPACES.
00077          05  HDG-ACTIVITY     PICTURE IS X(7)    VALUE 'ACT FEE'.
00078          05  FILLER           PICTURE IS X(2)    VALUE SPACES.
00079          05  HDG-SCHOLAR      PICTURE IS X(11)   VALUE 'SCHOLARSHIP'.
00080          05  FILLER           PICTURE IS X(2)    VALUE SPACES.
00081          05  HDG-TOTAL-BILL   PICTURE IS X(10)   VALUE 'TOTAL BILL'.
00082          05  FILLER          PICTURE IS X(36)  VALUE SPACES.
00083      PROCEDURE DIVISION.
00084      MAINLINE.
00085          OPEN INPUT CARD-FILE, OUTPUT PRINT-FILE.
00086          MOVE HEADER-LINE TO PRINT-LINE.
00087          WRITE PRINT-LINE AFTER ADVANCING PAGE.
00088          MOVE DASHED-LINE TO PRINT-LINE.
00089          WRITE PRINT-LINE AFTER ADVANCING 1 LINE.
00090          READ CARD-FILE
00091              AT END MOVE 'NO' TO DATA-REMAINS-SWITCH.
00092          PERFORM PROCESS-A-CARD
00093              UNTIL DATA-REMAINS-SWITCH = 'NO'.
00094          PERFORM WRITE-UNIVERSITY-TOTALS.
00095          CLOSE CARD-FILE, PRINT-FILE.
00096          STOP RUN.
00097
00098      PROCESS-A-CARD.
00099          COMPUTE TUITION = 80 * CREDITS.
00100          MOVE ZERO TO UNION-FEE.
00101          IF UNION-MEMBER = 'Y' MOVE 25 TO UNION-FEE.
00102          MOVE 25 TO ACTIVITY-FEE.
00103          IF CREDITS > 6 MOVE 50 TO ACTIVITY-FEE.
00104          IF CREDITS > 12 MOVE 75 TO ACTIVITY-FEE.
00105          COMPUTE INDIVIDUAL-BILL = TUITION + UNION-FEE + ACTIVITY-FEE
00106              - SCHOLARSHIP.
00107
00108      *** INCREMENT UNIVERSITY TOTALS
00109          ADD TUITION TO TOTAL-TUITION.
00110          ADD UNION-FEE TO TOTAL-UNION-FEE.
00111          ADD ACTIVITY-FEE TO TOTAL-ACTIVITY-FEE.
00112          ADD INDIVIDUAL-BILL TO TOTAL-IND-BILL.
00113          ADD SCHOLARSHIP TO TOTAL-SCHOLARSHIP.
00114
00115      *** WRITE DETAIL LINE
00116          MOVE SPACES TO PRINT-LINE.
00117          MOVE STUDENT-NAME TO PRINT-STUDENT-NAME.
00118          MOVE SOC-SEC-NO TO PRINT-SOC-SEC-NO.
00119          MOVE CREDITS TO PRINT-CREDITS.
00120          MOVE TUITION TO PRINT-TUITION.
00121          MOVE UNION-FEE TO PRINT-UNION-FEE.
00122          MOVE ACTIVITY-FEE TO PRINT-ACTIVITY-FEE.
00123          MOVE SCHOLARSHIP TO PRINT-SCHOLARSHIP.
00124          MOVE INDIVIDUAL-BILL TO PRINT-IND-BILL.
00125          WRITE PRINT-LINE AFTER ADVANCING 1 LINE.
00126
00127          READ CARD-FILE
00128              AT END MOVE 'NO' TO DATA-REMAINS-SWITCH.
00129
00130      WRITE-UNIVERSITY-TOTALS.
00131          MOVE DASHED-LINE TO PRINT-LINE.
00132          WRITE PRINT-LINE AFTER ADVANCING 1 LINE.
00133          MOVE SPACES TO PRINT-LINE.
00134          MOVE TOTAL-TUITION TO PRINT-TUITION.
00135          MOVE TOTAL-UNION-FEE TO PRINT-UNION-FEE.
00136          MOVE TOTAL-ACTIVITY-FEE TO PRINT-ACTIVITY-FEE.
00137          MOVE TOTAL-SCHOLARSHIP TO PRINT-SCHOLARSHIP.
00138          MOVE TOTAL-IND-BILL TO PRINT-IND-BILL.
00139          WRITE PRINT-LINE AFTER ADVANCING 2 LINES.
```

FIGURE 5.2 (continued)

```
12    IKF1004I-E    INVALID WORD SERECT . SKIPPING TO NEXT RECOGNIZABLE WORD.
30    IKF1056I-E    FILE-NAME NOT DEFINED IN A SELECT. DESCRIPTION IGNORED.
85    IKF3001I-E    PRINT-FILE NOT DEFINED. DELETING TILL LEGAL ELEMENT FOUND.
86    IKF3001I-E    PRINT-LINE NOT DEFINED. DISCARDED.
87    IKF3001I-E    PRINT-LINE NOT DEFINED. STATEMENT DISCARDED.
88    IKF3001I-E    PRINT-LINE NOT DEFINED. DISCARDED.
89    IKF3001I-E    PRINT-LINE NOT DEFINED. STATEMENT DISCARDED.
95    IKF3001I-E    PRINT-FILE NOT DEFINED. DELETING TILL LEGAL ELEMENT FOUND.
```

Diagnostics for Figure 5.2

```
116     IKF3001I-E        PRINT-LINE NOT DEFINED. DISCARDED.
117     IKF3001I-E        PRINT-STUDENT-NAME NOT DEFINED. DISCARDED.
118     IKF3001I-E        PRINT-SOC-SEC-NO NOT DEFINED. DISCARDED.
119     IKF3001I-E        PRINT-CREDITS NOT DEFINED. DISCARDED.
120     IKF3001I-E        PRINT-TUITION NOT DEFINED. DISCARDED.
121     IKF3001I-E        PRINT-UNION-FEE NOT DEFINED. DISCARDED.
122     IKF3001I-E        PRINT-ACTIVITY-FEE NOT DEFINED. DISCARDED.
123     IKF3001I-E        PRINT-SCHOLARSHIP NOT DEFINED. DISCARDED.
124     IKF3001I-E        PRINT-IND-BILL NOT DEFINED. DISCARDED.
125     IKF3001I-E        PRINT-LINE NOT DEFINED. STATEMENT DISCARDED.
131     IKF3001I-E        PRINT-LINE NOT DEFINED. DISCARDED.
132     IKF3001I-E        PRINT-LINE NOT DEFINED. STATEMENT DISCARDED.
133     IKF3001I-E        PRINT-LINE NOT DEFINED. DISCARDED.
134     IKF3001I-E        PRINT-TUITION NOT DEFINED. DISCARDED.
135     IKF3001I-E        PRINT-UNION-FEE NOT DEFINED. DISCARDED.
136     IKF3001I-E        PRINT-ACTIVITY-FEE NOT DEFINED. DISCARDED.
137     IKF3001I-E        PRINT-SCHOLARSHIP NOT DEFINED. DISCARDED.
138     IKF3001I-E        PRINT-IND-BILL NOT DEFINED. DISCARDED.
139     IKF3001I-E        PRINT-LINE NOT DEFINED. STATEMENT DISCARDED.
```

Diagnostics for Figure 5.2 *(continued)*

a fantastic number of operations in infinitesimal amounts of time; its weakness stems from the fact that it does exactly what it has been instructed to do. The machine cannot think for itself. The programmer must think for the machine. If you were to inadvertently instruct the computer to compute tuition by charging $8 instead of $80 per credit, then that is what it would do.

To give you an idea of what can happen, we have deliberately altered the original tuition billing problem of Chapter 4 and created a new program shown in Figure 5.3. That, in turn, created the output of Figure 5.4, which at first glance resembles the original output of Figure 4.9. There are, however, subtle errors as follows:

1. A row of dashes should appear prior to the total line.
2. The total of all individual bills in the total line appeared as $1,490 (the amount for the last record) rather than a running total.
3. The total for the individual union fees printed as 0, rather than $75.
4. The last record (for Benjamin Lee) was processed twice.
5. The ACTIVITY FEE for John Smith and Henry James printed as $50 rather than $75.
6. The SCHOLARSHIP amount for Henry James and Susan Baker printed as $0 rather than $500, although their individual bills were in fact reduced by $500.

Note well that Figure 5.3, the program that produced the output of Figure 5.4, compiled with only two *warning* diagnostics relating to lines 123 and 134. (These in turn created the difficulty in item 6, the scholarship amounts for Henry James and Susan Baker, as will be explained shortly.) Put another way, the errors inherent in Figure 5.4 are errors in execution, rather than compilation. The compiler successfully translated the COBOL program of Figure 5.3 into machine language because it (the program) was *syntactically correct*. Unfortunately, the program was *logically incorrect*, and hence the errors in Figure 5.4. Each error is discussed in detail:

1. Missing row of dashes: DASHED-LINE is defined in lines 61 to 64 and moved to PRINT-LINE in line 128. It was never written, however, as the original WRITE statement of line 129 was removed. PRINT-LINE is cleared in line 130, and eventually a total line is written.
2. The total amount of individual bills is incorrect in the total line: TOTAL-IND-BILL is defined in line 60 and correctly incremented for each record in line 112; so far, so good. However, when the total line is cleared in line 130, and built in lines 131 to 135, INDIVIDUAL-BILL rather than TOTAL-IND-BILL is moved to PRINT-IND-BILL in line 135.
3. The total for UNION-FEE is wrong: TOTAL-UNION-FEE is defined and initialized in line 59. However, when the other counters are incremented in lines 109 to 113, an ADD statement for TOTAL-UNION-FEE is conspicuously absent. (Unlike the previous error, TOTAL-UNION-FEE is moved to PRINT-UNION-FEE in line 132, except TOTAL-UNION-FEE never budged from its initial value of zero, owing to the missing ADD statement.)

```
00001        IDENTIFICATION DIVISION.
00002        PROGRAM-ID.  'TUITION'.
00003        AUTHOR.      THE BURSAR.
00004
00005        ENVIRONMENT DIVISION.
00006        CONFIGURATION SECTION.
00007        SOURCE-COMPUTER.  IBM-370.
00008        OBJECT-COMPUTER.  IBM-370.
00009        INPUT-OUTPUT SECTION.
00010        FILE-CONTROL.
00011            SELECT CARD-FILE ASSIGN TO UT-S-SYSIN.
00012            SELECT PRINT-FILE ASSIGN TO UT-S-SYSOUT.
00013
00014        DATA DIVISION.
00015        FILE SECTION.
00016        FD  CARD-FILE
00017            LABEL RECORDS ARE OMITTED
00018            RECORD CONTAINS 80 CHARACTERS
00019            DATA RECORD IS STUDENT-CARD.
00020        01  STUDENT-CARD.
00021            05   STUDENT-NAME          PICTURE IS A(20).
00022            05   SOC-SEC-NO            PICTURE IS 9(9).
00023            05   CREDITS               PICTURE IS 9(2).
00024            05   UNION-MEMBER          PICTURE IS A.
00025            05   SCHOLARSHIP           PICTURE IS 9(4).
00026            05   FILLER                PICTURE IS X(44).
00027        FD  PRINT-FILE
00028            LABEL RECORDS ARE OMITTED
00029            RECORD CONTAINS 133 CHARACTERS
00030            DATA RECORD IS PRINT-LINE.
00031        01  PRINT-LINE.
00032            05   FILLER                PICTURE IS X.
00033            05   PRINT-STUDENT-NAME    PICTURE IS A(20).
00034            05   FILLER                PICTURE IS X(2).
00035            05   PRINT-SOC-SEC-NO      PICTURE IS 999B99B9999.
00036            05   FILLER                PICTURE IS X(4).
00037            05   PRINT-CREDITS         PICTURE IS 99.
00038            05   FILLER                PICTURE IS X(3).
00039            05   PRINT-TUITION         PICTURE IS $$$$,$$9.
00040            05   FILLER                PICTURE IS X.
00041            05   PRINT-UNION-FEE       PICTURE IS $$$$,$$9.
00042            05   FILLER                PICTURE IS X(3).
00043            05   PRINT-ACTIVITY-FEE    PICTURE IS $$$$,$$9.      Picture clause
00044            05   FILLER                PICTURE IS X(8).        / is too small
00045            05   PRINT-SCHOLARSHIP     PICTURE IS    [$$9.]
00046            05   FILLER                PICTURE IS X(5).
00047            05   PRINT-IND-BILL        PICTURE IS $$$$,$$9.
00048            05   FILLER                PICTURE IS X(38).
00049
00050        WORKING-STORAGE SECTION.
00051        77  DATA-REMAINS-SWITCH       PICTURE IS X(2)   VALUE SPACES.
00052        77  TUITION                   PICTURE IS 9(4)   VALUE ZEROS.
00053        77  ACTIVITY-FEE              PICTURE IS 9(2)   VALUE ZEROS.
00054        77  UNION-FEE                 PICTURE IS 9(2)   VALUE ZEROS.
00055        77  INDIVIDUAL-BILL           PICTURE IS 9(6)   VALUE ZEROS.
00056        77  TOTAL-TUITION             PICTURE IS 9(6)   VALUE ZEROS.
00057        77  TOTAL-SCHOLARSHIP         PICTURE IS 9(6)   VALUE ZEROS.
00058        77  TOTAL-ACTIVITY-FEE        PICTURE IS 9(6)   VALUE ZEROS.
00059        77  TOTAL-UNION-FEE           PICTURE IS 9(6)   VALUE ZEROS.
00060        77  TOTAL-IND-BILL            PICTURE IS 9(6)   VALUE ZEROS.
00061        01  DASHED-LINE.
00062            05   FILLER         PICTURE IS X       VALUE SPACES.
00063            05   FILLER         PICTURE IS X(97)   VALUE ALL '-'.
00064            05   FILLER         PICTURE IS X(35)   VALUE SPACES.
00065        01  HEADER-LINE.
00066            05   FILLER         PICTURE IS X.
00067            05   HDG-NAME       PICTURE IS X(12)   VALUE 'STUDENT NAME'.
00068            05   FILLER         PICTURE IS X(10)   VALUE SPACES.
00069            05   HDG-SOC-SEC    PICTURE IS X(11)   VALUE 'SOC SEC NUM'.
00070            05   FILLER         PICTURE IS X(2)    VALUE SPACES.
00071            05   HDG-CREDITS    PICTURE IS X(7)    VALUE 'CREDITS'.
00072            05   FILLER         PICTURE IS X(2)    VALUE SPACES.
00073            05   HDG-TUITION    PICTURE IS X(7)    VALUE 'TUITION'.
00074            05   FILLER         PICTURE IS X(2)    VALUE SPACES.
00075            05   HDG-UNION-FEE  PICTURE IS X(9)    VALUE 'UNION FEE'.
00076            05   FILLER         PICTURE IS X(2)    VALUE SPACES.
00077            05   HDG-ACTIVITY   PICTURE IS X(7)    VALUE 'ACT FEE'.
```

FIGURE 5.3 *Errors in Execution*

```
00078                  05  FILLER              PICTURE IS X(2)    VALUE SPACES.
00079                  05  HDG-SCHOLAR         PICTURE IS X(11)   VALUE 'SCHOLARSHIP'.
00080                  05  FILLER              PICTURE IS X(6)    VALUE SPACES.
00081                  05  HDG-TOTAL-BILL      PICTURE IS X(10)   VALUE 'TOTAL BILL'.
00082                  05  FILLER              PICTURE IS X(36)   VALUE SPACES.
00083              PROCEDURE DIVISION.
00084              MAINLINE.
00085                  OPEN INPUT CARD-FILE, OUTPUT PRINT-FILE.
00086                  MOVE HEADER-LINE TO PRINT-LINE.
00087                  WRITE PRINT-LINE AFTER ADVANCING PAGE.
00088                  MOVE DASHED-LINE TO PRINT-LINE.
00089                  WRITE PRINT-LINE AFTER ADVANCING 1 LINE.
00090                  PERFORM PROCESS-A-CARD
00091                      UNTIL DATA-REMAINS-SWITCH = 'NO'.
00092                  PERFORM WRITE-UNIVERSITY-TOTALS.
00093                  CLOSE CARD-FILE, PRINT-FILE.
00094                  STOP RUN.
00095                                                            ┌─ READ statement is incorrectly placed
00096              PROCESS-A-CARD.
00097                  ┌────────────────────────────────────────┐
                       │ READ CARD-FILE                          │
00098                  │     AT END MOVE 'NO' TO DATA-REMAINS-SWITCH. │
                       └────────────────────────────────────────┘
00099                  COMPUTE TUITION = 80 * CREDITS.
00100                  MOVE ZERO TO UNION-FFE.
00101                  IF UNION-MEMBER = 'Y' MOVE 25 TO UNION-FEE.
00102                  MOVE 25 TO ACTIVITY-FEE.              ┌─ Order of IF statements
00103                  ┌──────────────────────────────────┐ │  is reversed
                       │ IF CREDITS > 12 MOVE 75 TO ACTIVITY-FEE. │
00104                  │ IF CREDITS > 6 MOVE 50 TO ACTIVITY-FEE. │
                       └──────────────────────────────────┘
00105                  COMPUTE INDIVIDUAL-BILL = TUITION + UNION-FEE + ACTIVITY-FEE
00106                      - SCHOLARSHIP.
00107
00108          ***  INCREMENT UNIVERSITY TOTALS            ┌─ ADD statement missing
00109                  ADD TUITION TO TOTAL-TUITION.        │  for TOTAL-UNION-FEE
00110                  ┌─────────────────────────────────┐
                       │                                 │
00111                  ADD ACTIVITY-FEE TO TOTAL-ACTIVITY-FEE.
00112                  ADD INDIVIDUAL-BILL TO TOTAL-IND-BILL.
00113                  ADD SCHOLARSHIP TO TOTAL-SCHOLARSHIP.
00114
00115          ***  WRITE DETAIL LINE
00116                  MOVE SPACES TO PRINT-LINE.
00117                  MOVE STUDENT-NAME TO PRINT-STUDENT-NAME.
00118                  MOVE SOC-SEC-NO TO PRINT-SOC-SEC-NO.
00119                  MOVE CREDITS TO PRINT-CREDITS.
00120                  MOVE TUITION TO PRINT-TUITION.
00121                  MOVE UNION-FEE TO PRINT-UNION-FEE.
00122                  MOVE ACTIVITY-FEE TO PRINT-ACTIVITY-FEE.
00123                  MOVE SCHOLARSHIP TO PRINT-SCHOLARSHIP.
00124                  MOVE INDIVIDUAL-BILL TO PRINT-IND-BILL.
00125                  WRITE PRINT-LINE AFTER ADVANCING 1 LINE.
00126
00127              WRITE-UNIVERSITY-TOTALS.                  ┌─ WRITE statement missing
00128                  MOVE DASHED-LINE TO PRINT-LINE.
00129                  ┌─────────────────────────────────┐
                       │                                 │
00130                  MOVE SPACES TO PRINT-LINE.
00131                  MOVE TOTAL-TUITION TO PRINT-TUITION.     Wrong field is moved to print line
00132                  MOVE TOTAL-UNION-FEE TO PRINT-UNION-FEE.
00133                  MOVE TOTAL-ACTIVITY-FEE TO PRINT-ACTIVITY-FEE.
00134                  MOVE TOTAL-SCHOLARSHIP TO PRINT-SCHOLARSHIP.
00135                  ┌─────────────────────────────────────┐
                       │ MOVE INDIVIDUAL-BILL TO PRINT-IND-BILL. │
                       └─────────────────────────────────────┘
00136                  WRITE PRINT-LINE AFTER ADVANCING 2 LINES.
```

FIGURE 5.3 *(continued)*

Activity fee should be $75

STUDENT NAME	SOC SEC NUM	CREDITS	TUITION	UNION FEE	ACT FEE	SCHOLARSHIP	TOTAL BILL
JOHN SMITH	123 45 6789	15	$1,200	$25	$50	$0	$1,275
HENRY JAMES	987 65 4321	15	$1,200	$0	$50	$0	$750
SUSAN BAKER	111 22 3333	09	$720	$0	$50	$0	$270
JOHN PART-TIMER	456 21 3546	03	$240	$25	$25	$0	$290
PEGGY JONES	456 45 6456	15	$1,200	$25	$50	$0	$1,275
H. HEAVY-WORKER	789 52 1234	18	$1,440	$0	$50	$0	$1,490
BENJAMIN LEE	876 87 6876	18	$1,440	$0	$50	$0	$1,490
BENJAMIN LEE	876 87 6876	18	$1,440	$0	$50	$0	$1,490
			$8,880	$0	$375	$0	$1,490

Row of dashes is missing

Last student appears twice

Union fee was not summed

Scholarship should be $500

Total is not correct

FIGURE 5.4 *Tuition Billing Output with Errors*

CHAPTER 5: DEBUGGING, I

4. The last record was processed twice: Recall that when the program structure was first presented in Chapter 4, there was an initial READ statement in the mainline paragraph, and a second READ, as the *last* statement in the performed routine. That structure was *correct*. In Figure 5.3, the initial READ statement was eliminated, and the second READ *incorrectly* moved to the beginning of the performed routine. To understand the effect, consider a file with only a single record, which will be read as the performed routine of Figure 5.3 is entered for the first time. When the end of the routine is reached, the end of file has not yet been sensed; hence PROCESS-A-CARD is entered a *second* time, even though there is only a single record. The end of file is sensed immediately in line 98, but the perform is not terminated until line 125. Consequently, the intermediate statements are executed a second time for the previous record. The problem is corrected by restoring an initial read in the mainline paragraph, between lines 89 and 90, and placing the existing READ statement of lines 97 and 98 after line 125.

5. ACTIVITY-FEE computations are incorrect: Consider the case of John Smith and his 15 credits. The value of ACTIVITY-FEE is initially set to 25 in line 102. Since Smith has more than 12 credits, ACTIVITY-FEE is reset to 75 in line 103 and again reset to 50 in line 104. The problem is simply that lines 103 and 104 are inverted, causing anyone with 6 credits or more to be charged $50. Reversing lines 103 and 104 will set the activity fee to $50 for students with 7 to 12 credits and to $75 for anyone with more than 12 credits.

6. Individual SCHOLARSHIP is incorrect: This is the *only* error caught by the compiler, which flagged lines 123 and 134 with the message, AN INTERMEDIATE RESULT OR A SENDING FIELD MAY HAVE ITS HIGH ORDER DIGIT POSITION TRUNCATED. In line 123, SCHOLARSHIP with picture 9(4) is moved to PRINT-SCHOLARSHIP with picture $$9. The largest value that can appear in the latter field is $99; hence any scholarship amounts in excess of $99 will have the high-order digit eliminated.

It is important to emphasize that these execution errors are not contrived, but typical of students and beginning programmers. Even the accomplished practitioner can be guilty of similar errors when rushed or careless. Realize also that execution errors occur without fanfare. There are no compiler diagnostics to warn of impending trouble. The program has compiled cleanly, and if it goes to a normal end of job, there is nothing to indicate a problem. A critical question, therefore, is how to best detect and prevent these errors.

ERROR DETECTION: THE STRUCTURED WALKTHROUGH

Although it is reasonable to expect errors, the programmer is also expected (reasonably) to find and correct them. Until recently, error detection and correction was a lonely activity. A programmer was encouraged to *desk check*, i.e., read and reread the code, in an attempt to discern logic errors *before* they occurred. Desk checking is still an important activity, but it is frequently supplemented by a newer technique, the *structured walkthrough.*

The walkthrough brings the evaluation into the open. It requires a programmer to formally, and periodically, have his or her work reviewed by a peer group. The theory is simple: a programmer is too close to his or her work to adequately see, and objectively evaluate, potential problems. The purpose of the walkthrough therefore is to ensure that all specifications are met, and that the logic and its COBOL implementation are correct.

The single most important objective of a walkthrough is *early error detection,* because the sooner an error is found, the easier it is to correct. This implies that walkthroughs occur at several stages during a project. They often begin during the design phase in which the work of a systems analyst is evaluated. The purpose then is to make sure that the analyst has adequately understood the user's requirements and that all necessary data will be made available. Walkthroughs can occur again after the programmer has received the analyst's specifications and developed the logic to implement the solution. Finally, they can occur during the coding stage during which the programmer presents actual code prior to testing.

Walkthroughs are usually scheduled by the person being reviewed, who also selects the reviewers. The reviewee distributes copies of the work (pseudocode or a COBOL program) prior to the session. Reviewers are supposed to study the material in advance so that they can discuss it intelligently. At the walkthrough itself, the reviewee presents the program, objectively, concisely, and dispassionately. He or she should encourage discussion and be genuinely glad when (not if) errors are discovered.

One of the reviewers should function as a moderator to keep the discussion on track. Another should act as a secretary, and maintain an action list of problems uncovered during the session. The action list is given to the reviewee at the end of the walkthrough who in turn is expected to correct the errors and notify attendees accordingly. However the objective of the walkthrough itself is only to find errors, not to correct them. The latter is accomplished by the reviewee upon receipt of the action list.

The preceding discussion may read well in theory, but programmers often dislike the walkthrough concept. The probable reason is that they dislike having their work reviewed, and regard criticism of code, intended or otherwise, as a personal affront. This attitude is natural and stems from years of working as individuals.

In addition, walkthroughs can and have become unpleasant and ego-deflating experiences. Only if the atmosphere is kept open and nondefensive, only if the discussion is restricted to major problems rather than trivial errors, and only if personality clashes are avoided can the walkthrough be an effective technique. To have any chance of success, programmers who function as both reviewer and reviewee must adhere to the following:

1. The program and *not* the programmer is reviewed. Structured walkthroughs are intended to find programming problems; they will not be used by management as an evaluation tool. No one should keep count of how many errors are found in an individual's work or how many errors one finds in someone else's. It is quite logical, therefore, to exclude the project manager, i.e., the individual in charge of salaries and promotions, from review sessions.

2. Emphasis is on error detection, *not* correction. It is simply assumed that the individual being reviewed will take the necessary corrective action. Reviewers should not harp on errors by discussing how to correct them; indeed, *no* corrections whatsoever are made during a walkthrough. Finally, reviewers should focus on major problems and omit trivial errors entirely.

3. Everyone, from senior analyst to trainee, has his or her work reviewed. This avoids singling out an individual and further removes any stigma from having one's work reviewed. It also promotes the give-and-take atmosphere that is so vital to making the concept work.

SUMMARY

Don't be discouraged if you have many compilation errors in your first few attempts, and don't be surprised if you have several pages of diagnostics. Remember that a single error in a COBOL program can result in many error messages and that the errors can be made to disappear in bunches. (Recall the invalid SELECT statement of Figure 5.2.)

Before leaving the subject of compilation errors, it is worthwhile to review a list of common errors and suggested ways to avoid them:

1. *Nonunique data names.* Occurs because the same data name is defined in two different records or twice within the same record. For example, CREDITS might be specified as input data in a CARD-FILE and printed as output in a PRINT-FILE. To avoid the problem of nonunique data names, it is best to prefix every data name within a file by a short prefix. CARD could be established as a prefix for CARD-FILE, and PRINT as the prefix for PRINT-FILE, as shown on page 84; this also helps locate data names while writing and debugging programs (see Chapter 6):

```
FD    CARD-FILE
                  .
                  .

      DATA RECORD IS CARD-RECORD.
01    CARD-RECORD.
      05    CARD-NAME             PIC X(20).
      05    CARD-SOC-SEC-NO       PIC 9(9).
                  .
                  .

FD    PRINT-FILE
                  .
                  .

      DATA RECORD IS PRINT-RECORD.
01    PRINT-RECORD.
      05    PRINT-NAME            PIC X(20).
      05    FILLER                PIC X(5).
      05    PRINT-SOC-SEC-NO      PIC 9(9).
```

2. *Omitted periods.* Every COBOL sentence should have a period; omission usually results in the compiler's assumption of a period.

3. *Omitted space before/after an arithmetic operator.* The arithmetic operators **, *, /, +, and − all require a blank before and after (a typical error for FORTRAN or PL/I programmers since the space is not required in those languages).

4. *Invalid picture for numeric entry.* All data names used in arithmetic statements must have numeric pictures consisting of 9's and an optional V. The only other permitted entry is a sign which is discussed in Chapter 8.

5. *Conflicting picture and value clause.* Numeric pictures must have numeric values (no quotes); nonnumeric data pictures must have nonnumeric values (must be enclosed in quotes). Both entries below are *invalid:*

```
05    TOTAL            PIC 9(3)    VALUE '123'.
05    TITLE-WORD       PIC X(3)    VALUE 123.
```

Another common error is to use value and picture clauses of different lengths. The entry

```
05    EMPLOYEE-NAME    PIC X(4)    VALUE 'R BAKER'.
```

causes a diagnostic for just that reason.

6. *Inadvertent use of COBOL reserved words.* COBOL has a list of some 300 reserved words that can only be used in their designated sense; any other use results in one or several diagnostics. Some reserved words are obvious, e.g., WORKING-STORAGE, IDENTIFIC-ATION, ENVIRONMENT, DATA, and PROCEDURE. Others, such as CODE, DATE, START, and REPORT, are less obvious. Instead of memorizing the list or continually referring to it, we suggest this simple rule of thumb. Always use a hyphen in every data name you create. This will work better than 99% of the time.

7. *Conflicting RECORD CONTAINS clause and FD record description.* A recurrent error, even for established programmers. It stems from sometimes careless addition in that the sum of the pictures in an FD does not equal the number of characters in the RECORD CONTAINS clause. It can also result from other errors within the data division, i.e., when an entry containing a picture clause is flagged. If an E-level diagnostic is present, that entry will be ignored, and the count is thrown off. This is often one of the last errors to disappear before a clean compile.

8. *Receiving field too small to accommodate sending field.* An extremely common error, often associated with edited pictures. Consider the entries

```
05   PRINT-TOTAL-PAY     PIC $$,$$$.
     .
     .
     .
05   WS-TOTAL-PAY     PIC 9(5).
     .
     .
     .
MOVE WS-TOTAL-PAY TO PRINT-TOTAL-PAY.
```

The MOVE statement would generate the warning that the receiving field may be too small to accommodate the sending field. The greatest possible value for WS-TOTAL-PAY is 99,999; the largest possible value that could be printed by PRINT-TOTAL-PAY is $9,999. Even though the print field contains five $'s, one $ must always print and hence the warning.

9. *Omitted hyphen in a data name.* A careless error but one that occurs too often. If in the data division we define PRINT-TOTAL-PAY and then reference PRINT TOTAL-PAY, the compiler objects violently. It doesn't state that a hyphen was omitted, but it flags both PRINT and TOTAL-PAY as undefined.

10. *Misspelled data names or reserved words.* Too many COBOL students are poor spellers. Sound strange? How do you spell environment? One or many errors can result, depending on which word was spelled incorrectly.

11. *Reading a record name or writing a file name.* The COBOL rule is very simple. One is supposed to read a file and write a record; many people get it confused. The entries below should clarify the situation:

```
FD   CARD-FILE
     .
     .
     DATA RECORD IS CARD-RECORD.
     .
     .
FD   PRINT-FILE
     .
     .
     DATA RECORD IS PRINT-RECORD.
```

Correct entries:
```
     READ CARD-FILE,.....
     WRITE PRINT-RECORD....
```
Incorrect entries:
```
     READ CARD-RECORD....
     WRITE PRINT-FILE...
```

12. *Going past column 72.* This error can cause any of the above errors as well as a host of others. A COBOL statement must end in column 72 or before; columns 73 to 80 are left blank or used for program identification. If one goes past column 72 in a COBOL statement, it is very difficult to catch because the COBOL listing contains columns 1 to 80 although the compiler interprets only columns 1 to 72. (The 72-column restriction does not apply to data cards.)

REVIEW EXERCISES

TRUE	FALSE	
☐	☐	**1.** If a program compiles with no diagnostics, it must execute correctly.
☐	☐	**2.** If a program compiles with warning diagnostics, execution will be suppressed.
☐	☐	**3.** If a program contains logical errors, but *not* syntactical errors, the compiler will print appropriate warnings.
☐	☐	**4.** A COBOL program is considered as data by the COBOL compiler.
☐	☐	**5.** An error in one COBOL statement can cause errors in several other, apparently correct, statements.
☐	☐	**6.** There are four distinct levels of IBM compiler diagnostics.
☐	☐	**7.** A C-level diagnostic is more severe than a W-level diagnostic.
☐	☐	**8.** Paragraph names begin in the A margin.
☐	☐	**9.** Spaces are required before and after arithmetic symbols.
☐	☐	**10.** Spaces are required before and after punctuation symbols.
☐	☐	**11.** A data name that appears in a COMPUTE statement can be defined with a picture of X's.
☐	☐	**12.** Data names may contain blanks.
☐	☐	**13.** The contents of columns 73 to 80 are ignored by the compiler.
☐	☐	**14.** In a COBOL program, one reads a record name and writes a file name.

PROBLEMS

1. A COBOL program is required to compute a company payroll. Incoming data are in the following format:

Columns	Field	Picture
1–25	CARD-NAME	A(25)
26–30	CARD-HOURS	9(3)V99
31–35	CARD-RATE	9(3)V99

An individual receives straight time for the first 40 hours worked, time and a half for the next 8 hours, and double time for each hour over 48. For example, an employee earning $7.00/hour and working 49 hours would receive

Straight time	40 hours @ $7.00	$280
Time and a half	8 hours @ $10.50	84
Double time	1 hour @ $14.00	14
	Gross pay	$378

Federal income taxes are computed according to the following schedule:

Gross Pay	Tax
$240 or less	16% of gross
More than $240, but less than $300	$42 + 20% of amount over $240
$300 or more	$60 + 22% of amount over $300

Thus individuals with gross wages of $200, $276, and $378 would pay $32.00, $49.20, and $77.16, respectively.

The completed program is to process a file of employee records and for each employee, compute, and print gross pay, federal tax, and net pay. Company totals are also required for these fields, as is a suitable heading line.

Figure 5.5 contains the first attempt at a COBOL program to solve the payroll program. Correct all compilation errors.

2. A corrected listing for the payroll program is shown in Figure 5.6. It compiled cleanly, but produced execution errors resulting in an incorrect report. Figure 5.7 contains the desired report followed by the erroneous report that was actually produced. Find and correct all logic errors. Finally, review the program specifications and see if you can find an inconsistency.

```
00001          IDENTIFICATION DIVISION.
00002          PROGRAM-ID. 'PAYROLL'.
00003          AUTHOR.
00004              MARION MILGROM.
00005
00006          ENVIRONMENT DIVISION.
00007          CONFIGURATION SECTION.
00008          SOURCE-COMPUTER.   IBM-370.
00009          OBJECT-COMPUTER.   IBM-370.
00010
00011          INPUT-OUTPUT SECTION.
00012          FILE-CONTROL.
00013              SELECT CARD-FILE ASSIGN TO UT-S-SYSIN.
00014              SELECT PRINT-FILE ASSIGN TO UT-S-SYSOUT.
00015
00016          DATA DIVISION.
00017          FILE SECTION.
00018          FD  CARD-FILE
00019              LABEL RECORDS ARE OMITTED
00020              RECORD CONTAINS 80 CHARACTERS
00021              DATA RECORD IS CARD.
00022          01  CARD.
00023              05  CARD-NAME              PIC A(25).
00024              05  CARD-HOURS             PIC 9(3)V99.
00025              05  CARD-RATE              PIC 9(3)V99.
00026              05  FILLER                 PIC X(44).
00027
00028          FD  PRINT-FILE
00029              LABEL RECORDS ARE OMITTED
00030              RECORD CONTAINS 133 CHARACTERS
00031              DATA RECORD IS PRINT-LINE.
00032          01  PRINT-LINE.
00033
00034              05  FILLER                 PIC X.
00035              05  PRINT-NAME             PIC X(25).
00036              05  FILLER                 PIC X(3).
00037              05  PRINT-HOURS            PIC ZZZZV99.
00038              05  FILLER                 PIC X(3).
00039              05  PRINT-RATE             PIC $$$$.99.
00040              05  FILLER                 PIC X(3).
00041              05  PRINT-GROSS            PIC $$$$$.99
00042              05  FILLER                 PIC X(5).
00043              05  PRINT-FED-TAX          PIC $$$$$.99.
00044              05  FILLER                 PIC X(4).
00045              05  PRINT-NET              PTC $$$$$.99.
00046              05  FILLER                 PIC X(51).
00047          WORKING-STORAGE SECTION.
00048          01  DATA-REMAINS-SWITCH        PIC X(3)    VALUE 'YES'.
00049
00050          01  INDIVIDUAL-COMPUTATIONS.
00051              05  IND-GROSS-PAY          PIC 9(4)V99.
00052              05  IND-FED-TAX            PIC 9(4)V99.
00053              05  IND-NET-PAY            PIC 9(4)V99.
00054
00055          01  COMPANY-TOTALS.
00056              05  COMP-GROSS-PAY         PIC 9(5)V99 VALUE ZEROS.
00057              05  COMP-FED-TAX           PIC 9(5)V99 VALUE ZEROS.
00058              05  COMP-NET-PAY           PIC 9(5)V99 VALUE ZEROS.
00059
00060          01  HEADING-LINE.
00061              05  FILLER                 PIC X(8)    VALUE SPACES.
00062              05  FILLER                 PIC X(4)    VALUE 'NAME'.
00063              05  FILLER                 PIC X(19)   VALUE SPACES.
00064              05  FILLER                 PIC X(5)    VALUE 'HOURS'.
00065              05  FILLER                 PIC X(5)    VALUE SPACES.
00066              05  FILLER                 PIC X(4)    VALUE 'RATE'.
00067              05  FILLER                 PIC X(6)    VALUE SPACES.
00068              05  FILLER                 PIC X(9)    VALUE 'GROSS PAY'.
00069              05  FILLER                 PIC X(5)    VALUE SPACES.
00070              05  FILLER                 PIC X(7)    VALUE 'FED TAX'.
00071              05  FILLER                 PIC X(5)    VALUE SPACES.
00072              05  FILLER                 PIC X(7)    VALUE 'NET PAY'.
00073              05  FILLER                 PIC X(50)   VALUE SPACES.
00074
```

FIGURE 5.5 *Payroll Program with Compilation Errors*

```
00075          01  TOTAL-LINE.
00076              05  FILLER                 PIC X(34)    VALUE SPACES.
00077              05  FILLER                 PIC X(13)    VALUE 'TOTAL'.
00078              05  PRINT-CO-GROSS         PIC $$$,$$$.99.
00079              05  FILLER                 PIC X(3)     VALUE SPACES.
00080              05  PRINT-CO-FED-TAX       PIC $$$,$$$.99.
00081              05  FILLER                 PIC X(3)     VALUE SPACES.
00082              05  PRINT-CO-NET           PIC $$$,$$$.99.
00083              05  FILLER                 PIC X(48)    VALUE SPACES.
00084      PROCEDURE DIVISION.
00085      MAINLINE.
00086          OPEN INPUT CARD-FILE
00087              OUTPUT PRINT-FILE.
00088          READ CARD-FILE
00089              AT END MOVE 'NO' TO DATA-REMAINS-SWITCH.
00090          MOVE HEADER-LINE TO PRINT-LINE.
00091          WRITE PRINT-LINE AFTER ADVANCING PAGE.
00092          PERFORM PROCESS-CARDS
00093              UNTIL DATA-REMAINS-SWITCH = 'NO'.
00094          PERFORM WRITE-TOTAL-LINE.
00095          CLOSE CARD-FILE
00096              PRINT-FILE.
00097          STOP RUN.
00098
00099      PROCESS-CARD.
00100          COMPUTE IND-GROSS-PAY = CARD-HOURS * CARD-RATE.
00101          IF CARD-HOURS>40
00102              COMPUTE IND-GROSS-PAY =
00103                  IND-GROSS-PAY + (CARD-HOURS  - 40) * .5 * CARD-RATE.
00104          IF CARD-HOURS > 48
00105              COMPUTE IND-GROSS-PAY =
00106                  IND-GROSS-PAY + (CARD-HOURS  - 48) * .5 * CARD-RATE.
00107          IF IND-GROSS-PAY > 300
00108            COMPUTE IND-FED-TAX = 60 + .22 * (IND-GROSS-PAY - 300)
00109          ELSE
00110              IF IND-GROSS-PAY > 240
00111                  COMPUTE IND-FED-TAX = 42 + .20 * (IND-GROSS-PAY - 240)
00112              ELSE
00113                  COMPUTE IND-FED-TAX = .16 * IND-GROSS-PAY.
00114
00115          SUBTRACT IND-FED-TAX FROM IND-GROSS-PAY
00116              GIVING IND-NET-PAY.
00117
00118          ADD IND-GROSS-PAY TO COMP-GROSS-PAY.
00119          ADD IND-FED-TAX TO COMP-FED-TAX.
00120          ADD IND-NET-PAY TO COMP-NET-PAY.
00121
00122          MOVE SPACES TO PRINT-LINE.
00123          MOVE CARD-NAME TO PRINT-NAME.
00124          MOVE CARD-HOURS TO PRINT-HOURS.
00125          MOVE CARD-RATE TO PRINT-RATE.
00126          MOVE IND-GROSS-PAY TO PRINT-GROSS.
00127          MOVE IND-FED-TAX TO PRINT-FED-TAX.
00128          MOVE IND-NET-PAY TO PRINT-NET-PAY.
00129          WRITE PRINT-LINE
00130              ADVANCING 2 LINES.
00131
00132          READ CARD
00133              AT END MOVE 'NO' TO DATA-REMAINS-SWITCH.
00134
00135      WRITE-TOTAL-LINE.
00136          MOVE COMP-GROSS-PAY TO PRINT-CO-GROSS.
00137          MOVE COMP-FED-TAX TO PRINT-CO-FED-TAX.
00138          MOVE COMP-NET-PAY TO PRINT-CO-NET.
00139          MOVE TOTAL-LINE TO PRINT-LINE.
00140          WRITE PRINT-FILE
00141              AFTER ADVANCING 2 LINES.
```

FIGURE 5.5 *(continued)*

13   IKF2146I-C   RECORD SIZE IN RECORD-CONTAINS CLAUSE DISAGREES WITH COMPUTED RECORD SIZE. 00079
             ASSUMED.
14   IKF2146I-C   RECORD SIZE IN RECORD-CONTAINS CLAUSE DISAGREES WITH COMPUTED RECORD SIZE. 00132
             ASSUMED.

Diagnostics for Figure 5.5

```
42      IKF1043I-W    END OF SENTENCE SHOULD PRECEDE 05 . ASSUMED PRESENT.
90      IKF3001I-E    HEADER-LINE NOT DEFINED. DISCARDED.
92      IKF3001I-E    PROCESS-CARDS NOT DEFINED. STATEMENT DISCARDED.
102     IKF1007I-W    GREATER NOT PRECEDED BY A SPACE. ASSUME SPACE.
102     IKF1007I-W    40 NOT PRECEDED BY A SPACE. ASSUME SPACE.
128     IKF3001I-E    PRINT-NET-PAY NOT DEFINED. DISCARDED.
129     IKF4003I-E    EXPECTING NEW STATEMENT. FOUND ADVANCING . DELETING TILL NEXT VERB OR
                      PROCEDURE-NAME.
132     IKF4050I-E    SYNTAX REQUIRES FILE-NAME . FOUND DNM=1-112 . STATEMENT DISCARDED.
140     IKF4050I-E    SYNTAX REQUIRES RECORD-NAME . FOUND DNM=1-198 . STATEMENT DISCARDED.
```

Diagnostics for Figure 5.5 *(continued)*

```
00001            IDENTIFICATION DIVISION.
00002            PROGRAM-ID. 'PAYROLL'.
00003            AUTHOR.
00004                MARION MILGROM.
00005
00006            ENVIRONMENT DIVISION.
00007            CONFIGURATION SECTION.
00008            SOURCE-COMPUTER.    IBM-370.
00009            OBJECT-COMPUTER.    IBM-370.
00010
00011            INPUT-OUTPUT SECTION.
00012            FILE-CONTROL.
00013                SELECT CARD-FILE ASSIGN TO UT-S-SYSIN.
00014                SELECT PRINT-FILE ASSIGN TO UT-S-SYSOUT.
00015
00016            DATA DIVISION.
00017            FILE SECTION.
00018            FD  CARD-FILE
00019                LABEL RECORDS ARE OMITTED
00020                RECORD CONTAINS 80 CHARACTERS
00021                DATA RECORD IS CARD.
00022            01  CARD.
00023                05  CARD-NAME            PIC A(25).
00024                05  CARD-HOURS           PIC 9(3)V99.
00025                05  CARD-RATE            PIC 9(3)V99.
00026                05  FILLER               PIC X(45).
00027
00028            FD  PRINT-FILE
00029                LABEL RECORDS ARE OMITTED
00030                RECORD CONTAINS 133 CHARACTERS
00031                DATA RECORD IS PRINT-LINE.
00032            01  PRINT-LINE.
00033
00034                05  PRINT-NAME           PIC X(25).
00035                05  FILLER               PIC X(3).
00036                05  PRINT-HOURS          PIC ZZZZ.99.
00037                05  FILLER               PIC X(3).
00038                05  PRINT-RATE           PIC $$$$.99.
00039                05  FILLER               PIC X(3).
00040                05  PRINT-GROSS          PIC $$$$$.99.
00041                05  FILLER               PIC X(5).
00042                05  PRINT-FED-TAX        PIC $$$$$.99.
00043                05  FILLER               PIC X(5).
00044                05  PRINT-NET-PAY        PIC $$$$$.99.
00045                05  FILLER               PIC X(51).
00046            WORKING-STORAGE SECTION.
00047            01  DATA-REMAINS-SWITCH      PIC X(3)    VALUE 'YES'.
00048
00049            01  INDIVIDUAL-COMPUTATIONS.
00050                05  IND-GROSS-PAY        PIC 9(4).
00051                05  IND-FED-TAX          PIC 9(4).
00052                05  IND-NET-PAY          PIC 9(4).
00053
00054            01  COMPANY-TOTALS.
00055                05  COMP-GROSS-PAY       PIC 9(5)V99 VALUE ZEROS.
00056                05  COMP-FED-TAX         PIC 9(5)V99 VALUE ZEROS.
00057                05  COMP-NET-PAY         PIC 9(5)V99 VALUE ZEROS.
00058
00059            01  HEADING-LINE.
00060                05  FILLER               PIC X(8)    VALUE SPACES.
00061                05  FILLER               PIC X(4)    VALUE 'NAME'.
00062                05  FILLER               PIC X(19)   VALUE SPACES.
```

FIGURE 5.6 *COBOL Program with Logic Errors*

```
00063              05   FILLER                        PIC X(5)    ·VALUE 'HOURS'.
00064              05   FILLER                        PIC X(5)    VALUE SPACES.
00065              05   FILLER                        PIC X(4)    VALUE 'RATE'.
00066              05   FILLER                        PIC X(6)    VALUE SPACES.
00067              05   FILLER                        PIC X(9)    VALUE 'GROSS PAY'.
00068              05   FILLER                        PIC X(5)    VALUE SPACES.
00069              05   FILLER                        PIC X(7)    VALUE 'FED TAX'.
00070              05   FILLER                        PIC X(5)    VALUE SPACES.
00071              05   FILLER                        PIC X(7)    VALUE 'NET PAY'.
00072              05   FILLER                        PIC X(50)   VALUE SPACES.
00073
00074        01   TOTAL-LINE.
00075              05   FILLER                        PIC X(34)   VALUE SPACES.
00076              05   FILLER                        PIC X(13)   VALUE 'TOTAL'.
00077              05   PRINT-CO-GROSS                PIC $$$,$$$.99.
00078              05   FILLER                        PIC X(3)    VALUE SPACES.
00079              05   PRINT-CO-FED-TAX              PIC $$$,$$$.99.
00080              05   FILLER                        PIC X(3)    VALUE SPACES.
00081              05   PRINT-CO-NET                  PIC $$$,$$$.99.
00082              05   FILLER                        PIC X(48)   VALUE SPACES.
00083        PROCEDURE DIVISION.
00084        MAINLINE.
00085              OPEN INPUT CARD-FILE
00086                   OUTPUT PRINT-FILE.
00087              READ CARD-FILE
00088                   AT END MOVE 'NO' TO DATA-REMAINS-SWITCH
00089              MOVE HEADING-LINE TO PRINT-LINE
00090              WRITE PRINT-LINE AFTER ADVANCING PAGE.
00091              PERFORM PROCESS-CARDS
00092                   UNTIL DATA-REMAINS-SWITCH = 'NO'.
00093              PERFORM WRITE-TOTAL-LINE.
00094              CLOSE CARD-FILE
00095                   PRINT-FILE.
00096              STOP RUN.
00097
00098        PROCESS-CARDS.
00099              COMPUTE IND-GROSS-PAY = CARD-HOURS * CARD-RATE.
00100              IF CARD-HOURS > 40
00101                   COMPUTE IND-GROSS-PAY =
00102                        IND-GROSS-PAY + (CARD-HOURS  - 40) * 1.5 * CARD-RATE.
00103              IF CARD-HOURS > 48
00104                   COMPUTE IND-GROSS-PAY =
00105                        IND-GROSS-PAY + (CARD-HOURS  - 48) * 2.0 * CARD-RATE.
00106              IF IND-GROSS-PAY > 300
00107                 COMPUTE IND-FED-TAX = 60 + .22 * (IND-GROSS-PAY - 300)
00108              ELSE
00109                   IF IND-GROSS-PAY > 240
00110                        COMPUTE IND-FED-TAX = 42 + .20 * (IND-GROSS-PAY - 240)
00111                   ELSE
00112                        COMPUTE IND-FED-TAX = .16 * IND-GROSS-PAY.
00113
00114              SUBTRACT IND-FED-TAX FROM IND-GROSS-PAY
00115                   GIVING IND-NET-PAY.
00116
00117              ADD IND-GROSS-PAY COMP-GROSS-PAY GIVING COMP-GROSS-PAY.
00118              ADD IND-FED-TAX TO COMP-FED-TAX.
00119              ADD IND-NET-PAY TO COMP-NET-PAY.
00120
00121              MOVE SPACES TO PRINT-LINE.
00122              MOVE CARD-NAME TO PRINT-NAME.
00123              MOVE CARD-HOURS TO PRINT-HOURS.
00124              MOVE CARD-RATE TO PRINT-RATE.
00125              MOVE IND-GROSS-PAY TO PRINT-GROSS.
00126              MOVE IND-FED-TAX TO PRINT-FED-TAX.
00127              MOVE COMP-NET-PAY TO PRINT-NET-PAY.
00128              WRITE PRINT-LINE
00129                   AFTER ADVANCING 2 LINES.
00130
00131              READ CARD-FILE
00132                   AT END MOVE 'NO' TO DATA-REMAINS-SWITCH.
00133
```

FIGURE 5.6 *(continued)*

```
00134          WRITE-TOTAL-LINE.
00135              MOVE COMP-GROSS-PAY TO PRINT-CO-GROSS.
00136              MOVE COMP-FED-TAX TO PRINT-CO-FED-TAX.
00137              MOVE COMP-NET-PAY TO PRINT-CO-NET.
00138              MOVE TOTAL-LINE TO PRINT-LINE.
00139              WRITE PRINT-LINE
00140                  AFTER ADVANCING 2 LINES.
```

FIGURE 5.6 *(continued)*

CORRECT REPORT:

NAME	HOURS	RATE	GROSS PAY	FED TAX	NET PAY
SMITH	40.00	$5.00	$200.00	$32.00	$168.00
JONES	44.00	$6.00	$276.00	$49.20	$226.80
PETERS	49.00	$7.00	$378.00	$77.16	$300.84
HANSEN	36.00	$5.55	$199.80	$31.96	$167.84
MILGROM	42.00	$10.14	$436.02	$89.92	$346.10
TATAR	40.00	$4.33	$173.20	$27.71	$145.49
		TOTAL	$1,663.02	$307.95	$1,355.07

ACTUAL REPORT:

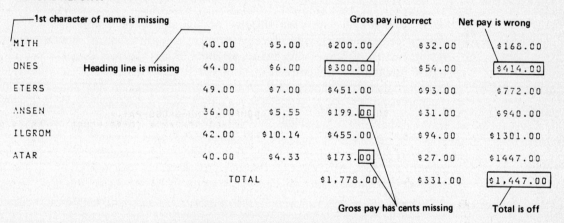

MITH	40.00	$5.00	$200.00	$32.00	$168.00
ONES	44.00	$6.00	$300.00	$54.00	$414.00
ETERS	49.00	$7.00	$451.00	$93.00	$772.00
ANSEN	36.00	$5.55	$199.00	$31.00	$940.00
ILGROM	42.00	$10.14	$455.00	$94.00	$1301.00
ATAR	40.00	$4.33	$173.00	$27.00	$1447.00
		TOTAL	$1,778.00	$331.00	$1,447.00

FIGURE 5.7 *Correct and invalid output*

CHAPTER 5: DEBUGGING, I   91

Chapter 6

PROGRAMMING STYLE, I

OVERVIEW

As a beginning student, your objective should simply be a working program. As an advanced student or professional, your objective is enlarged—an "efficient" program that is easily read and maintained by someone other than yourself. Further, the professional's program should conform to his installation's standards. It must be tested under a variety of conditions, including obviously improper data, and should include programming checks to flag potentially invalid transactions. In short, while the beginner is concerned with merely translating a working flowchart or pseudocode into COBOL, the professional requires straightforward logic, easy-to-read COBOL code, and a well-tested program.

Over time, an individual develops a collection of techniques, i.e., a style, to accomplish these objectives. Most introductory texts omit programming style entirely, or at best devote only a few pages to the subject near the end of the book. We believe that the topic is so important that it merits two entire chapters, and further that coverage should begin as soon as basic programming concepts have been established. We have found that an early awareness of "style" is highly beneficial to both student and professional. Individuals conscious of style tend to write programs that are easier to read, easier to debug, and more apt to be correct.

 In this chapter we are concerned with two elements of programming style: coding standards and structured programming. There are no absolute truths, i.e., no right or wrong, insofar as programming style is concerned. Different programmers develop slightly or even radically different styles that are consistent within the rules of COBOL and within the programmer's objective. Accordingly, the discussion that follows here and in Chapter 11 reflects the viewpoints of the authors and is necessarily subjective in parts.

CODING STANDARDS

In spite of what you may think of the COBOL compiler, COBOL is a relatively free-form language. There is considerable flexibility as to starting column for most entries (i.e., in or beyond column 12). The rules for paragraph and data names make for easy-to-write, but not necessarily easy-to-read, programs.

In a commercial installation, it is absolutely essential that programs be well documented, as the person who writes a program today may not be here tomorrow. Indeed, continuing success depends on someone other than the author being able to maintain a program. Accordingly, most

92

installations impose a set of coding standards, such as those described herein, which go beyond the requirements of COBOL. Such standards are optional for the student. However, they are typical of what is required in the real world.

Data Division

1. *Begin all PICTURE clauses in the same column,* usually between columns 36 and 52, but the choice is arbitrary. Further, choose one form of the PICTURE clause (PIC, PIC IS, PICTURE, or PICTURE IS) and follow it consistently. The actual starting column and form chosen are immaterial, but consistency is essential. Vertical alignment of the PICTURE clause greatly improves the overall appearance of a COBOL program. (Similar guidelines apply to the VALUE and USAGE clauses as well.)

2. *Prefix all data names within the same FD or 01,* e.g., two characters unique to the FD: CD-LAST-NAME, CD-FIRST-NAME, CD-ADDRESS, etc. The utility of this guideline becomes apparent in the procedure division if it is necessary to refer back to the definition of a data name. The prefix points you immediately to the proper record.

3. *Eliminate 77-level entries.* In theory, a 77-level entry is an independent data item having no relationship to any other data item in the program. In practice, few if any data items are truly independent, and related items should be grouped under a common 01 entry.

4. *Indent successive level numbers in an FD by a consistent amount,* e.g., two or four columns. Use the same level numbers from FD to FD and leave numerical gaps between successive levels: 05, 10, 15, 20 or 03, 07, 11, 15, etc.

5. *Choose mnemonically significant data names.* COBOL allows data names up to 30 characters, but two- and three-character cryptic names are used frequently. It is impossible for a maintenance programmer, or even the original author, to determine the meaning of CD-X, RF-P, etc. Moreover, meaningful names should be chosen; e.g., END-OF-EMPLOYEE-FILE-SWITCH is superior to SWITCH-1.

6. *Indent successive lines of the same entry.* If a given statement contains several clauses, it is usually not possible to fit the entire entry on one line. In those instances the continued line should be indented. Further, a clause should not be split over two lines (not always possible with VALUE clauses).

The following COBOL code summarizes these suggestions:

```
01   STUDENT-INPUT-RECORD.
     05   SR-STUDENT-NAME.
          10   SR-STUDENT-LAST-NAME      PIC   X(20).
          10   SR-STUDENT-FIRST-NAME     PIC   X(10).
     05   SR-BIRTH-DATE.
          10   SR-BIRTH-MONTH            PIC   99.
          10   SR-BIRTH-YEAR             PIC   99.



WORKING-STORAGE SECTION.
01   UNIVERSITY-TOTALS.
     05   UN-TUITION                     PIC   9(6).
     05   UN-SCHOLARSHIP                 PIC   9(6).
```

Procedure Division

1. *Do not put more than one statement on a line.* The COBOL compiler accepts a period as the delimiter between statements, but a new line is much easier for the eye to follow. Further, if a sentence extends past column 72, then continued lines should be indented by a consistent amount, e.g., four columns.

2. *Paragraph and section headers should be the only entries on a line.* Thus, the first statement in a section or paragraph should always begin a new line. In addition, a blank line before each paragraph or section name helps the entry to further stand out.

3. *Sequence all section and paragraph names,* e.g., 0010-HOUSEKEEPING, 0020-READ-A-CARD, etc. This technique makes it easy to locate paragraphs and/or section headers quickly and is particularly important for large programs.

4. *Highlight important verbs or clauses by indenting or inserting a blank line.* We like to indent all nested IF statements and also precede them by a blank line. Additional verbs, clauses, etc., are at programmer discretion.

5. *Align IF/ELSE statements with the ELSE portion under the relevant IF.* The compiler does not interpret ELSE clauses as the programmer writes them but *associates the ELSE clause with the closest unpaired previous IF.* Incorrect indentation in a listing conveys a programmer's intention, which is not recognized by the compiler. Consider the *misleading* example

```
IF CD-SEX IS EQUAL TO 'M'
    IF CD-AGE IS GREATER THAN 30
        MOVE CD-NAME TO MALE-OVER-30
ELSE MOVE CD-NAME TO REJECT.
```

The indentation implies that CD-NAME should be moved to REJECT if CD-SEX is not equal to 'M'. This is *not* the compiler interpretation. *The ELSE clause is associated with the closest previous IF that is not already paired with another ELSE.* Therefore, the compiler will move CD-NAME to REJECT if CD-SEX equals 'M' but CD-AGE is not greater than 30. The statement should be *rewritten* and guidelines for proper indentation are covered in depth in chapter 7.

6. *Stack, i.e., vertically align, similar portions of a statement or group of statements.* The MOVE statement provides a good example:

```
MOVE CD-NAME        TO PR-NAME.
MOVE CD-STUDENT-ID  TO PR-STUDENT-ID.
MOVE CD-AGE         TO PR-AGE.
MOVE CD-ADDRESS     TO PR-ADDRESS.
```

7. *Code in a straightforward manner.* This guideline is more of a stylistic nature, but of such concern to the authors that it is included anyway. Procedure division code should be kept as straightforward as possible and efforts at being cute or fancy, should be discouraged. Beginning programmers especially are notorious for trying to impress their peers with "clever" code. Compare, for example, the following IF statements, which are logically equivalent:

```
IF  HOURS-WORKED > 48
COMPUTE GROSS-PAY
    = 40 * HOURLY-RATE
    +  8 * HOURLY-RATE * 1.5
    + (HOURS-WORKED − 48) * HOURLY-RATE * 2.
```

versus

```
IF HOURS-WORKED > 48
    COMPUTE GROSS-PAY
        = 52 * HOURLY-RATE
        + (HOURS-WORKED − 48) * HOURLY-RATE * 2.
```

It is fairly easy to determine the method of payment from the first statement. Individuals working more than 48 hours receive straight time for the first 40 hours, time and a half for the next 8 hours, and double time for any hours over 48. The second statement produces equivalent results for GROSS-PAY and is a line shorter. It is, however, decidedly *poorer* code because it deviates significantly from the physical situation. A maintenance programmer would be hard pressed to understand the meaning of the constant 52. Lest the reader think this is a concocted example, it was written by a math major in COBOL 1. The student was an accomplished mathematician and FORTRAN programmer. His solution may be elegant in a mathematical sense, but it is certainly undesirable in a commercial environment.

Both Divisions

1. *Use blank lines, SKIP's, and EJECT's freely.* EJECT (restricted to IBM systems) causes the next statement in a COBOL listing to begin on top of a new page. SKIP1, SKIP2, and SKIP3 (also restricted to IBM) cause the listing to space one, two, or three lines, respectively, before the next statement. Blank lines, SKIP's, and EJECT's should be freely used prior to section and division headers, FD's, 01's, etc. (The ANS 74 standard uses a slash in column 7 for EJECT, and blank cards in lieu of SKIPs.)

2. *Make use of Columns 73 to 80.* Columns 73 to 80 are optional in COBOL, but can be put to good use, e.g., to indicate program corrections. Any statement that is added or altered could contain the modifier's initials and date of modification. Thus, RTG08/78 appearing in columns 73 to 80 would indicate that the programmer RTG modified (or added) this statement in August, 1978.

3. *Use appropriate comments.* Although there is growing disillusionment with comments in structured COBOL programs, good code does *not* eliminate their necessity. As Yourdon[1] has so eloquently stated, "no programmer, no matter how wise, no matter how experienced, no matter how hard pressed for time, no matter how well intentioned, should be forgiven an uncommented and undocumented program." The mere presence of comments, however, does not ensure a well-documented program, and poor comments are sometimes worse than no comments at all. The most common fault is redundancy with the source code. For example, in the code

```
*       CALCULATE NET PAY
        COMPUTE NET-PAY = GROSS-PAY − FEDERAL-TAX − VOLUNTARY-DEDUCTION.
```

the comment does not add to the readability of the program. It might even be said to detract from legibility because it breaks the logical flow as one is reading. Worse than redundant, comments may be obsolete or incorrect, i.e., inconsistent with the associated code. This happens if program statements are changed during debugging or maintenance and the comments are not correspondingly altered. The compiler, unfortunately, does not validate comments. Comments may also be correct, but incomplete and hence misleading. In sum, the presence of comments is essential, but great care, *more than is commonly exercised,* should be applied to developing and maintaining comments in a program.

As a general rule, comments should be provided whenever you are doing something that is not immediately obvious to another person. When considering a comment, imagine you are turning the program over for maintenance, and insert comments whenever you would pause to explain a feature in your program. Do assume, however, that the maintenance programmer is as competent in COBOL as you are. Thus your comments should be directed to *why* you are doing something, rather than to what you are doing.

4. *Avoid commas.* The compiler treats a comma as "noise"; i.e., a comma has no effect on the generated object code. Many programmers, the authors included, have acquired the habit (which they are trying to break) of inserting commas to increase legibility. While this works rather well with prose, it can have just the opposite effect in COBOL. This is because of blurred print chains, which make it difficult to distinguish a comma from a period. As we have already seen, the presence or absence of a period is critical. Hence, the inability to distinguish a period from a comma becomes rather annoying; consequently, try avoiding commas altogether.

STRUCTURED PROGRAMMING

This is the first mention of the term *structured programming,* although every program presented so far has been "structured." Structured programming is the discipline of making a program's logic easy to follow. This is accomplished by limiting a program to three basic logic structures: sequence, selection, and iteration, as depicted in Figure 6.1.

---

[1] Edward Yourdon, *Techniques of Program Structure and Design,* Prentice-Hall, Inc., Englewood Cliffs, N.J., 1975.

(a) SEQUENCE

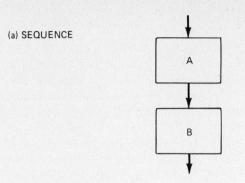

(b) SELECTION (IF THEN ELSE)

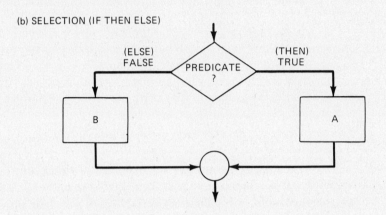

(c) ITERATION (DO WHILE)

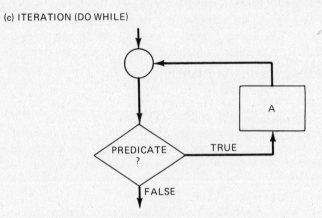

FIGURE 6.1 *The Logic Structures of a "Proper" Program*

The *sequence* structure formally specifies that program statements are executed sequentially, i.e., in the order in which they appear unless otherwise specified. The two blocks, A and B, may denote anything from single statements to complete programs.

Selection is the choice between two actions. A condition (known as a predicate) is tested. If the predicate is true, block A is executed; if it is false, block B is executed. A and B join in a single exit point from the structure. The predicate itself is the single entry point.

Iteration calls for repeated execution of code while a condition is true. The condition (predicate) is tested. If it holds true, block A is executed; if false, the structure relinquishes control to the next sequential statement. Again, there is exactly one entry point and exit point from the structure.

The logic structures of Figure 6.1 can be combined in a limitless variety of ways to produce any required logic. This is possible because an entire structure may be substituted anywhere block A or B appears. Figure 6.2 contains such a combination. The iteration structure contains a selection structure, which in turn contains a sequence. *Each of the structures contains one entry and one exit point.*

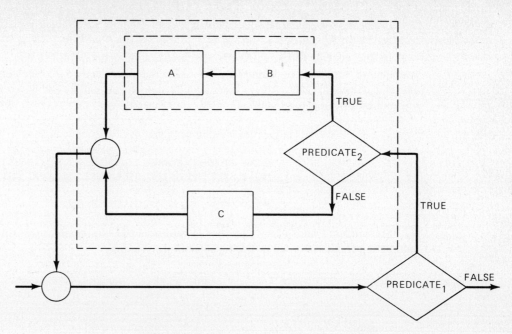

FIGURE 6.2 *Combination of Logic Structures*

Conspicuous by its absence in Figure 6.1 is the GO TO statement. This is *not* to say that structured programming is synonymous with "GO TO less" programming, nor is the goal of structured programming merely the removal of all GO TO statements. The discipline aims at making programs *understandable,* which in turn mandates the elimination of indiscriminate page turning brought on by abundant use of GO TO. (The procedure division of unstructured programs often consists of 10% GO TO statements.)

Implementation in COBOL

The sequence structure is implemented by coding statements sequentially, and no further explanation is necessary. The selection structure is implemented by the COBOL "IF THEN ELSE" statement, and the iteration structure by the COBOL "PERFORM UNTIL."

Selection Structure

The selection structure is implemented by the COBOL IF statement, which has the general format

```
IF condition
    statement 1
ELSE
    statement 2.
```

The condition generally tests the relationship between two items, e.g., equal, less than, etc. Statements 1 and 2 denote any COBOL statement (or group of statements) that are to be executed if the condition is true or false, respectively.

For example, consider the computation of the student union fee in the tuition billing problem. Union members (denoted by a 'Y' on the input card) are to be charged a fee of $25; nonmembers are not charged anything. This is coded as follows:

```
IF UNION-MEMBER IS EQUAL TO 'Y'
    MOVE 25 TO UNION-FEE
ELSE
    MOVE ZERO TO UNION-FEE.
```

The predicate tests whether 'Y' is contained in the field UNION-MEMBER. If so, 25 is moved to UNION-FEE; if not, 0 is moved to UNION-FEE.

In the general form of the IF statement, statements 1 and 2 can each denote a series of statements. Suppose, for example, that union members are to receive season tickets to football games and are also to have their names added to a member mailing list. These additional requirements are met by listing several actions under one IF as shown:

```
IF UNION-MEMBER IS EQUAL TO 'Y'
      MOVE 25                TO UNION-FEE
      MOVE STUDENT-NAME   TO FOOTBALL-TICKET-LIST
      MOVE STUDENT-NAME   TO MEMBER-MAILING-LIST
ELSE
      MOVE ZERO              TO UNION-FEE.
```

Statements 1 and 2 can also denote additional IF statements. Consider the specification for calculating the activity fee in the tuition billing example:

Credits Taken	Activity Fee
0–6	$25
7–12	$50
13 or more	$75

These instructions are represented by combining two selection structures as shown in Figure 6.3. (Note that credits must be 6 or less for a fee of $25.) It is now a simple matter to establish the correct COBOL code:

```
IF CREDITS > 12
      MOVE 75 TO ACTIVITY-FEE
ELSE
      IF CREDITS > 6
            MOVE 50 TO ACTIVITY-FEE
      ELSE
            MOVE 25 TO ACTIVITY-FEE.
```

Note that each ELSE is directly under its associated IF as described in the section on coding standards. This is not a COBOL requirement but rather a technique to improve clarity.

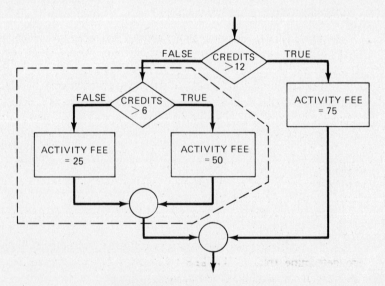

FIGURE 6.3 *Nested IF Structure*

Iteration Structure

The <u>iteration</u> structure is implemented by the COBOL PERFORM UNTIL. The perform statement was first introduced in Chapter 3. It was shown to transfer control to the paragraph specified, execute every statement in that paragraph, and return control to the statement immediately following, i.e., the statement after the perform itself.

It is important to emphasize that perform is *not* a fancy way of saying GO TO. A GO TO statement is a "one-way" ticket; i.e., control is transferred to another point in the program and never returns. Perform is a "round-trip" ticket in that control always returns after the designated procedure is completed.

Iteration is accomplished by including the UNTIL clause, specifying a condition, and modifying that condition during execution of the performed routine. For example,

```
MOVE 'YES' TO DATA-REMAINS-SWITCH.
READ STUDENT-FILE
    AT END MOVE 'NO' TO DATA-REMAINS-SWITCH.
PERFORM 020-PROCESS-A-RECORD
    UNTIL DATA-REMAINS-SWITCH = 'NO'.
    .
    .
    .
020-PROCESS-A-RECORD.
    .
    .
    .
    READ STUDENT-FILE
        AT END MOVE 'NO' TO DATA-REMAINS-SWITCH.
030-NEXT-PARAGRAPH.
```

The paragraph 020-PROCESS-A-RECORD will be executed repeatedly until the incoming file is empty. Note well the initialization of DATA-REMAINS-SWITCH and the presence of an initial read prior to the perform itself (as explained in Chapter 1). Realize also that the until condition is tested *before* the perform takes place. Thus, consider what would happen in the preceding code if STUDENT-FILE were empty. The initial read would sense the end of file and move NO to DATA-REMAINS-SWITCH. The until condition is immediately satisfied and hence 020-PROCESS-A-RECORD would never be performed.

AN IMPROVED TUITION BILLING PROGRAM

The tuition billing example of Figure 4.8 has been rewritten to reflect the ideas of this chapter. Although no objections were raised to Figure 4.8 at the time of its development, Figure 6.4 is superior because of the attention to programming style.

Many of the changes have to do with coding standards. The data names in STUDENT-FILE are now prefixed with SR-. Note the file name itself is more meaningful; STUDENT-FILE (in Figure 6.4) rather than CARD-FILE in Figure 4.8. The picture clause has been uniformly shortened to PIC and vertical alignment of this clause has been achieved.

77-Level entries have been eliminated in favor of multiple 01 entries that consist of group related items. Hence, IND-TUITION, IND-ACTIVITY-FEE, etc., appear together under the 01 entry INDIVIDUAL-CALCULATIONS, whereas TOTAL-TUITION, TOTAL-ACTIVITY-FEE, etc., are also grouped (lines 56 to 67). Note also the use of common prefixes.

Blank lines have been inserted before 01 entries and paragraph headers. The latter have also been sequenced.

The procedure division remains relatively unchanged. Note, however, the use of a nested IF to determine IND-ACTIVITY-FEE (lines 115 to 121) in lieu of two individual IF statements. Note well the associated indentation.

Finally, observe how the two read statements of Figure 4.8 have been replaced by performs,

```
00001          IDENTIFICATION DIVISION.
00002          PROGRAM-ID.    'TUITION'.
00003          AUTHOR.        THE BURSAR.
00004
00005          ENVIRONMENT DIVISION.
00006          CONFIGURATION SECTION.
00007          SOURCE-COMPUTER.  IBM-370.
00008          OBJECT-COMPUTER.  IBM-370.        ┌─ Data name of STUDENT-FILE is preferable to
00009          INPUT-OUTPUT SECTION.             │  CARD-FILE
00010          FILE-CONTROL.
00011              SELECT STUDENT-FILE ASSIGN TO UT-S-SYSIN.
00012              SELECT PRINT-FILE ASSIGN TO UT-S-SYSOUT.
00013
00014          DATA DIVISION.
00015          FILE SECTION.
00016          FD  STUDENT-FILE
00017              LABEL RECORDS ARE OMITTED
00018              RECORD CONTAINS 80 CHARACTERS    ┌─ Prefix STUDENT-RECORD entries
00019              DATA RECORD IS STUDENT-RECORD.
00020          01  STUDENT-RECORD.
00021              05  SR-STUDENT-NAME          PIC A(20).
00022              05  SR-SOC-SEC-NO            PIC 9(9).
00023              05  SR-CREDITS               PIC 9(2).
00024              05  SR-UNION-MEMBER          PIC A.
00025              05  SR-SCHOLARSHIP           PIC 9(4).
00026              05  FILLER                   PIC X(44).
00027
00028          FD  PRINT-FILE
00029              LABEL RECORDS ARE OMITTED
00030              RECORD CONTAINS 133 CHARACTERS
00031              DATA RECORD IS PRINT-LINE.
00032          01  PRINT-LINE.
00033              05  FILLER                   PIC X.
00034              05  PRINT-STUDENT-NAME       PIC A(20).
00035              05  FILLER                   PIC X(2).
00036              05  PRINT-SOC-SEC-NO         PIC 999B99B9999.
00037              05  FILLER                   PIC X(4).
00038              05  PRINT-CREDITS            PIC 99.
00039              05  FILLER                   PIC X(3).
00040              05  PRINT-TUITION            PIC $$$$,$$9.
00041              05  FILLER                   PIC X.
00042              05  PRINT-UNION-FEE          PIC $$$$,$$9.
00043              05  FILLER                   PIC X(3).
00044              05  PRINT-ACTIVITY-FEE       PIC $$$$,$$9.
00045              05  FILLER                   PIC X(3).
00046              05  PRINT-SCHOLARSHIP        PIC $$$$,$$9.
00047              05  FILLER                   PIC X(5).
00048              05  PRINT-IND-BILL           PIC $$$$,$$9.
00049              05  FILLER                   PIC X(38).
00050
00051          WORKING-STORAGE SECTION.              ── 77 level entries have been omitted
00052
00053          01  PROGRAM-SWITCHES.
00054              05  DATA-REMAINS-SWITCH      PIC X(2)    VALUE SPACES.
00055
00056          01  INDIVIDUAL-CALCULATIONS.
00057              05  IND-TUITION              PIC 9(4)    VALUE ZEROS.
00058              05  IND-ACTIVITY-FEE         PIC 9(2)    VALUE ZEROS.
00059              05  IND-UNION-FEE            PIC 9(2)    VALUE ZEROS.
00060              05  IND-STUDENT-BILL         PIC 9(6)    VALUE ZEROS.
00061                                                 ── Blank lines before 01 entries
00062          01  UNIVERSITY-TOTALS.
00063              05  TOTAL-TUITION            PIC 9(6)    VALUE ZEROS.
00064              05  TOTAL-SCHOLARSHIP        PIC 9(6)    VALUE ZEROS.
00065              05  TOTAL-ACTIVITY-FEE       PIC 9(6)    VALUE ZEROS.
00066              05  TOTAL-UNION-FEE          PIC 9(6)    VALUE ZEROS.
00067              05  TOTAL-IND-BILL           PIC 9(6)    VALUE ZEROS.
00068
00069          01  DASHED-LINE.
00070              05  FILLER                   PIC X       VALUE SPACES.
00071              05  FILLER                   PIC X(97)   VALUE ALL '-'.
00072              05  FILLER                   PIC X(35)   VALUE SPACES.
```

FIGURE 6.4 *Tuition Billing Program with Coding Standards*

```
00073
00074.        01  HEADER-LINE.
00075            05  FILLER                    PIC X.
00076            05  HDG-NAME                  PIC X(12)  VALUE 'STUDENT NAME'.
00077            05  FILLER                    PIC X(10)  VALUE SPACES.
00078            05  HDG-SOC-SEC               PIC X(11)  VALUE 'SOC SEC NUM'.
00079            05  FILLER                    PIC X(2)   VALUE SPACES.
00080            05  HDG-CREDITS               PIC X(7)   VALUE 'CREDITS'.
00081            05  FILLER                    PIC X(2)   VALUE SPACES.
00082            05  HDG-TUITION               PIC X(7)   VALUE 'TUITION'.
00083            05  FILLER                    PIC X(2)   VALUE SPACES.
00084            05  HDG-UNION-FEE             PIC X(9)   VALUE 'UNION FEE'.
00085            05  FILLER                    PIC X(2)   VALUE SPACES.
00086            05  HDG-ACTIVITY              PIC X(7)   VALUE 'ACT FEE'.
00087            05  FILLER                    PIC X(2)   VALUE SPACES.
00088            05  HDG-SCHOLAR               PIC X(11)  VALUE 'SCHOLARSHIP'.
00089            05  FILLER                    PIC X(2)   VALUE SPACES.
00090            05  HDG-TOTAL-BILL            PIC X(10)  VALUE 'TOTAL BILL'.
00091            05  FILLER                    PIC X(36)  VALUE SPACES.
00092        PROCEDURE DIVISION.
00093        0010-MAINLINE.
00094            OPEN INPUT STUDENT-FILE
00095                 OUTPUT PRINT-FILE.
00096            MOVE HEADER-LINE TO PRINT-LINE.
00097            WRITE PRINT-LINE AFTER ADVANCING PAGE.
00098            MOVE DASHED-LINE TO PRINT-LINE.
00099            WRITE PRINT-LINE AFTER ADVANCING 1 LINE.
00100            PERFORM 0040-READ-A-RECORD.
00101            PERFORM 0020-PROCESS-A-RECORD
00102                UNTIL DATA-REMAINS-SWITCH = 'NO'.
00103            PERFORM 0030-WRITE-UNIVERSITY-TOTALS.
00104            CLOSE STUDENT-FILE
00105                  PRINT-FILE.
00106            STOP RUN.
00107
00108        0020-PROCESS-A-RECORD.
00109            COMPUTE IND-TUITION = 80 * SR-CREDITS.
00110            IF SR-UNION-MEMBER = 'Y'
00111                MOVE 25 TO IND-UNION-FEE
00112            ELSE
00113                MOVE ZERO TO IND-UNION-FEE.
00114
00115            IF SR-CREDITS > 12
00116                MOVE 75 TO IND-ACTIVITY-FEE
00117            ELSE
00118                IF SR-CREDITS > 6
00119                    MOVE 50 TO IND-ACTIVITY-FEE
00120                ELSE
00121                    MOVE 25 TO IND-ACTIVITY-FEE.
00122
00123            COMPUTE IND-STUDENT-BILL = IND-TUITION + IND-ACTIVITY-FEE
00124                + IND-UNION-FEE - SR-SCHOLARSHIP.
00125
00126        *** INCREMENT UNIVERSITY TOTALS
00127            ADD IND-TUITION           TO TOTAL-TUITION.
00128            ADD IND-UNION-FEE         TO TOTAL-UNION-FEE.
00129            ADD IND-ACTIVITY-FEE      TO TOTAL-ACTIVITY-FEE
00130            ADD IND-STUDENT-BILL      TO TOTAL-IND-BILL.
00131            ADD SR-SCHOLARSHIP        TO TOTAL-SCHOLARSHIP.
00132
00133        *** WRITE DETAIL LINE
00134            MOVE SPACES               TO PRINT-LINE.
00135            MOVE SR-STUDENT-NAME      TO PRINT-STUDENT-NAME.
00136            MOVE SR-SOC-SEC-NO        TO PRINT-SOC-SEC-NO.
00137            MOVE SR-CREDITS           TO PRINT-CREDITS.
00138            MOVE IND-TUITION          TO PRINT-TUITION.
00139            MOVE IND-UNION-FEE        TO PRINT-UNION-FEE.
00140            MOVE IND-ACTIVITY-FEE     TO PRINT-ACTIVITY-FEE.
00141            MOVE SR-SCHOLARSHIP       TO PRINT-SCHOLARSHIP.
00142            MOVE IND-STUDENT-BILL     TO PRINT-IND-BILL.
00143            WRITE PRINT-LINE AFTER ADVANCING 1 LINE.
00144
00145            PERFORM 0040-READ-A-RECORD.
00146
```

Vertical alignment of PICTURE clause

READ is performed rather than coded in-line

A nested IF determines ACTIVITY FEE

To has been vertically aligned

FIGURE 6.4 (continued)

```
00147          0030-WRITE-UNIVERSITY-TOTALS.
00148              MOVE DASHED-LINE TO PRINT-LINE.
00149              WRITE PRINT-LINE AFTER ADVANCING 1 LINE.
00150              MOVE SPACES            TO PRINT-LINE.
00151              MOVE TOTAL-TUITION     TO PRINT-TUITION.
00152              MOVE TOTAL-UNION-FEE   TO PRINT-UNION-FEE.
00153              MOVE TOTAL-ACTIVITY-FEE TO PRINT-ACTIVITY-FEE.
00154              MOVE TOTAL-SCHOLARSHIP TO PRINT-SCHOLARSHIP.
00155              MOVE TOTAL-IND-BILL    TO PRINT-IND-BILL.
00156              WRITE PRINT-LINE AFTER ADVANCING 2 LINES.
00157
00158          0040-READ-A-RECORD.
00159              READ STUDENT-FILE
00160                  AT END MOVE 'NO' TO DATA-REMAINS-SWITCH.
```

Paragraph names are sequenced also blank lines appear before paragraph headers

FIGURE 6.4 *(continued)*

which in turn invoke a read paragraph (lines 100, 145, and 158 to 160). Program logic is unaffected, but many practitioners prefer a performed routine to duplicate read statements.

SUMMARY

A well-written program should be easily understood by someone other than the original author. Its logical flow should be readily apparent, and the program itself should be as self-documenting as possible. Legibility is one of the key aspects of a good program.

Structured programming and coding standards are both designed to accomplish this objective. These techniques can be used simultaneously, as in Figure 6.4, or individually (nondevotees of structured programming will use coding standards). Accordingly, a structured program is not in and of itself a good program, nor is a nonstructured program necessarily a poor one. Programming style is discussed further in Chapter 11.

REVIEW EXERCISES

TRUE   FALSE

☐   ☐   **1.** Structured programming is "GO TO less" programming.

☐   ☐   **2.** Program indentation affects compiler interpretation.

☐   ☐   **3.** Any COBOL program may be written *without* 77-level entries.

☐   ☐   **4.** Blank lines are permitted in a COBOL program.

☐   ☐   **5.** A comment is indicated by an asterisk in column 6.

☐   ☐   **6.** Program identification is required in columns 73 to 80.

☐   ☐   **7.** A perform statement with an UNTIL clause causes the designated paragraph to be executed *at least once.*

☐   ☐   **8.** The COBOL coding standards for programmers in IBM and AT&T are apt to be identical.

☐   ☐   **9.** An IF statement may contain two IFs, but only one ELSE.

☐   ☐   **10.** An IF statement may contain two ELSEs but only one IF.

☐   ☐   **11.** ANS 74 COBOL requires that paragraphs be sequenced.

☐   ☐   **12.** A slash in column 7 causes the next line in a compiler listing to begin on a new page.

☐   ☐   **13.** The GO TO and PERFORM statements are equivalent.

☐   ☐   **14.** Data names should be short to cut down on coding and keypunch effort.

☐   ☐   **15.** Where possible, several statements should appear on one line in the procedure division to save space.

☐   ☐   **16.** Indentation of COBOL statements is a waste of time.

☐   ☐   **17.** The logic of any program can be expressed with only three types of logic structures.

☐   ☐   **18.** Each of the logic structures of Figure 6.1 has only one entry and one exit.

□ □ **19.** A well-commented COBOL program should contain half as many comment lines as procedure division statements.

□ □ **20.** One should *never* code two COBOL statements if the same logic can be expressed in one.

PROBLEMS

1. Given the accompanying flowchart,
   (a) Construct a nested COBOL IF to accomplish this logic.
   (b) Respond true or false to the following based on the flowchart:
      1. If A > B and C > D, then *always* add 1 to J.
      2. If A > B, then *always* add 1 to G.
      3. If E > F, then *always* add 1 to H.
      4. If A < B and C < D, then *always* add 1 to J.
      5. There are no conditions under which 1 will be added to both G and J simultaneously.
      6. If C > D and E < F, then *always* add 1 to I.

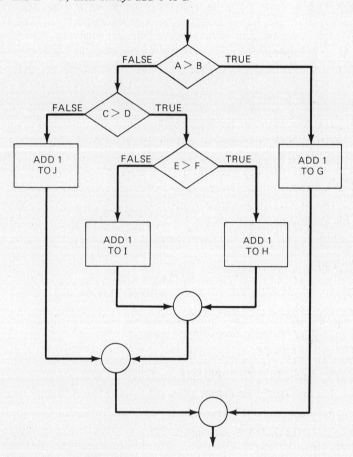

2. Given the following procedure division,

```
PROCEDURE DIVISION.
    PERFORM 010-FIRST.
    PERFORM 020-SECOND.
    PERFORM 040-FOURTH UNTIL FINAL-SUM > 20.
    STOP RUN.
010-FIRST.
    MOVE 1 TO N.
    MOVE ZERO TO FINAL-SUM.
020-SECOND.
    COMPUTE M = N * 2.
    COMPUTE X = N * 3.
    ADD 1 TO N.
    COMPUTE SUM-1 = M + N + X.
```

```
040-FOURTH.
    ADD SUM-1 TO FINAL-SUM.
050-FIFTH.
    ADD 1 TO N.
    ADD 1 TO X.
```

(a) What is the final value of SUM-1?

(b) What is the final value of FINAL-SUM?

(c) How many times is the paragraph 040-FOURTH executed?

(d) Are there any paragraphs that are not executed?

(e) Are there any paragraphs that are executed more than once?

3. Given the COBOL statement,

IF A > 100 MOVE 20 TO N, ELSE IF A = 100 MOVE 19 TO N,
ELSE IF B = 100 MOVE 30 TO N, ELSE MOVE 40 TO N.

(a) Rewrite the COBOL statement indenting the ELSE under the associated IF.

(b) Determine the value of N for the following pairs of A and B:

    1. A = 101, B = 100; N = ?

    2. A = 100, B = 100; N = ?

    3. A = 99, B = 100; N = ?

    4. A = 99, B = 99; N = ?

(c) Draw the flowchart corresponding to the IF statement.

4. Draw a flowchart corresponding to the following COBOL statements:

(a)
```
IF A > B
    IF C > D
        MOVE E TO F
        MOVE G TO H
    ELSE
        ADD I TO J
ELSE
    ADD K TO L
    ADD M TO N.
```

(b)
```
IF A > B
    IF C > D
        IF E > F
            MOVE 1 TO G
        ELSE
            ADD 1 TO H.
```

Section III

MORE COBOL

Chapter 7

MORE ABOUT
THE PROCEDURE DIVISION

OVERVIEW

This chapter begins the third section in our text. Section I (Chapters 1 and 2) consisted of a general introduction to computers and the programming process. In Section II (Chapters 3 to 6) we learned the rudiments of programming. We learned how to write a COBOL program, how to debug it, and were made aware of programming style. Now we are concerned with becoming proficient in COBOL.

This chapter is devoted entirely to the procedure division. Its objective is to introduce a somewhat disjoint set of procedure division elements to increase one's overall capability in COBOL. We shall study the IF and PERFORM statements in detail. We shall learn some new verbs to make life easier, e.g., ACCEPT, DISPLAY, and INSPECT. We shall learn new options for statements we already know something about, e.g., READ INTO, WRITE FROM, and MOVE CORRESPONDING. We shall also cover the ROUNDED and SIZE ERROR options of the arithmetic verbs.

There is so much material in this chapter that it is not possible to master it all in a first reading. We suggest you read initially for general content only and leave the details for later. Try to get a "feel" for the overall power of the material but do not attempt to memorize all the options. Instead, return to specific portions in the chapter as you need the material in your projects.

THE IF STATEMENT

The IF statement is often used incorrectly. Its importance is obvious, yet the large number of options make it one of the more difficult statements to master. The IF statement was introduced in Chapter 3. Now we shall extend the condition portion to include class tests, sign tests, and condition names (88-level entries). We shall consider compound and implied IF's using AND and OR. Finally, we shall take a good look at NEXT SENTENCE, ELSE, and nested IF's.

✳ Class Tests

If you haven't already realized, improper data are a frequent cause of a program's failure to execute. A numeric field can contain only the digits 0 to 9 (a sign is optional), while an alphabetic field can contain only the letters A to Z and/or blanks. Alphanumeric fields can contain anything, e.g., combinations of letters and numbers or special characters, e.g., +, &, etc.

The presence of nonnumeric data in a numeric field used for computation can cause some rather unpleasant results (see Chapter 13 on dump reading and the data exception). Class tests are an excellent way to ensure that numeric data are numeric, alphabetic data are alphabetic, etc. The general format is

$$\text{IF identifier IS [\underline{NOT}] } \left\{ \begin{array}{l} \text{NUMERIC} \\ \text{ALPHABETIC} \end{array} \right\}$$

The class test cannot be used indiscriminately. Specifically, a numeric test is used for data names defined with a numeric picture (i.e., a picture of 9's). An alphabetic test is valid for data names defined with a picture of A. However, either test may be performed on alphanumeric items. The validity of class tests is summarized in Table 7.1 and by examples in Figure 7.1.

TABLE 7.1 Valid Forms of Class Test

Data type and picture	Valid tests
Numeric (9)	NUMERIC, NOT NUMERIC
Alphabetic (A)	ALPHABETIC, NOT ALPHABETIC
Alphanumeric (X)	NUMERIC, NOT NUMERIC, ALPHABETIC, NOT ALPHABETIC

```
        05   NUMERIC-FIELD        PIC 9(5).
        05   ALPHABETIC-FIELD     PIC A(5).
        05   ALPHANUMERIC-FIELD   PIC X(5).
```

(valid)	IF NUMERIC-FIELD IS NUMERIC.....
(valid)	IF NUMERIC-FIELD IS NOT NUMERIC.....
(invalid)	IF NUMERIC-FIELD IS NOT ALPHABETIC.....
(invalid)	IF ALPHABETIC-FIELD IS NOT NUMERIC.....
(valid)	IF ALPHANUMERIC-FIELD IS NOT NUMERIC.....
(valid)	IF ALPHANUMERIC-FIELD IS NOT ALPHABETIC.....

FIGURE 7.1 *Examples of Class Test*

Relational Tests

The relational test was first discussed in Chapter 3 when we introduced the IF statement. The general form of the relational test is

$$\text{IF} \left\{ \begin{array}{l} \text{identifier-1} \\ \text{literal-1} \\ \text{expression-1} \end{array} \right\} \left\{ \begin{array}{l} \text{IS [\underline{NOT}] \underline{LESS} THAN} \\ \text{IS [\underline{NOT}] <} \\ \text{IS [\underline{NOT}] \underline{EQUAL} TO} \\ \text{IS [\underline{NOT}] =} \\ \text{IS [\underline{NOT}] \underline{GREATER} THAN} \\ \text{IS [\underline{NOT}] >} \end{array} \right\} \left\{ \begin{array}{l} \text{identifier-2} \\ \text{literal-2} \\ \text{expression-2} \end{array} \right\}$$

The action of the relational test is easily predictable when only numeric quantities are involved, but more explanation is required concerning alphabetic or alphanumeric items. Assume BAKER is compared to BROWN. BAKER is considered smaller since it is alphabetically before BROWN. Comparison proceeds from left to right one letter at a time. Both names begin with B, but the A in BAKER precedes the R in BROWN.

Now compare GREEN to GREENFIELD. GREEN is considered smaller. Comparison again proceeds from left to right. The first five characters, G, R, E, E, and N, are the same in both names. The shorter field, GREEN, is extended with blanks so that comparison may continue. A blank, however, is always considered smaller than any other letter so that GREEN is the smaller of the two names.

Comparison is possible on alphanumeric fields as well as alphabetic fields. In this instance, determination of the smaller field depends on the *collating sequence* of the machine. Collating

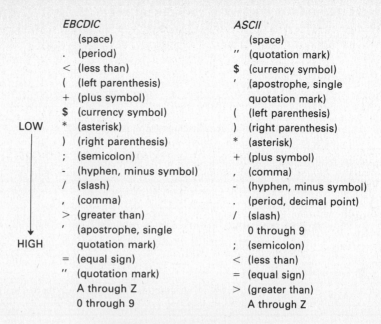

EBCDIC		ASCII	
	(space)		(space)
.	(period)	"	(quotation mark)
<	(less than)	$	(currency symbol)
(	(left parenthesis)	'	(apostrophe, single
+	(plus symbol)		quotation mark)
$	(currency symbol)	(	(left parenthesis)
LOW *	(asterisk)	)	(right parenthesis)
)	(right parenthesis)	*	(asterisk)
;	(semicolon)	+	(plus symbol)
-	(hyphen, minus symbol)	,	(comma)
/	(slash)	-	(hyphen, minus symbol)
,	(comma)	.	(period, decimal point)
>	(greater than)	/	(slash)
'	(apostrophe, single		0 through 9
	quotation mark)	;	(semicolon)
HIGH =	(equal sign)	<	(less than)
"	(quotation mark)	=	(equal sign)
	A through Z	>	(greater than)
	0 through 9		A through Z

FIGURE 7.2 *Collating Sequences*

sequence is defined as the ordered list (from low to high) of all valid characters. Collating sequence is a function of manufacturer; IBM uses EBCDIC, while most others use ASCII. Both sequences are shown in Figure 7.2 for selected characters.

As can be seen from Figure 7.2, 1 is greater than A for EBCDIC. Under ASCII, however, 1 is less than A. It is certainly not necessary for you to memorize either collating sequence. Simply learn which one applies to your machine and be aware of the conceptual significance.

✳ Sign Test

The sign test determines the sign of a numeric data field; the general format is

$$\underline{\text{IF}} \left\{ \begin{matrix} \text{identifier} \\ \text{arithmetic expression} \end{matrix} \right\} \left\{ \begin{matrix} \text{IS } [\underline{\text{NOT}}] \ \underline{\text{POSITIVE}} \\ \text{IS } [\underline{\text{NOT}}] \ \underline{\text{NEGATIVE}} \\ \text{IS } [\underline{\text{NOT}}] \ \underline{\text{ZERO}} \end{matrix} \right\}$$

A value is positive if it is greater than zero and negative if it is less than zero. This test is frequently used to validate incoming data or to verify the results of a calculation. Consider these examples:

```
IF NET-PAY IS NOT POSITIVE PERFORM TOO-MUCH-TAXES.
IF CHECK-BALANCE IS NEGATIVE PERFORM OVERDRAWN.
```

Condition Name Tests

The condition in the IF statement often tests the value of an incoming code, e.g., IF YEAR-CODE = '1'. . . . While such coding is quite permissible, and indeed commonplace, the meaning of the value '1' in YEAR-CODE is not immediately apparent. An alternative form of coding, condition names (88-level entries), provides superior documentation. 88-Level entries appear in the data division and can be applied only to elementary items.

```
05   YEAR-CODE             PIC   X.
     88 FRESHMAN           VALUE '1'.
     88 SOPHOMORE          VALUE '2'.
     88 JUNIOR             VALUE '3'.
     88 SENIOR             VALUE '4'.
     88 VALID-YEAR-CODES   VALUES '1', '2', '3', '4'.
```

If the preceding entries were made in the data division, one could code

IF FRESHMAN

as equivalent to

IF YEAR-CODE = ' 1 '

The advantage of condition names is threefold. First, they provide improved documentation; i.e., FRESHMAN is inherently clearer than YEAR-CODE = '1.' Second, they facilitate maintenance in that additions and/or changes to existing codes need be made in only one place. For example, suppose the code for freshman is subsequently changed to 'F'. Only a single change is required in the 88-level entry. If, however, condition names are not used, then one must find all occurrences of YEAR-CODE = '1' in the procedure division, and the chance of error is much greater. Finally, they permit grouping of several codes into a single entry; e.g., VALID-YEAR-CODES.

Condition names are discussed again in Chapter 8.

✳ Compound Tests

Any two "simple" tests (i.e., relational, class, condition name, or sign) may be combined to form a compound test. This is accomplished through the logical operators AND and OR. AND means both; i.e., two conditions must be satisfied for the IF to be considered true. OR means either; i.e., only one of the two conditions need be satisfied for the IF to be considered true. A flowchart is shown in Figure 7.3 depicting the AND condition. It requires that *both* A be greater than B *and* C be greater than D in order to proceed to TRUE. If either of these tests fails, the compound condition is judged false.

Figure 7.4 contains a flowchart for a compound OR. As can be seen from Figure 7.4, *only* one of two conditions need be met for the IF to be considered true. If either A is greater than B *or* C is greater than D, processing is directed to TRUE. In other words, the OR provides a second chance in that the first test can fail but the IF can still be considered true.

Beginning programmers are often carried away with compound conditions. Consider the statement

IF X > Y OR X = Z AND X < W . . .

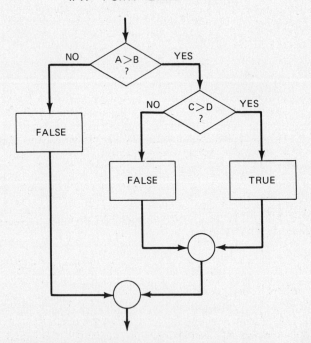

FIGURE 7.3 *Flowchart for the Condition A > B and C > D*

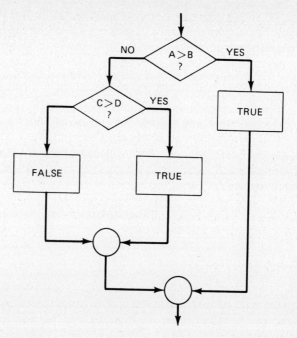

FIGURE 7.4 *Flowchart for the Condition A > B or C > D*

Surely the programmer knew what he intended at the time he first wrote this statement. A day later, however, he is apt to stare at it and wonder what will happen first; i.e., which takes precedence, AND or OR? To provide an unequivocal evaluation of compound conditions, the following hierarchy is established by COBOL:

1. Arithmetic expressions
2. Relational operators
3. NOT condition
4. AND (from left to right if more than one)
5. OR (from left to right if more than one)

Thus, for the preceding statement to be true either

$$X > Y$$

or

$$X = Z \underline{and} X < W$$

However, parentheses can and should be used to clarify the programmer's intent. The meaning of the above statement is made clearer if it is rewritten as

$$IF\ X > Y\ OR\ (X = Z\ AND\ X < W)\ .\ .\ .$$

Note well that parentheses can also *alter* meaning. Thus the following statement is *logically different* from the original code:

$$IF\ (X > Y\ OR\ X = Z)\ AND\ X < W\ .\ .\ .$$

 Implied Conditions

The compound condition can be further clouded by the use of implied subjects; i.e., if a compound condition has the same subject immediately before each relation, only the first occurrence of the subject need to be written. In other words;

IF SALARY > 30000 AND < 40000

is equivalent to

IF SALARY > 30000 AND SALARY < 40000

If both the subject and relational operator of the simple conditions within a compound condition are the same, then only the first occurrence of both need be written; i.e.,

IF DEPARTMENT = 10 OR 20

is equivalent to

IF DEPARTMENT = 10 OR DEPARTMENT = 20

Since implied conditions are often confusing, the following are provided as additional examples:

X = Y OR Z	is equivalent to	X = Y OR X = Z
A = B OR C OR D	is equivalent to	A = B OR A = C OR A = D
A = B AND > C	is equivalent to	A = B AND A > C

Nested IF's

The general format of the IF statement is

$$\underline{IF} \text{ condition} \begin{Bmatrix} \text{statement-1} \\ \underline{\text{NEXT}}\ \underline{\text{SENTENCE}} \end{Bmatrix} \left[\underline{\text{ELSE}} \begin{Bmatrix} \text{statement-2} \\ \underline{\text{NEXT}}\ \underline{\text{SENTENCE}} \end{Bmatrix} \right]$$

The condition may be any of the tests we have discussed, i.e., class, condition name, relational, sign, or compound. The NEXT SENTENCE clause causes execution to continue with the first statement following the period.

A *nested IF* results when either statement-1 or statement-2 is itself another IF statement; i.e., there are two or more IFs in one sentence. Consider Figure 7.5, which shows a flowchart and corresponding COBOL code to determine the largest of three quantities A, B, and C. (They are assumed to be unequal numbers.)

The code in Figure 7.5 is a nested IF statement because there are three IF clauses within one sentence. The rule for compiler interpretation bears repeating: *The ELSE clause is associated with the closest previous IF that is not already paired with another ELSE.*

The compiler, however, pays *no* attention to indentation in a nested IF statement, which is done strictly for programmer convenience. We strongly advocate careful attention to indentation and recommend the following guidelines:

1. Each nested IF should be indented four columns from the previous IF.
2. The word ELSE should appear on a line by itself and directly under its associated IF.
3. Detail lines should be indented four columns under both IF and ELSE.

These guidelines were used in Figure 7.5. A second example follows:

```
IF A > B
    IF C > D
        MOVE S TO W
        MOVE X TO Y
    ELSE
        ADD 1 TO Z.
```

Note that in this example Z is incremented by 1 if A is greater than B, but C is not greater than D. If, however, A is not greater than B, control passes to the next sentence with no further action being taken.

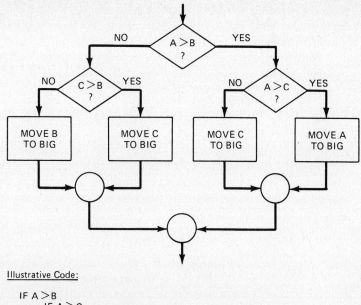

Illustrative Code:

```
IF A > B
    IF A > C
        MOVE A TO BIG
    ELSE
        MOVE C TO BIG
ELSE
    IF C > B
        MOVE C TO BIG
    ELSE
        MOVE B TO BIG.
```

FIGURE 7.5 *Flowchart and COBOL Code for Nested IF's*

✳ PERFORM

The PERFORM verb was introduced in Chapters 3 and 6 as the means of implementing the iteration structure. We now consider additional options available with this verb.

The procedure name in the PERFORM statement can be either a paragraph name or a section name. We already know what a paragraph is. A section consists of one or more paragraphs. If the procedure name in the PERFORM refers to a section name, then *every* paragraph in the section will be executed prior to returning control. Consider

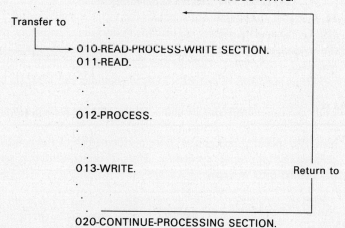

When the PERFORM statement references a section-name, control is transferred to the first sentence in the section. Control will not return to the sentence after the PERFORM until the

CHAPTER 7: MORE ABOUT THE PROCEDURE DIVISION

last statement in the section was executed. Notice that this results in the execution of several paragraphs. How does the compiler know when the section ends? Simply when a new section name is encountered.

Situations may arise when it is necessary to cease performing, i.e., prematurely exit a given routine. This is accomplished by the THRU option of the PERFORM and the EXIT statement. Consider an extended format of the PERFORM:

PERFORM procedure-name-1 [THRU procedure-name-2]

The THRU option causes all statements between the two procedure names to be executed. (Remember, the procedures may be either paragraphs or sections.) Common practice is to make procedure-name-2 a single-sentence paragraph consisting of the word EXIT. The EXIT statement causes no action to be taken; its function is to delineate the end of the PERFORM. Consider

PERFORM 010-READ-PROCESS THRU 020-READ-EXIT.

```
              .
              .
              .
   ┌─ 010-READ-PROCESS.
   │          .
   │          .
   │          .
   │          IF CARD-CODE = 'F', GO TO 020-READ-EXIT.
   │      015-ANOTHER-PARAGRAPH.
   │          .
Range of PERFORM   .
   │          .
   │          IF CARD-CODE = 'G', GO TO 020-READ-EXIT.
   │      018-STILL-ANOTHER-PARAGRAPH.
   │          .
   │          .
   │          .
   │          IF CARD-CODE = 'H', GO TO 020-READ-EXIT.
   │      020-READ-EXIT.
   └─        EXIT.
```

The PERFORM nominally causes execution of all statements within the two procedures. However, at various points within the PERFORM, we wish to return control to the statement after the PERFORM. This is readily accomplished by GO TO 020-READ-EXIT. The GO TO does *not* leave the PERFORM, but it does jump forward to the end of the PERFORM, i.e., to the EXIT statement. The PERFORM is terminated, and control returns to the statement after the PERFORM. Although the strictest definition of structured programming does not permit the use of GO TO, we believe its use in this fashion is completely permissible and indeed consistent with the overall goal of structured programming, greater legibility; i.e., we permit the use of GO TO provided it is a *forward* branch to an exit paragraph of a performed routine.

Another form of the PERFORM includes the UNTIL condition:

PERFORM procedure-name-1 [THRU procedure-name-2] [UNTIL condition]

The specified procedure(s) are performed until the condition is satisfied. *The condition is tested prior to performing the procedure.* Thus, if the condition is satisfied initially, the procedure is never performed. For example,

MOVE 10 TO N.
PERFORM PAR-A UNTIL N = 10.

Since the condition is satisfied immediately (i.e., N = 10), PAR-A will never be performed. Consider this example:

```
                              MOVE 1 TO N.
                              PERFORM PAR-A UNTIL N = 5.
                                       .
                                       .
                                       .
                      PAR-A.
                              ADD 1 TO N.
```

PAR-A will be performed four times, not five. After the fourth time through PAR-A, N = 5. Thus, when the condition is next tested, N = 5, and PAR-A is not performed. (If the paragraph is to be performed five times, change the condition to N > 5.)

INSPECT

The INSPECT verb is used to accomplish two things:

1. To count the number of times a specified character appears within a field.
2. To replace one character by another within a field.

The INSPECT verb has several formats: consider first

INSPECT identifier-1 REPLACING

$$\left\{\begin{array}{l} \text{CHARACTERS } \underline{BY} \left\{\begin{array}{l}\text{identifier-2}\\\text{literal-1}\end{array}\right\} \left[\left\{\begin{array}{l}\underline{BEFORE}\\\underline{AFTER}\end{array}\right\} \text{INITIAL}\left\{\begin{array}{l}\text{identifier-3}\\\text{literal-2}\end{array}\right\}\right] \\ \left\{\begin{array}{l}\underline{ALL}\\\underline{LEADING}\\\underline{FIRST}\end{array}\right\}\left\{\begin{array}{l}\text{identifier-4}\\\text{literal-3}\end{array}\right\} \underline{BY} \left\{\begin{array}{l}\text{identifier-5}\\\text{literal-4}\end{array}\right\}\left[\left\{\begin{array}{l}\underline{BEFORE}\\\underline{AFTER}\end{array}\right\}\text{INITIAL}\left\{\begin{array}{l}\text{identifier-6}\\\text{literal-5}\end{array}\right\}\right]\end{array}\right\}\dots$$

This format is extremely useful for editing reports and is often used in conjunction with the edit characters of Chapters 4 and 8. Assume, for example, that the social security number is stored as a nine-position field (i.e., with no hyphens), but we wish it to appear with hyphens in a printed report. This is accomplished as follows:

```
      01   CARD-IN.
               .
               .
               .
           05   SOC-SEC-NUM                          PIC 9(9).
      01   PRINT-LINE.
               .
               .
           05   SOC-SEC-NUM-OUT                      PIC 999B99B9999.

      PROCEDURE DIVISION.
               .
               .
           MOVE SOC-SEC-NUM TO SOC-SEC-NUM-OUT.
           INSPECT SOC-SEC-NUM-OUT REPLACING ALL ' ' BY '-'.
```

The MOVE statement transfers the incoming social security number to an 11-position field containing two blanks (denoted by B in the PICTURE clause). The INSPECT statement replaces every occurrence of a blank in SOC-SEC-NUM-OUT by the desired hyphen. (This technique is also used to insert /'s in date fields.)

Another frequent use of the INSPECT verb is the elimination of leading blanks in numeric fields. Numeric fields in COBOL should not contain anything other than the digits 0 to 9 and a sign over the rightmost (low-order) position, although the latter is infrequently used. Let us assume a lazy keypuncher did not punch the leading zeros but left blanks instead. Such data cards might not be acceptable in subsequent numeric calculations, and corrective action must be taken. (IBM systems will, however, accept blanks as leading zeros.) One alternative is to repunch the data; our choice is to use the INSPECT verb as follows:

INSPECT FIELD-WITH-BLANKS REPLACING LEADING ' ' BY '0'.

If the CHARACTERS option is chosen, no comparison takes place. Instead, each character in identifier-1 is replaced by literal-1 or identifier-2.

A second format of the INSPECT verb includes the TALLYING option:

INSPECT identifier-1 TALLYING

$$\left\{ \text{identifier-2 FOR} \left\{ \begin{matrix} \underline{ALL} \\ \underline{LEADING} \\ \underline{CHARACTERS} \end{matrix} \right\} \left\{ \begin{matrix} \text{identifier-3} \\ \text{literal-1} \end{matrix} \right\} \right\} \left[\left\{ \begin{matrix} \underline{BEFORE} \\ \underline{AFTER} \end{matrix} \right\} \text{INITIAL} \left\{ \begin{matrix} \text{identifier-4} \\ \text{literal-2} \end{matrix} \right\} \right] \right\} \dots$$

The TALLYING option counts the number of times a designated character appears. The count is contained in the data name defined by the programmer as identifier-2. The programmer is responsible for defining identifier-2 in the data division and for *initializing* its value prior to using the INSPECT statement. (This is *different* from the use of TALLY with the EXAMINE verb.)

A third format of the INSPECT verb combines TALLYING and REPLACING, but is not discussed here. Finally, realize that the INSPECT verb replaces the EXAMINE verb from the ANS 68 standard.

The INSPECT verb is summarized in Table 7.2.

TABLE 7.2 Use of the INSPECT Verb

INSPECT	FIELD-A before execution	FIELD-A after execution	Value of COUNTER-1
INSPECT FIELD-A REPLACING ALL ' ' BY '/'.	10 31 73	10/31/73	N/A
INSPECT FIELD-A TALLYING COUNTER-1 FOR ALL ' '.	10 31 73	10 31 73	2
INSPECT FIELD-A TALLYING COUNTER-1 FOR LEADING '1'.	32110	32110	0
INSPECT FIELD-A REPLACING LEADING ' ' BY '0'.	_ _ _123	000123	N/A
INSPECT FIELD-A TALLYING COUNTER-1 FOR CHARACTERS.	BENJAMIN	BENJAMIN	8
INSPECT FIELD-A REPLACING CHARACTERS BY 'A'.	BENJAMIN	AAAAAAAA	N/A

Notes: 1. N/A denotes not applicable.
2. The programmer is responsible for initializing COUNTER-1 prior to each INSPECT statement.

DUPLICATE DATA NAMES

Most programs require that the output contain some of the input, e.g., name, social security number, etc. COBOL permits duplicate data names to be defined in the data division provided all procedure division references to duplicate data names use qualification. We prefer not to use duplicate names in that they violate the prefix coding standard of Chapter 6. However, duplicate names are often used by others since they are conducive to the CORRESPONDING option, which results in fewer statements in the procedure division. Both qualification and the CORRESPONDING option are discussed in accordance with Figure 7.6.

```
01  CARD-IN.
    05  STUDENT-NAME            PIC A(20).
    05  SOCIAL-SECURITY-NUM     PIC 9(9).
    05  STUDENT-ADDRESS.
        10  STREET              PIC A(15).
        10  CITY-STATE          PIC A(15).
    05  ZIP-CODE                PIC X(5).
    05  CREDITS                 PIC 999.
    05  MAJOR                   PIC X(10).
    05  FILLER                  PIC X(3).


01  PRINT-LINE.
    10  STUDENT-NAME            PIC A(20).
    10  FILLER                  PIC X(2).
    10  CREDITS                 PIC ZZ9.
    10  FILLER                  PIC X(2).
    10  TUITION                 PIC $$,$$9.99.
    10  FILLER                  PIC X(2).
    10  STUDENT-ADDRESS.
        15  STREET              PIC A(15).
        15  CITY-STATE          PIC A(15).
        15  ZIP-CODE            PIC X(5).
    10  FILLER                  PIC X(2).
    10  SOCIAL-SECURITY-NUM     PIC 999B99B9999.
    10  FILLER                  PIC X(47).
```

FIGURE 7.6 *Data Division Code for Duplicate Data Names*

Qualification

The coding in Figure 7.6 has several data names contained in both CARD-IN and PRINT-LINE, e.g., CREDITS, and it is confusing to reference any of these data names in the procedure division.

Consider the statement

MULTIPLY CREDITS BY COST-PER-CREDIT GIVING CHARGE.

The use of CREDITS is ambiguous; i.e., the compiler does not know which CREDITS (i.e., in CARD-IN or PRINT-LINE) we are talking about. The solution is to qualify the data name, using OF or IN to clarify the reference. Thus the statement is rewritten as

MULTIPLY CREDITS OF CARD IN BY COST PER CREDIT GIVING CHARGE.

Qualifications may be required over several levels. For example, this statement is still ambiguous:

MOVE STREET OF STUDENT-ADDRESS TO OUTPUT-AREA.

Both STREET and STUDENT-ADDRESS are duplicate data names, so the qualification didn't help. We could use two levels to make our intent clear, e.g.,

MOVE STREET OF STUDENT-ADDRESS OF CARD-IN TO OUTPUT-AREA.

We could also skip the intermediate level and code

MOVE STREET IN CARD-IN TO OUTPUT-AREA.

Notice that OF and IN can be used interchangeably. Duplicate data names offer the advantage of not having to invent different names for the same item, e.g., an employee name appearing in both an input record and output report. They also permit the CORRESPONDING option.

CORRESPONDING Option

The general form of the CORRESPONDING option is

$$\text{MOVE} \begin{Bmatrix} \underline{\text{CORRESPONDING}} \\ \underline{\text{CORR}} \end{Bmatrix} \text{identifier-1} \ \underline{\text{TO}} \ \text{identifier-2}.$$

Notice that CORR is the abbreviated form of CORRESPONDING (analogous to PIC and PICTURE). Consider the record description in Figure 7.6 and the statement

MOVE CORRESPONDING CARD-IN TO PRINT-LINE.

The MOVE CORRESPONDING statement is equivalent to several individual MOVEs. It takes every data name of CARD-IN and looks for a duplicate data name in PRINT-LINE. Whenever a "match" is found, an individual MOVE is generated. Thus the preceding MOVE CORRESPONDING is equivalent to

```
MOVE STUDENT-NAME OF CARD-IN          TO STUDENT-NAME OF PRINT-LINE.
MOVE SOCIAL-SECURITY-NUM OF CARD-IN   TO SOCIAL-SECURITY-NUM OF PRINT-LINE.
MOVE STREET OF CARD-IN                TO STREET OF PRINT-LINE.
MOVE CITY-STATE OF CARD-IN            TO CITY-STATE OF PRINT-LINE.
MOVE CREDITS OF CARD-IN               TO CREDITS OF PRINT-LINE.
```

Notice that the level numbers of the duplicate data names do not have to match; it is only the data names themselves that must be the same in each record. Further, notice that the order of the data names is immaterial; e.g., SOCIAL-SECURITY-NUM is the second field in CARD-IN and the next to last in PRINT-LINE.

There are several restrictions pertaining to the use of the CORRESPONDING option. In particular,

1. At least one item in each pair of CORRESPONDING items must be an elementary item for the MOVE to be effective. Thus, in the example, STUDENT-ADDRESS of CARD-IN is *not* moved to STUDENT-ADDRESS of PRINT-LINE. (The elementary items STREET and CITY-STATE are moved instead.)
2. Corresponding elementary items will be moved only if they have the same name and qualifications up to but not including identifier-1 and identifier-2. Thus ZIP-CODE will *not* be moved.
3. Any elementary item containing a REDEFINES, RENAMES, OCCURS, or USAGE IS INDEX clause is not moved.

One additional point: The CORRESPONDING option is also available with the ADD and SUBTRACT statements (see COBOL formats, Appendix C). We shall not discuss this feature in the text and suggest you consult a COBOL manual at your installation for additional information.

DISPLAY

The DISPLAY verb is a convenient way of printing information without having to format a record description in the data division. The general form is

$$\text{DISPLAY} \begin{Bmatrix} \text{identifier-1} \\ \text{literal-1} \end{Bmatrix} \begin{bmatrix} \begin{Bmatrix} \text{identifier-2} \\ \text{literal-2} \end{Bmatrix} \end{bmatrix} \ \dots \ [\underline{\text{UPON}} \ \text{mnemonic-name}]$$

Some examples:

```
1. DISPLAY EMPLOYEE-NAME.
2. DISPLAY 'NAME = ' EMPLOYEE-NAME.
3. DISPLAY EMPLOYEE-NAME, EMPLOYEE-NUMBER.
4. DISPLAY 'IDENTIFICATION ', EMPLOYEE-NAME, EMPLOYEE-NUMBER.
```

Example 1 causes the value of the data name EMPLOYEE-NAME to print. Example 2 causes the literal 'NAME = ' to print, prior to the value of EMPLOYEE-NAME. Example 3 prints the values of two data names, and example 4 prints one literal and two data names.

The "UPON mnemonic-name" is an optional clause. If it is omitted, the information is displayed on the printer. If a mnemonic name is specified, then output goes to the referenced device, and the mnemonic name must have been defined in the SPECIAL-NAMES paragraph of the environment division. (Note, however, that IBM computers establish CONSOLE and SYSOUT as reserved words, so that one may display directly on these devices *without* defining a mnemonic name.) Consider

```
SPECIAL-NAMES.
    SYSOUT IS LINE-PRINTER.
    CONSOLE IS KEYBOARD.
```

```
PROCEDURE DIVISION.
    DISPLAY FIELD-A.
    DISPLAY FIELD-B UPON LINE-PRINTER.
    DISPLAY FIELD-C UPON KEYBOARD.
    DISPLAY FIELD-D UPON CONSOLE.
```

Both FIELD-A and FIELD-B would appear on the printer. FIELD-C and FIELD-D would appear on the console typewriter. It should be noted that many installations frown on sending messages to the operator. Indeed, within medium and large configurations, the operator is apt to miss or ignore such messages.

ACCEPT

The ACCEPT statement is a convenient way to "read" information without having to define the entire record. The general form is

ACCEPT identifier [FROM mnemonic-name]

As with the DISPLAY statement, the mnemonic name is optional. If the mnemonic name is omitted, then the input is taken from the card reader. If the mnemonic name is used, then it must be defined in the SPECIAL-NAMES paragraph. However, taking input directly from the operator via the console is specifically discouraged. First, the operator may not know the required response. Second, execution of the program is delayed waiting for the operator's response.

A second form of the ACCEPT verb is new to ANS 74 COBOL and is used to obtain the date and/or time of program execution. Consider

$$\text{ACCEPT identifier-1 FROM} \begin{Bmatrix} \text{DATE} \\ \text{DAY} \\ \text{TIME} \end{Bmatrix}$$

In all cases, identifier-1 is a programmer-defined work area to hold the information being accepted. If DATE is specified, then identifier-1 will receive a six-digit numeric field in the form yymmdd. The first two digits contain year, the next two month, and the last two, day of the month, e.g., 790316, denoting March 16, 1979. If DAY, rather than DATE is specified, a five-digit numeric field is returned to the work area. The first two digits represent year and the last three the day of the year, numbered from 1 to 366. March 16, 1979, would be represented as 79075, but March, 16, 1980, as 80076 since 1980 is a leap year.

TIME returns an eight-digit numeric field in a 24-hour system. It contains the number of elapsed hours, minutes, seconds, and hundredths of seconds after midnight, in that order, from left to right. 10:15 A.M. would return as 10150000; 10:15 P.M. as 22150000.

✳READ INTO

The general form of the READ statement is

READ file-name RECORD [INTO identifier] AT END imperative statement.

The READ INTO option stores the input record in the specified area and, in addition, moves it to the designated identifier following INTO. Consider

```
FD   CARD-FILE
    .
    .
    .
     DATA RECORD IS CARD-IN.
01   CARD-IN                    PIC X(80).
    .
    .
    .
     WORKING-STORAGE SECTION.
01   WS-CARD-AREA               PIC X(80).
    .
    .
    .
     PROCEDURE DIVISION.
     READ CARD-FILE INTO WS-CARD-AREA
        AT END PERFORM END-OF-JOB-ROUTINE.
```

The input data will be available in both CARD-IN and WS-CARD-AREA. Thus the single READ INTO statement is equivalent to both

```
READ CARD-FILE
   AT END PERFORM END-OF-JOB-ROUTINE.
```

and

```
MOVE CARD-IN TO WS-CARD-AREA.
```

✳WRITE FROM

WRITE FROM is analogous to READ INTO in that it combines a MOVE and WRITE statement into one. Note, however, that after a WRITE is executed one may not access the data in the FD area. In other words, do all your work on a given record *prior* to writing it out. Do not expect the record in the FD area to contain the current record after writing, as system I/O routines alter pointers. The general form of the WRITE statement is

$$\text{WRITE record-name } [\text{FROM identifier-1}] \left[\left\{ \begin{array}{l} \text{BEFORE} \\ \text{AFTER} \end{array} \right\} \text{ADVANCING} \left\{ \begin{array}{l} \text{identifier-2} \\ \text{integer} \\ \text{mnemonic-name} \\ \text{PAGE} \end{array} \right\} \left[\begin{array}{l} \text{LINE} \\ \text{LINES} \end{array} \right] \right]$$

WRITE FROM is particularly useful when writing heading lines. Consider

```
FD   PRINT-FILE
     .
     .
     .
     DATA RECORD IS PRINT-LINE.
01   PRINT-LINE                                    PIC X(133).
     .
     .
     .
     WORKING-STORAGE SECTION.
01   HEADING-LINE.
     05   FILLER     VALUE SPACES                   PIC X(20).

     05   FILLER     VALUE 'ACME WIDGETS'           PIC X(12).
     .
     .
     .
     WRITE PRINT-LINE FROM HEADING-LINE
          AFTER ADVANCING TOP-OF-PAGE LINES.
```

The single WRITE FROM statement is equivalent to

```
     MOVE HEADING-LINE TO PRINT-LINE.
     WRITE PRINT-LINE AFTER ADVANCING TOP-OF-PAGE LINES.
```

Note well that TOP-OF-PAGE must be defined in the SPECIAL-NAMES paragraph of the environment-division (see Figure 7.7). Figure 7.7 illustrates many procedure division features and is further described on page 124.

✳ROUNDED AND SIZE ERROR OPTIONS

The ROUNDED and SIZE ERROR options are available for the five arithmetic verbs ADD, SUBTRACT, MULTIPLY, DIVIDE, and COMPUTE. Both options are frequently used. Consider the general form of the COMPUTE statement:

COMPUTE identifier-1 [ROUNDED] = arithmetic expression . . . [ON SIZE ERROR imperative-statement]

The SIZE ERROR option is used to signal when the result of calculation is too large for the designated field. Consider

```
     05   HOURLY-RATE                              PIC 99.
     05   HOURS-WORKED                             PIC 99.
     05   GROSS-PAY                                PIC 999.
     .
     .
     .
     COMPUTE GROSS-PAY = HOURLY-RATE * HOURS-WORKED.
```

Assume that HOURLY-RATE and HOURS-WORKED are 25 and 40, respectively. The result of the multiplication should be 1000. Unfortunately, GROSS-PAY is defined as a three-position numeric field. Only the three rightmost digits are retained, and GROSS-PAY becomes 000. The computer goes merrily on its way, for it does not sense any kind of error. Indeed, the director of data processing will first be made aware of this happening only when the burly construction worker pounds on his door asking about his check.

The situation is prevented by the inclusion of the SIZE ERROR option:

```
     COMPUTE GROSS-PAY = HOURLY-RATE * HOURS-WORKED
          ON SIZE ERROR PERFORM ERROR-ROUTINE.
```

```
00001          IDENTIFICATION DIVISION.
00002          PROGRAM-ID.
00003              'CARS'.
00004          AUTHOR.
00005              ROBERT T. GRAUER.
00006
00007          ENVIRONMENT DIVISION.
00008          CONFIGURATION SECTION.
00009          SOURCE-COMPUTER.
00010              IBM-370.
00011          OBJECT-COMPUTER.          ┌─ SPECIAL-NAMES paragraph used for pagination
00012              IBM-370.
00013          ┌──────────────────────┐
00014          │ SPECIAL-NAMES.       │
               │    C01 IS TOP-OF-PAGE.│
00015          └──────────────────────┘
00016          INPUT-OUTPUT SECTION.
00017          FILE-CONTROL.
00018              SELECT RENTAL-RECORD-FILE
00019                  ASSIGN TO UT-S-SYSIN.
00020              SELECT PRINT-FILE
00021                  ASSIGN TO UT-S-SYSPRT.
00022
00023          DATA DIVISION.
00024          FILE SECTION.           Indicates blocksize is entered in JCL - see Chapter 18
00025
00026          FD   RENTAL-RECORD-FILE
00027          ┌──────────────────────────┐
               │ BLOCK CONTAINS 0 RECORDS │
00028          └──────────────────────────┘
               LABEL RECORDS ARE OMITTED
00029              RECORD CONTAINS 80 CHARACTERS
00030              DATA RECORD IS RENTAL-RECORD.
00031
00032          01   RENTAL-RECORD              PIC X(80).
00033
00034          FD   PRINT-FILE
00035              BLOCK CONTAINS 0 RECORDS
00036              LABEL RECORDS ARE OMITTED
00037              RECORD CONTAINS 133 CHARACTERS
00038              DATA RECORD IS PRINT-LINE.      Counters used with page heading routine
00039
00040          01   PRINT-LINE              PIC X(133).
00041
00042          WORKING-STORAGE SECTION.
00043          01   WS-END-OF-FILE-SWITCH   PIC XXX       VALUE 'NO'.
00044              88  WS-END-OF-FILE                     VALUE 'YES'.
00045          01   PAGE-AND-LINE-COUNTERS.
00046              05  WS-LINE-COUNT        PIC 99        VALUE 51.
00047              05  WS-PAGE-COUNT        PIC 99        VALUE ZERO.
00048          01   BILLINGS-CONSTANTS.
00049              05  WS-MILEAGE-RATE      PIC 9V99.
00050              05  WS-DAILY-RATE        PIC 99V99.
00051              05  WS-CUSTOMER-BILL     PIC 9999V99.
00052
00053          01   DATE-WORK-AREA.
00054              05  TODAYS-YEAR          PIC 99.       Used to hold date of execution
00055              05  TODAYS-MONTH         PIC 99.
00056              05  TODAYS-DAY           PIC 99.
00057
00058          01   WS-CARD-IN.
00059              05  SOC-SEC-NUM          PIC 9(9).
00060              05  NAME-FIELD           PIC A(25).
00061              05  DATE-RETURNED        PIC 9(6).
00062              05  CAR-TYPE             PIC X.
00063                  88  COMPACT                        VALUE 'C'.
00064                  88  INTERMEDIATE                   VALUE 'I'.
00065                  88  FULL-SIZE                      VALUE 'F'.
00066                  88  VALID-CODES                    VALUES ARE 'C'
00067                                                         'I' 'F'.
00068              05  DAYS-RENTED          PIC 99.
00069              05  MILES-DRIVEN         PIC 9(4).       Use of 88 level entries
00070              05  FILLER               PIC X(33).
00071
00072          01   WS-PRINT-LINE.
00073              05  FILLER               PIC X(4).
00074              05  SOC-SEC-NUM          PIC 999B99B9999.
00075              05  FILLER               PIC X(4).
```

FIGURE 7.7 *Car Billing Problem*

```
00076          05  NAME-FIELD              PIC A(25).
00077          05  FILLER                  PIC XX.
00078          05  CAR-TYPE                PIC X.
00079          05  FILLER                  PIC X(4).
00080          05  DAYS-RENTED             PIC Z9.
00081          05  FILLER                  PIC X(4).
00082          05  MILES-DRIVEN            PIC ZZZ9.
00083          05  FILLER                  PIC X(4).
00084          05  CUSTOMER-BILL           PIC $$,$$9.99.
00085          05  FILLER                  PIC X(59).
00086
00087      01  WS-HEADING-LINE-ONE.
00088          05  FILLER                  PIC X(65)      VALUE SPACES.
00089          05  FILLER                  PIC X(5)       VALUE 'PAGE '.
00090          05  WS-PAGE-PRINT           PIC ZZ9.
00091          05  FILLER                  PIC X(60)      VALUE SPACES.
00092
00093      01  WS-HEADING-LINE-TWO.
00094          05  FILLER                  PIC X(20)      VALUE SPACES.
00095          05  TITLE-INFO              PIC X(33).
00096          05  FILLER                  PIC XX         VALUE SPACES.
00097          05  TITLE-DATE.
00098              10  TITLE-MONTH         PIC 99.
00099              10  FILLER              PIC X          VALUE '/'.
00100              10  TITLE-DAY           PIC 99.
00101              10  FILLER              PIC X          VALUE '/'.
00102              10  TITLE-YEAR          PIC 99.
00103          05  FILLER                  PIC X(70)      VALUE SPACES.
00104
00105      01  WS-HEADING-LINE-THREE.
00106          05  FILLER                  PIC X(8)       VALUE SPACES.
00107          05  FILLER                  PIC X(11)      VALUE ' ACCT #'.
00108          05  FILLER                  PIC XX         VALUE SPACES.
00109          05  FILLER                  PIC X(4)       VALUE 'NAME'.
00110          05  FILLER                  PIC X(19)      VALUE SPACES.
00111          05  FILLER                  PIC X(4)       VALUE 'TYPE'.
00112          05  FILLER                  PIC XX         VALUE SPACES.
00113          05  FILLER                  PIC X(4)       VALUE 'DAYS'.
00114          05  FILLER                  PIC XX         VALUE SPACES.
00115          05  FILLER                  PIC X(5)       VALUE 'MILES'.
00116          05  FILLER                  PIC X(4)       VALUE SPACES.
00117          05  FILLER                  PIC X(6)       VALUE 'AMOUNT'.
00118          05  FILLER                  PIC X(60)      VALUE SPACES.
00119      PROCEDURE DIVISION.
00120
00121      A-MAINLINE.                                    ┌─Obtaining date of execution
00122          ACCEPT DATE-WORK-AREA FROM DATE.
00123          OPEN INPUT RENTAL-RECORD-FILE
00124               OUTPUT PRINT-FILE.
00125          READ RENTAL-RECORD-FILE INTO WS-CARD-IN
00126               AT END MOVE 'YES' TO WS-END-OF-FILE-SWITCH.
00127          PERFORM B-PROCESS-CUSTOMER-RECORDS
00128               UNTIL WS-END-OF-FILE.
00129          CLOSE RENTAL-RECORD-FILE PRINT-FILE.
00130          STOP RUN.
00131                                              ┌─Validation of incoming data
00132      B-PROCESS-CUSTOMER-RECORDS.
00133          IF VALID-CODES
00134              AND MILES-DRIVEN OF WS-CARD-IN IS POSITIVE
00135              AND DAYS-RENTED OF WS-CARD-IN IS POSITIVE
00136                  PERFORM C-COMPUTE-AND-WRITE
00137          ELSE
00138              DISPLAY 'ERROR IN DATA ' NAME-FIELD OF WS-CARD-IN.
00139          READ RENTAL-RECORD-FILE INTO WS-CARD-IN────Use of READ INTO
00140              AT END MOVE 'YES' TO WS-END-OF-FILE-SWITCH.
00141
00142      C-COMPUTE-AND-WRITE.
00143          IF COMPACT
00144              MOVE .08 TO WS-MILEAGE-RATE
00145              MOVE 7.00 TO WS-DAILY-RATE
00146          ELSE                                       Nested IF
00147              IF INTERMEDIATE
00148                  MOVE .10 TO WS-MILEAGE-RATE
00149                  MOVE 8.00 TO WS-DAILY-RATE
00150              ELSE
00151                  MOVE .12 TO WS-MILEAGE-RATE
00152                  MOVE 10.00 TO WS-DAILY-RATE.
00153
```

FIGURE 7.7 (continued)

```
00154                     COMPUTE WS-CUSTOMER-BILL ROUNDED =
00155                         MILES-DRIVEN OF WS-CARD-IN * WS-MILEAGE-RATE
00156                         + DAYS-RENTED OF WS-CARD-IN * WS-DAILY-RATE           SIZE ERROR option
00157                     ON SIZE ERROR
00158                         DISPLAY 'RECEIVING FIELD TOO SMALL FOR BILL'
00159                             NAME-FIELD OF WS-CARD-IN.
00160
00161                     IF WS-LINE-COUNT IS GREATER THAN 50        Test for Page Heading routine
00162                         PERFORM D-PAGE-HEADING-ROUTINE.
00163                     MOVE SPACES TO WS-PRINT-LINE.
00164                     MOVE CORRESPONDING WS-CARD-IN TO WS-PRINT-LINE.
00165                     INSPECT SOC-SEC-NUM OF WS-PRINT-LINE        Use of INSPECT verb
00166                         REPLACING ALL ' ' BY '-'.
00167                     MOVE WS-CUSTOMER-BILL TO CUSTOMER-BILL.
00168                     WRITE PRINT-LINE FROM WS-PRINT-LINE
00169                         AFTER ADVANCING 2 LINES.
00170                     ADD 2 TO WS-LINE-COUNT.
00171
00172             D-PAGE-HEADING-ROUTINE.
00173                     MOVE ZEROS TO WS-LINE-COUNT.
00174                     ADD 1 TO WS-PAGE-COUNT.
00175                     MOVE WS-PAGE-COUNT TO WS-PAGE-PRINT.        Use of SPECIAL-NAMES
00176                     WRITE PRINT-LINE FROM WS-HEADING-LINE-ONE   entry to begin on new page
00177                         AFTER ADVANCING TOP-OF-PAGE.
00178                     MOVE ' STACEY CAR RENTALS - REPORT DATE ' TO TITLE-INFO.
00179                     MOVE TODAYS-DAY TO TITLE-DAY.
00180                     MOVE TODAYS-MONTH TO TITLE-MONTH.
00181                     MOVE TODAYS-YEAR TO TITLE-YEAR.
00182                     WRITE PRINT-LINE FROM WS-HEADING-LINE-TWO   Use of WRITE FROM
00183                         AFTER ADVANCING 1 LINES.
00184                     WRITE PRINT-LINE FROM WS-HEADING-LINE-THREE
00185                         AFTER ADVANCING 1 LINES.
```

FIGURE 7.7 *(continued)*

Whenever the calculated result is too large, the SIZE ERROR clause will perform ERROR-ROUTINE. The latter consists of programmer-specified logic that should cause a warning message to print.

Realize also that SIZE ERROR can be activated by zero division since any attempt to divide by zero results in a quotient of infinity.

The ROUNDED clause causes the last decimal place to be rounded. Consider

```
COMPUTE GROSS-PAY ROUNDED = HOURLY-RATE * HOURS-WORKED
        ON SIZE ERROR PERFORM ERROR-ROUTINE.
```

If GROSS-PAY is defined to two decimal places [e.g., PIC 9(4)V99], then .005 is added to the result, and the third decimal place is truncated.

SUMMARY AND A COMPLETE EXAMPLE

In this chapter we covered several advanced procedure division capabilities. We began with the IF statement and all its ramifications. We studied the INSPECT verb and saw its use in editing data. We took another look at the I/O statements ACCEPT, DISPLAY, READ INTO, and WRITE FROM. We learned about nonunique data names, qualification, and the CORRESPONDING option. Arithmetic statements were expanded to include the ROUNDED and SIZE ERROR options. Finally, we took a second look at the PERFORM verb.

While we hope the material in this chapter has been understandable, we readily admit it can make for dry reading. Our fundamental approach throughout the text is to learn by doing. To that end we have developed a complete COBOL program that incorporates most of the material in this chapter. In addition, the program includes three "aspects of reality," validation of incoming data, dating the report, and a page heading routine.

Our illustrative program computes customer bills for Stacey Car Rental. Specifications are as follows:

INPUT: A file of customer records, in the following format:

Columns	Field	Picture
1–9	Soc-Sec-Num	9(9)
10–34	Name	A(25)
35–40	Date-Returned	9(6)
41	Car-Type	X
42–43	Days-Rented	99
44–47	Miles-Driven	9(4)

PROCESSING: Compute the money owed for each customer. The amount due is a function of car type, days rented, and miles driven. Compact cars (C in column 41) are billed at 8 cents per mile and $7.00 a day. Intermediate cars (I in column 41) cost 10 cents per mile and $8.00 per day. Full-size cars (F in column 41) cost 12 cents per mile and $10.00 per day. Each incoming record is to be checked for valid data. Car type must be C, I, or F, and both miles driven and days rented must be positive numbers. If any of these conditions is not met, the record should be bypassed and an appropriate error message indicated.

OUTPUT: One line of information is required for each valid record. Output is to be double-spaced, and a maximum of 26 customers is to appear on each page. Further, each page of output is to have an appropriate heading, including the date on which the program was executed.

The COBOL program is shown in Figure 7.7, and sample output is shown in Figure 7.8. Let us begin by discussing D-PAGE-HEADING-ROUTINE. Two counters, WS-LINE-COUNT and WS-PAGE-COUNT, are established in working storage. Every time D-PAGE-HEADING-ROUTINE is executed, WS-PAGE-COUNT is incremented by 1 so that the proper page number prints at the top of each page. Every time a detail line is written, WS-LINE-COUNT is incremented by 2 (COBOL line 170). D-PAGE-HEADING-ROUTINE is performed only if WS-LINE-COUNT is greater than 50 (COBOL line 161) so that 26 customers will be printed per page. Note that WS-LINE-COUNT is reset to zero each time the heading routine is entered (COBOL line 173).

The D-PAGE-HEADING-ROUTINE causes three heading lines to be printed: WS-HEADING-LINE-ONE, -TWO, and -THREE. The constant portions of heading lines 1 and 3 are established directly in working storage via the VALUE clause (e.g., COBOL lines 87 to 118). The constant portion of line 2 is established via the move of a nonnumeric literal (COBOL line 178). Both techniques are acceptable, but we prefer the former.

Figure 7.7 uses a different technique to begin output on the top of a new page for WS-HEADING-LINE-ONE. Recall that the WRITE statement may specify a mnemonic name in lieu of the reserved word PAGE. If a mnemonic name (e.g., TOP-OF-PAGE in line 177) is specified, it must be defined in the SPECIAL-NAMES paragraph of the environment division (lines 13 to 14) C01 is an IBM-defined implementor name, which directs the printer to the top of a new form. C01 is equated to the mnemonic name of the programmer's choosing in the SPECIAL-NAMES paragraph. Hence the WRITE statement of lines 176 to 177, in conjunction with the SPECIAL-NAMES paragraph, causes pagination, (i.e. jumping to a new page).

WS-HEADING-LINE-TWO requires the current report date. Accordingly, the date of execution is accepted (COBOL line 122) into a date work area, defined in working storage in COBOL lines 53 to 56. (While DATE is the specified ANS 74 reserved word, many IBM compilers recognize CURRENT-DATE instead. The latter is an eight-position field, also specifying date of execution, but in the form mm/dd/yy, and is not discussed further.)

The mainline portion of the program appears in COBOL statements 121 to 130. Compound IF's, condition names, and class tests are used to validate incoming data (COBOL lines 133 to 135).

Observe the nested IF/ELSE statement to determine appropriate rates (COBOL lines 143 to 152). Note the indentation conventions and the multiple statements after a condition is met. Finally, note the ROUNDED and SIZE ERROR options in the COMPUTE statement (COBOL lines

```
                                                              PAGE   3
                      STACEY CAR RENTALS - REPORT DATE  09/29/76
            ACCT #    NAME                      TYPE  DAYS  MILES   AMOUNT
      193-45-6789     SAMUELS,SH                 C     5    345     $62.60

      987-65-4391     SHERRY,KL                  I    10    9000    $980.00

      193-45-6789     BAKER,RG                   C     5    345     $62.60

                                                                    $924.00
```

```
                                                         PAGE   2
                   STACEY CAR RENTALS - REPORT DATE  09/29/76
         ACCT #    NAME                   TYPE  DAYS  MILES   AMOUNT
   999-77-7666     ELSINOR,TR              F     5    345     $91.40

   987-65-4390     SMITH,PG                I     3    9000    $924.00

   093-47-7777     BUTLER,JH               C     5    345     $62.60

                                                             $924.00
```

```
                                                    PAGE   1
                STACEY CAR RENTALS - REPORT DATE  09/29/76
      ACCT #    NAME                TYPE  DAYS  MILES   AMOUNT
123-45-6789     BAKER,RG             F     5    345     $91.40

987-65-4321     BROWN,PG             I    10    2000    $280.00

999-99-9999     JONES,PJ             I     5    345     $74.50

987-65-4555     BROWNING,PJ          I    10    2000    $280.00
```

FIGURE 7.8 *Illustrative Output for Car Billing Problem*

154 to 159), the MOVE CORRESPONDING (COBOL line 164), and the INSPECT REPLACING (COBOL lines 165 to 166).

A modified version of this program appears as a debugging exercise in R. Grauer, *A COBOL Book of Practice and Reference* (Englewood Cliffs, N.J.: Prentice Hall, Inc., 1981).

REVIEW EXERCISES

TRUE FALSE

☐ ☐ **1.** The INSPECT statement must contain the reserved word REPLACING.

☐ ☐ **2.** If the TALLYING form of the INSPECT statement is used, the programmer is responsible for initializing a counter.

☐ ☐ **3.** The INSPECT verb has more than one format.

☐ ☐ **4.** The numeric class test can be applied to alphanumeric data.

☐ ☐ **5.** The alphabetic class test can be applied to alphanumeric data.

☐ ☐ **6.** The numeric class test can be applied to alphabetic data.

☐ ☐ **7.** The alphabetic class test can be applied to numeric data.

□ □ **8.** Every machine has the same collating sequence.

□ □ **9.** BLOOM will be considered less than BLOOMBERG, independent of collating sequence.

□ □ **10.** XYZ will always be considered less than 123, independent of collating sequence.

□ □ **11.** Several data names can appear in the same DISPLAY statement.

□ □ **12.** The ACCEPT statement has two distinct forms.

□ □ **13.** Both literals and data names can appear in a DISPLAY statement.

□ □ **14.** COBOL requires that the DISPLAY statement direct its output to the printer.

□ □ **15.** COBOL requires that the ACCEPT statement receive its input from the console typewriter.

□ □ **16.** Either OF or IN may be used to qualify data names.

□ □ **17.** Qualification over a single level will always remove ambiguity of duplicate data names.

□ □ **18.** CORRESPONDING is allowed only in the MOVE statement.

□ □ **19.** ROUNDED and SIZE ERROR are allowed only in the COMPUTE statement.

□ □ **20.** ROUNDED and SIZE ERROR are mandatory in the COMPUTE statement.

□ □ **21.** CORR is permitted instead of CORRESPONDING.

□ □ **22.** For the CORRESPONDING option to work, both duplicate names must be at the same level.

□ □ **23.** DATE is a COBOL reserved word, containing the date of execution in the form yymmdd.

□ □ **24.** DAY and DATE produce the same results.

□ □ **25.** TIME returns a six-digit numeric field, indicating the time of program execution.

□ □ **26.** The EXIT statement is required to delineate the end of a performed routine.

□ □ **27.** Every PERFORM statement must contain at least one paragraph-name.

□ □ **28.** A paragraph consists of one or more sections.

□ □ **29.** It is permissible to "perform out of a perform."

□ □ **30.** The GO TO statement should *never* appear in a structured program.

PROBLEMS

1. Recode the following statements to show the ELSE indented under the relevant IF. Draw appropriate flowcharts, using the structures of Chapter 6.

(a) IF A > B, IF C > D, MOVE E TO F,
    ELSE MOVE G TO H.

(b) IF A > B, IF C > D, MOVE E TO F,
    ELSE MOVE G TO H, ELSE MOVE X TO Y.

(c) IF A > B, IF C > D, MOVE E TO F,
    ADD 1 TO E, ELSE MOVE G TO H,
    ADD 1 TO G.

(d) IF A > B, MOVE X TO Y, MOVE Z TO W,
    ELSE IF C > D MOVE 1 TO N,
    ELSE MOVE 2 TO Y, ADD 3 TO Z.

2. Given the code

```
PROCEDURE DIVISION.
MAINLINE SECTION.
FIRST-PARAGRAPH.
    PERFORM SEC-A.
    PERFORM PAR-C THRU PAR-E.
    MOVE 1 TO N.
    PERFORM PAR-G UNTIL N > 3.
    STOP RUN.
SEC-A SECTION.
    ADD 1 TO X.
    ADD 1 TO Y.
    ADD 1 TO Z.
PAR-B.
    ADD 2 TO X.
```

```
PAR-C.
    ADD 10 TO X.
PAR-D.
    ADD 10 TO Y.
    ADD 20 TO Z.
PAR-E.
    EXIT.
PAR-F.
    MOVE 2 TO N.
PAR-G.
    ADD 1 TO N.
    ADD 5 TO X.
```

(a) How many times is each paragraph executed?

(b) What is the final value of X, Y, and Z? (Assume they were all initialized to 0.)

(c) What would happen if the statement ADD 1 TO N were removed from PAR-G?

3. Code COBOL statements to correspond to the accompanying flowcharts.

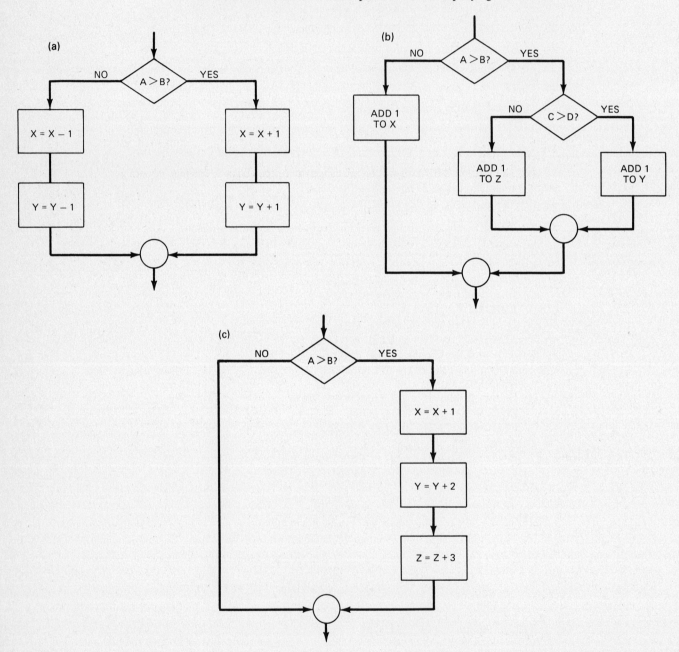

SECTION III: MORE COBOL

4. Given the following data division entries and the procedure division statement MOVE CORRESPONDING RECORD-ONE TO RECORD-TWO:

```
01  RECORD-ONE.
    05  FIELD-A      PIC X(4).
    05  FIELD-B      PIC X(4).
    05  FIELD-C.
        10  C-ONE    PIC X(4).
        10  C-TWO    PIC X(4).
    05  FIELD-D.
        10  D-ONE    PIC X(6).
        10  D-TWO    PIC X(6).
        10  D-THREE  PIC X(6).
01  RECORD-TWO.
    15  FIELD-E      PIC X(8).
    15  FIELD-D      PIC X(18).
    15  FIELD-C      PIC X(8).
    15  FIELD-B      PIC X(2).
    15  FIELD-A      PIC X(4).
    15  FIELD-F      PIC X(4).
    15  FIELD-G      PIC X(4).
    15  FIELD-H      PIC X(4).
```

Answer true or false (refer to the receiving field):

(a) The value of FIELD-E is unchanged.

(b) The value of FIELD-D is unchanged.

(c) No moves at all will take place since the corresponding level numbers are different in both records.

(d) The value of FIELD-A will be unchanged since it is the first entry in RECORD-ONE but the last entry in RECORD-TWO.

(e) The value of FIELD-B will be unchanged since the length is different in both records.

5. Take the tuition billing problem of Chapter 6 (Figure 6.4) and modify it to include a page-heading routine (print 45 lines per page). Print the current date at the top of each page.

6. Modify the tuition billing problem of Chapter 6 (Figure 6.4) to include an error-processing routine that will flag invalid data. We leave the decision of which errors to check for in your hands.

7. The following code is used to keep a separate count of four different types of employees. Describe why it *won't* work. Recode the example with condition names to accomplish the intended effect.

```
IF EMPL-CODE = 'A'
    ADD 1 TO WS-CNT-OF-ACTIVE-EMP
ELSE
    IF EMPL-CODE = 'P'
        ADD 1 TO WS-CNT-OF-PART-TIME-EMP
    ELSE
        IF EMPL-CODE = 'R'
            ADD 1 TO WS-CNT-OF-RETIRED-EMP.
            ADD 1 TO WS-CNT-OF-INACTIVE-EMP.
```

8. Given the nested IF statement

```
IF SEX = 'M'
    PERFORM PROCESS-MALE-RECORD
ELSE
    IF SEX = 'F'
        PERFORM PROCESS-FEMALE-RECORD
    ELSE
        PERFORM WRITE-ERROR-MESSAGE.
```

and the logically equivalent code:

```
            IF SEX = 'M'
                PERFORM PROCESS-MALE-RECORD.
            IF SEX = 'F'
                PERFORM PROCESS-FEMALE-RECORD.
            IF SEX NOT = 'M' AND SEX NOT = 'F'
                PERFORM WRITE-ERROR-MESSAGE.
```

(a) Discuss the relative efficiency of the two alternatives.

(b) What would be the effect of changing AND to OR in the third IF of the second set of statements?

(c) What would be the effect of removing the word ELSE wherever it occurs in the first set of IF statements?

9. Consider the following COBOL code and resulting output. The intent is to give customers with orders of $2000 or more a 2% discount. (Customers with orders of less than $2000 are *not* to receive any discount.) Explain the rather surprising output. (*Hint:* Count Columns.)

COBOL CODE:
```
            IF AMOUNT-ORDERED-THISWEEK < 2000
                MOVE ZEROS TO CUSTOMER-DISCOUNT
            ELSE
                COMPUTE CUSTOMER-DISCOUNT = AMOUNT-ORDERED-THISWEEK * .02.
            COMPUTE NET = AMOUNT-ORDERED-THISWEEK − CUSTOMER-DISCOUNT.
            DISPLAY AMOUNT-ORDERED-THISWEEK CUSTOMER-DISCOUNT NET.
```

OUTPUT:

Amount Ordered	Discount	Net
3000	60	2940
4000	80	3920
1000	0	3920
5000	100	4900
1500	0	4900

— Correct calculation

— Net is incorrect and equal to value of previous order

10. Are the two IF statements logically equivalent?

STATEMENT 1:
```
            IF  A > B
                IF C > D
                    ADD 1 TO X
                ELSE
                    ADD 1 TO Y.
```

STATEMENT 2:
```
            IF  A > B AND C > D
                ADD 1 TO X
            ELSE
                ADD 1 TO Y.
```

Try the following sets of values to aid in answering the question:

(a) A = 5, B = 1, C = 10, D = 15.

(b) A = 1, B = 5, C = 10, D = 15.

11. Consider the following code, intended to calculate an individual's age from a stored birth date and the date of execution.

```
            01  EMPLOYEE-RECORD.
                05  EMP-BIRTH-DATE.
                    10  BIRTH-MONTH           PIC 99.
                    10  BIRTH-YEAR            PIC 99.
```

```
      01  DATE-WORK-AREA.
          05  TODAYS-MONTH                    PIC 99.
          05  TODAYS-DAY                      PIC 99.
          05  TODAYS-YEAR                     PIC 99.
              .
              .

          PROCEDURE DIVISION.
              ACCEPT DATE-WORK-AREA FROM DATE.
                  .
                  .

          COMPUTE EMPLOYEE-AGE = TODAYS-YEAR – BIRTH-YEAR
              + TODAYS-MONTH – BIRTH-MONTH.
```

There are *two* distinct reasons why the code will not work as intended. Find and correct the errors.

PROJECTS

1. Develop a program that will process a customer file for TRUST TRICIA'S NEW CAR CENTER. Each record in the file contains data for a previous customer who purchased a new car from Tricia. Input records are in the following format:

Columns	Field	Picture
1–20	NAME	X(20)
21–40	STREET-ADDRESS	X(20)
41–60	CITY-STATE	X(20)
61–65	ZIP-CODE	9(5)
66	SEX	A
67–70	YEAR-OF-LAST-PURCHASE	9(4)
71–80	FILLER	X(10)

Your program is to print a list of only those customers who purchased a car in the last three years (i.e., in calendar year 1980, include customers from 1977, 1978, 1979; in 1981, take customers from 1978, 1979, 1980; etc. In addition, your program is to accommodate all the following requirements:

(a) Obtain today's date from the system, so that your program can continue from year to year without need of modification.

(b) Display invalid records with an appropriate error message. Records are deemed invalid if either date of last purchase or zip code is not numeric, or if column 66 is neither male nor female.

(c) Develop an appropriate page-heading routine that includes the date of execution. Limit output to eight valid customers per page and triple space between customers. (Invalid records should not appear in this report, but rather in separate DISPLAY messages as per item b.)

(d) Obtain totals for the number of valid and invalid records. Print both numbers on a separate page at the conclusion of the report.

Use the following test data.

ROBERT THOMAS	2133 NW 102 TERRACE	CORAL SPRINGS, FL	33065M1978
MARY ADAMS	103 NE 15 STREET	SUNRISE, FL	33313F1974
KATHY GARDNER	557 SW 21 LANE	FT LAUDERDALE, FL	33310F1979
WILLIAM JACOBS	2112 NW 67 AVENUE	LAUDERHILL, FL	33313X1980
DAVID HAMILTON	1001 SW 96 STREET	MIAMI, FL	33153M
EDWARD LEE	613 NE 9 AVENUE	BOCA RATON, FL	33432M1978
WAYNE MATTHEWS	941 SW 82 TERRACE	N LAUDERDALE, FL	33068M1977
LARRY BROWN	7431 SE 46 AVENUE	PLANTATION, FL	32670M1979
LISA MARTIN	675 NE 8 TERRACE	MARGATE, FL	33063F1979
JOSEPH HAYES	8001 SE 50 STREET	SUNRISE, FL	33313 1979
TRACI LOGAN	981 HALL AVENUE	FT LAUDERDALE, FL	33307F1977
LILLIAN MARCUS	504 KING AVENUE	BOCA RATON, FL	33432F1976
DANIEL EVANS	442 JAMES BOULEVARD	LAUDERHILL, FL	33313M1979
CHARLES JACKSON	583 SW 10 AVENUE	MIAMI, FL	M1979

MICHAEL CARLSON	477 NW 80 STREET	MARGATE, FL	33063M1980
STEVEN KAPLAN	812 NE 46 AVENUE	FT LAUDERDALE, FL	33310M1979
FRANK DAVIDSON	6003 WEST RHODES	BOCA RATON, FL	33432M1978
EVE WILLIAMS	751 NE 12 STREET	PLANTATION, FL	32670F1979

Note Well: Keypunch the test data exactly as shown, including obviously invalid records. Realize that your program should test for invalid data.

2. Write a program to print a list of patients seen by a doctor's office for one day. The day's patients are input from cards with the following format:

Columns	Field	Picture
1–15	LAST-NAME	X(15)
16–25	FIRST-NAME	X(10)
26–50	REASON-FOR-SEEING-DOCTOR	X(25)
51–55	AMOUNT-PAID	9(3)V99
56–80	FILLER	X(25)

The following items should be considered in developing your program:

(a) The amount paid has spaces in the high-order positions. Use the INSPECT verb with the REPLACING LEADING option to convert the leading spaces to zeros.

(b) Verify that the incoming amount paid is numeric. If not, display an error message followed by the card in error. Do not print a line for a card with a nonnumeric amount.

(c) Use the same data-names in the card file record layout as in the print file layout. Use one MOVE CORRESPONDING to move the card fields to the print line.

(d) Obtain today's date through an ACCEPT statement and move it to a heading line.

(e) Keep a count of the number of patients seen and a total of the amount paid. Print these on the total line.

(f) Use the COMPUTE verb and the ROUNDED option and calculate the cost of an average visit (TOTAL PAID divided by the number of patients).

(g) Use double spacing before each detail line. Only allow five detail lines per page.

Use the following test data. Punch *exactly* as shown.

JONES	TOM	HEAD COLD	1600
KING	SARAH	EARACHE	1400
WHITBECK	KENNETH	SORE SHOULDER	1600
DAY	BILL	UNEXPLAINED DIZZINESS	1000
POLLACK	MARY	HEADACHE	750
ARMSTRONG	LIZA	FOOT PROBLEMS	1075
SCHEUR	HELEN	PNEUMONIA REVISIT	1000
MCKEON	DICK	GENERAL PHYSICAL	8A

3. A television store in a large city guarantees that its antennas will stay on residents' roofs at least six years or else they will reinstall the antenna free. A punched card is made every time an installation is made, with the following data:

Columns	Field	Picture
1–25	NAME	X(25)
26–50	ADDRESS	X(25)
51–52	YEAR-OF-INSTALLATION	99
53–54	MONTH-OF-INSTALLATION	99
58–60	TYPE-OF-ANTENNA	XXX

Write a program that will print only the names of customers whose antennas were installed within the last six years. Put an asterisk next to the name of any customer whose antenna is at least four years old. Define your card record as PIC X(80) and your print record as X(133). Define a work record for the card file in Working-Storage and three work records for the print file (for heading, detail, and total line.) Keep a count of the number of guarantees in effect. Use (READ INTO) and (WRITE FROM). Use duplicate names in at least three fields of the detail-print-line and card records in Working-Storage. Use a MOVE CORRESPONDING when moving the card fields to the print record. Use an 88-level entry to define a switch to determine end of file.

Use the following test data:

WILLIAMS, JOAN	128 SECOND AVE.	7403	NNT
FIELDS, HENRY	11 MEADOW COURT	7812	RNT
HOURGLASS, GEORGE	17 TREE LANE	8004	RNT
MORGAN, HAROLD	11603 VALLEY LANE	7905	TRR
ADABAR, R	STONE ROAD	8012	NNT
COUNTER, VIVIAN	P.O. BOX 4301	7312	RNT
JONES, ROGER	14 POMQUAY AVE.	7610	NVT
RODRIGUEZ, VICTOR	38 GARDEN RD.	7203	RNT
TELLER, L	39 LODGE LANE	7711	TRR
COX, MAXINE	75 SANFORD RD.	7504	NVT

Chapter 8

THE DATA DIVISION

OVERVIEW

We return to the data division to cover some of the fine points used by professional programmers. We shall begin with an extended discussion of editing and condition names. We shall cover multiple record definitions for the same file and the COPY clause. We shall introduce tables (in this chapter we shall cover only one dimension; in Chapter 9 we shall discuss two and three dimensions). We shall present the OCCURS and REDEFINES clauses. We shall show how to establish a table of constant values and how to do a *table lookup*. We shall conclude with a discussion of subprograms and the linkage section.

EDITING

Editing involves a change in data format. We may add commas, insert a dollar sign, suppress leading zeros, indicate negative values by a credit sign, etc. Regardless of what we do, our purpose is to make reports easier to read.

The tuition billing problem of Chapter 4 introduced the concept of editing. Now we shall present a more complete discussion, beginning with Table 8.1, which contains the set of editing characters.

TABLE 8.1 Editing Characters

Symbol	Meaning
.	Actual decimal point
Z	Zero suppress
*	Check protection
CR	Credit symbol
DB	Debit symbol
+	Plus sign
−	Minus sign
$	Dollar sign
,	Comma
0	Zero
B	Blank
/	Slash

134

The blank (B) can be associated with any type of source field, i.e., alphabetic, numeric, or alphanumeric. The zero (0) is restricted to numeric or alphanumeric fields. All other symbols are for numeric source fields only. Realize, however, that any MOVE statement involving edited pictures is also affected by the rules discussed in Chapter 3 with regard to decimal alignment, truncation, etc.

The use of various editing characters is best explained by direct example. Consider Table 8.2.

TABLE 8.2 The $, Z, and * Edit Characters

	Source field		Receiving field	
	Picture	Value	Picture	Edited result
(a)	9999V99	000123	9999.99	0001.23
(b)	9999V99	000123	ZZZZ.99	1.23
(c)	9999V99	000123	$$$$$.99	$1.23
(d)	9999V99	000123	$ZZZZ.99	$ 1.23
(e)	9999V99	000123	$****.99	$***1.23

The concepts of source field, receiving field, and actual and assumed decimal point were covered in Chapter 4. The character Z will zero-suppress; i.e., it replaces leading zeros by blanks. The $ causes a dollar sign to print. If several dollar signs are strung together [example (c) in Table 8.2], the effect is a floating dollar sign; i.e., a dollar sign prints immediately to the left of the first significant digit. The $ can be used in conjunction with Z to cause a fixed dollar sign as in example (d) in Table 8.2. For obvious reasons, example (d) is not sound practice when "cutting" checks, and the asterisk is used for check protection as shown in example (e). The asterisks appear in the edited result in lieu of leading zeros or spaces.

SIGNED NUMBERS

Frequently, the picture of a numeric source field is preceded by an S to indicate a signed field. The S is immaterial if only positive numbers can occur but absolutely essential any time a negative number results as the consequence of an arithmetic operation. If the S is omitted, the result of the arithmetic operation will always assume a positive sign. Consider

```
05   FIELD-A       PIC S99   VALUE −20.
05   FIELD-B       PIC 99    VALUE  15.
05   FIELD-C       PIC S99   VALUE −20.
05   FIELD-D       PIC 99    VALUE  15.


          ADD FIELD-B TO FIELD-A.
          ADD FIELD-C TO FIELD-D.
```

Numerically, we expect the sum of −20 and +15 to be −5. If the result is stored in FIELD-A, there is no problem. However, if the sum is stored in FIELD-D (an unsigned field), it will assume a value of +5. Many programmers adopt the habit of always using signed fields to avoid any difficulty.

Table 8.3 illustrates the use of floating plus and minus signs. If a plus sign is used, the sign of the edited field will appear if the number is either positive, negative, or zero [examples (a), (b), and (c)]. However, if a minus sign is used, the sign appears only when the edited result is negative. Note also that the receiving field must be at least one character longer than the sending field to accommodate the sign; otherwise, a compiler warning message results.

Financial statements usually contain either the credit (CR) or debit (DB) symbol to indicate a negative number. The use of these characters is illustrated in Table 8.4.

CR and DB appear only when the sending field is negative [examples (b) and (d)]. If the

TABLE 8.3 Floating + and − Characters

Source field		Receiving field	
Picture	Value	Picture	Edited result
(a) S9(4)	1234	++,+++	+1,234
(b) S9(4)	0123	++,+++	+123
(c) S9(4)	−1234	++,+++	−1,234
(d) S9(4)	1234	−−,−−−	1,234
(e) S9(4)	0123	−−,−−−	123
(f) S9(4)	−1234	−−,−−−	−1,234

field is positive or zero, the symbols are replaced by blanks. The choice of CR or DB depends on the accounting system. COBOL treats both identically, i.e., CR and/or DB appear if and only if the sending field is negative.

TABLE 8.4 CR and DB Symbols

Source field		Receiving field	
Picture	Value	Picture	Value
(a) S9(5)	98765	$$$,999CR	$98,765
(b) S9(5)	−98765	$$$,999CR	$98,765CR
(c) S9(5)	98765	$$$,999DB	$98,765
(d) S9(5)	−98765	$$$,999DB	$98,765DB

CONDITION NAMES

In Chapter 7 we introduced 88-level entries. Now we shall consider them in greater detail by using the VALUES ARE option. The general format is

$$88 \text{ data-name } \begin{Bmatrix} \text{VALUE IS} \\ \text{VALUES ARE} \end{Bmatrix} \text{literal-1 [THRU literal-2] [literal-3 [THRU literal-4]]} \ldots$$

Condition names permit a given value to appear under more than one classification; e.g., records containing a 3 belong to JUNIOR, UPPER-CLASSMAN, and VALID-CODES.

```
05   YEAR-IN-SCHOOL              PIC 9.
     88   FRESHMAN                    VALUE 1.
     88   SOPHOMORE                   VALUE 2.
     88   JUNIOR                      VALUE 3.
     88   SENIOR                      VALUE 4.
     88   GRAD-STUDENT                VALUES ARE 5 THRU 8.
     88   UNDER-CLASSMAN              VALUES ARE 1, 2.
     88   UPPER-CLASSMAN              VALUES ARE 3, 4.
     88   VALID-CODES                 VALUES ARE 1 THRU 8.
```

In addition to documentation advantages, the VALUES ARE clause eliminates the need for compound conditions in an IF statement. Thus

IF GRAD-STUDENT . . .

is equivalent to

IF YEAR-IN-SCHOOL > 4 AND YEAR-IN-SCHOOL < 9 . . .

Further, the VALUES ARE clause makes it very easy to test for error conditions by grouping all valid codes together as shown.

MULTIPLE RECORDS

The commercial programmer frequently finds himself in situations where the same file contains different record formats. A customer file may contain two types of records, e.g., a single master card and several transaction cards. A print file may contain several print lines, e.g., heading, detail, and total lines. One way to handle this is to use the READ INTO and WRITE FROM options, which were discussed in Chapter 7, and then define multiple 01 entries in working storage. A widely used alternative is to use the DATA RECORDS ARE clause in the COBOL FD as shown in Figure 8.1.

Only one record is contained in storage at any given instant. The type of record is indicated by a code in column 80 (MAST-CARD-CODE and DET-CARD-CODE). If 'M' and 'D' denote a master and detail, respectively, we might find procedure division code of the form

```
IF MAST-CARD-CODE = 'M' PERFORM MASTER-PROCESSING.
IF DET-CARD-CODE = 'D' PERFORM DETAIL-PROCESSING.
```

It does not matter if we test MAST-CARD-CODE or DET-CARD-CODE, as both data names refer to position 80 in an incoming record. Thus, the two statements are completely equivalent:

```
IF DET-CARD-CODE = 'D' PERFORM DETAIL-PROCESSING.
IF MAST-CARD-CODE = 'D' PERFORM DETAIL-PROCESSING.
```

Of course, it is possible, and indeed desirable, to modify Figure 8.1 to accommodate 88-level entries for DETAIL-RECORD and MASTER-RECORD, respectively, to reflect a D or M in column 80.

```
FD   CUSTOMER-FILE
     RECORD CONTAINS 80 CHARACTERS
     LABEL RECORDS ARE OMITTED
     DATA RECORDS ARE MASTER-RECORD, DETAIL-RECORD.
01   MASTER-RECORD.
     05   MAST-NAME                            PIC X(25).
     05   MAST-ACCT-NUMBER                     PIC 9(9).
     05   MAST-ADDRESS.
          10   MAST-ADDRESS-LINE-ONE           PIC X(20).
          10   MAST-ADDRESS-LINE-TWO           PIC X(20).
     05   MAST-NUMBER-OF-DETAILS               PIC 99.
     05   FILLER                               PIC X(3).
     05   MAST-CARD-CODE                       PIC X.
01   DETAIL-RECORD.
     05   DET-ACCT-NUMBER                      PIC 9(9).
     05   DET-ITEM-DESCRIPTION                 PIC X(25).
     05   DET-AMOUNT                           PIC S99999V99.
     05   DET-TYPE                             PIC X.
          88   PURCHASE         VALUE IS 'P'.
          88   CREDIT           VALUE IS 'C'.
     05   DET-DATE                             PIC 9(6).
     05   FILLER                               PIC X(31).
     05   DET-CARD-CODE                        PIC X.
```

FIGURE 8.1 *Use of Multiple Records*

COPY CLAUSE

Commercial applications are frequently classified into systems, e.g., inventory, accounting, and payroll. Each system in turn consists of several programs, the files of which are interrelated. Indeed, the same file may appear in several programs. The COPY clause enables an installation to build a library of record descriptions and offers the following advantages:

1. Individual programmers need not code the extensive data division entries that can make COBOL so tedious. (This is particularly helpful in commercial programs where record

descriptions run into hundreds of lines.) Instead, a programmer codes an appropriate COPY clause. The COBOL compiler then searches a library and brings the proper entries into the COBOL program as though the programmer had written them himself.

2. Changes are made only in one place, i.e., in the library version. Although changes in a file or record description occur infrequently, they do happen. However, only the library version need be altered explicitly, as individual programs will automatically bring in the corrected version during compilation.

3. Programming errors are reduced, and standardization is promoted. Since an individual is coding fewer lines, his program will contain fewer errors. More importantly, all fields are defined correctly. Further, there is no chance of omitting an existing field or erroneously creating a new one. Finally, all programmers will be using identical record descriptions.

An abbreviated form of the ANS 74 COPY clause is

$$\text{COPY text-name} \left[\underline{\text{REPLACING}} \begin{Bmatrix} \text{word-1} \\ \text{literal-1} \\ \text{identifier-1} \end{Bmatrix} \underline{\text{BY}} \begin{Bmatrix} \text{word-2} \\ \text{literal-2} \\ \text{identifier-2} \end{Bmatrix} \dots \right]$$

The REPLACING option allows the programmer to substitute his data names for those in the original text, and is not further discussed.[1]

The COPY clause can be used anywhere in a COBOL program, except that the text being copied cannot contain another COPY statement. The most common use is to bring in FD's and/ or record descriptions in the data division. It is also frequently used in the procedure division to bring in entire sections and/or paragraphs.

Use of the COPY clause is shown in Figure 8.2.

A COMPLETE EXAMPLE

Thus far we have discussed the COPY clause, multiple records, condition names, signed fields, and report editing. The significance of these important capabilities is best illustrated in a complete COBOL program. Specifications are as follows:

INPUT: There are two types of incoming records, a master and detail, denoted by 'M' and 'D', respectively, in column 80. The master record contains customer name and address, and the number of detail records. Each detail record denotes either a purchase (P in column 42) or a credit (C in column 42) and contains an item description, date, and amount.

PROCESSING: A customer's balance is to be calculated for each set of master and detail records. The balance is computed by subtracting the sum of the credit transactions from the sum of the purchases. For example, if John Smith made two purchases of $100 and $200 and one payment (i.e., credit) of $50, his balance due should show as $250.

OUTPUT: Individual statements, one per page in suitable format.

The logic is straightforward, and the COBOL listing is contained in Figure 8.2. The sample output is shown in Figure 8.3.

Figure 8.2 illustrates several features discussed thus far. The FD for CUSTOMER-FILE is contained within the COBOL program, yet it was not coded explicitly by the COBOL programmer. COBOL line 14 contains the clause COPY CUSTFIL, which causes the compiler to bring in lines 15 to 41 from a user library. Note the presence of a C in each of lines 15 to 41, denoting a copied entry.

Multiple records are present in PRINT-FILE, as indicated by the DATA RECORDS ARE

---

[1] R. Grauer and M. Crawford, see *THE COBOL ENVIRONMENT*, Chapter 4, Prentice-Hall, Inc., Englewood Cliffs, N.J., 1979, for additional information on the COPY statement.

```
00001              IDENTIFICATION DIVISION.
00002              PROGRAM-ID. COPYEDIT.
00003              AUTHOR. MARSHAL A. CRAWFORD.
00004              ENVIRONMENT DIVISION.
00005              CONFIGURATION SECTION.
00006              SOURCE-COMPUTER. IBM-370.
00007              OBJECT-COMPUTER. IBM-370.
00008              INPUT-OUTPUT SECTION.
00009              FILE-CONTROL.
00010                  SELECT CUSTOMER-FILE ASSIGN TO UT-S-SYSIN.
00011                  SELECT PRINT-FILE ASSIGN TO UT-S-PRINT.
00012              DATA DIVISION.
00013              FILE SECTION.                    Use of COPY statement
00014              COPY CUSTFIL.
00015  C      FD   CUSTOMER-FILE
00016  C           LABEL RECORDS ARE OMITTED
00017  C           BLOCK CONTAINS 0 RECORDS
00018  C           RECORD CONTAINS 80 CHARACTERS
00019  C           DATA RECORDS ARE MASTER-RECORD, DETAIL-RECORD.
00020  C      01   MASTER-RECORD.
00021  C           05   MAST-NAME              PIC X(25).
00022  C           05   MAST-ACCT-NUMBER       PIC 9(9).
00023  C           05   MAST-ADDRESS.
00024  C                10   MAST-ADDR-LINE-1  PIC X(20).
00025  C                10   MAST-ADDR-LINE-2  PIC X(20).
00026  C           05   MAST-NUMBER-OF-DETAILS PIC 99.
00027  C           05   FILLER                 PIC XXX.
00028  C           05   MAST-CARD-CODE         PIC X.
00029  C      01   DETAIL-RECORD.                   Signed numeric field
00030  C           05   DET-ACCT-NUMBER        PIC 9(9).
00031  C           05   DET-ITEM-DESCRIPTION   PIC X(25).
00032  C           05   DET-AMOUNT             PIC S99999V99.
00033  C           05   DET-TYPE               PIC X.
00034  C                88   PURCHASE                   VALUE IS 'P'.
00035  C                88   CREDIT                     VALUE IS 'C'.
00036  C           05   DET-DATE               PIC 9(6).
00037  C           05   FILLER                 PIC X(31).
00038  C           05   DET-CARD-CODE          PIC X.   Use of 88 level entries
00039  C                88   VALID-CODES                VALUES ARE 'D', 'M'.
00040  C                88   MASTER-CODE                VALUE IS 'M'.
00041  C                88   DETAIL-CODE                VALUE IS 'D'.
00042         FD   PRINT-FILE
00043              LABEL RECORDS ARE OMITTED          Multiple 01 records
00044              RECORD CONTAINS 133 CHARACTERS
00045              DATA RECORDS ARE PRINT-LINE, PRINT-LINE-ONE, PRINT-LINE-TWO
00046              PRINT-LINE-THREE, PRINT-LINE-FOUR.
00047         01   PRINT-LINE                 PIC X(133).
00048         01   PRINT-LINE-ONE.
00049              05   FILLER                PIC X(5).   Use of blank editing character
00050              05   PRINT-NAME            PIC X(25).
00051              05   FILLER                PIC X(5).
00052              05   PRINT-ACCT-NUMBER     PIC 999B99B9999.
00053              05   FILLER                PIC X(87).
00054         01   PRINT-LINE-TWO.
00055              05   FILLER                PIC X(5).
00056              05   PRINT-ADDRESS         PIC X(20).
00057              05   FILLER                PIC X(108).
00058         01   PRINT-LINE-THREE.
00059              05   FILLER                PIC X(13).
00060              05   PRINT-DATE-HDG        PIC X(15).
00061              05   FILLER                PIC X.
00062              05   PRINT-CURRENT-DATE    PIC X(8).
00063              05   FILLER                PIC X(96).
00064         01   PRINT-LINE-FOUR.
00065              05   FILLER                PIC X(5).
00066              05   PRINT-DESCRIPTION     PIC X(25).
00067              05   FILLER                PIC X(2).
00068              05   PRINT-DATE.
00069                   10   PRINT-MO         PIC XX.
00070                   10   PRINT-SLASH-1    PIC X.
00071                   10   PRINT-DA         PIC XX.      Fixed dollar sign with
00072                   10   PRINT-SLASH-2    PIC X.       zero suppression
00073                   10   PRINT-YR         PIC XX.
00074              05   PRINT-DATE-EDIT REDEFINES PRINT-DATE
00075                                        PIC 99B99B99.
00076              05   FILLER                PIC X(2).
00077              05   PRINT-AMOUNT          PIC $ZZZZ9.99CR.
```

FIGURE 8.2 *COBOL Program to Illustrate Data Division Features*

```
00078                05  FILLER                    PIC X(80).
00079        WORKING-STORAGE SECTION.
00080        01  WS-END-OF-FILE               PIC X(3)     VALUE 'NO '.
00081        01  WS-RECORD-TOTAL              PIC S9(6)V99.
00082
00083        01  DATE-WORK-AREA.
00084                05  TODAYS-YEAR          PIC XX.
00085                05  TODAYS-MONTH         PIC XX.
00086                05  TODAYS-DAY           PIC XX.
00087                                                        Use of fill character
00088        01  WS-TOTAL-LINE.
00089                05  FILLER               PIC X(28)    VALUE SPACES.
00090                05  FILLER               PIC X(12)    VALUE 'BALANCE DUE '.
00091                05  WS-EDIT-TOTAL         PIC $***,***.99CR.
00092                05  FILLER               PIC X(80)    VALUE SPACES.
00093        01  WS-HEADING-LINE.
00094                05  FILLER               PIC X(9)     VALUE SPACES.
00095                05  FILLER               PIC X(5)     VALUE 'ITEM '.
00096                05  FILLER               PIC X(11)    VALUE 'DESCRIPTION'.
00097                05  FILLER               PIC X(10)    VALUE SPACES.
00098                05  FILLER               PIC X(4)     VALUE 'DATE'.
00099                05  FILLER               PIC X(11)    VALUE '      AMOUNT'.
00100                05  FILLER               PIC X(83)    VALUE SPACES.
00101        PROCEDURE DIVISION.
00102
00103        010-MAINLINE.
00104            ACCEPT DATE-WORK-AREA FROM DATE.
00105            OPEN INPUT CUSTOMER-FILE,
00106                 OUTPUT PRINT-FILE.
00107            PERFORM 060-READ-CUSTOMER-FILE.
00108            PERFORM 020-PROCESS-RECORDS
00109                UNTIL WS-END-OF-FILE = 'YES'.
00110            CLOSE CUSTOMER-FILE
00111                  PRINT-FILE.
00112            STOP RUN.
00113
00114        020-PROCESS-RECORDS.
00115            IF MASTER-CODE
00116                PERFORM 030-WRITE-NEW-MASTER
00117                PERFORM 040-ESTABLISH-DETAIL-LINE
00118                    MAST-NUMBER-OF-DETAILS TIMES
00119                PERFORM 050-WRITE-CUSTOMER-TOTAL
00120            ELSE
00121                DISPLAY 'FIRST CARD NOT MASTER ' MAST-NAME
00122                STOP RUN.
00123            PERFORM 060-READ-CUSTOMER-FILE.
00124
00125        030-WRITE-NEW-MASTER.
00126            MOVE ZEROS TO WS-RECORD-TOTAL.
00127            MOVE SPACES TO PRINT-LINE-ONE.
00128            MOVE MAST-NAME TO PRINT-NAME.
00129            MOVE MAST-ACCT-NUMBER TO PRINT-ACCT-NUMBER.
00130            INSPECT PRINT-ACCT-NUMBER REPLACING ALL ' ' BY '-'.
00131            WRITE PRINT-LINE-ONE AFTER ADVANCING PAGE.
00132                                                        Output begins on new page
00133            MOVE SPACES TO PRINT-LINE-TWO.
00134            MOVE MAST-ADDR-LINE-1 TO PRINT-ADDRESS.
00135            WRITE PRINT-LINE-TWO AFTER ADVANCING 1 LINES.
00136
00137            MOVE SPACES TO PRINT-LINE-TWO.
00138            MOVE MAST-ADDR-LINE-2 TO PRINT-ADDRESS.
00139            WRITE PRINT-LINE AFTER ADVANCING 1 LINES.
00140
00141            MOVE SPACES TO PRINT-LINE-THREE.
00142            MOVE 'STATEMENT DATE' TO PRINT-DATE-HDG.
00143            MOVE '/' TO PRINT-SLASH-1 PRINT-SLASH-2.
00144            MOVE TODAYS-MONTH TO PRINT-MO.
00145            MOVE TODAYS-DAY TO PRINT-DA.
00146            MOVE TODAYS-YEAR TO PRINT-YR.
00147            WRITE PRINT-LINE-THREE AFTER ADVANCING 1 LINES.
00148
00149            MOVE SPACES TO PRINT-LINE.                  Use of 88 level entry
00150            MOVE WS-HEADING-LINE TO PRINT-LINE.         (see line 35)
00151            WRITE PRINT-LINE AFTER ADVANCING 3 LINES.
00152
00153        040-ESTABLISH-DETAIL-LINE.
00154            PERFORM 060-READ-CUSTOMER-FILE.
00155            IF CREDIT
00156                COMPUTE DET-AMOUNT = DET-AMOUNT * (-1).
```

FIGURE 8.2 *(continued)*

```
00157              ADD DET-AMOUNT TO WS-RECORD-TOTAL.
00158              MOVE SPACES TO PRINT-LINE-FOUR.
00159              MOVE DET-ITEM-DESCRIPTION TO PRINT-DESCRIPTION.
00160              MOVE DET-DATE TO PRINT-DATE-EDIT.
00161              EXAMINE PRINT-DATE REPLACING ALL ' ' BY '/'.
00162              MOVE DET-AMOUNT TO PRINT-AMOUNT.
00163              WRITE PRINT-LINE-FOUR AFTER ADVANCING 1 LINES.
00164
00165          050-WRITE-CUSTOMER-TOTAL.
00166              MOVE WS-RECORD-TOTAL TO WS-EDIT-TOTAL.
00167              MOVE WS-TOTAL-LINE TO PRINT-LINE.
00168              WRITE PRINT-LINE AFTER ADVANCING 2 LINES.
00169
00170          060-READ-CUSTOMER-FILE.
00171              READ CUSTOMER-FILE
00172                  AT END MOVE 'YES' TO WS-END-OF-FILE.
```

FIGURE 8.2 *(continued)*

clause in COBOL lines 45 to 46. Note that each of the multiple records has an 01 record entry and appropriate record description.

Multiple record formats are also present in CUSTOMER-FILE; i.e., there is a single master card and a variable number of detail cards signified by MAST-NUMBER-OF-DETAILS. Note the use of this field to control a performed procedure in COBOL line 118. (This is rather dangerous in that we are assuming the value of MAST-NUMBER-OF-DETAILS is correct. It would be preferable, indeed mandatory, in a commercial situation to include some type of defensive checks to ensure that this is the case. However, the necessary logic is somewhat involved, and not considered at this time.)

Various editing characters are used (COBOL lines 52, 77, and 91). In particular, note the asterisk fill character in line 91 and the use of CR to indicate negative numbers in lines 77 and 91. Figure 8.3 shows that M. A. CRAWFORD made a purchase of $123.45 on 8/17 and a payment of $200.00 on 8/21. Thus he has a credit of $76.55. Study COBOL lines 155 to 157 to see how the proper arithmetic sign is obtained for purchase, credit, and balance. This technique was used because numeric data almost always come in unsigned. It is also possible to punch the sign over the low-order (rightmost) digit, although we believe this is not good practice.

```
CRAWFORD,M.A.                    987-65-4321
25 SUNSHINE STREET
ANYWHERE, USA
          STATEMENT DATE   09/29/76


     ITEM DESCRIPTION          DATE       AMOUNT
WIDGETS                      08/17/76   $   123.45
OVERPAYMENT                  08/21/76   $   200.00CR

               BALANCE DUE  $*****76.55CR
```

FIGURE 8.3 *Output Produced by Figure 8.2*

TABLES

A table is a grouping of similar data. The values in a table are stored in consecutive storage locations and assigned a single data name. Reference to individual items within a table is accomplished by subscripts that identify the location of the particular item.

For example, assume company XYZ tabulates its sales on a monthly basis and that the sales of each month have to be referenced within a COBOL program. Without tables, 12 data names are required: SALES-FOR-JANUARY, SALES-FOR-FEBRUARY, etc. With tables, however, we define only a single data name, e.g., SALES, and refer to individual months by an appropriate subscript. Thus SALES (2) would indicate sales for the second month, i.e., February.

TABLE 8.5 One-Dimension Table

Month	Sales
Jan.	$1000
Feb.	$2000
Mar.	$3000
April	$4000
May	$5000
June	$4000
July	$3000
Aug.	$2000
Sept.	$1000
Oct.	$2000
Nov.	$3000
Dec.	$6000

Note: SALES (3) = sales for 3rd month = $3000.

In this chapter we shall concentrate on one-dimension tables, as illustrated in Table 8.5. In Chapter 9 we shall consider both two- and three-dimension tables.

OCCURS Clause

The OCCURS clause specifies the number of entries in a table. The format of the OCCURS clause is simply

<u>OCCURS</u> integer <u>TIMES</u>

Thus, for the one-dimension table of Table 8.5, we might have the entry

    05 SALES   OCCURS 12 TIMES   PIC 9(6).

This entry would cause a 72-position table (12 entries × 6 positions per entry) to be established in the computer's memory, as shown:

There may be instances in which the OCCURS clause functions as a group item and does not contain a PICTURE clause. Consider

    05 SALES-TABLE OCCURS 12 TIMES.
        10 VOLUME   PIC 9(6).
        10 MONTH   PIC X(10).

SALES-TABLE as shown contains 192 (12 × 16) positions:

SALES-TABLE					
SALES-TABLE (1)		SALES-TABLE (2)			SALES-TABLE (12)
Vol	Month	Vol	Month	• • •	Vol	Month

One could reference either VOLUME (1) to refer to the sales volume of the first month, MONTH (1) to refer to the name of the first month, or SALES-TABLE (1) to refer collectively to the 16 positions of the first month.

Processing a Table

Once Table 8.5 has been established (via an OCCURS clause), we shall want to sum the 12 monthly totals and produce an annual total. We shall illustrate two approaches.

The first is brute force, i.e.,

```
COMPUTE ANNUAL-SALES = SALES (1)  + SALES (2)  + SALES (3)
                    + SALES (4)  + SALES (5)  + SALES (6)
                    + SALES (7)  + SALES (8)  + SALES (9)
                    + SALES (10) + SALES (11) + SALES (12).
```

This technique is cumbersome to code, but it does explicitly illustrate the concept of table processing. A more elegant procedure is to establish a *loop* through the use of a variable subscript. Consider the following:

```
MOVE ZERO TO ANNUAL-SALES.
MOVE 1 TO SUBSCRIPT.
PERFORM COMPUTE-ANNUAL-TOTALS UNTIL SUBSCRIPT > 12.
```

```
COMPUTE-ANNUAL-TOTALS.
ADD SALES (SUBSCRIPT) TO ANNUAL-SALES.
ADD 1 TO SUBSCRIPT.
```

The reader should convince himself that this code produces the same numeric result as the brute force technique. Even so, he or she is probably wondering why bother with the more complex code of a loop when a single COMPUTE statement is apparently shorter? Suppose, however, that instead of monthly sales we had weekly or even daily totals—end of debate. (A second argument in favor of a loop is the increased generality it provides, a subject to which we shall return in Chapter 11.)

There are two basic ways to control the value of a subscript within a loop. The first is for the programmer to explicitly vary the value, as was already shown. The second is to use the VARYING option of the PERFORM verb. Consider

```
MOVE ZERO TO ANNUAL-SALES.
PERFORM COMPUTE-ANNUAL-TOTALS
    VARYING SUBSCRIPT FROM 1 BY 1
        UNTIL SUBSCRIPT > 12.
```

```
COMPUTE-ANNUAL-TOTALS.
ADD SALES (SUBSCRIPT) TO ANNUAL-SALES.
```

The value of SUBSCRIPT is initialized to 1 and automatically incremented by 1 every time COMPUTE-ANNUAL-TOTALS is executed. In the next chapter, we shall consider this format in much greater detail.

Rules for Subscripts

COBOL subscripts may be either variable or constant. Either way, subscripts *must* adhere to the following rules:

1. A space may not precede the right parenthesis or follow the left parenthesis.

VALID: SALES (SUB)
VALID: SALES (2)
INVALID: SALES (2)
INVALID: SALES (2)

2. At least one space is required between the data name and left parenthesis.

INVALID: SALES(SUB)
VALID: SALES (2)
INVALID: SALES(2)

3. Multiple subscripts are separated by commas. The comma must be followed by, but cannot be preceded by, a space. A maximum of three subscripts is allowed.

VALID: SALES (1, 3)
INVALID: SALES (1 ,3)
INVALID: SALES (1, 2, 3, 4)   (limit 3 dimensions)

4. Subscript values must be positive (nonzero) integers. Violation will not cause compilation errors but almost certainly will cause difficulty during execution.

Suggestions

When defining a variable subscript in working storage, make it binary via the USAGE clause. This will not affect the correctness of a program, but strongly affects execution efficiency. The USAGE clause to specify a binary subscript can be any of the following:

```
05  SUBSCRIPT-1    PIC S9(4)    USAGE IS COMPUTATIONAL.
05  SUBSCRIPT-2    PIC S9(4)    COMPUTATIONAL.
05  SUBSCRIPT-3    PIC S9(4)    USAGE IS COMP.
05  SUBSCRIPT-4    PIC S9(4)    COMP.
```

Notice that each subscript was specified with a picture of S9(4). This should be standard practice under IBM, but this suggestion has to be taken on faith until the discussion on COBOL from the viewpoint of BAL in Section IV.

REDEFINES Clause

The REDEFINES clause is frequently used to establish constant values for a table. Assume, for example, that we wish to refer to the 12 months of the year by name. We know that MONTH (1) refers to January, MONTH (2) to February, etc., but the computer must be made aware of this explicitly. The OCCURS and REDEFINES clauses are used in conjunction with one another in working storage as shown in Figure 8.4.

The group item MONTH-NAMES has 12 FILLER entries, each 10 characters long. The VALUE clause is used with each FILLER entry to establish an initial value.

.
.
.

```
01  MONTH-TABLE.
    05  MONTH-NAMES.
        10  FILLER                    PIC X(10)  VALUE 'JANUARY    '.
        10  FILLER                    PIC X(10)  VALUE 'FEBRUARY   '.
        10  FILLER                    PIC X(10)  VALUE 'MARCH      '.
        10  FILLER                    PIC X(10)  VALUE 'APRIL      '.
        10  FILLER                    PIC X(10)  VALUE 'MAY        '.
        10  FILLER                    PIC X(10)  VALUE 'JUNE       '.
        10  FILLER                    PIC X(10)  VALUE 'JULY       '.
        10  FILLER                    PIC X(10)  VALUE 'AUGUST     '.
        10  FILLER                    PIC X(10)  VALUE 'SEPTEMBER  '.
        10  FILLER                    PIC X(10)  VALUE 'OCTOBER    '.
        10  FILLER                    PIC X(10)  VALUE 'NOVEMBER   '.
        10  FILLER                    PIC X(10)  VALUE 'DECEMBER   '.
    05  MONTH-SUB REDEFINES MONTH-NAMES.
        10  MONTH OCCURS 12 TIMES  PIC X(10).
```

FIGURE 8.4 *Initialization of a Table Using OCCURS and REDEFINES*

The REDEFINES clause says that MONTH-SUB is another name for the 120 positions of MONTH-NAMES. However, MONTH-SUB consists of a table, MONTH, with 12 entries. Thus, MONTH (1) refers to the first 10 positions in MONTH-NAMES ('JANUARY   '), MONTH (2) to the next 10 positions ('FEBRUARY   '), etc. This may appear somewhat confusing. However, it is made mandatory by a language restriction in COBOL: *a VALUE clause cannot be used in the same statement as an OCCURS clause.*

Note that an alternative way to accomplish the initialization is to define MONTH as a 12-element table and then use 12 MOVE statements in the procedure division, i.e.,

```
MOVE 'JANUARY     ' TO MONTH (1).
MOVE 'FEBRUARY    ' TO MONTH (2).
                         etc.
```

The latter approach requires additional machine instructions, and is not as clear from the viewpoint of documentation. Hence it is seldom used by sophisticated programmers.

Table Lookups

Data are almost invariably stored in coded rather than expanded format. The obvious advantage is that less space is required in the storage medium be it punched cards, magnetic tape, etc. Printed reports, however, rarely contain coded information. Thus, somewhere along the way, a conversion from a code to an expanded value has to take place. The conversion is known as a *table lookup* and is illustrated in Figure 8.5. In the next chapter we shall introduce the SEARCH verb, which simplifies the procedure division code of Figure 8.5. However, the logic in processing a table is so basic that the reader is well advised to study Figure 8.5 before looking for any shortcuts.

The coding in Figure 8.5 is extracted from the listing in Figure 8.7, which appears at the end of the chapter. The objective of Figure 8.5 is to take a four-digit code for major and convert it to an expanded value that will subsequently appear in a printed report. The table of codes and expanded values is established in working storage using the OCCURS, REDEFINES, and VALUE clauses discussed earlier. (Note that we are using a REDEFINES on the 01 level in working storage. REDEFINES *cannot* appear on the 01 level in the file section, where multiple records are used instead; i.e., the clause DATA RECORDS ARE corresponds conceptually to a REDEFINES at the 01 level. Nor can the VALUE clause appear in the file section except for 88-level entries.)

WORKING-STORAGE SECTION.

```
01  TABLE-PROCESSING-ELEMENTS.
    05  WS-MAJOR-SUB              PIC S9(4)   USAGE IS COMPUTATIONAL.
    05  WS-FOUND-MAJOR-SWITCH  PIC X(3)    VALUE 'NO'.
01  MAJOR-VALUE.
    05  FILLER                   PIC X(14)   VALUE '1234ACCOUNTING'.
    05  FILLER                   PIC X(14)   VALUE '1400BIOLOGY'.
    05  FILLER                   PIC X(14)   VALUE '1976CHEMISTRY'.
    05  FILLER                   PIC X(14)   VALUE '2100CIVIL ENG'.
    05  FILLER                   PIC X(14)   VALUE '2458E. D. P.'.
    05  FILLER                   PIC X(14)   VALUE '3245ECONOMICS'.
    05  FILLER                   PIC X(14)   VALUE '3960FINANCE'.
    05  FILLER                   PIC X(14)   VALUE '4321MANAGEMENT'.
    05  FILLER                   PIC X(14)   VALUE '4999MARKETING'.
    05  FILLER                   PIC X(14)   VALUE '5400STATISTICS'.
01  MAJOR-TABLE REDEFINES MAJOR-VALUE.
    05  MAJORS      OCCURS 10 TIMES.
        10  MAJOR-CODE          PIC X(4).
        10  MAJOR-NAME          PIC X(10).

*   DETERMINE MAJOR
        MOVE 1 TO WS-MAJOR-SUB.
        MOVE 'NO' TO WS-FOUND-MAJOR-SWITCH.
        PERFORM 030-FIND-MAJOR THRU 030-FIND-MAJOR-EXIT
            UNTIL WS-FOUND-MAJOR-SWITCH = 'YES'.




030-FIND-MAJOR.
    IF WS-MAJOR-SUB > 10
        MOVE 'YES' TO WS-FOUND-MAJOR-SWITCH
        MOVE 'UNKNOWN' TO HDG-MAJOR
    ELSE
        IF ST-MAJOR-CODE = MAJOR-CODE (WS-MAJOR-SUB)
            MOVE 'YES' TO WS-FOUND-MAJOR-SWITCH
            MOVE MAJOR-NAME (WS-MAJOR-SUB) TO HDG-MAJOR
        ELSE
            ADD 1 TO WS-MAJOR-SUB.
030-FIND-MAJOR-EXIT.
    EXIT.
```

FIGURE 8.5 *Table Lookup*

The logic in Figure 8.5 begins by setting a subscript to 1 and a switch to 'NO'. When the incoming code, ST-MAJOR-CODE, matches a code in the table, the switch, WS-FOUND-MAJOR-SWITCH, is set to 'YES' and processing is finished. Notice that we test the value of the subscript, WS-MAJOR-SUB, against the number of entries in the table. If we have gone through the entire table without finding a match, we signify an unknown major and terminate processing in the loop. This type of error checking is extremely important and is one way of distinguishing the professional from the student. If the check were not included and an unknown code did appear, the subscript would be incremented indefinitely until some type of fatal error occurred.

SUBPROGRAMS AND THE LINKAGE SECTION

The PERFORM statement can be utilized to divide a program into a series of routines that are called by the mainline portion of the program. In effect the PERFORM invokes a subroutine in a COBOL program. As such, the called routine must be coded, compiled, and debugged *within* the main program. There is, however, a way to make the subroutine an entirely separate entity from the main program. This technique requires the CALL and USING statements in the procedure division and the linkage section in the data division.

A subprogram (i.e., one which is independent of the main program) contains the four divisions of a regular program. In addition, it contains a linkage section in its data division that passes information to and from the main program. The same program may call several subprograms, and a subprogram may in turn call another subprogram.

Consider Figure 8.6, which contains code extracted from the listings at the end of the chapter. *The two programs are developed independently of one another.* The main program contains a CALL statement somewhere in its procedure division. At that point control is transferred from the main program to the subroutine. The CALL statement contains a USING clause, which specifies the data on which the subprogram is to operate. The subprogram in turn contains a USING clause in its procedure division header indicating which data it is to receive from an external program. Note that the data names in the two USING clauses are different. However, the *order* of data names within the USING clause is absolutely critical. The first item in the USING clause of the main program (STUDENT-RECORD) corresponds to the first item in the USING clause of the subprogram (DATA-PASSED-FROM-MAIN); both are 01 records with 80 characters. The second item in the main program (WS-GRADE-AVERAGE) matches the second item in the subroutine (LS-GRADE-AVERAGE), etc. Data names in the main program are defined in either the file section or working storage, whereas data names in the subprogram (which are passed from the main program) are defined in the linkage section.

When the CALL statement in the main program is executed, the subprogram is entered at the beginning of its procedure division. It executes exactly as a regular COBOL program except that it contains an EXIT PROGRAM statement instead of a STOP RUN. The EXIT PROGRAM terminates processing of the subprogram and returns control to the main program to the statement immediately after the CALL. (Note that it is possible for a subprogram to contain a STOP RUN statement as well. However, this would tend to obscure the mainline logic, as it would be difficult to tell where execution terminates.)

The data names passed to the subprogram are known as arguments. The ANS 74 standard requires that arguments be either 77 or 01 entries, but some IBM compilers permit passed parameters to be defined at any level. Finally, the main program is also known as a calling program, and the subprogram as a called program.

Table initialization, table lookups, and subprograms are illustrated in Figures 8.7, 8.8, and 8.9. The program specifications are as follows:

INPUT: A file of student records containing name, major code, and number of courses taken and, for each course, the course number, credits, and grade.

PROCESSING: Calculate a grade point average for each student. A four-point system is used in which A, B, C, D, and F are worth 4, 3, 2, 1, and 0, respectively. A subprogram is to be written that calculates the grade point average.

OUTPUT: A separate transcript is to be printed for each student record. The transcript should show each course taken, the number of credits, and the grade received. It should also show the calculated average and the student's major.

Figure 8.7 contains the main (calling) program, and Figure 8.8 contains the subprogram (called program). The main program calls the subprogram in COBOL lines 111 to 113 and passes two arguments, STUDENT-RECORD and WS-GRADE-AVERAGE. The subprogram in turn knows these arguments as STUDENT-RECORD and WS-CALCULATED-AVERAGE (subprogram lines 36 to 37). It defines these data names in its linkage section (subprogram lines 22 to 33). The data names in the main and subprogram can, but need not be, the same. It is good practice to use the same COPY clause in both programs for some or all of the passed parameters to ensure identical record descriptions. (See lines 27 and 24 in the main and subprograms respectively.)

The subprogram is concerned exclusively with calculating the grade point average. Notice the four simple IF statements in lines 60 to 68. These could of course have been written as a single nested IF, but we have chosen to use the four statements for variety. Which is preferable? There is no unequivocal answer. Some installations disallow nested IF's on the grounds they are

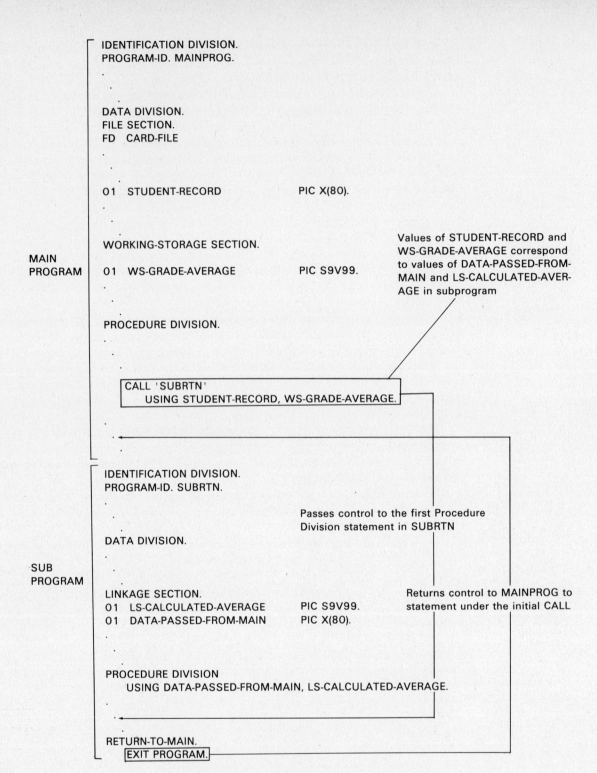

```
            IDENTIFICATION DIVISION.
            PROGRAM-ID. MAINPROG.
                 .
                 .
                 .
            DATA DIVISION.
            FILE SECTION.
            FD   CARD-FILE
                 .
                 .
                 .
            01   STUDENT-RECORD              PIC X(80).
                 .
                 .
                                                         Values of STUDENT-RECORD and
            WORKING-STORAGE SECTION.                     WS-GRADE-AVERAGE correspond
                                                         to values of DATA-PASSED-FROM-
            01   WS-GRADE-AVERAGE            PIC S9V99.  MAIN and LS-CALCULATED-AVER-
                 .                                       AGE in subprogram
                 .
            PROCEDURE DIVISION.
                 .
                 .
                 .
            CALL 'SUBRTN'
                USING STUDENT-RECORD, WS-GRADE-AVERAGE.

                 .
                 .

            IDENTIFICATION DIVISION.
            PROGRAM-ID. SUBRTN.
                 .                          Passes control to the first Procedure
                 .                          Division statement in SUBRTN
                 .
            DATA DIVISION.
                 .
                 .
                 .
            LINKAGE SECTION.                Returns control to MAINPROG to
            01   LS-CALCULATED-AVERAGE  PIC S9V99.   statement under the initial CALL
            01   DATA-PASSED-FROM-MAIN  PIC X(80).
                 .
                 .
                 .
            PROCEDURE DIVISION
                USING DATA-PASSED-FROM-MAIN, LS-CALCULATED-AVERAGE.
                 .
                 .

            RETURN-TO-MAIN.
            EXIT PROGRAM.
```

MAIN PROGRAM

SUB PROGRAM

FIGURE 8.6 *Illustration of Subprogram*

too difficult to read. Other installations encourage their use. We use both techniques in the text to give as broad exposure as possible, but we do favor nested IFs.

The subprogram also illustrates table processing via the PERFORM VARYING option (lines 49 to 51). Each student record contains a variable number of courses (ST-NUMBER-OF-COURSES), and hence the routine to include each course in the overall average must be performed a variable number of times. The VARYING option increments WS-COURSE-SUB by 1 prior to entering

```
00001              IDENTIFICATION DIVISION.
00002              PROGRAM-ID.
00003                  'MAINPROG'.
00004              AUTHOR.
00005                  ROBERT T. GRAUER.
00006
00007              ENVIRONMENT DIVISION.
00008              CONFIGURATION SECTION.
00009              SOURCE-COMPUTER.
00010                  IBM-370.
00011              OBJECT-COMPUTER.
00012                  IBM-370.
00013
00014              INPUT-OUTPUT SECTION.
00015              FILE-CONTROL.
00016                  SELECT STUDENT-FILE ASSIGN TO UT-S-CARDS.
00017                  SELECT PRINT-FILE ASSIGN TO UT-S-PRINT.
00018
00019              DATA DIVISION.
00020              FILE SECTION.
00021
00022          FD   STUDENT-FILE
00023               LABEL RECORDS ARE OMITTED
00024               RECORD CONTAINS 80 CHARACTERS
00025               BLOCK CONTAINS 0 RECORDS
00026               DATA RECORD IS STUDENT-RECORD.
00027               COPY STUDREC.
00028  C        01   STUDENT-RECORD.
00029  C             05   ST-NAME               PIC X(15).
00030  C             05   ST-MAJOR-CODE         PIC X(4).
00031  C             05   ST-NUMBER-OF-COURSES  PIC 9(2).
00032  C             05   ST-COURSE-TABLE OCCURS 8 TIMES.      ── Copied entry
00033  C                  10   ST-COURSE-NUMBER   PIC X(3).
00034  C                  10   ST-COURSE-GRADE    PIC X.
00035  C                  10   ST-COURSE-CREDITS  PIC 9.
00036  C             05   FILLER                PIC X(19).
00037
00038          FD   PRINT-FILE
00039               BLOCK CONTAINS 0 RECORDS        ── Indicates Blocksize will be entered in JCL
00040               LABEL RECORDS ARE OMITTED
00041               RECORD CONTAINS 133 CHARACTERS
00042               DATA RECORD IS PRINT-LINE.
00043          01   PRINT-LINE            PIC X(133).
00044          WORKING-STORAGE SECTION.                  Binary subscripts for efficiency
00045          01   WS-SUBSCRIPTS.
00046               05   WS-MAJOR-SUB     PIC S9(4)   COMP.       Different switches for
00047               05   WS-COURSE-SUB    PIC S9(4)   COMP.       different purposes
00048          01   PROGRAM-SWITCHES.
00049               05   WS-END-OF-FILE        PIC X(3)   VALUE 'NO '.
00050               05   WS-FOUND-MAJOR-SWITCH PIC X(3)   VALUE 'NO '.
00051          01   WS-GRADE-AVERAGE      PIC S9V99.
00052          01   HEADING-LINE-ONE.
00053               05   FILLER          PIC X(20)   VALUE SPACES.
00054               05   FILLER          PIC X(10)   VALUE 'TRANSCRIPT'.
00055               05   FILLER          PIC X(103)  VALUE SPACES.
00056          01   HEADING-LINE-TWO.
00057               05   FILLER          PIC X(6)    VALUE ' NAME:'.
00058               05   HDG-NAME        PIC X(15).
00059               05   FILLER          PIC X(5)    VALUE SPACES.
00060               05   FILLER          PIC X(6)    VALUE 'MAJOR:'.
00061               05   HDG-MAJOR       PIC X(10).
00062               05   FILLER          PIC X(91)   VALUE SPACES.
00063          01   HEADING-LINE-THREE.
00064               05   FILLER          PIC X(10)   VALUE SPACES.
00065               05   FILLER          PIC X(9)    VALUE 'COURSE#
00066               05   FILLER          PIC X(9)    VALUE 'CREDITS
00067               05   FILLER          PIC X(5)    VALUE 'GRADE'.
00068               05   FILLER          PIC X(100)  VALUE SPACES.
00069          01   DETAIL-LINE.
00070               05   FILLER          PIC X(13)   VALUE SPACES.
00071               05   DET-COURSE      PIC X(3).
00072               05   FILLER          PIC X(9)    VALUE SPACES.
00073               05   DET-CREDITS     PIC 9.
00074               05   FILLER          PIC X(5)    VALUE SPACES.
00075               05   DET-GRADE       PIC X.
```

FIGURE 8.7 *Main (Calling) Program*

```
00076                  05  FILLER                      PIC X(101)  VALUE SPACES.
00077            01  TOTAL-LINE.
00078                  05  FILLER                      PIC X(16)   VALUE SPACES.
00079                  05  FILLER                      PIC X(9)    VALUE 'AVERAGE: '.
00080                  05  TOT-GPA                     PIC 9.99.
00081                  05  FILLER                      PIC X(104)  VALUE SPACES.
00082            01  MAJOR-VALUE.
00083                  05  FILLER                      PIC X(14)   VALUE '1234ACCOUNTING'.
00084                  05  FILLER                      PIC X(14)   VALUE '1400BIOLOGY    '.
00085                  05  FILLER                      PIC X(14)   VALUE '1976CHEMISTRY  '.
00086                  05  FILLER                      PIC X(14)   VALUE '2100CIVIL ENG  '.
00087                  05  FILLER                      PIC X(14)   VALUE '2458E. D. P.  '.
00088                  05  FILLER                      PIC X(14)   VALUE '3245ECONOMICS  '.
00089                  05  FILLER                      PIC X(14)   VALUE '3960FINANCE    '.
00090                  05  FILLER                      PIC X(14)   VALUE '4321MANAGEMENT'.
00091                  05  FILLER                      PIC X(14)   VALUE '4999MARKETING  '.
00092                  05  FILLER                      PIC X(14)   VALUE '5400STATISTICS'.
00093            01  MAJOR-TABLE REDEFINES MAJOR-VALUE.
00094                  05  MAJORS     OCCURS 10 TIMES.
00095                      10  MAJOR-CODE      PIC X(4).
00096                      10  MAJOR-NAME      PIC X(10).
00097            PROCEDURE DIVISION.
00098
00099            010-MAINLINE.
00100                  OPEN INPUT STUDENT-FILE,
00101                       OUTPUT PRINT-FILE.
00102                  READ STUDENT-FILE,
00103                      AT END MOVE 'YES' TO WS-END-OF-FILE.
00104                  PERFORM 020-PROCESS-RECORDS THRU 025-PROCESS-RECORDS-EXIT
00105                      UNTIL WS-END-OF-FILE = 'YES'.
00106                  CLOSE STUDENT-FILE
00107                        PRINT-FILE.
00108                  STOP RUN.
00109
00110            020-PROCESS-RECORDS.
00111                  CALL 'SUBRTN'
00112                      USING STUDENT-RECORD
00113                            WS-GRADE-AVERAGE.
00114
00115                  WRITE PRINT-LINE FROM HEADING-LINE-ONE
00116                      AFTER ADVANCING PAGE.
00117                  MOVE 1 TO WS-MAJOR-SUB.
00118                  MOVE 'NO ' TO WS-FOUND-MAJOR-SWITCH.
00119                  PERFORM 030-FIND-MAJOR THRU 030-FIND-MAJOR-EXIT
00120                      UNTIL WS-FOUND-MAJOR-SWITCH = 'YES'.
00121
00122                  MOVE ST-NAME TO HDG-NAME.
00123                  WRITE PRINT-LINE FROM HEADING-LINE-TWO
00124                      AFTER ADVANCING 2 LINES.
00125                  WRITE PRINT-LINE FROM HEADING-LINE-THREE
00126                      AFTER ADVANCING 2 LINES.
00127                  PERFORM 040-WRITE-DETAIL-LINE THRU 040-WRITE-DETAIL-EXIT
00128                      VARYING WS-COURSE-SUB FROM 1 BY 1
00129                      UNTIL WS-COURSE-SUB > ST-NUMBER-OF-COURSES.
00130                  MOVE WS-GRADE-AVERAGE TO TOT-GPA.
00131                  WRITE PRINT-LINE FROM TOTAL-LINE
00132                      AFTER ADVANCING 2 LINES.
00133                  READ STUDENT-FILE,
00134                      AT END MOVE 'YES' TO WS-END-OF-FILE.
00135
00136            025-PROCESS-RECORDS-EXIT.
00137                  EXIT.
00138
00139            030-FIND-MAJOR.
00140                  IF WS-MAJOR-SUB > 10
00141                      MOVE 'YES' TO WS-FOUND-MAJOR-SWITCH
00142                      MOVE 'UNKNOWN   ' TO HDG-MAJOR
00143                  ELSE
00144                      IF ST-MAJOR-CODE = MAJOR-CODE (WS-MAJOR-SUB)
00145                          MOVE 'YES' TO WS-FOUND-MAJOR-SWITCH
00146                          MOVE MAJOR-NAME (WS-MAJOR-SUB) TO HDG-MAJOR
00147                      ELSE
00148                          ADD 1 TO WS-MAJOR-SUB.
00149
```

Use of REDEFINES and OCCURS clauses

Call to subprogram

Use of PERFORM VARYING

Check for unknown major

Expanded major is moved to output line

FIGURE 8.7 (continued)

```
00150          030-FIND-MAJOR-EXIT.
00151              EXIT.
00152
00153          040-WRITE-DETAIL-LINE.
00154              MOVE ST-COURSE-NUMBER (WS-COURSE-SUB) TO DET-COURSE.
00155              MOVE ST-COURSE-CREDITS (WS-COURSE-SUB) TO DET-CREDITS.
00156              MOVE ST-COURSE-GRADE (WS-COURSE-SUB) TO DET-GRADE.
00157              WRITE PRINT-LINE FROM DETAIL-LINE
00158                  AFTER ADVANCING 1 LINES.
00159          040-WRITE-DETAIL-EXIT.
00160              EXIT.
```

FIGURE 8.7 *(continued)*

```
00001          IDENTIFICATION DIVISION.
00002          PROGRAM-ID.
00003              'SUBRTN'.
00004          AUTHOR.
00005              EDWARD RAMSEY.
00006
00007          ENVIRONMENT DIVISION.
00008          CONFIGURATION SECTION.
00009          SOURCE-COMPUTER.
00010              IBM-370.
00011          OBJECT-COMPUTER.
00012              IBM-370.
00013
00014          DATA DIVISION.
00015          WORKING-STORAGE SECTION.
00016          01   TRANSCRIPT-TOTALS.
00017               05   WS-TOTAL-CREDITS          PIC 999.
00018               05   WS-TOTAL-QUALITY-POINTS   PIC 999.
00019          01   WS-MULTIPLIER                  PIC 9.
00020          01   WS-COURSE-SUB                  PIC S9(4)    COMP.
00021          ********************************************************
00022          LINKAGE SECTION.──── Linkage Section appears in called program
00023          01   WS-CALCULATED-AVERAGE          PIC S9V99.
00024               COPY STUDREC.
00025 C        01   STUDENT-RECORD.
00026 C             05   ST-NAME                   PIC X(15).
00027 C             05   ST-MAJOR-CODE             PIC X(4).
00028 C             05   ST-NUMBER-OF-COURSES      PIC 9(2).  ⟋One Dimension Table
00029 C             05   ST-COURSE-TABLE OCCURS 8 TIMES.
00030 C             10   ST-COURSE-NUMBER   PIC X(3).
00031 C             10   ST-COURSE-GRADE    PIC X.
00032 C             10   ST-COURSE-CREDITS  PIC 9.
00033 C             05   FILLER                    PIC X(19).
00034          ********************************************************
00035          PROCEDURE DIVISION                   ⟍Data Names in called program can,
00036              USING STUDENT-RECORD              but need not be, the same as calling
00037                    WS-CALCULATED-AVERAGE.      program
00038          ********************************************************
00039          * ROUTINE TO COMPUTE GRADE POINT AVERAGE
00040          * WEIGHTS: A=4, B=3, C=2, D=1, F=0
00041          * NO PLUS OR MINUS GRADES
00042          * QUALITY POINTS FOR A GIVEN COURSE = WEIGHT X CREDITS
00043          * GRADE POINT AVERAGE = TOTAL QUALITY POINTS / TOTAL CREDITS
00044          ********************************************************
00045
00046          001-MAINLINE.
00047              MOVE ZERO TO WS-TOTAL-QUALITY-POINTS.
00048              MOVE ZERO TO WS-TOTAL-CREDITS.
00049              PERFORM 010-COMPUTE-QUALITY-POINTS
00050                  VARYING WS-COURSE-SUB FROM 1 BY 1
00051                  UNTIL WS-COURSE-SUB > ST-NUMBER-OF-COURSES.
00052              COMPUTE WS-CALCULATED-AVERAGE ROUNDED
00053                  = WS-TOTAL-QUALITY-POINTS / WS-TOTAL-CREDITS.
00054
00055          005-RETURN-TO-MAIN.
00056              EXIT PROGRAM.
00057
00058          010-COMPUTE-QUALITY-POINTS.
```

FIGURE 8.8 *Sub (Called) Program*

```
00059          MOVE ZERO TO WS-MULTIPLIER.
00060          IF ST-COURSE-GRADE (WS-COURSE-SUB) = 'A'
00061              MOVE 4 TO WS-MULTIPLIER.
00062          IF ST-COURSE-GRADE (WS-COURSE-SUB) = 'B'
00063              MOVE 3 TO WS-MULTIPLIER.
00064          IF ST-COURSE-GRADE (WS-COURSE-SUB) = 'C'
00065              MOVE 2 TO WS-MULTIPLIER.
00066          IF ST-COURSE-GRADE (WS-COURSE-SUB) = 'D'
00067              MOVE 1 TO WS-MULTIPLIER.
00068
00069          COMPUTE WS-TOTAL-QUALITY-POINTS = WS-TOTAL-QUALITY-POINTS
00070              + ST-COURSE-CREDITS (WS-COURSE-SUB) * WS-MULTIPLIER.
00071          ADD ST-COURSE-CREDITS (WS-COURSE-SUB) TO WS-TOTAL-CREDITS.
```

FIGURE 8.8 *(continued)*

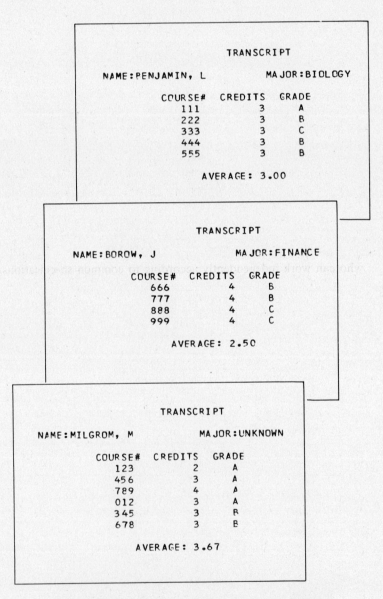

FIGURE 8.9 *Output from Student Transcript Problem*

010-COMPUTE-QUALITY-POINTS. The UNTIL clause terminates the PERFORM when all courses have been processed. Finally, note the running total of quality points in 010-COMPUTE-QUALITY-POINTS and the use of subscripting in conjunction with the table of student courses.

After the subprogram has been executed, control returns to the main program (line 115), where generation of output begins. Notice the table lookup (lines 139 to 151), which again illustrates subscripts and table processing.

A modified version of this program appears as a debugging exercise in R. Grauer, *A COBOL Book of Practice and Reference,* Prentice-Hall, Inc., Englewood Cliffs, N.J., 1981.

SUMMARY

This chapter has dealt exclusively with the data division. We began by amplifying points introduced in earlier chapters, i.e., editing and condition names. We then moved to new material: multiple records, COPY, tables, and subprograms.

Multiple records are used in the file section when there are different formats in a given file (e.g., a master card and several detail cards). They are not a requirement. Many programmers prefer to use the READ INTO and WRITE FROM options and define multiple records in working-storage.

The advantages of the COPY clause are obvious. Earlier versions of COBOL limited the use of the COPY, but now it is permitted anywhere within the COBOL program. A direct consequence is the use of COPY to duplicate procedure division code. In this way entire modules may be copied directly from a library. The REPLACING option of the COPY verb is used to make the data names in the library version conform to those of the specific program.

Tables are extremely important, and this chapter has merely scratched the surface. In the next chapter we shall introduce two- and three-dimension tables. In Chapter 9 we shall also present the SEARCH verb, in an extended discussion on table processing.

Subprograms are an important concept and are extremely useful in modular programming. A primary advantage of this technique in a commercial setting is the capability to divide a large program into several smaller ones. These may in turn be divided among several programmers, who can work independently according to common specifications.

REVIEW EXERCISES

TRUE FALSE

☐   ☐   **1.** The COPY clause is permitted only in the data division.

☐   ☐   **2.** The VALUE clause cannot be used in the file section.

☐   ☐   **3.** Several record descriptions are permitted for the same file.

☐   ☐   **4.** Tables in COBOL may contain one, two, or three dimensions.

☐   ☐   **5.** The REDEFINES clause must be used when defining a table.

☐   ☐   **6.** The same entry may not contain both an OCCURS clause and a PICTURE clause.

☐   ☐   **7.** The same entry may not contain both an OCCURS clause and a VALUE clause.

☐   ☐   **8.** The REDEFINES clause cannot be used at the 01 level.

☐   ☐   **9.** The USAGE clause is required when defining a subscript in working-storage.

☐   ☐   **10.** Subscripts can assume a zero value.

☐   ☐   **11.** The edit characters $ and * may not appear in the same PICTURE clause.

☐   ☐   **12.** The linkage section appears in the main program.

☐   ☐   **13.** The linkage section appears in the called program.

☐   ☐   **14.** Data names in 'CALL . . . USING' and 'PROCEDURE DIVISION USING . . .' must be the same.

□ □ 15. A subprogram contains only the data and procedure divisions.

□ □ 16. The COPY clause can be used on an FD only.

□ □ 17. Subscripts may be constant or variable.

□ □ 18. A program can contain only one CALL statement.

□ □ 19. The same program may be simultaneously considered a "called" and a "calling" program.

□ □ 20. 88-Level entries are allowed in the file section.

PROBLEMS

1. Indicate which entries are incorrectly subscripted. Assume SUB1 = 5 and that the following entry applies:

05   SALES-TABLE   OCCURS 12 TIMES   PIC 9(5).

(a) SALES-TABLE (1)
(b) SALES-TABLE (15)
(c) SALES-TABLE (0)
(d) SALES-TABLE (SUB1)
(e) SALES-TABLE(SUB1)
(f) SALES-TABLE (5)
(g) SALES-TABLE (SUB1, SUB2)
(h) SALES-TABLE (3)
(i) SALES-TABLE (3)

2. Show the edited results for each entry:

	Source field		Receiving field	
	Picture	Value	Picture	Edited result
(a)	S9(4)V99	−45600	$$$$$.99CR	
(b)	S9(4)V99	45600	$$,$$$.99DB	
(c)	S9(4)	4567	$$,$$$.00	
(d)	S9(6)	122577	99B99B99	
(e)	S9(6)	123456	++++,+++	
(f)	S9(6)	−123456	++++,+++	
(g)	S9(6)	123456	----,---	
(h)	S9(6)	−123456	----,---	
(i)	9(6)V99	567890	$$$$,$$$.99	
(j)	9(6)V99	567890	$ZZZ,ZZZ.99	
(k)	9(6)V99	567890	$***,***.99	

3. Rewrite the car billing problem of Figure 7.7 to contain a subprogram that calculates the customer bills. The following arguments are to be passed: car type, mileage driven, days rented, and calculated bill.

4. Consider the subprogram of Figure 8.8 in which WS-TOTAL-QUALITY-POINTS and WS-TOTAL-CREDITS are initialized in the first two lines of the procedure division. What would be the effect (if any) of removing these statements and replacing them with VALUE ZERO clauses in the data division? What would be the effect (if any) of removing the periods in the IF statements of lines 61, 63, and 65?

5. Modify the input for the car billing problem of Figure 7.7 to include a three-position field denoting the car type on the incoming data card (e.g., CHE for Chevrolet, PON for Pontiac, etc.). Include a table lookup routine that will print expanded car type on each line of output. Use your own table of abbreviations.

6. Write procedure division statements to do a table lookup in a table called CODE-NAME-TABLE for an entry that matches THIS-CODE. If a match is found, perform paragraph FOUND; if no match is found, perform paragraph NO-MATCH.

```
01  THIS-CODE           PIC 9(5).
01  SUB                 PIC S9(4) COMP.
01  CODE-NAME-TABLE.
    02  TABLE-VALUES OCCURS 100 TIMES.
        03  CODE-TAB    PIC 9(5).
        03  NAME-TAB    PIC X(20).
```

7. Recode the four simple IF statements in the program of Figure 8.8 as a single nested IF. Which would execute more efficiently? Could a knowledge of grade distributions be used to further increase efficiency? (Hint: see Chapter 11 on efficiency considerations!)

8. Company XYZ has four corporate functions: manufacturing, marketing, financial, and administrative. Each function in turn has several departments, as shown:

Function	Departments
MANUFACTURING	10, 12, 16–30, 41, 56
MARKETING	6–9, 15, 31–33
FINANCIAL	60–62, 75
ADMINISTRATIVE	1–4, 78

Establish condition name entries so that, given a value of EMPLOYEE-DEPARTMENT, we can determine the function. Include an 88-level entry, VALID-CODES, to verify that the incoming department is indeed a valid department (any department number not shown is invalid).

PROJECTS

1. Write a subprogram that will become part of a larger system that processes medical claims. Input to your program consists of a work record that is passed from another program. Include a COPY clause in your LINKAGE SECTION, with COPY member name MEDCPY03, to obtain the record description. If, however, the COPY facility is unavailable, code the record longhand as follows:

```
01  MED-COPY-03.
    05  M3-LAST-NAME            PIC X(13).
    05  M3-FIRST-NAME           PIC X(10).
    05  M3-CLAIM-NO             PIC S9(11).
    05  M3-SYSTEM-CODE          PIC XX.
    05  M3-SYSTEM-NUMERIC-CODE  PIC S9(3).
    05  FILLER                  PIC X(41).
```

Your program is to convert the two-position system code, M3-SYSTEM-CODE, to a three-digit numeric code, M3-SYSTEM-NUMERIC-CODE, as per the following table:

List of Alphanumeric Codes and Corresponding Values

AX	001
BN	001
BR	003
CN	001
FE	004
FN	001
LP	003
LX	013
NA	002
NB	008
PS	007
TN	002
ZZ	001

It will be necessary to establish a table of system codes and corresponding numeric codes. The following code might be helpful, as will the example in Figure 8.5 under table lookups.

```
01  TABLE-VALUES.
    05  FILLER      PIC X(5)  VALUE 'AX001'.
    05  FILLER      PIC X(5)  VALUE 'BN001'.
```

```
01  TABLE-WITH-SUBSCRIPTS  REDEFINES TABLE-VALUES.
   05  ALPHA-AND-NUMERIC  OCCURS 13 TIMES.
      10  ALPHA-CODE       PIC X(2).
      10  NUMERIC-CODE     PIC 9(3).
```

To test your program, you will have to code an additional COBOL program (i.e., main program) that reads the incoming file of claims records, passes appropriate data to your program, and prints adequate data to indicate whether the subprogram worked as intended. The preparation of test data and print formats is left to the reader.

2. Write a subprogram to accept a 2-position abbreviation for state name and return a 20-position expanded name. Include the table of abbreviations and state names in your subprogram.

AL — Alabama	MT — Montana
AK — Alaska	NB — Nebraska
AZ — Arizona	NV — Nevada
AR — Arkansas	NH — New Hampshire
CA — California	NJ — New Jersey
CO — Colorado	NM — New Mexico
CT — Connecticut	NY — New York
DE — Delaware	NC — North Carolina
DC — District of Columbia	ND — North Dakota
FL — Florida	OH — Ohio
GA — Georgia	OK — Oklahoma
HI — Hawaii	OR — Oregon
ID — Idaho	PA — Pennsylvania
IL — Illinois	RI — Rhode Island
IN — Indiana	SC — South Carolina
IA — Iowa	SD — South Dakota
KS — Kansas	TN — Tennessee
KY — Kentucky	TX — Texas
LA — Lousiana	UT — Utah
ME — Maine	VT — Vermont
MD — Maryland	VA — Virginia
MA — Massachusetts	WA — Washington
MI — Michigan	WV — West Virginia
MN — Minnesota	WI — Wisconsin
MS — Mississippi	WY — Wyoming
MO — Missouri	

3. A large photo album company sells photographs to school children in two counties. They collect the following information for each student: name, grade, a preassigned number for the school, and an indication of up to three types of picture package(s) the parents wish to buy. There are seven types of packages, numbers 1 to 7, but the parent buys only *one* of each type desired. The input record contains the following data:

Columns	Field	Picture
1–25	NAME	X(25)
26–29	SCHOOL	X(4)
31–32	GRADE	XX
34	PACKAGE-1	9
36	PACKAGE-2	9
38	PACKAGE-3	9

The values appearing in columns 34, 36, and 38 indicate the type (not quantity) of respective picture package(s); e.g., a 4 in column 34, a 6 in column 36, and a blank in column 38 indicate that the parent will buy 1 package of type 4 and 1 package of type 6. Your job is to write a program to print the total amount due from individuals who have purchased pictures.

Do not print the names of children ordering no packages. For those students ordering packages, i.e., those with numeric entries in column 34, 36, or 38, check for a valid number from 1 to 7 (use an 88-level entry with a VALUES ARE clause). If the number is invalid, display a message and the person's name, school, and grade.

If the value in column 34, 36, or 38 is numeric and between 1 and 7, use it as a subscript and move the appropriate cost from the following table. Code this table into your program.

Package Number	Cost
1	$7.50
2	$4.00
3	$3.75
4	$2.50
5	$2.50
6	$8.00
7	$10.50

Print the total due for each child as it occurs as well as a grand total on a total line.

The following test data are provided:

WATSON, AMY	0023 02 1 7
HOLMES, ANDREW	0023 02 1
STUCHELL, MARION	0023 02
MITCHUM, MARY	0023 03 2
HEDIN, SAM	0023 04 3 4 5
FLETCHER, RAYMOND	0023 04 1
FOSTER, ED	0023 05 1 8
GORE, JEAN	0023 06
HARDING, ZACHARY	0023 07 2
JACOBSON, SUE	0023 07 6 1

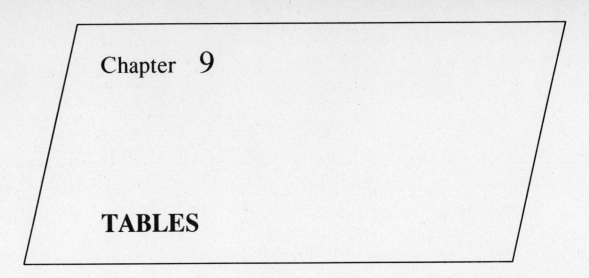

Chapter 9

TABLES

OVERVIEW

Tables are of paramount importance. In the previous chapter, we introduced subscripts and one-dimension tables. In this chapter we shall extend those concepts to two- and three-dimension tables. We shall also introduce indexes, which are conceptually the same as subscripts; however, the use of indexes in lieu of subscripts leads to more efficient machine code.

We shall present two distinct search techniques: linear and binary. We shall also discuss direct access to table entries and various means of initializing a table. Finally, we shall present the necessary COBOL to implement these procedures. We shall cover the SEARCH, SEARCH ALL, and SET verbs as well as associated clauses in the data division.

SUBSCRIPTING VERSUS INDEXING

Figure 8.5 contained a table lookup routine to determine a student major given a major code. Although the table lookup of Figure 8.5 is logically correct, it is not efficient in terms of the generated object code. Execution speed is increased if indexes and the SEARCH verb are used in lieu of subscripting. Consider Figure 9.1.

Let us highlight the differences between Figures 8.5 and 9.1. Figure 8.5 uses a *subscript*, WS-MAJOR-SUB; Figure 9.1 uses an *index*, MAJOR-INDEX. The subscript is defined in working-storage; the index is defined with the table. Figure 8.5 uses the PERFORM verb for the table lookup; Figure 9.1 uses the SEARCH verb. In actuality, however, the most significant difference is in the generated machine code, and this is not overtly visible from a simple comparison of the two figures. We must further differentiate between a subscript and an index.

A subscript and an index are conceptually the same in that they both reference an entry in a table. An index, however, represents a *displacement* into the table, whereas a subscript is an *occurrence*. Consider the following sketch with respect to Figure 9.1:

MAJORS							
OCCURRENCE (1)		OCCURRENCE (2)			OCCURRENCE (10)		
MAJOR CODE	MAJOR NAME	MAJOR CODE	MAJOR NAME		MAJOR CODE	MAJOR NAME	
				...			

158

```
01  MAJOR-VALUE.
    05  FILLER            PIC X(14)  VALUE  '1234ACCOUNTING'.
    05  FILLER            PIC X(14)  VALUE  '1400BIOLOGY'.
    05  FILLER            PIC X(14)  VALUE  '1976CHEMISTRY'.
    05  FILLER            PIC X(14)  VALUE  '2100CIVIL ENG'.
    05  FILLER            PIC X(14)  VALUE  '2458E. D. P.'.
    05  FILLER            PIC X(14)  VALUE  '3245ECONOMICS'.
    05  FILLER            PIC X(14)  VALUE  '3960FINANCE'.
    05  FILLER            PIC X(14)  VALUE  '4321MANAGEMENT'.
    05  FILLER            PIC X(14)  VALUE  '4999MARKETING'.
    05  FILLER            PIC X(14)  VALUE  '5400STATISTICS'.
01  MAJOR-TABLE REDEFINES MAJOR-VALUE.
    05  MAJORS      OCCURS 10 TIMES
                    INDEXED BY MAJOR-INDEX.
        10  MAJOR-CODE     PIC 9(4).
        10  MAJOR-NAME     PIC X(10).
*  DETERMINE MAJOR
    SET MAJOR-INDEX TO 1.
    SEARCH MAJORS
        AT END
            MOVE 'UNKNOWN   ' TO HDG-MAJOR
        WHEN ST-MAJOR-CODE = MAJOR-CODE (MAJOR-INDEX)
            MOVE MAJOR-NAME (MAJOR-INDEX) TO HDG-MAJOR.
```

FIGURE 9.1 *Illustration of the SEARCH Verb (Linear Search)*

Figure 9.1 establishes a table with 10 entries, MAJORS, occupying a total of 140 positions. Valid *subscripts* for MAJOR-CODE are 1, 2, 3, . . . , 10; i.e., MAJOR-CODE can occur 10 times. Valid *displacements* for MAJOR-CODE are 0, 14, 28, . . . , 126; e.g., the second value of MAJOR-CODE begins in position 15, a displacement of 14 positions into the table, etc. Thus the first value in the table is denoted by a subscript of 1 or a displacement (i.e., an index) of 0, the second value by a subscript of 2 or an index of 14, the last value by a subscript of 10 or an index of 126. The COBOL programmer, however, explicitly codes index values of 1, 2, etc., which correspond to *internal* displacements of 0, 14, etc.

In most instances, the COBOL programmer need not concern himself with the actual value of an index; instead he should regard it conceptually as a subscript. Accordingly, COBOL provides the capability to adjust an index to its proper value through the SET, SEARCH, and PERFORM verbs. Indeed these are the *only* verbs that can be used to modify an index. The only time a programmer need be concerned with the actual value of an index is in debugging (i.e., dump reading).

Let us return to Figure 9.1 and consider the action of the SET and SEARCH verbs. The statement SET MAJOR-INDEX TO 1 is analogous to MOVE 1 TO WS-MAJOR-SUB and initiates the point in the table where the search is to begin. The SET verb must be used to modify an index; i.e., it is *incorrect* to say MOVE 1 TO MAJOR-INDEX.

When the SEARCH verb is executed, it compares in sequence the entries in the MAJORS table to ST-MAJOR-CODE. If no match is found, i.e., the AT END condition is reached, then UNKNOWN is moved to HDG-MAJOR. However, if a match does occur, i.e., ST-MAJOR-CODE = MAJOR-CODE (MAJOR-INDEX), the appropriate major is moved to HDG-MAJOR, and the search is terminated, with control passing to the statement following the SEARCH.

BINARY SEARCH

The coding in both Figures 8.5 and 9.1 represents a linear or sequential search. The incoming code is compared to the first entry in the table, then the second entry, the third entry, etc. The number of comparisons that have to be made depends on where in the table we find our match.

Obviously, if the incoming code is near the beginning of the table, fewer comparisons are needed than if the code is at the end of the table.

✳ A binary search is a way to reduce the number of necessary comparisons and further to make the number of comparisons "relatively" independent of where in the table the match occurs. *It requires, however, that the entries in the table be in sequence (either ascending or descending).* The action of a binary search is illustrated in Figure 9.2.

Note: Incoming value is 3960

Position	Table Entries	
1	1234	
2	1400	
3	1976	
4	2100	
5	2458 ←——— 1st guess	
6	3245	
7	3960 ←————————————— 3rd guess	
8	4321 ←————— 2nd guess	
9	4999	
10	5400	

FIGURE 9.2 *Illustration of a Binary Search*

✳ A binary search eliminates half the table with every comparison. In Figure 9.2 there are ten entries in the table and we are looking for a match on 3960. We begin in the middle of the table at the fifth entry; the logic flow is as follows:

1. There are ten entries in the table; examine the middle (i.e., fifth entry). Is the incoming entry (3960) greater than the fifth entry (2458)? Yes; therefore eliminate table entries 1 to 5.
2. There are five remaining entries (positions 6 to 10). Select the middle (i.e., the eighth entry). Is the incoming entry (3960) greater than the eighth entry (4321)? No; therefore eliminate table entries 9 and 10.
3. There are three remaining entries (positions 6 to 8). Select the middle (i.e., the seventh) entry; with a value of 3960, a match is found, and the search is terminated.

Individual programmers vary the implementation of a binary search as to the type of test, i.e., high or low. Further, it is sometimes necessary to include a second test (equal) at a given guess. Indeed steps 1, 2, and 3 are perhaps a little hazy in that we skip over this completely, for our objective is to present only the flavor of a binary search. However, it is a good exercise to try to program these considerations into your own binary search routine in COBOL.

Notice that a total of three comparisons was required to match 3960. (If 3245 had been the incoming entry, four comparisons would have been needed, but this is the *maximum* number that would ever be required for a ten-position table; see Table 9.1.) A linear search, on the other

TABLE 9.1 Required Number of Comparisons for Binary Search

Number of elements		Maximum number of comparisons
8–15	(less than 2^4)	4
16–31	(less than 2^5)	5
32–63	(less than 2^6)	6
64–127	(less than 2^7)	7
128–255	(less than 2^8)	8
256–511	(less than 2^9)	9
512–1023	(less than 2^{10})	10
1024–2047	(less than 2^{11})	11
2048–4095	(less than 2^{12})	12

hand, would require seven comparisons until a match was found on 3960. Thus, if all ten entries in the table have an equal chance of occurring, the *average* number of comparisons for a linear search on a table of ten entries is five, which is greater than the *maximum* number for a binary search. Indeed, as table size increases, the advantage of the binary search increases dramatically. Table 9.1 shows the maximum number of comparisons for tables with 8 to 4095 entries.

Although the number of comparisons is less for a binary search, additional machine time is required for individual comparisons. Thus, as a rule of thumb, the binary search should not be used for small tables, i.e., those with 25 elements or less.

Figure 9.3 illustrates the implementation of a binary search in COBOL. The differences between Figures 9.1 and 9.3 are slight. SEARCH ALL is used in lieu of SEARCH to denote a binary search. Further, the ASCENDING KEY clause is needed in the table definition to indicate that MAJORS is in ascending sequence by MAJOR-CODE. Remember, a table *must* be in sequence (either ascending or descending) if a binary search is to be applied. Finally, the SET verb is not needed to initiate a binary search, as SEARCH ALL calculates its own starting position.

```
01   MAJOR-VALUE.
     05   FILLER                      PIC X(14)   VALUE   '1234ACCOUNTING'.
     05   FILLER                      PIC X(14)   VALUE   '1400BIOLOGY'.
     05   FILLER                      PIC X(14)   VALUE   '1976CHEMISTRY'.
     05   FILLER                      PIC X(14)   VALUE   '2100CIVIL ENG'.
     05   FILLER                      PIC X(14)   VALUE   '2458E. D. P.'.
     05   FILLER                      PIC X(14)   VALUE   '3245ECONOMICS'.
     05   FILLER                      PIC X(14)   VALUE   '3960FINANCE'.
     05   FILLER                      PIC X(14)   VALUE   '4321MANAGEMENT'.
     05   FILLER                      PIC X(14)   VALUE   '4999MARKETING'.
     05   FILLER                      PIC X(14)   VALUE   '5400STATISTICS'.
01   MAJOR-TABLE REDEFINES MAJOR-VALUE.
     05   MAJORS OCCURS 10 TIMES
               ASCENDING KEY IS MAJOR-CODE
               INDEXED BY MAJOR-INDEX.
          10   MAJOR-CODE      PIC 9(4).
          10   MAJOR-NAME      PIC X(10).
*  DETERMINE MAJOR
     SEARCH ALL MAJORS
          AT END
               MOVE 'UNKNOWN    ' TO HDG-MAJOR
          WHEN MAJOR-CODE (MAJOR-INDEX) = ST-MAJOR-CODE
               MOVE MAJOR-NAME (MAJOR-INDEX) TO HDG-MAJOR.
```

FIGURE 9.3 *Illustration of the SEARCH ALL Verb (Binary Search)*

DIRECT ACCESS TO TABLE ENTRIES

The *binary* search is a substantial improvement over the *linear* search, as it reduces the number of required comparisons. *Direct access* to table entries is better yet in that it requires no comparisons whatsoever. It is not really a search but rather a table lookup that uses the key of a record to indicate its position in a table. Consider the table of student majors used to illustrate the linear and binary searches of Figures 9.1 and 9.3. MAJOR-CODE is a four-digit numeric code, presumably with values of 1 to 9999. Both the linear and binary searches vary MAJOR-INDEX and compare the incoming code, ST-MAJOR-CODE, to various codes in the table until a match is found. Suppose, however, that the MAJORS table is defined to occur 9999 times. We no longer have to search for the matching code but instead can look it up directly. The SEARCH can be replaced by a single statement:

MOVE MAJOR-NAME (ST-MAJOR-CODE) TO HDG-MAJOR.

This assumes ST-MAJOR-CODE is a valid subscript, i.e., with a value from 1 to 9999. ST-MAJOR-CODE could also be defined as an index, instead of a subscript, provided

1. The OCCURS clause for the table MAJOR-NAME contains the clause INDEXED BY ST-MAJOR-CODE, and
2. The value of ST-MAJOR-CODE has been established by a SET statement.

Direct access is desirable in that it eliminates a search entirely. Its primary drawback is one of storage requirements; e.g., the major code example requires a table of 9999 entries even though there are only a few valid codes. Tables of this size are apt to be prohibitive in terms of storage requirements. The table would be defined as shown:

```
01  MAJOR-TABLE.
    05  MAJOR-NAME OCCURS 9999 TIMES     PIC X(10).
```

Notice that the MAJOR-CODE is not defined explicitly in the table, as the position in the table corresponds to the code. A second requirement of direct access is that the incoming code be strictly numeric so that it can be treated as a subscript. Even with these constraints, the direct "search" is a widely used technique and should be utilized where possible.

COBOL FORMATS

We have established three common approaches for searching, i.e., linear, binary, and direct. We have also discussed the difference between a subscript and an index. In this section we shall discuss the necessary COBOL for searching and indexing.

OCCURS Clause

The general format of the OCCURS clause is

$$\underline{\text{OCCURS}} \quad \left\{ \begin{array}{l} \text{integer-1 } \underline{\text{TO}} \text{ integer-2 TIMES } [\underline{\text{DEPENDING}} \text{ ON data-name-1}] \\ \text{integer-2 TIMES} \end{array} \right\}$$

$$\left[\left\{ \begin{array}{l} \underline{\text{ASCENDING}} \\ \underline{\text{DESCENDING}} \end{array} \right\} \text{ KEY IS data-name-2 [data-name-3] } \ldots \right]$$

$$[\underline{\text{INDEXED}} \text{ BY index-name-1 [index-name-2] } \ldots]$$

The OCCURS clause defines a table as explained in Chapter 8. Until now, all tables have been fixed length; i.e., they contained a constant number of entries. The DEPENDING ON option provides for variable-length tables. For example, consider the entries:

```
05  BILLING-TABLE OCCURS 1 TO 7 TIMES
                  DEPENDING ON NUMBER-OF-BILLS-SENT
                  INDEXED BY BILL-INDEX.
    10  INVOICE-NUMBER          PIC 9(4).
    10  INVOICE-AMOUNT          PIC 9(3)V99.
```

This establishes a variable-length table with 1 to 7 entries, depending on the number of bills sent. The table length will vary from 9 to 63 positions.

The ASCENDING (DESCENDING) KEY is required for tables that will utilize a binary search. The INDEXED BY clause denotes an index and is required anytime a table is processed with an index (either through the SEARCH verb and/or through indexing). Data names referenced in this clause are not defined elsewhere in the data division.

SET Verb

The SET verb is used to manipulate indexes. Two formats are available:

1. Format 1:

$$\text{\underline{SET}} \quad \begin{Bmatrix} \text{index-name-1 [index-name-2]} \\ \text{identifier-1 [identifier-2]} \end{Bmatrix} \ldots \text{\underline{TO}} \begin{Bmatrix} \text{index-name-3} \\ \text{identifier-3} \\ \text{literal-1} \end{Bmatrix}$$

2. Format 2:

$$\text{\underline{SET}} \quad \text{index-name-1 [index-name-2]} \ldots \begin{Bmatrix} \text{\underline{UP BY}} \\ \text{\underline{DOWN} BY} \end{Bmatrix} \begin{Bmatrix} \text{identifier-1} \\ \text{literal-1} \end{Bmatrix}$$

The SET verb can convert an index to an occurrence (i.e., subscript), and vice versa. However, the rules for such conversion can get tricky, and we refer the reader to an appropriate COBOL manual. We use the SET verb primarily to initialize an index and/or increment its value. ✳

The following code is a simple illustration of the SET verb and its use in processing a table. Assume BILLING-TABLE was previously defined to contain a variable number of entries and to be indexed by BILL-INDEX. The total amount due is to be computed and stored in the entry WS-TOTAL-BILL-AMOUNT. Note the use of the SET verb to both initialize and increment the index, BILL-INDEX.

```
MOVE ZERO TO WS-TOTAL-BILL-AMOUNT.
SET BILL-INDEX TO 1.
PERFORM COMPUTE-INVOICE-AMOUNT NUMBER-OF-BILLS TIMES.
       .
       .
       .
COMPUTE-INVOICE-AMOUNT.
    ADD INVOICE-AMOUNT (BILL-INDEX) TO WS-TOTAL-BILL-AMOUNT.
    SET BILL-INDEX UP BY 1.
```

Note well that indexing is *not* required in COBOL. Thus it is syntactically correct in the preceding code to define a 77 level entry, BILL-SUBSCRIPT, and replace the two SET statements by MOVE 1 TO BILL-SUBSCRIPT and ADD 1 TO BILL-SUBSCRIPT. Such changes have no effect on the complexity of the source code. Their impact can only be measured by examining the generated object code. ✳

USAGE Clause

The general format of the USAGE clause is:

$$\text{\underline{USAGE} IS} \begin{Bmatrix} \text{\underline{DISPLAY}} \\ \text{\underline{COMPUTATIONAL}} \\ \text{\underline{COMPUTATIONAL}-3} \\ \text{\underline{INDEX}} \end{Bmatrix}$$

The differences among DISPLAY, COMPUTATIONAL, and COMPUTATIONAL-3 are fully discussed in Chapters 12 and 14 under internal representation of data (the reader should consult a vendor's manual for information on additional forms of the USAGE clause, e.g., COMPUTA-TIONAL-1, COMPUTATIONAL-2). USAGE IS INDEX designates indexes rather than subscripts. Appropriate specification in the USAGE clause causes more efficient object code to be generated. However, the clause does not affect a program's logic and thus it is often ignored by those unconcerned with machine efficiency, e.g., students. We shall say no more about the subject until Chapters 12 and 14.

SEARCH Verb

There are two formats of the SEARCH verb, for linear and binary searches, respectively:

Format 1:

$$\text{SEARCH} \quad \text{identifier-1} \left[\underline{\text{VARYING}} \begin{Bmatrix} \text{index-name-1} \\ \text{identifier-2} \end{Bmatrix} \right]$$

[AT END imperative-statement-1]

$$\underline{\text{WHEN}} \quad \text{condition-1} \begin{Bmatrix} \text{imperative-statement-2} \\ \underline{\text{NEXT SENTENCE}} \end{Bmatrix}$$

$$\left[\underline{\text{WHEN}} \quad \text{condition-2} \begin{Bmatrix} \text{imperative-statement-3} \\ \underline{\text{NEXT SENTENCE}} \end{Bmatrix} \right] \ldots$$

Format 2:

$$\underline{\text{SEARCH}} \ \underline{\text{ALL}} \ \text{identifier-1}$$

[AT END imperative-statement-1]

$$\underline{\text{WHEN}} \quad \text{condition-1} \begin{Bmatrix} \text{imperative-statement-2} \\ \underline{\text{NEXT SENTENCE}} \end{Bmatrix}$$

✳   SEARCH ALL denotes a binary search; SEARCH by itself specifies a linear search. Identifier-1, in both formats, designates a table defined in the data division containing OCCURS and INDEXED BY clauses. If a binary search is specified (i.e., SEARCH ALL), then identifier-1 must also contain an ASCENDING (DESCENDING) KEY clause.

    The AT END clause is optional in both formats. If it is omitted, control passes to the next sentence following the SEARCH if the end of the table has been reached and no match was found. If the AT END clause is supplied but it does not contain a GO TO, control will also pass to the next sentence.

    The WHEN clause specifies a condition and imperative sentence. Note that more than one of these clauses may be contained in a linear search; e.g., we are searching a table for one of two keys and the required action depends on which key is matched. If the WHEN clause does not contain a GO TO statement, control will pass to the statement immediately following the SEARCH whenever the WHEN condition is satisfied.

    A VARYING option is also possible with a linear search but is not discussed here.

TWO-DIMENSION TABLES

✳Two-dimension tables require two subscripts to specify a particular entry. Consider Figure 9.4, which shows a two-dimension table to determine entry-level salaries in Company X. Personnel has established a policy that starting salary is a function of both responsibility level (values 1 to 10) and experience (values 1 to 5). Thus an employee with responsibility level of 4 and experience level of 1 would receive $10,000. An employee with responsibility of 1 and experience of 4 would receive $9,000.

    Establishment of space for this table in COBOL requires data division entries as follows:

```
01  SALARY-TABLE.
    05  SALARY-RESPONSIBILITY OCCURS 10 TIMES.
        10  SALARY-EXPERIENCE OCCURS 5 TIMES      PIC 9(5).
```

These entries would cause a total of 250 consecutive storage positions to be allocated (10 × 5 × 5) as shown:

SALARY-TABLE									
SALARY – RESPONSIBILITY (1)					SALARY – RESPONSBILITY (2)				
Exp 1	Exp 2	Exp 3	Exp 4	Exp 5	Exp 1	Exp 2	Exp 3	Exp 4	Exp 5

    Each of the 10 salary responsibility levels has 5 experience levels associated with it. Once we realize that the first 25 storage positions refer to the first responsibility level, the next 25 to the second responsibility level, etc., we know how to initialize the table using the VALUE and REDE-

Experience

Responsibility	1	2	3	4	5
1	6,000	7,000	8,000	9,000	10,000
2	7,000	8,000	9,000	10,000	11,000
3	8,000	9,000	10,000	11,000	12,000
4	10,000	12,000	14,000	16,000	18,000
5	12,000	14,000	16,000	18,000	20,000
6	14,000	16,000	18,000	20,000	22,000
7	16,000	19,000	22,000	25,000	28,000
8	19,000	22,000	25,000	28,000	31,000
9	22,000	25,000	28,000	31,000	34,000
10	26,000	30,000	34,000	38,000	42,000

Responsibility level = 4
Experience level = 1

Responsibility level = 1
Experience level = 4

FIGURE 9.4 *Entry-Level Salary (Illustration of Two-Dimension Table)*

FINES clauses. (See the COBOL listing in Figure 9.5.) Note that the level number for experience (10) is higher than for responsibility (05), indicating that experience belongs to responsibility. Indeed, if the level numbers were the same, SALARY-TABLE would not be two-dimensional.

Any reference to SALARY-EXPERIENCE in a program requires two subscripts, e.g., SALARY-EXPERIENCE (4, 1). Realize that SALARY-EXPERIENCE (10, 5) is a valid reference, but that SALARY-EXPERIENCE (5, 10) is invalid. The former denotes responsibility and experience levels of 10 and 5, respectively. However, the latter denotes a responsibility level of 5 and an experience level of 10 which does not exist.

TABLE LOOKUPS: A COMPLETE EXAMPLE

We are ready to incorporate the discussion on searching and two-dimension tables into a complete COBOL program. We shall utilize three table lookup techniques: linear search, binary search, and direct access to table entries. We shall also illustrate three ways of initializing a table: reading it from a file, redefinition and VALUE clauses, and use of the COPY clause. Specifications are as follows:

INPUT: A file of employee records containing name, location code, job code, and two salary determinants—experience and responsibility. There is also a second file containing data to initialize the table of job codes and expanded values.

PROCESSING: Establish tables for location, title, and salary determinants. For each employee record, determine expanded values of job title and location using a binary and linear search, respectively. Determine starting salary as a function of responsibility and experience (via direct access to the appropriate entry) as per the two-level table in Figure 9.4.

OUTPUT: One line per employee containing name, location, job title, and starting salary. Headings, page counts, line counts, etc., are not required.

```
00001          IDENTIFICATION DIVISION.
00002          PROGRAM-ID.
00003              'SEARCH'.
00004          AUTHOR.
00005              ROBERT T. GRAUER.
00006
00007          ENVIRONMENT DIVISION.
00008          CONFIGURATION SECTION.
00009          SOURCE-COMPUTER.
00010              IBM-370.
00011          OBJECT-COMPUTER.
00012              IBM-370.
00013
00014          INPUT-OUTPUT SECTION.
00015          FILE-CONTROL.
00016              SELECT EMPLOYEE-FILE  ASSIGN TO UT-S-SYSIN.
00017              SELECT PRINT-FILE ASSIGN TO UT-S-PRINT.
00018              SELECT TITLE-FILE ASSIGN TO UT-S-TITLES.
00019
00020          DATA DIVISION.
00021          FILE SECTION.          ⎯ This file will be used to initialize the title table
00022          FD  TITLE-FILE
00023              LABEL RECORDS ARE OMITTED
00024              RECORD CONTAINS 80 CHARACTERS
00025              DATA RECORD IS TITLE-IN.
00026          01  TITLE-IN.
00027              05  CARD-TITLE-CODE              PIC X(4).
00028              05  CARD-TITLE-NAME              PIC X(15).
00029              05  FILLER                       PIC X(61).
00030          FD  EMPLOYEE-FILE
00031              LABEL RECORDS ARE OMITTED
00032              RECORD CONTAINS 80 CHARACTERS
00033              DATA RECORD IS EMPLOYEE-RECORD.
00034          01  EMPLOYEE-RECORD.
00035              05  EMP-NAME                     PIC X(20).
00036              05  EMP-TITLE-CODE               PIC X(4).
00037              05  EMP-LOC-CODE                 PIC X(3).
00038              05  EMP-SALARY-DETERMINANTS.
00039                  10  EMP-RESPONSIBILITY       PIC 99.
00040                  10  EMP-EXPERIENCE           PIC 9.
00041              05  FILLER                       PIC X(50).
00042          FD  PRINT-FILE
00043              LABEL RECORDS ARE OMITTED
00044              RECORD CONTAINS 133 CHARACTERS
00045              DATA RECORD IS PRINT-LINE.
00046          01  PRINT-LINE.
00047              05  FILLER                       PIC X.
00048              05  DET-NAME                     PIC X(20).
00049              05  FILLER                       PIC XX.
00050              05  DET-LOCATION                 PIC X(13).
00051              05  FILLER                       PIC XX.
00052              05  DET-TITLE                    PIC X(14).
00053              05  FILLER                       PIC XX.
00054              05  DET-SALARY                   PIC $ZZ,ZZZ.00.
00055              05  FILLER                       PIC X(69).
00056          WORKING-STORAGE SECTION.
00057          01  WS-END-OF-FILE-SWITCHES.   ⎯ Different switches are defined for different files
00058              05  WS-END-OF-TITLE-FILE         PIC X(3)     VALUE 'NO'.
00059                  88  NO-MORE-TITLES                        VALUE 'YES'.
00060              05  WS-END-OF-EMPLOYEE-FILE      PIC X(3)     VALUE 'NO'.
00061                  88  NO-MORE-EMPLOYEES                     VALUE 'YES'.
00062          01  TITLE-TABLE-VARIABLES.
00063              05  WS-NUMBER-OF-TITLES          PIC 999      VALUE ZEROS.
00064              05  WS-TITLE-SUB                 PIC S9(4)
00065                  USAGE COMP                                VALUE ZEROS.
00066          COPY LOCVAL.
00067 C        01  LOCATION-VALUE.
00068 C            05  FILLER      PIC X(16)   VALUE 'ATLATLANTA      '.
00069 C            05  FILLER      PIC X(16)   VALUE 'BOSBOSTON       '.
00070 C            05  FILLER      PIC X(16)   VALUE 'CHICHICAGO      '.
00071 C            05  FILLER      PIC X(16)   VALUE 'DETDETROIT      '.
00072 C            05  FILLER      PIC X(16)   VALUE 'KC KANSAS CITY  '.
00073 C            05  FILLER      PIC X(16)   VALUE 'LA LOSANGELES   '.
00074 C            05  FILLER      PIC X(16)   VALUE 'MINMINEAPOLIS   '.
```

FIGURE 9.5 *Illustration of SEARCH Techniques*

```
00075 C          05   FILLER        PIC X(16)    VALUE 'NY NEW YORK       '.
00076 C          05   FILLER        PIC X(16)    VALUE 'PHIPHILADELPHIA '.
00077 C          05   FILLER        PIC X(16)    VALUE 'SF SAN FRANCISCO'.
00078     01  LOCATION-TABLE REDEFINES LOCATION-VALUE.
00079         05   LOCATIONS OCCURS 10 TIMES          ——— Indexed clause required for subsequent SEARCH
00080              INDEXED BY LOCATION-INDEX.
00081              10   LOCATION-CODE          PIC X(3).
00082              10   LOCATION-NAME          PIC X(13).
00083     01  TITLE-TABLE.
00084         05   TITLES OCCURS 1 TO 999 TIMES
00085              DEPENDING ON WS-NUMBER-OF-TITLES
00086              ASCENDING KEY IS TITLE-CODE ———— Required for binary search
00087              INDEXED BY TITLE-INDEX.
00088              10   TITLE-CODE             PIC X(4).
00089              10   TITLE-NAME             PIC X(15).
00090                                             ———— Initialization of two dimension table
00091     01  SALARY-MIDPOINTS.
00092         05   FILLER    PIC X(25)    VALUE '06000070000800009000 10000'.
00093         05   FILLER    PIC X(25)    VALUE '07000080000900010000 11000'.
00094         05   FILLER    PIC X(25)    VALUE '08000090001000011000 12000'.
00095         05   FILLER    PIC X(25)    VALUE '10000120001400016000 18000'.
00096         05   FILLER    PIC X(25)    VALUE '12000140001600018000 20000'.
00097         05   FILLER    PIC X(25)    VALUE '14000160001800020000 22000'.
00098         05   FILLER    PIC X(25)    VALUE '16000190002200025000 28000'.
00099         05   FILLER    PIC X(25)    VALUE '19000220002500028000 31000'.
00100         05   FILLER    PIC X(25)    VALUE '22000250002800031000 34000'.
00101         05   FILLER    PIC X(25)    VALUE '26000300003400038000 42000'.
00102     01  SALARY-TABLE REDEFINES SALARY-MIDPOINTS.
00103         05   SALARY-RESPONSIBILITY OCCURS 10 TIMES.
00104              10   SALARY-EXPERIENCE OCCURS 5 TIMES
00105                                             PIC 9(5).
00106
00107     PROCEDURE DIVISION.          ———— Allocation of space for two dimension table
00108
00109     005-MAINLINE.
00110         PERFORM 010-INITIALIZE-TITLES.
00111         OPEN INPUT EMPLOYEE-FILE
00112              OUTPUT PRINT-FILE.
00113         READ EMPLOYEE-FILE
00114              AT END MOVE 'YES' TO WS-END-OF-EMPLOYEE-FILE.
00115         PERFORM 020-PROCESS-EMPLOYEE-RECORDS
00116              UNTIL NO-MORE-EMPLOYEES.
00117         CLOSE EMPLOYEE-FILE
00118               PRINT-FILE.
00119         STOP RUN.          ———— Routine to initialize title table by reading
00120                                 value from a file
00121     010-INITIALIZE-TITLES.
00122         OPEN INPUT TITLE-FILE.
00123         READ TITLE-FILE
00124              AT END MOVE 'YES' TO WS-END-OF-TITLE-FILE.
00125         PERFORM 015-READ-TITLE-FILE
00126              UNTIL NO-MORE-TITLES.
00127         CLOSE TITLE-FILE.
00128
00129     015-READ-TITLE-FILE.
00130         ADD 1 TO WS-NUMBER-OF-TITLES.
00131         ADD 1 TO WS-TITLE-SUB.
00132         MOVE CARD-TITLE-CODE TO TITLE-CODE (WS-TITLE-SUB).
00133         MOVE CARD-TITLE-NAME TO TITLE-NAME (WS-TITLE-SUB).
00134         READ TITLE-FILE
00135              AT END MOVE 'YES' TO WS-END-OF-TITLE-FILE.
00136
00137     020-PROCESS-EMPLOYEE-RECORDS.
00138
00139     *CLEAR PRINT LINE
00140         MOVE SPACES TO PRINT-LINE.
00141                                             ———— Binary search
00142     *DETERMINE TITLE USING BINARY SEARCH
00143         SEARCH ALL TITLES
00144              AT END MOVE 'UNKNOWN' TO DET-TITLE
00145              WHEN EMP-TITLE-CODE = TITLE-CODE (TITLE-INDEX)
00146                   MOVE TITLE-NAME (TITLE-INDEX) TO DET-TITLE.
00147
```

FIGURE 9.5 *(continued)*

```
00148                *DETERMINE LOCATION USING LINEAR SEARCH          Linear search
00149                     SET LOCATION-INDEX TO 1.
00150                     SEARCH LOCATIONS
00151                         AT END MOVE 'UNKNOWN' TO DET-LOCATION
00152                         WHEN EMP-LOC-CODE = LOCATION-CODE (LOCATION-INDEX)
00153                             MOVE LOCATION-NAME (LOCATION-INDEX) TO DET-LOCATION.
00154
00155                *USE DIRECT TABLE LOOKUP - NO SEARCH
00156                     MOVE SALARY-EXPERIENCE (EMP-RESPONSIBILITY, EMP-EXPERIENCE)
00157                         TO DET-SALARY.
00158
00159                * WRITE DETAIL LINE              Direct access to table entries
00160                     MOVE EMP-NAME TO DET-NAME.
00161                     WRITE PRINT-LINE AFTER ADVANCING 2 LINES.
00162
00163                * READ NEXT RECORD
00164                     READ EMPLOYEE-FILE
00165                         AT END MOVE 'YES' TO WS-END-OF-EMPLOYEE-FILE.
```

FIGURE 9.5 *(continued)*

Figure 9.5 contains the COBOL listing to illustrate table lookups. Three distinct tables are established and searched. The values for location codes and expanded names are brought in via a COPY clause (COBOL lines 66 to 77). The locations table itself is established in COBOL lines 78 to 82 and searched via a linear search in lines 149 to 153. Notice the SET verb in line 149, immediately prior to the SEARCH instruction, used to establish the starting position for the search.

The titles table is defined in COBOL lines 83 to 89, with the OCCURS DEPENDING clause used to indicate a variable-length table. Observe the ASCENDING KEY clause to subsequently enable a binary search. The titles table is initialized by reading a file of title records (FD in lines 22 to 29). After each record is read, the number of titles is incremented by 1 in an ADD statement (COBOL line 130) as is WS-TITLE-SUB in COBOL line 131. The table itself is searched (via a binary search) in COBOL lines 143 to 146.

The table of starting salaries is initialized in lines 91 to 101. SALARY-TABLE contains 250 positions (10 responsibilities × 5 experience levels × 5 positions per elementary item) and is initialized one row per COBOL line. Verify the correspondence with Figure 9.4. Study COBOL line 156 to see the implementation of a direct table lookup; i.e., the incoming values EMP-RESPONSIBILITY and EMP-EXPERIENCE are used as subscripts, and no search is required.

Notice that incoming data are coming from two distinct files (EMPLOYEE-FILE and TITLE-FILE) and that two distinct end-of-file switches are established in working storage (lines 58 to 61). The first file contains the values to initialize the title table; the second contains the employee data.

A modified version of Figure 9.6 appears as a debugging exercise in R. Grauer, *A COBOL Book of Practice and Reference* (Englewood Cliffs, N.J.: Prentice-Hall Inc, 1981).

TWO-DIMENSION TABLES: A COMPLETE EXAMPLE

We further develop the concept of two-dimension tables by considering requirements for another COBOL program. A survey of ten questions has been distributed, answered, and keypunched. Every question has three possible answers: yes, no, and not sure (denoted by Y, N, or X, respectively). The answers to all questions on a given survey were punched in columns 1 to 10 of a single data card. There are as many data cards as there are survey respondents; i.e., each card contains ten responses from one individual.

Figure 9.6 shows various ways of representing a two-dimension table. Figure 9.6a illustrates the way the survey tabulations would probably appear in a report. Note that the object of the COBOL program is to process the completed questionnaires and compute the numbers in Figure 9.6 (which contains hypothetical values for 50 surveys).

Figure 9.6b contains the COBOL entries for establishing a two-dimension table of 10 rows and 3 columns. Realize that Figure 9.6b merely allocates space but does *not* assign values to the table.

Question No.	Number of Responses		
	Yes	No	Not Sure
1	15	20	15
2	20	18	12
3	6	23	21
4	24	21	5
5	38	11	1
6	16	32	2
7	10	20	20
8	35	10	5
9	4	39	7
10	46	3	1

└ Six people responded yes to the third question, i.e. the
element in row 3, column 1, has a value of 6.

(a)

```
01  SURVEY-RESPONSES.
    05  QUESTION-NUMBER      OCCURS 10 TIMES.
        10  ANSWERS          OCCURS 3 TIMES      PIC 99.
```
(b)

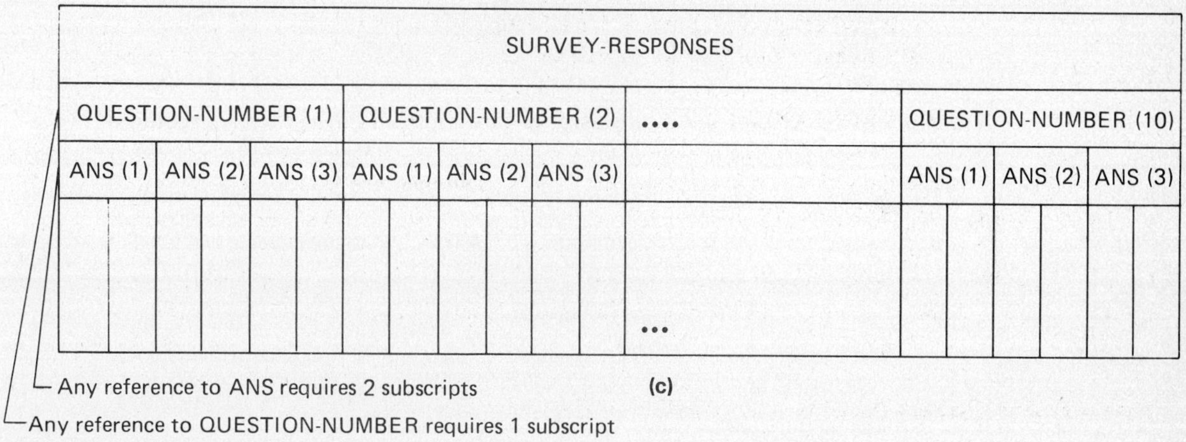

└ Any reference to ANS requires 2 subscripts   **(c)**
└ Any reference to QUESTION-NUMBER requires 1 subscript

FIGURE 9.6 *Two-Dimension Tables: (a) Conceptual View; (b) COBOL Entries (Allocates Space But Does Not Assign Values); (c) Storage Allocation*

Figure 9.6c shows the storage allocation resulting from Figure 9.6b. A total of 60 storage positions are allocated, 2 for each of the 30 table entries. Each reference to QUESTION-NUMBER requires only a single subscript; e.g., QUESTION-NUMBER (2) refers collectively to the three answers for the second question. Each reference to ANSWER, however, requires two subscripts denoting the question number and answer, i.e., yes, no, or not sure. Hence, the value contained in the table element ANSWER (4, 2) is the number of "no" answers to the fourth question.

Consider now Figure 9.7, the COBOL program for processing the surveys. Lines 53 to 55 contain the two-dimension table to hold the survey responses, as explained in conjunction with Figure 9.6. Note also COBOL line 24, which defines a one-dimension table, SURVEY-RESPONSE, to reference the ten responses for each survey.

```
00001          IDENTIFICATION DIVISION.
00002          PROGRAM-ID. SURVEY.
00003          AUTHOR.
00004             ROBERT T. GRAUER.
00005
00006          ENVIRONMENT DIVISION.
00007          CONFIGURATION SECTION.
00008          SOURCE-COMPUTER.
00009             IBM-370.
00010          OBJECT-COMPUTER.
00011           . IBM-370.
00012          INPUT-OUTPUT SECTION.
00013          FILE-CONTROL.
00014             SELECT SURVEY-FILE ASSIGN TO UT-S-SYSIN.
00015             SELECT PRINT-FILE ASSIGN TO UT-S-PRINT.
00016
00017          DATA DIVISION.
00018          FILE SECTION.
00019          FD   SURVEY-FILE
00020               LABEL RECORDS ARE OMITTED
00021               RECORD CONTAINS 80 CHARACTERS
00022               DATA RECORD IS SURVEY-RECORD.   Definition of one dimension table
00023          01   SURVEY-RECORD.
00024               05   SURVEY-RESPONSE OCCURS 10 TIMES    PIC X.
00025               05   FILLER                             PIC X(70).
00026          FD   PRINT-FILE
00027               LABEL RECORDS ARE OMITTED
00028               RECORD CONTAINS 133 CHARACTERS
00029               DATA RECORDS ARE DETAIL-LINE, HEADING-LINE.
00030          01   HEADING-LINE.
00031               05   FILLER                             PIC X(4).
00032               05   HEADING-INFORMATION                PIC X(30).
00033               05   FILLER                             PIC X(99).
00034          01   DETAIL-LINE.
00035               05   FILLER                             PIC X(7).
00036               05   QUESTION                           PIC ZZ.
00037               05   FILLER                             PIC X(6).
00038               05   PRINT-YES                          PIC ZZ.
00039               05   FILLER                             PIC XXX.
00040               05   PRINT-NO                           PIC ZZ.
00041               05   FILLER                             PIC X(6).
00042               05   NOT-SURE                           PIC ZZ.
00043               05   FILLER                             PIC X(103).
00044          WORKING-STORAGE SECTION.
00045          01   WS-EOF-SWITCH                           PIC X(3)
00046                                              VALUE SPACES.
00047               88   WS-END-OF-FILE            VALUE 'YES'.
00048          01   SURVEY-SUBSCRIPTS.      Binary subscript for more efficient processing
00049               05   WS-ANSWER-SUB                      PIC S9(4)
00050                    USAGE IS COMP        VALUE ZEROS.
00051               05   WS-QUESTION-SUB                    PIC S9(4)
00052                    USAGE IS COMP        VALUE ZEROS.
00053          01   SURVEY-RESPONSES.
00054               05   QUESTION-NUMBER OCCURS 10 TIMES.
00055                    10 ANSWER      OCCURS  3 TIMES  PIC 9(2).
00056
00057          PROCEDURE DIVISION.            Definition of two dimension table
00058
00059          000-MAINLINE.
00060               OPEN INPUT SURVEY-FILE
00061                    OUTPUT PRINT-FILE.
00062               READ SURVEY-FILE
00063                    AT END MOVE 'YES' TO WS-EOF-SWITCH.
00064               PERFORM 005-INITIALIZE-SURVEY-TOTALS
00065                    VARYING WS-QUESTION-SUB FROM 1 BY 1        Performed routine is executed
00066                    UNTIL WS-QUESTION-SUB > 10                 a total of 30 times
00067                    AFTER WS-ANSWER-SUB FROM 1 BY 1
00068                    UNTIL WS-ANSWER-SUB > 3.
00069
00070               PERFORM 010-PROCESS-SURVEYS
00071                    UNTIL WS-END-OF-FILE.
00072               PERFORM 018-WRITE-HEADING.
00073               PERFORM 020-WRITE-RESPONSES
00074                    VARYING WS-QUESTION-SUB FROM 1 BY 1        Performed routine is executed
00075                    UNTIL WS-QUESTION-SUB > 10.                a total of 10 times
```

FIGURE 9.7 *COBOL Program for Two Dimension Table*

```
00076            CLOSE SURVEY-FILE
00077                  PRINT-FILE.
00078            STOP RUN.
00079                                           ANSWER must be referenced with two
00080       005-INITIALIZE-SURVEY-TOTALS.        subscripts
00081            MOVE ZERO TO ANSWER (WS-QUESTION-SUB, WS-ANSWER-SUB).
00082
00083       010-PROCESS-SURVEYS.
00084            PERFORM 015-TABULATE-ANSWERS
00085                VARYING WS-QUESTION-SUB FROM 1 BY 1
00086                    UNTIL WS-QUESTION-SUB > 10.
00087            READ SURVEY-FILE
00088                AT END MOVE 'YES' TO WS-EOF-SWITCH.
00089                                           Determines appropriate column
00090       015-TABULATE-ANSWERS.                for two dimension table
00091            IF SURVEY-RESPONSE (WS-QUESTION-SUB) = 'Y'
00092                MOVE 1 TO WS-ANSWER-SUB
00093            ELSE
00094                IF SURVEY-RESPONSE (WS-QUESTION-SUB) = 'N'
00095                    MOVE 2 TO WS-ANSWER-SUB
00096                ELSE
00097                    MOVE 3 TO WS-ANSWER-SUB.
00098            ADD 1 TO ANSWER (WS-QUESTION-SUB, WS-ANSWER-SUB).
00099
00100       018-WRITE-HEADING.
00101            MOVE SPACES TO HEADING-LINE.
00102            MOVE 'QUESTION   YES    NO    NOT SURE'
00103                TO HEADING-INFORMATION.
00104            WRITE HEADING-LINE AFTER PAGE.
00105
00106       020-WRITE-RESPONSES.
00107            MOVE SPACES TO DETAIL-LINE.
00108            MOVE WS-QUESTION-SUB TO QUESTION.
00109            MOVE ANSWER (WS-QUESTION-SUB, 1) TO PRINT-YES.
00110            MOVE ANSWER (WS-QUESTION-SUB, 2) TO PRINT-NO.
00111            MOVE ANSWER (WS-QUESTION-SUB, 3) TO NOT-SURE.
00112            WRITE DETAIL-LINE AFTER ADVANCING 1 LINE.
```

FIGURE 9.7 (continued)

The procedure division begins by opening files and reading the first survey. The 30 elements in the SURVEY-RESPONSE table are initialized through a PERFORM VARYING statement, which causes the paragraph 005-INITIALIZE-SURVEY-TOTALS to be executed 30 times, once for each of 30 elements. The routine 010-PROCESS-SURVEYS is performed until there are no more surveys to process. It in turn invokes the routine 015-TABULATE-ANSWERS 10 times, i.e., once for each question on the survey. (The PERFORM VARYING of lines 84 to 86 automatically increments the value of WS-QUEST-SUB from 1 to 10.) The nested IF of lines 91 to 97 determines the appropriate column in which to enter the particular response, i.e., yes, no, or not sure for columns 1, 2, and 3, respectively. When the end of file is reached, and the perform of lines 70 and 71 is terminated, the computed responses are printed by the routine 020-WRITE-RESPONSES.

The PERFORM VARYING statement is explained more fully in a following section.

THREE-DIMENSION TABLES

Three-dimension tables require three subscripts to specify a particular entry. Consider a university with three colleges, five schools (e.g., engineering, business, etc.) within each college, and four years within each school. We define a three-dimension table of enrollments as follows:

```
01  ENROLLMENTS.
    05  COLLEGE OCCURS 3 TIMES.
        10  SCHOOL OCCURS 5 TIMES.
            15  YEAR OCCURS 4 TIMES    PIC S9(4).
```

There are 60 (3 × 5 × 4) elements in the table. Note that YEAR is the only elementary item, and hence it is the only entry with a PICTURE clause. The COBOL compiler allocates a total of 240 positions (60 elements × 4 positions per element), as indicated in Figure 9.8.

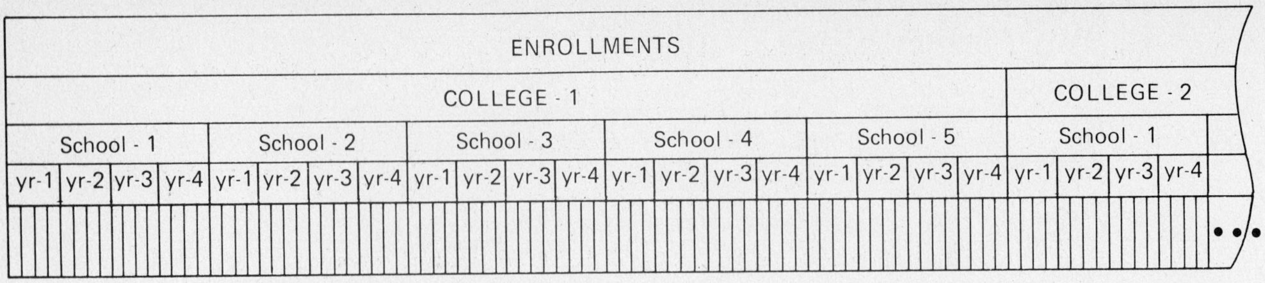

FIGURE 9.8 *Storage Allocation for Three-Dimension Table*

As can be implied from Figure 9.8, table positions 1 to 80 refer to the first college, positions 81 to 160 to the second college, and positions 161 to 240 to the third college. Positions 1 to 16 refer to the first school in the first college, positions 81 to 96 refer to the first school in the second college, and positions 161 to 176 refer to the first school in the third college. Finally, positions 1 to 4 refer to the first year in the first school in the first college, positions 81 to 84 refer to the first year in the first school in the second college, and so on.

Returning to the COBOL definition of the three-dimension table,

YEAR (1, 2, 3)   Refers to the enrollment in the first college, second school, third year. Note that in Figure 9.8 any reference to year must also specify school and college to remove ambiguity; hence YEAR must always be referenced with 3 subscripts.

YEAR (4, 3, 2)   Is incorrect since there are only 3 colleges (i.e., COLLEGE OCCURS 3 TIMES). Reference to YEAR (4, 3, 2) may not cause a compilation error, but could present problems in execution.

COBOL provides additional flexibility to reference data at different hierarchical levels. In effect definition of a three-dimension table automatically allows reference to one- and two-dimension tables as well. Thus,

SCHOOL (1, 2)   Refers to the enrollment in college 1, school 2; in effect it references the four years of college 1, school 2 collectively. Figure 9.8 implies that one must state the college in which a school occurs in order to pinpoint the school under discussion; hence SCHOOL requires two subscripts.

COLLEGE (3)   Refers to the enrollment in the third college; it references the 20 fields of the third college collectively. COLLEGE must always be used with one subscript.

ENROLLMENTS   Refers to the entire table of 60 elements. ENROLLMENTS may not be referenced with a subscript.

PERFORM VARYING

The VARYING option of the PERFORM verb is extremely convenient for manipulating subscripts and/or indexes. It was used in Figure 8.7 for one-dimension tables; it is extended to two and three dimensions:

PERFORM procedure-name-1 [THRU procedure-name-2]

$$\text{VARYING} \left\{ \begin{array}{l} \text{identifier-1} \\ \text{index-1} \end{array} \right\} \text{FROM} \left\{ \begin{array}{l} \text{identifier-2} \\ \text{literal-2} \\ \text{index-2} \end{array} \right\} \text{BY} \left\{ \begin{array}{l} \text{identifier-3} \\ \text{literal-3} \end{array} \right\} \text{UNTIL condition-1}$$

$$\left[\underline{\text{AFTER}} \left\{ \begin{array}{l} \text{identifier-4} \\ \text{index-4} \end{array} \right\} \underline{\text{FROM}} \left\{ \begin{array}{l} \text{identifier-5} \\ \text{literal-5} \\ \text{index-5} \end{array} \right\} \underline{\text{BY}} \left\{ \begin{array}{l} \text{identifier-6} \\ \text{literal-6} \end{array} \right\} \underline{\text{UNTIL}} \text{ condition-2} \right]$$

$$\left[\underline{\text{AFTER}} \left\{ \begin{array}{l} \text{identifier-7} \\ \text{index-7} \end{array} \right\} \underline{\text{FROM}} \left\{ \begin{array}{l} \text{identifier-8} \\ \text{literal-8} \\ \text{index-8} \end{array} \right\} \underline{\text{BY}} \left\{ \begin{array}{l} \text{identifier-9} \\ \text{literal-9} \end{array} \right\} \underline{\text{UNTIL}} \text{ condition-3} \right]$$

As an illustration, consider the following PERFORM statement:

```
PERFORM 010-READ-ENROLLMENT-RECORDS
    VARYING COLLEGE-SUB
        FROM 1 BY 1 UNTIL COLLEGE-SUB > 3
    AFTER SCHOOL-SUB
        FROM 1 BY 1 UNTIL SCHOOL-SUB > 5
    AFTER YEAR-SUB
        FROM 1 BY 1 UNTIL YEAR-SUB > 4.
```

The procedure 010-READ-ENROLLMENT-RECORDS will be performed a total of 60 times. Initially, COLLEGE-SUB, SCHOOL-SUB, and YEAR-SUB are all set to 1, and the first perform is done. Then YEAR-SUB is incremented by 1 and becomes 2 (COLLEGE-SUB and SCHOOL-SUB remain at 1), and a second perform is done. YEAR-SUB is incremented to 3 and then to 4, resulting in two additional performs. YEAR-SUB temporarily becomes 5, but no perform is realized since YEAR-SUB $>$ 4. SCHOOL-SUB is then incremented to 2, YEAR-SUB drops to 1, and we go merrily on our way. (See Figure 9.10 for further illustration.)

THREE-DIMENSION TABLES: A COMPLETE EXAMPLE

Figure 9.9 is a COBOL listing containing a three-dimension table and the PERFORM VARYING option. It utilizes the enrollments table defined earlier. Figure 9.10 depicts the input, and Figure 9.11 has generated output.

INPUT: A file of enrollment records; each record contains the enrollment for a specific year, in a given school and college. There are 60 (3 colleges $\times$ 5 schools $\times$ 4 years) records in all. The records are arranged by college, school, and year; i.e., the first 4 records contain enrollments for the first school in the first college, the next 4 records contain the enrollments for the second school in the first college, etc. Thus the order of the incoming records corresponds directly to the storage arrangement of Figure 9.8.

PROCESSING: Read the file of enrollment records. Compute the total enrollment for each school in each college.

OUTPUT: Display the enrollments in each college, one college per page. Show the calculated totals for each school as well.

A three-dimension enrollments table is established in COBOL lines 41 to 44. Subscripts to reference the table are grouped under a common 01 entry in working storage and defined as binary (i.e., COMPUTATIONAL) entries in lines 37 to 40. The PERFORM VARYING statement of lines 95 to 101 reads the 60 elements of the table. Year is varied first, followed by school, then college. The variation in subscripts is depicted by Figure 9.10. Note well the correspondence between the input data of Figure 9.10 and the output in Figure 9.11.

One-dimension tables are defined for school and college names in lines 48 to 64. Note also the OCCURS clause in the detail print line and the use of editing characters for printing enrollments (lines 85 and 87).

Notice the PERFORM VARYING statements in lines 102 to 104 and 121 to 123. The former

```
00001          IDENTIFICATION DIVISION.
00002          PROGRAM-ID.
00003              'SUBS'.
00004          AUTHOR.
00005              ROBERT T. GRAUER.
00006
00007          ENVIRONMENT DIVISION.
00008          CONFIGURATION SECTION.
00009          SOURCE-COMPUTER.
00010              IBM-370.
00011          OBJECT-COMPUTER.
00012              IBM-370.
00013
00014          INPUT-OUTPUT SECTION.
00015          FILE-CONTROL.
00016              SELECT ENROLLMENT-FILE
00017                  ASSIGN TO UT-S-SYSIN.
00018              SELECT PRINT-FILE
00019                  ASSIGN TO UT-S-PRINT.
00020
00021          DATA DIVISION.        This file contains 60 records
00022          FILE SECTION.         (see lines 41-44)
00023
00024          FD  ENROLLMENT-FILE
00025              LABEL RECORDS ARE OMITTED
00026              RECORD CONTAINS 80 CHARACTERS
00027              DATA RECORD IS ENROLLMENT-RECORD.
00028          01  ENROLLMENT-RECORD.
00029              05  ENROLLMENT-DATA          PIC 9(4).
00030              05  FILLER                   PIC X(76).
00031          FD  PRINT-FILE
00032              LABEL RECORDS ARE OMITTED
00033              RECORD CONTAINS 133 CHARACTERS
00034              DATA RECORD IS PRINT-LINE.
00035          01  PRINT-LINE                   PIC X(133).   Definition of 3 binary subscripts
00036          WORKING-STORAGE SECTION.
00037          01  WS-SUBSCRIPTS.
00038              05  COLLEGE-SUB     COMP     PIC S9(4).
00039              05  SCHOOL-SUB      COMP     PIC S9(4).
00040              05  YEAR-SUB        COMP     PIC S9(4).
00041          01  ENROLLMENT-TABLE.                         Definition of 3 dimension table
00042              05  COLLEGE OCCURS 3 TIMES.
00043                  10  SCHOOL OCCURS 5 TIMES.
00044                      15  YEAR OCCURS 4 TIMES  PIC S9(4).
00045
00046          01  SCHOOL-TOTAL                 PIC S9(6).
00047
00048          01  SCHOOL-VALUES.
00049              05  FILLER              PIC X(12) VALUE 'BUSINESS     '.
00050              05  FILLER              PIC X(12) VALUE 'EDUCATION    '.
00051              05  FILLER              PIC X(12) VALUE 'ENGINEERING '.
00052              05  FILLER              PIC X(12) VALUE 'FINE ARTS    '.
00053              05  FILLER              PIC X(12) VALUE 'LIBERAL ARTS'.
00054
00055          01  SCHOOL-NAMES REDEFINES SCHOOL-VALUES.    Table of college names with assigned values
00056              05  SCH-NAME  OCCURS 5 TIMES PIC X(12).
00057
00058          01  COLLEGE-VALUES.
00059              05  FILLER              PIC X(8)  VALUE 'ATLANTIC'.
00060              05  FILLER              PIC X(8)  VALUE 'MID-WEST'.
00061              05  FILLER              PIC X(8)  VALUE 'PACIFIC '.
00062
00063          01  COLLEGE-NAMES REDEFINES COLLEGE-VALUES.
00064              05  COL-NAME OCCURS 3 TIMES  PIC X(8).
00065
00066          01  HEADING-LINE-ONE.
00067              05  FILLER              PIC X(20) VALUE SPACES.
00068              05  FILLER              PIC X(9)  VALUE 'COLLEGE: '.
00069              05  COLLEGE-NAME        PIC X(8).
00070              05  FILLER              PIC X(96) VALUE SPACES.
00071
00072          01  HEADING-LINE-TWO.
00073              05  FILLER              PIC X(12) VALUE '   SCHOOL    '.
00074              05  FILLER              PIC X(12) VALUE '   FRESHMAN  '.
00075              05  FILLER              PIC X(12) VALUE '   SOPHOMORE '.
```

FIGURE 9.9 *COBOL Program for Three-Dimension Table*

SECTION III: MORE COBOL

```
00076              05  FILLER                    PIC X(12) VALUE '   JUNIOR     '.
00077              05  FILLER                    PIC X(12) VALUE '   SENIOR     '.
00078              05  FILLER                    PIC X(12) VALUE '   TOTAL      '.
00079              05  FILLER                    PIC X(12) VALUE SPACES.
00080
00081          01  DETAIL-LINE.                      1 dimension table used in output line
00082              05  FILLER                    PIC X.
00083              05  DET-NAME                  PIC X(12).
00084              05  DET-OUTPUT   OCCURS 4 TIMES.
00085                  10  DET-YEAR              PIC ZZZZ,999.
00086                  10  FILLER                PIC X(4).
00087              05  DET-TOTAL                 PIC ZZZZ,999.
00088              05  FILLER                    PIC X(64).
00089
00090          PROCEDURE DIVISION.
00091
00092          005-MAINLINE.
00093              OPEN INPUT ENROLLMENT-FILE,
00094                   OUTPUT PRINT-FILE.
00095              PERFORM 010-READ-ENROLLMENT-RECORDS
00096                  VARYING COLLEGE-SUB
00097                      FROM 1 BY 1 UNTIL COLLEGE-SUB > 3        PERFORM VARYING statement
00098                  AFTER SCHOOL-SUB                             with 3 variables
00099                      FROM 1 BY 1 UNTIL SCHOOL-SUB > 5
00100                  AFTER YEAR-SUB
00101                      FROM 1 BY 1 UNTIL YEAR-SUB > 4.
00102              PERFORM 015-PRINT-DATA-FOR-ONE-COLLEGE
00103                  VARYING COLLEGE-SUB
00104                      FROM 1 BY 1 UNTIL COLLEGE-SUB > 3.
00105              CLOSE ENROLLMENT-FILE, PRINT-FILE.
00106              STOP RUN.
00107
00108          010-READ-ENROLLMENT-RECORDS.
00109              READ ENROLLMENT-FILE
00110                  AT END DISPLAY 'ERROR - RAN OUT OF DATA'
00111                      STOP RUN.
00112              MOVE ENROLLMENT-DATA TO
00113                  YEAR (COLLEGE-SUB, SCHOOL-SUB, YEAR-SUB).
00114
00115          015-PRINT-DATA-FOR-ONE-COLLEGE.
00116              MOVE COL-NAME (COLLEGE-SUB) TO COLLEGE-NAME.
00117              WRITE PRINT-LINE FROM HEADING-LINE-ONE
00118                  AFTER ADVANCING PAGE.
00119              WRITE PRINT-LINE FROM HEADING-LINE-TWO
00120                  AFTER ADVANCING 2 LINES.
00121              PERFORM 020-PRINT-DATA-FOR-ONE-SCHOOL
00122                  VARYING SCHOOL-SUB
00123                      FROM 1 BY 1 UNTIL SCHOOL-SUB > 5.
00124
00125          020-PRINT-DATA-FOR-ONE-SCHOOL.                  PERFORM VARYING statement
00126              MOVE ZERO TO SCHOOL-TOTAL.                  with 1 variable
00127              ADD YEAR (COLLEGE-SUB, SCHOOL-SUB, 1)
00128                  YEAR (COLLEGE-SUB, SCHOOL-SUB, 2)
00129                  YEAR (COLLEGE-SUB, SCHOOL-SUB, 3)
00130                  YEAR (COLLEGE-SUB, SCHOOL-SUB, 4)
00131                  GIVING SCHOOL-TOTAL.
00132                                                          YEAR is referenced with
00133              MOVE SPACES TO DETAIL-LINE.                 3 subscripts
00134              MOVE SCH-NAME (SCHOOL-SUB) TO DET-NAME.
00135              MOVE YEAR (COLLEGE-SUB, SCHOOL-SUB, 1) TO DET-YEAR (1).
00136              MOVE YEAR (COLLEGE-SUB, SCHOOL-SUB, 2) TO DET-YEAR (2).
00137              MOVE YEAR (COLLEGE-SUB, SCHOOL-SUB, 3) TO DET-YEAR (3).
00138              MOVE YEAR (COLLEGE-SUB, SCHOOL-SUB, 4) TO DET-YEAR (4).
00139              MOVE SCHOOL-TOTAL TO DET-TOTAL.
00140              WRITE PRINT-LINE FROM DETAIL-LINE
00141                  AFTER ADVANCING 2 LINES.
```

FIGURE 9.9 *(continued)*

statement invokes 015-PRINT-DATA-FOR-ONE-COLLEGE 3 times. The second perform is contained within the 015-PRINT-DATA-FOR-ONE-COLLEGE procedure and calls 020-PRINT-DATA-FOR-ONE-SCHOOL 5 times. Thus the procedure 020-PRINT-DATA-FOR-ONE-SCHOOL is effectively called 15 (3 colleges × 5 schools) times in all.

The output of Figure 9.11 is straightforward and should contain no surprises. The reader

		FRESHMAN (YEAR-SUB = 1)	2000 – **First data card**
	BUSINESS (SCHOOL-SUB = 1)	SOPHOMORE (YEAR-SUB = 2)	1900
		JUNIOR (YEAR-SUB = 3)	1800
		SENIOR (YEAR-SUB = 4)	1700
	EDUCATION (SCHOOL-SUB = 2)	FRESHMAN (YEAR-SUB = 1)	4000
		SOPHOMORE (YEAR-SUB = 2)	3900
		JUNIOR (YEAR-SUB = 3)	3800
		SENIOR (YEAR-SUB = 4)	3700
ATLANTIC (COLLEGE-SUB = 1)	ENGINEERING (SCHOOL-SUB = 3)	FRESHMAN (YEAR-SUB = 1)	3600
		SOPHOMORE (YEAR-SUB = 2)	2500
		JUNIOR (YEAR-SUB = 3)	2450
		SENIOR (YEAR-SUB = 4)	2300
	FINE ARTS (SCHOOL-SUB = 4)	FRESHMAN (YEAR-SUB = 1)	2250
		SOPHOMORE (YEAR-SUB = 2)	2200
		JUNIOR (YEAR-SUB = 3)	2100
		SENIOR (YEAR-SUB = 4)	2000
	LIBERAL ARTS (SCHOOL-SUB = 5)	FRESHMAN (YEAR-SUB = 1)	3900
		SOPHOMORE (YEAR-SUB = 2)	3850
		JUNIOR (YEAR-SUB = 3)	3800
		SENIOR (YEAR-SUB = 4)	3700
	BUSINESS (SCHOOL-SUB = 1)	FRESHMAN (YEAR-SUB = 1)	1000
		SOPHOMORE (YEAR-SUB = 2)	0900
		JUNIOR (YEAR-SUB = 3)	0800
		SENIOR (YEAR-SUB = 4)	0700
	EDUCATION (SCHOOL-SUB = 2)	FRESHMAN (YEAR-SUB = 1)	3000
		SOPHOMORE (YEAR-SUB = 2)	2900
		JUNIOR (YEAR-SUB = 3)	2800
		SENIOR (YEAR-SUB = 4)	2700
MIDWEST (COLLEGE-SUB = 2)	ENGINEERING (SCHOOL-SUB = 3)	FRESHMAN (YEAR-SUB = 1)	1600
		SOPHOMORE (YEAR-SUB = 2)	1500
		JUNIOR (YEAR-SUB = 3)	1450
		SENIOR (YEAR-SUB = 4)	1300
	FINE ARTS (SCHOOL-SUB = 4)	FRESHMAN (YEAR-SUB = 1)	1150
		SOPHOMORE (YEAR-SUB = 2)	1100
		JUNIOR (YEAR-SUB = 3)	1100
		SENIOR (YEAR-SUB = 4)	1000
	LIBERAL ARTS (SCHOOL-SUB = 5)	FRESHMAN (YEAR-SUB = 1)	3900
		SOPHOMORE (YEAR-SUB = 2)	3850
		JUNIOR (YEAR-SUB = 3)	3800
		SENIOR (YEAR-SUB = 4)	3700
	BUSINESS (SCHOOL-SUB = 1)	FRESHMAN (YEAR-SUB = 1)	1400
		SOPHOMORE (YEAR-SUB = 2)	1300
		JUNIOR (YEAR-SUB = 3)	1200
		SENIOR (YEAR-SUB = 4)	1100
	EDUCATION (SCHOOL-SUB = 2)	FRESHMAN (YEAR-SUB = 1)	2800
		SOPHOMORE (YEAR-SUB = 2)	2700
		JUNIOR (YEAR-SUB = 3)	2600
		SENIOR (YEAR-SUB = 4)	2500
PACIFIC (COLLEGE-SUB = 3)	ENGINEERING (SCHOOL-SUB = 3)	FRESHMAN (YEAR-SUB = 1)	3600
		SOPHOMORE (YEAR-SUB = 2)	3500
		JUNIOR (YEAR-SUB = 3)	3450
		SENIOR (YEAR-SUB = 4)	3300
	FINE ARTS (SCHOOL-SUB = 4)	FRESHMAN (YEAR-SUB = 1)	3350
		SOPHOMORE (YEAR-SUB = 2)	3300
		JUNIOR (YEAR-SUB = 3)	3100
		SENIOR (YEAR-SUB = 4)	3000
	LIBERAL ARTS (SCHOOL-SUB = 5)	FRESHMAN (YEAR-SUB = 1)	4900
		SOPHOMORE (YEAR-SUB = 2)	4850
		JUNIOR (YEAR-SUB = 3)	4800
		SENIOR (YEAR-SUB = 4)	4700 – **Last data card**

FIGURE 9.10 *Input for Three-Dimension Table (Illustration of PERFORM VARYING)*

```
                                                                     Page 3
            COLLEGE: PACIFIC

    SCHOOL      FRESHMAN    SOPHOMORE    JUNIOR     SENIOR      TOTAL

    BUSINESS     1,400       1,300       1,200      1,100       5,000

    EDUCATION    2,800       2,700       2,600      2,500      10,600

    ENGINEERING  3,600       3,500       3,450      3,300      13,850

    FINE ARTS    3,350       3,300       3,100      3,000      12,750

    LIBERAL ARTS 4,900       4,850       4,800      4,700      19,250

            COLLEGE: MID-WEST

    SCHOOL      FRESHMAN    SOPHOMORE    JUNIOR     SENIOR      TOTAL

    BUSINESS     1,000        900         800        700       3,400

    EDUCATION    3,000       2,900       2,800      2,700      11,400     Page 2

    ENGINEERING  1,600       1,500       1,450      1,300       5,850

    FINE ARTS    1,150       1,100       1,100      1,000       4,350

    LIBERAL ARTS 3,900       3,850       3,800      3,700      15,250

            COLLEGE: ATLANTIC

    SCHOOL      FRESHMAN    SOPHOMORE    JUNIOR     SENIOR      TOTAL

    BUSINESS     2,000       1,900       1,800      1,700       7,400

    EDUCATION    4,000       3,900       3,800      3,700      15,400     Page 1

    ENGINEERING  3,600       2,500       2,450      2,300      10,850

    FINE ARTS    2,250       2,200       2,100      2,000       8,550

    LIBERAL ARTS 3,900       3,850       3,800      3,700      15,250
```

FIGURE 9.11 *Output from Three-Dimension Table Program*

should, however, be able to verify the numbers in Figure 9.11 as being derived from the input of Figure 9.10.

SUMMARY

An entire chapter has been devoted to table processing. In COBOL, tables may be one, two, or three dimensions. Individual elements are accessed by either subscripts or indexes. An index is conceptually the same as a subscript but results in more efficient machine code. If indexes are established, they can be referenced only by a SET, SEARCH, or PERFORM verb.

Three distinct methods for table lookups—linear, binary, and direct—were covered with associated COBOL implementation. The SEARCH and SEARCH ALL verbs are available for linear and binary searches, respectively.

Three distinct means of initializing a table were presented through the COBOL listing of Figure 9.5. These included use of the COPY clause, reading values from a file, and use of REDEFINES and VALUE clauses.

Finally, three complete programs were developed to illustrate the use of two- and three-dimension tables.

REVIEW EXERCISES

☐ ☐ **1.** A binary search over a table of 500 elements requires 10 or less comparisons.

☐ ☐ **2.** A linear search over a table of 500 elements could require 500 comparisons.

☐ ☐ **3.** Direct access to table entries requires no comparisons.

☐ ☐ **4.** The SEARCH verb requires an index.

☐ ☐ **5.** SEARCH ALL denotes a binary search.

☐ ☐ **6.** There are no additional requirements of table organization in order to implement a binary rather than linear search.

☐ ☐ **7.** An index (i.e. displacement) of zero refers to the first element in a table.

☐ ☐ **8.** A subscript of zero refers to the first element in a table.

☐ ☐ **9.** An index cannot be manipulated by a MOVE statement.

☐ ☐ **10.** PERFORM VARYING can manipulate both indexes and subscripts.

☐ ☐ **11.** The working size of a table can be adjusted at execution time to be less than its maximum allotted size.

☐ ☐ **12.** A SEARCH verb can contain only a single WHEN clause.

☐ ☐ **13.** The ASCENDING (DESCENDING) KEY clause is required whenever the SEARCH verb is applied to a table.

☐ ☐ **14.** The INDEXED BY clause is required whenever the SEARCH verb is applied to a table.

PROBLEMS

1. Write out the 12 pairs of values that will be assumed by SUB-1 and SUB-2 as a result of the statement

```
PERFORM 10-READ-CARDS
    VARYING SUB-1 FROM 1 BY 1
        UNTIL SUB-1 > 4
    AFTER SUB-2 FROM 1 BY 1
        UNTIL SUB-2 > 3.
```

2. Write out the 24 pairs of values that will be assumed by SUB-1, SUB-2, and SUB-3 as a result of the statement

```
PERFORM 10-READ-CARDS
    VARYING SUB-3 FROM 1 BY 1
        UNTIL SUB-3 > 3
    AFTER SUB-2 FROM 1 BY 1
        UNTIL SUB-2 > 2
    AFTER SUB-1 FROM 1 BY 1
        UNTIL SUB-1 > 4.
```

3. How many storage positions are allocated for each of the following table definitions? Show an appropriate schematic indicating storage assignment for each table.

```
(a)   01  STATE-TABLE.
          05  STATE-NAME OCCURS 50 TIMES        PIC A(15).
          05  STATE-POPULATION OCCURS 50 TIMES  PIC 9(8).
(b)   01  STATE-TABLE.
          05  NAME-POPULATION OCCURS 50 TIMES.
              10  STATE-NAME                    PIC A(15).
              10  STATE-POPULATION              PIC 9(8).
(c)   01  ENROLLMENTS.
          05  COLLEGE OCCURS 4 TIMES.
              10  SCHOOL OCCURS 5 TIMES.
                  15  YEAR OCCURS 4 TIMES       PIC 9(4).
(d)   01  ENROLLMENTS.
          05  COLLEGE OCCURS 4 TIMES.
              10  SCHOOL OCCURS 5 TIMES         PIC 9(4).
              10  YEAR OCCURS 4 TIMES           PIC 9(4).
```

4. Show procedure division code to determine the largest and smallest population in POPULATION-TABLE. Move these values to BIGGEST and SMALLEST, respectively. Move the state names to BIG-STATE and SMALL-STATE, respectively. POPULATION-TABLE is defined as follows:

```
01  POPULATION-TABLE.
    05  POPULATION-AND-NAME OCCURS 50 TIMES INDEXED BY POP-INDEX.
        10  POPULATION                PIC 9(8).
        10  STATE-NAME                PIC A(15).
```

5. Modify the COBOL listing in Figure 8.7 to use the SEARCH verb to determine the student major, given the student major code. Further modify the program to initialize the table of student majors by reading a file of codes, rather than initializing directly in the program.

6. Given the following table definition:

```
01  LOCATION-VALUE.
    05  FILLER          PIC X(16)   VALUE '010ATLANTA       '.
    05  FILLER          PIC X(16)   VALUE '020BOSTON        '.
    05  FILLER          PIC X(16)   VALUE '030CHICAGO       '.
    05  FILLER          PIC X(16)   VALUE '040DETROIT       '.
    05  FILLER          PIC X(16)   VALUE '050KANSAS CITY   '.
    05  FILLER          PIC X(16)   VALUE '060LOS ANGELES   '.
    05  FILLER          PIC X(16)   VALUE '070NEW YORK      '.
    05  FILLER          PIC X(16)   VALUE '080PHILADELPHIA  '.
    05  FILLER          PIC X(16)   VALUE '090SAN FRANCISCO'.
    05  FILLER          PIC X(16)   VALUE '045DENVER        '.
01  LOCATION-TABLE REDEFINES LOCATION-VALUE.
    05  LOCATION OCCURS 10 TIMES
        ASCENDING KEY IS LOCATION-CODE
        INDEXED BY LOCATION-INDEX.
        10  LOCATION-CODE   PIC X(3).
        10  LOCATION-NAME   PIC X(13).
```

and the following procedure division code:

```
SET LOCATION-INDEX TO 1.
SEARCH LOCATION
    AT END DISPLAY   '*ERROR IN LINEAR SEARCH FOR DENVER'
    WHEN LOCATION-CODE (LOCATION-INDEX) = '045'
    DISPLAY 'LINEAR SEARCH OK FOR DENVER'.
SEARCH LOCATION
    AT END DISPLAY   '*ERROR IN LINEAR SEARCH FOR NEW YORK'
    WHEN LOCATION-CODE (LOCATION-INDEX) = '070'
    DISPLAY 'LINEAR SEARCH OK FOR NEW YORK'.
```

(a) Indicate the output that will be produced.

(b) Code a *binary* search statement to expand code 045 for Denver. Do you expect any trouble in the execution of that statement?

7. Modify the program of Figure 9.7 to determine the question with the most positive responses (i.e., the highest number of yes answers). Also determine the question with the most negative responses. (For simplicity, assume no ties.)

PROJECTS

1. Acme Widgets Inc., has branch offices in New York, Los Angeles, and Miami (locations 1, 2, and 3, respectively). Each location has five departments: 10, 11, 12, 13, and 14. A deck of cards has been prepared for each employee in Acme containing the following information:

Field	Columns	Picture
NAME	1–20	X(20)
LOCATION	21	X
DEPARTMENT	22–23	99

Write a COBOL program to read the file of data cards and compute and print
(a) The total number of employees in each location.
(b) The total number of employees in each department throughout the company (five totals in all).
(c) The total number of employees in each department in each location.
Use any suitable format to print the totals; make up your own test data.

2. A large film company has decided to make a war movie requiring hundreds of people outside the 10 or 15 main actors and actresses. An hourly pay scale is used and based on both the type of role and the experience in previous movies. The following chart represents their pay scale:

		Previous experience (number of movies)						
		0	1	2	3	4	5–7	8–UP
	A	20.00	25.00	30.00	32.00	34.00	38.00	40.00
	B	14.00	17.00	18.00	19.00	21.00	23.00	24.00
Type	C	7.00	7.50	8.00	8.00	8.50	8.50	9.00
Role	D	4.00	5.00	5.50	5.50	5.50	6.00	6.00
	E	3.75	4.50	5.00	5.00	5.25	5.50	5.50
	F	3.50	3.50	3.50	3.75	3.75	3.75	4.00

A punched card was prepared for every extra containing the following information:

Columns	Field	Picture
1–9	SOC-SEC-NUMBER	9(9)
10–34	NAME	X(25)
35–36	MOVIE-EXPERIENCE	99
38	TYPE-ROLE	X
40–43	HOURS-WORKED	999V9
45–46	EXPANDED-ROLE	XX

A program is required to process incoming records and print one line for each extra, showing name, social security number, movie experience, type of role, hours worked, and amount earned.

Note well that the wage table must be coded into the program, and we suggest the technique of Figure 9.5. Realize, however, that the number of previous movies for an individual must be converted into a number from 1 to 7 so that it can be used as a subscript for access into the table.

In addition, your program is to accommodate all the following:
(a) Verify that the value in MOVIE-EXPERIENCE is numeric; if not, display an error message and do no further processing for that record.
(b) Verify that the value in TYPE-ROLE is valid (i.e., A, B, C, D, E, or F); if not, display an error message and do no further processing for that record.
(c) Print a heading line(s) from a performed routine for every four records. Include a page number and date of execution.

Finally, use the following test data:

```
000000001JONES, J.                00 C  0800 CN
000000002JONES, ROY               02 F  0450 FA
000000003WILLIAMS, JOHN           01 E  0450 EA
000000004FOSTER, RAYMOND          11 B  0425 BN
000000005HIGH, LUCY               08 A  0450 AR
000000006HARDING, HOWARD          04 A  0450 AV
000000007ZHE, KEVEN               05 D  0450 DN
000000008JENNINGS, VIVIAN            D  0200 DA
000000009ROOSEVELT, TIMOTHY       07 E  0230 XX
000000010TRUELOVE, BILL           09 G  0450 EN
```

3. Write a subprogram that will interface with Project 2. The director of the film has decreed that all employees will automatically get a bonus by paying each employee for a variable number of hours not appearing on their time record. A table was set up in ascending sequence by expanded role. The value opposite this field determines the number of extra hours. The table is as follows:

Expanded Role	Extra Hours
AA	01
AV	01
BA	03
BN	05
CA	05
CN	04
DA	08
DN	08
DR	09
EA	14
EN	03
ER	03
FA	01
FN	06

Set this table up in working storage. Set up a linkage section and pass the entire incoming record to the subprogram. Do a binary search on the table looking for match on expanded-role. If a match is found, take the hours shown in the table and add it to the hours in the incoming record. If no match is found display an appropriate error message, but do not add any extra hours. Modify the previous project to include a call to this program for valid records only. Use the test data from the previous project.

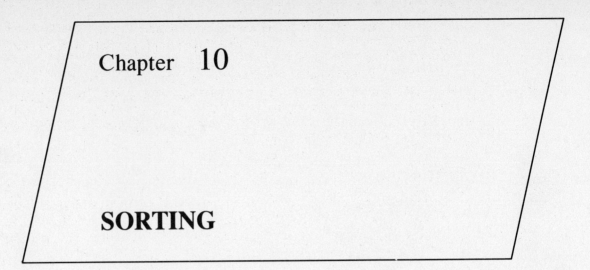

Chapter 10

SORTING

OVERVIEW

Sorting, i.e., the rearrangement of data, is one of the most frequent operations in data processing. Reports are presented in a variety of ways, depending on the analysis required. Transactions may be listed alphabetically, alphabetically within location, numerically, etc.

Sorting is typically accomplished in one of three ways:

1. Internal sort, in which the programmer develops his own logic within his application program.
2. Utility sort, in which the sort program is called independently of the application program as a separate job step.
3. COBOL SORT verb, in which the utility sort program is called directly from a COBOL program.

Regardless of which method is used, the objective is the same: rearrange a file according to the requirements of a particular application. Our discussion deals exclusively with the third approach, i.e., the COBOL SORT verb.

We shall begin the chapter by developing necessary vocabulary. Next we shall consider COBOL requirements. Finally, we shall present two complete programs to illustrate the concepts of the chapter and the variations within the COBOL SORT verb.

VOCABULARY

A sort *key* is a field within a record that determines how the file is to be arranged. Several keys may be specified in a single sort. For example, assume an unsorted file is to be used in preparing a department census in which employees are to appear alphabetically within department. In other words, the file is to be rearranged, i.e. sorted, so that all employees in the same department appear together, and further that employees in a given department appear alphabetically. Department is a more important key than employee-name; thus department is considered the *major* key and employee-name the *minor* key. (Other, equally correct, terminology refers to department as the *primary* key and name as the *secondary* key.)

Sorting is done in one of two sequences: *ascending* (low to high) or *descending* (high to low). If sequence is not specified, an ascending sort is assumed. Thus, employees listed alphabetically is an *ascending* sort on name. However, employees listed by age, with the oldest first, denotes a *descending* sort on age.

182

To be absolutely sure of this terminology, consider Figure 10.1. Figure 10.1(a) lists unsorted data for 12 students. Figure 10.1(b) sorts these records by name only; i.e., students with different majors and different years are mixed together in a single list. Figure 10.1(c) shows a primary sort on year (descending) and a secondary sort on name. Thus all students in year 4 are listed first (in alphabetical order), then all students in year 3, etc. Finally, Figure 10.1(d) illustrates primary, secondary, and tertiary sorts. All business majors are listed first, then all engineering majors, and finally all liberal arts majors. Within a major, students are listed by year in descending order and listed alphabetically within year.

COBOL IMPLEMENTATION

We shall now introduce four COBOL statements used exclusively with sorting: SD (sort description), SORT, RELEASE, and RETURN. The SD is present in the data division, and the other three are procedure division verbs. Implementation revolves around the SORT verb, which has the general form

Name	Year	Major
Smith	1	Liberal arts
Jones	4	Engineering
Adams	3	Business
Howe	2	Liberal arts
Frank	1	Engineering
Epstein	2	Engineering
Zev	4	Business
Benjamin	4	Business
Grauer	3	Liberal arts
Crawford	2	Engineering
Deutsch	4	Business
Makoske	1	Business

FIGURE 10.1(a) *Unsorted Data*

Primary Sort—Name (Ascending)

Name	Year	Major
Adams	3	Business
Benjamin	4	Business
Crawford	2	Engineering
Deutsch	4	Business
Epstein	2	Engineering
Frank	1	Engineering
Grauer	3	Liberal arts
Howe	2	Liberal arts
Jones	4	Engineering
Makoske	1	Business
Smith	1	Liberal arts
Zev	4	Business

FIGURE 10.1(b) *Sorted Data*

Primary Sort—Year (Descending)
Secondary Sort—Name (Ascending)

Name	Year	Major
Benjamin	4	Business
Deutsch	4	Business
Jones	4	Engineering
Zev	4	Business
Adams	3	Business
Grauer	3	Liberal arts
Crawford	2	Engineering
Epstein	2	Engineering
Howe	2	Liberal arts
Frank	1	Engineering
Makoske	1	Business
Smith	1	Liberal arts

FIGURE 10.1(c) *Sorted Data*

Primary Sort—Major (Ascending)
Secondary Sort—Year (Descending)
Tertiary Sort—Name (Ascending)

Name	Year	Major
Benjamin	4	Business
Deutsch	4	Business
Zev	4	Business
Adams	3	Business
Makoske	1	Business
Jones	4	Engineering
Crawford	2	Engineering
Epstein	2	Engineering
Frank	1	Engineering
Grauer	3	Liberal arts
Howe	2	Liberal arts
Smith	1	Liberal arts

FIGURE 10.1(d) *Sorted Data*

SORT file-name-1

    ON $\begin{Bmatrix} \text{DESCENDING} \\ \text{ASCENDING} \end{Bmatrix}$ KEY data-name-1 [data-name-2] . . .

    $\left[\text{ON} \begin{Bmatrix} \text{DESCENDING} \\ \text{ASCENDING} \end{Bmatrix} \text{KEY data-name-3 [data-name-4] . . .} \right]$ . . .

    [COLLATING SEQUENCE IS alphabet-name]

    $\begin{Bmatrix} \text{INPUT PROCEDURE IS section-name-1} \left[\begin{Bmatrix} \text{THRU} \\ \text{THROUGH} \end{Bmatrix} \text{section-name-2} \right] \\ \text{USING file-name-2} \end{Bmatrix}$

    $\begin{Bmatrix} \text{OUTPUT PROCEDURE IS section-name-3} \left[\begin{Bmatrix} \text{THRU} \\ \text{THROUGH} \end{Bmatrix} \text{section-name-4} \right] \\ \text{GIVING file-name-3} \end{Bmatrix}$

As can be seen, the word SORT is always required. Multiple keys are listed in the order of importance. Thus the statement

        SORT file-name-1   ASCENDING MAJOR
                          DESCENDING YEAR
                          ASCENDING NAME . . .

corresponds to the keys of Figure 10.1(d) (MAJOR is the primary sort and NAME the tertiary sort). File-name-1 refers to the file designated by an SD (sort description) in the data division.

The SORT verb has several formats. One can use INPUT PROCEDURE in combination with OUTPUT PROCEDURE or USING in conjunction with GIVING. Both methods are equally valid and are illustrated through sample programs (Figures 10.2 and 10.3.). *However, INPUT PROCEDURE is a more general technique in that it permits sorting on a calculated field.* For example, assume an incoming record has both an employee's present and previous salary. The USING option permits a sort on either field but not on percent of salary increase. The latter field is a calculated field; i.e., it is not contained in an incoming record per se but is calculated from two fields that are.

It is also possible to use INPUT PROCEDURE with GIVING or USING with OUTPUT PROCEDURE. However, these combinations are not illustrated with sample programs. The former combination permits sorting on a calculated field; the latter does not.

Inclusion of the clause COLLATING SEQUENCE makes it possible to sort on a sequence other than EBCDIC, e.g., ASCII (see discussion in Chapter 7). If this option is chosen, additional entries are required in the SPECIAL-NAMES paragraph of the environment division.

The RELEASE and RETURN verbs are required with the INPUT PROCEDURE/OUTPUT PROCEDURE format. The RELEASE verb appears in the INPUT PROCEDURE and has the format

                RELEASE record-name [FROM identifier]

We shall see in the sample program in Figure 10.2 that RELEASE is analogous to WRITE.

The RETURN statement appears in the OUTPUT PROCEDURE and has the form

                RETURN file-name [INTO identifier] AT END statement

We shall see in Figure 10.2 that RETURN is analogous to READ.

File-name-1 of the SORT verb requires an SD in the data division, which has the format

    SD file-name $\left[\text{RECORD CONTAINS [integer-1 TO] integer-2 CHARACTERS} \right]$

        $\left[\text{DATA} \begin{Bmatrix} \text{RECORD IS} \\ \text{RECORDS ARE} \end{Bmatrix} \text{data-name-1 [data-name-2] . . .} \right]$

Two illustrative programs are shown in Figures 10.2 and 10.3, which are further described on page 190.

```
00001          IDENTIFICATION DIVISION.
00002          PROGRAM-ID.
00003              'CARSORT'.
00004          AUTHOR.
00005              ROBERT T. GRAUER.
00006
00007          ENVIRONMENT DIVISION.
00008          CONFIGURATION SECTION.
00009          SOURCE-COMPUTER.
00010              IBM-370.
00011          OBJECT-COMPUTER.
00012              IBM-370.
00013           SPECIAL-NAMES.
00014              C01 IS TOP-OF-PAGE.
00015
00016          INPUT-OUTPUT SECTION.        SELECT for SORT-FILE
00017          FILE-CONTROL.
00018              SELECT SORT-FILE
00019                  ASSIGN TO UT-S-SORTWK01.
00020              SELECT RENTAL-RECORD-FILE
00021                  ASSIGN TO UT-S-SYSIN.
00022              SELECT PRINT-FILE
00023                  ASSIGN TO UT-S-SYSPRT.
00024
00025          DATA DIVISION.              SD for SORT-FILE
00026          FILE SECTION.
00027          SD  SORT-FILE
00028              RECORD CONTAINS 53 CHARACTERS
00029              DATA RECORD IS SORT-RECORD.
00030          01  SORT-RECORD.
00031              05  SOC-SEC-NUM      PIC 9(9).
00032              05  NAME-FIELD       PIC A(25).
00033              05  DATE-RETURNED    PIC 9(6).
00034              05  CAR-TYPE         PIC X.
00035              05  DAYS-RENTED      PIC 99.
00036              05  MILES-DRIVEN     PIC 9999.
00037              05  CUSTOMER-BILL    PIC 9(4)V99.
00038
00039          FD  RENTAL-RECORD-FILE            Indicates blocksize is entered
00040              BLOCK CONTAINS 0 RECORDS      in JCL - see Chapter 18
00041              LABEL RECORDS ARE OMITTED
00042              RECORD CONTAINS 80 CHARACTERS
00043              DATA RECORD IS RENTAL-RECORD.
00044
00045          01  RENTAL-RECORD          PIC X(80).
00046
00047          FD  PRINT-FILE
00048              BLOCK CONTAINS 0 RECORDS
00049              LABEL RECORDS ARE OMITTED
00050              RECORD CONTAINS 133 CHARACTERS
00051              DATA RECORD IS PRINT-LINE.
00052
00053          01  PRINT-LINE             PIC X(133).
00054
00055          WORKING-STORAGE SECTION.
00056          01  WS-SWITCHES.
00057              05  WS-END-OF-INPUT-SWITCH  PIC XXX       VALUE 'NO'.
00058                  88  WS-END-OF-INPUT                   VALUE 'YES'.
00059              05  WS-END-OF-SORTED-FL-SW  PIC XXX       VALUE 'NO '.
00060                  88  WS-END-OF-SORTED-FILE             VALUE 'YES'.
00061          01  PAGE-AND-LINE-COUNTERS.
00062              05  WS-LINE-COUNT      PIC 99            VALUE 51.
00063              05  WS-PAGE-COUNT      PIC 99            VALUE ZERO.
00064          01  BILLING-CONSTANTS.
00065              05  WS-MILEAGE-RATE    PIC 9V99.
00066              05  WS-DAILY-RATE      PIC 99V99.
00067              05  WS-CUSTOMER-BILL   PIC 9999V99.
00068
00069          01  DATE-WORK-AREA.
00070              05  TODAYS-YEAR        PIC 99.
00071              05  TODAYS-MONTH       PIC 99.
00072              05  TODAYS-DAY         PIC 99.
00073
00074          01  WS-CARD-IN.
```

FIGURE 10.2 *SORT Verb (INPUT PROCEDURE/OUTPUT PROCEDURE)*

```
00075          05  SOC-SEC-NUM          PIC 9(9).
00076          05  NAME-FIELD           PIC A(25).
00077          05  DATE-RETURNED        PIC 9(6).
00078          05  CAR-TYPE             PIC X.
00079              88  COMPACT                      VALUE 'C'.
00080              88  INTERMEDIATE                 VALUE 'I'.
00081              88  FULL-SIZE                    VALUE 'F'.
00082              88  VALID-CODES                  VALUES ARE 'C'
00083                                                   'I' 'F'.
00084          05  DAYS-RENTED          PIC 99.
00085          05  MILES-DRIVEN         PIC 9(4).
00086          05  FILLER               PIC X(33).
00087
00088      01  WS-PRINT-LINE.
00089          05  FILLER               PIC X(4).
00090          05  SOC-SEC-NUM          PIC 999B99B9999.
00091          05  FILLER               PIC X(4).
00092          05  NAME-FIELD           PIC A(25).
00093          05  FILLER               PIC XX.
00094          05  CAR-TYPE             PIC X.
00095          05  FILLER               PIC X(4).
00096          05  DAYS-RENTED          PIC Z9.
00097          05  FILLER               PIC X(4).
00098          05  MILES-DRIVEN         PIC ZZZ9.
00099          05  FILLER               PIC X(4).
00100          05  CUSTOMER-BILL        PIC $$,$$9.99.
00101          05  FILLER               PIC X(59).
00102
00103      01  WS-HEADING-LINE-ONE.
00104          05  FILLER               PIC X(65)     VALUE SPACES.
00105          05  FILLER               PIC X(5)      VALUE 'PAGE '.
00106          05  WS-PAGE-PRINT        PIC ZZ9.
00107          05  FILLER               PIC X(60)     VALUE SPACES.
00108
00109      01  WS-HEADING-LINE-TWO.
00110          05  FILLER               PIC X(20)     VALUE SPACES.
00111          05  TITLE-INFO           PIC X(33).
00112          05  FILLER               PIC XX        VALUE SPACES.
00113          05  TITLE-DATE.
00114              10  TITLE-MONTH       PIC 99.
00115              10  FILLER            PIC X         VALUE '/'.
00116              10  TITLE-DAY         PIC 99.
00117              10  FILLER            PIC X         VALUE '/'.
00118              10  TITLE-YEAR        PIC 99.
00119          05  FILLER               PIC X(70)     VALUE SPACES.
00120
00121      01  WS-HEADING-LINE-THREE.
00122          05  FILLER               PIC X(8)      VALUE SPACES.
00123          05  FILLER               PIC X(11)     VALUE ' ACCT #'.
00124          05  FILLER               PIC XX        VALUE SPACES.
00125          05  FILLER               PIC X(4)      VALUE 'NAME'.
00126          05  FILLER               PIC X(19)     VALUE SPACES.
00127          05  FILLER               PIC X(4)      VALUE 'TYPE'.
00128          05  FILLER               PIC XX        VALUE SPACES.
00129          05  FILLER               PIC X(4)      VALUE 'DAYS'.
00130          05  FILLER               PIC XX        VALUE SPACES.
00131          05  FILLER               PIC X(5)      VALUE 'MILES'.
00132          05  FILLER               PIC X(4)      VALUE SPACES.
00133          05  FILLER               PIC X(6)      VALUE 'AMOUNT'.
00134          05  FILLER               PIC X(60)     VALUE SPACES.
00135      PROCEDURE DIVISION.
00136
00137      A-MAINLINE SECTION.
00138      A010-DRIVER.
00139          ACCEPT DATE-WORK-AREA FROM DATE.
00140          OPEN INPUT RENTAL-RECORD-FILE
00141               OUTPUT PRINT-FILE.
00142          READ RENTAL-RECORD-FILE INTO WS-CARD-IN
00143               AT END MOVE 'YES' TO WS-END-OF-INPUT-SWITCH.
00144          SORT SORT-FILE
00145              ON DESCENDING KEY CUSTOMER-BILL OF SORT-RECORD
00146              ON ASCENDING KEY NAME-FIELD    OF SORT-RECORD
00147                  INPUT PROCEDURE IS B-SORT-INPUT
00148                  OUTPUT PROCEDURE IS F-SORT-OUTPUT
00149          CLOSE RENTAL-RECORD-FILE PRINT-FILE.          SORT statement
00150          STOP RUN.
```

FIGURE 10.2 *(continued)*

SECTION III: MORE COBOL

```
00151
00152    B-SORT-INPUT SECTION.    ──INPUT PROCEDURE is a section
00153    B010-DRIVER.
00154        READ RENTAL-RECORD-FILE INTO WS-CARD-IN
00155            AT END MOVE 'YES' TO WS-END-OF-INPUT-SWITCH.
00156        PERFORM B020-PROCESS-CUSTOMER-RECORDS
00157            UNTIL WS-END-OF-INPUT.
00158        GO TO B040-EXIT.
00159    B020-PROCESS-CUSTOMER-RECORDS.
00160        IF VALID-CODES
00161            AND MILES-DRIVEN OF WS-CARD-IN IS POSITIVE
00162            AND DAYS-RENTED OF WS-CARD-IN IS POSITIVE
00163                PERFORM B030-COMPUTE-AND-WRITE
00164        ELSE
00165            DISPLAY 'ERROR IN DATA ' NAME-FIELD OF WS-CARD-IN.
00166        READ RENTAL-RECORD-FILE INTO WS-CARD-IN
00167            AT END MOVE 'YES' TO WS-END-OF-INPUT-SWITCH.
00168    B030-COMPUTE-AND-WRITE.
00169        IF COMPACT
00170            MOVE .08 TO WS-MILEAGE-RATE
00171            MOVE 7.00 TO WS-DAILY-RATE
00172        ELSE
00173            IF INTERMEDIATE
00174                MOVE .10 TO WS-MILEAGE-RATE
00175                MOVE 8.00 TO WS-DAILY-RATE
00176            ELSE
00177                MOVE .12 TO WS-MILEAGE-RATE
00178                MOVE 10.00 TO WS-DAILY-RATE.
00179        COMPUTE WS-CUSTOMER-BILL ROUNDED =
00180            MILES-DRIVEN OF WS-CARD-IN * WS-MILEAGE-RATE
00181            + DAYS-RENTED OF WS-CARD-IN * WS-DAILY-RATE
00182        ON SIZE ERROR
00183            DISPLAY 'RECEIVING FIELD TOO SMALL FOR BILL '
00184                NAME-FIELD OF WS-CARD-IN.
00185        MOVE CORR WS-CARD-IN TO SORT-RECORD.
00186        MOVE WS-CUSTOMER-BILL TO CUSTOMER-BILL OF SORT-RECORD.
00187        RELEASE SORT-RECORD.    ──Validated records are written to SORT file
00188    B040-EXIT.                              •
00189        EXIT.
00190
00191    F-SORT-OUTPUT SECTION.    ──OUTPUT PROCEDURE is a section
00192    F010-DO-OUTPUT-RTN.
00193        RETURN SORT-FILE
00194            AT END
00195                MOVE 'YES' TO WS-END-OF-SORTED-FL-SW.
00196        PERFORM F020-PROCESS-OUTPUT
00197            UNTIL WS-END-OF-SORTED-FILE.
00198        GO TO F040-EXIT.
00199    F020-PROCESS-OUTPUT.
00200        IF WS-LINE-COUNT > 50                          RETURN statement reads a
00201            PERFORM F030-PAGE-HEADING-ROUTINE.          record from sorted file
00202        MOVE SPACES TO WS-PRINT-LINE.
00203        MOVE CORRESPONDING SORT-RECORD TO WS-PRINT-LINE.
00204        INSPECT SOC-SEC-NUM OF WS-PRINT-LINE
00205            REPLACING ALL ' ' BY '-'.
00206        WRITE PRINT-LINE FROM WS-PRINT-LINE
00207            AFTER ADVANCING 2 LINES.
00208        ADD 2 TO WS-LINE-COUNT.
00209        RETURN SORT-FILE
00210            AT END
00211                MOVE 'YES' TO WS-END-OF-SORTED-FL-SW.
00212    F030-PAGE-HEADING-ROUTINE.
00213        MOVE ZEROS TO WS-LINE-COUNT.
00214        ADD 1 TO WS-PAGE-COUNT.
00215        MOVE WS-PAGE-COUNT TO WS-PAGE-PRINT.
00216        WRITE PRINT-LINE FROM WS-HEADING-LINE-ONE
00217            AFTER ADVANCING TOP-OF-PAGE.
00218        MOVE ' STACEY CAR RENTALS - REPORT DATE ' TO TITLE-INFO.
00219        MOVE TODAYS-DAY TO TITLE-DAY.
00220        MOVE TODAYS-MONTH TO TITLE-MONTH.
00221        MOVE TODAYS-YEAR TO TITLE-YEAR.
00222        WRITE PRINT-LINE FROM WS-HEADING-LINE-TWO
00223            AFTER ADVANCING 1 LINES.
00224        WRITE PRINT-LINE FROM WS-HEADING-LINE-THREE
00225            AFTER ADVANCING 1 LINES.
00226    F040-EXIT.
00227        EXIT.
```

FIGURE 10.2 *(continued)*

CHAPTER 10: SORTING

```
00001          IDENTIFICATION DIVISION.
00002          PROGRAM-ID.
00003              'CARSORT'.
00004          AUTHOR.
00005              ROBERT T. GRAUER.
00006
00007          ENVIRONMENT DIVISION.
00008          CONFIGURATION SECTION.
00009          SOURCE-COMPUTER.
00010              IBM-370.
00011          OBJECT-COMPUTER.
00012              IBM-370.
00013           SPECIAL-NAMES.
00014              C01 IS TOP-OF-PAGE.
00015
00016          INPUT-OUTPUT SECTION.
00017          FILE-CONTROL.
00018              SELECT SORT-FILE
00019                  ASSIGN TO UT-S-SORTWK01.
00020              SELECT RENTAL-RECORD-FILE                  Record lengths and field
00021                  ASSIGN TO UT-S-SYSIN.                  positions are identical
00022              SELECT PRINT-FILE                          for these files
00023                  ASSIGN TO UT-S-SYSPRT.
00024              SELECT ORDER-FILE
00025                  ASSIGN TO UT-S-ORDER.
00026
00027          DATA DIVISION.
00028          FILE SECTION.
00029          SD  SORT-FILE                         Sort work file
00030              RECORD CONTAINS 80 CHARACTERS
00031              DATA RECORD IS SORT-RECORD.
00032          01  SORT-RECORD.
00033              05  FILLER              PIC 9(9).
00034              05  NAME-FIELD          PIC A(25).
00035              05  FILLER              PIC X(46).
00036          FD  RENTAL-RECORD-FILE
00037              BLOCK CONTAINS 0 RECORDS
00038              LABEL RECORDS ARE OMITTED
00039              RECORD CONTAINS 80 CHARACTERS
00040              DATA RECORD IS RENTAL-RECORD.
00041
00042          01  RENTAL-RECORD.
00043              05  SOC-SEC-NUM         PIC 9(9).
00044              05  NAME-FIELD          PIC A(25).
00045              05  DATE-RETURNED       PIC 9(6).
00046              05  CAR-TYPE            PIC X.
00047              05  DAYS-RENTED         PIC 99.
00048              05  MILES-DRIVED        PIC 9999.
00049              05  FILLER              PIC X(33).
00050
00051
00052          FD  PRINT-FILE                         Indicates block size is entered in JCL -
00053              BLOCK CONTAINS 0 RECORDS            see Chapter 18
00054              LABEL RECORDS ARE OMITTED
00055              RECORD CONTAINS 133 CHARACTERS
00056              DATA RECORD IS PRINT-LINE.
00057
00058          01  PRINT-LINE              PIC X(133).
00059          FD  ORDER-FILE
00060              BLOCK CONTAINS 0 RECORDS
00061              LABEL RECORDS ARE OMITTED
00062              RECORD CONTAINS 80 CHARACTERS
00063              DATA RECORD IS ORDERED-RECORD.
00064          01  ORDERED-RECORD          PIC X(80).
00065
00066          WORKING-STORAGE SECTION.
00067          01  WS-SWITCHES.
00068              05  WS-END-OF-INPUT-SWITCH PIC XXX        VALUE 'NO'.
00069                  88  WS-END-OF-INPUT                   VALUE 'YES'.
00070          01  PAGE-AND-LINE-COUNTERS.
00071              05  WS-LINE-COUNT       PIC 99           VALUE 51.
00072              05  WS-PAGE-COUNT       PIC 99           VALUE ZERO.
00073          01  BILLING-CONSTANTS.
00074              05  WS-MILEAGE-RATE     PIC 9V99.
00075              05  WS-DAILY-RATE       PIC 99V99.
```

FIGURE 10.3 *SORT Verb (USING/GIVING)*

```
00076                05  WS-CUSTOMER-BILL            PIC 9999V99.
00077
00078         01  DATE-WORK-AREA.
00079                05  TODAYS-YEAR                 PIC 99.
00080                05  TODAYS-MONTH                PIC 99.
00081                05  TODAYS-DAY                  PIC 99.
00082
00083         01  WS-CARD-IN.
00084                05  SOC-SEC-NUM                 PIC 9(9).
00085                05  NAME-FIELD                  PIC A(25).
00086                05  DATE-RETURNED               PIC 9(6).
00087                05  CAR-TYPE                    PIC X.
00088                     88  COMPACT                              VALUE 'C'.
00089                     88  INTERMEDIATE                         VALUE 'I'.
00090                     88  FULL-SIZE                            VALUE 'F'.
00091                     88  VALID-CODES                          VALUES ARE 'C'
00092                                                                 'I' 'F'.
00093                05  DAYS-RENTED                 PIC 99.
00094                05  MILES-DRIVEN                PIC 9(4).
00095                05  FILLER                      PIC X(33).
00096
00097         01  WS-PRINT-LINE.
00098                05  FILLER                      PIC X(4).
00099                05  SOC-SEC-NUM                 PIC 999B99B9999.
00100                05  FILLER                      PIC X(4).
00101                05  NAME-FIELD                  PIC A(25).
00102                05  FILLER                      PIC XX.
00103                05  CAR-TYPE                    PIC X.
00104                05  FILLER                      PIC X(4).
00105                05  DAYS-RENTED                 PIC Z9.
00106                05  FILLER                      PIC X(4).
00107                05  MILES-DRIVEN                PIC ZZZ9.
00108                05  FILLER                      PIC X(4).
00109                05  CUSTOMER-BILL               PIC $$,$$9.99.
00110                05  FILLER                      PIC X(59).
00111
00112         01  WS-HEADING-LINE-ONE.
00113                05  FILLER                      PIC X(65)     VALUE SPACES.
00114                05  FILLER                      PIC X(5)      VALUE 'PAGE '.
00115                05  WS-PAGE-PRINT               PIC ZZ9.
00116                05  FILLER                      PIC X(60)     VALUE SPACES.
00117
00118         01  WS-HEADING-LINE-TWO.
00119                05  FILLER                      PIC X(20)     VALUE SPACES.
00120                05  TITLE-INFO                  PIC X(33).
00121                05  FILLER                      PIC XX        VALUE SPACES.
00122                05  TITLE-DATE.
00123                     10  TITLE-MONTH            PIC 99.
00124                     10  FILLER                 PIC X         VALUE '/'.
00125                     10  TITLE-DAY              PIC 99.
00126                     10  FILLER                 PIC X         VALUE '/'.
00127                     10  TITLE-YEAR             PIC 99.
00128                05  FILLER                      PIC X(70)     VALUE SPACES.
00129
00130         01  WS-HEADING-LINE-THREE.
00131                05  FILLER                      PIC X(8)      VALUE SPACES.
00132                05  FILLER                      PIC X(11)     VALUE ' ACCT #'.
00133                05  FILLER                      PIC XX        VALUE SPACES.
00134                05  FILLER                      PIC X(4)      VALUE 'NAME'.
00135                05  FILLER                      PIC X(19)     VALUE SPACES.
00136                05  FILLER                      PIC X(4)      VALUE 'TYPE'.
00137                05  FILLER                      PIC XX        VALUE SPACES.
00138                05  FILLER                      PIC X(4)      VALUE 'DAYS'.
00139                05  FILLER                      PIC XX        VALUE SPACES.
00140                05  FILLER                      PIC X(5)      VALUE 'MILES'.
00141                05  FILLER                      PIC X(4)      VALUE SPACES.
00142                05  FILLER                      PIC X(6)      VALUE 'AMOUNT'.
00143                05  FILLER                      PIC X(60)     VALUE SPACES.
00144         PROCEDURE DIVISION.
00145
00146         A-SORT-INPUT.                                  SORT statement
00147                ACCEPT DATE-WORK-AREA FROM DATE.
00148          ┌─────────────────────────────────────────────┐
00149          │ SORT SORT-FILE                              │
00150          │     ASCENDING KEY NAME-FIELD OF SORT-RECORD │
00151          │          USING RENTAL-RECORD-FILE           │
               │          GIVING ORDER-FILE.                 │
               └─────────────────────────────────────────────┘
```

FIGURE 10.3 (continued)

```
00152              OPEN INPUT ORDER-FILE
00153                   OUTPUT PRINT-FILE.
00154              READ ORDER-FILE INTO WS-CARD-IN
00155                   AT END MOVE 'YES' TO WS-END-OF-INPUT-SWITCH.
00156              PERFORM B-PROCESS-CUSTOMER-RECORDS
00157                   UNTIL WS-END-OF-INPUT.
00158              CLOSE ORDER-FILE PRINT-FILE.
00159              STOP RUN.
00160          B-PROCESS-CUSTOMER-RECORDS.
00161              IF VALID-CODES
00162                   AND MILES-DRIVEN OF WS-CARD-IN IS POSITIVE
00163                   AND DAYS-RENTED OF WS-CARD-IN IS POSITIVE
00164                       PERFORM C-COMPUTE-AND-WRITE
00165              ELSE
00166                   DISPLAY 'ERROR IN DATA ' NAME-FIELD OF WS-CARD-IN.
00167              READ ORDER-FILE INTO WS-CARD-IN
00168                   AT END
00169                       MOVE 'YES' TO WS-END-OF-INPUT-SWITCH.
00170          C-COMPUTE-AND-WRITE.
00171              IF COMPACT
00172                   MOVE .08 TO WS-MILEAGE-RATE
00173                   MOVE 7.00 TO WS-DAILY-RATE
00174              ELSE
00175                   IF INTERMEDIATE
00176                       MOVE .10 TO WS-MILEAGE-RATE
00177                       MOVE 8.00 TO WS-DAILY-RATE
00178                   ELSE
00179                       MOVE .12 TO WS-MILEAGE-RATE
00180                       MOVE 10.00 TO WS-DAILY-RATE.
00181              COMPUTE WS-CUSTOMER-BILL ROUNDED =
00182                   MILES-DRIVEN OF WS-CARD-IN * WS-MILEAGE-RATE
00183                   + DAYS-RENTED OF WS-CARD-IN * WS-DAILY-RATE
00184                ON SIZE ERROR
00185                   DISPLAY 'RECEIVING FIELD TOO SMALL FOR BILL
00186                       NAME-FIELD OF WS-CARD-IN.
00187              IF WS-LINE-COUNT > 50
00188                       PERFORM D-PAGE-HEADING-ROUTINE.
00189              MOVE SPACES TO WS-PRINT-LINE.
00190              MOVE CORRESPONDING WS-CARD-IN TO WS-PRINT-LINE.
00191              MOVE WS-CUSTOMER-BILL TO CUSTOMER-BILL OF WS-PRINT-LINE.
00192              INSPECT SOC-SEC-NUM OF WS-PRINT-LINE
00193                   REPLACING ALL ' ' BY '-'.
00194              WRITE PRINT-LINE FROM WS-PRINT-LINE
00195                   AFTER ADVANCING 2 LINES.
00196              ADD 2 TO WS-LINE-COUNT.
00197          D-PAGE-HEADING-ROUTINE.
00198              MOVE ZEROS TO WS-LINE-COUNT.
00199              ADD 1 TO WS-PAGE-COUNT.
00200              MOVE WS-PAGE-COUNT TO WS-PAGE-PRINT.
00201              WRITE PRINT-LINE FROM WS-HEADING-LINE-ONE
00202                   AFTER ADVANCING TOP-OF-PAGE.
00203              MOVE ' STACEY CAR RENTALS - REPORT DATE ' TO TITLE-INFO.
00204              MOVE TODAYS-DAY TO TITLE-DAY.
00205              MOVE TODAYS-MONTH TO TITLE-MONTH.
00206              MOVE TODAYS-YEAR TO TITLE-YEAR.
00207              WRITE PRINT-LINE FROM WS-HEADING-LINE-TWO
00208                   AFTER ADVANCING 1 LINES.
00209              WRITE PRINT-LINE FROM WS-HEADING-LINE-THREE
00210                   AFTER ADVANCING 1 LINES.
```

FIGURE 10.3 *(continued)*

Now that you are aware of the COBOL statements used in connection with sorting, we have incorporated this material in actual programs and have chosen the car billing problem of Chapter 7 for this purpose. In the initial listing (Figure 7.7), customer bills were listed in the order they came in. The SORT verb is used to list customers in order of decreasing bill (Figure 10.2) and in alphabetical order (Figure 10.3). Since the customer bill is a calculated field, Figure 10.2 utilizes the INPUT PROCEDURE/OUTPUT PROCEDURE option of the SORT verb. However, since name is contained on the input record and is therefore not a *calculated* field, the USING/GIVING option is shown in Figure 10.3.

Regardless of which option is chosen, the COBOL program must accomplish three things:

1. Read incoming data (e.g., from a customer file) and transfer it to a sort file.
2. Rearrange the sort file.
3. Read the sorted data and transfer it to an output file (e.g., a print file).

SORT VERB: INPUT PROCEDURE/OUTPUT PROCEDURE

Figure 10.2 is a modified version of the car billing problem in Chapter 7. COBOL lines 144 to 148 contain the SORT statement itself in which SORT-FILE (line 144) is the file actually used for sorting. It requires a SELECT statement (COBOL line 18) and an SD (COBOL lines 27 to 29). The INPUT PROCEDURE specifies a *section name*, B-SORT-INPUT, which processes incoming data and writes records to the sort file. The OUTPUT PROCEDURE also specifies a section name, F-SORT-OUTPUT, which reads records from the sorted file and writes records to the print file.

The mainline of the COBOL program is contained in lines 137 to 150. The program begins by opening RENTAL-RECORD-FILE and PRINT-FILE (SORT-FILE is *not* opened explicitly in the program). The SORT verb transfers control to the INPUT PROCEDURE, which does the input and calculates the bills. After the incoming data have been validated and the individual bill computed, information is first moved to the SORT-RECORD (lines 185 to 186) and then written to the SORT-FILE via the RELEASE statement in line 187.

When the entire RENTAL-RECORD-FILE has been processed and the INPUT PROCEDURE is completed, control passes to the sort utility, which rearranges records in the SORT-FILE. After the sort is completed, control passes to the OUTPUT PROCEDURE, which reads data from the sort file via the RETURN statement and prints them. After the entire sort file has been read, control passes to the statement after the SORT verb. The files are closed (line 149), and the processing is terminated (line 150).

The INPUT and OUTPUT PROCEDURES both contain a GO TO statement (lines 158 and 198), and indeed this is the first occurrence of a program containing GO TO in the entire book. Note well, however, that in both cases a *forward* branch to an EXIT paragraph is used. Further, due to the nature of the SORT verb itself, the authors see no easy way of eliminating the GO TO, nor do they see its use in this instance as harmful.

When the SORT verb is executed, control is transferred to the INPUT PROCEDURE, which is responsible for reading the unsorted input file and releasing its records to the sort file. The INPUT PROCEDURE has its own mainline routine, B010-DRIVER, containing an initial read, and a perform statement to process the remainder of the file. When that perform is satisfied, the INPUT PROCEDURE is essentially finished; hence the *forward* GO TO of line 158. A similar explanation holds for the OUTPUT PROCEDURE. In summary, the authors maintain that a structured program can include *limited* use of the GO TO, provided it is a *forward* branch to an EXIT paragraph.

SORT VERB: USING/GIVING

The USING/GIVING format simplifies the job of the COBOL programmer in that COBOL automatically does the I/O to and from the SORT. The price we pay is twofold. First, the option cannot sort on a calculated field. Second, an extra file is required. Thus Figure 10.3 contains SELECT statements for four files (COBOL lines 18 to 25) and sorts on a noncalculated field.

The procedure division begins immediately with the SORT statement (COBOL lines 148 to 151). Notice that RENTAL-RECORD-FILE is not opened explicitly since the SORT verb itself performs the necessary I/O. The data in RENTAL-RECORD-FILE are read, written, and returned in sorted sequence in the file ORDER-FILE. After the sort has been completed, control returns to line 152, and the remaining logic closely parallels the original listing in Figure 7.7. The essential difference between this program and the one in Figure 7.7 is that data are read from a file that has been sorted. Thus, the program in Figure 10.3 will cause bills to print alphabetically, while in Figure 7.7 bills were printed in the order they came in.

INPUT PROCEDURE/OUTPUT PROCEDURE VERSUS
USING/GIVING

Figures 10.2 and 10.3 illustrate two versions of the SORT verb, and it is useful to highlight the differences:

1. Figure 10.2 sorts on CUSTOMER-BILL, a calculated field. Figure 10.3 sorts on NAME-FIELD, which is contained on the incoming record.
2. Figure 10.2 requires the programmer to do his own I/O to and from the SORT. In Figure 10.3, the SORT verb causes RENTAL-RECORD-FILE to be opened, copied to SORT-FILE, and then closed.
3. Figure 10.2 uses the RELEASE and RETURN verbs to write to and read from SORT-FILE. These verbs are not used in Figure 10.3 since the USING/GIVING option does the I/O automatically.
4. Figure 10.2 requires only three files. Figure 10.3 uses four. (Compare SELECT statements.) The extra file is necessary since the sorted data are placed on a separate file (ORDER-FILE).
5. Record lengths in Figure 10.3 of RENTAL-RECORD-FILE, ORDER-FILE, and SORT-FILE must be the same (80 bytes). The record lengths of SORT-FILE and RENTAL-RECORD-FILE in Figure 10.2 are different.
6. Figure 10.2 *requires* section names for the INPUT PROCEDURE and OUTPUT PROCEDURE. Sections are optional in Figure 10.3.

SUMMARY

Sorting is an integral part of data processing. If the COBOL SORT verb is used to accomplish this task, four formats are possible. INPUT PROCEDURE/OUTPUT PROCEDURE and USING/GIVING were illustrated in Figures 10.2 and 10.3, respectively. INPUT PROCEDURE permits sorting on a calculated field; USING does not.

The chapter began with a definition of terms. Specifically, we discussed *key, ascending* versus *descending* sorts, and *major* versus *minor* sorts. Next we covered the COBOL implementation of sorting to include the SORT, SD, RELEASE, and RETURN statements.

We believe that the reader can readily adapt either Figure 10.2 or 10.3 to any problem with which he is confronted. As an additional aid, however, we shall list three basic rules associated with COBOL implementation. Should any of these points appear unclear, return to the examples in the chapter.

1. File-name-1 of the SORT verb must be described in an SD. Further, each key (i.e., data-name) appearing in the SORT verb must be described in the sort record.
2. If the USING/GIVING option is used, file-name-2 and file-name-3 each require an FD. Further, the record sizes of file-names 1, 2, and 3 must all be the same.
3. If INPUT PROCEDURE/OUTPUT PROCEDURE is used, both must be section names. Further, the INPUT PROCEDURE must contain a RELEASE statement to transfer records to the sort; the OUTPUT PROCEDURE must contain a RETURN statement to read the sorted data.

REVIEW EXERCISES

TRUE FALSE

☐   ☐   **1.** The SORT verb cannot be used on a calculated field.

☐   ☐   **2.** If USING is specified in the SORT verb, then GIVING must be specified also.

☐   ☐   **3.** If INPUT PROCEDURE is specified in the SORT verb, then OUTPUT PROCEDURE is also required.

☐   ☐   **4.** Only one ascending and one descending key are permitted in the SORT verb.

☐   ☐   **5.** Major sort and primary sort are synonymous.

SECTION III: MORE COBOL

☐ ☐ **6.** The USING/GIVING option requires one less file than the INPUT PROCEDURE/OUTPUT PROCEDURE format.

☐ ☐ **7.** RELEASE and RETURN are associated with the USING/GIVING option.

☐ ☐ **8.** RELEASE is present in the INPUT PROCEDURE.

☐ ☐ **9.** RETURN is specified in the OUTPUT PROCEDURE.

☐ ☐ **10.** Both the INPUT and OUTPUT PROCEDURES must be paragraph names.

☐ ☐ **11.** If a record is "released," it is written to the sort file.

☐ ☐ **12.** If a record is "returned," it is read from the sort file.

☐ ☐ **13.** If USING/GIVING is used, the sorted file *must* contain every record in the input file.

☐ ☐ **14.** If INPUT PROCEDURE/OUTPUT PROCEDURE is used, the sorted file *must* contain one record for every record in the input file.

PROBLEMS

1. Given the following data,

Name	Location	Department
Milgrom	New York	1000
Samuel	Boston	2000
Isaac	Boston	2000
Chandler	Chicago	2000
Lavor	Los Angeles	1000
Elsinor	Chicago	1000
Tater	New York	2000
Craig	New York	2000
Borow	Boston	2000
Kenneth	Boston	2000
Renaldi	Boston	1000
Gulfman	Chicago	1000

rearrange the data according to the following sorts:
(a) Major field:—department (descending); minor field:—name (ascending).
(b) Primary field:—department; secondary field:—location; tertiary field:—name.
Note: If neither ascending nor descending is specified, an ascending sequence should be used.

2. Given the statement

```
SORT SORT-FILE
    ASCENDING KEY STUDENT-NAME
    DESCENDING YEAR-IN-SCHOOL
    ASCENDING MAJOR
USING FILE-ONE
GIVING FILE-TWO.
```

(a) What is the major key?
(b) What is the minor key?
(c) Which file will be specified in an SD?
(d) Which file will contain the sorted output?
(e) Which file(s) will be specified in a SELECT?
(f) Which file contains the input data?
(g) Which file must contain the data-names STUDENT-NAME, YEAR-IN-SCHOOL, and MAJOR?

3. Modify the tuition billing problem of Chapter 6 (Figure 6.4) to print students in alphabetical order.

4. Modify the tuition billing problem of Chapter 6 (Figure 6.4) to print students in order of computed charges (from high to low). Use name as the secondary sort.

5. Modify the program in Figure 8.2 to print customer statements in alphabetical order.

6. Modify the main and subprograms of Figures 8.7 and 8.8 to print a list of students in order of descending grade point average.

7. The following code is intended to sort a file of employee records in order of age, listing the oldest first:

```
FD   EMPLOYEE-FILE
        .
        .
        .
01   EMPLOYEE-RECORD.
        05   EMP-NAME                     PIC X(25).
        05   EMP-BIRTH-DATE
                10   EMP-BIRTH-MONTH       PIC 99.
                10   EMP-BIRTH-YEAR        PIC 99.
        05   FILLER                        PIC X(51).
SD   SORT-FILE
        .
        .
        .
01   SORT-RECORD.
        05   FILLER                        PIC X(20).
        05   SORT-BIRTH-DATE.
                10   SORT-BIRTH-MONTH      PIC 99.
                10   SORT-BIRTH-YEAR       PIC 99.
        05   FILLER                        PIC X(56).
        .
        .
        .
PROCEDURE DIVISION.
        SORT SORT-FILE
              DESCENDING KEY SORT-BIRTH-MONTH SORT-BIRTH-YEAR
              USING EMPLOYEE-FILE
              GIVING ORDERED-FILE.
```

There are three distinct reasons why the intended code will not work. Find and correct the errors.

PROJECTS

1. A small company has a deck of cards, one card for each employee in the company. There are only four fields on each card, as per the record description:

```
01   EMPL-NAME-REC.
        05   EMPL-TYPE              PIC X.
        05   EMPL-LAST-NAME         PIC X(15).
        05   EMPL-FIRST-NAME        PIC X(10).
        05   EMPL-BIRTH-DATE        PIC X(8).
        05   FILLER                 PIC X(46).
```

The first field of each record (EMPL-TYPE) contains either a '1' or a '2'. The '2' is for management; the '1' is for nonmanagement. The vice-president has requested that you (you're the only member of their D.P. staff) write a program to print a list of employees. He wants an appropriate heading to appear at the top of each page in your report (use your imagination), and he wants the list to be in sequence by last name, except that he wants all the management employees to appear before the nonmanagement employees. In other words, the management/nonmanagement field is to be the major sort and last name the minor sort. In addition, accommodate the following:

(a) Both the management and nonmanagement listings are to begin at the top of a new page.
(b) Limit the number of employees on any given page to seven.
(c) Maintain two counters, for management and nonmanagement, respectively. Print each total at the end of the appropriate listing.
(d) Use the USING/GIVING option of the SORT verb.
A sample list of input records is provided.

```
2MILLER        DEBORAH       07/04/53
1BRANNIGAN     JOHN          10/14/51
2DUDLEY        BILL          08/13/45
1MODER         JOE           08/12/29
```

1FINK	MARCIA	03/02/52
1ADABAR	TRICIA	06/11/55
1TROWELL	ROY	09/30/38
1TROWELL	ROBERT	10/18/50
1JENNINGS	CARL	12/24/41
2CHENEY	RALPH	01/28/45
1CRAWFORD	MIKE	08/05/47
1GERRARD	JEAN	04/29/45
2GERRARD	JOHN	11/24/45
2COOPER	ROBERT	10/31/53
1COOPER	JESSICA	03/16/51
2JOHNSON	MARILYN	04/19/50
1HANSON	ROGER	02/21/47
1SIMPSON	GEORGE	05/23/52
2LARSON	KAREN	06/27/48
1MATTHEWS	CHARLES	10/22/51

2. Use the identical specifications as for Project 1, except use age as the minor key to list the oldest employee first (retain management/nonmanagement as the major key). Realize that you will have to *calculate* age from birth date, and consequently the INPUT PROCEDURE/OUTPUT PROCEDURE option is required.

3. Develop a program to process a file of employee records with the following information:

Columns	Field	Picture
1–15	LAST-NAME	X(15)
16–20	PRESENT-SALARY	9(5)
21–24	PRESENT-SALARY-DATE (mmyy)	9(4)
25–29	PREVIOUS-SALARY	9(5)
30–33	PREVIOUS-SALARY-DATE (mmyy)	9(4)

Two reports are required. The first is to contain new hires, i.e., those with a present salary but no previous salary. (List these employees in alphabetical order.) The second report is to list employees in order of percent of salary increase, with the biggest increase appearing first. Design different, but appropriate, print formats for each report. Use the following test data:

SMITH	180001080
JONES	090000980080000679
MILLER	140000680
BAKER	220000680200000679
BENJAMIN	190000980150000179
MILGROM	240000780
SPAIDE	215000780200000180
GOMBERG	120000680110000380
CATALANO	130000980

Chapter 11

PROGRAMMING STYLE, II

OVERVIEW

Although the systems analyst is responsible for defining the "specs" of a program, a good programmer is more than just a computer that does only what it is told. Depending on the degree of standards enforcement, the programmer has varying leeway to determine how the problem is to be solved and what the final product will look like; in short, he has a definite opportunity to exert an influence.

In Chapter 6 we introduced programming style and presented structured programming and coding standards. Now that you are further along in your study of COBOL, we shall present additional elements of programming style. We shall offer specific COBOL techniques to facilitate debugging and improve efficiency and maintainability. We shall discuss what a "good" program should and should not do in terms of generality and error detection. We shall extend the discussion of structured programming to include the case structure, and discuss the techniques of stepwise refinement and top down testing. Finally, we shall present two complete examples incorporating many of our ideas on programming style and emphasizing the advantages of the structured technique.

We expect this chapter to be understandable to you now. However, the more you read, and the more programs you write, the clearer it will become. This is a *substantial* chapter in that the examples are *not* trivial. The material on stepwise refinement and top down testing often requires more than one reading. Hence, we hope that this is one chapter to which you will continually refer. Bear in mind that the techniques we offer are sound programming practices, but they need not be used 100% of the time. Undoubtedly, situations will occur where techniques are not applicable and should be avoided.

We expect you and/or your instructor to disagree with some of our ideas on style. That is a perfectly acceptable, and perhaps even desirable, reaction. Our objective is to teach you COBOL, to expose you to a wide variety of practical situations, and to teach you to think your way through programming applications. If you have sound reasons against elements of our style, so be it; you are on your way toward developing your own. There are many ways to solve a problem, and that is one of the aspects which makes programming interesting.

DEBUGGING

Debugging is a part of life, so much so that we include two entire chapters on the subject. In addition to the material in Chapters 5 and 13, we have adopted the following techniques as an integral part of our overall style:

196

1. *Always use the RECORD CONTAINS clause in the COBOL FD.* Although this clause is optional (e.g., the information can be entered through JCL under IBM OS as described in Chapter 18), its inclusion is highly desirable. The RECORD CONTAINS clause causes the compiler to indicate an error at compile time if the record description, i.e., the sum of the PICTURE clauses, does not match the RECORD CONTAINS entry. If the clause is omitted, such an error will not manifest itself until execution time when it is much more difficult to detect. Moreover, any future programmer is saved from the task of adding individual PICTURE clauses to determine record size.

2. *Include the following two nonnumeric literals as the first and last entries of the working-storage section:*

```
01  FILLER    PICTURE X(27)
               VALUE 'WORKING-STORAGE BEGINS HERE'.



01  FILLER    PICTURE X(25)
               VALUE 'WORKING-STORAGE ENDS HERE'.
```

These entries will appear in all dumps of the program and will clearly delineate the working-storage section. (We shall discuss dumps further in Chapter 13.)

3. *Use READ INTO and WRITE FROM options and do all processing from working-storage.* First, this technique simplifies debugging since working-storage areas are generally easier to find in a dump than I/O buffer areas (especially if the preceding suggestion is followed). Second, if blocked records are processed (see Section V on file processing), it is much easier to determine the particular record in the block that was being processed. Next, the READ INTO option allows access to the last record after the end-of-file condition has been reached. Finally, since the WRITE FROM option specifies an area in working-storage, initial values can be assigned to output fields, and as a result it is often unnecessary to move spaces to the output area.

MAINTAINABILITY

Programs can be more easily understood, and hence maintained, if techniques such as the following are practiced:

1. *Use condition names (88-level entries) for all codes that are checked.* This technique is absolutely essential. As a review of the material in Chapters 7 and 8, consider:

```
05  DEPARTMENT-CODE    PICTURE 99.
    88  ACCOUNTING              VALUE IS 11.
    88  DATA-PROCESSING         VALUE IS 13.
    88  PERSONNEL               VALUE IS 43.



    88  VALID-CODES     VALUES ARE 11, 13, 43 THRU 99.
```

Use of condition names permits such procedure division statements as IF ACCOUNTING . . . or IF PERSONNEL . . . , etc. Omission of 88-level entries requires procedure division entries of the form IF DEPARTMENT-CODE IS EQUAL TO 11, ... Obviously, when condition names are used, the procedure division is easier to read. More importantly, if codes have to be changed, 88-level entries allow all changes to be made in only one easy-to-find place, the data division. If condition names were not used, changes would have to be made throughout the procedure division, and the chance for error would be much higher, particularly if the same condition were tested more than once. Finally, 88 level entries permit the grouping of many codes under the same entry, e.g., VALID-CODES, and thereby eliminate confusing compound conditions in an IF statement.

✳   2. *Consider the THRU option when performing paragraphs.* The THRU procedure should consist of a single sentence, EXIT, whose sole function is to signal the end of the perform. The paragraph name of the THRU option could be identical to the entry paragraph with –EXIT appended. Thus

```
        PERFORM 020-READ-A-CARD THRU 020-READ-A-CARD-EXIT.
                    .
                    .
                    .
        020-READ-A-CARD.
                    .
                    .
                    .
        020-READ-A-CARD-EXIT.
            EXIT.
```

The THRU option accomplishes two things. First, it makes the range of the perform explicitly clear. Second, it reduces the chance for error on subsequent maintenance. Consider, for example, omission of the EXIT paragraph and further that the entry paragraph subsequently had to be broken into two paragraphs. The maintenance programmer would have to examine the entire program to determine whether the original paragraph appeared in any perform statements (without the THRU clause), and if so, to modify those statements to include the THRU clause.

Note well the use of the word *consider* in this guideline. Opinion is highly divided as to whether THRU should be employed at all. Opponents contend that only single paragraphs should be performed to emphasize functionality and to avoid accidental execution of unwanted paragraphs.

ERROR PROCESSING

A well-written program is not limited to computing answers; it also includes checks for erroneous data. Indeed, a sizable percentage of commercial programs is usually dedicated to error detection. The requirements of precisely what to check for are included in the specs given to the programmer, but in the course of coding, other situations will suggest themselves. These should be brought to the attention of the analyst and included in the program.

Installations frequently develop program standards that specify overall requirements for error processing. We offer Murphy's law: "if something can go wrong, it will—and at the worst possible time," and suggest that you can't check too much. Incoming transactions are often processed by a separate edit program whose sole function is to "scrub the data." In this instance most of the programming checks suggested next are done in the edit program and need not be repeated. However, the essential point is that incoming data are apt to be in error and must be checked; when and how this is done is of secondary importance. The following are typical error checks:

1. *Check for proper order in sequenced files.* Do not assume a file is in order just because it is supposed to have been sorted. Print appropriate error messages for out-of-sequence records.
2. *Flag invalid codes.* If a table is searched, the at-end condition usually specifies a no-match condition and should branch to an error routine. If a code has two permissible values, do not assume the second if it is not the first. The field may have been left blank or miscoded; either way an error message should be printed.
3. *Numeric data should be numeric.* Use class tests prior to calculations and bypass invalid data, e.g.,

```
        IF CREDITS NOT NUMERIC PERFORM ERROR-ROUTINE.
```

A strong advantage of this technique is the avoidance of data exceptions that prevent the normal end of job. Also, many errors can be caught in one execution instead of the many individual jobs that would be required for each data exception and corresponding ABEND.
4. *Include checks on the range of computed values.* In a payroll problem, for example, one might check that net pay does not exceed a specified amount and print a warning message

when this condition is violated. The excess amount need not signal an error, but better "safe than sorry."

5. *Eliminate duplicate transactions.* Often the same transaction is entered twice, either from different sources or twice from the same source at different times. This type of error is usually not caught in an edit program since it requires historical information from the master file.

6. *Check for invalid subscripts.* This is one of the most common, and indeed hardest to find, causes of a program's failure to execute. Consider

```
DATA DIVISION.
        .
        .
        .
    05   STATE-NAME     OCCURS 48 TIMES     PIC X(20).
        .
        .

PROCEDURE DIVISION.
        .
        .

    PERFORM STATE-PROCESSING VARYING SUB FROM 1 BY 1 UNTIL SUB > 50.
        .
        .

    STATE-PROCESSING.
       MOVE STATE-NAME (SUB) TO . . .
```

This apparently simple code will probably result in a fatal error and dump. STATE-NAME was defined as a table with 48 entries, yet in the procedure division we attempt to reference STATE-NAME (49) and (50). The compiler merely allocates sufficient storage for 48 entries in the table. During execution, the computer will reference the next contiguous locations for the 49th and 50th entries. Such situations occur frequently when table sizes are altered or subscripts are computed incorrectly. It is highly desirable to include additional code such as "IF SUB IS GREATER THAN 48 PERFORM ERROR-ROUTINE" as a check.

Obviously, error checking requires additional time for both programming and execution. Is it worth it? We believe so, especially if you've ever received a call at home asking why your program didn't work.

GENERALITY

In addition to checking for invalid data, a good program must most of all be a general program. It should be parameter driven, i.e., written in terms of variables rather than constants. Adherence to this technique simplifies maintenance and also minimizes the invalid subscript error, which can be so damaging. Consider:

```
DATA DIVISION.
        .
        .
        .
    05   STATE-NAME     OCCURS 1 TO 50 TIMES
                        DEPENDING ON NUMBER-OF-STATES
                        PIC X(20).
        .
        .

PROCEDURE DIVISION.
        .
        .

    PERFORM STATE-PROCESSING NUMBER-OF-STATES TIMES.
```

Of course, if the number of states ever exceeds 50, the constant in the OCCURS clause must be altered. However, the procedure division entries need not be changed since all processing is a function of the variable NUMBER-OF-STATES, which can be input at execution. Indeed, even the data division entry need not be altered if the table is initially made larger than necessary.

The desirability of generality cannot be overemphasized.

EFFICIENCY

Commercial data processing imposes the additional requirement of efficiency, i.e., having programs run as quickly as possible. Suggestions on achieving efficiency are generally directed to coding techniques revolving around the USAGE clause, decimal alignment, etc. Indeed we do our share of "preaching" in this area in Chapter 14 when we discuss COBOL from the viewpoint of BAL. However, many people get carried away with machine considerations and neglect entirely *algorithmic* efficiency.

The algorithm employed to solve a problem is especially important in that it is machine independent. Further, an efficient algorithm, coded inefficiently, is often preferable to an inefficient algorithm painstakingly coded to take advantage of every machine idiosyncrasy. This is not to say that machine considerations are superfluous; they definitely are not, but there is a point of diminishing returns. We do believe that algorithmic considerations are entirely essential and certainly deserve more treatment than is commonly afforded them.

A general suggestion is "think before you code." After learning the requirements of a program, concentrate on the method you will use to solve it. Do no coding for a period of time, whether five minutes or five days. Determine first the best way to approach the problem. Then, and only then, should you begin to code. Two suggestions for achieving algorithmic efficiency are as follows:

1. *Use a linear search only as a last resort.* Direct and binary searches are quicker (see Chapter 9). The SEARCH ALL verb provides easy implementation of the binary search. The advantage of a binary search is obvious; it greatly reduces the number of comparisons, and hence the execution time, to find a match. For example, a linear search over a table of 500 entries requires an *average of 250* comparisons if each entry is equally likely. A binary search over the same table requires a *maximum of 9* comparisons.

2. *Test most likely conditions first.* Assume, for example, that in a file of 10,000 records three types of transaction codes are possible: A (addition), C (correction), and D (deletion). Further assume that 7000 records are corrections, 2500 are additions, and 500 are deletions and that this distribution remains fairly constant from run to run. If the most likely condition, i.e., corrections, is tested first, then a total of 13,500 comparisons are required, as shown:

```
IF IN-CODE = 'C' . . .        (executed 10,000 times)
ELSE IF IN-CODE = 'A' . . .   (executed  3,000 times)
ELSE IF IN-CODE = 'D' . . .   (executed    500 times)
```

If, on the other hand, the least likely condition is tested first, then 26,500 comparisons are necessary:

```
IF IN-CODE = 'D' . . .        (executed 10,000 times)
ELSE IF IN-CODE = 'A' . . .   (executed  9,500 times)
ELSE IF IN-CODE = 'C' . . .   (executed  7,000 times)
```

Although this technique requires some knowledge of file characteristics, it is used far too infrequently in our estimation.

Techniques for machine efficiency are obviously machine dependent. Accordingly, these suggestions are deferred to Chapter 14.

MORE ON STRUCTURED PROGRAMMING

Structured programming was formally introduced in Chapter 6 as one element of programming style. Additional elements of the structured discipline are now introduced. These are the case structure and the techniques of stepwise refinement and top-down development. Finally, two complete programs are developed to firmly present the advantages of the methodology.

Case Structure (GO TO DEPENDING)

Structured programming is often referred to as 'GO TO-less' programming, which, in fact, is a slight misrepresentation. No special effort is made to avoid the GO TO, even if there are valid reasons for not using it. The GO TO statement just never occurs if the three standard logic structures are adhered to. However, situations can occur in which the GO TO may actually improve clarity, as in the case structure.

Although all programs can be developed as a function of the three basic control structures, it is useful to include the case structure as a fourth permissible logic form. This structure conveniently expresses a multibranch situation. The value of a variable is tested to determine which of several routines is to be executed. Its flowchart is shown in Figure 11.1. As with the other building blocks of structured programming, there is exactly one entry and one exit point. Implementation is through the GO TO DEPENDING statement and is illustrated in Figure 11.2.

The GO TO DEPENDING statement tests the value of a code, in this instance INCOMING-YEAR-CODE. If it is equal to 1, control passes to the first paragraph specified, i.e., FRESHMAN. If INCOMING-YEAR-CODE is equal to 2, control passes to the second paragraph, i.e., SOPHO-MORE, etc. If the code has any value other than 1, 2, 3, 4, or 5 (since five paragraphs were specified), control passes to the next statement immediately following the GO TO DEPENDING, which should be an error routine. Indentation in the GO TO DEPENDING is strictly for legibility; it is not required by COBOL.

Figure 11.2 also contains five "villainous" GO TO statements, but their use is completely acceptable (to us, if not to the most rigid advocate of structured programming). If the GO TO statement is used in a structured program, it should appear only within the range of a perform statement and should always branch *forward* to the end of the perform. This in turn is a "dummy" paragraph consisting of a single EXIT statement. We believe that such usage adds to, rather than detracts from, clarity.

Of course, the GO TO DEPENDING may be omitted entirely in favor of a series of 'IF THEN PERFORM' statements, but we opt for the case structure. Indeed the larger the number of acceptable codes, the clearer the GO TO DEPENDING becomes, particularly if the paragraphs are stacked and an EXIT paragraph is used as in Figure 11.2.

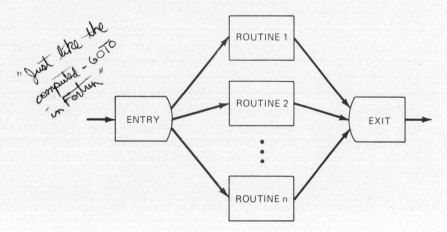

FIGURE 11.1 *The Case Structure*

```
YEAR-IN-COLLEGE.
    GO TO
        FRESHMAN
        SOPHOMORE
        JUNIOR
        SENIOR
        GRAD-SCHOOL
    DEPENDING ON INCOMING-YEAR-CODE.
    ... process error ...
    GO TO YEAR-IN-COLLEGE-EXIT.
FRESHMAN.
    ... process ...
    GO TO YEAR-IN-COLLEGE-EXIT.
SOPHOMORE.
    ... process ...
    GO TO YEAR-IN-COLLEGE-EXIT.
JUNIOR.
    ... process ...
    GO TO YEAR-IN-COLLEGE-EXIT.
SENIOR.
    ... process ...
    GO TO YEAR-IN-COLLEGE-EXIT.
GRAD-SCHOOL.
    ... process ...
YEAR-IN-COLLEGE-EXIT.
    EXIT.
```

FIGURE 11.2 *COBOL Implementation of the Case Structure*

A RATIONALE FOR STRUCTURED PROGRAMMING

Structured programming did not gain immediate and unqualified acceptance in the programming community. The authors at first did not completely embrace the concept, nor did they rewrite all their old programs. Even Yourdon, one of the foremost advocates, has talked about the "failure of the first structured revolution."

However, it has been more than 10 years since Dijkstra[1] wrote his now famous letter in which he suggested the quality of a program is inversely proportional to the number of GO TO statements it contains. The passage of time has *proved* him correct, and the impact of his work is probably far greater than even he imagined. As the 1970s ended, the bulk of the data-processing community has indeed "gone structured," in thought, if not always practice!

Regardless of what we say now, the arguments for structured programming, and the severe restriction on the use of the GO TO statement, have a somewhat nebulous and perhaps unconvincing quality. Further, a primary advantage of the structured approach, that it facilitates the development of logically difficult problems, has not yet been adequately demonstrated in our text. All the illustrative programs to date suffer from the fact that they were "logically simple"; i.e., our objective in Sections I to III was to teach the COBOL language per se, not to present complex logical situations. Accordingly, any programming difficulties you have encountered should have been primarily restricted to COBOL problems, and once a "clean" compile was achieved, a completed program was not far behind.

We believe, therefore, that the most convincing argument for structured programming is presentation of problems with substantial logic. Accordingly, we consider two problems with more imposing

[1] E. Dijkstra, "GO TO Statement Considered Harmful," Letter to the Editor, *Communications of the ACM*, March 1968.

SECTION III: MORE COBOL

requirements. The first involves control breaks; the second merges two files. Both problems are developed through techniques associated with the structured discipline. These include topdown development and testing, stepwise refinement, hierarchy charts, and pseudocode.

TOP DOWN VERSUS BOTTOM UP PROGRAMMING

Simply stated, top down development concentrates on the highest levels of logic first and leaves✶ the details for later. While this may sound reasonable, it is typically the opposite of what many programmers are used to; i.e., they begin, or are told to begin, with the detail and proceed from the bottom up. To amplify the distinction, let us consider the problem of Continental University.

Continental University consists of several colleges; each college has freshmen, sophomores, juniors, and seniors, and each year has several majors; e.g., business, liberal arts, etc. A punched card, showing the number of students in a given major, year, and college has been prepared (see Figure 11.3). These cards have been sorted by college (primary sort) and year (secondary sort). The problem is to

1. Sum the majors in a given year to provide enrollment totals for each year.

	Year in School	College	Major	Enrollment
	FRESHMAN	ATLANTIC	BUSINESS	000150
	FRESHMAN	ATLANTIC	EDUCATION	000100
	FRESHMAN	ATLANTIC	ENGINEERING	000025
	FRESHMAN	ATLANTIC	LIBERAL ARTS	000203
Single control break on year	SOPHOMORE	ATLANTIC	BUSINESS	000143
	SOPHOMORE	ATLANTIC	EDUCATION	000094
	SOPHOMORE	ATLANTIC	ENGINEERING	000018
	SOPHOMORE	ATLANTIC	LIBERAL ARTS	000202
	JUNIOR	ATLANTIC	BUSINESS	000141
	JUNIOR	ATLANTIC	EDUCATION	000092
	JUNIOR	ATLANTIC	ENGINEERING	000014
Single control break on year	JUNIOR	ATLANTIC	LIBERAL ARTS	000218
	SENIOR	ATLANTIC	BUSINESS	000138
	SENIOR	ATLANTIC	EDUCATION	000087
	SENIOR	ATLANTIC	ENGINEERING	000015
Double control break on year and college	SENIOR	ATLANTIC	LIBERAL ARTS	000188
	FRESHMAN	MIDWEST	BUSINESS	000231
	FRESHMAN	MIDWEST	EDUCATION	000134
	FRESHMAN	MIDWEST	ENGINEERING	000088
	FRESHMAN	MIDWEST	LIBERAL ARTS	000152
	SOPHOMORE	MIDWEST	BUSINESS	000226
	SOPHOMORE	MIDWEST	EDUCATION	000131
	SOPHOMORE	MIDWEST	ENGINEERING	000084
	SOPHOMORE	MIDWEST	LIBERAL ARTS	000141
	JUNIOR	MIDWEST	BUSINESS	000221
	JUNIOR	MIDWEST	EDUCATION	000127
	JUNIOR	MIDWEST	ENGINEERING	000078
	JUNIOR	MIDWEST	LIBERAL ARTS	000125
	SENIOR	MIDWEST	BUSINESS	000220
	SENIOR	MIDWEST	EDUCATION	000118
	SENIOR	MIDWEST	ENGINEERING	000074
Double control break on year and college	SENIOR	MIDWEST	LIBERAL ARTS	000118
	FRESHMAN	PACIFIC	BUSINESS	000115
	FRESHMAN	PACIFIC	EDUCATION	000066
	FRESHMAN	PACIFIC	ENGINEERING	000045
	FRESHMAN	PACIFIC	LIBERAL ARTS	000078
	SOPHOMORE	PACIFIC	BUSINESS	000114
	SOPHOMORE	PACIFIC	EDUCATION	000064
	SOPHOMORE	PACIFIC	ENGINEERING	000043
	SOPHOMORE	PACIFIC	LIBERAL ARTS	000068
	JUNIOR	PACIFIC	BUSINESS	000109
	JUNIOR	PACIFIC	EDUCATION	000065
	JUNIOR	PACIFIC	ENGINEERING	000043
	JUNIOR	PACIFIC	LIBERAL ARTS	000064
	SENIOR	PACIFIC	BUSINESS	000114
	SENIOR	PACIFIC	EDUCATION	000054
	SENIOR	PACIFIC	ENGINEERING	000043
	SENIOR	PACIFIC	LIBERAL ARTS	000059

FIGURE 11.3 *Data for Continental University*

2. Sum the year totals in each college to provide a college total.
3. Sum the college totals to provide a single university total.

The specifications call for two control breaks, on year and college. A control break is defined as a change in a designated field. Hence, as we go from freshman to sophomore, or sophomore to junior, there is a single control break on year in school. However, as we go from senior in Atlantic College, to freshman in Midwest College, there is a double control break on both year and college.

In the *bottom-up* approach one begins coding immediately and develops the report format. A manager is often generally satisfied, but requests that column headings be altered, notes added, etc. These modifications continue for several weeks before the manager is totally happy. Meanwhile, the deadline is drawing near and the programmer has yet to concern himself with the substantial logic of the problem, i.e., the control breaks. In all likelihood he will go into production with "beautiful" reports but inaccurate year and college totals. Errors will be discovered with an abundance of panic, overtime, etc.

By contrast, *top down* development recognizes that the actual report formating is *trivial* in comparison to the overall program logic. The discipline requires that one defer coding and concentrate instead on program development, beginning with the highest level of logic. The solution is developed through stepwise refinement.

STEPWISE REFINEMENT

Stepwise refinement is a technique in which a complicated problem is continually divided into smaller and more manageable pieces until the programmer can easily write a COBOL program. The double control break program for Continental University is too complex to begin coding immediately. Consequently we begin by breaking the problem into three steps: initialization, processing, and termination. These three instructions are also too comprehensive, and they in turn are further decomposed. Figure 11.4 shows the first "real" attempt for structuring the problem.

In Figure 11.4, initialization consists of opening files and general housekeeping. Processing involves a repetitive set of instructions for each college. Termination causes the university total to be written and the files closed.

Figure 11.5 amplifies the processing segment of Figure 11.4. It indicates a new loop for each year in each college to process all the majors in that year. (Recall that incoming data are sorted by college and year within college, as shown in Figure 11.3.)

Figure 11.6 further expands the processing function for each year. The year total is zeroed out; then all majors in that year are processed to (1) increment the year total, (2) increment the university total, and (3) write a detail line for a specific major in a specific year.

Figures 11.4, 11.5, and 11.6 are successive iterations in the stepwise refinement of a double-control-break problem. The earliest attempt, i.e., Figure 11.4, is the most general and, consequently, closest to the original problem specifications. Successive iterations, i.e., Figures 11.5 and 11.6, describe the problem in finer detail, until entries in the last iteration (Figure 11.6) are easily translated into pseudocode and eventually a program.

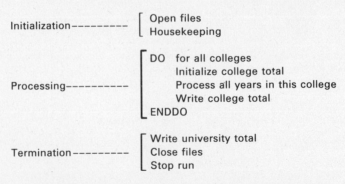

Initialization ————— ⌈ Open files
                      ⌊ Housekeeping

Processing ————— ⌈ DO for all colleges
                         Initialize college total
                         Process all years in this college
                         Write college total
                ⌊ ENDDO

Termination ————— ⌈ Write university total
                       Close files
                ⌊ Stop run

FIGURE 11.4 *Two-Level Control Break Program—Step 1*

```
Initialization--    Open files
                    Housekeeping

                    DO   for all colleges                Initialization for each year
                         Initialize college total        DO   for all majors in this year
Processing---            Process all years in this college---      Process record
                         Write college total            ENDDO
                    ENDDO                                Termination for each year

Termination--       Write university total
                    Close files
                    Stop run
```

FIGURE 11.5 *Two-Level Control Break Program—Step 2*

```
Initialization--    Open files
                    Housekeeping

                                                        Initialization  --------  Zero this year's total
                    DO   for all colleges
                         Initialize college total       DO   for all majors      Update year total
Processing---            Process all years in-----           in this year        Update university total
                         this college                        Process record---   Write detail line
                         Write college total            ENDDO
                    ENDDO                                Termination  ---------   Write year total
                                                                                  Update college total

Termination--       Write university total
                    Close files
                    Stop run
```

FIGURE 11.6 *Two-Level Control Break Program—Step 3*

```
Initialize
OPEN files
READ STUDENT-FILE at end of file indicate no more data
zero university total
PERFORM UNTIL there is no more data
   zero college total
   move CD-COLLEGE to WS-PREVIOUS-COLLEGE
   PERFORM UNTIL CD-COLLEGE is not equal to WS-PREVIOUS-COLLEGE
       or there is no more data
           zero year's total
           move CD-YEAR to WS-PREVIOUS-YEAR
           PERFORM UNTIL CD-COLLEGE is not equal to WS-PREVIOUS-COLLEGE
               or CD-YEAR is not equal to WS-PREVIOUS-YEAR
               or there is no more data
                   Increment year total
                   Increment university total
                   Write detail line for one major
                   READ STUDENT-FILE at end of file indicate no more data
           ENDPERFORM
           print year's total
           increment college total
   ENDPERFORM
   print college total
ENDPERFORM
print university total
CLOSE files
STOP RUN
```

FIGURE 11.7 *Pseudocode for Double-Control-Break Program*

PSEUDOCODE

The use of traditional flowchart as a design aid and/or documentation technique has been in a steady decline for several years. Programmers have, almost universally, written the program first, and then drawn the flowchart only to satisfy their manager. Hence, the main use for which the flowchart was intended, i.e., as a guide in writing the program, was destroyed. Moreover, its usefulness as documentation is practically nil, particularly as problems become larger and more complex. Structured programming, therefore, has given rise to its own documentation techniques of which pseudocode is the most common.

As was initially stated in Chapter 1, pseudocode enables a programmer to express his thoughts in a natural, English-like manner. It frees him from concerns about the syntax of a programming language and the constraints that such rigor imposes. Consequently, pseudocode enables an individual to concentrate on the method of solution without worrying about its (i.e., the solution's) eventual implementation. Pseudocode is particularly well suited to expressing "structured" logic in that it flows naturally from top to bottom. It meshes easily, therefore, with stepwise refinement. Figure 11.7 contains pseudocode corresponding to the last iteration, i.e., Figure 11.6.

CONTROL BREAKS: A COMPLETED PROGRAM

It is now an easy matter to convert the pseudocode of Figure 11.7 into the COBOL program of Figure 11.8. Output produced by that program is shown in Figure 11.9.

The mainline routine of Figure 11.8 invokes PROCESS-ONE-COLLEGE (until all records have been processed). PROCESS-ONE-COLLEGE invokes PROCESS-ONE-YEAR (until college changes), which in turn calls PROCESS-ONE-MAJOR (until year changes).

The procedure division is straightforward. The PROCESS-ONE-COLLEGE module writes a page heading and zeros out the college total for each new college. It then invokes a lower-level routine to process all years in that college until a control break occurs on college; i.e., CD-COLLEGE-NAME is not equal to WS-PREV-COLLEGE-NAME (line 78). After that control break has occurred, a total is written for the college.

The PROCESS-ONE-YEAR routine zeros the total for each new year. It then processes all the majors in that year until there is a break on year; i.e., CD-YEAR is not equal to WS-PREV-YEAR-NAME (line 90). When this control break occurs, a total is written for the year in question.

Coding standards are followed throughout. Picture and value clauses are uniformly aligned; record and paragraph names are prefixed. The beginning and end of working storage are delineated through appropriate literals. Note also the attention paid to indentation in the various perform statements.

Although Figure 11.8 adheres to all our suggested guidelines for good programming, it is still somewhat difficult to follow. This is not because of any shortcoming in the program, but because the problem itself is non-trivial. An alternative approach is presented in Appendix A on *Report Writer*.

TOP DOWN DEVELOPMENT

We now pose a second problem, on inventory control, to illustrate the technique of top down development. This philosophy parallels stepwise refinement and requires that the highest-level routines in a program be coded and tested first. The lower-level modules, containing the detailed but trivial logic, are developed last. Before proceeding further, consider the following specifications:

Two distinct input files, an old master and a transaction file, are to be matched against one another to produce an inventory status report. Each old master record contains a part number, quantity on hand, and date of last activity. Each transaction record contains a part number, the quantity received (if any), the quantity shipped or ordered by customers (if any), and an authorization code for new parts.

Any part appearing in *both* files is to appear on the inventory status report with the following information: quantity on hand, amount received, amount shipped or ordered, and the new quantity

```
00001          IDENTIFICATION DIVISION.
00002          PROGRAM-ID.
00003              TOTALS.
00004          AUTHOR.
00005              ROBERT T. GRAUER.
00006          ENVIRONMENT DIVISION.
00007          CONFIGURATION SECTION.
00008          SOURCE-COMPUTER. IBM-370.
00009          OBJECT-COMPUTER. IBM-370.
00010          INPUT-OUTPUT SECTION.
00011          FILE-CONTROL.
00012              SELECT STUDENT-FILE    ASSIGN TO UT-S-SYSIN.
00013              SELECT PRINT-FILE      ASSIGN TO UT-S-SYSOUT.
00014          DATA DIVISION.
00015          FILE SECTION.
00016          FD   STUDENT-FILE
00017              LABEL RECORDS ARE OMITTED        ┐Indicates blocksize will be
00018              BLOCK CONTAINS 0 RECORDS          entered in JCL (see Chapter 18)
00019              RECORD CONTAINS 80 CHARACTERS
00020              DATA RECORD IS CARD-REC.
00021          01   CARD-REC              PIC X(80).
00022          FD   PRINT-FILE
00023              LABEL RECORDS ARE OMITTED
00024              BLOCK CONTAINS 0 RECORDS
00025              RECORD CONTAINS 133 CHARACTERS          Identifies the start of
00026              DATA RECORD IS PRINT-LINE.             Working Storage in the
00027          01   PRINT-LINE            PIC X(133).     event of a dump
00028          WORKING-STORAGE SECTION.
00029          01   WS-BEGINS             PIC X(16)    VALUE ' WS BEGINS HERE'.
00030          01   WS-END-OF-FILE-SW     PIC XXX      VALUE SPACE.
00031              88  WS-END-OF-FILE                  VALUE 'YES'.
00032          01   WS-UNIVERSITY-TOTAL   PIC S9(6)    VALUE ZERO.
00033          01   WS-THIS-COLLEGE-TOTAL PIC S9(6)    VALUE ZERO.
00034          01   WS-PREV-COLLEGE-NAME  PIC X(10)    VALUE SPACE.
00035          01   WS-THIS-YEAR-TOTAL    PIC S9(6)    VALUE ZERO.
00036          01   WS-PREV-YEAR-NAME     PIC X(9)     VALUE SPACE.
00037          01   PR-PRINT-LINE.
00038              05   FILLER           PIC X.
00039              05   PR-COLLEGE       PIC X(10).
00040              05   FILLER           PIC XX.
00041              05   PR-MAJOR         PIC X(19).
00042              05   FILLER           PIC XX.
00043              05   PR-YEAR          PIC X(9).
00044              05   PR-YEAR-TOTAL    PIC ZZZ,ZZ9.
00045              05   FILLER           PIC X(81).
00046          01   CD-CARD-IN.
00047              05   CD-YEAR          PIC X(9).
00048              05   FILLER           PIC X(11).
00049              05   CD-COLLEGE-NAME  PIC X(10).
00050              05   CD-MAJOR-NAME    PIC X(19).
00051              05   CD-MAJOR-TOTAL   PIC S9(6).
00052              05   FILLER           PIC X(25).
00053          01   TL-TOTAL-LINE.
00054              05   FILLER           PIC X(23)    VALUE SPACES.
00055              05   FILLER           PIC X(10)    VALUE 'TOTAL FOR '.
00056              05   TL-HEADING       PIC X(10).
00057              05   FILLER           PIC XX       VALUE '- '.
00058              05   TL-TOTAL         PIC ZZZ,ZZ9.
00059              05   FILLER           PIC X(81)    VALUE SPACES.
00060          01   WS-END-OF-WORKING-STOR PIC X(16)  VALUE ' WS ENDS HERE  '.
00061          PROCEDURE DIVISION.
00062          A-MAINLINE.
00063              OPEN INPUT STUDENT-FILE              Literal to facilitate debugging
00064                  OUTPUT PRINT-FILE.
00065              READ STUDENT-FILE INTO CD-CARD-IN
00066                  AT END MOVE 'YES' TO WS-END-OF-FILE-SW.
00067              PERFORM B-PROCESS-ONE-COLLEGE
00068                  UNTIL WS-END-OF-FILE.
00069              PERFORM E-PRINT-UNIVERSITY-TOTALS.
00070              CLOSE STUDENT-FILE
00071                  PRINT-FILE.
00072              STOP RUN.
00073          B-PROCESS-ONE-COLLEGE.
00074              PERFORM F-PRINT-HEADING.
```

FIGURE 11.8 *Double Control Break Program*

```
00075                  MOVE ZEROS TO WS-THIS-COLLEGE-TOTAL.        Signifies control break on college
00076                  MOVE CD-COLLEGE-NAME TO WS-PREV-COLLEGE-NAME.         /
00077                  PERFORM C-PROCESS-ONE-YEAR
00078                     UNTIL CD-COLLEGE-NAME NOT EQUAL TO WS-PREV-COLLEGE-NAME
00079                        OR WS-END-OF-FILE.
00080                  MOVE WS-PREV-COLLEGE-NAME TO TL-HEADING.
00081                  MOVE WS-THIS-COLLEGE-TOTAL TO TL-TOTAL.
00082                  WRITE PRINT-LINE FROM TL-TOTAL-LINE AFTER ADVANCING 2 LINES.
00083                  MOVE SPACES TO PRINT-LINE.
00084                  WRITE PRINT-LINE AFTER ADVANCING 2 LINES.
00085              C-PROCESS-ONE-YEAR.
00086                  MOVE ZERO TO WS-THIS-YEAR-TOTAL.
00087                  MOVE CD-YEAR TO WS-PREV-YEAR-NAME.
00088                  PERFORM D-PROCESS-ONE-MAJOR
00089                     UNTIL CD-COLLEGE-NAME NOT EQUAL TO WS-PREV-COLLEGE-NAME
00090                        OR CD-YEAR IS NOT EQUAL TO WS-PREV-YEAR-NAME
00091                        OR WS-END-OF-FILE.          Signifies control break on year
00092                  MOVE WS-PREV-YEAR-NAME TO TL-HEADING.
00093                  MOVE WS-THIS-YEAR-TOTAL TO TL-TOTAL.
00094                  WRITE PRINT-LINE FROM TL-TOTAL-LINE AFTER ADVANCING 2 LINES.
00095                  ADD WS-THIS-YEAR-TOTAL TO WS-THIS-COLLEGE-TOTAL.
00096              D-PROCESS-ONE-MAJOR.
00097                  MOVE SPACES TO PR-PRINT-LINE.
00098                  MOVE CD-COLLEGE-NAME TO PR-COLLEGE.
00099                  MOVE CD-YEAR TO PR-YEAR.
00100                  MOVE CD-MAJOR-NAME TO PR-MAJOR.
00101                  MOVE CD-MAJOR-TOTAL TO PR-YEAR-TOTAL.
00102                  WRITE PRINT-LINE FROM PR-PRINT-LINE AFTER ADVANCING 1.
00103                  ADD CD-MAJOR-TOTAL TO WS-THIS-YEAR-TOTAL.
00104                  ADD CD-MAJOR-TOTAL TO WS-UNIVERSITY-TOTAL.
00105                  READ STUDENT-FILE INTO CD-CARD-IN
00106                     AT END MOVE 'YES' TO WS-END-OF-FILE-SW.
00107              E-PRINT-UNIVERSITY-TOTALS.
00108                  MOVE 'UNIVERSITY' TO TL-HEADING.
00109                  MOVE WS-UNIVERSITY-TOTAL TO TL-TOTAL.
00110                  WRITE PRINT-LINE FROM TL-TOTAL-LINE AFTER ADVANCING 2 LINES.
00111              F-PRINT-HEADING.
00112                  MOVE ' COLLEGE        MAJOR                  YEAR        ENROLLMENT'
00113                           TO PRINT-LINE.
00114                  WRITE PRINT-LINE AFTER ADVANCING PAGE.
00115                  MOVE '--------------------------------------------------------
00116        -            '-----' TO PRINT-LINE.
00117                  WRITE PRINT-LINE AFTER ADVANCING 2 LINES.
```

FIGURE 11.8 *(continued)*

on hand. Any part appearing *only* in the old master file should be checked to see if it is still an active part. This is done by checking the date of last activity and flagging as inactive any part whose last activity was more than 18 months ago. Any part appearing *only* in the transaction file represents either a miscopied number for an existing part or a new part not yet entered in the master file. (The determination is made from the new part code in the transaction record.)

The logic to solve this problem requires that the program read from two distinct input files, a situation not previously encountered. The solution is amenable to the stepwise refinement methodology, and the resulting logic is easily expressed in pseudocode. Both are left as exercises for the reader. We will emphasize top down testing and introduce the hierarchy chart as a design and documentation aid.

Hierarchy Charts

The COBOL program capable of the required problem logic will consist of several readily identifiable routines. The relationship among these modules (i.e., COBOL paragraphs or sections) is best expressed in a *hierarchy chart,* as shown in Figure 11.10. This figure depicts the *function* of each routine and the relationship among functions. It does not show decision-making logic or program flow as does pseudocode.

A hierarchy chart is developed from the top down. One module, PREPARE-INVENTORY-REPORT, sits alone at the top of the chart and controls all others. The next lower level breaks the overall nature of the program into smaller, more readily identifiable functions, e.g., COMPARE-

```
COLLEGE     MAJOR                   YEAR        ENROLLMENT
-----------------------------------------------------------------
PACIFIC     BUSINESS                FRESHMAN       115
PACIFIC     EDUCATION               FRESHMAN        66
PACIFIC     ENGINEERING             FRESHMAN        45
PACIFIC     LIBERAL ARTS            FRESHMAN        78
                        TOTAL FOR FRESHMAN  -      304
PACIFIC     BUSINESS                SOPHOMORE      114
PACIFIC     EDUCATION               SOPHOMORE       64
                                    SOPHOMORE       43
                                    SOPHOMORE       68
                         FOR SOPHOMORE -           289
                                    JUNIOR         109
                                    JUNIOR          65
                                    JUNIOR          43
                                    JUNIOR          64
                         FOR JUNIOR    -           281
                                    SENIOR         114
                                    SENIOR          54
                                    SENIOR          43
                                    SENIOR          59
                         FOR SENIOR    -           270
                         FOR PACIFIC   -         1,144

                         FOR UNIVERSITY-         5,240
```

```
COLLEGE     MAJOR              YEAR        ENROLLMENT
--------------------------------------------------------
MIDWEST     BUSINESS           FRESHMAN       231
MIDWEST     EDUCATION          FRESHMAN       134
MIDWEST     ENGINEERING        FRESHMAN        88
MIDWEST     LIBERAL ARTS       FRESHMAN       152
                   TOTAL FOR FRESHMAN  -       605
MIDWEST     BUSINESS           SOPHOMORE      226
MIDWEST     EDUCATION          SOPHOMORE      131
                               SOPHOMORE       84
                               SOPHOMORE      141
                    FOR SOPHOMORE -           582
                               JUNIOR         221
                               JUNIOR         127
                               JUNIOR          78
                               JUNIOR         125
                    FOR JUNIOR    -           551
                               SENIOR         220
                               SENIOR         118
                               SENIOR          74
                               SENIOR         118
                    FOR SENIOR    -           530
                    FOR MIDWEST   -         2,268
```

```
COLLEGE    MAJOR              YEAR        ENROLLMENT
-------------------------------------------------------
ATLANTIC   BUSINESS           FRESHMAN       150
ATLANTIC   EDUCATION          FRESHMAN       100
ATLANTIC   ENGINEERING        FRESHMAN        25
ATLANTIC   LIBERAL ARTS       FRESHMAN       203
                  TOTAL FOR FRESHMAN  -       478
ATLANTIC   BUSINESS           SOPHOMORE      143
ATLANTIC   EDUCATION          SOPHOMORE       94
ATLANTIC   ENGINEERING        SOPHOMORE       18
ATLANTIC   LIBERAL ARTS       SOPHOMORE      202
                  TOTAL FOR SOPHOMORE -       457
ATLANTIC   BUSINESS           JUNIOR         141
ATLANTIC   EDUCATION          JUNIOR          92
ATLANTIC   ENGINEERING        JUNIOR          14
ATLANTIC   LIBERAL ARTS       JUNIOR         218
                  TOTAL FOR JUNIOR    -       465
ATLANTIC   BUSINESS           SENIOR         138
ATLANTIC   EDUCATION          SENIOR          87
ATLANTIC   ENGINEERING        SENIOR          15
ATLANTIC   LIBERAL ARTS       SENIOR         188
                  TOTAL FOR SENIOR    -       428
                  TOTAL FOR ATLANTIC  -     1,828
```

FIGURE 11.9 *Output Produced by Control Break Program*

IDS. These in turn can be broken into still lower level modules with increasing detailed function, e.g., ADD-NEW-PART, UPDATE-EXISTING-PART, etc.

Each module in a hierarchy chart should be *independent* of all others. This allows any module to be modified without affecting the workings of another. For example, if the criteria for an inactive master record changed, then only the coding in CHECK-INACTIVE-MASTER need change. Inde-

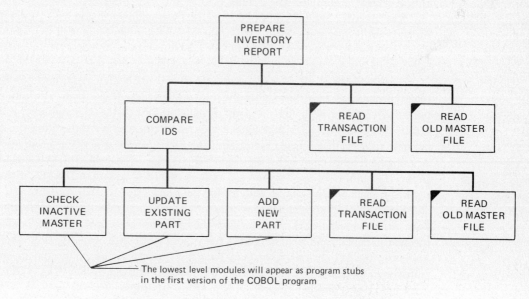

The lowest level modules will appear as program stubs in the first version of the COBOL program

FIGURE 11.10 *Hierarchy Chart for Inventory Control Problem*

pendence can best be achieved by restricting each module to a single *function,* e.g., adding a new record or comparing record numbers. One way of verifying function is in the name of the module; use only a single verb, one, two or three adjectives, and a one-word object, e.g., UPDATE-EXIST-ING-PART. If you can't name modules in this way, they are probably not functional.

There are also attempts at quantitative definition; e.g., a module should not contain more than 50 statements. Thus, if a module cannot be made to fit on a single page of a program listing, it is probably programming more than one function, in which case it should be divided into more than one module. Since many programmers welcome quantitative guidelines, we endorse the 50-line restriction.

Finally, *each module in a hierarchy chart can only be called by the module immediately above it, and must in turn return control to that module.* Some modules, however, may be called from different parts of a program, and consequently appear twice in a hierarchy chart. This is indicated by shading the upper left-hand corner, as was done in Figure 11.10.

Top Down Testing

It is not necessary to code every module in the hierarchy chart before testing begins. While the traditional approach required that a program be completely coded before testing could start, it is preferable to begin testing much earlier, and well before coding is finished. This is accomplished by testing modules in a hierarchy chart in the order in which they are developed, i.e., from the top down. It is made possible by initially coding lower-level modules as *program stubs,* i.e., single-sentence routines consisting of a DISPLAY statement to indicate only that the module has been entered.

A major advantage of top down testing is that bugs are detected earlier, and easier, than with conventional testing. It ensures the higher-level modules, which typically contain the more complex logic, are tested more frequently than lower-level routines. It allows testing and coding to become parallel activities that provide early feedback to the programmer.

To fully appreciate the significance of top down testing, a partially completed program (Figure 11.11) for the inventory problem will be developed. It will provide for all the modules in the hierarchy chart of Figure 11.10, but the three lowest-level routines will appear only as program stubs. It will be shown that significant testing can take place *without* providing the details of these procedures. In other words, one is initially more concerned with the interaction of these modules, and the higher-level routines that call them, than with the specifics of adding a new record or checking an existing, but inactive, old record. Once this interaction has been tested, it becomes almost trivial to complete the details.

Test data for the program of Figure 11.11 are shown in Figure 11.12. Figure 11.12b contains the old master file, and Figure 11.12a, the transaction file. Note well that both files are in sequence by part number. The reader should be convinced that Figure 11.12 contains sufficient data to adequately test a program to prepare the Inventory Status Report.

The program of Figure 11.11 begins with an OPEN statement, and immediately reads the first record from both the transaction and old master files. It performs the module, COMPARE-ID-NUMBERS, until both files are out of data, i.e., until the ID number on both files is equal to HIGH-VALUES. (HIGH-VALUES is a COBOL reserved word denoting the highest numeric value possible.) When that routine is finished, the files are closed and the program terminated.

Figure 11.11 is driven by the nested IF statement in the COMPARE-ID-NUMBERS module. If the ID number of the current old master record is less than the ID of the current transaction record, it means there was no activity for the old master record. Accordingly, the CHECK-INAC-TIVE-MASTER paragraph is invoked, after which a new record is read from the old master only. If, however, the ID numbers on the two files are equal, the UPDATE-EXISTING-PART module is called, and a new record read from both files. Finally, if neither of these conditions hold, i.e., the ID on the transaction record is less than that of the old master, it means that the transaction file contains an ID number not found in the old master. The ADD-NEW-PART routine is executed, and another record is taken from the transaction file only.

```
00001          IDENTIFICATION DIVISION.
00002          PROGRAM-ID.
00003              MERGE001.
00004          AUTHOR.
00005              MARSHAL A. CRAWFORD.
00006

00007          ENVIRONMENT DIVISION.
00008          CONFIGURATION SECTION.
00009          SOURCE-COMPUTER.
00010              IBM-370.
00011          OBJECT-COMPUTER.
00012              IBM-370.
00013

00014          INPUT-OUTPUT SECTION.
00015          FILE-CONTROL.
00016              SELECT OLD-MASTER-FILE   ASSIGN TO UT-S-OLDMAST.
00017              SELECT TRANS-FILF        ASSIGN TO UT-S-TRANS.
00018

00019          DATA DIVISION.
00020          FILE SECTION.
00021

00022          FD   OLD-MASTER-FILE              Indicates block size will be entered in JCL -
00023               BLOCK CONTAINS 0 RECORDS     see Chapter 18
00024               LABEL RECORDS ARE OMITTED
00025               RECORD CONTAINS 80 CHARACTERS
00026               DATA RECORD IS OLD-MASTER-RECORD.
00027          01   OLD-MASTER-RECORD            PIC X(80).
00028

00029          FD   TRANS-FILE
00030               BLOCK CONTAINS 0 RECORDS
00031               LABEL RECORDS ARE OMITTED
00032               RECORD CONTAINS 80 CHARACTERS
00033               DATA RECORD IS TRANSACTION-RECORD.
00034          01   TRANSACTION-RECORD           PIC X(80).
00035
00036          WORKING-STORAGE SECTION.                  Literal to facilitate debugging
00037          01   FILLER                       PIC X(16)
00038                             VALUE IS ' WS BEGINS HERE '.
00039
00040          01   MO-OLD-MAST-RECORD.
00041               05   MO-OLD-MAST-ID          PIC X(6).
00042               05   MO-OLD-QUAN-ON-HAND       PIC S9(6).
00043               05   MO-DATE-OF-LAST-ACTIVITY.
00044                    10   MO-LAST MONTH       PIC 99.
00045                    10   MO-LAST-YEAR        PIC 99.
00046               05   FILLER                   PIC X(56).
00047
00048          01   TR-TRANS-RECORD.                     I/O area is defined in
00049               05   TR-TRAN-ID               PIC X(6).   Working Storage to
00050               05   FILLER                   PIC X(13). accommodate READ INTO
00051               05   TR-TRAN-RECEIVED         PIC S9(4).
00052               05   FILLER                   PIC X(6).
00053               05   TR-TRAN-SHIPPED          PIC S9(4).
00054               05   TR-NEW-PART-CODE         PIC X.
00055                    88   TR-NEW-PART-AUTHORIZED           VALUE 'Y'.
00056               05   FILLER                   PIC X(46).
00057
00058
00059          PROCEDURE DIVISION.
00060
00061          010-PREPARE-INVENTORY-REPORT.
00062              OPEN INPUT TRANS-FILE
00063                         OLD-MASTER-FILE.        Initial read statements for each file
00064
00065              PERFORM 080-READ-TRANSACTION-FILE.
00066              PERFORM 090-READ-OLD-MASTER-FILE.
00067
00068              PERFORM 040-COMPARE-ID-NUMBERS
00069                  UNTIL TR-TRAN-ID IS EQUAL TO HIGH-VALUES
00070                      AND MO-OLD-MAST-ID IS EQUAL TO HIGH-VALUES.
00071
00072              CLOSE TRANS-FILE
00073                    OLD-MASTER-FILE.
00074              STOP RUN.
```

FIGURE 11.11 *Partially Completed (Stubs) Program*

```
00075
00076                 040-COMPARE-ID-NUMBERS.
00077
00078                     DISPLAY ' '.                                    ┐ Nested IF determines
00079                     DISPLAY 'RECORDS BEING PROCESSED'.               │ relationship of old
00080                     DISPLAY 'OLD MASTER: ' MO-OLD-MAST-ID.          ⟋ master and transaction
00081                     DISPLAY 'TRANSACTION:' TR-TRAN-ID.                 records
00082                     IF MO-OLD-MAST-ID IS LESS THAN TR-TRAN-ID
00083                         PERFORM 050-CHECK-INACTIVE-MASTER
00084                         PERFORM 090-READ-OLD-MASTER-FILE
00085                     ELSE
00086                         IF MO-OLD-MAST-ID IS EQUAL TO TR-TRAN-ID
00087                             PERFORM 060-UPDATE-EXISTING-PART
00088                             PERFORM 080-READ-TRANSACTION-FILE
00089                             PERFORM 090-READ-OLD-MASTER-FILE
00090                         ELSE
00091                             PERFORM 070-ADD-NEW-PART
00092                             PERFORM 080-READ-TRANSACTION-FILE.
00093
00094                 050-CHECK-INACTIVE-MASTER.
00095                     DISPLAY '050-CHECK-INACTIVE-MASTER'.             ┐
00096                                                                      │
00097                 060-UPDATE-EXISTING-PART.                            ├─ Program stubs
00098                     DISPLAY '060-UPDATE-EXISTING-PART'.              │
00099                                                                      │
00100                 070-ADD-NEW-PART.                                    │
00101                     DISPLAY '070-ADD-NEW-PART'.                      ┘
00102
00103                 080-READ-TRANSACTION-FILE.
00104                     READ TRANS-FILE INTO TR-TRANS-RECORD
00105                         AT END MOVE HIGH-VALUES TO TR-TRAN-ID.
00106
00107                 090-READ-OLD-MASTER-FILE.
00108                     READ OLD-MASTER-FILE INTO MO-OLD-MAST-RECORD
00109                         AT END MOVE HIGH-VALUES TO MO-OLD-MAST-ID.
```

FIGURE 11.11 (continued)

To better appreciate how the program works, consider Figure 11.13 containing output produced by the program of Figure 11.11 with the data of Figure 11.12. The first old master and transaction records have ID numbers of 000010 and 000015, respectively. The nested IF of lines 82 to 92 causes the paragraph 050-CHECK-INACTIVE-MASTER to be executed, which in turn does nothing except display a message that it (i.e., the paragraph 050-CHECK-INACTIVE-MASTER) was entered. The nested IF also causes a new record to be read from the old master file only, leading to identical ID numbers (000015) on both files. This condition invokes the routine 060-UPDATE-EXISTING-PART, after which records are read from both files. This time the ID numbers for the old master and transaction are 000021 and 000016, respectively, which invoke 070-ADD-NEW-PART.

Thus far, the nested IF statement of lines 82 to 92 has been executed three times. No substantial processing has resulted, because the lower-level routines performed by this statement are only program stubs, i.e., DISPLAY statements. However, the reader has gotten the feeling that the program is working correctly because the appropriate stub has always been called. Moreover, the program seems to handle the difficult decision of which (or both) input file to read next, depending on the result of the previous comparison. In short, the highest-level (and most difficult) module 040-COMPARE-ID-NUMBERS, has been tested and apparently proved correct. Further, this testing has been accomplished early in the development cycle, and produced valuable feedback for both the programmer and user. It is now a relatively simple manner to produce the finished program as shown in Figure 11.14. The remainder of Figure 9.13 is left as an exercise.

Merging Files: A Completed Program

Figure 11.14 reflects the completed Inventory Status Program. The most obvious difference between this program and its predecessor is in number of statements, 173 versus 109. The better than 50% increase in length is directly attributable to the expansion of the three stubs in the earlier program.

```
            000015        0015      0020
            000016        0003      0000Y
            000017        0024      0013
            000045        0123      0076
            000095        3200      0100
```

(a)

```
            0000100000211178
            0000150000041078
            0000210000561278
            0000350001031178
            0000450000020978
            0000500000070678
            0000650000670277
            0000950015460878
```

(b)

FIGURE 11.12 *Test Data for Inventory Status Program*
(a) Transaction File
(b) Old Master File

```
RECORDS BEING PROCESSED
OLD MASTER: 000010
TRANSACTION:000015                 Old master < transaction; hence
050-CHECK-INACTIVE-MASTER          050-CHECK-INACTIVE-MASTER
                                   is entered

RECORDS BEING PROCESSED
OLD MASTER: 000015
TRANSACTION:000015
060-UPDATE-EXISTING-PART

RECORDS BEING PROCESSED
OLD MASTER: 000021
TRANSACTION:000016                 Transaction < old master; hence
070-ADD-NEW-PART                   070-ADD-NEW-PART is entered

RECORDS BEING PROCESSED
OLD MASTER: 000021
TRANSACTION:000017
070-ADD-NEW-PART

RECORDS BEING PROCESSED
OLD MASTER: 000021
TRANSACTION:000045
050-CHECK-INACTIVE-MASTER

RECORDS BEING PROCESSED
OLD MASTER: 000035
TRANSACTION:000045
050-CHECK-INACTIVE-MASTER

RECORDS BEING PROCESSED
OLD MASTER: 000045
TRANSACTION:000045                 Old master = transaction; hence
060-UPDATE-EXISTING-PART           060-UPDATE-EXISTING-PART
                                   is entered

RECORDS BEING PROCESSED
OLD MASTER: 000050
TRANSACTION:000095
050-CHECK-INACTIVE-MASTER

RECORDS BEING PROCESSED
OLD MASTER: 000065
TRANSACTION:000095
050-CHECK-INACTIVE-MASTER

RECORDS BEING PROCESSED
OLD MASTER: 000095
TRANSACTION:000095
060-UPDATE-EXISTING-PART
```

FIGURE 11.13 *Output of Stubs Program*

```
00001          IDENTIFICATION DIVISION.
00002          PROGRAM-ID.
00003              MERGE001.
00004          AUTHOR.
00005              MARSHAL A. CRAWFORD.
00006
00007          ENVIRONMENT DIVISION.
00008          CONFIGURATION SECTION.
00009          SOURCE-COMPUTER.
00010              IBM-370.
00011          OBJECT-COMPUTER.
00012              IBM-370.
00013
00014          INPUT-OUTPUT SECTION.
00015          FILE-CONTROL.
00016              SELECT OLD-MASTER-FILE    ASSIGN TO UT-S-OLDMAST.
00017              SELECT TRANS-FILE         ASSIGN TO UT-S-TRANS.
00018              SELECT PRINT-FILE         ASSIGN TO UT-S-PRINT.
00019                                                  └ Print-file has been added
00020          DATA DIVISION.
00021          FILE SECTION.
00022
00023          FD   OLD-MASTER-FILE
00024               BLOCK CONTAINS 0 RECORDS
00025               LABEL RECORDS ARE OMITTED
00026               RECORD CONTAINS 80 CHARACTERS
00027               DATA RECORD IS OLD-MASTER-RECORD.
00028          01   OLD-MASTER-RECORD         PIC X(80).
00029
00030          FD   TRANS-FILE                    ┌ Indicates blocksize will be
00031               BLOCK CONTAINS 0 RECORDS         entered in JCL - see
00032               LABEL RECORDS ARE OMITTED        Chapter 18
00033               RECORD CONTAINS 80 CHARACTERS
00034               DATA RECORD IS TRANSACTION-RECORD.
00035          01   TRANSACTION-RECORD        PIC X(80).
00036
00037          FD   PRINT-FILE
00038               BLOCK CONTAINS 0 RECORDS
00039               LABEL RECORDS ARE OMITTED
00040               RECORD CONTAINS 133 CHARACTERS
00041               DATA RECORD IS PRINT-LINE.
00042          01   PRINT-LINE                PIC X(133).
00043
00044          WORKING-STORAGE SECTION.
00045          01   FILLER                    PIC X(16)
00046                         VALUE IS 'WS BEGINS HERE'.
00047          01   WS-NEW-QUAN-ON-HAND        PIC S9(6)
00048                         VALUE IS ZERO.
00049          01   DATE-WORK-AREA.
00050               05  WS-YEAR              PIC 99.
00051               05  WS-MONTH             PIC 99.
00052               05  WS-DAY               PIC 99.
00053
00054          01   WS-COMPUTED-MONTHS        PIC S9(5)    COMP-3    VALUE ZERO.
00055
00056          01   MO-OLD-MAST-RECORD.
00057               05  MO-OLD-MAST-ID       PIC X(6).
00058               05  MO-OLD-QUAN-ON-HAND  PIC S9(6).
00059               05  MO-DATE-OF-LAST-ACTIVITY.
00060                   10  MO-LAST-MONTH    PIC 99.
00061                   10  MO-LAST-YEAR     PIC 99.
00062               05  FILLER               PIC X(56).
00063
00064          01   TR-TRANS-RECORD.
00065               05  TR-TRAN-ID           PIC X(6).
00066               05  FILLER               PIC X(13).
00067               05  TR-TRAN-RECEIVED     PIC S9(4).
00068               05  FILLER               PIC X(6).
00069               05  TR-TRAN-SHIPPED      PIC S9(4).
00070               05  TR-NEW-PART-CODE     PIC X.
00071                   88  TR-NEW-PART-AUTHORIZED           VALUE 'Y'.
00072               05  FILLER               PIC X(46).
00073
```

FIGURE 11.14 *The Completed Inventory Status Program*

SECTION III: MORE COBOL

```
00074        01  HDG-LINE-1.
00075            05  FILLER                      PIC X(36)      VALUE SPACES.
00076            05  FILLER                      PIC X(22)
00077                    VALUE 'UPDATED MASTER RECORDS'.
00078
00079        01  HDG-LINE-2.
00080            05  FILLER                      PIC X(19)      VALUE SPACES.
00081            05  FILLER                      PIC X(6)       VALUE '  ID  '.
00082            05  FILLER                      PIC X(8)       VALUE ' OLD AMT'.
00083            05  FILLER                      PIC X(4)       VALUE SPACES.
00084            05  FILLER                      PIC X(9)       VALUE ' RECEIVED'.
00085            05  FILLER                      PIC X(3)       VALUE SPACES.
00086            05  FILLER                      PIC X(9)       VALUE '  SHIPPED'.
00087            05  FILLER                      PIC XX         VALUE SPACES.
00088            05  FILLER                      PIC X(9)       VALUE ' NEW AMT'.
00089
00090        01  PL-PRINT-LINE.                                             ─── Print lines have been added
00091            05  FILLER                      PIC X(19).
00092            05  PL-MAST-ID                  PIC X(6).
00093            05  FILLER                      PIC XX.
00094            05  PL-OLD-QUAN-ON-HAND         PIC ZZZZZ9.
00095            05  FILLER                      PIC X(4).
00096            05  PL-RECEIVED                 PIC Z(8)9.
00097            05  FILLER                      PIC XXX.
00098            05  PL-SHIPPED                  PIC Z(8)9.
00099            05  FILLER                      PIC XXX.
00100            05  PL-NEW-QUAN-ON-HAND         PIC Z(8)9.
00101            05  FILLER                      PIC XX.
00102            05  PL-BACKLOG                  PIC X(9).
00103            05  FILLER                      PIC X(52).
00104
00105        PROCEDURE DIVISION.
00106
00107        010-PREPARE-INVENTORY-REPORT.
00108            OPEN INPUT TRANS-FILE              Date of execution required to
00109                       OLD-MASTER-FILE         check on inactive master
00110                 OUTPUT PRINT-FILE.
00111            ACCEPT DATE-WORK-AREA FROM DATE.
00112
00113            WRITE PRINT-LINE FROM HDG-LINE-1 AFTER ADVANCING PAGE.
00114            WRITE PRINT-LINE FROM HDG-LINE-2 AFTER ADVANCING 2.
00115            PERFORM 080-READ-TRANSACTION-FILE.
00116            PERFORM 090-READ-OLD-MASTER-FILE.
00117
00118            PERFORM 040-COMPARE-ID-NUMBERS
00119                UNTIL TR-TRAN-ID IS EQUAL TO HIGH-VALUES
00120                    AND MO-OLD-MAST-ID IS EQUAL TO HIGH-VALUES.
00121
00122            CLOSE TRANS-FILE
00123                  OLD-MASTER-FILE
00124                  PRINT-FILE.
00125            STOP RUN.                           Higher level routine was completely tested
00126                                                in stubs program
00127        040-COMPARE-ID-NUMBERS.
00128            IF MO-OLD-MAST-ID IS LESS THAN TR-TRAN-ID
00129                PERFORM 050-CHECK-INACTIVE-MASTER
00130                PERFORM 090-READ-OLD-MASTER-FILE
00131            ELSE
00132                IF MO-OLD-MAST-ID IS EQUAL TO TR-TRAN-ID
00133                    PERFORM 060-UPDATE-EXISTING-PART
00134                    PERFORM 080-READ-TRANSACTION-FILE
00135                    PERFORM 090-READ-OLD-MASTER-FILE
00136                ELSE
00137                    PERFORM 070-ADD-NEW-PART             Expanded from
00138                    PERFORM 080-READ-TRANSACTION-FILE.   earlier stub
00139
00140        050-CHECK-INACTIVE-MASTER.
00141            COMPUTE WS-COMPUTED-MONTHS = ((12 * WS-YEAR) + WS-MONTH)
00142                - ((12 * MO-LAST-YEAR) + MO-LAST-MONTH).
00143            IF WS-COMPUTED-MONTHS IS GREATER THAN 18
00144                DISPLAY '18 MONTHS WITHOUT ACTIVITY FOR ' MO-OLD-MAST-ID.
00145
```

FIGURE 11.14 (continued)

```
00146        060-UPDATE-EXISTING-PART.
00147            COMPUTE WS-NEW-QUAN-ON-HAND = MO-OLD-QUAN-ON-HAND
00148                + TR-TRAN-RECEIVED - TR-TRAN-SHIPPED.
00149
00150            MOVE SPACES TO PL-PRINT-LINE.
00151            MOVE MO-OLD-QUAN-ON-HAND TO PL-OLD-QUAN-ON-HAND.
00152            MOVE TR-TRAN-RECEIVED TO PL-RECEIVED.
00153            MOVE TR-TRAN-SHIPPED TO PL-SHIPPED.
00154            MOVE WS-NEW-QUAN-ON-HAND TO PL-NEW-QUAN-ON-HAND.
00155            MOVE TR-TRAN-ID TO PL-MAST-ID.
00156
00157            IF WS-NEW-QUAN-ON-HAND IS LESS THAN ZERO
00158                MOVE '*BACKLOG*' TO PL-BACKLOG.
00159            WRITE PRINT-LINE FROM PL-PRINT-LINE AFTER ADVANCING 2 LINES.
00160
00161        070-ADD-NEW-PART.                                  ←── Expanded from earlier stub
00162            IF TR-NEW-PART-AUTHORIZED
00163                DISPLAY TR-TRAN-ID ' MUST BE ADDED TO MASTER FILE'
00164            ELSE
00165                DISPLAY 'NO MATCH FOR ' TR-TRAN-ID.
00166
00167        080-READ-TRANSACTION-FILE.                         ←── Expanded from earlier stub
00168            READ TRANS-FILE INTO TR-TRANS-RECORD
00169                AT END MOVE HIGH-VALUES TO TR-TRAN-ID.
00170
00171        090-READ-OLD-MASTER-FILE.
00172            READ OLD-MASTER-FILE INTO MO-OLD-MAST-RECORD
00173                AT END MOVE HIGH-VALUES TO MO-OLD-MAST-ID.
```

FIGURE 11.14 *(continued)*

The CHECK-INACTIVE-MASTER routine computes the time since the particular master record was updated and prints an appropriate message if necessary. It requires a DATE-WORK-AREA in working storage (lines 49 to 52) and the date of execution (line 111). The UPDATE-EXISTING-PART module produces the requested report and requires additional data division entries for a PRINT-FILE. Finally, the ADD-NEW-PART paragraph differentiates between a transaction that is to be added to the master file versus one whose ID number was merely miscopied. However, to restate the philosophy of top down development, the logic in any of these modules is less difficult than the higher-level module that calls them. Hence it is essential to test the higher-level routine, COMPARE-ID-NUMBERS, earlier and more often than any of the lower-level modules. Witness, for example, the several MOVE statements in the lower-level routine UPDATE-EXISTING-PART. While these statements are certainly necessary to build a print line, they should not tax anyone's programming ability. On the other hand, the nested IF in the COMPARE-ID-NUMBERS module merits some serious thought and embodies more powerful logic.

Output from the completed program is shown in Figure 11.15. (The program was run in December, 1979, and hence only part 000065 on the master file shows no activity in 18 months.)

```
                          UPDATED MASTER RECORDS
      ID    OLD AMT      RECEIVED       SHIPPED      NEW AMT
   000015        4            15            20            1    *BACKLOG*
   000045        2           123            76           49
   000095     1546          3200           100         4646
```

└─ Inventory Status Report

```
   000016 MUST BE ADDED TO MASTER FILE
   NO MATCH FOR 000017
   18 MONTHS WITHOUT ACTIVITY FOR 000065
```

└─ Display messages

FIGURE 11.15 *Output of Completed Program*

SUMMARY

This chapter concludes the discussion of programming style begun in Chapter 6. Generality, efficiency, error checking, and ease of maintenance are essential characteristics of good commercial programs. Techniques for achieving these goals were presented as part of an overall discussion on programming style.

The material on structured programming was extended to include the case structure, pseudocode, hierarchy charts, stepwise refinement, and top down development. Top down development is closely tied to structured programming and requires that one concentrate on the highest levels of logic first and bring in the details later. It assumes that the top-level logic is the most crucial and therefore should receive the most testing. It allows testing to begin *before* coding is finished. Programs developed in this manner can be read in sequence, from top to bottom without a lot of skipping around, and this makes it far easier to understand the overall program logic.

One final point: This chapter contained what we believe are two excellent arguments for structured techniques, i.e., the COBOL listings of Figures 11.8 and 11.14. These programs dealt with the logically difficult topics of control breaks and multiple input files. As anyone who has ever written either kind of program will attest, the logical requirements are imposing, yet the structured programs are remarkably simple. In conclusion, we believe the top down structured approach facilitates program development to such an extent that we can no longer code any other way.

REVIEW EXERCISES

TRUE   FALSE

☐   ☐   **1.** A program must be completely coded before any testing can begin.

☐   ☐   **2.** Individual modules (i.e., paragraphs) in a program should perform *many* functions for efficiency purposes.

☐   ☐   **3.** Hierarchy charts and pseudocode depict the same thing.

☐   ☐   **4.** Flowcharts and pseudocode depict the same thing.

☐   ☐   **5.** The technique of stepwise refinement allows a program's logic to be completely developed in a single pass.

☐   ☐   **6.** READ-WRITE-AND-COMPUTE is probably a good name for a COBOL paragraph.

☐   ☐   **7.** Substitution of a binary search for a linear search is an example of algorithmic efficiency.

☐   ☐   **8.** The USAGE clause can be employed to take advantage of machine efficiency.

☐   ☐   **9.** The lowest-level modules in a hierarchy chart should be coded first.

☐   ☐   **10.** The lowest-level modules in a hierarchy chart generally contain the most complex logic.

☐   ☐   **11.** The case structure can be implemented in COBOL by the GO TO DEPENDING verb.

☐   ☐   **12.** A structured program should *never* contain a GO TO statement.

☐   ☐   **13.** A programmer can logically assume that input to his program will always be valid.

☐   ☐   **14.** Incoming data to a program processing control breaks need not be in any special order.

☐   ☐   **15.** Control-break processing must be restricted to a single level.

☐   ☐   **16.** A module in a hierarchy chart can only be called from a module on its own level.

☐   ☐   **17.** A module in a hierarchy chart can be called from more than one module.

☐   ☐   **18.** It is reasonable to restrict all paragraphs to a maximum of 50 lines of code.

PROBLEMS

1. XYZ Corporation stocks four sizes of widgets: small (S), medium (M), large (L), and extra large (X). Sixty percent of all incoming orders are for medium widgets, 25% for large, 10% for small, and 5% for extra large.

(a) Rewrite the following COBOL code to reflect 88-level entries and realign the IF statement:

DATA DIVISION.

       .

05   IN-CODE   PICTURE IS X.

       .

PROCEDURE DIVISION.

       .

```
IF IN-CODE IS EQUAL TO 'S', PERFORM SMALL-SIZE
ELSE IF IN-CODE IS EQUAL TO 'M', PERFORM MEDIUM-SIZE
ELSE IF IN-CODE IS EQUAL TO 'L', PERFORM LARGE-SIZE
ELSE IF IN-CODE IS EQUAL TO 'X', PERFORM EXTRA-LARGE-SIZE.
```

(b) In a file of 10,000 transactions, how many comparisons would be saved if the IF statements were reordered to check for transactions in the order M, L, S, and X?

(c) What would have to be done in order to apply the GO TO DEPENDING in lieu of the series of IF statements?

2. Given Figure 11.2 illustrating the use of GO TO DEPENDING:

(a) What would happen if all the GO TO statements were removed and INCOMING-YEAR-CODE were equal to 1?

(b) What would happen if INCOMING-YEAR-CODE were equal to 6?

(c) Suppose the codes of interest were 10, 20, 30, 40, and 50 in lieu of 1, 2, 3, 4, and 5. Explain how the GO TO DEPENDING construct could still be used.

(d) Assume the codes of interest were 11, 17, 23, 46, and 59. Develop alternative code (i.e., a nested IF to accommodate the logic of Figure 11.2).

3. The program[1] in Figure 11.16 is designed to process an invoice file that has been *presorted* by location and by salesman. Each incoming record contains the salesman's name, amount of sale, invoice number, and location name. There can be many records, i.e., invoices, for one salesman. The program was designed to list all invoices in the file, with salesmen in the same location appearing on the same page. Individual totals are required for each salesman. Location totals are required as well. The program was tested with the following data and produced the output in Figure 11.17.

JOHN JONES	0500	123456	ATLANTA
JOHN JONES	2000	222222	ATLANTA
PETER SMITH	2800	100000	ATLANTA
PETER SMITH	3000	200000	ATLANTA
THOMAS TAYLOR	1500	300000	ATLANTA
JEFFRY BOROW	5000	373737	BOSTON
STEVEN GULFMAN	4300	424242	BOSTON
CHANDLER LLAVOR	8000	151100	CHICAGO
CRAIG TATER	0500	050000	CHICAGO

(a) Circle the errors in the printed report of Figure 11.17. Indicate what the report should look like.

(b) Circle and correct the errors in the COBOL program of Figure 11.16.

(c) Develop pseudocode and a hierarchy chart corresponding to the corrected program.

(d) Indicate how the top down approach to testing could be applied to this program; i.e., work backward and indicate a skeletal version of Figure 11.16 that could have been used in testing.

PROJECTS

1. Do Project 1, Chapter 15. This exercise is a typical sequential update and requires that input be taken from two files. Its logic will be similar to that of the inventory example in this chapter.

2. The personnel office of Gentle Electric Company requires some summary data on employee salaries. This large corporation has offices in several cities in the nation. Its personnel are also grouped into functional

[1] This is one of 17 problems on debugging that appears in R. Grauer, *A COBOL Book for Practice and Reference* (Englewood Cliffs, N.J.: Prentice-Hall, Inc., 1981).

```
00001               IDENTIFICATION DIVISION.
00002               PROGRAM-ID.   TWOLEVEL.
00003               AUTHOR.   R GRAUER.
00004               ENVIRONMENT DIVISION.
00005               CONFIGURATION SECTION.
00006               SOURCE-COMPUTER.    IBM-370.
00007               OBJECT-COMPUTER.    IBM-370.
00008               INPUT-OUTPUT SECTION.
00009               FILE-CONTROL.
00010                   SELECT SALES-FILE ASSIGN TO UT-S-SYSIN.
00011                   SELECT PRINT-FILE ASSIGN TO UT-S-SYSOUT.
00012
00013               DATA DIVISION.
00014               FILE SECTION.
00015               FD   SALES-FILE
00016                    LABEL RECORDS ARE OMITTED
00017                    RECORD CONTAINS 80 CHARACTERS
00018                    DATA RECORD IS TRANSACTION-RECORD.
00019               01   TRANSACTION-RECORD        PIC X(80).
00020               FD   PRINT-FILE
00021                    LABEL RECORDS ARE OMITTED
00022                    RECORD CONTAINS 133 CHARACTERS
00023                    DATA RECORD IS PRINT-LINE.
00024               01   PRINT-LINE                PIC X(133).
00025               WORKING-STORAGE SECTION.
00026               01   WS-PREVIOUS-SALESMAN      PIC X(20) VALUE SPACES.
00027               01   WS-PREVIOUS-LOCATION      PIC X(20) VALUE SPACES.
00028               01   WS-DATA-FLAG              PIC X(3)  VALUE SPACES.
00029                    88  NO-MORE-DATA                    VALUE 'NO '.
00030
00031               01   INTERMEDIATE-TOTALS.
00032                    05   THIS-LOCATION-SALES  PIC S9(6) VALUE ZEROS.
00033                    05   THIS-SALESMAN-SALES  PIC S9(4).
00034
00035               01   HEADING-LINE-ONE.
00036                    05   FILLER               PIC X(80) VALUE SPACES.
00037                    05   FILLER               PIC X(5)  VALUE 'PAGE '.
00038                    05   PAGE-NUMBER           PIC 9(4)  VALUE ZEROS.
00039                    05   FILLER               PIC X(44) VALUE SPACES.
00040
00041               01   HEADING-LINE-TWO.
00042                    05   FILLER               PIC X(10) VALUE SPACES.
00043                    05   FILLER               PIC X(20) VALUE 'SALESMAN NAME'.
00044                    05   FILLER               PIC X(10) VALUE SPACES.
00045                    05   FILLER               PIC X(15) VALUE 'LOCATION'.
00046                    05   FILLER               PIC X(10) VALUE SPACES.
00047                    05   FILLER               PIC X(13) VALUE 'TRANSACTION #'.
00048                    05   FILLER               PIC X(5)  VALUE SPACES.
00049                    05   FILLER               PIC X(4)  VALUE 'SALE'.
00050                    05   FILLER               PIC X(46) VALUE SPACES.
00051
00052               01   TRANSACTION-AREA.
00053                    05   TR-SALESMAN-NAME      PIC X(20).
00054                    05   TR-AMOUNT             PIC S9(4).
00055                    05   FILLER                PIC XX.
00056                    05   TR-NUMBER             PIC X(6).
00057                    05   FILLER                PIC X(18).
00058                    05   TR-SALESMAN-LOCATION  PIC X(20).
00059                    05   FILLER                PIC X(10).
00060
00061               01   SALESMAN-DETAIL-LINE.
00062                    05   FILLER                PIC X(10)   VALUE SPACES.
00063                    05   DETAIL-NAME           PIC X(20).
00064                    05   FILLER                PIC X(10)   VALUE SPACES.
00065                    05   DETAIL-LOCATION       PIC X(15).
00066                    05   FILLER                PIC X(12).
00067                    05   DETAIL-TRANSACTION    PIC X(6).
00068                    05   FILLER                PIC X(8).
00069                    05   DETAIL-SALES          PIC $Z,ZZ9.
00070                    05   FILLER                PIC X(46).
00071
00072               01   SALESMAN-TOTAL-LINE.
00073                    05   FILLER                PIC X(71) VALUE SPACES.
00074                    05   FILLER                PIC X(14) VALUE 'SALESMAN TOTAL'.
00075                    05   FILLER                PIC X(4)  VALUE SPACES.
```

FIGURE 11.16 *Two-Level Control Break Program with Execution Errors*

```
00076                       05   TOTAL-LINE-SALES      PIC $Z,ZZ9.
00077                       05   FILLER                PIC X(74) VALUE SPACES.
00078
00079                  01   LOCATION-TOTAL-LINE.
00080                       05   FILLER                PIC X(81) VALUE SPACES.
00081                       05   FILLER                PIC X(15) VALUE 'LOCATION TOTAL'.
00082                       05   FILLER                PIC X(9)  VALUE SPACES.
00083                       05   PRINT-LOCATION-SALES  PIC $$$$,999.
00084                       05   FILLER                PIC X(20) VALUE SPACES.
00085
00086              PROCEDURE DIVISION.
00087              0010-CREATE-REPORTS.
00088                  OPEN INPUT SALES-FILE
00089                       OUTPUT PRINT-FILE.
00090                  READ SALES-FILE INTO TRANSACTION-AREA
00091                       AT END MOVE 'NO ' TO WS-DATA-FLAG.
00092                  PERFORM A000-PROCESS-ALL-LOCATIONS UNTIL NO-MORE-DATA.
00093                  CLOSE SALES-FILE
00094                        PRINT-FILE.
00095                  STOP RUN.
00096
00097              A000-PROCESS-ALL-LOCATIONS.
00098                  MOVE TR-SALESMAN-LOCATION TO WS-PREVIOUS-LOCATION.
00099                  PERFORM A300-WRITE-LOCATION-HEADER.
00100                  PERFORM A100-PROCESS-ONE-LOCATION
00101                       UNTIL TR-SALESMAN-LOCATION NOT = WS-PREVIOUS-LOCATION
00102                          OR NO-MORE-DATA.
00103                  MOVE THIS-LOCATION-SALES TO PRINT-LOCATION-SALES.
00104                  WRITE PRINT-LINE FROM LOCATION-TOTAL-LINE
00105                       AFTER ADVANCING 2 LINES.
00106
00107              A100-PROCESS-ONE-LOCATION.
00108                  MOVE ZEROS TO THIS-SALESMAN-SALES.
00109                  MOVE TR-SALESMAN-NAME TO WS-PREVIOUS-SALESMAN.
00110                  PERFORM A310-PROCESS-ONE-SALESMAN
00111                       UNTIL TR-SALESMAN-NAME NOT = WS-PREVIOUS-SALESMAN
00112                          OR NO-MORE-DATA.
00113                  MOVE TR-AMOUNT TO TOTAL-LINE-SALES.
00114                  ADD THIS-SALESMAN-SALES TO THIS-LOCATION-SALES.
00115                  WRITE PRINT-LINE FROM SALESMAN-TOTAL-LINE
00116                       AFTER ADVANCING 2 LINES.
00117
00118              A300-WRITE-LOCATION-HEADER.
00119                  ADD 1 TO PAGE-NUMBER.
00120                  WRITE PRINT-LINE FROM HEADING-LINE-ONE
00121                       AFTER ADVANCING PAGE.
00122                  WRITE PRINT-LINE FROM HEADING-LINE-TWO
00123                       AFTER ADVANCING 2 LINES.
00124
00125              A310-PROCESS-ONE-SALESMAN.
00126                  MOVE SPACES TO SALESMAN-DETAIL-LINE.
00127                  MOVE TR-SALESMAN-NAME TO DETAIL-NAME.
00128                  MOVE TR-SALESMAN-LOCATION TO DETAIL-LOCATION.
00129                  MOVE TR-AMOUNT TO DETAIL-SALES.
00130                  MOVE TR-NUMBER TO DETAIL-TRANSACTION.
00131                  ADD TR-AMOUNT TO THIS-SALESMAN-SALES.
00132                  WRITE PRINT-LINE FROM SALESMAN-DETAIL-LINE
00133                       AFTER ADVANCING 2 LINES.
00134                  READ SALES-FILE INTO TRANSACTION-AREA
00135                       AT END MOVE 'NO ' TO WS-DATA-FLAG.
```

FIGURE 11.16 (continued)

departments, and a given department can appear in more than one city. The employee file has been sorted by location and by department within location. It contains a record for every employee in the company with the following data:

Columns	Field	Picture
1–15	LAST-NAME	X(15)
16–20	SALARY	9(5)
21–23	DEPARTMENT	9(3)
24–35	LOCATION	X(12)

```
                                                    PAGE 0003
   SALESMAN NAME              LOCATION          TRANSACTION #      SALE
   CHANDLER LLAVOR            CHICAGO             151100        $8,000
                                                  SALESMAN TOTAL    $  500
   CRAIG TATER               CHICAGO             050000       $  500
                                                  SALESMAN TOTAL    $  500
                                                      LOCATION TOTAL        $27,600
```

```
                                                    PAGE 0002
   SALESMAN NAME           LOCATION            TRANSACTION #     SALE
   JEFFRY BOROW            BOSTON               373737        $5,000
                                                SALESMAN TOTAL    $4,300
   STEVEN GULFMAN          BOSTON               424242        $4,300
                                                SALESMAN TOTAL    $8,000
                                                   LOCATION TOTAL       $19,100
```

```
                                                 PAGE 0001
   SALESMAN NAME         LOCATION           TRANSACTION #      SALE
   JOHN JONES            ATLANTA             123456        $  500
   JOHN JONES            ATLANTA             222222        $2,000
                                             SALESMAN TOTAL    $2,800
   PETER SMITH           ATLANTA             100000        $2,800
   PETER SMITH           ATLANTA             200000        $3,000
                                             SALESMAN TOTAL    $1,500
   THOMAS TAYLOR         ATLANTA             300000        $1,500
                                             SALESMAN TOTAL    $5,000
                                                LOCATION TOTAL       $9,800
```

FIGURE 11.17 *Incorrect Output of Double Control Break Program*

Write a program to compute the total salary for each location, as well as the various department subtotals within a location. Print a detail line showing all information for each employee. Begin the output for each location on a new page. Use the following test data:

ADAMS	15000100ATLANTA
BAKER	18000100ATLANTA
CHARLES	17000100ATLANTA
ALLEN	20000200ATLANTA
SMITH	14000200ATLANTA
JONES	25000100BOSTON
TYLER	26000250BOSTON
WEBER	18000300BOSTON
WHEELER	14000350BOSTON
GOODMAN	12000100CHICAGO
GORDON	12500100CHICAGO
DAVIS	15000150CHICAGO
ELSWORTH	18000150CHICAGO
HAYWARD	21000150CHICAGO
JACKSON	16000150CHICAGO
BABSON	14000150DETROIT

```
LEWIS          12000150DETROIT
HAYES          17000300DETROIT
JOHNSON        18000300DETROIT
KELLER         19000300DETROIT
```

As an *extra*, develop a subprogram that will accept department code and return a department name, which can then appear in the salary report. Use the following table of department codes:

Department Code	Department Name
100	DATA PROCESSING
150	LEGAL
200	FINANCIAL
250	MARKETING
300	MANUFACTURING
350	ACCOUNTING

Section IV

THE ROLE OF BAL
IN DEEPER
UNDERSTANDING

❋ Final Grades & Cum. Possibilities

LIKELY TO
OCCUR

CUM

A - COBOL
C - STATISTICS or B - COBOL
                    B - STATISTICS } 3.500   1ST

                    B - COBOL
                    C - STATISTICS } 3.333   2ND

                    A - COBOL
                    B - STATISTICS } 3.667   3RD

WORK-ON   WORK-ORDER

Nov. 16th, 17-21, 24-25, 29-30th   Dec. 2nd - Statistics Report Due (Two weeks from Nov. 18th) (Tues)

Nov. 22nd, 23rd, Dec 2-4th   Dec. 4th - (Last Day of Class) COBOL Program #5 Due
                                        (can also be turned in @ Final)

                              Dec 11th - COBOL Final (cumulative)

                              Dec 16th - STATISTICS Final.

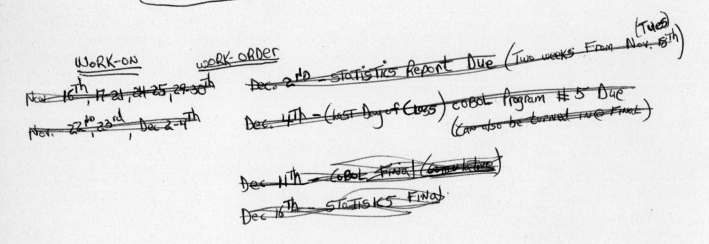

Chapter 12

NECESSARY BACKGROUND

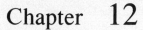

OVERVIEW

One of the reasons for using COBOL rather than a machine language is machine independence; i.e., a program written in ANS COBOL for an IBM system should run equally well, ideally with no modification, and practically with minimum modification on a Univac, Honeywell, or any other configuration. The concept of machine independence facilitates the learning of COBOL, or for that matter any other compiler language, in that knowledge of machine architecture is unnecessary. *Although the COBOL programmer need not know machine language, the authors are of the firm belief that even a superficial knowledge of the machine on which one is working greatly enhances the capabilities of the individual.* This is readily appreciated when one realizes the computer does not execute COBOL instructions per se but rather the machine language instructions generated by the COBOL compiler.

The next three chapters are designed to increase competence in COBOL through study of Assembler. In this chapter we shall introduce number systems, base/displacement addressing, internal representation, and instruction formats. In Chapter 13 we shall develop elementary capability in dump reading, and in Chapter 14 give an insight into the working of the COBOL compiler. The material may seem somewhat removed from COBOL, and perhaps it is. We maintain, however, that the best COBOL programmers are those who know a little more than COBOL.

NUMBER SYSTEMS

Fundamental to the next three chapters is a thorough understanding of number systems. A number system is merely a set of symbols controlled by a well-defined set of rules for measuring quantities. The value of every digit is determined by its position; as one moves from right to left (i.e., away from the decimal point), each succeeding digit is multiplied by a higher power of the base in which one is working. For example, the number 1976 in base 10 is equal to

$$1000 + 900 + 70 + 6$$
$$= 1 \times 10^3 + 9 \times 10^2 + 7 \times 10^1 + 6 \times 10^0$$

We commonly use the decimal number system (base 10), but the choice of a base is actually quite arbitrary. Ten was picked a few thousand years ago, probably because man has ten fingers and ten toes. The advent of digital computers has forced consideration of bases other than 10, and that is what this section is all about.

Number systems are easily understood if one approaches the subject from existing knowledge, i.e., base 10. Everything about any other base can be related back to base 10. *All concepts are identical.* Thus, the decimal system has 10 digits, 0 to 9; the octal (base 8) system has 8 digits, 0 to 7; and the binary (base 2) system has 2 digits, 0 and 1; etc. Engineering considerations make it impractical to build a "base 10" computer because 10 different physical levels would be required to represent each of the 10 digits. On the other hand, a binary machine is very easy to build, as only two values are required. A current may be on or off, a switch up or down, a magnetic field right or left, etc. All computers are built as binary machines, and for this reason we shall begin our study of number systems with base 2. To indicate which base we are talking about, we shall surround the number by ( )'s and use a subscript to indicate the base. If the parentheses are omitted, base 10 is assumed.

Binary

Base 2 has two digits, 0 and 1. The value of a digit is determined by its position, which represents some power of 2. The binary number $(10110)_2 = (22)_{10}$. The decimal value is obtained by expanding digits in the binary number by increasing powers of 2 as one moves away from the decimal point; thus,

$$
\begin{aligned}
(10110)_2 \\
0 \times 2^0 = 0 \times 1 &= 0 \\
1 \times 2^1 = 1 \times 2 &= 2 \\
1 \times 2^2 = 1 \times 4 &= 4 \\
0 \times 2^3 = 0 \times 8 &= 0 \\
1 \times 2^4 = 1 \times 16 &= 16 \\
&\overline{(22)_{10}}
\end{aligned}
$$

Easy enough? Try the following examples as practice:

$$(11011)_2 = (27)_{10} \quad \text{and} \quad (100101)_2 = (37)_{10}$$

Decimal to Binary

The reader should now be able to convert from binary to decimal; how does one go from decimal to binary? For example, what does $(18)_{10}$ equal in binary? One approach is to determine by trial and error which powers of 2 make up 18. After a few seconds, or minutes, we arrive at 16 and 2 and the binary number 10010. That approach is fine for small decimal numbers but doesn't work very well for large numbers. A more systematic way to go from decimal to binary is to repeatedly divide the decimal number by 2 until a quotient of zero is reached. The remainders, read in reverse order, constitute the binary number. Returning to the example, $(18)_{10} = (?)_2$,

$$
\begin{array}{ll}
2\underline{\big/\,18} & \\
2\underline{\big/\,9} & \text{remainder of 0} \\
2\underline{\big/\,4} & \text{remainder of 1} \\
2\underline{\big/\,2} & \text{remainder of 0} \\
2\underline{\big/\,1} & \text{remainder of 0} \\
\,0 & \text{remainder of 1}
\end{array}
\qquad \text{Answer} = (10010)_2
$$

As practice, consider the examples

$$(35)_{10} = (100011)_2 \quad \text{and} \quad (71)_{10} = (1000111)_2$$

Binary Addition

Just as one adds in decimal, one can add in binary. Binary addition is no more complicated than decimal addition; it just takes a little getting used to. However, the principles of addition in either base are identical, and if one truly understands decimal arithmetic, it should not be too difficult to work in binary, or, for that matter, in any other base. Consider first the following addition in base 10:

$$\begin{array}{r} 38 \\ +46 \\ \hline 84 \end{array}$$

If you add like most people, your thoughts begin with "8 + 6 = 14; write down 4 and carry 1." Now analyze that statement. We are working in base 10 with valid digits 0 to 9. "14" cannot be written as a single digit; thus, we subtract 10 (i.e., the base) from 14, and the result of 4 is valid as a single digit; we subtracted once and hence have a carry of 1. Involved? Yes, but that is precisely the process we follow. Addition in base 10 has become so ingrained over the years that we do all of that automatically. Now let's translate that thought process to the binary system:

$$\begin{array}{r} (10)_2 \\ +(11)_2 \\ \hline = \quad ? \end{array}$$

First, determine the result by converting each number to base 10, adding in base 10, and then converting the sum back to binary:

$$\begin{array}{r} (10)_2 \dashrightarrow (2)_{10} \\ (11)_2 \dashrightarrow (3)_{10} \\ \hline (101)_2 \leftarrow\!- (5)_{10} \end{array}$$

We need, however, to be able to perform the addition directly in binary without having to go through decimal, so let us add in binary, one column at a time. First, $(0)_2 + (1)_2 = (1)_2$. In the next column, we add 1 and 1 to get 2, except we can't write 2 as a single binary digit. Therefore, we subtract 2 from 2 and get zero, which is acceptable; we subtracted once and hence have a carry of 1. Returning to the initial example,

$$\begin{array}{r} \text{Carry} = \quad 1 \\ (10)_2 \\ (11)_2 \\ \hline (101)_2 \end{array}$$

It takes a little getting used to. To check your understanding and also to gain a little practice, consider Table 12.1 in which the binary equivalents of the decimal numbers 1 to 10 are obtained through repeated addition.

If you have been paying attention, you should now be able to convert from binary to decimal and from decimal to binary. You should also be able to do binary addition.

Hexadecimal

Although all computers function as binary machines, one never sees the internal contents displayed as binary numbers, simply because binary is too cumbersome. Nor does one see internal contents displayed as decimal numbers because binary-to-decimal conversion is time consuming and can be inexact with fractional numbers. The hexadecimal (base 16) number system solves both problems.

TABLE 12.1 Binary and Decimal Equivalents

Decimal		Binary
1	⟵————————⟶	1
		+ 1
2	⟵————————⟶	10
		+ 1
3	⟵————————⟶	11
		+ 1
4	⟵————————⟶	100
		+ 1
5	⟵————————⟶	101
		+ 1
6	⟵————————⟶	110
		+ 1
7	⟵————————⟶	111
		+ 1
8	⟵————————⟶	1000
		+ 1
9	⟵————————⟶	1001
		+ 1
10	⟵————————⟶	1010

It is much more concise than binary and provides direct and exact conversions to and from binary; i.e., four binary digits are exactly equal to one hex digit ($2^4 = 16$).

Just as base 10 has 10 digits, 0 to 9, base 16 has 16 digits, 0 to 15. The letter A represents 10, B represents 11, C is 12, D is 13, E is 14, and F is 15. In a decimal number each digit represents a power of 10; in a hex number each digit represents a power of 16. Consider the hex number $(12AB)_{16}$ and obtain its decimal equivalent:

$$(12AB)_{16}$$

$$B \times 16^0 = 11 \times \quad 1 = \quad 11$$
$$A \times 16^1 = 10 \times \quad 16 = \quad 160$$
$$2 \times 16^2 = \quad 2 \times 256 = \quad 512$$
$$1 \times 16^3 = \quad 1 \times 4096 = \underline{4096}$$
$$(4779)_{10}$$

Decimal to Hexadecimal

Conversion from decimal to hex is accomplished much the same as conversion from decimal to binary, except that we divide by 16 instead of 2. For example, $(1000)_{10} = (?)_{16}$:

$$16 \,\underline{/\, 1000}$$
$$16 \,\underline{/\,\quad 62} \quad \text{remainder of } 8$$
$$16 \,\underline{/\,\quad\quad 3} \quad \text{remainder of } 14 = E$$
$$\quad\quad 0 \quad \text{remainder of } 3$$

Answer $= (3E8)_{16}$

The remainders are read from the bottom up. Note that the remainder of 14 in decimal is converted to E in hex. As a check, we can convert $(3E8)_{16}$ to a decimal number and arrive at $(1000)_{10}$:

$$(3E8)_{16}$$

$$8 \times 16^0 = \quad 8 \times \quad 1 = \quad 8$$
$$E \times 16^1 = 14 \times \quad 16 = \quad 224$$
$$3 \times 16^2 = \quad 3 \times 256 = \underline{768}$$
$$(1000)_{10}$$

Hexadecimal Addition

Hexadecimal addition is made simple if we again use the thought processes of decimal arithmetic. Consider

$$
\begin{array}{r}
\text{Carry} = \ 1 \\
(39)_{16} \\
+\ (59)_{16} \\
\hline
(92)_{16}
\end{array}
$$

Nine and 9 are 18; hex cannot express 18 as a single-digit number; therefore, subtract 16 and get 2. Two is valid; we subtracted once and hence have a carry of 1. It seems complicated only because we are so used to decimal arithmetic. The concepts of addition are identical in both bases, and it should only be a matter of time and practice to be comfortable in both.

Since hexadecimal includes some "strange-looking" digits, i.e., A, B, C, D, E, and F, perhaps another example will be helpful. Consider

$$
\begin{array}{r}
\text{Carry} = \ 1 \\
(AB)_{16} \\
+\ (3\,7)_{16} \\
\hline
(E\,2)_{16}
\end{array}
$$

B and 7 are 18 (remember, B denotes 11). Hex cannot express 18 as a single digit; thus subtract 16, get 2, and carry 1. Now A, 3, and 1 (the carry) equal 14, which is represented to E in hex.

Binary to Hexadecimal Conversion

A computer functions internally as a binary machine, but its contents are often displayed as hex numbers. How does the conversion take place? Consider

$$(10110100)_2 = (??)_{16}$$

One way is to convert the binary number to a decimal number by expanding powers of 2 and then to convert the decimal number to its hex equivalent by repeated division by 16. Thus, $(10110100)_2 = (180)_{10} = (B4)_2$.

There is, however, a shortcut. Since $2^4 = 16$, there are exactly four binary digits to one hex digit. Simply take the binary number and divide it into groups of four digits; begin at the decimal point and work right to left, i.e., 1011   0100. Then take each group of four digits and mentally convert to hex. Thus, $(0100)_2 = (4)_{10} = (4)_{16}$ and $(1011)_2 = (11)_{10} = (B)_{16}$. The answer is then B4 in hex, which was obtained earlier.

The process works in reverse as well. The hex number ABC can be immediately converted to the binary number 101010111100. As verification, convert ABC to decimal and then go from decimal to binary.

The advantages of hex notation should now be apparent. It is a more concise representation of the internal workings of a machine than binary, yet unlike decimal conversion, it is immediate and exact. It should also occur to you that octal (base 8) would also be suitable as a shorthand, and indeed several computers use octal notation in lieu of hex.

INTERNAL DATA REPRESENTATION

The smallest addressable unit of storage is the *byte*. Each byte consists of 9 bits, 8 of which are used to represent data and a ninth bit, known as the parity bit, which is used for internal checking of data. The parity bit is of no concern to the programmer and is not discussed further.

TABLE 12.2 EBCDIC Configuration for Letters, Numbers, and Some Special Characters

Letters Character	EBCDIC Binary	EBCDIC Hex
A	1100 0001	C1
B	1100 0010	C2
C	1100 0011	C3
D	1100 0100	C4
E	1100 0101	C5
F	1100 0110	C6
G	1100 0111	C7
H	1100 1000	C8
I	1100 1001	C9
J	1101 0001	D1
K	1101 0010	D2
L	1101 0011	D3
M	1101 0100	D4
N	1101 0101	D5
O	1101 0110	D6
P	1101 0111	D7
Q	1101 1000	D8
R	1101 1001	D9
S	1110 0010	E2
T	1110 0011	E3
U	1110 0100	E4
V	1110 0101	E5
W	1110 0110	E6
X	1110 0111	E7
Y	1110 1000	E8
Z	1110 1001	E9

Numbers Character	EBCDIC Binary	EBCDIC Hex
0	1111 0000	F0
1	1111 0001	F1
2	1111 0010	F2
3	1111 0011	F3
4	1111 0100	F4
5	1111 0101	F5
6	1111 0110	F6
7	1111 0111	F7
8	1111 1000	F8
9	1111 1001	F9

Special Characters Character	EBCDIC Binary	EBCDIC Hex
Blank	0100 0000	40
.	0100 1011	4B
(	0100 1101	4D
+	0100 1110	4E
$	0101 1011	5B
*	0101 1100	5C
)	0101 1101	5D
—	0110 0000	60
/	0110 0001	61
,	0110 1011	6B
'	0111 1101	7D
=	0111 1110	7E

Three internal formats are of use to the COBOL programmer: EBCDIC, packed, and binary. (A fourth form, floating point, is useful in scientific languages, e.g., FORTRAN, but is not discussed here.[1])

Data represented according to EBCDIC (Extended Binary Coded Decimal Interchange Code) use specific byte combinations of 0's and 1's to denote different characters. Since a byte contains 8 data bits, each of which can assume either a 0 or 1, there are $2^8 = 256$ different combinations for a given byte. Table 12.2 displays the bit combinations for letters, numbers, and some special characters.

Yes, reader, there is a rhyme and reason to Table 12.2, at least where the letters and numbers are concerned. The 8 bits of a byte are divided into a zone and numeric portion as shown:

$$\boxed{\text{XXXX} \mid \text{XXXX}}$$

Zone   Digit

The 4 leftmost bits constitute the zone portion; the 4 rightmost bits make up the digit portion. Notice from Table 12.2 that the letters A to I all have the same zone (1100 in binary or C in hex). Note further that the letters J to R and S to Z and the digits 0 to 9 also have the same zones: D, E, and F, respectively.

Consider the word "COMPUTE" in EBCDIC. Since COMPUTE contains 7 characters, 7 bytes of storage are required. By Table 12.2, COMPUTE would appear internally as shown in Figure 12.1.

[1] See R. Grauer and M. Crawford, *The COBOL Environment*, Chapter 7 (Englewood Cliffs, N.J.: Prentice-Hall, Inc., 1979).

(Binary)	11000011	11010110	11010100	11010111	11100100	11100011	11000101
(Hex)	C3	D6	D4	D7	E4	E3	C5

FIGURE 12.1 *EBCDIC Representation of COMPUTE*

(Binary)	11110001	11110010	11110011	11110100	11110101
(Hex)	F1	F2	F3	F4	F5

FIGURE 12.2 *EBCDIC Representation of 12345*

Now suppose we wanted to represent the number "12345" in EBCDIC. This time, 5 bytes are required, and, again by Table 12.2, we get Figure 12.2. The "zone" portion of each byte is the same in Figure 12.2, and doesn't it seem inherently wasteful to use half of each byte for the zone when, in a numeric field, that zone is always 1111?

Packed Numbers

The packed format is used to represent numeric data more concisely. Essentially, it stores two numeric digits in 1 byte by eliminating the zone. This is done throughout except in the rightmost byte, which contains a numeric digit in the zone portion and the sign of the entire number in the digit portion. A "C" or "F" denotes a positive number, and a "D" represents a negative number. Figure 12.3 shows both positive and negative packed representations of the numbers 12345 and 67. Only 3 bytes are required to represent the number 12345 in packed format compared to 5 bytes in EBCDIC in Figure 12.2. Note, however, that the packed representation of numbers with an even number of digits, e.g., 67, always contains an extra half byte of zeros.

Both the EBCDIC and packed formats are said to represent variable-length fields in that the number of bytes required depends on the data that are stored. "COMPUTE" requires 7 bytes for EBCDIC representation and "IBM" only 3 bytes. "12345" take 3 bytes in packed format but "67" only 2 bytes.

Positive configuration (12345)

00010010	00110100	01011100	(Binary)
12	34	5C	(Hex)

Negative configuration (12345)

00010010	00110100	01011101	(Binary)
12	34	5D	(Hex)

Positive configuration (67)

00000110	01111100	(Binary)
06	7C	(Hex)

Negative configuration (67)

00000110	01111101	(Binary)
06	7D	(Hex)

FIGURE 12.3 *Packed Representation*

Binary Numbers

Numeric data can also be stored in fixed-length units as binary numbers. Two bytes (half-word), 4 bytes (word), or 8 bytes (double-word) are used depending on the size of a decimal number according to the rule

Up to 4 decimal digits	2 bytes
5–9 decimal digits	4 bytes
10–18 decimal digits	8 bytes

Some explanation is in order. Consider a half-word (16 bits). The largest positive number that can be represented is a 0 and fifteen 1's (the high-order zero indicates a plus sign), which equals $2^{15} - 1$ or 32,767. Any four-digit decimal number will fit in a half-word since the largest four-digit decimal number is only 9999. However, not all five-digit numbers will fit, and hence the limitation to four digits in a half-word.

The largest binary number that can be stored in a full word is $2^{31} - 1$, or 2,147,483,647 in decimal, and hence the limit of 9 decimal digits in a full-word. In similar fashion, a limit of 18 decimal digits is obtained for a double-word.

Two's Complement Notation

The sign of a binary number is indicated by its leftmost (high-order) bit. This is true regardless of whether the number occupies a half-word, word, or double-word. A "0" in the sign bit indicates a positive number; a "1" means the number is negative and stored in two's complement notation.

The two's complement of a number is obtained in two steps:

1. Reverse all bits; i.e., wherever there is a 0, make it 1, and wherever a 1 occurs, make it 0.
2. Add 1 to your answer from step 1.

For example, suppose we want the two's complement of 00101011:

Step 1:	Reverse all bits	11010100
Step 2:	Add 1 to answer from step 1	+ 1
		11010101

Thus, the two's complement of 00101011 is 11010101. As a check on the answer, simply add the original number and its calculated complement. The result should be all 0's and a high-order carry of 1:

Check: 00101011
                          +11010101
High-order carry → 1/00000000

Now that we can determine the sign of a number in storage and calculate its two's complement if necessary, consider the following half-words in storage:

(a) ⌐Sign
     | 0 | 0000000 | 00110001 |

(b) ⌐Sign
     | 1 | 1111111 | 11001111 |

In the example (a), the number is positive, as indicated by the high-order bit. Accordingly, its decimal value is simply +49. Example (b), however, has a sign bit of 1, indicating a negative number and further that the number itself is stored in two's complement. To get its decimal value, we must first get the two's complement of the number and then put a minus sign in front of our answer. You should get −49.

The COBOL USAGE Clause and Data Formats

We have stated that the COBOL programmer is typically concerned with three types of data format: EBCDIC, packed, and binary. The COBOL USAGE clause allows the programmer to explicitly specify how data are to be stored internally. (Omission of the clause causes default to EBCDIC, which often results in inefficient object code, as explained in Chapter 14.) Consider the following COBOL entries:

```
05   FIELD-A          PICTURE IS S9(3)
                 USAGE IS DISPLAY          VALUE IS +1.

05   FIELD-B          PICTURE IS S9(3)
                 USAGE IS COMPUTATIONAL-3   VALUE IS +1.

05   FIELD-C          PICTURE IS S9(3)
                 USAGE IS COMPUTATIONAL     VALUE IS +1.
```

In each instance we define a numeric constant of +1; however, each entry has a different usage specified, and hence the fields will have very different internal formats. In particular, USAGE IS DISPLAY indicates storage in zoned decimal (EBCDIC) format, COMPUTATIONAL-3 indicates packed format, and COMPUTATIONAL indicates binary format.

FIELD-A occupies 3 bytes of storage and stores the constant +1 in zoned decimal format, with high-order zeros. The internal representation of FIELD-A (shown in hex) is as follows:

F0	F0	C1

The reader may have expected F0F0F1, rather than F0F0C1. Recall that FIELD-A was defined with PIC S9(3). The specification of a sign in the picture clause causes the zone in the low-order position of the numeric field to be C rather than F. The reader could, however, think of C and F as being interchangeable plus signs, with no great loss of generality.

FIELD-B occupies 2 bytes of storage and stores the constant +1 in packed format, again with high-order zeros. Internal representation of FIELD-B (shown in hex) is as follows:

00	1C

FIELD-C is stored as a binary number with the number of bytes determined as per previous discussion. Thus, FIELD-C will occupy 2 bytes of storage as follows:

in binary: | 00000000 | 00000001 | in hex: | 00 | 01 |

BASE/DISPLACEMENT ADDRESSING

Since the byte is the smallest addressable unit of storage, every byte in main storage is assigned an address. The 360/370/303X/4300 are designed to reach a maximum address of 16,776,216, the equivalent of a 24-bit binary number. This implies that an instruction referencing two addresses in storage would require 6 bytes (48 bits) for the addresses alone, and clearly this is far too costly in terms of storage requirements. The solution is known as base/displacement addressing.

The addressing scheme uses the CPU's general-purpose registers (GPR's) to reduce storage requirements. A GPR is a hardware device capable of holding information during processing. Information is transferred to or from a register much faster than from main storage. There are 16 GPR's numbered from hex 0 to F. Each GPR contains 32 bits.

In the base/displacement method, memory is divided into units of 4096 (2^{12}) bytes. A 24-bit base address is loaded into a register, which is then designated as a *base* register. A 12-bit *displacement* is calculated for each location. (The displacement of a location is defined as the number of bytes higher, i.e., greater, than the base address.) The address of a particular location is determined by specifying a base register and displacement from that base. Since it takes only 4 bits to designate a base register (0 to F) and 12 bits for a displacement, we are effectively providing a 24-bit address in only 16 bits.

Consider the following example: GPR 7 has been designated as the base register. A program is to be stored beginning at core location $(8000)_{16}$, which is loaded into the 24 low-order bits of register 7 as the base address. It is required to reference core location $(8500)_{16}$. Given a base address of $(8000)_{16}$, the displacement for location $(8500)_{16}$ is calculated to be $(500)_{16}$. Now we have the 16 bits to specify the address of memory location $(8500)_{16}$, as shown in Figure 12.4. Four bits are used to designate GPR 7, and 12 bits are used for the hex displacement 500.

There is another major advantage to the base/displacement method in addition to economy of space. All programs are easily *relocatable;* i.e., all addresses in a given program are easily changed by altering only the contents of the base register(s).

Assumptions:
1. GPR 7 is the base register.
2. $(8000)_{16}$ is the base address, which is loaded into register 7.
3. $(500)_{16}$ is the calculated displacement.

	Base	Displacement		
(Binary)	0111	0101	0000	0000
(Hex)	7	5	0	0

FIGURE 12.4 *Base/Displacement Representation of Address* $(8500)_{16}$

INSTRUCTION FORMATS

The 360/370/303X/4300 series have different, but parallel, instructions for different data types. The instruction to add two packed numbers is different from the instruction to add two binary numbers; indeed the instruction to add binary half-words is different from that for binary full-words. The instruction set is designed in such a way that the instruction's length and format are dependent on the type and location of data on which it is to operate. Specifically, there are five types of instructions:

RR   Register to register (2 bytes long)
RX   Register to indexed storage (4 bytes long)
RS   Register to storage (4 bytes long)
SI   Storage immediate (4 bytes long)
SS   Storage to storage (6 bytes long)

Any of these instruction types provides the following information to the computer:

1. The operation to be performed, e.g., addition or subtraction.
2. The location of the operands, e.g., in registers, storage, or immediate (i.e., in the instruction).
3. The nature of the data, i.e., fixed or variable in length, and if the latter, then the length of the data field(s).

Machine instruction formats are displayed in Figure 12.5. Although Figure 12.5 may not make much sense now, it will assume greater importance in Chapters 13 and 14 when *dump reading* and efficiency considerations are studied. An explanation of the notation of Figure 12.5 is helpful:

OP   Operation code
B   Base register

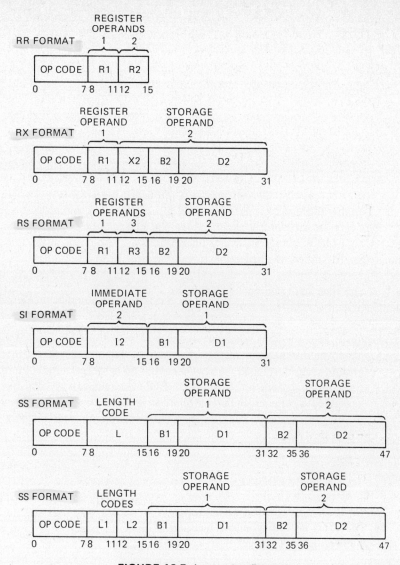

FIGURE 12.5 *Instruction Formats*

D   Displacement
X   Register designated as an index register (RX only)
R   Register designated as an operand
I   Immediate data; i.e., the operand is contained in the instruction itself (SI only)
L   Length; used only for variable-length operands in SS format

In later chapters, it will become necessary to disect a machine instruction into its component parts. Consider the instruction D205A0103050.

Using Figure 12.5, we must somehow decipher this cryptic combination of characters. The key is the first byte of the instruction, which contains the op code, D2. Armed with this essential piece of information, we go to Appendix D, 360/370 Assembler Instructions, and find that D2 is the machine op code for MVC (move characters), an SS instruction. We are therefore able to separate the essential components of the instruction according to Figure 12.5:

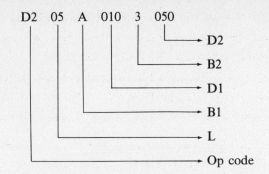

Essentially, the instruction is moving 6 bytes (always 1 more than the length code) beginning at the address specified in the second operand to the address specified in the first operand. Both addresses are derived according to the base/displacement scheme.

The workings of several instructions are explained in the first part of Chapter 14. Appreciation for the different instruction formats comes from the realization that data are stored internally in varying formats. Thus the instruction to add two binary numbers is necessarily different from the one that adds two packed numbers.

SUMMARY

Much of the material in this chapter may seem somewhat removed from COBOL. However, the groundwork developed here is essential to a deeper understanding of COBOL, especially since the computer does not execute COBOL instructions as such but rather the machine instructions generated by the COBOL compiler. It is imperative that the reader be familiar with the material on number systems, base/displacement addressing, and instruction formats before proceeding to Chapters 13 and 14.

REVIEW EXERCISES

TRUE   FALSE

☐   ☐   **1.** Every instruction must contain an op code.

☐   ☐   **2.** Mathematically, there are 256 possible op codes.

☐   ☐   **3.** The op code is the second byte in the instruction.

☐   ☐   **4.** Instructions are 2, 4, 6, or 8 bytes in length.

☐   ☐   **5.** Instructions are a half-word, word, or double-word in length.

☐   ☐   **6.** There are 16 general-purpose registers in the 360/370/303X/4300 series.

☐   ☐   **7.** If the COBOL USAGE clause is omitted, the default is to COMPUTATIONAL.

☐   ☐   **8.** Mathematically, there are 256 possible EBCDIC characters.

☐   ☐   **9.** The EBCDIC character for the letter A is D1.

☐   ☐   **10.** The displacement takes 12 bits in an instruction.

☐   ☐   **11.** The base/displacement scheme provides for an effective address of 24 bits.

☐   ☐   **12.** 123 is a valid number in base 16.

☐   ☐   **13.** 123 is a valid number in base 3.

☐   ☐   **14.** There are five different instruction types.

☐   ☐   **15.** USAGE IS COMP-3 corresponds to the packed format.

☐   ☐   **16.** Binary data are stored internally in 2, 4, or 6 bytes.

☐   ☐   **17.** There are two formats for the SS instruction.

☐   ☐   **18.** The high-order bit of a binary number denotes its sign.

□ □ **19.** The high-order 4 bits of a packed field denote its sign.

□ □ **20.** For packed numbers, either C or F indicates a plus sign.

□ □ **21.** For packed numbers, D indicates a minus sign.

□ □ **22.** A three-digit decimal number requires 2 bytes if USAGE is specified as COMP or COMP-3.

□ □ **23.** A five-digit decimal number requires 4 bytes if USAGE is specified as COMP or COMP-3.

□ □ **24.** The two's complement of a number is obtained just by switching 0's and 1's.

PROBLEMS

1. Indicate the instruction type that
(a) Has an operand contained in the instruction itself.
(b) Uses two registers to calculate a storage address.
(c) References two storage locations.
(d) Is 6 bytes long.
(e) Does not reference a storage location.
(f) Is 2 bytes long.
(g) Contains one length code.
(h) Contains two length codes.

2. Show internal representation for the following entries:

```
05  FIELD-A   PIC 9(5) COMP     VALUE 67.
05  FIELD-B   PIC 9(5) COMP-3   VALUE 67.
05  FIELD-C   PIC 9(5) DISPLAY  VALUE 67.
05  FIELD-D   PIC 9(5)          VALUE 67.
```

3. What is the EBCDIC representation for "COBOL"? (Show both hex and binary configurations.)

4. (a) $(1001101)_2$
$+(0111111)_2$
$\overline{\qquad ?}$

(b) $(1001101)_2$
$-(0111111)_2$
$\overline{\qquad ?}$

Check your answers to parts (a) and (b) by converting to decimal, performing the indicated operation, and converting the decimal answer back to binary.

5. (a) $(ABCD)_{16}$
$+(1\,2\,3\,4)_{16}$
$\overline{\qquad ?}$

(b) $(ABCD)_{16}$
$-(1\,2\,3\,4)_{16}$
$\overline{\qquad ?}$

Check your answers as in Problem 4.

6. (a) $(1010110)_2 = (?)_{10} = (?)_{16}$.
(b) $(?)_2 = (49)_{10} = (?)_{16}$.
(c) $(?)_2 = (?)_{10} = (49)_{16}$.

7. Although we have studied only bases 2, 10, and 16, the concepts are applicable to any base. Accordingly, you should be able to do the following:
(a) $(432)_5 = (?)_{10}$.
(b) $(100)_{10} = (?)_6$.
(c) $(2222)_3 = (?)_7$.
(d) $(1100110)_2 = (?)_4 = (?)_8 = (?)_{16}$.
(e) $(1234)_9$
$+(5678)_9$
$\overline{\qquad ?}$

8. What is the decimal value of the following half-words in storage?
(a) 11111111 11111111
(b) 01111111 11111111
(c) 10000000 00000000

9. Assume the contents of register 3 are $(00001234)_{16}$ and the contents of register 10 are $(00005678)_{16}$. Given the instruction D2023123A500:
(a) What is the effective address of the second operand?
(b) What is the effective address of the first operand?
(c) What is the nature of the instruction?

Chapter 13

DEBUGGING, II

OVERVIEW

Should the COBOL applications programmer have a knowledge of Assembler language? We answer with an emphatic yes, but there are those who would disagree. Although one can invariably find someone to debug a program, self-sufficiency and complete understanding demand at least some knowledge of Assembler and machine architecture.

As you have undoubtedly learned by now, there are many ways for your program not to work. Errors can be broadly separated into those which occur in compilation and those occurring during execution. The latter are further divided into two classes:

1. Errors that do not prevent execution of the entire job but that produce calculated results different from what the programmer expected.
2. Errors that result in the machine's inability to execute a particular instruction, thus causing an abnormal end (ABEND) of the job.

Chapter 5 dealt with compilation errors and execution errors of the first kind. This chapter is devoted to debugging the second type of execution error with emphasis placed on the *data exception*. We shall focus on two errors commonly made by beginning programmers: (1) failure to initialize a counter and (2) invalid input data.

When a program ABENDs, it is because the computer was instructed to do something it found impossible to perform. At that point, the COBOL program relinquishes control to the operating system, which then prints a rather cryptic message indicating the reason for the ABEND. Unfortunately, that message is rarely enough to indicate the exact cause or location of the problem. One's primary recourse is to the memory dump and related information. This type of debugging relies heavily on the concepts of number systems, base/displacement addressing, and instruction formats developed in Chapter 12. OS listings are used for all illustrations in this chapter, but the differences between OS and DOS are not great at the level of our discussion. The principal difference relates to finding the entry point of the main program, and this is discussed at the chapter's end.

THE MEMORY DUMP

Figure 13.1 illustrates a dump. The contents of internal storage are strictly binary but are displayed in hex for conciseness. A dump appears somewhat foreboding to the uninitiated, but as with everything else, a little practice goes a long way. The essential thing to remember in analyzing Figure

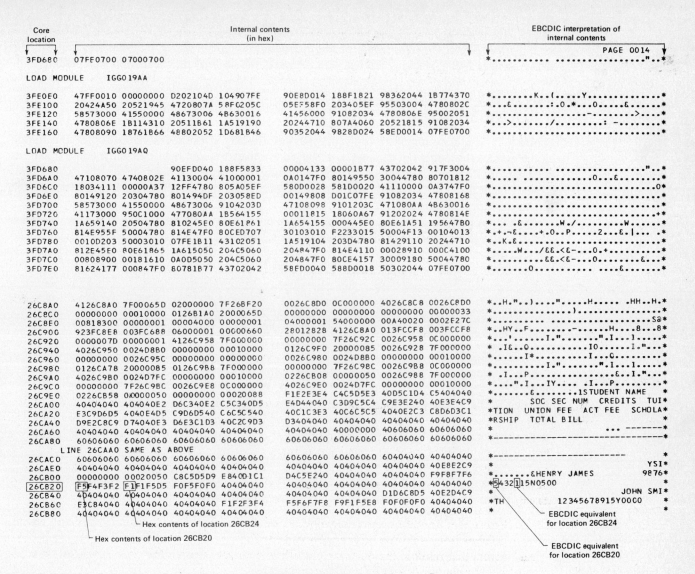

Core location	Internal contents (in hex)	EBCDIC interpretation of internal contents

FIGURE 13.1 *Illustrative Memory Dump*

13.1 is that a dump is merely a picture of memory contents at a given instant of time. The leftmost column of the dump indicates the internal location number. Subsequent digits are the contents of that location and others. Since the smallest addressable location is the byte (8 bits or 2 hex digits), every 2 hex digits indicate the contents of a particular byte.

Go down the first column in Figure 13.1 until you read 26CB20. The 2 hex digits immediately following are F5, indicating that the contents of byte 26CB20 are F5. The next 2 hex digits, F4, are the contents of the next sequential location, 26CB21. In similar fashion, F3 is the contents of 26CB22, F2 is the contents of 26CB23, etc. There are a total of 64 hex digits on the line beginning with 26CB20. Accordingly, the contents of 32 bytes beginning at 26CB20 and continuing to 26CB3F are shown on the same line. The first 2 hex digits on the next line will be the contents of location 26CB40.

Immediately following the 64 hex digits on a given line is the corresponding alphabetic interpretation of those digits. According to the EBCDIC configurations of Table 12.2, F5 is the representation for 5, F4 for 4, and so forth. Many of the interpretation columns are blank because the contents of the corresponding locations are hex 40's, which is the internal representation of a blank.

DUMP READING: EXAMPLE 1
(FAILURE TO INITIALIZE A COUNTER)

Figure 13.2 is a close duplicate (only line 63 was altered) of the COBOL listing for the tuition billing example introduced in Chapter 4, debugged in Chapter 5, and rewritten with coding standards in Chapter 6. Execution terminated after printing only the heading line and the message "COMPLETION CODE SYSTEM = 0C7," followed by pages of semiintelligible data culminating in a dump. Where do we go from here?

First, look up the meaning of an "0C7" error in the IBM manual *Operating System: Messages and Codes* and find that 0C7 is a data exception, indicating that an attempt was made to do

```
00001          IDENTIFICATION DIVISION.
00002          PROGRAM-ID.  'TUITION'.
00003          AUTHOR.      THE BURSAR.
00004
00005          ENVIRONMENT DIVISION.
00006          CONFIGURATION SECTION.
00007          SOURCE-COMPUTER.  IBM-370.
00008          OBJECT-COMPUTER.  IBM-370.
00009          INPUT-OUTPUT SECTION.
00010          FILE-CONTROL.
00011              SELECT STUDENT-FILE ASSIGN TO UT-S-SYSIN.
00012              SELECT PRINT-FILE ASSIGN TO UT-S-SYSOUT.
00013
00014          DATA DIVISION.
00015          FILE SECTION.
00016          FD  STUDENT-FILE
00017              LABEL RECORDS ARE OMITTED
00018              RECORD CONTAINS 80 CHARACTERS
00019              DATA RECORD IS STUDENT-RECORD.
00020          01  STUDENT-RECORD.
00021              05  SR-STUDENT-NAME      PIC A(20).
00022              05  SR-SOC-SEC-NO        PIC 9(9).
00023              05  SR-CREDITS           PIC 9(2).
00024              05  SR-UNION-MEMBER      PIC A.
00025              05  SR-SCHOLARSHIP       PIC 9(4).
00026              05  FILLER               PIC X(44).
00027
00028          FD  PRINT-FILE
00029              LABEL RECORDS ARE OMITTED
00030              RECORD CONTAINS 133 CHARACTERS
00031              DATA RECORD IS PRINT-LINE.
00032          01  PRINT-LINE.
00033              05  FILLER               PIC X.
00034              05  PRINT-STUDENT-NAME   PIC A(20).
00035              05  FILLER               PIC X(2).
00036              05  PRINT-SOC-SEC-NO     PIC 999B99B9999.
00037              05  FILLER               PIC X(4).
00038              05  PRINT-CREDITS        PIC 99.
00039              05  FILLER               PIC X(3).
00040              05  PRINT-TUITION        PIC $$$$,$$9.
00041              05  FILLER               PIC X.
00042              05  PRINT-UNION-FEE      PIC $$$$,$$9.
00043              05  FILLER               PIC X(3).
00044              05  PRINT-ACTIVITY-FEE   PIC $$$$,$$9.
00045              05  FILLER               PIC X(3).
00046              05  PRINT-SCHOLARSHIP    PIC $$$$,$$9.
00047              05  FILLER               PIC X(5).
00048              05  PRINT-IND-BILL       PIC $$$$,$$9.
00049              05  FILLER               PIC X(38).
00050
00051          WORKING-STORAGE SECTION.
00052
00053          01  PROGRAM-SWITCHES.
00054              05  DATA-REMAINS-SWITCH  PIC X(2)   VALUE SPACES.
```

FIGURE 13.2 *COBOL Listing for Tuition Billing Problem Causing ABEND*

```
00055
00056          01   INDIVIDUAL-CALCULATIONS.
00057              05    IND-TUITION           PIC 9(4)    VALUE ZEROS.
00058              05    IND-ACTIVITY-FEE      PIC 9(2)    VALUE ZEROS.
00059              05    IND-UNION-FEE         PIC 9(2)    VALUE ZEROS.
00060              05    IND-STUDENT-BILL      PIC 9(6)    VALUE ZEROS.
00061                                                              ┌─Value zeros
00062          01   UNIVERSITY-TOTALS.                             │ missing
00063              05    TOTAL-TUITION         PIC 9(6).  ┌─────────┘
00064              05    TOTAL-SCHOLARSHIP     PIC 9(6)    VALUE ZEROS.
00065              05    TOTAL-ACTIVITY-FEE    PIC 9(6)    VALUE ZEROS.
00066              05    TOTAL-UNION-FEE       PIC 9(6)    VALUE ZEROS.
00067              05    TOTAL-IND-BILL        PIC 9(6)    VALUE ZEROS.
00068
00069          01   DASHED-LINE.
00070              05    FILLER                PIC X       VALUE SPACES.
00071              05    FILLER                PIC X(97)   VALUE ALL '-'.
00072              05    FILLER                PIC X(35)   VALUE SPACES.
00073
00074          01   HEADER-LINE.
00075              05    FILLER                PIC X.
00076              05    HDG-NAME              PIC X(12)   VALUE 'STUDENT NAME'.
00077              05    FILLER                PIC X(10)   VALUE SPACES.
00078              05    HDG-SOC-SEC           PIC X(11)   VALUE 'SOC SEC NUM'.
00079              05    FILLER                PIC X(2)    VALUE SPACES.
00080              05    HDG-CREDITS           PIC X(7)    VALUE 'CREDITS'.
00081              05    FILLER                PIC X(2)    VALUE SPACES.
00082              05    HDG-TUITION           PIC X(7)    VALUE 'TUITION'.
00083              05    FILLER                PIC X(2)    VALUE SPACES.
00084              05    HDG-UNION-FEE         PIC X(9)    VALUE 'UNION FEE'.
00085              05    FILLER                PIC X(2)    VALUE SPACES.
00086              05    HDG-ACTIVITY          PIC X(7)    VALUE 'ACT FEE'.
00087              05    FILLER                PIC X(2)    VALUE SPACES.
00088              05    HDG-SCHOLAR           PIC X(11)   VALUE 'SCHOLARSHIP'.
00089              05    FILLER                PIC X(2)    VALUE SPACES.
00090              05    HDG-TOTAL-BILL        PIC X(10)   VALUE 'TOTAL BILL'.
00091              05    FILLER                PIC X(36)   VALUE SPACES.
00092          PROCEDURE DIVISION.
00093          0010-MAINLINE.
00094              OPEN INPUT STUDENT-FILE
00095                   OUTPUT PRINT-FILE.
00096              MOVE HEADER-LINE TO PRINT-LINE.
00097              WRITE PRINT-LINE AFTER ADVANCING PAGE.
00098              MOVE DASHED-LINE TO PRINT-LINE.
00099              WRITE PRINT-LINE AFTER ADVANCING 1 LINE.
00100              PERFORM 0040-READ-A-RECORD.
00101              PERFORM 0020-PROCESS-A-RECORD
00102                   UNTIL DATA-REMAINS-SWITCH = 'NO'.
00103              PERFORM 0030-WRITE-UNIVERSITY-TOTALS.
00104              CLOSE STUDENT-FILE
00105                    PRINT-FILE.
00106              STOP RUN.
00107
00108          0020-PROCESS-A-RECORD.
00109              COMPUTE IND-TUITION = 80 * SR-CREDITS.
00110              IF SR-UNION-MEMBER = 'Y'
00111                  MOVE 25 TO IND-UNION-FEE
00112              ELSE
00113                  MOVE ZERO TO IND-UNION-FEE.
00114
00115              IF SR-CREDITS > 12
00116                  MOVE 75 TO IND-ACTIVITY-FEE
00117              ELSE
00118                  IF SR-CREDITS > 6
00119                      MOVE 50 TO IND-ACTIVITY-FEE
00120                  ELSE
00121                      MOVE 25 TO IND-ACTIVITY-FEE.
00122
00123              COMPUTE IND-STUDENT-BILL = IND-TUITION + IND-ACTIVITY-FEE
00124                   + IND-UNION-FEE - SR-SCHOLARSHIP.
00125
00126      *** INCREMENT UNIVERSITY TOTALS
00127              ADD IND-TUITION        TO TOTAL-TUITION.
00128              ADD IND-UNION-FEE      TO TOTAL-UNION-FEE.
00129              ADD IND-ACTIVITY-FEE   TO TOTAL-ACTIVITY-FEE.
```

FIGURE 13.2 (continued)

```
00130                 ADD IND-STUDENT-BILL      TO TOTAL-IND-BILL.
00131                 ADD SR-SCHOLARSHIP        TO TOTAL-SCHOLARSHIP.
00132
00133         *** WRITE DETAIL LINE.
00134                 MOVE SPACES               TO PRINT-LINE.
00135                 MOVE SR-STUDENT-NAME      TO PRINT-STUDENT-NAME.
00136                 MOVE SR-SOC-SEC-NO        TO PRINT-SOC-SEC-NO.
00137                 MOVE SR-CREDITS           TO PRINT-CREDITS.
00138                 MOVE IND-TUITION          TO PRINT-TUITION.
00139                 MOVE IND-UNION-FEE        TO PRINT-UNION-FEE.
00140                 MOVE IND-ACTIVITY-FEE     TO PRINT-ACTIVITY-FEE.
00141                 MOVE SR-SCHOLARSHIP       TO PRINT-SCHOLARSHIP.
00142                 MOVE IND-STUDENT-BILL     TO PRINT-IND-BILL.
00143                 WRITE PRINT-LINE AFTER ADVANCING 1 LINE.
00144
00145                 PERFORM 0040-READ-A-RECORD.
00146
00147         0030-WRITE-UNIVERSITY-TOTALS.
00148                 MOVE DASHED-LINE TO PRINT-LINE.
00149                 WRITE PRINT-LINE AFTER ADVANCING 1 LINE.
00150                 MOVE SPACES               TO PRINT-LINE.
00151                 MOVE TOTAL-TUITION        TO PRINT-TUITION.
00152                 MOVE TOTAL-UNION-FEE      TO PRINT-UNION-FEE.
00153                 MOVE TOTAL-ACTIVITY-FEE TO PRINT-ACTIVITY-FEE.
00154                 MOVE TOTAL-SCHOLARSHIP   TO PRINT-SCHOLARSHIP.
00155                 MOVE TOTAL-IND-BILL       TO PRINT-IND-BILL.
00156                 WRITE PRINT-LINE AFTER ADVANCING 2 LINES.
00157
00158         0040-READ-A-RECORD.
00159                 READ STUDENT-FILE
00160                     AT END MOVE 'NO' TO DATA-REMAINS-SWITCH.
```

FIGURE 13.2 *(continued)*

arithmetic on invalid, i.e., nondecimal, data. Next, we turn to various aids supplied for these situations and try to determine the exact nature of the data exception. In particular, consider the data division map (Figure 13.3), register assignments (Figure 13.4), and procedure division map (Figure 13.5).

Figure 13.3 is a truncated data division map for Figure 13.2. A data division map lists all the data names in a given program and ties them to internal addresses by specifying a base locator (later tied to a base register) and a displacement. All data names within one file are assigned the same base locator. Thus, BL = 1 for all entries in STUDENT-FILE and BL = 2 for PRINT-FILE. All entries in working-storage are assigned BL = 3.

The base locators are tied to specific base registers by a table of register assignments shown in Figure 13.4. BL = 1 points to register 7, BL = 2 to register 8, and BL = 3 to register 6.[1]

Figure 13.5 is a truncated procedure division map corresponding to Figure 13.2. It contains information about the actual machine language statements generated by the compiler. Reading from left to right in Figure 13.5, the four columns denote

1. The COBOL statement number.
2. The COBOL verb referenced in the statement number.
3. The relative location, in hex, of the machine instruction.
4. The actual machine instruction.

Recall that the "instruction explosion" effect causes a single COBOL instruction to generate several machine language statements; e.g., COBOL statement 123 (COMPUTE) spawned nine machine language statements; statement 127 (ADD), five statements; etc.

A large amount of data is supplied in conjunction with a dump. The utility of this information varies with the experience of the individual, but certain portions are of immediate use. We have extracted some of the more essential information and grouped it into Figure 13.6, which contains (1) the cause of the ABEND, (2) the contents of the program status word (PSW) at ABEND, (3) the entry point address (EPA) of the COBOL program, and (4) the contents of the registers at ABEND.

---

[1] A more complete explanation of the role of base locators can be found in R. Grauer and M. Crawford, *The COBOL Environment,* Chapter 8 (Englewood Cliffs, N.J.: Prentice-Hall, Inc., 1979).

```
COBOL
level #        COBOL data name                           Pointer
                                                        to GPR  Displacement

           LVL  SOURCE NAME                             BASE   DISPL
           FD   STUDENT-FILE                            DCB=01
           01   STUDENT-RECORD                          BL=1   000
           02   SR-STUDENT-NAME                         BL=1   000
           02   SR-SOC-SEC-NO                           BL=1   014
           02   SR-CREDITS                              BL=1   01D
           02   SR-UNION-MEMBER                         BL=1   01F
           02   SR-SCHOLARSHIP                          BL=1   020
           02   FILLER                                  BL=1   024
           FD   PRINT-FILE                              DCB=02
           01   PRINT-LINE                              BL=2   000
           02   FILLER                                  BL=2   000
           02   PRINT-STUDENT-NAME                      BL=2   001
           02   FILLER                                  BL=2   015
           02   PRINT-SOC-SEC-NO                        BL=2   017
           02   FILLER                                  BL=2   022
           02   PRINT-CREDITS                           BL=2   026
           02   FILLER                                  BL=2   028
           02   PRINT-TUITION                           BL=2   02B
           02   FILLER                                  BL=2   033
           02   PRINT-UNION-FEE                         BL=2   034
           02   FILLER                                  BL=2   03C
           02   PRINT-ACTIVITY-FEE                      BL=2   03F
           02   FILLER                                  BL=2   047
           02   PRINT-SCHOLARSHIP                       BL=2   04A
           02   FILLER                                  BL=2   052
           02   PRINT-IND-BILL                          BL=2   057
           02   FILLER                                  BL=2   05F
           01   PROGRAM-SWITCHES                        BL=3   000
           02   DATA-REMAINS-SWITCH                     BL=3   000
           01   INDIVIDUAL-CALCULATIONS                 BL=3   003
           02   IND-TUITION                             BL=3   003
           02   IND-ACTIVITY-FEE                        BL=3   00C
           02   IND-UNION-FEE                           BL=3   00E
           02   IND-STUDENT-BILL                        BL=3   010
           01   UNIVERSITY-TOTALS                       BL=3   018
           02   TOTAL-TUITION                           BL=3   018
           02   TOTAL-SCHOLARSHIP                       BL=3   01E
           02   TOTAL-ACTIVITY-FEE                      BL=3   024
           02   TOTAL-UNION-FEE                         BL=3   02A
           02   TOTAL-IND-BILL                          BL=3   030
```

FIGURE 13.3 *Truncated Data Division Map for Figure 13.2*

```
                    REGISTER ASSIGNMENT

                    REG 6    BL =3
                    REG 7    BL =1
                    REG 8    BL =2
```

FIGURE 13.4 *Register Assignment for Figure 13.2*

We shall now begin the analysis of a dump. The last 3 bytes (6 hex digits) of the PSW provide the location of the interrupt. Subtraction of the entry point address (EPA) of the COBOL program from the 3 bytes in the PSW yields the *relative* address, i.e., the location within the COBOL program of the error. Thus, using Figure 13.6,

Address from PSW	096 8 B 2
− Entry point of COBOL program	− 095DA 8
Relative address	B 0 A

All addresses in a dump are specified in hexadecimal; thus the subtraction is also in hex. Now take the relative address (B0A) to the procedure division map and find that B0A occurs within COBOL statement 127, indicating that program execution terminated within this COBOL statement. The instruction at B0A is the next instruction that would have been executed had the

ABEND not occurred; the instruction that caused the problem is the one immediately before at B04. However, both machine instructions are contained within the COBOL ADD instruction of line 127.

To determine the exact cause of the error, we examine the machine language instruction at B04, which failed to execute. It has an op code of FA, and from the material on instruction formats in Chapter 12, we dissect the instruction as follows:

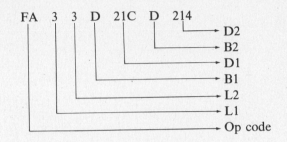

From Appendix D, we learn that FA is the op code for *add packed*. The instruction at B04 will add the contents of the second operand to the contents of the first operand and store the results in the first operand. The addresses of both operands are calculated in accordance with the base displacement addressing scheme discussed in Chapter 12.

We see that both operands use general register D (i.e., GPR 13) as a base register. The first operand has a displacement of 21C and the second a displacement of 214. From Figure 13.6 the address in register 13 is found to be 096250. Simple addition (in hex) locates both operands:

$$\begin{array}{rl} \text{Contents of register 13} & = 096250 \\ + \text{ 1st displacement} & = + \quad 21\text{C} \\ \hline \text{Location of 1st operand} & = 09646\text{C} \end{array}$$

$$\begin{array}{rl} \text{Contents of register 13} & = 096250 \\ + \text{ 2nd displacement} & = + \quad 214 \\ \hline \text{Location of 2nd operand} & = 096464 \end{array}$$

The first operand begins at location 09646C. Its length code in the add packed instruction is 3, so that the first operand extends 3 bytes past 09646C; i.e., the first operand is in location 09646C through 09646F. (Remember, the actual number of bytes is always one more than the corresponding length code.) In similar fashion, the second operand is located in 096464 through 096467.

The dump of Figure 13.7 is used to get the actual operands. The first, located in 09646C through 09646F, has a value of 0001200F, a valid packed number. The second operand, located in 096464 through 096467, is equal to 00000000, an invalid packed field; hence the data exception and dump.

In effect, we have determined the precise cause of the ABEND, i.e., invalid data in the second operand, but it seems somewhat removed from the COBOL program. Let us examine the entire sequence of machine instructions generated for COBOL statement 127 and try to get a more satisfying explanation.

COBOL statement 127 and its associated machine language instructions through B0A (see Figure 13.5) are as follows:

ADD IND-TUITION TO TOTAL-TUITION.

Location	Instruction
AF8	F2 73 D 218 6 008
AFE	F2 75 D 210 6 018
B04	FA 33 D 21C D 214
B0A	F3 53 6 018 D 21C

COBOL statement #	COBOL Verb	Relative location	Machine Instruction
108	*0020-PROCESS-A-RECORD		
		000A46	
		000A46	58 F0 C 014
		000A4A	05 1F
		000A4C	0000006C
109	COMPUTE	000A50	F2 71 D 210 7 01D
		000A56	FC 31 D 214 C 0B0
		000A5C	F3 32 6 008 D 215
		000A62	96 F0 6 00B
110	IF	000A66	58 20 C 054
		000A6A	95 E8 7 01F
		000A6E	07 72
111	MOVE	000A70	D2 01 6 00E C 0B2
		000A76	58 10 C 058
		000A7A	07 F1
113	MOVE	000A7C	
		000A7C	D2 01 6 00E C 0B4
115	IF	000A82	
		000A82	F2 71 D 210 7 01D
		000A88	F9 11 D 216 C 0B6
		000A8E	58 F0 C 05C
		000A92	07 DF
116	MOVE	000A94	D2 01 6 00C C 0B8
		000A9A	58 10 C 060
		000A9E	07 F1
118	IF	000AA0	
		000AA0	F2 71 D 210 7 01D
		000AA6	F9 10 D 216 C 0BA
		000AAC	58 F0 C 064
		000AB0	07 DF
119	MOVE	000AB2	D2 01 6 00C C 0B3
		000AB8	58 10 C 060
		000ABC	07 F1
121	MOVE	000ABE	
		000ABE	D2 01 6 00C C 0B2
123	COMPUTE	000AC4	
		000AC4	F2 71 D 210 6 00C
		000ACA	F2 73 D 218 6 008
		000AD0	FA 22 D 215 D 21D
		000AD6	F2 71 D 218 6 00E
		000ADC	FA 22 D 21D D 215
		000AE2	F2 73 D 210 7 020
		000AE8	FB 22 D 21D D 215
		000AEE	F3 52 6 010 D 21D
		000AF4	96 F0 6 015
127	ADD	000AF8	F2 73 D 218 6 008
		000AFF	F2 75 D 210 6 018
		000B04	FA 33 D 21C D 214
		000B0A	F3 53 6 018 D 21C
		000B10	96 F0 6 01D
128	ADD	000B14	F2 71 D 218 6 00E
		000B1A	F2 75 D 210 6 02A
		000B20	FA 33 D 21C D 214
		000B26	F3 53 6 02A D 21C
		000B2C	96 F0 6 02F

FIGURE 13.5 *Truncated Procedure Division Map for Figure 13.2*

Data division entries for IND-TUITION and TOTAL-TUITION are provided in COBOL statements 57 and 63 of Figure 13.2:

```
05  IND-TUITION      PIC 9(4)     VALUE IS ZEROS.
05  TOTAL-TUITION    PIC 9(6).
```

Consider the machine instructions generated for the COBOL statement. The programmer specifies that IND-TUITION is to be added to TOTAL-TUITION. Since the data division entries for these data names do not specify a USAGE clause, both are taken as display. The compiler must, therefore, convert the incoming DISPLAY data to packed format prior to addition. Referring to

JOB SSTBERN1   STEP GO   TIME 085641   DATE (79 158)   ID = 000   PAGE 0001

COMPLETION CODE   [SYSTEM = 0C7]——System Completion Code

PSW AT ENTRY TO ABEND   078D1000 00[0968B2]   ILC 6   INTC 0007
                                     └Last 3 bytes of PSW

CDE
                                                         Entry point address of main (COBOL) program
    80CA90   NCDE 00000000   RBP 007E1908 NM MAIN   [EPA 00095DA8]   XL/MJ 0080E040   USE 00010000   ATTR 0B20000
    FE35D0   NCDE 00FCCBD0   RBP 00000000 NM IGG019DK EPA 00F9A000   XL/MJ 00FE35F0   USE 00030000   ATTR B122000
    FFAB88   NCDE 00FD2348   RBP 00000000 NM IGG019AQ EPA 00ED0A70   XL/MJ 00FFABA8   USE 00070000   ATTR B122000
    FF8128   NCDE 00FFAAB8   RBP 00000000 NM IGG019DJ EPA 00AD2488   XL/MJ 00FF8148   USE 000B0000   ATTR B922000

                                                                          Contents of GPR 6
FLTR 0-6   0000000000000000   0000000000000000   000000000000000U   0000000000000000

REGS 0-7   000966DC   0009686C   00096824   00800634   000960B0   00096BC0   [00095E48]   000944F0
REGS 8-15 000961C8   00096C1C   00095DA8   00095DA8   000964E8   [00096250] 000967F8   00096848
                                                                      └Contents of GPR 13   *EBCDIC Table
                                                                       "D" register   on page 230

FIGURE 13.6 *Information Associated with Memory Dump, Example 1*

EBCDIC
Interpretation

```
095DA0              90ECD00C 185D05F0   4580F010 E3E4C9E3 C9D6D540 E5E2D9F1  *        ......0...0.TUITION VSR1*
095DC0  0700989F F02407FF 96021034 07FE41F0   000107FE 00096C1C 00095DA8 00095DA8  *....0..........0........*
095DE0  000964E8 00096250 000965CA 00096BDC   00000000 00000000 00000000 00000000  *...Y....................*
095E00  00000000 00000000 00000000 00000000   00000000 00000000 00000000 00000000  *........................*
095E20  U0000000 00000000 U0000000 00000000   40F84BF5 F64BF2F2 D1E4D540 40F76B40  *............ 8.56.22JUN 7. *
095E40  F1F9F7F9 00000000 40400000 00000000   F1F2F0F0 F7F5F2F5 F0F0F1F3 F0F00000  *1979.... ......12007525001300..*
095E60  [00000000 0000]F0F0 F0F0F0F0 F0F0F0F0   F0F0F0F0 F0F0F0F0 F0F0F0F0 F0F00000  *......00000000000000000000..*
095E80  40606060 60606060 60606060 60606060   60606060 60606060 60606060 60606060  *........................*
095EA0  60606060 60606060 60606060 60606060   60606060 60606060 60606060 60606060  *........................*
        LINE 095EC0 SAME AS ABOVE
095EE0  60604040 40404040 40404040 40404040   40404040 40404040 40404040 40404040  *..                      *
095F00  40404040 40000000 00E2E3E4 C4C5D5E3   40D5C1D4 C5404040 40404040 404040E2  *OC   ....STUDENT NAME        S*
095F20  D6C340E2 C5C340D5 E4D44040 C3D9C5C4   C9E3E240 40E3E4C9 E3C9D6D5 4040E4D5  *OC SEC NUM CREDITS TUITION UN*
095F40  09D6D540 C6C5C540 40C1C3E3 40C6C5C5   4040E2C3 C8D6D3C1 D9E2C8C9 D74040E3  *ION FEE ACT FEE SCHOLARSHIP T*
095F60  D6E3C1D3 40C2C9D3 D3404040 40404040   40404040 40404040 40404040 40404040  *OTAL BILL                   *
095F80  40404040 40404040 40404040 40000000   00000000 00000000 00000000 00000000  *           .............*
095FA0  00U00000 05097C2E 00095DCE 00000001   00000001 00000000 U0000000 00000000  *........................*
095FC0  00000000 00000000 80000000 00000000   00000000 00000000 00000000 00000000  *........................*
095FE0  050944E8 00504000 00094938 4609837A   80095F94 00A44800 007D1F88 12AD2494  *...Y....................*
096000  00ED0A70 00000001 08090050 00000000   000947E8 00094540 000944F0 00000050  *...........Y... ..0.....*

096300  00000040 00800634 02F0F000 00000000   00000000 00000000 00000000 00000000  *........00.............*
096320  00000000 00000000 06097478 00096250   000962F1 00000000 00000000 00000000  *...............1........*
096340  00000000 00000000 00000000 00000000   00000000 00000000 00000000 00000000  *........................*
096360  00000000 00000000 00000000 00000000   00000000 00000000 000103F8 00097C2E  *.....................8..*
096380  00000000 8F096DE8 00096DE8 00800634   000960B0 50096C6C 00095E48 00000000  *...Y...Y......Y.........*
0963A0  000961C8 00096C1C 00095DA8 00095DA8   000964E8 00000000 00000000 00000000  *...H........Y...........*
0963C0  00000000 00000000 00000000 00000000   00000000 00000000 00000000 00000000  *........................*
0963E0  00000000 00000000 00000000 00000000   00000000 00000000 00096B90 40095AD2  *.......................K*
096400  00095DA8 00000724 00099968 E2E8E2D6   E4E34040 C100000C 00095E30 00000000  *...........SYSOUT A.....*
096420  00000000 00000000 00000000 00000000   00000000 00000000 00000000 00000000  *........................*
096440  00000000 00000000 00000000 00000000   000944F0 000961C8 00095E48 00000000  *...........0..H........*
096460  00000000 [00000000] 00000000 [0001200F]   00000000 00000000 00096BC6 00096A5A  *........F......F...*
096480  00000000 00000000 00096BC6 00096A5A   00000000 00000000 00096BC6 00000000  *.......F.......F....*
0964A0  000966DC 00000000 00096B80 00000000   00095CCC 8F0960E8 00000000 140961C8  *............Y.......H*
0964C0  00000001 800960E8 00000000 05000E34   00000000 00096CBE 00096DC2 00096DCC  *...Y.......B...*
0964E0  00000000 00000000 00098F9A 00096E02   00097C92 000981E6 00098F9A 00097C96  *...W.....*
096500  00096E12 00097C2E 000988CA 000981E2   00098F9E 000967EE 00096A5A 00096B80  *.........S..........*
096520  00096BC6 0009667A 000966AE 000966C4   000966DC 000966EE 0009670C 00096324  *...F.......D...*
```
                                                      │Value of IND-TUITION before packing
                                                      │(locations 95E50-95E53)
                                            │Value of first operand in add packed instruction
                                            │(locations 09646C-09646F)
                              │Value of second operand in add packed instruction
                              │(locations 096464-096467)
          │Value of TOTAL-TUITION before packing;
          │(locations 95E60-95E65)

FIGURE 13.7 *Memory Dump for Example 1*

Figure 12.5, instruction formats, we can break the first machine instruction into its component parts as shown:

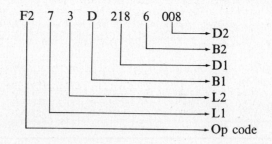

Appendix D, 360/370 Assembler Instructions, shows F2 to be the op code for PACK. A pack instruction converts data in the second operand to packed data and stores the result in the first operand. The second operand has a base register of 6 and a displacement of 008. From the data division map (Figure 13.3) and table of base register assignments (Figure 13.4), we conclude that the second operand is IND-TUITION. Analogous reasoning shows that the next machine instruction packs TOTAL-TUITION into a second compiler work area.

The third instruction in the sequence, the one at relative location B04, is the instruction that caused the ABEND. It has an op code of FA (add packed) and is supposed to add IND-TUITION to TOTAL-TUITION and store the result in TOTAL-TUITION. Instead, it caused a data exception, which occurs only when an arithmetic field does not contain valid arithmetic data. The culprit is either IND-TUITION or TOTAL-TUITION. We go into the dump (Figure 13.7) to find which of the two it is.

Both the data division map and first pack instruction show the address of IND-TUITION as 6 008 (base register 6, displacement 008). The address in GPR 6 at the time of the ABEND is 095E48. Since IND-TUITION is 4 bytes, its value is found in the 4 bytes from 095E50 to 095E53 (i.e., the address in register 6 plus the displacement of 008, points to the first byte, the one at 095E50). Figure 13.7 shows IND-TUITION to be F1F2F0F0. It is packed into a compiler work area via the instruction at AF8 and becomes 1200F, a valid decimal number.

The first byte of TOTAL-TUITION is at 6 018; its calculated address is, therefore, $(095E48) + (018)_{16} = (095E60)_{16}$. TOTAL-TUITION has a length of 6 bytes, so that its contents are found in the 6 bytes from 095E60 to 095E65 as 000000000000. TOTAL-TUITION is defined in line 63 of the COBOL program, but was never initialized. The first time the computer went to access TOTAL-TUITION, it took whatever happened to be there, i.e., whatever was in locations 095E60 to 095E65. The field was not initialized, the contents were binary rather than packed zeros, and the 0C7 resulted. The add pack instruction at B04 failed to execute because 0 is an invalid sign.

DUMP READING: EXAMPLE 2 (BAD INPUT DATA)

The COBOL program of Figure 13.2 was rerun (after line 63 was amended to include a VALUE IS ZERO clause) but another 0C7 occurred, resulting in a second ABEND. Figures 13.2 to 13.5 from the first example are applicable for this example as well. Figure 13.8 shows the PSW, entry point, and contents of the GPR's for Example 2. Figure 13.9 shows the relevant portion of the dump. We shall follow the procedure used in Example 1.

First, subtract the entry point of the COBOL program from the address where the data exception occurred:

Address from PSW	096 8 9 6
− Entry point of COBOL program	− 095DA 8
Relative address	AEE

Next take the relative location AEE, and using the procedure division map (Figure 13.5) establish

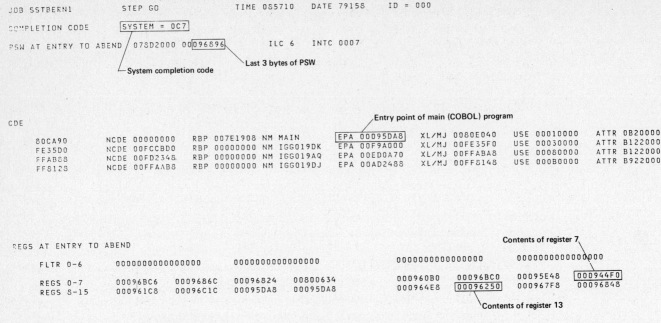

FIGURE 13.8 *Information Associated with Memory Dump, Example 2*

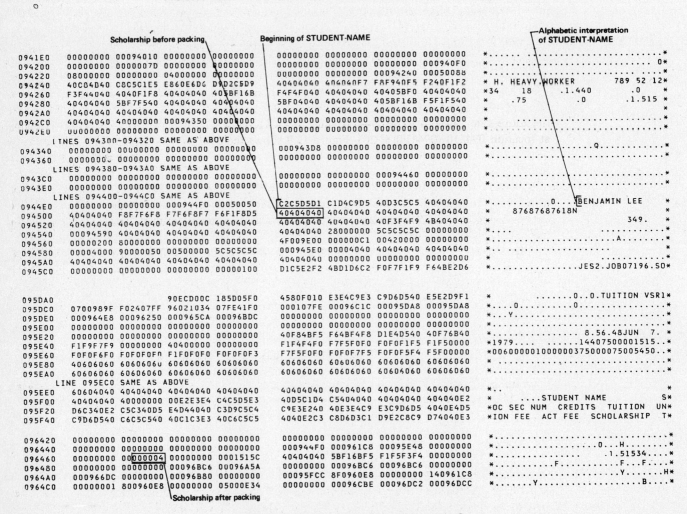

FIGURE 13.9 *Memory Dump for Example 2*

SECTION IV: THE ROLE OF BAL IN DEEPER UNDERSTANDING

which COBOL statement failed to execute. Location AEE is found to be within the COBOL COM-PUTE statement of line 123. The instruction at AEE is the one that would have executed next if the ABEND did not occur. The instruction that actually caused the ABEND is the one immediately preceding, i.e., the one at relative location AE8. The COMPUTE statement and machine instructions through AE8 are repeated here:

COMPUTE IND-STUDENT-BILL = IND-TUITION + IND-ACTIVITY-FEE + IND-UNION-FEE − SR-SCHOLARSHIP.

Location	Instruction
AC4	F2 71 D 210 6 00C
ACA	F2 73 D 218 6 008
AD0	FA 22 D 215 D 21D
AD6	F2 71 D 218 6 00E
ADC	FA 22 D 21D D 215
AE2	F2 73 D 210 7 020
AE8	FB 22 D 21D D 215

The COBOL compiler adds and subtracts two fields at a time from left to right within the COMPUTE. IND-TUITION is first added to IND-ACTIVITY-FEE; IND-UNION-FEE is added to that intermediate sum; finally, SR-SCHOLARSHIP is subtracted. Since the USAGE clause was not specified in the definition of any of the operands, they are all packed prior to any arithmetic.

The first two machine instructions pack IND-ACTIVITY-FEE and IND-TUITION into compiler work areas, which are then added via the third instruction (op code FA—add packed). IND-UNION-FEE is packed and added to the intermediate sum via the fourth and fifth instructions. SR-SCHOLARSHIP is packed in instruction 6 (op code F2—pack) and subtracted from the intermediate sum in the seventh instruction where the data exception occurred. Everything worked well until the attempt to subtract SR-SCHOLARSHIP.

The data division map (Figure 13.3) shows that SR-SCHOLARSHIP is stored in the base register designated by BL = 1 (i.e., register 7), with displacement of hex 20. Figure 13.8 shows the address in register 7 to be 0944F0; thus, SR-SCHOLARSHIP is stored in the 4 bytes beginning at location 094510 (0944F0 + 20). Figure 13.9 shows the contents of SR-SCHOLARSHIP to be 40404040, which is EBCDIC for a blank field. We conclude that in the last data card that was processed SR-SCHOLARSHIP was left blank.

Which student had the invalid data? SR-STUDENT-NAME is 20 bytes in length and tied to BL = 1 (i.e., register 7) with displacement of 000. Hence, the name of student with the invalid data is found in the 20 bytes beginning at 0944F0. Going into the dump, the bug is found to be in the data associated with BENJAMIN LEE.

One last point: We examined the value of SR-SCHOLARSHIP as it resided in the input area. As a check, we should also observe its value after it has been packed into a compiler work area. The subtract instruction had as its second operand the 3 bytes beginning at location D 215. Thus, the beginning address is

Contents of register 13	096250
+ Displacement	+ 215
Address of first byte	096465

Examining Figure 13.9, we see that the second operand contains 000004. (Reader, this is not an error. It is exactly what should be there as the result of a pack instruction on a blank field.) Since 4 is an invalid sign, the data exception occurred.

The STATE and FLOW Options

One might logically, or perhaps hopefully, ask: Is this really necessary to determine the cause of an ABEND? We answer with an equivocal "maybe," because there are other aids that can sometimes lead to an answer more quickly. Two of these are the STATE and FLOW options, which are requested at compile time (see Table 18.1).

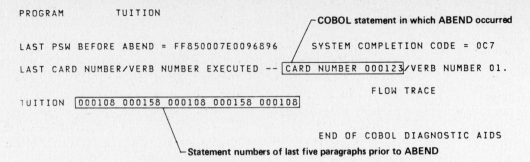

PROGRAM   TUITION

                   COBOL statement in which ABEND occurred

LAST PSW BEFORE ABEND = FF850007E0096896 SYSTEM COMPLETION CODE = 0C7

LAST CARD NUMBER/VERB NUMBER EXECUTED -- CARD NUMBER 000123/VERB NUMBER 01.

                   FLOW TRACE

TUITION   000108 000158 000108 000158 000108

            END OF COBOL DIAGNOSTIC AIDS
      Statement numbers of last five paragraphs prior to ABEND

FIGURE 13.10 *Illustration of STATE and FLOW Options*

Consider Figure 13.10, which shows additional output produced by the second example on dump reading. The STATE option displays the number of the last COBOL statement executed, statement number 123 in Figure 13.10. This is the same conclusion that was reached by subtracting the Entry Point Address from the last three bytes in the PSW and relating the answer to the PMAP. An experienced programmer would know immediately that an 0C7 can only be caused by an invalid packed field and conclude that one of the operands in the COBOL COMPUTE was invalid. The programmer would not know, however, which field was bad, and consequently would still require the dump to identify both the field and the record in which it is contained.

On the other hand, if the STATE option were available for the first example, in which a counter was not initialized, no further analysis would be needed. The STATE option would have identified COBOL statement 127 as the one causing the ABEND. It in turn contains only two operands, IND-TUITION and TOTAL-TUITION, and it would be a simple matter to go directly to the COBOL listing and discover the missing VALUE clause in the definition of TOTAL-TUI-TION.

Figure 13.10 also illustrates the FLOW option, which shows the number of the first statement in the last *n* procedures executed. (The value of *n* is specified through JCL at compile time as will be explained in Chapter 18; in this case *n* = 5.) As can be seen from Figure 13.10, execution has switched back and forth between the paragraph beginning in line 108, 0020-PROCESS-A-RECORD, and the one in line 158, 0040-READ-A-RECORD. No conclusion of any substance can be drawn from this, save that the program appeared to execute successfully for at least two records prior to the ABEND. The FLOW option will on other occasions help to pinpoint the nature of errors by showing unexpected paths of execution.

In conclusion, use of the STATE and FLOW options will often, but not always, facilitate ABEND debugging. The programmer should realize, however, that these options are not "free" in the sense that they require execution of additional operating system routines (which are transparent to the programmer). This in turn increases execution time. Consequently, many shops restrict use of these options to the testing phase and discourage it in production.

MVS IMPLICATIONS

The alert reader may have noticed that the Entry Point address was the same in Examples 1 and 2 (095DA8 in both instances). This is *not* coincidence and implies that these listings were run under MVS (as opposed to MFT, MVT, VS1, or early releases of VS2).

Under the MVS operating system, every job is given the entire 16 megabytes of storage. Each time a COBOL program is loaded for execution, it will be assigned the *same* storage locations, provided neither it, nor the operating system, were modified since the previous submission. This is not true under other versions of OS in which the available storage is shared among all jobs. This in turn causes a program to be loaded in different locations whenever it is run, i.e., whichever locations are available.

None of the other features of MVS need concern us here; consequently the material in this chapter is applicable to any version of OS.

EXTENSION TO DOS

The examples in this chapter have been drawn from OS. At our level of discussion almost everything about OS pertains to DOS as well, with the exception of the COBOL program's entry point and the relative address of the instruction causing the ABEND. Accordingly, DOS procedures for reading procedure and data division maps, core dumps, etc., are the same as those in this chapter.

Figure 13.11 illustrates the linkage editor map for DOS. Only the LABEL and REL-FR (relocation factor) columns are of interest here. The key to using Figure 13.11 is the PROGRAM-ID statement in the COBOL identification division. Assume, for example, the following COBOL statement in conjunction with Figure 13.11:

PROGRAM-ID. 'BILLING'.

To determine the entry point for the COBOL program BILLING, search the LABEL column in Figure 13.11 for BILLING and then read across under REL-FR and find 2640 as the entry point (in hex) of the COBOL program. (The other, rather cryptic, names in the label column are IBM-supplied programs that are required by the COBOL program. Most of these routines are for I/O processing.)

Finally, under OS the subtraction of the Entry Point Address from the address in the PSW points to the instruction that *would* have been executed rather than the one causing the dump. Under DOS, however, the subtraction generally points *directly* to the instruction which caused the ABEND.

PHASE	XFR-AD	LOCORE	HICORE	DSK-AD	ESD TYPE	LABEL	LOADED	REL-FR
PHASE***	002DC4	002000	003DBF	5D 03 2	CSECT	IHD02200	002000	002000
					ENTRY	IHD02201	002000	
					CSECT	IJJCPD1	002018	002018
					ENTRY	IJJCPD1N	002018	
				* ENTRY	IJJCPD3	002018	
					CSECT	IHD02800	002210	002210
					ENTRY	IHD02801	002210	
					ENTRY	IHD02802	002246	
					CSECT	IHD03700	002388	002388
				* ENTRY	IHD03701	002388	
				* ENTRY	IHD03702	002398	
					ENTRY	IHD03704	002524	
					CSECT	BILLING	002640	002640
					CSECT	IJCFZII1	003C18	003C18
					CSECT	IJDFADIZ	003CA8	003CA8
				* ENTRY	IJDFAZIZ	003CA8	

— Entry point for COBOL program

FIGURE 13.11 *DOS Linkage Editor Map*

SUMMARY

The beginning programmer is often guilty of two practices that result in a data exception:

1. Failure to initialize a counter (Example 1).
2. Use of bad, i.e., nonnumeric, data as input (Example 2).

It is sound technique to always initialize a counter with the VALUE clause regardless of whether or not the entry is initialized or calculated in the procedure division. It is not as easy to eliminate the second error. Incoming numeric fields are not allowed to contain decimal points, commas, $ signs, or special characters. Further, high- and low-order zeros should be punched and not left blank. Even after this is done, there is still the possibility for error if data are punched in the wrong columns. The record layout in the data division and the incoming data must correspond exactly. The computer does not know what you intended; it only knows what you did.

If a data exception does occur, the procedure to determine its exact cause is as follows:

1. Get the address of the data exception from the last 3 bytes of the PSW.
2. Get the entry point of the main program.
3. Subtract the address in step 2 from the address in step 1. The result is the relative location (within the COBOL program) of the next statement that would have been executed.

 4. Use the procedure division map and relative location determined from step 3 to pinpoint the machine instruction causing the error.
5. Determine the COBOL instruction that contained the machine instruction that failed to execute.
6. Examine the operands in the COBOL instruction using the COBOL listing first (easy way out) or the dump if the answer is not readily apparent.
7. If steps 1 to 6 fail, ask for help.

PROBLEMS

1. Take a program that you have written and debugged and cause it to ABEND. (This is best accomplished by failing to initialize a counter or blanking out a numeric field in a data card.) Analyze the data and procedure division maps and the dump, and find the cause of the error. After all, it is easiest to go through a dump if you know what you are looking for, and this exercise is a good one to build confidence. To have the appropriate material after an ABEND, the JCL from Chapter 2 is modified as follows (the OS JCL may vary slightly at your facility):

> OS: (a) // EXEC COBUCLG,PARM.COB = (PMAP,DMAP,STATE,'FLOW = 5')
> (replace existing EXEC card)
>
> (b) //GO.SYSUDUMP DD SYSOUT = A
> (new card before GO.SYSIN card)
>
> DOS: (a) // OPTION LINK,DUMP,SYM,LISTX
> (replace existing OPTION card)

The meaning of these JCL modifications is covered in the chapters on JCL in the next section.

2. Use the COBOL listing, register assignments, and maps of Figures 13.2 to 13.5 with the accompanying dump (Figure 13.12) to determine the cause of the ABEND. A series of leading questions is provided to help.
   i. *Determine where the ABEND occurred.*
      a. At what machine location did the ABEND occur?
      b. At what location was the program loaded?
      c. What is the relative location within the COBOL program of the instruction that would have executed if there were no ABEND?
      d. What machine instruction is at that location?
      e. What is the actual machine address of the instruction in part d?
      f. What is the corresponding COBOL instruction?
   ii. *Examine the machine instruction that failed to execute.*
      The instruction that actually produced the ABEND is the one immediately before the instruction determined in part c.
      g. What is the machine instruction that actually caused the ABEND?
      h. What is its op code?
      i. Which base register is associated with the first operand?
      j. What is the displacement of the first operand?
      k. What is the effective address of the first operand?
      l. How many bytes are associated with the first operand *(careful)?*
      m. What are the internal contents of the first operand; are they valid as a decimal number?

```
JOB SSTBERN1        STEP GO            TIME 085830   DATE 79158   ID = 000

COMPLETION CODE     SYSTEM = 0C7

PSW AT ENTRY TO ABEND  078D1000 00096804          ILC 6   INTC 0007



CDE

    80CA90    NCDE 00000000   RBP 007E1908 NM MAIN      EPA 00095DA8   XL/MJ 0080E040   USE 00010000   ATTR 0B20000
    FE35D0    NCDE 00FCCBD0   RBP 00000000 NM IGG019DK  EPA 00F9A000   XL/MJ 00FE35F0   USE 00030000   ATTR B122000
    FFABS8    NCDE 00FD2348   RBP 00000000 NM IGG019AQ  EPA 00ED0A70   XL/MJ 00FFABA8   USE 00080000   ATTR B122000
    FF8128    NCDE 00FFAAB8   RBP 00000000 NM IGG019DJ  EPA 00AD2488   XL/MJ 00FF8148   USE 000B0000   ATTR B922000


REGS AT ENTRY TO ABEND

    FLTR 0-6   0000000000000000      0000000000000000        0000000000000000      0000000000000000

    REGS 0-7   00096BC6   500967F4   000966EE   00800634      000960B0   00096BC0   00095E48   000944F0
    REGS 8-15  000961C8   00096C1C   00095DA8   00095DA8      000964E8   00096250   000967F8   00097C96


094220   08000000 00000000 04000000 00000000    00000000 00000000 00094240 00050088   *.........................*
094240   40C8C5D5 D9E840D1 C1D4C5E2 40404040    40404040 404040F9 F8F740F6 F540F4F3   * HENRY JAMES        987 65 43*
094260   F2F14040 4040F1F5 40404040 405BF16B    F2F0F040 40404040 40405BF0 40404040   *21    15    .1.200    .0  *
094280   40404040 5BF7F540 40404040 40405BF5    F0F04040 40404040 40404040 F7F7F540   *   .75      .500      .775 *
0942A0   40404040 40404040 40404040 40404040    40404040 40404040 40404040 40404040   *                          *
0942C0   40404040 40000000 00094350 00000000    00000000 00000000 00000000 00000000   *                          *
0942E0   00000000 00000000 00000000 00000000    00000000 00000000 00000000 00000000   *.........................*
         LINES 094300-094320 SAME AS ABOVE
094340   00000000 00000000 00000000 00000000    000943D8 00000000 00000000 00000000   *................Q........*
094360   00000000 00000000 00000000 00000000    00000000 00000000 00000000 00000000   *.........................*
         LINES 094380-0943A0 SAME AS ABOVE
0943C0   00000000 00000000 00000000 00000000    00000000 00000000 00094460 00000000   *.........................*
0943E0   00000000 00000000 00000000 00000000    00000000 00000000 00000000 00000000   *.........................*
         LINES 094400-0944C0 SAME AS ABOVE
0944E0   00000000 00000000 00094460 00050050    E2E4E2C1 D540C2C1 D2C5D940 40404040   *.........O...SUSAN BAKER    *
094500   40404040 F1F1F1F2 F2F3F3F3 F34040D5    F0F5F0F0 40404040 40404040 40404040   *    111223333  N0500       *
094520   40404040 40404040 40404040 40404040    40404040 40404040 40F6F9F5 4B404040   *                    695.   *
094540   00094590 40404040 40404040 40404040    40404040 28000000 5C5C5C5C 00000000   *....                      *
094560   00000200 80000000 00000000 00000000    4F009E00 000000C1 00420000 00000000   *.....................A...*
094580   00004000 90000050 00500000 5C5C5C5C    000945E0 00000000 40404040 40404040   *..  ..........             *
0945A0   40404040 40404040 40404040 40404040    40404040 00000000 00000000 00000000   *                          *
0945C0   00000000 00000000 00000000 00000100    D1C5E2F2 4BD1D6C2 F0F7F1F9 F64BE2D6   *................JES2.JOB07196.SO*


096440   00000000 00000000 00000000 0000775F    000944F0 000961C8 00095E48 00000000   *.................O...H......*
096460   00000000 00000004 00000000 00000000    40404040 40405BF7 F7F5F2F1 00000000   *....................77521...*
096480   00000000 00000000 00096BC6 00096A5A    00000000 00096BC6 00096BC6 00000000   *.........F......F..F...*
0964A0   000966DC 00000000 00096B80 00000000    00095FCC 8F0960E8 00000000 140961C8   *......Y.....H*
0964C0   00000001 800960E8 00000000 05000E34    00000000 00096CBE 00096DC2 00096DCC   *......Y.......B...*
0964E0   00000000 00000000 00098F9A 00096E02    00097C92 000981E6 00098F9A 00097C96   *..................W.......*
096500   00096E12 00097C2E 000988CA 000981E2    00098F9E 000967EE 00096A5A 00096B80   *.............S..........*
096520   00096BC6 0009667A 000966AE 000966C4    000966DC 00096EEE 0009670C 00096824   *..F..........D.........*
096540   0009682A 00096848 0009686C 00096866    00096A36 00096A4C 00096A98 00096B7A   *.........................*
096560   00096BBA 00096BC0 000967A8 000967E2    000967E8 00096BB4 00095FCC 000960E8   *.............S..Y......Y*
096580   00096BC6 00000000 00096A5A 00000000    00096B80 00000000 080CF2F5 F0F0012C   *.F...............2500..*
0965A0   F7F56CF0 21202040 20204020 20202040    205B2020 206B2021 20100000 001C0000   *75.0....  ..   .........*
0965C0   0001D5D6 00481400 000058F0 C014051F    0000005D 58F0C018 05EF5810 C0905840   *..NO......O.......O......*
0965E0   1024D202 4011C01D 5010D260 9200D260    581UCU94 D2031094 C0205840 1024D202   *..K....K....K..........K.*
096600   4011C01D 5010D264 920FD264 9680D264    4110D260 D203D060 C0D158F0 C02405EF   *....K...K....K.K.....J.0..*
096620   5810C090 D203D060 C0D558F0 C02405EF    5870D200 5810C094 D203D060 C0D558F0   *..K...N.0......K.......K...N.0*
096640   C02405EF 5880D204 D2848000 60C058F0    C01805EF 5810C094 1821D203 D26CD204   *.......K.K....O........K.K.K.*
096660   9254D26C D203D274 C094D203 D270C0D6    4110D26C 58F020D4 05EFD284 80006038   *..K.K.K...K.K..O..K..O.M..K......*
```

FIGURE 13.12 Dump for Problem 2

CHAPTER 13: DEBUGGING, II   253

n. Which base register is associated with the second operand?
o. What is the displacement of the second operand?
p. How many bytes are associated with the second operand?
q. What are the internal contents of the second operand; are they valid as a decimal number?

iii. *Determine the record that contained the invalid data.*
r. Which base register is associated with STUDENT-FILE?
s. What is the address contained in that base register when the ABEND occurred?
t. What is the displacement of SR-CREDITS?
u. What is the internal location of SR-CREDITS?
v. What value was read from the record for SR-CREDITS?
w. Which student had the invalid data?

3. Explain how a data exception need not occur, even though a 77-level entry used as a counter was not initialized; specifically, consider the first example in this chapter in which TOTAL-TUITION was not set to zero. What would be the consequences of *not* getting a data exception, even if TOTAL-TUITION was not initialized?

4. a. A blank in a one-position numeric field causes a data exception, if arithmetic is performed in that field, and the USAGE for that field is DISPLAY. Assume that we define a four-position numeric field, with USAGE DISPLAY, that is also used in arithmetic calculations. Further assume that this four-position field has a valid low-order digit but is punched with leading (high-order) blanks. Will a data exception result? Why or why not?
b. Explain why an incoming numeric field (USAGE DISPLAY) will cause a data exception if a decimal point is actually punched in the field.
Note: A period is 4B in EBCDIC; a space is 40 in EBCDIC. (See Table 12.2)

5. Can you think of any reason for *not* using the STATE and/or FLOW options in the testing phase of program development? In the production phase?

6. Answer the following with respect to Figure 13.1:
(a) What are the hex contents of location 3FD7CO?
(b) What are the hex contents of location 3FD7C7?
(c) What are the hex contents of location 3FD7CF?
(d) What are the hex contents of location 3FD6FO?
(e) What are the hex contents of location 3FD6F6?
(f) What are the hex contents of location 3FD6FF?
(g) What are the hex contents of the 8 bytes beginning at 26CB80?
(h) What is the alphabetic interpretation of your answer in part (g)?
(i) What are the hex contents of the 5 bytes beginning at 26CA47?
(j) What is the alphabetic interpretation of your answer to part (i)?

Chapter 14

INSIGHT INTO THE COBOL COMPILER

OVERVIEW

The COBOL compiler is a remarkably sophisticated program that translates COBOL into Assembler language. Unfortunately, many practicing programmers know little more about the compiler. While such knowledge is unnecessary in terms of being able to write a COBOL program, it is invaluable in raising the overall capabilities of the individual.

The compiler-generated instructions to add two COMPUTATIONAL fields are different from those which add two COMPUTATIONAL-3 fields. Further, if COBOL operands are of different data types and/or decimal alignment, additional machine instructions are generated to convert and/or shift the data. How does this relate to COBOL, since the programmer is permitted to mix data types or decimal alignments in the same COBOL instruction? The compiler, and not the programmer, is responsible for generating proper machine code to convert, shift, and do arithmetic. If the programmer is "lazy" or unaware, the compiler will bail him out. The COBOL programmer can, however, simplify the job of the compiler and thereby ensure more efficient machine code by specifying appropriate data types, decimal alignments, etc. That is the focus of this chapter. We shall examine in close detail machine language instructions generated by the COBOL compiler and see how apparently insignificant changes in COBOL code produce very different machine instructions. We shall show that even brief consideration of machine characteristics results in more efficient COBOL code and a *better understanding of the COBOL logic.*

The chapter begins with elementary coverage of some Assembler instructions. (We assume the material on instruction formats and machine architecture from Chapter 12 has been well digested.) A superficial level is maintained, for the present objective is to establish a link between COBOL and Assembler and not to provide in-depth coverage of BAL coding. As in previous chapters, emphasis is on IBM, but the concepts are applicable to any manufacturer. After the necessary Assembler has been covered, we shall concoct a COBOL program in which the procedure division consists entirely of ADD instructions for different data types, signs, and decimal alignments. We shall then examine the procedure and data division maps associated with this program to accomplish our objective.

This chapter may appear somewhat removed from COBOL to the casual reader. We hope, however, that the serious student finds these concepts well worth the effort as he or she progresses through advanced courses and perhaps an eventual career.

CONVERSION INSTRUCTIONS

The reader may refer to Chapter 12 to review instruction formats and the addressing scheme. We shall begin with two instructions that convert from character to packed format and packed to character format, the PACK and UNPK instructions, respectively. First the PACK instruction:

Name	Pack
Mnemonic op code	PACK
Machine op code	F2
Type	SS
Assembler format	PACK D 1(L1,B1),D2(L2,B2)

Essentially, the PACK instruction takes the data in the second operand, packs them, and moves the result into the first operand. The contents of the second operand are unchanged.

Example 14.1

    PACK FIELDA,FIELDB

Before execution: FIELDA [?? | ?? | ??]   FIELDB [F1 | F2 | F3]

After execution: FIELDA [00 | 12 | 3F]   FIELDB [F1 | F2 | F3]

Observe that, since FIELDA was larger than necessary, high-order zeros are generated. The initial contents of FIELDA, i.e., the receiving field, are overwritten, and the final contents of FIELDB, i.e., the sending field, are not changed.

The UNPK (unpack) instruction is the reverse of the PACK instruction in that a packed field is converted to character format:

Name	Unpack
Mnemonic op code	UNPK
Machine op code	F3
Type	SS
Assembler format	UNPK D 1(L1,B1),D2(L2,B2)

Example 14.2

    UNPK FIELDC,FIELDD

Before execution: FIELDC [?? | ?? | ??]   FIELDD [32 | 1F]

After execution: FIELDC [F3 | F2 | F1]   FIELDD [32 | 1F]

As before, the final contents of the sending field, i.e., FIELDD, are unchanged, and the initial contents of the receiving field, i.e., FIELDC, are destroyed. Further note that the receiving field is larger than the sending field to accommodate the expanded results of the unpacking operation.

Next, consider two instructions that convert binary to decimal data (i.e., packed) and decimal to binary, the convert to decimal and convert to binary instructions:

Name	Convert to binary
Mnemonic op code	CVB
Machine op code	4F
Type	RX
Assembler format	CVB R1,D2(X2,B2)

The convert to binary (CVB) instruction requires that the second operand be in packed decimal format. The result of the conversion is stored in the general register specified as R1.

Example 14.3

```
CVB   8,FIELDC
```

Before execution: FIELDC | 00 | 00 | 00 | 00 | 00 | 00 | 12 | 3C |

Register 8 | ?? | ?? | ?? | ?? |

After execution: FIELDC | 00 | 00 | 00 | 00 | 00 | 00 | 12 | 3C |

Register 8 | 00   00   00   7B | *Note:* $(123)_{10} = (7B)_{16}$.

The convert to decimal (CVD) instruction works in reverse; i.e., it takes the binary contents of a general-purpose register, converts it to decimal, and stores the result in the packed field specified in the instruction.

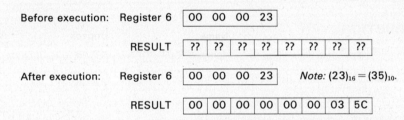

Name	Convert to decimal
Mnemonic op code	CVD
Machine op code	4E
Type	RX
Assembler format	CVD R1,D2(X2,B2)

Example 14.4

```
CVD   6,RESULT
```

Before execution: Register 6 | 00   00   00   23 |

RESULT | ?? | ?? | ?? | ?? | ?? | ?? | ?? | ?? |

After execution: Register 6 | 00   00   00   23 | *Note:* $(23)_{16} = (35)_{10}$.

RESULT | 00 | 00 | 00 | 00 | 00 | 00 | 03 | 5C |

Execution of the CVD instruction leaves the contents of the designated register unchanged. The original contents of the register are converted to a packed number and stored in the second operand.

INSTRUCTIONS THAT MOVE DATA

Data are constantly transferred from one storage location to another, or from storage to a register, or from a register to storage. In this section two instructions are introduced that are used to move data, but there are several others in the complete instruction set.

Load instructions bring data from a storage location to a register, while store instructions transfer data from a register to storage. A load instruction does not alter the initial contents of the storage address. A store instruction does not change the contents of a register. We shall consider two instructions that manipulate a full word.

Name	Load
Mnemonic op code	L
Machine op code	58
Type	RX
Assembler format	L R1,D2(X2,B2)

Example 14.5

    L 5,FIELDA

Before execution: Register 5 | ?? | ?? | ?? | ?? | FIELDA | 00 | 00 | 00 | 01 |

After execution: Register 5 | 00 | 00 | 00 | 01 | FIELDA | 00 | 00 | 00 | 01 |

FIELDA is a full word, and after the load instruction has been executed, the contents of FIELDA are unchanged. The initial contents of register 5 have been replaced by the contents of FIELDA.

    The store instruction causes the contents of a register to be placed in storage. The contents of the register are unaltered, and what was originally in storage is overwritten.

Name	Store
Mnemonic op code	ST
Machine op code	50
Type	RX
Assembler format	ST R1,D2(X2,B2)

Example 14.6

    ST 6,FIELDB

Before execution: Register 6 | 00 | 00 | 12 | 34 | FIELDB | ?? | ?? | ?? | ?? |

After execution: Register 6 | 00 | 00 | 12 | 34 | FIELDB | 00 | 00 | 12 | 34 |

ADD INSTRUCTIONS

Any one of several BAL instructions can be used to add data depending on the length, type, and location of the operands. The add packed (AP) instruction is for decimal data with both operands in storage. The add full word (A) instruction is for binary data when one operand is contained in a register and the other in a full word in storage. Consider the add packed instruction:

Name	Add packed
Mnemonic op code	AP
Machine op code	FA
Type	SS
Assembler format	AP D1(L1,B1),D2(L2,B2)

    The contents of the second operand are added to the contents of the first operand, and the results are placed in the first operand. Both fields must be valid decimal fields, i.e., packed; otherwise a data exception will occur. The sum is in packed format, and its sign is stored in the low-order byte of the first operand.

Example 14.7

    AP FIELDA,FIELDB

Before execution: FIELDA | 01 | 23 | 4C | FIELDB | 05 | 67 | 8C |

After execution: FIELDA | 06 | 91 | 2C | FIELDB | 05 | 67 | 8C |

The initial contents of the first operand are overwritten, and the contents of the second operand are unchanged.

The add full word instruction adds (in binary) the contents of a full word in storage to the contents of a register and places the results in the designated register.

Name	Add full word
Mnemonic op code	A
Machine op code	5A
Type	RX
Assembler format	A R1,D2(X2,B2)

Example 14.8

A   5,FIELDC

Before execution: Register 5 | 00 | 00 | 00 | 07 | FIELDC | 00 | 00 | 00 | 01 |

After execution: Register 5 | 00 | 00 | 00 | 08 | FIELDC | 00 | 00 | 00 | 01 |

The contents of FIELDC, a full word in storage, are added to the value of register 5, and the result is placed in register 5. (Note that both operands are binary.) The initial contents of register 5 are destroyed, and the contents of FIELDC are unaltered.

COBOL FROM THE VIEWPOINT OF BAL

The intent of Figure 14.1 is to illustrate a variety of COBOL and corresponding object formats for different data types, lengths, signs, decimal alignments, etc. The working-storage section defines 12 data names that are used in various combinations in the procedure division. Of primary interest in this example is the machine language code generated from the COBOL statements. In the ensuing sections, we shall consider only a few of the COBOL statements in Figure 14.1, but the reader is well advised to consider the entire listing as an exercise.

Figure 14.2 shows the data division map, Figure 14.3 the literal pool and register assignment, and Figure 14.4 the procedure division map for Figure 14.1.

Data Division Map

Figure 14.2 is the data division map or glossary. A partial explanation of the various entries is given here, but the reader is referred to the *IBM COBOL Programmer's Guide* for a more detailed description.

Internal name	The internal name generated by the compiler and used in the object code listing to represent data names in the source program. This column appears twice for legibility.
Level number	A normalized level number in that the first level for any hierarchy is always kept at 01 but the other levels are incremented by 1. Levels 66, 77, and 88 are unaffected. Thus the level numbers in the data division map need not match those in the data division. (See Figures 13.2 and 13.3 for clarification.)
Source name	Data name as it appears in the source program.
Base	Contains information about the base register used for each data name. In general, every file has its own base locator. In our example all 77-level entries have a base locator of 1, which is tied to register 6 in Figure 14.3.
Displ	Indicates the displacement, in hexadecimal, from the base register for each data name.

```
00001          IDENTIFICATION DIVISION.
00002          PROGRAM-ID.   COBOLBAL.
00003          AUTHOR.   GRAUER AND CRAWFORD.
00004          ENVIRONMENT DIVISION.
00005          CONFIGURATION SECTION.
00006          SOURCE-COMPUTER.   IBM-370.
00007          OBJECT-COMPUTER.   IBM-370.
00008          DATA DIVISION.
00009          WORKING-STORAGE SECTION.
00010          77  BINARY-FIELD-ONE          PICTURE IS S9(3)
00011              USAGE IS COMPUTATIONAL.
00012          77  BINARY-FIELD-TWO          PICTURE IS S9(5)
00013              USAGE IS COMPUTATIONAL.
00014          77  BINARY-FIELD-UNSIGNED     PICTURE IS 9(3)
00015              USAGE IS COMPUTATIONAL.
00016          77  BINARY-FIELD-WITH-POINT   PICTURE IS S9(3)V9
00017              USAGE IS COMPUTATIONAL.
00018          77  ZONED-DECIMAL-FIELD-ONE   PICTURE IS S9(3)
00019              USAGE IS DISPLAY.
00020          77  ZONED-DECIMAL-FIELD-TWO   PICTURE IS S9(5)
00021              USAGE IS DISPLAY.
00022          77  ZONED-DECIMAL-UNSIGNED    PICTURE IS 9(3)
00023              USAGE IS DISPLAY.
00024          77  ZONED-DECIMAL-WITH-POINT  PICTURE IS S9(3)V9
00025              USAGE IS DISPLAY.
00026          77  PACKED-FIELD-ONE          PICTURE IS S9(3)
00027              USAGE IS COMPUTATIONAL-3.
00028          77  PACKED-FIELD-TWO          PICTURE IS S9(5)
00029              USAGE IS COMPUTATIONAL-3.
00030          77  PACKED-FIELD-UNSIGNED     PICTURE IS 9(3)
00031              USAGE IS COMPUTATIONAL-3.
00032          77  PACKED-FIELD-WITH-POINT   PICTURE IS S9(3)V9
00033              USAGE IS COMPUTATIONAL-3.
00034          PROCEDURE DIVISION.
00035
00036          ***************************************************************************
00037          *    COMPARISON OF ADD INSTRUCTIONS FOR ALL COMBINATIONS OF DATA TYPES   *
00038          *    ALL DATA NAMES ARE SIGNED                                           *
00039          *    ALL DATA NAMES HAVE SIMILAR DECIMAL ALIGNMENTS                      *
00040          ***************************************************************************
00041
00042
00043          *    COMBINING SIMILAR DATA TYPES
00044              ADD BINARY-FIELD-ONE TO BINARY-FIELD-TWO.
00045              ADD ZONED-DECIMAL-FIELD-ONE TO ZONED-DECIMAL-FIELD-TWO.
00046              ADD PACKED-FIELD-ONE TO PACKED-FIELD-TWO.
00047
00048
00049          * COMBINING PACKED FIELDS WITH ZONED DECIMAL FIELDS
00050              ADD PACKED-FIELD-ONE TO ZONED-DECIMAL-FIELD-ONE.
00051              ADD ZONED-DECIMAL-FIELD-ONE TO PACKED-FIELD-ONE.
00052
00053          * COMBINING PACKED FIELDS WITH BINARY FIELDS
00054              ADD PACKED-FIELD-ONE TO BINARY-FIELD-ONE.
00055              ADD BINARY-FIELD-ONE TO PACKED-FIELD-ONE.
00056
00057          * COMBINING ZONED DECIMAL FIELDS WITH BINARY FIELDS
00058              ADD ZONED-DECIMAL-FIELD-ONE TO BINARY-FIELD-ONE.
00059              ADD BINARY-FIELD-ONE TO ZONED-DECIMAL-FIELD-ONE.
00060
00061          ***************************************************************************
00062          *    COMPARISON OF ADD INSTRUCTIONS FOR SIMILAR DATA TYPES               *
00063          *    ONE OPERAND IS UNSIGNED                                             *
00064          *    ALL DATA NAMES HAVE SIMILAR DECIMAL ALIGNMENTS                      *
00065          ***************************************************************************
00066
00067              ADD ZONED-DECIMAL-UNSIGNED TO ZONED-DECIMAL-FIELD-ONE.
00068              ADD ZONED-DECIMAL-FIELD-ONE TO ZONED-DECIMAL-UNSIGNED.
00069              ADD BINARY-FIELD-UNSIGNED TO BINARY-FIELD-ONE.
00070              ADD BINARY-FIELD-ONE TO BINARY-FIELD-UNSIGNED.
00071              ADD PACKED-FIELD-UNSIGNED TO PACKED-FIELD-ONE.
00072              ADD PACKED-FIELD-ONE TO PACKED-FIELD-UNSIGNED.
00073
```

FIGURE 14.1 *COBOL Listing to Illustrate Efficiency Considerations*

```
00074              ***************************************************************************
00075              *     COMPARISON OF ADD INSTRUCTIONS FOR SIMILAR DATA TYPES            *
00076              *     ALL DATA NAMES ARE SIGNED                                        *
00077              *     DATA NAMES HAVE DIFFERENT DECIMAL ALIGNMENTS                     *
00078              ***************************************************************************
00079
00080              ADD ZONED-DECIMAL-WITH-POINT TO ZONED-DECIMAL-FIELD-ONE.
00081              ADD ZONED-DECIMAL-FIELD-ONE TO ZONED-DECIMAL-WITH-POINT.
00082              ADD BINARY-FIELD-ONE TO BINARY-FIELD-WITH-POINT.
00083              ADD BINARY-FIELD-WITH-POINT TO BINARY-FIELD-ONE.
00084              ADD PACKED-FIELD-ONE TO PACKED-FIELD-WITH-POINT.
00085              ADD PACKED-FIELD-WITH-POINT TO PACKED-FIELD-ONE.
00086              STOP RUN.
```

FIGURE 14.1 *(continued)*

Definition	Defines storage requirements for each data item in Assembler-like terminology. Observe the various storage assignments and how they correspond to the specific COBOL USAGE and PICTURE clauses.
Usage	Indicates the usage of the data name as defined in the COBOL program.
ROQM	Four columns, each with special significance:

R—data name redefines another data name.
O—OCCURS clause has been specified.
Q—DEPENDING ON clause was specified.
M—format of the records in the file; fixed, variable, etc.

INTRNL NAME	LVL	SOURCE NAME	BASE	DISPL	INTRNL NAME	DEFINITION	USAGE	R	O	Q	M
DNM=1-032	77	BINARY-FIELD-ONE	BL=1	000	DNM=1-032	DS 2C	COMP				
DNM=1-058	77	BINARY-FIELD-TWO	BL=1	002	DNM=1-058	DS 4C	COMP				
DNM=1-084	77	BINARY-FIELD-UNSIGNED	BL=1	006	DNM=1-084	DS 2C	COMP				
DNM=1-115	77	BINARY-FIELD-WITH-POINT	BL=1	008	DNM=1-115	DS 2C	COMP				
DNM=1-148	77	ZONED-DECIMAL-FIELD-ONE	BL=1	00A	DNM=1-148	DS 3C	DISP-NM				
DNM=1-181	77	ZONED-DECIMAL-FIELD-TWO	BL=1	00D	DNM=1-181	DS 5C	DISP-NM				
DNM=1-214	77	ZONED-DECIMAL-UNSIGNED	BL=1	012	DNM=1-214	DS 3C	DISP-NM				
DNM=1-246	77	ZONED-DECIMAL-WITH-POINT	BL=1	015	DNM=1-246	DS 4C	DISP-NM				
DNM=1-280	77	PACKED-FIELD-ONE	BL=1	019	DNM=1-280	DS 2P	COMP-3				
DNM=1-306	77	PACKED-FIELD-TWO	BL=1	01B	DNM=1-306	DS 3P	COMP-3				
DNM=1-332	77	PACKED-FIELD-UNSIGNED	BL=1	01E	DNM=1-332	DS 2P	COMP-3				
DNM=1-363	77	PACKED-FIELD-WITH-POINT	BL=1	020	DNM=1-363	DS 3P	COMP-3				

FIGURE 14.2 *Data Division Map*

Literal Pool and Register Assignment

Figure 14.3 contains the literal pool and register assignment for Figure 14.1. The literal pool lists ✳ the collection of literals in the program. It includes those specified by the programmer as in a move statement and those generated by the compiler, e.g., those needed for decimal alignment. Use of these literals is made clearer in the section on nonaligned fields. The PGT, or program global table, contains the remaining addresses and literals used by the object program. Its use is not discussed further.

The register assignment shows that BL 1 (base locator 1) is assigned to general register 6.

Procedure Division Map

The procedure division map (Figure 14.4) contains information about the generated object code. Reading from left to right, we see

1. Compiler-generated statement number.
2. The COBOL verb referenced in the statement number under item 1.
3. The relative location, in hexadecimal, of the object instruction.
4. The actual object code instruction.
5. The object code instruction in a form that most closely resembles the Assembler language.
6. Compiler-generated information about the operands.

002F8 (LIT + 0)   000A0000   0000000A

PGT	002E0
OVERFLOW CELLS	002E0
VIRTUAL CELLS	002E0
PROCEDURE NAME CELLS	002F4
GENERATED NAME CELLS	002F4
DCB ADDRESS CELLS	002F8
VNI CELLS	002F8
LITERALS	002F8
DISPLAY LITERALS	00300

REGISTER ASSIGNMENT

REG 6   BL = 1

FIGURE 14.3 *Literal Pool and Register Assignment*

```
44  ADD  000300                      START  EQU  *
         000300  48 30 6 000               LH    3,000(0,6)           DNM=1-32
         000304  5A 30 6 002               A     3,002(0,6)           DNM=1-58
         000308  50 30 6 002               ST    3,002(0,6)           DNM=1-58
45  ADD  00030C  F2 72 D 1F8 6 00A         PACK  1F8(8,13),00A(3,6)   TS=01       DNM=1-148
         000312  F2 74 D 200 6 00D         PACK  200(8,13),00D(5,6)   TS=09       DNM=1-181
         000318  FA 32 D 1FC D 205         AP    1FC(4,13),205(3,13)  TS=05       TS=014
         00031E  F3 43 6 00D D 1FC         UNPK  00D(5,6),1FC(4,13)   DNM=1-181   TS=05
46  ADD  000324  FA 21 6 01B 6 019         AP    01B(3,6),019(2,6)    DNM=1-306   DNM=1-280
50  ADD  00032A  F2 72 D 200 6 00A         PACK  200(8,13),00A(3,6)   TS=09       DNM=1-148
         000330  FA 21 6 205 6 019         AP    205(3,13),019(2,6)   TS=014      DNM=1-280
         000336  F3 22 6 00A D 205         UNPK  00A(3,6),205(3,13)   DNM=1-148   TS=014
51  ADD  00033C  F2 72 D 200 6 00A         PACK  200(8,13),00A(3,6)   TS=09       DNM=1-148
         000342  FA 11 6 019 D 206         AP    019(2,6),206(2,13)   DNM=1-280   TS=015
54  ADD  000348  F8 71 D 200 6 019         ZAP   200(8,13),019(2,6)   TS=09       DNM=1-280
         00034E  4F 30 D 200               CVB   3,200(0,13)          TS=09
         000352  4A 30 6 000               AH    3,000(0,6)           DNM=1-32
         000356  40 30 6 000               STH   3,000(0,6)           DNM=1-32
55  ADD  00035A  48 30 6 000               LH    3,000(0,6)           DNM=1-32
         00035E  4E 30 D 200               CVD   3,200(0,13)          TS=09
         000362  FA 11 6 019 D 206         AP    019(2,6),206(2,13)   DNM=1-280   TS=015
58  ADD  000368  F2 72 D 200 6 00A         PACK  200(8,13),00A(3,6)   TS=09       DNM=1-148
         00036E  4F 30 D 200               CVB   3,200(0,13)          TS=09
         000372  4A 30 6 000               AH    3,000(0,6)           DNM=1-32
         000376  40 30 6 000               STH   3,000(0,6)           DNM=1-32
59  ADD  00037A  F2 72 D 200 6 00A         PACK  200(8,13),00A(3,6)   TS=09       DNM=1-148
         000380  48 30 6 000               LH    3,000(0,6)           DNM=1-32
         000384  4E 30 D 1F8               CVD   3,1F8(0,13)          TS=01
         000388  FA 21 D 1FD D 206         AP    1FD(3,13),206(2,13)  TS=06       TS=015
         00038E  F3 22 6 00A D 1FD         UNPK  00A(3,6),1FD(3,13)   DNM=1-148   TS=06
67  ADD  000394  F2 72 D 200 6 012         PACK  200(8,13),012(3,6)   TS=09       DNM=1-214
         00039A  F2 72 D 1F8 6 00A         PACK  1F8(8,13),00A(3,6)   TS=01       DNM=1-148
         0003A0  FA 21 D 205 D 1FE         AP    205(3,13),1FE(2,13)  TS=014      TS=07
         0003A6  F3 22 6 00A D 205         UNPK  00A(3,6),205(3,13)   DNM=1-148   TS=014
68  ADD  0003AC  F2 72 D 200 6 00A         PACK  200(8,13),00A(3,6)   TS=09       DNM=1-148
         0003B2  F2 72 D 1F8 6 012         PACK  1F8(8,13),012(3,6)   TS=01       DNM=1-214
         0003B8  FA 21 D 205 D 1FE         AP    205(3,13),1FE(2,13)  TS=014      TS=07
         0003BE  F3 22 6 012 D 205         UNPK  012(3,6),205(3,13)   DNM=1-214   TS=014
         0003C4  96 F0 6 014               OI    014(6),X'F0'         DNM=1-214+2
69  ADD  0003C8  48 30 6 006               LH    3,006(0,6)           DNM=1-84
         0003CC  4A 30 6 000               AH    3,000(0,6)           DNM=1-32
         0003D0  40 30 6 000               STH   3,000(0,6)           DNM=1-32
70  ADD  0003D4  48 30 6 000               LH    3,000(0,6)           DNM=1-32
         0003D8  4A 30 6 006               AH    3,006(0,6)           DNM=1-84
         0003DC  10 33                     LPR   3,3
         0003DE  40 30 6 006               STH   3,006(0,6)           DNM=1-84
71  ADD  0003E2  FA 11 6 019 6 01E         AP    019(2,6),01E(2,6)    DNM=1-280   DNM=1-332
72  ADD  0003E8  FA 11 6 01E 6 019         AP    01E(2,6),019(2,6)    DNM=1-332   DNM=1-280
         0003EE  96 0F 6 01F               OI    01F(6),X'0F'         DNM=1-332+1
80  ADD  0003F2  F2 73 D 200 6 015         PACK  200(8,13),015(4,6)   TS=09       DNM=1-246
         0003F8  F2 72 D 1F8 6 00A         PACK  1F8(8,13),00A(3,6)   TS=01       DNM=1-148
         0003FE  F0 20 D 1FD 0 001         SRP   1FD(3,13),001(0),0   TS=06
         000404  FA 22 D 205 D 1FD         AP    205(3,13),1FD(3,13)  TS=014      TS=06
         00040A  F1 76 D 200 D 200         MVO   200(8,13),200(7,13)  TS=09       TS=09
         000410  F3 22 6 00A D 205         UNPK  00A(3,6),205(3,13)   DNM=1-148   TS=014
81  ADD  000416  F2 72 D 200 6 00A         PACK  200(8,13),00A(3,6)   TS=09       DNM=1-148
         00041C  F2 73 D 1F8 6 015         PACK  1F8(8,13),015(4,6)   TS=01       DNM=1-246
         000422  F0 20 D 205 0 001         SRP   205(3,13),001(0),0   TS=014
         000428  FA 22 D 205 D 1FD         AP    205(3,13),1FD(3,13)  TS=014      TS=06
         00042E  F3 32 6 015 D 205         UNPK  015(4,6),205(3,13)   DNM=1-246   TS=014
82  ADD  000434  48 30 6 000               LH    3,000(0,6)           DNM=1-32
         000438  4C 30 C 018               MH    3,018(0,12)          LIT+0
         00043C  4A 30 6 008               AH    3,008(0,6)           DNM=1-115
         000440  40 30 6 008               STH   3,008(0,6)           DNM=1-115
```

FIGURE 14.4 *Procedure Division Map*

SECTION IV: THE ROLE OF BAL IN DEEPER UNDERSTANDING

```
83    ADD       000444  48 30 6 000              LH     3,000(0,6)          DNM=1-32
                000448  4C 30 C 018              MH     3,018(0,12)         LIT+0
                00044C  4A 30 6 008              AH     3,008(0,6)          DNM=1-115
                000450  18 23                    LR     2,3
                000452  8E 20 0 020              SRDA   2,020(0)
                000456  5D 20 C 01C              D      2,01C(0,12)         LIT+4
                00045A  40 30 6 000              STH    3,000(0,6)          DNM=1-32
84    ADD       00045E  F8 71 D 200 6 019        ZAP    200(8,13),019(2,6)  TS=09               DNM=1-280
                000464  F0 20 D 205 0 001        SRP    205(3,13),001(0),0  TS=014
                00046A  FA 22 6 020 D 205        AP     020(3,6),205(3,13)  DNM=1-363           TS=014
                000470  94 0F 6 020              NI     020(6),X'0F'        DNM=1-363
85    ADD       000474  F8 71 D 200 6 019        ZAP    200(8,13),019(2,6)  TS=09               DNM=1-280
                00047A  F0 20 D 205 0 001        SRP    205(3,13),001(0),0  TS=014
                000480  FA 22 D 205 6 020        AP     205(3,13),020(3,6)  TS=014              DNM=1-363
                000486  F1 76 D 200 D 200        MVO    200(8,13),200(7,13) TS=09               TS=09
                00048C  F8 11 6 019 D 206        ZAP    019(2,6),206(2,13)  DNM=1-280           TS=014+1
86    STOP      000492  58 F0 C 00C              L      15,00C(0,12)        V(ILBODBG4)
                000496  05 EF                    BALR   14,15
                000498                  GN=01    EQU    *
                000498  58 F0 C 010              L      15,010(0,12)        V(ILBOSRV1)
                00049C  07 FF                    BCR    15,15
                00049E  50 D0 5 008     INIT2    ST     13,008(0,5)
                0004A2  50 50 D 004              ST     5,004(0,13)
                0004A6  50 E0 D 054              ST     14,054(0,13)
                0004AA  91 20 D 048              TM     048(13),X'20'       SWT+0
                0004AE  47 E0 F 02E              BC     14,02E(0,15)
                0004B2  58 20 D 1B8              L      2,1B8(0,13)
                0004B6  91 40 D 049              TM     049(13),X'40'       SWT+1
```

FIGURE 14.4 *(continued)*

COBOL ADD INSTRUCTIONS WITH SIMILAR DATA TYPES

DISPLAY TO DISPLAY: We return to Figure 14.1 and shall examine three COBOL add statements and generated object code. In each example both operands are signed, of the same data type, and have identical decimal alignment. Consider first COBOL statement 45, as well as statements 18 to 21 in the working-storage section.

ADD ZONED-DECIMAL-FIELD-ONE TO ZONED-DECIMAL-FIELD-TWO.

77   ZONED-DECIMAL-FIELD-ONE   PICTURE IS S9(3)
     USAGE IS DISPLAY.

77   ZONED-DECIMAL-FIELD-TWO   PICTURE IS S9(5)
     USAGE IS DISPLAY.

From the procedure division map, we extract four lines associated with COBOL statement 45:

```
45  ADD  F2 72 D 1F8 6 00A     PACK ... TS = 01     DNM = 1-148
         F2 74 D 200 6 00D     PACK ... TS = 09     DNM = 1-181
         FA 32 D 1FC D 205     AP   ... TS = 05     TS = 014
         F3 43 6 00D D 1FC     UNPK ... DNM = 1-181 TS = 05
```

The COBOL programmer simply wants to add two numeric fields. However, since the fields are DISPLAY, i.e., stored as zoned decimal numbers, they must first be packed, and then after the addition, the sum must be unpacked. The first object instruction packs DNM = 1-148, i.e., ZONED-DECIMAL-FIELD-ONE (check the data division map), into a temporary storage area 8 bytes in length. In like manner, DNM = 1-181, i.e., ZONED-DECIMAL-FIELD-TWO, is packed into TS = 09, also a temporary storage area of 8 bytes. Notice how the length, base register, and displacement match the data division map. The contents of the two temporary storage areas are then added via the add packed instruction, and finally the sum is unpacked into DNM = 1-181, i.e., ZONED-DECIMAL-FIELD-TWO. (Observe the length codes associated with each instruction.)

PACKED TO PACKED: Consider now COBOL statement 46 and its relevant 77-level entries (lines 26 to 29).

ADD PACKED-FIELD-ONE TO PACKED-FIELD-TWO.

77   PACKED-FIELD-ONE   PICTURE IS S9(3)
     USAGE IS COMPUTATIONAL-3.

CHAPTER 14: INSIGHT INTO THE COBOL COMPILER

```
77  PACKED-FIELD-TWO                      PICTURE IS S9(5)
        USAGE IS COMPUTATIONAL-3.
```

This time only a single add packed instruction is generated by the compiler:

```
46  ADD    FA 21 6 01B 6 019    AP ... DNM = 1–306    DNM = 1–280
```

Observe that the operands DNM = 1–306 and DNM = 1–280 correspond to PACKED-FIELD-TWO and PACKED-FIELD-ONE, respectively. Further note the displacement for each operand, 01B and 019, and the correspondence in the data division map. Finally, the sum of the add packed instruction is stored in the first operand, i.e., DNM = 1–306 corresponding to PACKED-FIELD-TWO, as intended by the COBOL programmer. Compare this single instruction to the four instructions and 24 bytes of code required in the previous example. The saving is realized because the operands are defined as packed fields by the programmer; hence, there is no need for the compiler to pack and subsequently unpack.

BINARY TO BINARY: Addition of two binary operands is illustrated in COBOL statement 44 with the relevant 77-level entries defined in statements 10 to 13.

```
ADD BINARY-FIELD-ONE TO BINARY-FIELD-TWO.

77  BINARY-FIELD-ONE                      PICTURE IS S9(3)
        USAGE IS COMPUTATIONAL.
77  BINARY-FIELD-TWO                      PICTURE IS S9(5)
        USAGE IS COMPUTATIONAL.
```

Object instructions generated by the compiler are shown:

```
44  ADD    48 30 6 000    LH ... DNM = 1–32
           5A 30 6 002    A  ... DNM = 1–58
           50 30 6 002    ST ... DNM = 1–58
```

Since we are dealing with binary operands, the add packed instruction is no longer appropriate. Instead the compiler generates either an AH (add half word) or A (add full word) instruction depending on the size of the binary operands. The LH (load half word) instruction brings BINARY-FIELD-ONE into register 3. The A (add full word) instruction adds the value of BINARY-FIELD-TWO to register 3. Finally, the store instruction moves the contents of register 3 to BINARY-FIELD-TWO.

Careful analysis of this section shows how three apparently similar COBOL instructions in Figure 14.1, statements 44, 45, and 46, produce vastly different object instructions. In each instance, the programmer was adding a three-position signed field to a five-position signed field of similar data type and decimal alignment. Addition of two COMPUTATIONAL-3 fields required one instruction (6 bytes); addition of two DISPLAY fields took four instructions (24 bytes); and addition of two COMPUTATIONAL fields took three instructions (12 bytes).

COBOL ADD INSTRUCTIONS
WITH DISSIMILAR DATA TYPES

We shall concentrate on combinations of packed and binary data and leave the reader to work through other examples in Figure 14.1.

BINARY TO DECIMAL: BINARY-FIELD-ONE is added to PACKED-FIELD-ONE in COBOL statement 55. Both fields are defined as signed three-digit fields with no decimal point, as shown:

```
ADD BINARY-FIELD-ONE TO PACKED-FIELD-ONE.

77  BINARY-FIELD-ONE                      PICTURE IS S9(3)
```

```
                    USAGE IS COMPUTATIONAL.
        77  PACKED-FIELD-ONE                    PICTURE IS S9(3)
                    USAGE IS COMPUTATIONAL-3.
```

Since a binary field is added to a packed field, it is necessary to first convert the binary data to packed data. Consider the three machine language statements generated:

```
    55  ADD     48 30 6 000         LH  ... DNM = 1–32
                4E 30 D 200         CVD ... TS = 09
                FA 11 6 019 D 206   AP  ... DNM = 1–280  TS = 015
```

BINARY-FIELD-ONE (i.e., DNM = 1–32) is loaded into register 3 via the load half-word instruction. Next it is converted to a packed field and stored on a double word boundary by the CVD instruction. Finally, the newly created packed field is added to DNM = 1–280, i.e., PACKED-FIELD-ONE, and the results are stored there. (If the reader is paying attention, he or she should question why the displacement associated with register D changed from 200 to 206 in the second and third instructions.)

DECIMAL TO BINARY: COBOL statement 54 is identical to statement 55 except the results are stored in the binary field. The reasoning in the Assembler sequence is analogous to the previous example.

```
    54  ADD     F8 71 D 200 6 019   ZAP ... TS = 09        DNM = 1–280
                4F 30 D 200         CVB ... TS = 09
                4A 30 6 000         AH  ... DNM = 1–32
                40 30 6 000         STH ... DNM = 1–32
```

The CVB instruction must operate on a double word boundary, and since PACKED-FIELD-ONE is only 2 bytes in length, it is necessary to fill the high-order bytes of the double word with zeros. The ZAP (zero and add packed) instruction takes the second operand DNM = 1–280, i.e., PACKED-FIELD-ONE, moves it to a double word boundary, and fills the high-order bytes with binary zeros. The newly moved decimal field is then converted to binary and stored in register 3. BINARY-FIELD-ONE is added to the contents of register 3, with the sum remaining in register 3. The sum is finally stored in BINARY-FIELD-ONE via the STH. Seem complicated? Yes, it is, but that is exactly the point. It is unnecessarily complex because the COBOL programmer, perhaps inadvertently, is adding a packed field to a binary field. Compare the four instructions and 18 bytes of code in this example to the single add packed instruction needed for addition of two decimal fields.

ADDITION OF SIMILAR DATA TYPES WITH AN UNSIGNED OPERAND

PACKED TO PACKED: When the data division and picture clause were first studied, we stated that any numeric field should be preceded by an "S" or otherwise the sign would be lost. That rule is still valid. Now let's learn what the compiler does. Consider COBOL statement 72 and relevant 77-level entries, lines 26, 27, 30, and 31.

```
        ADD PACKED-FIELD-ONE TO PACKED-FIELD-UNSIGNED.

    77  PACKED-FIELD-ONE                PICTURE IS S9(3)
            USAGE IS COMPUTATIONAL-3.
    77  PACKED-FIELD-UNSIGNED           PICTURE IS 9(3)
            USAGE IS COMPUTATIONAL-3.
```

The generated instructions are

```
    72  ADD     FA 11 6 01E 6 019   AP ... DNM = 1–332      DNM = 1–280
                96 0F 6 01F         OI ... DNM = 1–332 + 1
```

The add packed instruction works exactly as the one generated by COBOL statement 46, considered earlier in the addition of packed fields. DNM = 1–332 is 2 bytes in length and stored in bytes 01E and 01F displaced from register 6. The AP instruction always produces a sign of "C" (plus) or "D" (minus) and stores it in the low-order byte of the sum, in this case byte 01F displaced from register 6.

The OI (or immediate) instruction is an SI instruction that takes the value of the "I" operand, "0F," and does a bit-by-bit *logical or* upon the storage address, altering the value of the storage location DNM = 1–332 + 1 (base register 6, displaced by 01F). In effect, it changes the sign from either "C" or "D" to "F" while the rest of the field remains undistrubed. Thus, since PACKED-FIELD-UNSIGNED was declared unsigned, an OI instruction was generated to remove the sign. This is not true in COBOL statement 71, as shown:

ADD PACKED-FIELD-UNSIGNED TO PACKED-FIELD-ONE.

Generated instructions:

71   ADD   FA 11 6 019 6 01E   AP ... DNM = 1–280   DNM = 1–332

Here the sum is stored in PACKED-FIELD-ONE, which was declared as a signed field. Thus, there is only a single AP instruction generated, and the sign remains intact.

BINARY TO BINARY: Similar reasoning holds for binary operands, except a different instruction is used to remove the sign. Recall that the sign of a binary number is stored in the high-order bit. (A "0" indicates a positive number, and a "1" indicates a negative number stored in two's complement.) If the receiving field is unsigned, then an LPR (load positive register) instruction is generated in the series of instructions. Consider COBOL statement 70 and relevant 77-level entries 10, 11, 14, and 15.

ADD BINARY-FIELD-ONE TO BINARY-FIELD-UNSIGNED.

77	BINARY-FIELD-ONE	PICTURE IS S9(3)
	USAGE IS COMPUTATIONAL.	
77	BINARY-FIELD-UNSIGNED	PICTURE IS 9(3)
	USAGE IS COMPUTATIONAL.	

The generated instructions are

70   ADD   48 30 6 000   LH   ... DNM = 1–32
              4A 30 6 006   AH   ... DNM = 1–84
              10 33   LPR ...
              40 30 6 006   STH ... DNM = 1–84

These instructions parallel those generated for COBOL statement 44 except that an AH (add half-word) and STH (store half-word) are generated in lieu of an A (add full word) and ST (store full word), respectively. Why? Further note the instruction LPR 3,3 after the addition. The effect of this instruction is to load the absolute value of register 3 into register 3, thereby destroying a minus sign if it were present.

COBOL statement 69 also involves an unsigned operand, except that it is not the receiving field; hence, there is no LPR instruction, and the generated code is comparable to that of COBOL statement 44.

ADDING OPERANDS THAT ARE NOT ALIGNED

The addition of operands with nonsimilar decimal alignment produces extensive and often confusing object code. COBOL statements 80 to 85 in Figure 14.1 illustrate several combinations for nonaligned fields. However, only statement 82 is covered in detail, as the others require introduction of several new instructions that go beyond the scope of this chapter. The reader should also realize that as complicated as the object instructions appear, they would be substantially more involved if different data types were mixed in the same instruction.

Consider COBOL statement 82 and relevant 77-level entries, statements 10, 11, 16, 17.

ADD BINARY-FIELD-ONE TO BINARY-FIELD-WITH-POINT.

77	BINARY-FIELD-ONE	PICTURE IS S9(3)
	USAGE IS COMPUTATIONAL.	
77	BINARY-FIELD-WITH-POINT	PICTURE IS S9(3)V9
	USAGE IS COMPUTATIONAL.	

The generated object code is

```
82   ADD     48 30 6 000     LH  ... DNM = 1–32
             4C 30 C 018     MH  ... LIT + 0
             4A 30 6 008     AH  ... DNM = 1–115
             40 30 6 008     STH ... DNM = 1–115
```

Let us first consider conceptually what is and is not required. Both operands are binary, so there is no need for conversion of data type; both operands are signed, and thus no instructions need be generated to remove the sign. However, the decimal alignments are different, and they must first be made identical before addition can occur. BINARY-FIELD-WITH-POINT is the receiving field with an implied decimal point, which in effect makes it larger by a factor of 10 than BINARY-FIELD-ONE; thus BINARY-FIELD-ONE will be multiplied by 10 prior to addition. (Note the presence of a divide instruction in the Assembler sequence for COBOL statement 83 in which the same two operands are combined but where BINARY-FIELD-ONE is the receiving field.)

First, DNM = 1–32, i.e., BINARY-FIELD-ONE, is loaded into register 3. The contents of register 3 are then multiplied by the contents of a half-word, beginning at LIT + 0, which equals "000A" in hexadecimal and "10" in decimal (see Figure 14.3). The results of the multiplication are stored in register 3. Next, DNM = 1–115, i.e., BINARY-FIELD-WITH-POINT, is added to the contents of register 3, and the sum is placed in register 3. Finally, the contents of register 3 are stored in BINARY-FIELD-WITH-POINT.

As can be seen from this example, the combination of nonaligned fields in a source program necessitates the generation of extra instructions in the object program. COBOL statements 80 to 85 present a sufficient variety of new BAL instructions to acquaint the reader with alignment logic. In actual practice, situations arise in which incompatible formats are unavoidable. In such instances one must comply with the "specs" as given, and efficiency considerations are shunted aside.

SUMMARY

The following Assembler instructions were introduced as background for efficiency considerations:

PACK	Pack
UNPK	Unpack
CVB	Convert to binary
CVD	Convert to decimal
L	Load (full word)
ST	Store (full word)
AP	Add packed
A	Add (full word)

Next, a COBOL program, consisting of ADD statements using various combinations of data types and decimal alignments, was used to illustrate basic workings of the COBOL compiler. The procedure and data division maps, register assignments, and literal pool were examined in detail. Several sets of COBOL and generated object instructions were compared. Initially, both operands in the COBOL instruction were of the same data type and sign and were similarly aligned. Subsequently, these restrictions were removed to consider combinations of packed and binary data, non-aligned binary fields, and unsigned binary and decimal fields.

The COBOL listing of Figure 14.1 and its associated output can be used to provide intuitive justification for some commonplace efficiency considerations. These include the following:

1. Where possible, arithmetic should be performed on packed fields, i.e., those defined as COMPUTATIONAL-3. Arithmetic should not be performed on zoned decimal fields, i.e., those with no clause or with USAGE IS DISPLAY, as additional instructions are required to convert these fields to packed data prior to arithmetic. With respect to Figure 14.1, the statement

    ADD PACKED-FIELD-ONE TO PACKED-FIELD-TWO

    is preferable to

    ADD DISPLAY-FIELD-ONE TO DISPLAY-FIELD-TWO.

    As can be seen from Figure 14.1, addition of packed fields requires one instruction, addition of binary fields takes three instructions, and addition of zoned decimal fields, four.

2. Regardless of what usage is specified, all data names in the same instruction should contain the same number of decimal places. Thus the statement

    ADD PACKED-FIELD-ONE TO PACKED-FIELD-TWO

    is preferable to

    ADD PACKED-FIELD-ONE TO PACKED-FIELD-WITH-POINT.

    The second statement, involving addition of two operands with different numbers of decimal places, requires additional machine instructions to align the data prior to the arithmetic.

3. The receiving operand, whether packed, binary, or display, should always be signed. Omission of the sign in the picture clause causes an extra instruction that removes the sign generated as the result of the arithmetic operation. Further, omission of a sign in the picture clause of the receiving data name could cause algebraic errors in cases where negative numbers could legitimately be present. Thus the statement

    ADD PACKED-FIELD-ONE TO PACKED-FIELD-TWO

    is preferable to

    ADD PACKED-FIELD-ONE TO PACKED-FIELD-UNSIGNED.

4. Arithmetic should be performed on fields with like usage clauses to avoid conversion from one format to another; thus the statement

    ADD PACKED-FIELD-ONE TO PACKED-FIELD-TWO

    is superior to

    ADD PACKED-FIELD-ONE TO BINARY-FIELD-ONE.

In reviewing these suggestions, the reader must remember they are only guidelines and consequently cannot be implemented 100% of the time. Since the problem specifications may, in and of themselves, prohibit implementation, the guidelines must be subservient to the problem itself. Second, all suggestions are based solely on the number of generated machine instructions. Thus the alternative with fewer instructions is presumed superior in that it requires less storage.

In conclusion, the COBOL programmer can and does function with no knowledge of the machine. However, a little knowledge in this area goes a long way toward genuine understanding of debugging and efficiency considerations. We hope this point has been effectively made in both this chapter and the entire section. We have found that the best COBOL programmers are those who also know, or at least have a fundamental understanding of, Assembler.

REVIEW EXERCISES

TRUE FALSE

☐ ☐ **1.** A load instruction changes the contents of a register.

☐ ☐ **2.** A store instruction does not change the contents of a storage location.

☐ ☐ **3.** DISPLAY data must be packed before they can be added.

☐ ☐ **4.** Data must be in binary format before they can be added.

☐ ☐ **5.** The COBOL programmer is not permitted to mix data types in the same COBOL instruction.

☐ ☐ **6.** An add half-word instruction could be used in conjunction with packed data.

☐ ☐ **7.** The CVD instruction converts binary data to packed format.

☐ ☐ **8.** The CVB instruction changes the contents of a register.

☐ ☐ **9.** The PACK instruction must operate on two fields of identical length.

☐ ☐ **10.** The AP instruction has only one length field.

☐ ☐ **11.** AP (add packed) is a storage-to-storage instruction.

☐ ☐ **12.** The CVB instruction works directly on DISPLAY data.

☐ ☐ **13.** The addition of two COMPUTATIONAL-3 fields requires fewer machine instructions than the addition of two DISPLAY fields.

☐ ☐ **14.** A minimum of four machine instructions is required to add two DISPLAY fields.

☐ ☐ **15.** The COBOL programmer is not permitted to combine data names of different decimal alignments in the same instruction.

☐ ☐ **16.** Regardless of the data types involved, object code is more efficient if COBOL operands have identical decimal alignments.

☐ ☐ **17.** If both a signed and unsigned operand appear in the same COBOL instruction, the answer will be unsigned.

☐ ☐ **18.** If both COMP and COMP-3 operands appear in the same COBOL statement, the answer will be in packed format.

PROBLEMS

1. Consider the data division map of Figure 14.2. Show how the displacement and definition columns are consistent with the definitions in the working-storage section of Figure 14.1.

2. Consider the object instructions generated for COBOL statement 45. Show that the length codes in both the machine and Assembler instructions are consistent with the definitions in working-storage. Also show consistency of base registers and displacement between the machine and Assembler instructions.

3. Consider the following COBOL statement:

ADD COMP3-DATA-NAME TO DISPLAY-DATA-NAME.

where

05 COMP3-DATA-NAME PICTURE IS S9(4)
USAGE IS COMPUTATIONAL-3.

and
05 DISPLAY-DATA-NAME PICTURE IS S9(4).

are the definitions for the respective data names. The following statements were found in a corresponding procedure division map:

```
F2 F3 3168 A009    (PACK)
FA F2 3168 A021    (AP)
.F3 3F A009 3168   (UNPK)
```

(a) Where is the compiler work area? How many bytes does it contain?
(b) What is the location associated with each COBOL data name? (*Do not guess,* but explain how the structure of the COBOL and BAL ADD statements gives you an unambiguous answer.)

4. Given the data division entries

```
05  FIELD-A  PIC 9(3)   VALUE 456.
05  FIELD-B  PIC 9(3)   VALUE 123.
05  FIELD-C  PIC S9(3)  VALUE -100.
05  SUM1     PIC 9(3)   VALUE 0.
05  SUM2     PIC S9(3)  VALUE 0.
05  SUM3     PIC S9(3)  VALUE 25.
05  SUM4     PIC 9(4)   VALUE 25.
```

and the procedure division entries

```
ADD FIELD-A, FIELD-B GIVING SUM1.
ADD FIELD-A, FIELD-B GIVING SUM2.
ADD FIELD-C TO SUM3.
ADD FIELD-C TO SUM4.
```

(a) Explain why SUM1 would print as 579 but SUM2 might print as 57I.
(b) Explain why SUM3 would retain the value −75, but SUM4 would become +75. *Hint:* Remember the Or Immediate instruction.

5. Given the following data division entries:

```
01  FIRST-SET-OF-COUNTERS.
    05  COUNTER-A    DISPLAY    PIC 9(3).
    05  COUNTER-B    DISPLAY    PIC 9(3).
    05  COUNTER-C    DISPLAY    PIC 9(3).

01  SECOND-SET-OF-COUNTERS.
    05  COUNTER-D    COMP       PIC S9(4).
    05  COUNTER-E    COMP       PIC S9(4).
    05  COUNTER-F    COMP       PIC S9(4).

01  THIRD-SET-OF-COUNTERS.
    05  COUNTER-G    COMP-3     PIC 9(5).
    05  COUNTER-H    COMP-3     PIC 9(5).
    05  COUNTER-I    COMP-3     PIC 9(5).
```

Is there anything 'wrong' with the following?[1]
(a) MOVE ZEROS TO FIRST-SET-OF-COUNTERS.
(b) MOVE ZEROS TO SECOND-SET-OF-COUNTERS.
(c) MOVE ZEROS TO THIRD-SET-OF-COUNTERS.

[1] A discussion of the peculiar results associated with parts (b) and (c) is found in R. Grauer and M. Crawford, *The COBOL Environment,* Chapter 7 (Englewood Cliffs, N.J.: Prentice-Hall, Inc., 1979).

Section V

FILE PROCESSING

Chapter 15

MAGNETIC TAPE: CONCEPTS AND COBOL IMPLICATIONS

OVERVIEW

The punched card has enjoyed a long and successful reign since its introduction by Herman Hollerith. However, beginning in the late 1950s, as electronic computers gained in capability and acceptance, it became impractical to store entire files on cards. This is not to say that the punched card has outlived its usefulness, for even today it serves as a primary means of data input. Data are recorded on cards, but after initial entry are transferred to auxiliary storage such as tape or disk. In this chapter we shall discuss concepts of magnetic tape and associated COBOL implications. The COBOL discussion adheres strictly to the ANS 74 standard, which introduced several changes and new capabilities.

We discuss various kinds of record formats, e.g., blocked versus unblocked and fixed versus variable length. The chapter concludes with a discussion of sequential file maintenance, culminating in a COBOL program to accomplish this function. Since the logical requirements of this program are relatively complex, we include pseudocode and a hierarchy chart to facilitate the discussion.

TAPE CHARACTERISTICS AND CAPACITY

We begin by considering the physical aspects of magnetic tape. This is a good place to distinguish between a reel of tape and a tape drive. The typical reel of magnetic tape is 2400 feet long, ½ inch wide, and weighs about 4 pounds. The tape drive is the unit that reads (writes) information from the reel. The reel is easily portable; the drive is obviously confined to the machine room. See Figure 15.1.

Tapes are generally classified as either 7 or 9 track, depending on how data are stored internally. Recall from Chapter 12 that IBM systems use EBCDIC (an 8-bit code), whereas most other manufacturers use ASCII (a 6-bit code). Both codes employ parity checking and hence the extension to either 9 or 7 track. A 9-track tape can be viewed as having 9 rows extending for the entire length of the tape, i.e., 2400 feet. Each individual character is stored in a vertical column. Each column contains 9 bits, one for each track. The individual bits may be "on" or "off," i.e., 1 or 0. The presence or absence of these bits in a particular column denotes a character much like the punched holes in a card column. Figure 15.2 shows schematics of 7- and 9-track tapes.

The amount of data that can be stored on a given reel is dependent on three factors: tape density, blocking factor, and interrecord gap (also known as interblock gap). Tape *density* is a

FIGURE 15.1 *IBM Tape Drive (Courtesy IBM).*

measure of how close the columns are to one another. It is usually specified as characters or *bytes per inch (bpi).* Common densities are 800, 1600, and 6250 bpi.

The next time you are in the computer center, watch the operation of the tape drive and notice an uneven rather than smooth motion. This is produced by gaps, i.e., lengths of blank tape, between each record on the reel. These gaps are required for the system to distinguish between different physical records. In reality the tape drive continually stops and starts every time it encounters a gap, producing the irregular motion.

The *interrecord gap (IRG)* profoundly affects the storage capacity of a tape. It is typically anywhere from .3 to .75 inch. Consider a tape with a density of 1600 bpi and an IRG of ½ inch. If we are recording card images, each tape record consists of 80 bytes and takes 80/1600 or 1/20 inch. However, an IRG of ½ inch is present between each record. Thus we are left with the somewhat incongruous situation of having 10 times as much empty space as data.

Blocking offers a way out of this dilemma. If blocking is used, several *logical records* are grouped into one block (known as a *physical record*), and the entire block is read (written) at

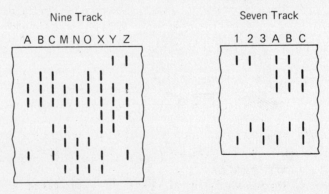

FIGURE 15.2 *7- and 9-Track Schematics*

SECTION V: FILE PROCESSING

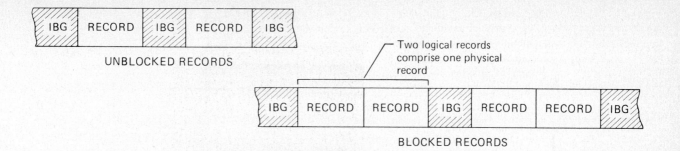

UNBLOCKED RECORDS

Two logical records comprise one physical record

BLOCKED RECORDS

FIGURE 15.3 *Blocked and Unblocked Records*

one time. The *blocking factor* is the number of logical records in one physical record. The interrecord ✳ gap is still required, but only between physical records. Figure 15.3 shows blocked and unblocked records, with an arbitrary blocking factor of 2 chosen for illustration.

To appreciate the effect of blocking on capacity, return to our example with card images, 1600 bpi and an IRG of ½ inch, and assume a blocking factor of 5. Each physical record contains 400 bytes (5 × 80) and requires ¼ inch (400/1600). We have effected a fivefold improvement in terms of wasted space, but the tape still contains twice as much empty space as data.

Obviously, blocking is a good thing. The higher the blocking factor, the more economical the tape storage. Why not increase the blocking factor to 10, 100, or 1000, or, better yet, consider the entire file as a single block. The limitation on blocking is determined by internal storage capacity. The entire block must be taken into storage at the same time. Card images, blocked by 100, would require an I/O area in storage of 8000 (80 × 100) bytes, which may not be available. Accordingly, the blocking factor is limited by storage considerations, and the programmer must operate within these constraints.

Example 15.1

How many card images can fit on a 2400-foot reel? Assume a density of 1600 bpi, IRG = ½ inch, and a blocking factor of 30.

SOLUTION
1. Since the blocking factor is 30, there are 30 logical records to 1 physical record. Each physical record contains 30 × 80 = 2400 bytes.
2. Each physical record takes 1½ inches (2400/1600).
3. Associated with each physical record is an IRG of ½ inch. Thus we may say that each physical record requires 2 inches (1½ for data and ½ for the IRG).
4. Since each physical record takes 2 inches, the entire tape can accommodate 14,400 physical records: (2400 ft/tape × 12 inches/ft) ÷ 2 inches/record.
5. Since there are 30 logical records per physical record, and since the tape holds 14,400 physical records, it can take 432,000 cards (14,400 × 30).

OBSERVATIONS
1. There are 2000 cards in a box. Thus a reel of tape with 432,000 cards is equivalent to 216 boxes. Which would you rather carry?
2. One box of cards weighs approximately 10 pounds; 216 boxes would weigh a little over 1 ton.
3. When stacked vertically, there are 140 cards to the inch. Thus a stack of 432,000 cards would stand approximately 252 feet tall [432,000/(140 × 12)] or the equivalent of a 25-story building.
4. Tapes with density of 6250 bpi and an IRG of .3 inch are commonly available. Consider these implications to items 1 through 3.

Example 15.2

The inventory file of ACME Wigdets, Inc., contains 36,000 records, each 800 bytes long. Determine whether the entire file will fit on a single 2400 foot reel of tape (use 1600 bpi and IRG = .5 inch). Consider no blocking and then a blocking factor of 3.

SOLUTION: NO BLOCKING
1. Each logical record takes ½ inch (800/1600).
2. Each record has an associated gap of ½ inch. Since there is no blocking, each physical record requires 1 inch (½ for data and ½ for the IRG).
3. The entire file of 36,000 records takes 36,000 inches or 3000 feet (36,000/12).
4. The entire file does not fit on one reel if blocking is not used.

SOLUTION: BLOCKING FACTOR OF 3
1. Each logical record still takes ½ inch.
2. Each physical record consists of three logical records or 2400 bytes (800 × 3). Each physical record takes 1½ inches (2400/1600).
3. Each physical record has an associated gap of ½ inch. The total requirement for a physical record is 2 inches (1½ inches for data and ½ inch for IRG).
4. 36,000 logical records in the file and a blocking factor of 3 means 12,000 physical records.
5. Since each physical record takes 2 inches, the entire file takes 24,000 inches or 2000 feet.
6. The entire file will fit on one reel if a blocking factor of 3 is used.

Vendors are constantly improving tape capabilities, and the numbers used herein may possibly be obsolete when you read them. However, that is immaterial. The concepts and methods of calculation are of primary importance; the actual numbers may add to the interest of the problem but are of secondary value from a pedagogical viewpoint.

TIMING CONSIDERATIONS

For purposes of this discussion, reading and writing on tape are assumed to take equal amounts of time. The time required to pass a file (i.e., read or write) is dependent on two factors: *transfer rate* and *start/stop time.* Transfer rate is a function of the actual speed of the tape. Start/stop time is the time associated with passing an interrecord gap. The tape actually stops and starts everytime it encounters an IRG, producing the irregular motion noted earlier. These concepts are clarified in Example 15.3.

Example 15.3

How long would it take to pass a file of 12,000 records, if each record is 400 bytes long? Use 800 bpi, a tape speed of 200 inches per second, and a start/stop time of 10 milliseconds (.01 second). Answer for both no blocking and a blocking factor of 3.

SOLUTION: NO BLOCKING
1. A tape speed of 200 inches per second and a density of 800 bpi are equivalent to a transfer rate of 160,000 bytes per second (200 × 800).
2. The file contains a total of 4,800,000 bytes (12,000 records × 400 bytes per record).
3. Thirty seconds are required for transfer time (4,800,000/160,000). This is the time to actually read the file; it does not include the time to pass the IRG's.
4. With no blocking, there are 12,000 IRG's, one for each record.
5. Since start/stop time is .01 second for 1 IRG, the start/stop time for the entire file is 120 seconds (.01 × 12,000).
6. The total time to pass the file is 150 seconds (transfer time of 30 seconds plus start/stop time of 120 seconds).

SECTION V: FILE PROCESSING

SOLUTION: BLOCKING FACTOR OF 3

1. The transfer time of 30 seconds is unaffected by blocking; i.e., the file still contains 4,800,000 bytes, and the tape still moves at 200 inches per second.
2. Start/stop time is reduced. A blocking factor of 3 means there are now only 4000 IRG's (12,000/3). Start/stop time is now 40 seconds (.01 × 4000).
3. The total time is 70 seconds (30 seconds transfer plus 40 seconds start/stop).

OBSERVATIONS

1. A moderately fast card reader can process 1000 cards per minute. A file of 12,000 records, each record 400 bytes long, requires 5 cards per record or 60,000 cards total. At 1000 cards per minute, it would take 1 hour to read the entire file.
2. A significant advantage of blocking is the reduction in the time required to read or write a file. This consideration outweighs the benefits of increased storage capacity.

IDENTIFYING FILES ON TAPE

The files contained on a tape are identified by means of internal *labels*, i.e., information stored on the tape before and after the file. Each reel contains a volume label and each file contains both a header and trailer label. A given reel may contain several files (multifile volume), or a single file may stretch over several volumes (multivolume file). All volumes contain both a load point and end of tape marker, which are aluminum strips located 10 feet from either end. The load point signals where information begins, and the end of tape marker signals where information ends (see Figure 17.4 and the related discussion).

When the COBOL phrase LABEL RECORDS ARE STANDARD is included in the FD for a tape file, the system checks the internal labels of a file to assure that the proper volume has been mounted and that it contains the proper file. This is accomplished in conjunction with the JCL and is discussed in detail in Chapters 17 and 18, with the bulk of the discussion in Chapter 17.

COBOL REQUIREMENTS

The COBOL statements for processing tape are remarkably similar to those which process other *sequential* files, e.g. card. Nevertheless, there are required extensions in the environment, data, and procedure divisions. Since sequential files may be stored on either tape or disk, the ensuing discussion pertains to files stored on either medium.

Environment Division

Our discussion of tape requirements revolves about the FILE-CONTROL and I-O-CONTROL paragraphs. The SELECT statement appears in the FILE-CONTROL paragraph and has the general form

SELECT [OPTIONAL] file-name ASSIGN TO tape-unit-1[tape-unit-2] . . .

[ORGANIZATION IS SEQUENTIAL]

[ACCESS MODE IS SEQUENTIAL]

$$\left[\text{RESERVE} \begin{Bmatrix} \text{integer} \\ \text{NO} \end{Bmatrix} \text{ALTERNATE} \begin{bmatrix} \text{AREA} \\ \text{AREAS} \end{bmatrix} \right]$$

[FILE STATUS IS data-name]

The OPTIONAL phrase can be specified for sequential files only. It means that the file need not be present when the program is run, e.g., the first cycle of sequential maintenance during which the old master file does not exist.

* The ORGANIZATION and ACCESS MODE clauses default to sequential if omitted. Consequently, these clauses are often left out with sequential (e.g., tape) processing, but are required for other types of file organization as described in Chapter 16.

The RESERVE clause in the SELECT statement increases processing efficiency through overlap. Modern computer systems include hardware devices, called *channels,* which permit *overlap,* i.e., simultaneous processing and I/O (see Chapter 17). Under overlap the CPU processes data from one I/O area while the channel simultaneously operates on an alternate area called an I/O buffer. Unless instructed otherwise, most compilers reserve one alternate area to permit overlap, but this will vary from system to system. If the phrase RESERVE NO ALTERNATE AREAS is specified, *overlap is prevented. Processing is substantially slowed, but an amount of core storage equal to the I/O buffer is saved. Usually, RESERVE NO ALTERNATE AREAS is specified only on smaller systems if core storage is a problem.

The FILE STATUS clause allows the user to monitor the execution of each I/O request for a file. It is further discussed in Chapter 16.

* The I-O-CONTROL paragraph specifies points for rerun, common memory areas for different files, and the location of multiple files on tape. It has the general form

I-O-CONTROL.

$$\left[\text{RERUN} \left[\text{ON} \begin{Bmatrix} \text{file-name-1} \\ \text{implementor-name} \end{Bmatrix} \right] \right.$$

$$\left. \text{EVERY} \begin{Bmatrix} \begin{Bmatrix} \text{[END OF]} \begin{Bmatrix} \underline{\text{REEL}} \\ \underline{\text{UNIT}} \end{Bmatrix} \\ \text{integer-1} \underline{\text{RECORDS}} \end{Bmatrix} \text{OF file-name-2} \\ \text{integer-2} \underline{\text{CLOCK-UNITS}} \\ \text{condition-name} \end{Bmatrix} \right] \dots$$

$$\left[\underline{\text{SAME}} \begin{bmatrix} \underline{\text{RECORD}} \\ \underline{\text{SORT}} \\ \underline{\text{SORT-MERGE}} \end{bmatrix} \text{AREA FOR file-name-3} \quad \{, \text{file-name-4}\} \dots \right] \dots$$

[$\underline{\text{MULTIPLE}}$ $\underline{\text{FILE}}$ TAPE CONTAINS file-name-5 [$\underline{\text{POSITION}}$ integer-3] . . .]

The RERUN clause is used to establish a checkpoint, i.e., a snapshot of a program's status *at a given point during execution. The intended use is for *long-running* programs, so that if a program terminates abnormally, it can be restarted from the checkpoint, rather than the beginning. It is relatively easy to create a checkpoint, but often difficult to restart the job from the checkpoint. Moreover, the problem may have occurred *before* the checkpoint was taken, in which case the restart would be worthless. The facility is there, but should be used with discretion.

The SAME AREA clause causes the listed files to share the same storage locations for their I/O routines. While that capability may have been useful 10 or 15 years ago, when storage was * at a premium, it is less essential today. Moreover, its use may introduce unnecessary complications in program logic in that the listed files cannot be open at the same time.

The MULTIPLE FILE clause is used when there are multiple files on a given reel to indicate the position of the file in question. The identical function can also be accomplished through the LABEL parameter in OS JCL; see Chapter 18.

Data Division

Extension from card and print files to tape centers on the COBOL FD, with the general format.

FD file-name

$$\left[\underline{\text{BLOCK}} \text{ CONTAINS } \left[\text{integer-1 } \underline{\text{TO}} \right] \text{ integer-2 } \left\{ \begin{array}{l} \underline{\text{RECORDS}} \\ \underline{\text{CHARACTERS}} \end{array} \right\} \right]$$

[RECORD CONTAINS [integer-3 TO] integer-4 CHARACTERS]

$$\text{LABEL } \left\{ \begin{array}{l} \underline{\text{RECORDS}} \text{ ARE} \\ \underline{\text{RECORD}} \text{ IS} \end{array} \right\} \left\{ \begin{array}{l} \underline{\text{STANDARD}} \\ \underline{\text{OMITTED}} \end{array} \right\}$$

$$\left[\underline{\text{VALUE}} \ \underline{\text{OF}} \left\{ \text{implementor-name IS } \left\{ \begin{array}{l} \text{data-name-1} \\ \text{literal-1} \end{array} \right\} \right\} \cdots \right]$$

$$\left[\underline{\text{DATA}} \left\{ \begin{array}{l} \underline{\text{RECORD}} \text{ IS} \\ \underline{\text{RECORDS}} \text{ ARE} \end{array} \right\} \text{record-name-1 [record-name-2]} \cdots \right]$$

Until now, all records have been the same (i.e., *fixed*) length. Note, however, the *variable* lengths implied by RECORD (or BLOCK) CONTAINS integer-1 TO integer-2 CHARACTERS. In practice, records are often of varying length. For example, in a file of student records, a senior has completed more courses than a sophomore and requires a larger record to store his transcript. It is, of course, possible to provide a uniform maximum length for all, but this entails a large amount of wasted space. Accordingly, variable-length records are permitted and specified in the COBOL FD. Variable-length records can employ the OCCURS DEPENDING ON clause in the record description as shown in Figure 15.4.

```
FD   STUDENT-TRANSCRIPT-FILE
     RECORD CONTAINS 42 TO 342 CHARACTERS
     LABEL RECORDS ARE STANDARD
     DATA RECORD IS STUDENT-RECORD.
01   STUDENT-RECORD.
     05   ST-NAME                              PIC X(30).
     05   ST-YEAR-IN-SCHOOL                    PIC X(10).
     05   ST-COURSES-COMPLETED                 PIC 99.
     05   ST-COURSE-GRADE OCCURS 0 TO 60 TIMES
          DEPENDING ON ST-COURSES-COMPLETED.
          10   ST-COURSE-NUMBER                PIC 9999.
          10   ST-GRADE                        PIC X.
```

FIGURE 15.4 *Illustration of Variable-Length Record Description*

Every record contains a minimum of 42 characters (30 for name, 10 for year, and 2 for number of courses). If the student is an entering freshman, then no courses were completed, and the entire record consists of 42 characters. Records for upperclassmen contain an additional 5 bytes for every completed course. A maximum of 60 courses (300 bytes) is permitted in a record. There is considerable flexibility in the COBOL FD, and care must be taken to express one's exact intent. Thus the following pairs of entries are *not* equivalent:

BLOCK CONTAINS 5 RECORDS
RECORD CONTAINS 42 TO 342 CHARACTERS

vs.

BLOCK CONTAINS 210 TO 1710 CHARACTERS
RECORD CONTAINS 42 TO 342 CHARACTERS

The first pair states that the block contains exactly 5 records. The second pair states that the block contains from 210 to 1710 characters and thus could contain many more than 5 records if most of the records are of the smaller size.

Omission of the BLOCK CONTAINS clause causes the compiler to assume that the records are unblocked and is equivalent to BLOCK CONTAINS 1 RECORD. Note also that the entry

BLOCK CONTAINS 0 RECORDS is valid and common under OS. It means that the block size will be entered in the JCL; see Chapter 18.

The LABEL RECORDS clause is the only required clause in the FD. LABEL RECORDS ARE STANDARD implies that standard labels are used and label processing is to be performed. LABEL RECORDS ARE OMITTED means either labels are omitted or they are nonstandard (i.e., user labels); in either case no label processing is to be performed (see Chapters 17 and 18).

When labels are used, the system must have additional information supplied to enable it to perform label processing. Under an IBM operating system, the information is specified in the JCL (see Chapters 17 and 18). In other systems it is supplied in the VALUE clause of the FD. Consider the entry

```
FD   TAPE-FILE
     .
     .
     .
     LABEL RECORDS ARE STANDARD
     VALUE OF TAPE-LABEL IS 123456.
```

TAPE-LABEL is an implementor-name (i.e., a system-name that refers to a particular feature available in a given vendor's system. The SPECIAL-NAMES paragraph of the environment division relates implementor names to programmer-specified mnemonic names). The intent of these entries is to ensure that the COBOL file, TAPE-FILE, will be read from a specific tape volume.

Procedure Division

Procedure division extensions involve the OPEN and CLOSE statements. General formats for sequential files are shown:

$$
\text{OPEN} \left\{ \begin{array}{l} \underline{\text{INPUT}} \text{ file-name-1} \left[\begin{array}{l} \underline{\text{REVERSED}} \\ \text{WITH } \underline{\text{NO}} \text{ REWIND} \end{array} \right] \cdots \\ \underline{\text{OUTPUT}} \text{ file-name-2 [WITH } \underline{\text{NO}} \text{ REWIND] } \cdots \\ \underline{\text{EXTEND}} \text{ file-name-3} \end{array} \right\} \cdots
$$

$$
\underline{\text{CLOSE}} \left\{ \text{file-name-1} \left[\left\{ \begin{array}{l} \underline{\text{REEL}} \\ \underline{\text{UNIT}} \end{array} \right\} \left[\begin{array}{l} \text{WITH } \underline{\text{NO}} \text{ REWIND} \\ \text{FOR } \underline{\text{REMOVAL}} \end{array} \right] \right] \cdots \right\}
$$

The action of the OPEN and CLOSE verbs depends on the specifications of the LABEL RECORDS clause in the file FD. If standard labels are used, the OPEN initiates label processing. In an input file, the header label is checked against information in the JCL (IBM systems) or in the FD VALUE clause (non-IBM). When an output file is opened, an appropriate header label is written. The CLOSE initiates similar procedures for trailer labels; i.e., it checks the trailer label of an input file and causes a new trailer label to be written for an output file. No label processing is performed if the FD contains LABEL RECORDS ARE OMITTED.

The simplest form of an OPEN for an input file is OPEN INPUT file-name, which automatically causes the tape to be rewound. If NO REWIND is specified, the rewinding is suppressed. The latter is used when many files are contained on the same reel. The REVERSED option causes the file to be processed in reverse order, starting with the last record. (This is not possible on all tape drives; further, the option is available only for single-reel files.)

The EXTEND option in the OPEN statement is restricted to single-reel files. If this mode is specified, subsequent write statements will add records after the last existing record in the file, as though the file were in the OUTPUT mode. (The same effect can be accomplished by coding DISP = MOD in OS JCL; see Chapter 18.)

The simplest form of the CLOSE is CLOSE file-name, which automatically rewinds the tape at the end of processing. The NO REWIND option is used for multifile volumes and prevents the automatic rewinding associated with the CLOSE. The REEL or UNIT specification causes the volume, but not the file, to close and is used with multivolume files.

The READ and WRITE verbs are conceptually the same as for card files, but when blocking is used, the physical process is different. Assume, for illustration, a blocking factor of 5. When the first READ is executed, the entire block of 5 records is read into a storage buffer, but only the first record is made available to the program. The next time a READ is executed the second record is made available to the program, but no physical I/O takes place. In similar fashion, no physical I/O occurs for the 3rd, 4th, and 5th READ. The 6th, 11th, etc., execution of the READ all cause a new physical record to be brought into the I/O buffer, but there is no physical I/O for the 7th through 10th, 12th through 15th, etc., execution of the READ.

RECORD FORMATS

It is useful to review the various record formats as shown in Figure 15.5:

Fixed unblocked	Every record in the file is the same length; there is one record per block.
Fixed blocked	Every record in the file is the same length; there are many records per block.
Variable unblocked	Records are of different lengths; there is one record per block.
Variable blocked	Records are of different lengths; there are many records per block.

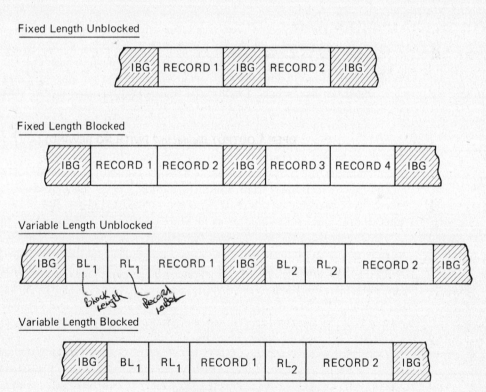

FIGURE 15.5 *Record Formats*

FILE MAINTENANCE

A large proportion of data-processing activity is devoted to file maintenance. Although printed reports are a more visible result of data processing, files must be maintained to reflect the changing nature of the physical environment. In a payroll system, for example, new employees can be added,

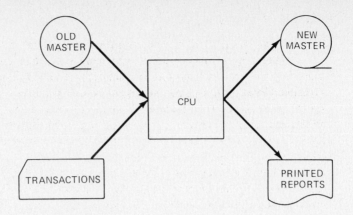

FIGURE 15.6 *Sequential Update System Flowchart*

while existing employees may be terminated or receive salary increases. Every physical system requires file maintenance, but the question of how often depends on the application. A file of student transcripts is updated only a few times a year. An airline reservation system, however, is continuously updated as seats on individual flights are booked.

Files can be processed either *sequentially* or *nonsequentially*. Sequential processing means that every single record is accessed in a given run. Nonsequential processing requires that only records which are actually changed be accessed. Tape processing is *always* sequential. Nonsequential processing is possible only with direct-access storage devices and is discussed in Chapter 16.

A sequential file update is shown schematically in Figure 15.6. Input to a sequential update consists of an old master file and a transaction file. Output will be a new master file and a series of printed reports reflecting the update. Figure 15.6 depicts both the old and new master files as being on tape. In actuality, the files could be contained on magnetic disk as well, as long as they were organized sequentially. Finally, the transaction file need not be physically on cards provided it is in sequential order.

Sequential maintenance is usually done periodically. Let us assume a payroll system is updated monthly and begin with a current master file on January 1. Transactions are collected *(batched)* during the month of January. Then, on February 1, we take the master file of January 1 (now the old master), the transactions accrued during January, and produce a new master as of February 1. The process continues from month to month. Transactions are collected during February. On March 1, we take the file created February 1 as the old master, run it against the February transactions, and produce a new master as of March 1. Figure 15.7 illustrates this discussion.

In Figure 15.7 the master files for January, February, and March are physically contained on different reels of tape. Further, since the January master gave rise to the February master, which in turn spawned the March master, the files are known as grandfather, father, and son, respectively.

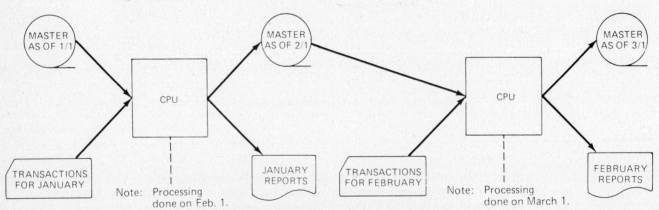

FIGURE 15.7 *Two-Period Sequential Update*

BACKUP

Murphy's law states that "if something can go wrong, it will—and at the worst possible time." (The corollary to this law, by an unknown author, is that Murphy was an optimist.) Data processing is certainly not exempt from this law, and it is absolutely essential that we provide as much backup as feasible. What if the tape containing the February master were inadvertently destroyed on February 27, just prior to the next update? If we were prudent enough to keep both the January 1 master and transactions for January, it is a simple matter to recreate the February 1 master file. A generally accepted practice is to keep at least the last three historical levels, i.e., the grandfather, father, and son.

How could information on tape be destroyed in the first place? The most likely way is that the operator incorrectly mounted a tape containing live data as a scratch tape. The *file protect ring* is a precautionary measure, designed to make the operator "think twice" before mounting a given reel as an output tape. The file protect ring fits into a groove on the tape. When it is in place either reading or writing can occur; when the ring is removed, only reading can take place. All reels containing live data should be stored *without* the file protect ring.

CASE STUDY

We shall now proceed to a COBOL program for a sequential update. The COBOL per se is not difficult, but the logic is as complex as anything we have yet tackled. Processing specifications are

1. Input: a master file and transaction file, both in ascending sequence by social security number.
2. Output: a master file and printed error report; the latter is to list invalid incoming transactions as described in item 5.
3. Each record in both master and transaction files contains three fields: name, social security number, and salary. In addition, each transaction record contains a transaction code.
4. There are three types of transactions: additions, deletions, and salary changes, denoted by A, D, and C, respectively. Incoming transactions with a code of A are to be added to the file. Transactions with a code of D are to be removed from the master, and transactions with a code of C are to have the salary corrected.
5. The incoming data have been *scrubbed* via a previous edit program. Thus the transactions can be assumed to be in sequential order, to contain all three fields, and to have a valid transaction code. However, the edit run could not check for two types of errors: (a) *no matches* in which a salary correction or deletion is indicated for a record not in the file, and (b) *duplicate additions* for records already in the file. An appropriate error message is to be printed whenever either of these situations occurs.

Figure 15.8 contains the logic of the program expressed in pseudocode, Figure 15.9 contains a hierarchy chart indicating the necessary COBOL modules, and Figure 15.10 a flowchart of the COMPARE-IDs routine. (Hierarchy charts were first introduced in Chapter 11 as a method of dividing a program into *functional* components. Pseudocode and/or flow charts indicate logic flow and are *procedural* in nature.) Any or all of these techniques can be used for program development and documentation. The authors lean toward the first two and deemphasize the flowchart.

The COMPARE-IDS procedure drives the entire program. It compares the social security numbers of the current records in both the old master and transaction files. If the former is lower, the COPY routine is performed. If the social security numbers are equal, the MATCH routine is performed; otherwise the ADD routine is performed. Regardless of which of the three routines is called, two switches are tested to determine from which file another record should be read.

The COPY routine copies an existing record from the old master as is and sets the switch to read another record from the old master. The MATCH routine checks for the type of transaction, A, D, or C, and processes accordingly. Note that a code of A in the MATCH routine causes an error message. Finally, the MATCH routine sets switches to read from both records. The ADD routine writes the incoming transaction record to the new master. If, however, the incoming code

```
Initialize
Open Files
Initial reads for OLD-MASTER and TRANSACTION files
┌PERFORM until no more data on both files
│   ┌IF OLD-MASTER social security number < TRANSACTION social security number
│   │   ┌PERFORM
│   │   │    Copy old master record to new master record
│   │   │    Set switch to read OLD-MASTER only
│   │   └ENDPERFORM
│   │ ELSE IF OLD-MASTER social security number = TRANSACTION social security number
│   │   ┌PERFORM
│   │   │    IF addition-write error indicating duplicate addition
│   │   │    ELSE IF deletion-delete old master record
│   │   │    ELSE IF salary-change-do salary update
│   │   │    ENDIF
│   │   │    Set switches to read both OLD-MASTER and TRANSACTION files
│   │   └ENDPERFORM
│   │ ELSE IF OLD-MASTER social security number > TRANSACTION social security number
│   │   ┌PERFORM
│   │   │    IF addition-add record to NEW-MASTER-FILE
│   │   │    ELSE write error indicating no match
│   │   │    ENDIF
│   │   │    Set switch to read TRANSACTION-FILE only
│   │   └ENDPERFORM
│   └ENDIF
│  Read OLD-MASTER and/or TRANSACTION files as appropriate
└ENDPERFORM
Close files
Stop run
```

FIGURE 15.8 *Pseudocode for Sequential Update*

is not an A, an appropriate error message is printed. The ADD routine sets the switch to read another record from the transaction file.

The resulting COBOL program is shown in Figure 15.11, which utilizes standards advocated in Chapters 6 and 11. Observe the use of record prefixing, paragraph sequencing, uniform columns for PICTURE, etc. The READ INTO and WRITE FROM options are used, and the reads for both old master and transaction files are performed rather than coded in line. All ELSE clauses are aligned under the relevant IF, with associated detail clauses indented further. Proper indentation is critical! Finally, note the use of 88-level conditional entries.

Figure 15.12 shows illustrative data for the program of Figure 15.11. The new master file has NEW EMPLOYEE and NEW EMPLOYEE II since the transaction file contained valid "adds"

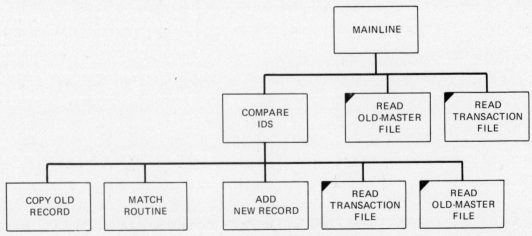

Note: Shaded blocks indicate a module is called from one place.

FIGURE 15.9 *Hierarchy Chart for Sequential Update*

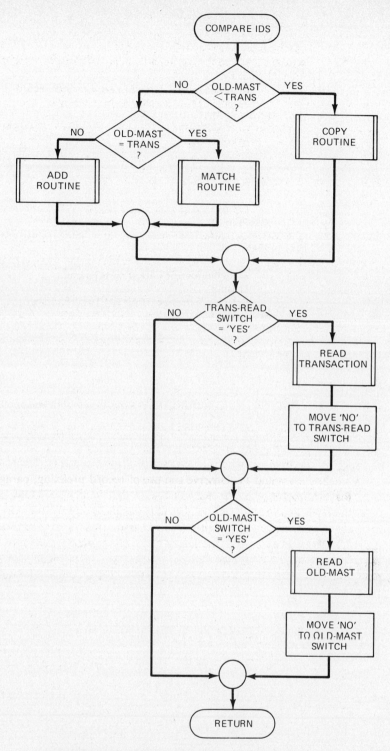

FIGURE 15.10 *COMPARE IDs Routine of Sequential Update*

for these employees. SHERRY (social security number 666666666) has been deleted from the new master, while BAKER and BOROW had their salaries changed. The transaction for JONES was invalid in that we attempted to change the salary of a record that was absent from the old master. The transaction for JAMES was also invalid since it tried to add a record already in the master file.

```
00001          IDENTIFICATION DIVISION.
00002          PROGRAM-ID.        UPDATE.
00003          AUTHOR.            GRAUER.
00004          ENVIRONMENT DIVISION.
00005          CONFIGURATION SECTION.
00006          SOURCE-COMPUTER.   IBM-370.
00007          OBJECT-COMPUTER.   IBM-370.
00008          INPUT-OUTPUT SECTION.              Program requires four files
00009          FILE-CONTROL.
00010              SELECT TRANSACTION-FILE ASSIGN TO UT-S-TRANS.
00011              SELECT ERROR-FILE ASSIGN TO UT-S-PRINT.
00012              SELECT OLD-MASTER-FILE ASSIGN TO UT-S-OLD.
00013              SELECT NEW-MASTER-FILE ASSIGN TO UT-S-NEW.
00014          DATA DIVISION.
00015          FILE SECTION.            Label processing - see Chapters 17 and 18
00016          FD  OLD-MASTER-FILE
00017              LABEL RECORDS ARE STANDARD
00018              BLOCK CONTAINS 0 RECORDS
00019              RECORD CONTAINS 40 CHARACTERS
00020              DATA RECORD IS OLD-MAST-RECORD.
00021          01  OLD-MAST-RECORD        PIC X(40).
00022          FD  NEW-MASTER-FILE
00023              LABEL RECORDS ARE STANDARD    Indicates block size will be entered in JCL
00024              BLOCK CONTAINS 0 RECORDS
00025              RECORD CONTAINS 40 CHARACTERS
00026              DATA RECORD IS NEW-MAST-RECORD.
00027          01  NEW-MAST-RECORD        PIC X(40).
00028          FD  TRANSACTION-FILE
00029              LABEL RECORDS ARE OMITTED
00030              RECORD CONTAINS 80 CHARACTERS
00031              DATA RECORD IS TRANS-RECORD.
00032          01  TRANS-RECORD           PIC X(80).
00033          FD  ERROR-FILE
00034              LABEL RECORDS ARE OMITTED
00035              RECORD CONTAINS 132 CHARACTERS
00036              DATA RECORD IS ERROR-RECORD.
00037          01  ERROR-RECORD           PIC X(132).
00038          WORKING-STORAGE SECTION.
00039          01  FILLER                 PIC X(14)   VALUE 'WS BEGINS HERE'.
00040          01  WS-OLD-MAST-READ-SWITCH PIC X(3)   VALUE 'NO'.
00041          01  WS-TRANS-READ-SWITCH   PIC X(3)    VALUE 'NO'.
00042          01  WS-OLD-MAST-RECORD.
00043              05  WS-OLDMAST-ID      PIC X(9).   Switches indicate which file is read next
00044              05  WS-OLDMAST-NAME    PIC X(25).
00045              05  WS-OLDMAST-SALARY  PIC 9(6).
00046          01  WS-NEW-MAST-RECORD.
00047              05  WS-NEWMAST-ID      PIC X(9).
00048              05  WS-NEWMAST-NAME    PIC X(25).
00049              05  WS-NEWMAST-SALARY  PIC 9(6).
00050          01  WS-TRANS-RECORD.
00051              05  WS-TRANS-ID        PIC X(9).
00052              05  WS-TRANS-NAME      PIC X(25).  Condition names used for
00053              05  WS-TRANS-SALARY    PIC 9(6).   transaction codes
00054              05  WS-TRANS-CODE      PIC X.
00055                  88  ADDITION                   VALUE 'A'.
00056                  88  DELETION                   VALUE 'D'.
00057                  88  SALARY-CHANGE              VALUE 'C'.
00058              05  FILLER             PIC X(39).
00059          01  WS-PRINT-RECORD.
00060              05  WS-PRINT-MESSAGE   PIC X(40).
00061              05  WS-PRINT-ID        PIC X(9).
00062              05  FILLER             PIC X(5)    VALUE SPACES.
00063              05  WS-PRINT-NAME      PIC X(25).
00064              05  FILLER             PIC X(53)   VALUE SPACES.
00065          PROCEDURE DIVISION.
00066          005-MAINLINE.
00067              OPEN INPUT TRANSACTION-FILE
00068                         OLD-MASTER-FILE
00069                   OUTPUT NEW-MASTER-FILE   Initial reads are performed
00070                         ERROR-FILE.
00071              PERFORM 080-READ-TRANSACTION.
00072              PERFORM 090-READ-OLD-MASTER.
00073              PERFORM 010-COMPARE-IDS
00074                  UNTIL WS-TRANS-ID = HIGH-VALUES
00075                  AND WS-OLDMAST-ID = HIGH-VALUES.
```

FIGURE 15.11 *COBOL Listing for Sequential Update*

```
00076                    CLOSE TRANSACTION-FILE
00077                          OLD-MASTER-FILE
00078                          NEW-MASTER-FILE
00079                          ERROR-FILE.
00080                    STOP RUN.                        ┌ Nested IF drives program
00081                                                    /
00082           010-COMPARE-IDS.                        /
00083           ┌──IF WS-OLDMAST-ID < WS-TRANS-ID──────────────┐
00084           │     PERFORM 050-COPY-OLD-REC                 │
00085           │  ELSE                                        │
00086           │     IF WS-OLDMAST-ID = WS-TRANS-ID           │
00087           │        PERFORM 060-MATCH-ROUTINE             │
00088           │     ELSE                                     │
00089           │        PERFORM 070-NEW-RECORD.               │
00090           └──────────────────────────────────────────────┘
00091           ┌──IF WS-TRANS-READ-SWITCH = 'YES'─────────────┐
00092           │     MOVE 'NO ' TO WS-TRANS-READ-SWITCH        │          ┐ Switches are tested and reset
00093           │     PERFORM 080-READ-TRANSACTION.             │─────────/
00094           └──────────────────────────────────────────────┘
00095           ┌──IF WS-OLD-MAST-READ-SWITCH = 'YES'──────────┐
00096           │     MOVE 'NO ' TO WS-OLD-MAST-READ-SWITCH     │
00097           │     PERFORM 090-READ-OLD-MASTER.              │
00098   Copy routine └───────────────────────────────────────────┘
00099
00100        ┌─050-COPY-OLD-REC.
00101        │    WRITE NEW-MAST-RECORD FROM WS-OLD-MAST-RECORD.
00102        └─  │MOVE 'YES' TO WS-OLD-MAST-READ-SWITCH.│
00103                                      └ Switch set to read from old master only
00104        ┌─060-MATCH-ROUTINE.
00105        │    IF ADDITION
00106        │       MOVE WS-TRANS-NAME          TO WS-PRINT-NAME
00107        │       MOVE WS-TRANS-ID            TO WS-PRINT-ID
00108   Match │       MOVE 'ERROR - RECORD IN FILE' TO WS-PRINT-MESSAGE
00109   routine│       WRITE ERROR-RECORD FROM WS-PRINT-RECORD
00110        │       WRITE NEW-MAST-RECORD FROM WS-OLD-MAST-RECORD
00111        │    ELSE
00112        │       IF SALARY-CHANGE
00113        │          MOVE WS-TRANS-SALARY TO WS-OLDMAST-SALARY
00114        │          WRITE NEW-MAST-RECORD FROM WS-OLD-MAST-RECORD
00115        │       ELSE
00116        │          IF DELETION
00117        │             NEXT SENTENCE.
00118        │
00119        │    MOVE 'YES' TO WS-TRANS-READ-SWITCH.
00120        └─  MOVE 'YES' TO WS-OLD-MAST-READ-SWITCH.
00121
00122        ┌─070-NEW-RECORD.
00123        │    IF ADDITION
00124   New record  WRITE NEW-MAST-RECORD FROM WS-TRANS-RECORD
00125   routine│    ELSE
00126        │       MOVE WS-TRANS-NAME          TO WS-PRINT-NAME
00127        │       MOVE WS-TRANS-ID            TO WS-PRINT-ID
00128        │       MOVE 'ERROR - NO MATCH'     TO WS-PRINT-MESSAGE
00129        │       WRITE ERROR-RECORD FROM WS-PRINT-RECORD.
00130        └─  │MOVE 'YES' TO WS-TRANS-READ-SWITCH.│
00131                                    └ Switch set to read from transaction file only
00132           080-READ-TRANSACTION.
00133                READ TRANSACTION-FILE INTO WS-TRANS-RECORD
00134                   AT END MOVE HIGH-VALUES TO WS-TRANS-RECORD.
00135
00136           090-READ-OLD-MASTER.
00137                READ OLD-MASTER-FILE INTO WS-OLD-MAST-RECORD
00138                   AT END MOVE HIGH-VALUES TO WS-OLD-MAST-RECORD.
```

FIGURE 15.11 *(continued)*

SUMMARY

Magnetic tape was introduced as a medium for data storage. Several problems were presented to illustrate tape capacity and timing. The necessary COBOL extensions for tape processing were covered. The extensions per se are not difficult, but the logic inherent in file maintenance can get very involved. In addition, four types of record formats were discussed: fixed-length blocked, fixed-length unblocked, variable-length blocked, and variable-length unblocked.

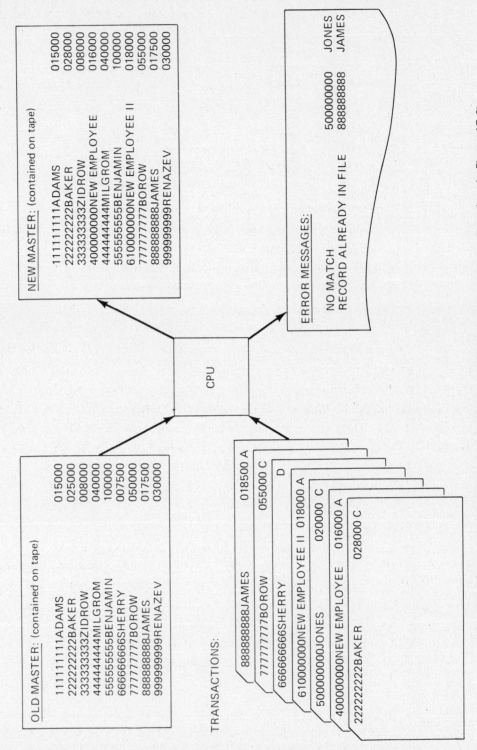

OLD MASTER: (contained on tape)

111111111ADAMS	015000
222222222BAKER	025000
333333333ZIDROW	008000
444444444MILGROM	040000
555555555BENJAMIN	100000
666666666SHERRY	007500
777777777BOROW	050000
888888888JAMES	017500
999999999RENAZEV	030000

NEW MASTER: (contained on tape)

111111111ADAMS	015000
222222222BAKER	028000
333333333ZIDROW	008000
400000000NEW EMPLOYEE	016000
444444444MILGROM	040000
555555555BENJAMIN	100000
610000000NEW EMPLOYEE II	018000
777777777BOROW	055000
888888888JAMES	017500
999999999RENAZEV	030000

CPU

TRANSACTIONS:

888888888JAMES	018500	A
777777777BOROW	055000	C
666666666SHERRY		D
610000000NEW EMPLOYEE II	018000	A
500000000JONES	020000	C
400000000NEW EMPLOYEE	016000	A
222222222BAKER	028000	C

ERROR MESSAGES:

NO MATCH	500000000 JONES
RECORD ALREADY IN FILE	888888888 JAMES

FIGURE 15.12 *Illustrative Data for Sequential Update (Corresponds to System Flowchart in Figure 15.6)*

Concepts of sequential file maintenance were covered in detail. The grandfather–father–son hierarchy was introduced as a means of backup. A COBOL program for sequential updating was developed using techniques of structured programming, and the importance of checking incoming data was emphasized. The reader may also review the discussion on merging files from Chapter 11. The use of top down testing, program stubs, hierarchy charts, and pseudocode is especially relevant.

REVIEW EXERCISES

TRUE FALSE

☐ ☐ **1.** The capacity of a tape increases as the length of the IRG increases.

☐ ☐ **2.** The capacity of a tape increases as the density increases.

☐ ☐ **3.** A tape will start and stop many times as it processes a file.

☐ ☐ **4.** Thirty is the absolute limit to the blocking factor.

☐ ☐ **5.** Doubling the blocking factor will halve the transfer rate.

☐ ☐ **6.** Doubling the blocking factor will halve the storage requirements of a file.

☐ ☐ **7.** Density is commonly expressed in bytes per inch.

☐ ☐ **8.** Doubling the blocking factor will halve the number of IRG's.

☐ ☐ **9.** As the blocking factor increases, the start/stop time decreases.

☐ ☐ **10.** More than one file can appear on a single reel of tape.

☐ ☐ **11.** One file can stretch over several reels of tape.

☐ ☐ **12.** There is more than one kind of internal label.

☐ ☐ **13.** If the RESERVE clause is omitted in the SELECT statement, no alternate areas will be established.

☐ ☐ **14.** The OPEN statement makes the first record in an input file available for processing.

☐ ☐ **15.** Every record in a given file must contain the same number of bytes.

☐ ☐ **16.** The OPEN statement causes a tape to rewind unless specification is made to the contrary.

☐ ☐ **17.** The CLOSE statement causes the tape to rewind unless specification is made to the contrary.

☐ ☐ **18.** If blocking is used, every READ statement causes a new block to be taken from tape.

☐ ☐ **19.** Both input and output files can be opened in the same statement.

☐ ☐ **20.** The OPEN statement will always initiate label processing.

☐ ☐ **21.** Variable-length records cannot be blocked.

☐ ☐ **22.** Nonsequential processing is possible using magnetic tape.

☐ ☐ **23.** The file protect ring must be on the reel to enable writing on a tape.

☐ ☐ **24.** In a sequential update, the transaction file must be in the same sequence as the master file.

☐ ☐ **25.** The ORGANIZATION and ACCESS MODE clauses are required in the SELECT statement for sequential files.

☐ ☐ **26.** The SAME AREA clause should be used whenever possible to conserve storage space.

☐ ☐ **27.** The functions of EXTEND and MULTIPLE FILE can also be accomplished through OS JCL.

☐ ☐ **28.** BLOCK CONTAINS 0 RECORDS is a valid entry under OS.

☐ ☐ **29.** Omission of the BLOCK CONTAINS clause in a COBOL FD will cause a compiler diagnostic.

PROBLEMS

1. How many boxes of cards (2000 cards per box) are required for a file of 20,000 records, if each record contains 200 bytes? (Do *not* split records; i.e., one card cannot contain information for two different logical records.) How long will it take to read the entire file assuming the card reader can process 1000 cards per minute?

2. How much space on tape does the file of Problem 1 require? (Assume 800 bpi and IRG = .75 inch.) Answer for no blocking and a blocking factor of 5. Answer for 1600 bpi and IRG = .375.

3. How long will it take to pass the file of Problem 1? Assume a start/stop time of 10 milliseconds and a transfer rate of 200,000 bytes per second. Answer for no blocking and a blocking factor of 5.

4. Use the "old master" of Figure 15.12 and the following transactions:

```
                  111111111ADAMS      017000  ...A
                  222222222BAKER              ...D
                  300000000BROWN      028000  ...A
                  444444444MILGROM    045000  ...C
                  600000000SHERRY     010000  ...C
                  888888888JAMES      020000  ...C
```

Show the "new master" and error listing that would be produced using the COBOL program in Figure 15.11.

5. Modify the COBOL program of Figure 15.11 to accommodate the following:
   (a) New fields for LOCATION-CODE (PIC 99) and TITLE-CODE (PIC 999) in the old master, new master, and transaction records.
   (b) Process two additional transaction codes, L and T, to process location and title changes, respectively. These should function in a manner analogous to a salary change.
   (c) Flag as an error any attempted addition that does not have all the following: name, salary, location, and title codes.
   (d) Flag as an error any transaction record with a code other than A, C, D, L, or T.
   (e) Write deleted records to a new file for possible recovery at a later date.

PROJECTS

1. Write a sequential maintenance program that will read a transaction and an old master file, and produce a corresponding new master. Include pseudocode and a hierarchy chart as program documentation. Use the top down approach to testing (see Chapter 11). Code a stubs version of the program first and begin testing immediately.[1]

   Record layouts are given next: (The new master file has a layout identical to that of the old master.)

```
OLD-MASTER FILE
01  EMPLOYEE-RECORD.
    05  EMP-SOC-SEC-NUMBER              PIC X(9).
    05  EMP-NAME-AND-INITIALS           PIC X(15).
    05  EMP-DATE-OF-BIRTH.
        10  EMP-BIRTH-MONTH             PIC 99.
        10  EMP-BIRTH-YEAR              PIC 99.
    05  EMP-DATE-OF-HIRE.
        10  EMP-HIRE-MONTH              PIC 99.
        10  EMP-HIRE-YEAR               PIC 99.
    05  EMP-LOCATION-CODE               PIC 99.
    05  EMP-EDUCATION-CODE              PIC 9.
    05  EMP-TITLE-DATA.
        10  EMP-TITLE-CODE              PIC 9(3).
        10  EMP-TITLE-DATE              PIC 9(4).
        10  EMP-PERFORMANCE             PIC 9.
    05  EMP-SALARY-DATA OCCURS 3 TIMES.
        10  EMP-SALARY                  PIC 9(5).
        10  EMP-SALARY-TYPE             PIC X.
        10  EMP-SALARY-DATE.
            15  EMP-SALARY-MONTH        PIC 99.
            15  EMP-SALARY-YEAR         PIC 99.
        10  EMP-SALARY-GRADE            PIC 9.
    05  FILLER                          PIC X(4).


TRANSACTION FILE:
01  TRANSACTION-RECORD.
    05  TRANS-SOC-SEC-NUMBER            PIC X(9).
    05  TRANS-NAME-AND-INITIALS         PIC X(15).
    05  TRANS-DATE-OF-BIRTH.
        10  TRANS-BIRTH-MONTH           PIC 99.
```

[1] This project is developed completely in R. Grauer, *COBOL: A Vehicle for Information Systems,* Chapter 11 (Englewood Cliffs, N.J.: Prentice-Hall, Inc., 1981.

```
              10    TRANS-BIRTH-YEAR              PIC 99.
        05  TRANS-DATE-OF-HIRE.
              10    TRANS-HIRE-MONTH              PIC 99.
              10    TRANS-HIRE-YEAR               PIC 99.
        05  TRANS-LOCATION-CODE                   PIC 99.
        05  TRANS-EDUCATION-CODE                  PIC 9.
        05  TRANS-TITLE-DATA.
              10    TRANS-TITLE-CODE              PIC 9(3).
              10    TRANS-TITLE-DATE              PIC 9(4).
              10    TRANS-PERFORMANCE             ·PIC 9.
        05  TRANS-SALARY-DATA.
              10    TRANS-SALARY                  PIC 9(5).
              10    TRANS-SALARY-TYPE             PIC X.
              10    TRANS-SALARY-DATE.
                    15  TRANS-SALARY-MONTH        PIC 99.
                    15  TRANS-SALARY-YEAR         PIC 99.
              10    TRANS-SALARY-GRADE            PIC 9.
        05  FILLER                                PIC X(25).
        05  TRANS-CODE                            PIC X.
              88  ADDITION        VALUE "A".
              88  CORRECTION      VALUE "C".
              88  DELETION        VALUE "D".
              88  SALARY-UPDATE   VALUE "U".
```

As can be seen from the transaction record, four types of transactions are possible:

1. An *addition* means that the transaction record is to be added to the new master in its entirety. (The salary data on the transaction is to be moved to the first occurrence in the new master.) No error checking is required, save for preventing a duplicate addition, i.e., adding a record which already exists in the old master.
2. A *deletion* means simply that an existing record in the old master is to be deleted from the new master. No error processing is required, other than to print a message if the record intended for deletion does not exist in the old master.
3. A *correction* applies to the following fields: name, date of birth, date of hire, location, education, all title data, and the first occurrence of salary data. This transaction type should move data in any of these fields from the transaction record to the corresponding field in the new master record. The transaction record contains the social security number and only those fields which actually *change;* e.g., if date of birth is to be corrected, the transaction would contain only social security number and date of birth. All other fields are to be copied, as is, from the old master. As with the deletion transaction type, check that the social security number of the record intended for correction exists in the old master; if not, print a suitable error message.
4. A *salary-update* indicates an increase in salary. The salary data in the transaction record is to become the first occurrence of salary data in the new master; the first occurrence of salary data in the old master becomes the second occurrence in the new master; the second occurrence in the old master becomes the third occurrence in the new master. For example, assume an existing record has three salary occurrences of $13,000, $12,000 and $10,000, respectively. The transaction indicates a new salary of $14,000. The new master would then contain $14,000, $13,000 and $12,000. Again, as with a correction and a deletion, verify that the transaction social security number is present in the old master.

Use the following test data:

OLD MASTER:

```
100000000DOE            J  12441177303155117723000M11787215OOH1177500000
200000000WILCOX         P  10481177303145117721900OM1178517500H1177400000
300000000SMITH          J  11550776404145077621500OM0778514000M0777513200H01775
400000000LEVINE         S  01500876304145087621900OH0876500000        00000
500000000CRAWFORD       M  03460172404160117722800OM0876726500M0575725000M05746
600000000SUPERPROG      S  04571077405145107713900OH1077900000        00000
700000000LEE            B  10530276306145027712000OP0578510000H0277400000
800000000PERSNICKETY    P  08510378403145037810900OH0378600000        00000
900000000MILGROM        MB11550977303145097721000OM0578309000H0977300000
```

TRANSACTION:

```
100000000DOE            J                     23000M11787                     U
200000000WILCOX         PA                                                    C
211111111ADAMS          JJ035002792133330279110000H02793                      A
```

```
300000000SMITH                                                                           D
400000000LEVINE        S                  0878                                           C
444444444LOWELL        S 0150117830414511782180000H11785                                 A
500000000SMITHERS      M                                                                 C
600000000SUPERPROG     S 0457107740514510771390000H10779                                 A
654321000JONES         GR     0378                                                       C
800000000PERSNICKETY   P 0855                   2               3                         C
878787878PETERS        SM                       20000M02797                              U
900000000MILGROM       MB                       12000M11784                              U
```

As an aid to understanding the problem specifications, we show the intended output given the previous input data.

INTENDED NEW MASTER:

```
100000000DOE           J 124411773031551177223000M1178721500H1177500000
200000000WILCOX        PA104811773031451177219000M1178517500H1177400000
211111111ADAMS         JJ035002792133330279110000H0279300000          00000
400000000LEVINE        S 015008763041450878219000H0876500000          00000
444444444LOWELL        S 015011783041451178218000H1178500000          00000
500000000SMITHERS      M 034601724041601177228000M0876726500M0575725000M05746
600000000SUPERPROG     S 045710774051451077139000H1077900000          00000
700000000LEE           B 105302763061450277120000P0578510000H0277400000
800000000PERSNICKETY   P 085503784031450378209000H0378300000          00000
900000000MILGROM       MB115509773031450977212000M1178410000M0578309000H09773.
```

INTENDED ERROR MESSAGES:

```
ERROR - UPDATE ALREADY DONE        100000000    DOE          J
ERROR - RECORD IN FILE             600000000    SUPERPROG    S
ERROR - NO MATCH                   654321000    JONES        GR
ERROR - NO MATCH                   878787878    PETERS       SM
```

Chapter 16

MAGNETIC DISK: CONCEPTS AND COBOL IMPLICATIONS

OVERVIEW

In Chapter 15 we covered magnetic tape and sequential file organization. Sequential processing is adequate when a significant number of records in a file have activity but totally impractical in situations where only a limited number of records are to be accessed. The physical characteristics of magnetic tape, however, dictate sequential processing as the only means of file organization possible with that device. One starts at the beginning of a file and interrogates every record (in sequential order) until the desired one is reached.

A direct capability can be provided only by devices with physical characteristics different from those of magnetic tape. Such units include the drum or data cell, but the most common device by far is the magnetic disk. This chapter begins with a discussion of the physical characteristics of the magnetic disk. Next, indexed files are discussed in detail and illustrated with appropriate listings. We include a program on nonsequential file maintenance, which parallels the requirements of the one in Chapter 15 and provide pseudocode to facilitate documentation. The chapter concludes with formal discussion of the ANS 74 COBOL elements for nonsequential files, and contrasts the requirements of ISAM and VSAM processing.

MAGNETIC DISK: PHYSICAL CHARACTERISTICS

A disk pack is the device on which data are recorded. It consists of a series of platters (disks) permanently attached to a central spindle. The disk pack is mounted on a disk drive, which is the unit that reads or writes information from the pack. Disk drives in turn can be grouped into a direct-access storage facility, shown in Figure 16.1.

Figure 16.2(a) shows a 2314 disk pack, with 11 disks, enclosed in a protective cover. Data can be recorded on both sides of 9 of the 11 platters; it cannot be recorded on the top surface of the top disk or the bottom surface of the bottom disk, making a total of 20 surfaces on which data can be recorded. This design concept was also used in the 3330 disk except that the number of recording surfaces changed.

The 3340 (Figure 16.2(b)) employed a new concept in that the pack itself contains read/write heads and access arms in addition to the recording surfaces. This approach is intended to reduce exposure to outside contamination by keeping the data in a sealed container.

All disk devices utilize a comb-type access mechanism as shown in Figure 16.3. Each recording surface (ten in all) has its own read/write head. Each pair of read/write heads (five pairs in all)

FIGURE 16.1 *Direct-Access Storage Facility (Courtesy IBM)*

is attached to an access arm, which in turn is attached to an access assembly. Figure 16.3 illustrates a typical access mechanism, but realize the number of recording surfaces varies from device to device.

Every recording surface is divided into concentric circles, known as tracks, on which data are recorded (Figure 16.4). Interestingly enough, each track has *identical* storage capacity. Thus the innermost concentric circle (track 199 in Figure 16.4) has the same capacity as the outermost concentric circle (track 0). The number of tracks that can be accessed in a single position of the access assembly is known as a cylinder. Figures 16.3 and 16.5 illustrate the cylinder concept. The device shown has ten recording surfaces or ten tracks per cylinder. Each surface has 200 tracks, hence the device has 200 cylinders.

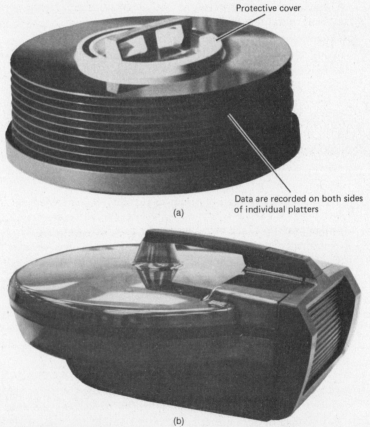

Protective cover

Data are recorded on both sides
of individual platters

(a)

(b)

FIGURE 16.2 *(a) IBM 2314 Disk Pack (Courtesy IBM) (b) 3340 Disk Storage Facility (Courtesy IBM)*

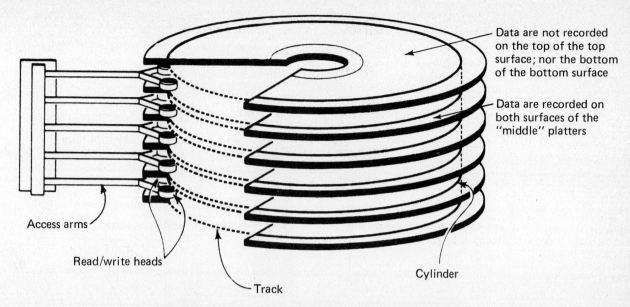

Data are not recorded on the top of the top surface; nor the bottom of the bottom surface

Data are recorded on both surfaces of the "middle" platters

Access arms

Read/write heads

Track

Cylinder

FIGURE 16.3 *Comb-Type Access Mechanism (Courtesy IBM)*

Capacity

The maximum capacity of a disk pack is a function of three factors: (1) density (i.e., the number of bytes per track), (2) the number of recording surfaces (i.e., the number of tracks per cylinder), and (3) the number of tracks per surface (i.e., the number of cylinders). Capacity increases as any of these factors increases. As an illustration, consider the 2314 disk pack with density of 7294 bytes per track, 20 tracks per cylinder, and 200 cylinders. Maximum capacity is calculated to be

$$7294 \frac{\text{bytes}}{\text{track}} \times 20 \frac{\text{tracks}}{\text{cylinder}} \times 200 \frac{\text{cylinders}}{\text{device}} = 29{,}176{,}000 \frac{\text{bytes}}{\text{device}}$$

In similar fashion, the maximum capacity of a single-density 3330 pack is calculated as approximately 100 million bytes (13,030 bytes per track, 19 tracks per cylinder, and 404 cylinders). As with other calculations in this chapter and in Chapter 15, the numbers themselves are of secondary importance compared to the underlying concepts. The maximum capacity of devices other than the 2314 and 3330 is shown in Table 18.3.

In actual practice the achieved capacity is somewhat less than the calculated maximum. Each track requires certain fields to identify itself to the system, and these areas detract from the capacity available to the user. The addition of keys to permit direct access also reduces capacity. Finally,

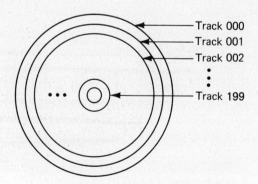

Track 000
Track 001
Track 002
Track 199

FIGURE 16.4 *Tracks on a Disk Surface*

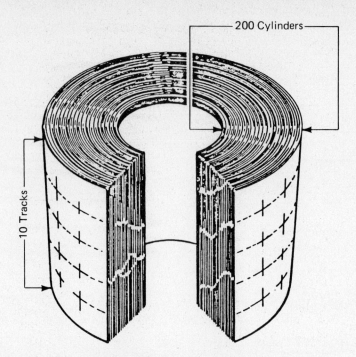

200 Cylinders

10 Tracks

FIGURE 16.5 *The Cylinder Concept*

if more than one record is present per track, interrecord gaps are needed. Thus, while one track of a 2314 can contain one 7294-byte record (without keys), it *cannot* contain two records of 3647 bytes but is restricted to two records of 3521 bytes. Effective track capacity is further reduced as the number of records per track increases, as can be seen in the table of track capacities (Table 16.1).

Yet another factor further reduces track capacity. Direct-access devices are designed to permit a straight path to a specified record but require that an additional field (key) be present. The key itself requires space and an additional gap that decreases capacity. Using Table 16.1, we find that when keys are used on a 2314, each track can contain two *physical* records of 3476 bytes each. This is contrasted to two records of 3521 bytes with no keys. These concepts should be clarified by the following examples:

Example 16.1: Use of Track Capacity Table (2314)

Given physical records of 150 bytes each, how many such records, with and without keys, will fit on a single track of a 2314?

SOLUTION

From Table 16.1 we find that, with no keys, either twenty-eight 157-byte records or twenty-nine 148-byte records fit on a single track; i.e., 29 records will fit per track only if the record length is 148 bytes or less. Since this example is concerned with 150-byte records, each track will hold only 28 records.

With keys, twenty-four 156-byte or twenty-five 144-byte records fit per track. Thus 24 is the answer.

Example 16.2: Use of Track Capacity Table (3330)

Given physical records of 400 bytes each, how many such records, with and without keys, will fit on a single track of a 3330?

TABLE 16.1 Track Capacity

Maximum bytes per physical record formated without keys		Records per track	Maximum bytes per physical record formated with keys	
2314	3330		2314	3330
7294	13030	1	7249	12974
3521	6447	2	3476	6391
2298	4253	3	2254	4197
1693	3156	4	1649	3100
1332	2498	5	1288	2442
1092	2059	6	1049	2003
921	1745	7	878	1689
793	1510	8	750	1454
694	1327	9	650	1271
615	1181	10	571	1125
550	1061	11	506	1005
496	962	12	452	906
450	877	13	407	821
411	805	14	368	749
377	742	15	333	686
347	687	16	304	631
321	639	17	277	583
298	596	18	254	540
276	557	19	233	501
258	523	20	215	467
241	491	21	198	435
226	463	22	183	407
211	437	23	168	381
199	413	24	156	357
187	391	25	144	335
176	371	26	133	315
166	352	27	123	296
157	335	28	114	279
148	318	29	105	262
139	303	30	96	247

Note: Calculation of track capacities requires the use of formulas to determine physical record size from logical record size. The material in this table is *not* intended as complete coverage; rather we present a mere taste of what is involved.

SOLUTION

Without keys, either twenty-four 413-byte records or twenty-five 391-byte records fit per track; thus 24 is the answer. With keys, only twenty-two 400-byte records will fit per track.

Example 16.3: Calculation of File Storage Requirements

Given a file of 6000 records, how many cylinders on a 2314 are required to store the file if records are formated without keys? (There are 20 tracks per cylinder.) Assume no blocking and that each physical record is 2000 bytes.

SOLUTION

Using Table 16.1, we find each track of a 2314 can hold three records, each 2298 bytes long, so that we can fit three records per track. Since there are 20 tracks per cylinder, each cylinder holds 60 (i.e., 20 × 3) records. A 6000-record file requires 100 (6000/60) cylinders.

Timing

Timing calculations are more complex with disk than with tape. Accordingly, we shall discuss timing from a conceptual viewpoint and shall not work any problems. Illustrative numbers are used for the 2314 to give an overall appreciation.

The time required to access data on a magnetic disk consists of four parts: access motion, head selection, rotational delay, and data transfer. (See Figure 16.3.) First, the access assembly is positioned over the proper cylinder. If the assembly is already over the proper cylinder, access time is zero. A movement of one cylinder on the 2314 requires 24 milliseconds; a movement of 200 cylinders takes 130 milliseconds. Access time requires an initial acceleration, but it is essentially a function of the number of cylinders moved. Once the arm is over the proper cylinder, a negligible time is required to activate the correct read/write head. Rotational delay is the time required for the data to rotate under the read/write head. This can range from 0 to 25 milliseconds. Finally, data are transferred between the device and main storage at the rate of 312,000 bytes per second.

File Organization

Three types of file organization are recognized in the ANS 74 standard: sequential, relative, and indexed. The latter two are permitted only with direct-access devices.

In a sequential file, records are processed in the same order in which they appear; e.g., the 50th record is used only after the 49th, etc. Individual records cannot be located quickly, and as with magnetic tape, the entire file has to be rewritten when records are added or deleted. Thus sequential organization should be used only when a significant number of records in a file are to be processed. It is one of several methods commonly available on direct devices, but the "only game in town" for magnetic tape.

Relative organization depends on a definitive relationship between the key of a record and its location on the device. It enables individual records to be directly accessed; e.g., the 50th record in the file can be accessed without processing the first 49. This method is used when the time to locate individual records must be kept at an absolute minimum, and is not discussed further.

Indexed organization permits both sequential and direct access. Sequential processing is less rapid than with strict sequential files, and location of individual records generally takes longer than with relative organization. Indexed files utilize a set of indexes, which allow new records to be added without rewriting the entire file and which provide its direct-access capability.

SEQUENTIAL PROCESSING

Although disk devices are capable of nonsequential processing, they are frequently used for sequential processing as well. Indeed, the maintenance program of Figure 15.11 would run just as well if the files were on disk instead of tape, because the SELECT statements were written to be device independent. (See Chapter 18.) Consider the significance of this statement: A COBOL program that processes sequential files can run on either tape or disk with no modification whatsoever. Obviously, something has to change, but that something is the JCL submitted with the program.

The point we are trying to make is that sequential processing is conceptually the same whether the incoming files are contained on tape, disk, or even cards; i.e., the storage medium is immaterial to the COBOL program. Information on the type of file, its location, etc., is supplied through control cards submitted with the program.

Every program in the text to this point has involved sequential processing. We shall not present any examples of sequential processing using disk, simply because we have already covered this material. We shall concentrate instead on examples using indexed files. Admittedly, the beginner is more comfortable with cards than with disk or tape, simply because he can touch his files; however, this reluctance to utilize mass storage devices is soon overcome.

INDEXED ORGANIZATION (IBM/ISAM IMPLEMENTATION)

Indexed organization requires that records be loaded sequentially so that indexes can be established ✻ for direct access of individual records. There is one *cylinder index* for the entire file and many *track indexes*, one for each cylinder in the file. The cylinder index contains the key of the *highest* record contained in every cylinder in the file. The track index (for a given cylinder) contains the ✻ key of the *highest* record for every track in that cylinder. As an illustration, assume an indexed file was loaded on cylinders 100 to 115 of a device with ten tracks per cylinder. A hypothetical cylinder index (Table 16.2) for this file contains 16 entries (one for each cylinder in the file).

TABLE 16.2 Cylinder Index

Cylinder number	Highest key
100	130
101	249
102	800
103	1240
104	1410
105	1811
106	2069
107	2410
108	2811
109	3040
110	3400
111	3619
112	4511
113	4900
114	5213
115	6874

A hypothetical track index for cylinder 102 is shown in Table 16.3. Although there are ten tracks per cylinder, each track index contains only seven entries. The first track, i.e., track 0, contains the track index itself. The last two tracks, tracks 8 and 9, are typically reserved as a cylinder overflow area, whose function is described in the next section. Note that the highest key for all of cylinder 102 is 800, which occurs on track 7, and that this corresponds to the highest key for cylinder 102 in Table 16.2.

TABLE 16.3 Track Index for Cylinder 102

Track number	Highest key
1	312
2	346
3	449
4	598
5	642
6	717
7	800

Note: 1. Track 0 contains the track index.
2. Tracks 8 and 9 contain the cylinder overflow area.

Suppose we seek the record whose key is 400. The record key, 400, is first compared to entries in the cylinder index. Since an indexed file is loaded sequentially, we conclude record 400, *if it is present,* is on cylinder 102. (The highest key in cylinder 101 is 249, and the highest key in cylinder 102 is 800; therefore, key 400 must be contained in cylinder 102.) Next we examine the track index for cylinder 102 (Table 16.3). Each entry in the track index contains the highest key for that track. We conclude that the key 400, if it is present, is contained on track 3 of cylinder 102. We now know both the cylinder and track on which the record resides and may proceed directly to it.

When an indexed file is accessed in a COBOL program, the I/O routines of the operating system perform the search for the programmer. The cylinder and track indexes are established automatically by the system when the file is loaded. The COBOL necessary to create and access indexed files is straightforward and should present little difficulty when introduced later in this chapter.

Let us now consider what happens when a new record is added to an existing indexed file. A major disadvantage of sequential organization is that the entire file has to be rewritten if even a single record is added. One might logically ask that, since indexed files are loaded sequentially, shouldn't a similar requirement pertain. Fortunately, the answer is no. Indexed files solve the problem by establishing an overflow area and appropriate linkages. When an indexed file is initially loaded, the programmer provides, through the JCL, a prime data area and an overflow area. (Usually two tracks of every cylinder are reserved as a cylinder overflow area, as was done in Table 16.3. It is also possible to designate entire cylinders as an independent overflow area.)

Table 16.4 is an expanded version of Table 16.3 to reflect both prime and overflow areas for cylinder 102. In addition, we have appended the hypothetical record keys of every record in every track (assume four records per track).

The track index of Table 16.4 reflects the file immediately after creation; i.e., all records are stored in the prime data area, and the overflow area is entirely empty. This is denoted by identical entries in the overflow and prime portions of the track index.

What happens when a new record with key 410 is added to the file? The existing indexes indicate this record belongs in cylinder 102, track 3. The new record with key 410 is put in its proper place and "bumps" record 449 to an overflow area. No change is required in the cylinder index, for the highest key in cylinder 102 is still 800. However, changes are made in the track index for cylinder 102. The highest record in the prime area of track 3 is no longer 449 but 410; the overflow area is no longer empty but contains record 449. The overflow entries for track 3 now contain a key of 449 and a pointer to the overflow area, i.e., track 8, record 1.

Table 16.5 reflects the track index of Table 16.4 after three new records with keys 410, 730, and 289 were added in that order. The cylinder overflow area (tracks 8 and 9) contains the three bumped records in the order in which they were bumped. Thus the first record in track 8 is 449, the second is 800, and the last is 312.

Suppose another record, with key 380, is added to the file. Logically, 380 belongs in track 3, and as in the previous example, it will bump a record in the prime area to overflow. The prime area for track 3 now consists of records 377, 380, 394, and 400. The bumped record, key 410, is written in the first available space in overflow, i.e., track 8, record 4. Consider carefully the contents of the overflow area: records 449, 800, 312, and 410. Both 449 and 410 logically belong to track 3. They are physically separated from track 3 and indeed from each other. They must be logically reconnected, and this is done via link fields in the overflow area. Each record in overflow has an associated link field that points to the next logical record in the track. Table 16.6 is an updated

TABLE 16.4 Track Index Plus Record Keys for Cylinder 102

Prime		Overflow					
Track	Key	Track	Key	Actual record keys			
1	312	1	312	251	269	280	312
2	346	2	346	318	327	345	346
3	449	3	449	377	394	400	449
4	598	4	598	469	500	502	598
5	642	5	642	617	619	627	642
6	717	6	717	658	675	700	717
7	800	7	800	722	746	748	800

SECTION V: FILE PROCESSING

TABLE 16.5 Track Index of Table 16.4 with Three Additions

	Prime		Overflow					
	Track	Key	Track	Key	Actual record keys			
	1	289	T8, R3	312	251	269	280	289
	2	346	2	346	318	327	345	346
	3	410	T8, R1	449	377	394	400	410
	4	598	4	598	469	500	502	598
	5	642	5	642	617	619	627	642
	6	717	6	717	658	675	700	717
	7	748	T8, R2	800	722	730	746	748
Overflow	8	No entries			449	800	312	
	9	No entries			No entries			

version of Table 16.5 to reflect the addition of record 380 to track 3 and the linkage fields in overflow. (Table 16.6 also contains two new additions, records 311 and 635, as additional examples.)

Let us trace through track 3 in Table 16.6. The prime area contains keys 377, 380, 394, and 400. The overflow area begins on track 8, record 4, i.e., key 410. This in turn has a link field to track 8, record 1, key 449. The link associated with key 449 is ***, indicating the logical end of the chain.

As more and more records are added to the file, the overflow area becomes increasingly full and processing necessarily slows. Periodically, the file will be reorganized. It is read sequentially, i.e., via overflow linkages, and then rewritten to a work file. Finally, the work file is reloaded as a new indexed file, with all records in strict physical order and overflow areas empty.

TABLE 16.6 Track Index Plus Overflow Linkages

	Prime		Overflow					
	Track	Key	Track	Key	Actual record keys			
	1	289	T9, R1	312	251	269	280	289
	2	346	2	346	318	327	345	346
	3	400	T8, R4	449	377	380	394	400
	4	598	4	598	469	500	502	598
	5	635	T9, R2	642	617	619	627	635
	6	717	6	717	658	675	700	717
	7	748	T8, R2	800	722	730	746	748
		Key	Link	Key	Link	Key	Link	Key	Link
Overflow	8	449	***	800	***	312	***	410	T8, R1
	9	311	T8, R3	642	***				

COBOL Implications

Indexed files are recognized in the ANS 74 standard and widely used by all vendors. IBM has *two* distinct implementations: ISAM (Indexed Sequential Access Method) and VSAM (Virtual Storage Access Method).[1]

Very little in the way of additional COBOL is required to process indexed files of either type. We have included two COBOL listings to illustrate considerations of ISAM processing. Figure 16.6 creates an ISAM file from sequential input, and Figure 16.8 demonstrates random (direct) access of an ISAM file.

We follow the listing of Figure 16.8 with a discussion of ISAM/VSAM coding differences. *Note well that the COBOL requirements for IBM's ISAM implementation do not adhere to the*

[1] The reader is referred to R. Grauer and M. Crawford, *The COBOL Environment,* Chapter 5, Prentice-Hall, Inc., Englewood Cliffs, N.J., 1979, for a complete discussion of their differences.

```
00001            IDENTIFICATION DIVISION.
00002            PROGRAM-ID.
00003               CREATE.
00004            AUTHOR.
00005               ROBERT T. GRAUER.
00006            ENVIRONMENT DIVISION.
00007            CONFIGURATION SECTION.
00008            SOURCE-COMPUTER.
00009               IBM-370.
00010            OBJECT-COMPUTER.
00011               IBM-370.
00012            INPUT-OUTPUT SECTION.
00013            FILE-CONTROL.
00014               SELECT TRANSACTION-FILE ASSIGN TO UT-S-SYSIN.
00015               SELECT NEW-MASTER-FILE ASSIGN TO DA-I-NEWMAST
00016                  ACCESS IS SEQUENTIAL
00017                  RECORD KEY IS ISAM-ID-NUMBER.          This field is contained in ISAM record
00018            DATA DIVISION.
00019            FILE SECTION.
00020
00021            FD  NEW-MASTER-FILE
00022                LABEL RECORDS ARE STANDARD           Indicates blocking factor
00023                BLOCK CONTAINS 3 RECORDS
00024                RECORD CONTAINS 41 CHARACTERS
00025                DATA RECORD IS ISAM-MAST-RECORD.        First byte indicates active/inactive
00026            01  ISAM-MAST-RECORD.                        record (Non ANS standard)
00027                05  ISAM-DELETE-CODE        PIC X.
00028                05  ISAM-ID-NUMBER          PIC X(9).
00029                05  ISAM-NAME               PIC X(25).
00030                05  ISAM-SALARY             PIC X(6).
00031
00032            FD  TRANSACTION-FILE
00033                LABEL RECORDS ARE OMITTED
00034                RECORD CONTAINS 80 CHARACTERS
00035                DATA RECORD IS TRANS-RECORD.
00036            01  TRANS-RECORD.
00037                05  TR-ID-NUMBER            PIC X(9).
00038                05  TR-NAME                 PIC X(25).
00039                05  TR-SALARY               PIC X(6).
00040                05  FILLER                  PIC X(40).
00041            WORKING-STORAGE SECTION.
00042            01  WS-EOF-INDICATOR            PIC X(3)        VALUE 'NO '.
00043
00044            PROCEDURE DIVISION.
00045                OPEN INPUT TRANSACTION-FILE,
00046                     OUTPUT NEW-MASTER-FILE.
00047                READ TRANSACTION-FILE,
00048                    AT END MOVE 'YES' TO WS-EOF-INDICATOR.
00049                PERFORM 010-READ-A-CARD
00050                    UNTIL WS-EOF-INDICATOR = 'YES'.
00051                CLOSE TRANSACTION-FILE, NEW-MASTER-FILE.
00052                STOP RUN.                              Denotes an active record
00053                                                        (Non ANS 74 standard)
00054            010-READ-A-CARD.
00055                MOVE LOW-VALUES TO ISAM-DELETE-CODE.
00056                MOVE TR-ID-NUMBER TO ISAM-ID-NUMBER.
00057                MOVE TR-SALARY TO ISAM-SALARY.          Use of INVALID KEY clause
00058                WRITE ISAM-MAST-RECORD
00059                    INVALID KEY DISPLAY 'RECORD OUT OF SEQUENCE OR ',
0.0060                        'DUPLICATE', TR-ID-NUMBER.
00061                READ TRANSACTION-FILE,
00062                    AT END MOVE 'YES' TO WS-EOF-INDICATOR.
```

FIGURE 16.6 *Creation of an ISAM File*

ANS 74 standard, whereas VSAM coding does conform. We conclude with a formal presentation
of the ANS 74 elements for indexed files which are used in conjunction with VSAM.

Creation of an ISAM File

Figure 16.6 contains a COBOL program to create an ISAM file. The only new material is in the
SELECT statement (lines 15 to 17), the MOVE statement (line 55), and the WRITE statement

(lines 58 to 60). The program utilizes two files. It reads an incoming transaction file and creates ✳ an ISAM file as output. *The incoming file must be in sequential order.*

The SELECT statement contains the clause ACCESS IS SEQUENTIAL (line 16), indicating ✳ that in this particular run we are accessing the ISAM file sequentially. It also contains a RECORD KEY clause (line 17), which specifies the field within the ISAM record that serves as a key. Note that ISAM-ID-NUMBER, the field specified in the RECORD KEY, [must] be defined within the ISAM record itself.

✳ ISAM files do not physically delete inactive records. Instead a 1-byte field is established at the beginning of each record (line 27) with the convention that LOW-VALUES denote an active record and HIGH-VALUES an inactive record. When a file is created, all records are initially active, thus the MOVE statement of line 55. Subsequent processing, e.g., file maintenance, may "delete" specified records by moving HIGH-VALUES to this field (see Figure 16.8).

The WRITE statement (lines 58 to 60) contains an INVALID KEY clause. As was explained earlier, the key of every record in a file must be unique. Further, ISAM files must be written in *logical* sequential order. The INVALID KEY clause is a check on these two conditions; i.e., it ✳ ensures that the RECORD KEY of the present record is not a duplicate and, further, that it is higher than the key of the previous record.

Random (Direct) Access of an ISAM File

In Chapter 15 we introduced the concepts of file maintenance and sequential processing; in particular, Figure 15.11 contained a maintenance program to take a transaction file and an old master file as input and create a new master file as output. *Since processing was strictly sequential, every record in the old master had to be read and rewritten regardless of whether or not it was changed.* Obviously, if only a "small" percentage of records is changed, sequential processing is an inefficient means of file maintenance. *ISAM files provide the capability to do file maintenance on a direct basis; i.e.,* ✳ *only new or changed records are written—unchanged records are left alone.* Thus, while sequential processing required two distinct master files, an old and a new, direct processing uses a single ✳ master file from which records are both read and written to.

Figure 16.7 contains pseudocode for a nonsequential update and Figure 16.8 has the corresponding COBOL listing.

Unlike the sequential update of Figure 15.11, which is driven by the *relationship* between the old master and transaction files, a nonsequential update is driven solely by the transaction file; ✳ i.e., it processes transactions until no more remain.

The program of Figure 16.8 contains only three files: an input transaction file, an output error file, and an ISAM file, which is used for *both* input and output. We are familiar with the first two kinds of files and have used them throughout the text. An I/O file is a file that is both read from and written to. When a direct-access file is updated, we are not required to write every ✳ single record, as is the case in a sequential file. Instead only new and/or changed records are written, and these are written to the original file. Hence the same file is both input and output. Further, the altered records are *rewritten;* i.e., they were present in the original file and thus the necessity of the REWRITE statement (lines 111 and 115). The reader should realize that the I/O and REWRITE options make sense for ISAM files, but are not permitted with strict sequential organization.

The SELECT statement for the ISAM file (COBOL lines 12 to 15) has three clauses: ACCESS IS RANDOM, NOMINAL KEY, and RECORD KEY. The NOMINAL KEY denotes a field in working-storage, whereas RECORD KEY specifies the key of each ISAM record and as such is contained in the record itself.

After a record is read from the transaction file, its ID number is moved to the NOMINAL KEY (MOVE statement in line 89). The ISAM file is accessed by the READ statement in lines 90 to 91. The READ in turn searches the ISAM file and attempts to find a record whose key is ✳ the same as the value just moved to the NOMINAL KEY. The INVALID KEY clause in line 91 will be activated only if the read does not find a record containing the NOMINAL KEY. (Under random access of an ISAM file, however, the system will return "deleted" records, i.e.,

```
Initialize
Open files
READ TRANSACTION-FILE at end indicate no more data
PERFORM until no more data
      MOVE TRANSACTION-ID to nominal-key
      READ ISAM-FILE
          INVALID KEY means transaction record does not exist
    IF transaction record does not exist
        PERFORM new record routine
            IF TRANSACTION-CODE is addition
                WRITE new record on ISAM-FILE
            ELSE write error message for no match
        ENDPERFORM
    ELSE
        PERFORM match routine
            IF TRANSACTION-CODE is addition
                WRITE error message for duplicate add
            ELSE
                IF TRANSACTION-CODE is deletion
                    Remove record
                ELSE do salary change
        ENDPERFORM
    ENDIF
      READ TRANSACTION-FILE at end indicate no more data
ENDPERFORM
Close files
Stop run
```

FIGURE 16.7 *Pseudocode for Random Update*

those records with HIGH-VALUES in the first byte. An additional routine could be inserted in Figure 16.8 to check for this possibility.) If the INVALID KEY is activated, it means either a new record or a "no match." Either way it causes a perform of 070-NEW-RECORD. If INVALID KEY is not activated, then 060-MATCH-ROUTINE is performed instead. In other words, the data name contained in the NOMINAL KEY clause (WS-MATCH-NUMBER) holds the key of the current transaction, i.e., the record we are trying to find. When an ISAM file is read, the COBOL program searches the ISAM file to find an existing record that has a RECORD KEY that matches the NOMINAL KEY.

Figure 16.8 utilizes many of the procedure division techniques advocated in Chapter 11. In particular, note the use of READ INTO, WRITE FROM, and PERFORM THRU. Figure 16.8 was tested with the same data used for Figure 15.11 and, as expected, produced identical results (see Figure 15.12).

ISAM/VSAM Coding Differences

Recall that IBM has two distinct implementations for indexed files—ISAM and VSAM. Physically the two methods are very different, but that is of little concern here. Our present needs are restricted solely to the COBOL implementation. Consequently, Figure 16.8 requires modification to process a VSAM rather than an ISAM file. (Realize, however, that the JCL requirements are considerably different and beyond the scope of the JCL chapters in this book.[1])

The first change in Figure 16.8 concerns the SELECT statement. VSAM requires insertion of a new clause, ORGANIZATION IS INDEXED, after line 12. In addition, the NOMINAL KEY clause is no longer required, and consequently line 14 of Figure 16.8 is eliminated. Correspondingly, the working-storage definition in line 40 is also removed. A random read to a VSAM file is accomplished by first moving the desired key to the data name specified in the RECORD KEY clause. Hence line 89 of Figure 16.8 becomes MOVE WS-TRANS-ID TO VSAM-ID-NUMBER.

---

[1] The reader is referred to R. Grauer and M. Crawford, *The COBOL Environment*, Chapter 10 (Englewood Cliffs, N.J.: Prentice-Hall, Inc., 1979).

304

```
00001          IDENTIFICATION DIVISION.
00002          PROGRAM-ID.    UPDATE2.
00003          AUTHOR.          GRAUER.
00004          ENVIRONMENT DIVISION.
00005          CONFIGURATION SECTION.
00006          SOURCE-COMPUTER.   IBM-370.
00007          OBJECT-COMPUTER.   IBM-370.
00008          INPUT-OUTPUT SECTION.
00009          FILE-CONTROL.
00010              SELECT TRANSACTION-FILE ASSIGN TO UT-S-TRANS.
00011              SELECT ERROR-FILE ASSIGN TO UT-S-SYSOUT.
00012             ┌SELECT ISAM-FILE ASSIGN TO DA-I-ISAMMAST
00013              │  ACCESS IS RANDOM
00014              │  NOMINAL KEY IS WS-MATCH-NUMBER
00015              │  RECORD KEY IS ISAM-ID-NUMBER.
00016          DATA DIVISION.                                    ┌──────────────────────────
00017          FILE SECTION.                                     SELECT statement for ISAM file
00018          FD  ISAM-FILE                                     (non-ANS-74 standard)
00019              LABEL RECORDS ARE STANDARD
00020              RECORD CONTAINS 41 CHARACTERS
00021              DATA RECORD IS ISAM-RECORD.
00022          01  ISAM-RECORD.                                    ┌──RECORD KEY
00023              05 ISAM-DELETE-CODE        PIC X.
00024             ┌05 ISAM-ID-NUMBER          PIC X(9).┐
00025              05 ISAM-NAME               PIC X(25).
00026              05 ISAM-SALARY             PIC X(6).
00027          FD  TRANSACTION-FILE
00028              LABEL RECORDS ARE OMITTED
00029              RECORD CONTAINS 80 CHARACTERS
00030              DATA RECORD IS TRANS-RECORD.
00031          01  TRANS-RECORD               PIC X(80).
00032          FD  ERROR-FILE
00033              LABEL RECORDS ARE OMITTED
00034              RECORD CONTAINS 133 CHARACTERS
00035              DATA RECORD IS ERROR-RECORD.
00036          01  ERROR-RECORD               PIC X(133).
00037          WORKING-STORAGE SECTION.
00038          77  FILLER                     PIC X(14)
00039                                    VALUE 'WS BEGINS HERE'.
00040         ┌77  WS-MATCH-NUMBER           PIC X(9).┐
00041          77  WS-EOF-INDICATOR           PIC·X(3)        Definition of NOMINAL KEY
00042                                    VALUE 'NO '.          in working storage
00043          77  WS-INVALID-SWITCH          PIC X(3).        (non-ANS-74 standard)
00044              88 NO-MATCH-OR-NEW-RECORD        VALUE 'YES'.
00045          01  WS-TRANS-RECORD.
00046              05 WS-TRANS-ID             PIC X(9).
00047              05 WS-TRANS-NAME           PIC X(25).
00048              05 WS-TRANS-SALARY         PIC 9(6).
00049              05 FILLER                  PIC X(39).
00050              05 WS-TRANS-CODE           PIC X.
00051                 88 ADDITION        VALUE 'A'.
00052                 88 DELETION        VALUE 'D'.
00053                 88 SALARY-CHANGE   VALUE 'C'.
00054          01  WS-ERROR-MESSAGE-1         PIC X(40)
00055                                    VALUE ' RECORD ALREADY IN FILE '.
00056          01  WS-ERROR-MESSAGE-2         PIC X(40)
00057                                    VALUE ' NO MATCH '.
00058          01  WS-PRINT-RECORD.
00059              05 WS-PRINT-MESSAGE        PIC X(40).
00060              05 WS-PRINT-ID             PIC X(9).
00061              05 FILLER                  PIC X(5)
00062                                    VALUE SPACES.
00063              05 WS-PRINT-NAME           PIC X(25).
00064              05 FILLER                  PIC X(53)
00065                                    VALUE SPACES.
00066          01  WS-ISAM-RECORD.
00067              05 WS-ISAM-DELETE-CODE     PIC X.
00068              05 WS-ISAM-ID              PIC X(9).
00069              05 WS-ISAM-NAME            PIC X(25).
00070              05 WS-ISAM-SALARY          PIC X(6).
00071
00072          01  FILLER                     PIC X(12)
00073                                    VALUE 'WS ENDS HERE'.
00074          PROCEDURE DIVISION.
00075              MOVE 'NO ' TO WS-INVALID-SWITCH.
```

FIGURE 16.8 *Random Update of ISAM File*

CHAPTER 16: MAGNETIC DISK: CONCEPTS AND COBOL IMPLICATIONS

```
00076              OPEN INPUT TRANSACTION-FILE
00077                   I-O ISAM-FILE
00078                   OUTPUT ERROR-FILE.
00079              READ TRANSACTION-FILE INTO WS-TRANS-RECORD
00080                   AT END MOVE 'YES' TO WS-EOF-INDICATOR.
00081              PERFORM 010-READ-ISAM-FILE THRU 010-READ-ISAM-FILE-EXIT
00082                   UNTIL WS-EOF-INDICATOR = 'YES'.
00083              CLOSE TRANSACTION-FILE
00084                   ISAM-FILE
00085                   ERROR-FILE.
00086              STOP RUN.                          Transaction key moved to NOMINAL KEY
00087                                                 (non-ANS-74 standard)
00088          010-READ-ISAM-FILE.
00089              MOVE WS-TRANS-ID TO WS-MATCH-NUMBER.        INVALID KEY clause
00090              READ ISAM-FILE INTO WS-ISAM-RECORD          turns switch on
00091                  INVALID KEY MOVE 'YES' TO WS-INVALID-SWITCH.
00092              IF NO-MATCH-OR-NEW-RECORD
00093                  PERFORM 070-NEW-RECORD THRU 070-NEW-RECORD-EXIT
00094              ELSE
00095                  PERFORM 060-MATCH-ROUTINE THRU 060-MATCH-ROUTINE-EXIT.
00096              READ TRANSACTION-FILE INTO WS-TRANS-RECORD
00097                  AT END MOVE 'YES' TO WS-EOF-INDICATOR.
00098
00099          010-READ-ISAM-FILE-EXIT.
00100              EXIT.
00101
00102          060-MATCH-ROUTINE.
00103              IF ADDITION
00104                  MOVE WS-TRANS-NAME      TO WS-PRINT-NAME
00105                  MOVE WS-TRANS-ID        TO WS-PRINT-ID
00106                  MOVE WS-ERROR-MESSAGE-1 TO WS-PRINT-MESSAGE
00107                  WRITE ERROR-RECORD FROM WS-PRINT-RECORD
00108              ELSE                         HIGH-VALUES signify an inactive record
00109                  IF DELETION              (non-ANS-74 standard)
00110                      MOVE HIGH-VALUES TO WS-ISAM-DELETE-CODE
00111                      REWRITE ISAM-RECORD FROM WS-ISAM-RECORD
00112                  ELSE
00113                      IF SALARY-CHANGE
00114                          MOVE WS-TRANS-SALARY TO WS-ISAM-SALARY
00115                          REWRITE ISAM-RECORD FROM WS-ISAM-RECORD.
00116                                             REWRITE statement
00117          060-MATCH-ROUTINE-EXIT.
00118              EXIT.
00119
00120          070-NEW-RECORD.                      INVALID-SWITCH is turned off
00121              MOVE 'NO ' TO WS-INVALID-SWITCH.
00122              IF ADDITION
00123                  MOVE LOW-VALUES      TO WS-ISAM-DELETE-CODE
00124                  MOVE WS-TRANS-ID     TO WS-ISAM-ID
00125                  MOVE WS-TRANS-NAME   TO WS-ISAM-NAME
00126                  MOVE WS-TRANS-SALARY TO WS-ISAM-SALARY
00127                  WRITE ISAM-RECORD FROM WS-ISAM-RECORD
00128              ELSE
00129                  MOVE WS-TRANS-NAME      TO WS-PRINT-NAME
00130                  MOVE WS-TRANS-ID        TO WS-PRINT-ID
00131                  MOVE WS-ERROR-MESSAGE-2 TO WS-PRINT-MESSAGE
00132                  WRITE ERROR-RECORD FROM WS-PRINT-RECORD.
00133
00134          070-NEW-RECORD-EXIT.
00135              EXIT.
```

— Routine to process new records or no matches

FIGURE 16.8 *(continued)*

The second major change stems from the fact that inactive records are removed immediately from a VSAM file. Thus there is no reason to reserve the first byte of a VSAM record as a delete byte, with LOW or HIGH VALUES denoting active and inactive records, respectively. This leads to the elimination of COBOL lines 23, 110, and 123 in Figure 16.8. Finally, inactive records are removed through the DELETE verb, causing line 111 to read DELETE VSAM-FILE, in which the file-name of the indexed file is coded.

There are more similarities than differences between the two types of file organizations. Both permit sequential as well as nonsequential organization through the ACCESS MODE clause. Both require the indexed file to be opened as I/O. Both use the READ verb with the INVALID KEY clause; both use the same WRITE and REWRITE statements.

ADDITIONAL COBOL ELEMENTS
(VSAM AND THE ANS 74 STANDARD)

As previously mentioned, the IBM implementation for ISAM does *not* conform to the ANS 74 standard, whereas the VSAM implementation does. The discussion that follows pertains to IBM's OS/VS COBOL compiler, which meets the standard, and hence is restricted to VSAM.

The SELECT statement for ANS 74 indexed files is shown:

```
SELECT file-name
    ASSIGN TO implementor-name-1 [, implementor-name-2]...

    [                    ⌈ AREA  ⌉ ]
    [ RESERVE integer-1  ⌊ AREAS ⌋ ]

    ORGANIZATION IS INDEXED

    [                   ⌈ SEQUENTIAL ⌉ ]
    [ ACCESS MODE IS  ⎰ RANDOM      ⎱ ]
    [                   ⌊ DYNAMIC    ⌋ ]

    RECORD KEY IS data-name-1
    [ ALTERNATE RECORD KEY IS data-name-2 [WITH DUPLICATES]]...
    [ FILE STATUS IS data-name-3].
```

Note that only three clauses, ASSIGN, ORGANIZATION IS INDEXED, and RECORD KEY are required. The ACCESS MODE defaults to sequential if omitted, and all remaining clauses are optional.

The ALTERNATE RECORD KEY provides a second direct path into a file. However, unlike the RECORD KEY, which must be unique for each record, the ALTERNATE KEY need not be unique. This capability is extremely powerful and gives COBOL some limited facility for data base management. Thus it is possible to retrieve not only individual records, but also groups of records. Consider, for example,

```
SELECT EMPLOYEE-FILE
          .
          .

          .
          .

    RECORD KEY IS EMPLOYEE-NUMBER
    ALTERNATE RECORD KEY IS LOCATION WITH DUPLICATES.
```

This statement permits us to access *directly* the first employee with a given location, and then all the rest of the employees in the same location.

FILE STATUS defines a 2-byte area that indicates results of each I/O operation. Its use is optional. Status keys and their meanings for indexed (VSAM) files are shown in Table 16.7.

FILE STATUS is commonly used in conjunction with DECLARATIVES to facilitate the processing of I/O errors. DECLARATIVES must immediately follow the procedure division header and must end with the sentence END DECLARATIVES. This is illustrated in Figure 16.9.

Consider the action taken on an INVALID KEY condition. If FILE STATUS is specified in the SELECT statement for a file, a value is placed into the designated 2-byte area after every I/O operation for that file. If the INVALID KEY option is specified in the statement causing the condition, control is transferred to the imperative statement following INVALID KEY. Any declarative procedure for this file is *not* executed.

If, however, INVALID KEY is not specified and the condition occurs, control passes to the declarative procedure for that file. Control returns to the statement immediately following the

TABLE 16.7 I/O Status Codes

Key-1	Key-2	Cause	
0	0	Successful completion	
1	0	End-of-file	
2	1	Invalid key:	Sequence error
	2		Duplicate key
	3		No record found
	4		Boundary violation
3	0	Permanent I/O error:	No further information
	4		Boundary violation
9	1	Other error:	Password failure
	2		Logic error
	3		Resource not available
	4		Sequential record not available
	5		Invalid or incomplete file information
	6		No DD statement

one causing the error after the action specified in declaratives has been taken. Thus, if an INVALID KEY condition was raised as a consequence of the WRITE in Figure 16.9, control would pass to the appropriate DECLARATIVES section and return to the statement immediately under WRITE. The advantage of the STATUS field over the INVALID KEY clause is that the cause of an I/O error is known more precisely.

VSAM files can specify ACCESS IS DYNAMIC in lieu of RANDOM or SEQUENTIAL. This permits records to be accessed both sequentially and/or randomly in the same program. The form of the READ statement determines the access method. For sequential access, READ file-name NEXT . . . must be specified; for random access NEXT is omitted.

ACCESS IS DYNAMIC is often used in conjunction with ALTERNATE KEY. Consider for example an online billing system which defines customer account number as the *unique* RECORD

```
SELECT VSAM-FILE
    ASSIGN TO DA-VSAMMAST
    ORGANIZATION IS INDEXED
    RECORD KEY IS VSAM-KEY
    STATUS IS STATUS-FILE-ONE.
        .
        .
        .

WORKING-STORAGE SECTION.
01   STATUS-FILE-ONE.
     05   FIRST-KEY            PIC X.
     05   SECOND-KEY           PIC X.
PROCEDURE DIVISION.
DECLARATIVES.
D010-INVALID-KEY SECTION.
     USE AFTER ERROR-PROCEDURE ON VSAM-FILE.
     IF FIRST-KEY = '2' AND SECOND-KEY = '1'
       DISPLAY 'SEQUENCE ERROR — VSAM-FILE'.
     IF FIRST-KEY = '2' AND SECOND-KEY = '2'
       DISPLAY 'DUPLICATE KEY — VSAM-FILE'.
        .
        .
        .

END DECLARATIVES.
REST-OF-PROCEDURE-DIVISION.
     WRITE VSAM-FILE.
        .
        .
```

FIGURE 16.9 *Use of FILE STATUS and DECLARATIVES*

KEY, and customer name as an ALTERNATE KEY WITH DUPLICATES. A customer, e.g. Smith, calls in without knowing his customer number. The program could execute a *random* read to find the first Smith, and then process *sequentially* until the proper record is found.

The START statement causes the file to be positioned to the first record whose value is equal to, greater than, or not less than the value contained in the identifier. INVALID KEY is raised if no record is found that meets the specified criterion. Syntactically, the START statement has the form

$$\underline{\text{START}}\ \text{file-name}\ [\text{KEY IS}\ \begin{Bmatrix} \underline{\text{EQUAL}}\ \text{TO} \\ = \\ \underline{\text{GREATER}}\ \text{THAN} \\ > \\ \underline{\text{NOT}}\ \underline{\text{LESS}}\ \text{THAN} \\ \underline{\text{NOT}} < \end{Bmatrix}\ \text{identifier}]$$

[INVALID KEY imperative statement]

SUMMARY

The chapter was primarily concerned with indexed file organization. As such, it began with a discussion of magnetic disk, a device that physically permits this type of organization. Next, the conceptual framework of indexed files was presented through an extended example.

Two COBOL listings were shown to create and randomly update an ISAM file. The latter contained parallel requirements of the sequential update program of Chapter 15 and was accompanied by pseudocode. The COBOL similarities and differences between ISAM and VSAM were discussed; the latter adheres to the ANS 74 standard, whereas the former does not.

Additional COBOL elements of the ANS 74 standard were presented. These included DYNAMIC ACCESS, FILE STATUS, and ALTERNATE RECORD KEY in the SELECT statement, use of DECLARATIVES, and the START verb.

One final point on file organization: the inherent characteristics of a file should determine its method of organization. Perhaps the most important consideration is file activity. If the file is inactive, i.e., a "low" percentage of records are processed in a given run, then file organization should permit individual records to be located quickly. Alternatively, a highly active file should be processed sequentially. Unfortunately, quantitative guidelines as to the percentage of activity that constitutes an active file are difficult to define.

REVIEW EXERCISES

TRUE   FALSE

☐   ☐   **1.** The number of cylinders on a disk pack is equal to the number of tracks on a recording surface.

☐   ☐   **2.** The number of read/write heads on the assembly arm is equal to the number of tracks per cylinder.

☐   ☐   **3.** An increase in the density per track decreases the overall capacity of the disk pack.

☐   ☐   **4.** If one track on a disk device can hold a single 10,000-byte record, it is logical to assume it could hold two records each of 5000 bytes.

☐   ☐   **5.** Sequential organization is not possible on a direct-access device.

☐   ☐   **6.** An ISAM file can be accessed either sequentially or directly.

☐   ☐   **7.** Head selection is the most time-consuming process in retrieving a record from a disk pack.

☐   ☐   **8.** If two records are located on the same cylinder, access time for the second will be zero.

☐   ☐   **9.** If two records are located on different tracks of the same recording surface, access time for the second will be zero.

☐   ☐   **10.** It is not possible to have a zero rotational delay.

☐   ☐   **11.** Indexed files are an IBM extension to the ANS 74 standard.

☐   ☐   **12.** An ISAM file has more than one track index.

☐   ☐   **13.** In an ISAM file, records are physically in sequential order.

☐ ☐ **14.** The same COBOL program can be used to process sequential files, irrespective of whether the files are stored on tape or disk.

☐ ☐ **15.** The START verb allows sequential access of an indexed file to begin at a record other than the first.

☐ ☐ **16.** ISAM and VSAM are two distinct IBM implementations for indexed files.

☐ ☐ **17.** Device type must be specified in a SELECT statement.

☐ ☐ **18.** The REWRITE verb can be used only on a file that was opened as I/O.

☐ ☐ **19.** The clause, ORGANIZATION IS INDEXED, is required for indexed files according to the ANS 74 standard.

☐ ☐ **20.** The ACCESS MODE clause must always be specified.

☐ ☐ **21.** The NOMINAL KEY is always required for ISAM files.

☐ ☐ **22.** LOW-VALUES commonly denote active records for ISAM files.

☐ ☐ **23.** WRITE and REWRITE may be used interchangeably.

☐ ☐ **24.** The INVALID KEY clause of the WRITE statement cannot be used for sequential files.

☐ ☐ **25.** A given READ statement can contain both the INVALID KEY and AT END clauses.

PROBLEMS

1. Calculate the maximum storage capacity of a hypothetical disk device with 16 recording surfaces, 400 cylinders, and a recording density of 10,000 bytes per track.

2. Consider a file of 10,000 physical records, each 400 bytes long. How many cylinders are required to store the file (sequentially with no keys) on a 2314? On a 3330?

3. Consider the file of Problem 2, i.e., 10,000 records, each 400 bytes long. This time assume keys and determine how many cylinders are required to store this file as an ISAM file on both a 2314 and a 3330. Further assume that one track in each cylinder is used for the track index and two additional tracks are used for overflow.

4. Extend Table 16.6 to reflect the addition of record keys 747 and 701.

5. Indicate whether the following statements apply to ISAM only, VSAM only, or both:

ISAM	VSAM	BOTH	
☐	☐	☐	(a) Uses the first byte to denote active or inactive status.
☐	☐	☐	(b) Removes inactive records through the DELETE verb.
☐	☐	☐	(c) Requires the RECORD KEY clause in its SELECT statement.
☐	☐	☐	(d) Has the NOMINAL KEY clause in its SELECT statement.
☐	☐	☐	(e) Requires ORGANIZATION IS INDEXED in its SELECT statement.
☐	☐	☐	(f) Conforms to the ANS 74 standard.
☐	☐	☐	(g) Can access records either sequentially or nonsequentially.
☐	☐	☐	(h) Can access records either sequentially or nonsequentially in the *same* program.
☐	☐	☐	(i) Can be opened as an I/O file.
☐	☐	☐	(j) Uses the REWRITE verb to change existing records.
☐	☐	☐	(k) Can specify ACCESS IS DYNAMIC.
☐	☐	☐	(l) Contains track and cylinder indexes.
☐	☐	☐	(m) Has its records in logically sequential, but not necessarily physically sequential, order.
☐	☐	☐	(n) Can be accessed through the START verb.
☐	☐	☐	(o) Can have an ALTERNATE RECORD KEY.
☐	☐	☐	(p) Requires a "virtual" operating system.

6. Incorporate the modifications of Problem 5 in Chapter 15 into the program of Figure 16.8.

PROJECTS

1. See Project 1, Chapter 15. Develop a COBOL program for *nonsequential* maintenance with otherwise identical specifications to the project in Chapter 15. Realize, however, that a single file will be both input and output in this project. Consequently, only those records that actually change will be written to the new master. Use the data provided in Chapter 15, except rearrange the transaction file so that transactions are not in order.

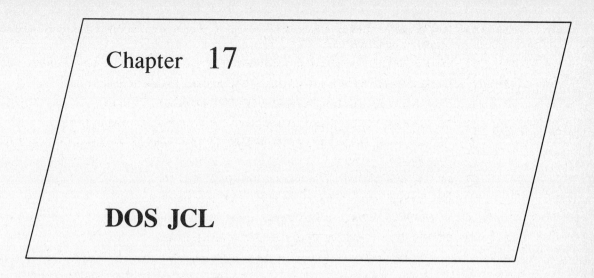

Chapter 17

DOS JCL

OVERVIEW

An operating system is a complex set of programs, supplied by the mainframe manufacturer, to improve the effectiveness of a computer. Communication with the operating system is accomplished through user-prepared control cards known as job control language, or simply JCL. Chapters 17 and 18 are directed at the COBOL programmer (in an "IBM shop") who continually utilizes the facilities of an operating system but whose knowledge of JCL is typically below his or her COBOL capability. "Just give me the control cards" is a phrase heard far too often.

In this chapter and the next we shall discuss the two most widely used operating systems, DOS and OS. The chapters may be read independently of one another, and we suggest you concentrate on the operating system in use at your installation. This chapter begins with an overview of the programs constituting the operating system. This is followed by substantial coverage of JCL. At the conclusion of either chapter the reader should have acquired sufficient JCL to manipulate tape and disk files in conjunction with the COBOL covered in Chapters 15 and 16.

DOS COMPONENTS

The disk-operating system is composed of three sets of programs: control programs, language translators, and service programs (Table 17.1).

Control programs supervise the execution of all other programs as well as controlling the location, storage, and retrieval of data. The *initial program loader (IPL)* loads the supervisor into main storage when the system is initiated. It is used only at the start of operations or after a system crash when the system has to be reinitiated. The *supervisor* is the most important control program, and part of it resides in main storage at all times. It handles all I/O operations, program interrupts, and any other functions required by a problem program. *Job control* interprets JCL statements and provides for continuity between jobs and job steps. It is called by the supervisor whenever necessary.

A *language translator* accepts statements in a higher-level language and translates them into machine language. We are familiar with COBOL and Assembler. FORTRAN is a widely used language that is best suited to problems with a large amount of calculations and limited I/O. PL/I is a general-purpose language that combines features of COBOL, FORTRAN, and other languages. RPG is a report program generator designed especially for report writing and file maintenance applications.

TABLE 17.1 Programs Comprising DOS

I. Control programs
    Supervisor
    Job control
    Initial program loader (IPL)
II. Language translators
    Assembler (BAL)
    COBOL
    FORTRAN
    PL/I
    RPG
III. Service programs
    Linkage-editor
    Librarian
    Sort/merge
    Utilities
    Autotest
    POWER (DOS/VS)

Service programs perform a variety of functions required by the user. The *linkage-editor* combines object modules (i.e., the output of a language translator) with modules from a system library to produce an executable program. The *sort/merge* programs allow the user to sort a file of randomly ordered records or to merge several sequenced files into one. *Autotest* provides aid in testing and debugging programs. *Utility* programs are used to copy files from one device to another, e.g., tape to disk, card to tape, etc. *POWER* is a service program designed to facilitate spooling.[1]

The *librarian* is used to maintain the three system libraries. A given program can be stored (cataloged) in a different form in all three libraries. The *source statement library* contains programs in the form in which they were written. The *relocatable library* contains object modules that are the results of a compilation. Programs in the relocatable library have been translated into machine language but have not yet been tied to specific addresses or combined with other required modules; hence they are not yet executable. The *core image library* contains fully executable programs. Each program in this library has been processed by the linkage editor. A *procedure library* is also available in DOS/VS and DOS/VSE.

We proceed to a discussion of DOS JCL.

A BASIC JOB STREAM

The JCL to compile, link-edit, and execute a COBOL program is shown in Figure 17.1.

All JCL statements consist of up to four components, with blanks as the delimiters between components. Every statement begins with // in columns 1 and 2, with the exception of /*, denoting end of file, * indicating a comment, and /&, denoting end of job. The second component indicates the operation, e.g., EXEC, OPTION, etc., and may be up to eight characters long. Operands follow next. A statement may have none, e.g., the last EXEC card, or several, as in the OPTION statement. Comments are last and follow the last operand, as illustrated in the JOB statement.

Presentation of JCL statements is facilitated through notation similar to that used in explaining COBOL. Thus

Uppercase letters   Are required to appear in a JCL statement exactly as shown in the sample format.

Lowercase letters   Denote generic terms that are replaced in the actual JCL statement.

[ ]   Indicate an optional specification; i.e., the contents of the brackets appear at the discretion of the programmer in conjunction with his requirements.

---

[1] See Appendix A, R. Grauer and M. Crawford, *The COBOL Environment,* Prentice-Hall, Inc., Englewood Cliffs, N.J., 1979.

SECTION V: FILE PROCESSING

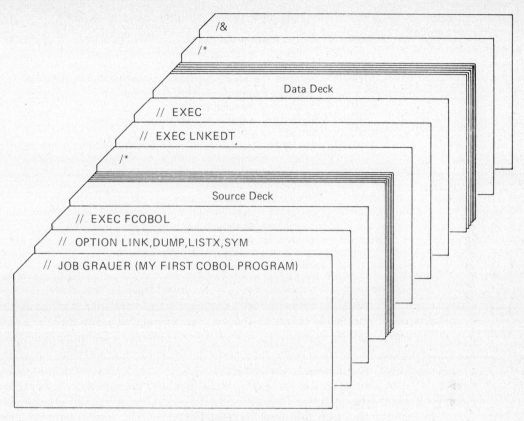

FIGURE 17.1 *Basic DOS JCL*

{   }   Require that a choice be made among the items stacked within.

. . .   Denote repetition, at programmer discretion, of the last syntactical element.

We proceed to an explanation of the JOB, OPTION, EXEC, /*, and /& statements.

JOB Statement

Format: // JOB jobname
Example: // JOB GRAUER (MY FIRST COBOL PROGRAM)

The jobname is a programmer-defined name consisting of one to eight alphanumeric characters, the first of which must be alphabetic. User comments may appear on the JOB card following the jobname through column 72.

OPTION Statement

Format: // OPTION option1,option2,option3 . . .
Example: // OPTION LINK

Default values for all options are established when the system is generated (SYSGEN time). The OPTION statement permits one to temporarily, i.e., for the duration of the job, override the standard options. Table 17.2 contains a partial list of DOS options, which are listed for the most part in mutually exclusive pairs, e.g., DUMP and NODUMP.

TABLE 17.2 Partial List of DOS Options

DUMP	Causes a dump of main storage and registers to be printed in case of abnormal program termination, e.g., a data exception.
NODUMP	Suppresses the DUMP option.
LINK	Indicates the object module is to be link-edited. This option must be present prior to the EXEC FCOBOL statement.
NOLINK	Suppresses the LINK option.
DECK	Causes the compiler to punch an object deck.
NODECK	Suppresses the DECK option.
LISTX	Generates a procedure division map. In addition, other information, such as register assignments and the literal pool, is also printed.
NOLISTX	Suppresses the LISTX option.
XREF	Provides a cross-reference list.
NOXREF	Suppresses the XREF option.
SYM	Generates a data division map. In addition, other information, such as register assignments and the literal pool, is also printed.
NOSYM	Suppresses the SYM option.
ERRS	Causes compiler diagnostics to be listed.
NOERRS	Suppresses the ERRS option.
CATAL	Causes the cataloging of the program in the core image library.

Note: The LINK and CATAL options may *not* appear in the same statement.

The CATAL option does not appear in a mutually exclusive pair. This option will *catalog* a program in the core image library. If the option is not specified, no cataloging will take place; however, it is *incorrect* to say NOCATAL.

As an illustration, assume we want data and procedure division maps, a dump in the event of ABEND, and for the object module to be link-edited. All this is accomplished by the statement

// OPTION LISTX,SYM,DUMP,LINK

Options may be listed in any order. What about the options of Table 17.2 not specified in the OPTION statement; i.e., which is, in effect, DECK or NODECK, ERRS or NOERRS, etc.? The answer depends on the options included in the system generation. Typically, NODECK and ERRS are default options, and hence there is no reason to specify them explicitly. The purpose of the OPTION card is to *temporarily* override the default options. Common practice, therefore, is to specify only those options which differ from the SYSGEN, but it is certainly not incorrect to explicitly specify all options.

EXEC Statement

Format: // EXEC prog-name
Example: // EXEC FCOBOL

The EXEC statement causes the execution of a program. A given job stream can contain several EXEC statements, each of which produces a job step. The program-name field must be specified when the program to be executed is in the core image library, e.g., FCOBOL or LNKEDT. It is not specified if the COBOL program was freshly compiled and link-edited as in the third EXEC statement of Figure 17.1.

The EXEC statement can also invoke a procedure under DOS/VS or VSE by specifying // EXEC PROC=procedure name.[1]

---

[1] The reader is referred to R. Grauer and M. Crawford, *The COBOL Environment,* Chapter 12 (Englewood Cliffs, N.J.: Prentice-Hall, Inc., 1979), for additional information.

/* (Slash Asterisk) Statement

The /* control card signifies that the end of data has been reached. It appears after the COBOL source deck in Figure 17.1, since the COBOL source deck is the data for the COBOL compiler. It also appears after the data cards.

/& (Slash Ampersand) Statement

This statement denotes the end of a job, and it is the last statement in a job stream. A given job may contain several /* statements, but it must contain one and only one /& card.

DEVICE ASSIGNMENTS

A computer is connected to its I/O devices through a *channel* (a hardware device with limited logic circuitry.) A channel permits overlap, i.e., simultaneous I/O and processing, and is therefore essential to maximize overall utilization of a system's resources. Each I/O device is attached to a channel through a control unit. There can be several control units hooked to one channel and several I/O devices tied to one control unit. Each type of I/O device, however, requires its own control unit. To the user the functions of the control unit are indistinguishable from the functions of the I/O device itself. Indeed, some control units are physically housed within the device itself, while others (e.g., tape drives) require a separate piece of equipment in the machine room.

The JCL ASSGN statement ties an I/O device to a symbolic address. The COBOL SELECT statement links the programmer-defined file name to the symbolic address of an I/O device. The two statements in combination relate COBOL-defined file names to specific I/O devices. (Disk files require an additional JCL statement, the EXTENT statement, covered in a later section in this chapter, to specify the exact location of a file on the disk pack.)

A three-digit number of the form 'cuu' is used in the ASSGN statement to specify the address of the I/O device. The 'c' denotes the channel number; the first 'u' denotes the control unit, and the second 'u' the device. Figure 17.2 is a schematic diagram of an installation with four tape drives, four disk drives, a card reader and punch, printer, and keyboard. Note the boxes denoting the tape and disk drive control units. Further note that the tapes and disks are all on the same channel. There are two control units hooked to this channel, one for the tape drives and one for the disk drives. The card reader, punch, printer, and keyboard are all on a second channel. The reader, punch, and printer share a common control unit; the control unit for the console is housed within the device itself.

The four tape drives are addressed by 181, 182, 183, and 184, respectively. Each of these drives is on channel 1. The disk drives have addresses 191, 192, 193 and 194 and are all on channel 1. The card reader, punch, printer, and keyboard are 00C, 00D, 00E, and 01F, respectively.

The COBOL programmer does not refer to an I/O device by its address. Instead he uses a symbolic name that causes programs to be dependent on a device type rather than a particular device. At execution time, the symbolic name is tied to the specific device by a table of permanent assignments established at SYSGEN or by individual ASSGN statements that override permanent assignments. Symbolic names are divided into system and programmer units, as shown in Table 17.3.

We have discussed the symbolic addresses and permanent assignments of I/O devices. Both are tied to COBOL through the SELECT statement. Consider

SELECT INPUT-FILE ASSIGN TO SYS004-UR-2540R-S.

The programmer specifies that INPUT-FILE is to come from SYS004 and further that SYS004 is a card reader. According to Table 17.3, SYS004 is permanently assigned to the card reader, and there is no need for further JCL. We could, however, optionally provide an ASSGN card, which temporarily (for the duration of the JOB or until another ASSGN card is read) overrides the permanent assignment of Table 17.3.

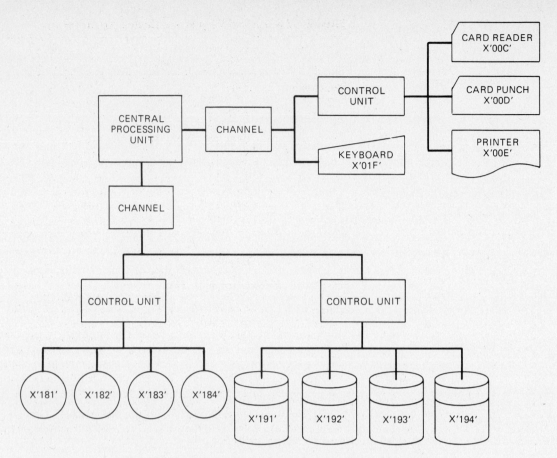

FIGURE 17.2 *Schematic Illustration of a Typical Installation*

ASSGN Statement

Format: // ASSGN SYSnnn,X'cuu'
Example: // ASSGN SYS004,X'00C'

In this example SYS004 is assigned to the device whose address is 00C. Since the temporary and permanent assignments match, the ASSGN card has no effect. It is common practice, however, to explicitly specify all assignments in the JCL to avoid any ambiguity. Moreover, in a majority of instances, ASSGN statements are mandatory rather than optional. Consider the COBOL SELECT statements:

```
SELECT OLD-TAPE-MASTERFILE ASSIGN TO SYS010-UT-3400-S.
SELECT NEW-TAPE-MASTERFILE ASSIGN TO SYS011-UT-3400-S.
```

The programmer specifies SYS010 and SYS011 for **OLD-TAPE-MASTERFILE** and **NEW-TAPE-MASTERFILE**, respectively. These symbolic names are permanently assigned to tape drives 181 and 182. Assume, however, that one of these drives, 181, is unavailable. Are we to wait until it becomes available before our program can be executed? That would hardly be practical. We bypass the problem by assigning SYS010 to an available drive via an ASSGN statement: // ASSGN SYS010, X'183'.

GENERIC ASSIGNMENTS: Generic assignments specify a device type, rather than a particular device, and are available only under DOS/VS or VSE. Consider the difference between

```
                          // ASSGN SYS010,X'180'
and                       // ASSGN SYS011,TAPE,VOL=123456
```

TABLE 17.3 Typical Permanent Device Assignments

	Symbolic name	Address	Device type
Programmer	SYS004	X'00C'	Card reader
logical	SYS005	X'00D'	Card punch
units	SYS006	X'00E'	Printer
	SYS010	X'181'	Tape drive
	SYS011	X'182'	Tape drive
	SYS012	X'183'	Tape drive
	SYS013	X'184'	Tape drive
	SYS014	X'191'	Disk drive
	SYS015	X'192'	Disk drive
	SYS016	X'193'	Disk drive
	SYS017	X'194'	Disk drive

	Symbolic name	Address	Function
System	SYSRDR	X'00C'	Input for JCL
logical	SYSIPT	X'00C'	Input for programs
units	SYSPCH	X'00D'	Punched output
	SYSLST	X'00E'	Printed output
	SYSLOG	X'01F'	Operator messages
	SYSLNK	X'191'	Input to linkage editor
	SYSRES	X'192'	Contains operating system

Note: These assignments are representative of permanent assignments established at system generation. They will, of course, vary from installation to installation.

The first example is the "old-fashioned" assign statement that *requires* device 180 for SYS010. The second example assigns SYS011 to any tape drive that has a tape mounted with a volume number of 123456.

Generic assignments for other kinds of devices are also permitted. Thus the statements

```
// ASSGN SYS009,PRINTER
// ASSGN SYS010,READER
// ASSGN SYS011,PUNCH
```

would assign SYS009, SYS010, and SYS011 to any available printer, card reader, or punch, respectively.

Generic assignments also make it possible to *share* a disk device across partitions; i.e., programs executing concurrently in separate partitions can access the same physical device at the same time. This is accomplished via the SHR parameter as shown:

```
// ASSGN SYS012,DISK,VOL=WORK01,SHR
```

The generic assignment causes each disk in a ready status to be examined until a disk with a volume ID of WORK01 is found. SYS012 is then assigned to that device. Inclusion of the SHR parameter allows the particular disk drive to be simultaneously assigned to any other job. Realize, however, that SHR has no meaning for other device types; e.g., it is meaningless to share a tape or printer among two jobs.

IGNORING ASSIGNMENTS: It is possible to negate (ignore) I/O operations through the command // ASSGN SYSXXX,IGN. This causes logical IOCS commands to the specified SYS number to be ignored. The effect in COBOL is that an end-of-file condition is registered on the first read for an input file and/or that output records are not written to any device. This capability is extremely useful as follows.

Assume a new system is being implemented with three files: an old master, a new master, and a transaction file. However, there is no old master file available as input for the first cycle. This problem is easily circumvented by assigning the input file to IGN.

On the output side, there are many instances where a file is required only under specific conditions. Creation of the file is controlled by the IGN parameter.

PAUSE Statement

Format: // PAUSE   comments
Example: // PAUSE   MOUNT TAPE REEL   # 123456 ON 183

The PAUSE statement allows one to instruct the operator between job steps. It is a convenient way to request that a particular reel of tape, disk pack, print form, etc., be mounted. The example requests the operator to mount reel # 123456 from the tape library on 183. (Of course, the programmer must coordinate his PAUSE, SELECT, and ASSGN statements.)

When a PAUSE statement is encountered by the operating system, its message prints on the keyboard, and processing is suspended. The operator complies with the request, then hits the end-of-block or enter key on the console, whereupon processing resumes. A variety of messages can be given via the PAUSE statement. Most commonly, instructions are given to mount specific volumes (tape, reels, or disk packs) and special forms for the printer (e.g., payroll checks, multiple part paper, etc.).

PROCESSING TAPE FILES

The tape library of a typical installation consists of hundreds or even thousands of reels. When the programmer requests a specific reel via a PAUSE statement or other instruction, he is referring to an *external* label, i.e., a piece of paper pasted on the reel of tape for visual identification. Unfortunately, it is far too easy to inadvertently mount the wrong reel, and the consequences of such an action can be disastrous. *Internal* labels, consisting of information written on the tape itself, are used as a precaution.

There are three standard DOS labels: volume, header, and trailer. The volume label appears at the beginning of each volume (i.e., reel) and contains a six-digit serial number to uniquely identify the volume. A header label is an 80-byte record that appears before each file on the tape. The trailer label, also 80 bytes, appears at the end of each file. The header and trailer labels contain identical information, with the exception of a block count field (in the trailer label) that indicates the number of records contained in the file.

Every volume may contain one and only one volume label. It can contain several sets of header and trailer labels depending on the number and size of the files on the reel. The COBOL programmer indicates label processing is desired by the clause "LABEL RECORDS ARE STANDARD" in the FD for the file. If this clause is included for a tape file, then supporting JCL, i.e., the LBLTYP and TLBL statements, are also required.

Volume, header, and trailer labels are illustrated schematically in Figure 17.3. Figure 17.3 is

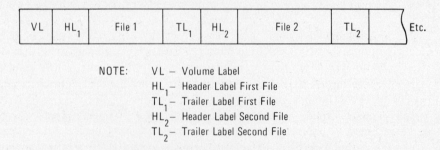

NOTE: VL — Volume Label
         HL$_1$— Header Label First File
         TL$_1$— Trailer Label First File
         HL$_2$— Header Label Second File
         TL$_2$— Trailer Label Second File

FIGURE 17.3 *Volume, Header, and Trailer Labels*

an example of a multifile volume; i.e., several files are contained on the same volume (reel). It is also possible to have a multivolume file in which the same file extends over several volumes.

LBLTYP Statement

Format: // LBLTYP $\begin{Bmatrix} \text{TAPE} \\ \text{NSD(nn)} \end{Bmatrix}$

Example: // LBLTYP TAPE

The NSD (nonsequential disk) option is used only when processing nonsequential disk files and is discussed in that section. The LBLTYP statement must appear immediately before the // EXEC LNKEDT statement. It specifies that an amount of storage is to be allocated for label processing.

TLBL Statement

Format: // TLBL filename[,'file-identifier'] [,date]
[,file-serial-number] [,volume-sequence-number]
[,file-sequence-number] [,generation-number]
[,version-number]

Example: // TLBL SYS010,,99/365,111111

The TLBL statement is used when tape label processing is desired. It is a complex statement in that a number of parameters may optionally be specified. Observe that only one parameter, the file name (derived from the COBOL SELECT statement), is mandatory. If a parameter is omitted and others follow, an extra comma is used. In the example, file-identifier was skipped; thus two commas follow the file name. If, however, a parameter is omitted and no further parameters appear to its right, the extra commas are not used. Since file-serial-number was the last specified parameter, all other commas were skipped. Each of the entries in the TLBL statement is explained as follows:

Filename	From 1 to 7 characters in length. It identifies the file to the control program and is taken directly from the COBOL SELECT statement. If SELECT TAPE-FILE ASSIGN TO SYS010-UT-3400-S appears in the COBOL program, then SYS010 must be the file name in the TLBL statement.
File-identifier	Consists of 1 to 17 characters and is contained within apostrophes. If omitted on output files, then the file name is used. If it is omitted on input files, no checking is done.
Date	Consists of 1 to 6 characters in the form yy/ddd indicating the expiration date of the file. Output files may specify an alternative format, dddd, indicating the number of days the file is to be retained.
File-serial-number	Consists of 1 to 6 characters indicating the volume serial number of the first (often only) reel of the file.
Volume-sequence-number	Consists of 1 to 4 characters indicating the sequence number of a multi-volume file (i.e., a large file extending over several reels).
File-sequence-number	Consists of 1 to 4 characters indicating the sequence number of the file on a multifile volume (i.e., several short files contained on one volume).
Generation-number	Consists of 1 to 4 digits indicating the number of a particular edition of the file.
Version-number	Consists of 1 or 2 digits that modify the generation-number.

All parameters in the TLBL card correspond directly to entries in the standard tape labels shown in Figure 17.4. Header and trailer labels for a given file are identical except for the label

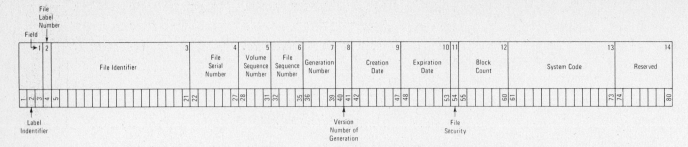

FIGURE 17.4 *Standard Tape Label (Courtesy IBM)*

identifier (indicating the type of label) and the block count field (showing the number of physical records in the file). If an output file is processed, header and trailer labels are written on the tape according to specifications in the TLBL card. If an input file is processed, the label information on the tape is checked against the TLBL card to ensure that the proper reel has been mounted.

Information on tape processing is summarized via Figure 17.5. It shows JCL for a COBOL program to update an existing tape file from transactions punched on cards. The program creates a new tape file and a printed exception report. Label processing is done for both input and output tapes. The OPTION card provides for the linkage-editor, procedure and data division maps, and a dump in the event of an ABEND. Label processing is called for by the phrase "LABEL RECORDS ARE STANDARD" in the COBOL program. Note the tie between the COBOL SELECT and the ASSGN and TLBL statements; also note the use of generic assignments that permit any available drives to be used. Finally, note the use of the PAUSE statements to provide instructions to the operator.

Some changes of technique are possible, and common, in connection with Figure 17.5. The first has to do with using multiple comment cards and a single PAUSE, rather than two PAUSE statements. As Figure 17.5 now stands, the operator is required to respond to two PAUSE statements, i.e., the "end of block" must be hit twice for processing to continue. An alternative is to stack all instructions to the operator in comment statements, followed by a single PAUSE to give the operator a chance to respond. (A comment statement has an asterisk in column 1, with the rest of the card available for comments.) For example,

```
* MOUNT TAPE #123456
* MOUNT TAPE #654321
// PAUSE
```

The advantage of a single pause is that the operator only has to respond once. This may not seem like much of a difference in Figure 17.5, but it does add up when stretched over a shift. The second change in technique has to do with altering the TLBL statements. As Figure 17.5 stands now, the use of unique label names for the input and output (i.e., old and new master) versions of the same file is not practical. This is because production job streams would have to change each cycle. Accordingly, the TLBL statements would most likely appear as

```
// TLBL SYS010,'PAYROLL YTD MAST' INPUT
// TLBL SYS011,'PAYROLL YTD MAST' OUTPUT
```

These statements would still offer some protection in that the file identifier would be checked for 'PAYROLL YTD MAST'. However, it would be an *external* control function to ensure that the correct version of the file was mounted for SYS010 and SYS011. Realize that instructions on which tape to mount would be specified by production control in a job sheet rather than on JCL statements; otherwise, one is back to ground zero (OS circumvents this problem nicely through generation data groups; see Chapter 18).

Some programmers have really become extreme and begun to use TLBL statements of the form // TLBL SYS011. This statement, although functional, allows any tape to be read as input and effectively bypasses label processing. It may be useful at times, but in most cases it is *undesirable*.

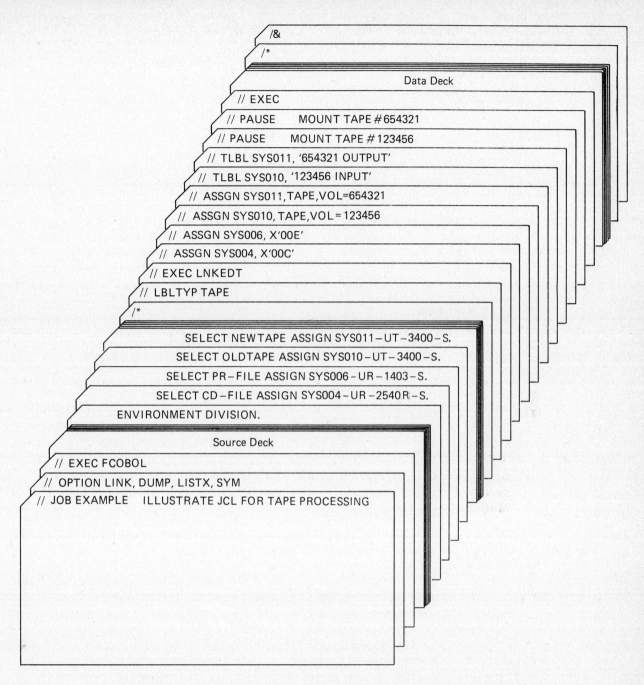

FIGURE 17.5 *Job Stream for Tape Processing (Generic Assignments Imply DOS/VS)*

PROCESSING DISK FILES

The concepts of label processing are applicable to disk as well as tape. Just as there is a TLBL statement, there is a DLBL statement. There is also one major extension for disk files. Tape processing is strictly sequential, whereas disk processing may be either sequential or nonsequential. Thus the DLBL statement contains an additional parameter indicating the type of file organization. In addition, the EXTENT statement, required for disk files, specifies the address of the file on the disk device by providing a cylinder and track number where the first record in the file may be found. The EXTENT statement also specifies the size (extent) of the file by stating the number of tracks allocated for its storage.

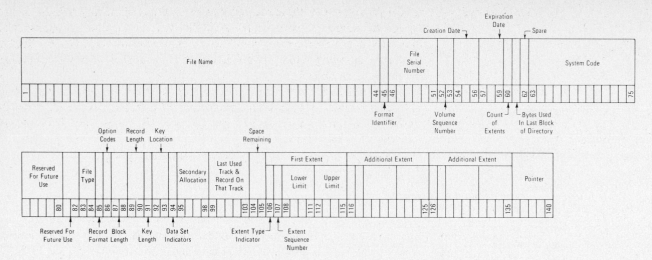

FIGURE 17.6 *Standard Disk Label (Courtesy IBM)*

DLBL Statement

Format: // DLBL filename [,'file-identifier'] [,date] [,codes]
Example: // DLBL SYS013,'THIS IS DISK FILE',99/365,SD

The DLBL statement provides the necessary information for processing disk labels. As with tape processing, if an input file is referenced, label checking is done to ensure that the proper volume was mounted. If an output file is specified, a disk label is created in accordance with Figure 17.6. Only the filename parameter is required on the DLBL card; and it is tied to the COBOL SELECT, as was the filename in the TLBL statement. All parameters are explained as follows:

Filename   Consists of 1 to 7 characters in length and is tied directly to the SELECT statement; i.e., the SYS number matches in both statements. However, the file name in the DLBL card need not match the symbolic name on the ASSGN or EXTENT statements (more on this in the next section).

File-identifier   File name as it appears in the volume label; consists of 1 to 44 characters.

Date   One of two formats as in the TLBL statement. Omission of this parameter causes the file to be retained for seven days.

Codes   A two- or three-character field indicating the type of file, as follows:
    SD—sequential disk
    DA—direct access
    ISC—create ISAM file
    ISE—existing ISAM file
    Omission of this parameter causes a default to sequential disk.

EXTENT Statement

Format: // EXTENT [symbolic-unit] [,serial-number] [,type]
             [,sequence-number] [,relative-track] [,number-of-tracks]
             [split-cylinder-track] [,B-bins]
Example: // EXTENT SYS014,111111,1,,200,20

The EXTENT statement specifies the exact location of a file, the number of tracks in the file, and other information associated with the file. One or more EXTENT statements *must* follow the corresponding DLBL card. Parameters are as follows:

SECTION V: FILE PROCESSING

Symbolic-unit	The SYS number of the device on which the file is physically located. It must match the symbolic name on the ASSGN card (or standard assignment) and may, but is not required to, match the SYS number on the COBOL SELECT and corresponding DLBL card. (Stay with us—we shall clarify the statement in ensuing examples.)
Serial-number	Consists of 1 to 6 characters specifying the volume serial number. If omitted, the volume serial number of the preceding EXTENT card is used. If omitted entirely, the serial number is not checked, and the programmer runs the risk of processing the wrong volume.

Type	A one-character field indicating the type of extent, as follows:
	   1—data area
	   2—overflow area (ISAM)
	   4—index area (ISAM)
	   8—split cylinder data area (split cylinders are not covered in the text)

Sequence-number	One to three digits indicating the sequence number of the extent within a multiextent file. Its use is optional for sequential (code = SD on DLBL) or direct-access (code = DA on DLBL) files, but mandatory for ISAM files.
Relative-track	A 1- to 5-digit number indicating the sequential number of the track (relative to zero) where the file begins. A simple calculation is required to convert a cylinder and track address to a relative track. The calculation is device dependent and is shown in Table 17.4.
Number-of-tracks	A 1- to 5-digit number specifying the number of tracks allocated to the file.

Split cylinder and bin parameters are not discussed further in the text. (The reader is referred to the *DOS Programmer's Guide* for information.)

TABLE 17.4 Conversion of Cylinder and Track Address to Relative Track

The formula is device dependent as shown:

Device	Formula
2311	Relative track = 10 * cylinder + track
2314	Relative track = 20 * cylinder + track
3330	Relative track = 19 * cylinder + track
3340	Relative track = 12 * cylinder + track

Sometimes it is necessary to go in reverse, i.e., calculate a cylinder and track address given a relative track. Again, the formula is device dependent as shown:

Device	Formula	
2311	(Relative track)/10	quotient = cylinder, remainder = track
2314	(Relative track)/20	quotient = cylinder, remainder = track
3330	(Relative track)/19	quotient = cylinder, remainder = track
3340	(Relative track)/12	quotient = cylinder, remainder = track

SEQUENTIAL PROCESSING

Figure 17.7 shows the JCL necessary to update a sequential disk file from card transactions. A new master file is created, as is a printed exception report. Both disk files are stored on the same pack. Among other points, the example emphasizes relationships among the SELECT, ASSGN, DLBL, and EXTENT statements.

The files OLD-MAST and NEW-MAST are assigned to SYS014 and SYS016, respectively, via COBOL SELECT statements. There are corresponding DLBL statements for each of these file names. Both DLBL cards are followed by EXTENT statements specifying the physical device where the file is located, in this instance SYS010 for both. Both files are on the same device,

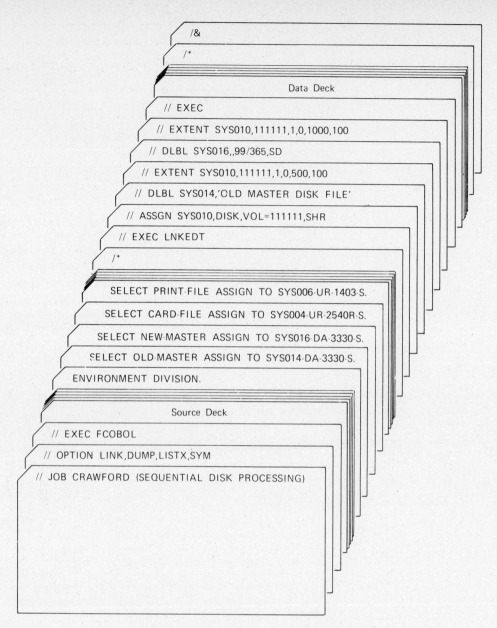

FIGURE 17.7 *JCL for Sequential Disk Processing (Generic Assignments Imply DOS/VS)*

SYS010, which in turn is assigned to any available drive by the generic ASSGN statement. The file NEW-MAST will be retained until the last day of 1999 as per the entry on its DLBL statement. It begins on relative track 1000 and continues for 100 tracks (EXTENT statement).

Label processing will be performed, but the LBLTYP card is omitted, as that statement is not used with sequential disk files. The ASSGN statements have been omitted for CARD-FILE and PRINT-FILE, since those SELECT statements match the permanent assignments in Table 17.3.

Sequential processing has been discussed for both tape and disk. We now proceed to JCL for nonsequential processing, in particular ISAM reorganization.

NONSEQUENTIAL PROCESSING

ISAM processing becomes less efficient as new records are added and old records are logically deleted (ISAM organization was discussed in Chapter 16). Accordingly, an ISAM file is periodically reorganized whereby the logically deleted records are physically dropped from the file, and the

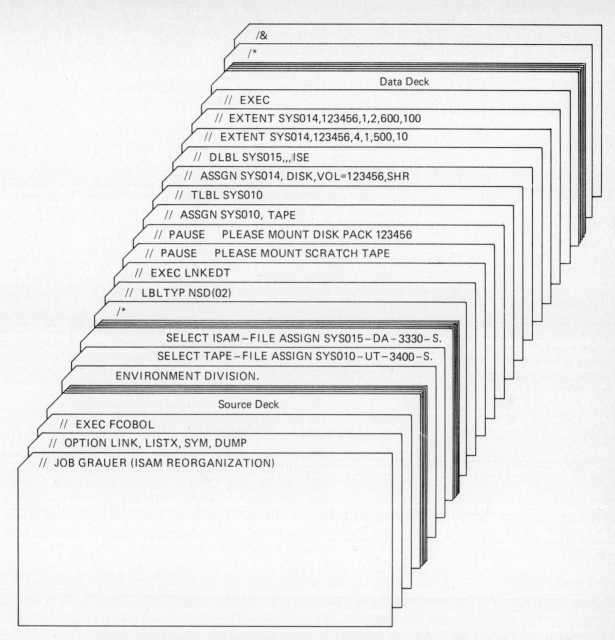

FIGURE 17.8 *JCL for ISAM Reorganization (Generic Assignments Imply DOS/VS)*

additions are transferred from the overflow to the prime data area. The decision of how often this is to be done is made by a systems analyst and is not discussed here.

Reorganization is generally a two-step process. First, the ISAM file is read sequentially and dumped on tape. Next, the newly created tape is used as input to a second COBOL (or utility) program, which restores the ISAM file on disk. The restored file is logically equivalent to the original; however, its records have been physically rearranged to make processing more efficient. Figure 17.8 shows the JCL needed for the first step.

Much of Figure 17.8 has already been reviewed in Figures 17.5 and 17.7, and that discussion will not be repeated here. Note, however, the NSD parameter in the LBLTYP statement. The 02 in parentheses indicates the number of EXTENT cards associated with the nonsequential disk file. The type and sequence parameters in the EXTENT statements assume importance. In this example, the first EXTENT has a type of 4, indicating the EXTENT for the cylinder index. The second EXTENT has a type of 1, indicating EXTENTs for the prime data area.

SUMMARY

Job control language (JCL) is the means whereby the programmer communicates with an operating system. Sufficient JCL for DOS was presented to enable the programmer to do basic file processing. A synopsis of the various statements and their functions follows:

JOB	Indicates a new job and its job name.
OPTION	Specifies the options to be in effect for the duration of the job. Any options included in this statement override those established at SYSGEN. Any omitted options default to those of the SYSGEN.
EXEC	Causes the execution of a program.
/*	Indicates the end of a file or data set. (This statement appears at the end of a COBOL deck because the COBOL deck is the data for the program FCOBOL.)
/&	Indicates the end of a job.
*	Indicates a comment.
ASSGN	Links a symbolic device to a physical device. It is required only if the temporary assignment is different from the permanent assignment.
PAUSE	Temporarily suspends execution; it enables the programmer to make requests of the operator, such as mounting a particular volume.
LBLTYP	Required for label processing of tape and nonsequential disk files. It is not used when processing sequential disk files.
TLBL	Contains information for the label processing of tape files.
DLBL	Contains information for the label processing of disk files.
EXTENT	Specifies the exact location(s) of a file on disk.

The JOB statement is always the first in a job stream. It is followed by an OPTION statement, if one is present. ASSGN, DLBL, and EXTENT cards *precede* their associated EXEC statement in the order listed. The LBLTYP statement is required before EXEC LNKEDT if label processing is requested for tape and nonsequential disk; it is *not* used with sequential disk processing.

The link between the TLBL, DLBL, and COBOL SELECT statements was discussed, as were elementary concepts of the disk-operating system. DOS JCL is relatively easy, and only a little practice is necessary to become thoroughly comfortable with it. You should expect, however, to make several errors, especially in the beginning. As a guide to understanding your mistakes, and also as a teaching aid, we offer a list of JCL *errors to avoid:*

1. Incorrect format: *All* statements (except for /*, and /&) require // in columns 1 and 2 and a space in column 3. Too often, this simple rule is violated, as in //JOB.
2. Misspelling of key words: TLBL, DLBL, ASSGN, LNKEDT, and LBLTYP are correct spellings. Beginners, and accomplished programmers as well, are guilty of many variations.
3. Incomplete information for label processing: A TLBL or DLBL statement is required for label processing of tape and disk files, respectively. The LBLTYP card is also required for tape and nonsequential disk files. Finally, the phrase "LABEL RECORDS ARE STANDARD" must be present in the COBOL FD if label processing is desired.
4. Incorrect placement of LBLTYP: This statement, if present, must immediately precede the EXEC LNKEDT card.
5. Incorrect correspondence between COBOL SELECT and JCL: The SYS number in the COBOL SELECT must match with appropriate TLBL and DLBL statements.
6. Invalid extents: All disk files require one or more EXTENT statements, and frequently this information is incorrect or miscopied. This error may produce a cryptic message "LOGICAL TRANSIENT AREA NOT ASSIGNED."
7. Incorrect volume (i.e., tape reel or disk pack): This can result from several causes. The programmer might request the wrong volume, or the operator may fail to mount the volume requested by the programmer. Even if neither of these situations occurs, the system may still think it has the wrong volume because incorrect (i.e., nonmatching) label information was supplied in the TLBL or DLBL statement.

8. Omission of OPTION LINK with EXEC LNKEDT: NOLINK is usually established as the default option at SYSGEN. Thus, if a program is to be link-edited after compilation, OPTION LINK must be specified.

9. Omission of ASSGN statement(s): An ASSGN statement is not necessary if the temporary assignment matches the permanent assignment. In the majority of instances, this is not the case, and a separate ASSGN card is required for every device where the assignments do not match.

REVIEW EXERCISES

TRUE FALSE

☐ ☐ **1.** Every JCL statement begins with // in columns 1 and 2.

☐ ☐ **2.** Every job stream must contain one and only one /& card.

☐ ☐ **3.** Every job stream must contain one and only one /* card.

☐ ☐ **4.** There may be more than one EXEC statement within a job stream.

☐ ☐ **5.** The /* statement is the last card in a deck.

☐ ☐ **6.** Comments are not permitted on JCL statements.

☐ ☐ **7.** The PAUSE statement suspends processing for 2 minutes.

☐ ☐ **8.** The LBLTYP statement must be present whenever label processing is performed.

☐ ☐ **9.** The ASSGN statement is required only when a permanent assignment matches a temporary assignment.

☐ ☐ **10.** The COBOL SELECT statement matches the SYS number in a DLBL or TLBL card.

☐ ☐ **11.** A TLBL card is mandatory whenever a tape file is processed.

☐ ☐ **12.** The SYS number in the DLBL statement must match the SYS number in the EXTENT card that follows it.

☐ ☐ **13.** A given file can have more than one EXTENT statement.

☐ ☐ **14.** The formula to calculate the relative track from a cylinder and track address is device dependent.

☐ ☐ **15.** The expiration date of a file is specified on its EXTENT card.

☐ ☐ **16.** The ASSGN statement equates a logical (symbolic) device to a physical device.

☐ ☐ **17.** There is only one type of internal label.

☐ ☐ **18.** The LBLTYP statement (if required) immediately follows the EXEC LNKEDT statement.

☐ ☐ **19.** The code parameter in the DLBL card must always be specified.

☐ ☐ **20.** The COBOL compiler is considered a "control program."

☐ ☐ **21.** The job control program remains in main storage at all times.

☐ ☐ **22.** DOS has three distinct system libraries.

☐ ☐ **23.** The FORTRAN compiler is not a part of the disk-operating system.

☐ ☐ **24.** A multivolume tape file extends over several reels.

☐ ☐ **25.** Parameters in the OPTION statement may be listed in any order.

☐ ☐ **26.** Parameters in the TLBL statement may be listed in any order.

PROBLEMS
1. Show the DOS JCL to compile, link-edit, and execute a COBOL program. The program reads a deck of cards (CARD-FILE) and writes them on tape (TAPE-FILE). Your JCL must accommodate all the following:

1. Suppress procedure and data division maps as well as the COBOL listing. A dump is required in the event of an ABEND.
2. Perform label processing as follows:
   a. Assign an expiration date of 1/1/82 to the tape file.
   b. Assign file and volume identifiers of "NEW TAPE MASTER" and 123456, respectively.

3. Cause the operator to mount a scratch tape, which will be saved as student tape #1 (external label).
4. Use 00C and 183 as the addresses of the card reader and tape drive, respectively.
5. Show appropriate COBOL SELECT statements.

2. Show the DOS JCL to compile, link-edit, and execute a COBOL program that will create an ISAM file from cards. You are to accommodate all the following:

1. Procedure division and data division maps are required, as is a dump in the event of an unplanned termination.
2. An object deck is to be produced.
3. Show COBOL SELECTS for CARD-FILE, PRINT-FILE, and DISK-FILE; the latter is the ISAM file to be created.
4. The cylinder index is to be the first five tracks of cylinder 60. Independent overflow is to take all of cylinders 61 and 62. The prime data area is to extend for all cylinders 63 to 72. (Volume ID is 222222.) Assume a 3330.
5. 00C, 00F, and 191 are the addresses of the card reader, printer, and disk device, respectively.
6. Retain the newly created ISAM file for 2 weeks.
7. Create standard labels (supply necessary DLBL parameters).

3. Show the DOS JCL to execute a COBOL program UPDATE, which has been cataloged in the core image library. The program UPDATE merges transactions from a tape file (SYS010) and a sequential disk file (SYS014) to create a new sequential disk file (SYS015). Accommodate all the following:

1. Produce a dump in the event of an ABEND.
2. Perform label processing:
   a. Existing tape file: File serial number is 111111.
   b. Existing disk file: Volume serial number is 222222.
      File identifier is 'DISK-MASTER'.
   c. New disk file: File identifier is 'NEW-FILE'.
      Retain 100 days.
      Volume serial number is 222222.
3. The old disk file begins at cylinder 30, track 0, and goes for 100 tracks. The new disk file begins at cylinder 60 and goes for 100 tracks. (Assume a 2314 device.)
4. Use 181 and 291 as the tape and disk address, respectively.

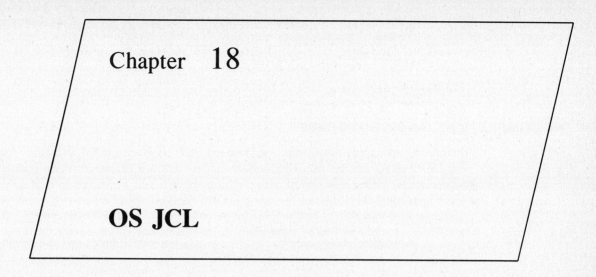

Chapter 18

OS JCL

OVERVIEW

Although COBOL is a higher-level language, and as such is theoretically machine independent, the COBOL programmer cannot function in a vacuum. He is required to surround his deck with control cards that are unique to the system on which he is running. In other words, whether we like it or not, the programmer is forced to interact with an operating system. Communication with the operating system is accomplished through user-prepared control cards known as job control language, or simply JCL.

An *effective* COBOL programmer must be thoroughly comfortable with the job control language. Unfortunately, OS JCL retains a mystique that too often makes both students and practicing programmers shy away. Admittedly, the multipage collection of /'s, X's, etc., is somewhat foreboding, but given half a chance, it becomes thoroughly understandable. In this chapter we shall attempt to remove this apprehension and instill in the reader an appreciation for OS JCL.

The chapter begins with a classification of various versions of OS, followed by an overview of the "compile, link, and go" process. Next we shall consider syntactical rules, basic statements (JOB, EXEC, DD, /*, and //), key-word and positional parameters, and system output. Our objective is to develop JCL capability corresponding to the COBOL in the first 16 chapters. Thus material is included to support subprograms, SORT, COPY, and file maintenance.

CLASSIFICATION OF OS SYSTEMS

Several different operating systems fall under the general heading of OS. Two versions, MFT and MVT, were originally introduced with the 360.

In MFT, main storage is divided into an area for the control program and as many as 15 predefined areas of contiguous core called partitions. Individual programs are loaded into specific partitions. Under MVT, a portion of main storage is allocated for control programs, and the remainder is considered a dynamic storage area. MVT dynamically allocates core storage for each job as it is run. Storage space in MVT is determined by individual program requirements rather than by predefined partition sizes as in MFT.

Two new operating systems, VS1 and VS2, were provided with the 370, and evolved from MFT and MVT, respectively. VS2, however, is further classified into SVS and MVS. SVS represents release 1 of VS2, and MVS denotes all subsequent releases. Under SVS, the total system including *all* user partitions and/or regions cannot exceed 16 million bytes. Under MVS, however, *each individual* region is allowed up to 16 million bytes.

The specific differences of the various operating systems need not concern the reader. All one need know, or indeed care about, is that the JCL covered in the chapter is applicable to *any* of these operating systems.

THE COMPILE, LINK, AND GO PROCESS

Before beginning the actual discussion of OS JCL, it is important to realize exactly what the typical COBOL job entails. When a job is submitted for execution, three distinct processes (or steps) occur. First, the COBOL program is compiled, i.e., translated into machine language. In the second step, the output of the compile (known as an object module) is combined with various IBM supplied subroutines that are needed to complete COBOL I/O statements (READ, WRITE, etc.). This is accomplished by a program called the linkage editor. In the third and final step, the output of the linkage editor (known as a load module) gains control and is executed. It is only in the third step that the COBOL program takes over. The three-step process is illustrated in Figure 18.1.

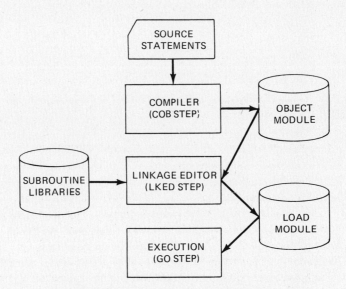

FIGURE 18.1 *Execution of a Typical COBOL Job*

BASIC JOB STREAM

Figure 18.2 is a typical job stream to compile, link-edit, and execute a COBOL program. It also illustrates key-word and positional parameters, and the rules for JCL continuation. The discussion uses the words *file* and *data set* interchangeably.

Figure 18.2 contains five types of statements: JOB, EXEC, DD, /*, and //. Our entire discussion of OS JCL revolves around variation in the first three. The JOB, EXEC, and DD statements each consist of up to five parts in specified order: //, name, operation, parameter, and comments. If the name is supplied, it must begin in column 3 immediately following //. Whether or not a name is used depends on the type of statement and whether subsequent references are made back to the statement. In Figure 18.2 names are given to the JOB and three DD statements but not to the EXEC statement. The operation (i.e., JOB, EXEC, or DD) follows next. Optional parameters (e.g., MSGLEVEL or PARM) follow the operation. A blank separates the name, operation, and parameter fields. However, if the name is omitted, as in the EXEC statement, then a blank separates the // and operation. A comma delineates individual parameters. Comments may follow the last parameter, but none are shown in Figure 18.2.

Parameters are of two types: *key-word* and *positional*. Key-word parameters may appear in

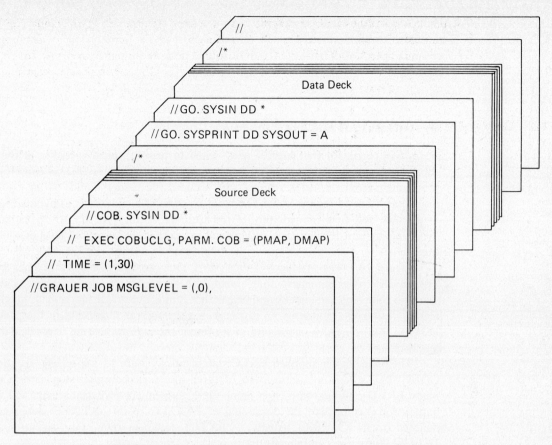

FIGURE 18.2 *Compile, Link-Edit, and Execute a COBOL Program*

any order within a statement; it is the key word itself that conveys meaning to the system. Positional ✳ parameters, as the name implies, are required to appear in a specified order. If a positional parameter is omitted, its absence must be denoted by a comma, unless no additional positional parameters follow in the statement.

The JOB statement in Figure 18.2 contains both key-word and positional parameters.✳ MSGLEVEL and TIME are key words, and their order could be reversed. However, the subparameters appearing in parentheses are positional and must appear in the order shown. (1,30) indicates 1 minute and 30 seconds. If the minute's parameter were omitted, i.e., if only 30 seconds were desired, then the comma would still be required (,30). If, however, only the *last* positional parameter, i.e., seconds, is omitted, then no comma is required. For example, if the time were specified as 1 minute, with no mention of seconds, one would code TIME=(1), or more simply TIME=1.

The JOB statement also illustrates the rules for continuation. Coding begins in column 1 and continues up to and including column 71. If additional space is needed, one stops somewhere before column 71 and continues on a second, third, etc., card. The continued cards (all cards but ✳ the first) require // in columns 1 and 2 and a blank in column 3. Coding on the continued card must begin between columns 4 and 16. The statement that was continued, i.e., the first card, must end with a comma. Earlier versions of OS also required that a nonblank character be inserted in column 72 of the first card, but this is not shown in Figure 18.2.

The EXEC statement of Figure 18.2 invokes the procedure COBUCLG, which will compile, ✳ link-edit, and execute a COBOL program. (The procedure concept is explained in the next section.) The PARM parameter in this statement will generate procedure and data division maps with the COBOL compilation.

There are three DD (data definition) statements in Figure 18.2, each of which supplies infor-✳ mation about an input or output file. The ✳ is a positional parameter that means the file immediately follows in the job stream. Thus COBOL source and data decks follow the COB.SYSIN and

GO.SYSIN DD cards, respectively. In the DD statement for SYSPRINT, SYSOUT=A means the file is to appear on a class A output device, i.e., a printer. The /* denotes the end of a data set and appears after both the COBOL source deck and input data cards. The // statement denotes end of job.

System Output and the Procedure Concept

A COBOL program that merely goes "card to print" typically results in the series of messages shown in Figure 18.3. (Figure 18.3 was *not* produced by Figure 18.2, as can be seen by the different job names. However, after reading this section, the reader could, as an exercise, determine the input jobstream to Figure 18.3.) The reaction of most beginners is to bypass Figure 18.3 as quickly as possible and turn immediately to the COBOL listing. We try to do better. We do, however, avoid line-by-line detailed explanations and instead aim at an overall level of conceptual understanding.

Figure 18.3 was produced under MVT and consists primarily of lines beginning with XX, //, or IEF.[1] Any statement that starts with // means the line originated in the programmer-supplied JCL. Any statement beginning with XX indicates a JCL statement pulled from the procedure COBUCLG. (XX represents // in the JCL statement as it appears in the procedure.) The letters IEF are the first three characters in a system message indicating a particular action the system has taken.

The programmer-supplied EXEC statement of Figure 18.3 specifies execution of the procedure COBUCLG, which in turn consists of three job steps: compile (step name COB), link-edit (step name LKED), and execute (step name GO). Subsequent JCL statements will reference these step names; for example, see the discussion of PARM.COB in the EXEC statement. Each job step is denoted by an XX EXEC (really // EXEC) statement requesting execution of a program, e.g., IKFCBL00 for the compile (COB) step.

At the conclusion of each job step a completion message, perhaps of the form "STEP WAS EXECUTED—COND CODE 0000", appears. The value of the condition code indicates the success encountered during that step. In the compile step, for example, a condition code of 0000 indicates no diagnostics, a code of 0004 indicates that a warning was the most severe level of error, 0008 means a C-level diagnostic, and 0012 an E-level diagnostic. If a step is abnormally terminated, i.e., ABENDs, the condition code is replaced by a completion code stating the reason for the termination. In Figure 18.3 the first two steps executed with condition codes of 0004 and 0000, respectively. The GO step ABENDed due to a data exception (completion code 0C7). Thus, by examining the system output, we can tell the highest severity error encountered during the execution of each job step. We can also tell how far the COBOL program went in the compile, link-edit, and execute sequence.

The DD statements of Figure 18.2 are also made clearer by a conceptual understanding of Figure 18.3. Consider the components of the statement //GO.SYSIN DD *. // is followed by the step-name.file-name, i.e., GO.SYSIN. GO is the step name for the execute step of COBUCLG, SYSIN indicates the file name and is tied to the COBOL SELECT statement, DD indicates the operation, and * says the file (i.e., data cards) follows immediately in the job stream.

The concept of a procedure (or proc) is fundamental to OS. It is perfectly permissible, albeit impractical, for the COBOL programmer to submit the entire job stream, i.e., procedure, with his program. Common practice is to catalog the necessary JCL into a procedure and then invoke the procedure. In this way the job of the individual is simplified, and every programmer has convenient access to identical job streams. Installations usually establish a procedure library, with many of the actual procs (procedures) supplied by IBM, e.g., COBUCLG.

[1] A listing produced under MVS will contain substantially the same information, but slightly rearranged; see R. Grauer and M. Crawford, *The COBOL Environment*, Chapter 10 (Englewood Cliffs, N.J.: Prentice-Hall, Inc., 1979).

```
//DANBB142 JOB  TIME=(1,30)                                    Programmer supplied
// EXEC COBUCLG,PARM.COB=(PMAP,DMAP)                           EXEC statement
XXCOBUCLG PROC SUT1=15,SOBJ=15,SLUT1=50,SLUT2=20,SLMOD1=50,SLMOD2=20,    00000100
XX              ADDLIB='SYS1.ADDLIB',STEPLIB='SYS1.ADDLIB'              00000200
XXCOB    EXEC PGM=IKFCBL00                                             00000300
XXSYSPRINT DD  SYSOUT=A,DCB=BLKSIZE=1936         IBM program - COBOL compiler  00000400
XXSYSUT1  DD   UNIT=3330,SPACE=(TRK,(&SUT1,5))                         00000500
IEF653I SUBSTITUTION JCL - UNIT=3330,SPACE=(TRK,,(15,5))
XXSYSUT2  DD   UNIT=3330,SPACE=(TRK,(&SUT1,5))                         00000600
IEF653I SUBSTITUTION JCL - UNIT=3330,SPACE=(TRK,,(15,5))
XXSYSUT3  DD   UNIT=3330,SPACE=(TRK,(&SUT1,5))                         00000700
IEF653I SUBSTITUTION JCL - UNIT=3330,SPACE=(TRK,,(15,5))
XXSYSUT4  DD   UNIT=3330,SPACE=(TRK,(&SUT1,5))                         00000800
IEF653I SUBSTITUTION JCL - UNIT=3330,SPACE=(TRK,,(15,5))
XXSYSUT5  DD   UNIT=3330,SPACE=(TRK,(&SUT1,5)),DISP=(,PASS)            00000900
IEF653I SUBSTITUTION JCL - UNIT=3330,SPACE=(TRK,(15,5)),DISP=(,PASS)
XXSYSLIN  DD   DSNAME=&LOADSET,DCB=BLKSIZE=3120,DISP=(MOD,PASS),       00001000
XX             UNIT=3330,SPACE=(6400,(&SOBJ,10))                       00001100
IEF653I SUBSTITUTION JCL - UNIT=3330,SPACE=(6400,(15,10))
//COB.SYSIN DD *
IEF236I ALLOC. FOR DANBB142 COB
IEF237I 77E    ALLOCATED TO SYSPRINT       Step name - COB
IEF237I 268    ALLOCATED TO SYSUT1         (Beginning of compile step)
IEF237I 268    ALLOCATED TO SYSUT2
IEF237I 268    ALLOCATED TO SYSUT3
IEF237I 268    ALLOCATED TO SYSUT4
IEF237I 269    ALLOCATED TO SYSUT5
IEF237I 268    ALLOCATED TO SYSLIN
IEF237I 784    ALLOCATED TO SYSIN
IEF142I - STEP WAS EXECUTED - COND CODE 0004       End of compile step
IEF285I    SYS76273.T113030.RV001.DANBB142.ASP0A001    DELETED
IEF285I    VOL SER NOS= ASP77E.
IEF285I    SYS76273.T113030.RV001.DANBB142.R0002648    DELETED
IEF285I    VOL SER NOS= SCR001.
IEF285I    SYS76273.T113030.RV001.DANBB142.R0002649    DELETED
IEF285I    VOL SER NOS= SCR001.
IEF285I    SYS76273.T113030.RV001.DANBB142.R0002650    DELETED
IEF285I    VOL SER NOS= SCR001.
IEF285I    SYS76273.T113030.RV001.DANBB142.R0002651    DELETED
IEF285I    VOL SER NOS= SCR001.
IEF285I    SYS76273.T113030.RV001.DANBB142.R0002652    PASSED
IEF285I    VOL SER NOS= SCR002.
IEF285I    SYS76273.T113030.RV001.DANBB142.LOADSET     PASSED
IEF285I    VOL SER NOS= SCR001.
IEF285I    SYS76273.T113030.RV001.DANBB142.ASPIO001    DELETED
IEF285I    VOL SER NOS= 016948.


 ** START - STEP=COB        JOB=DANBB142    DATE= 9/29/76   CLOCK=11.30.40   PGM=IKFCBL00
 ** END   -                                 DATE= 9/29/76   CLOCK=11.31.18   CPU=   0.81 SEC; CC=    4 **
 ** EXCPS - DISK=   240,  CTC=   210,   TAPE=     0,  TOTAL=   450;  REGION USED=  120K OF  130K **

    DDNAME      EXCP COUNT    PCI COUNT
    LINK/SVC:       78          447
    SYSPRINT:       53
    SYSUT1  :       31
    SYSUT2  :       37
    SYSUT3  :       50
    SYSUT4  :       32
    SYSUT5  :        0        Step name - LKED
    SYSLIN  :       12        (Beginning of link step)
    SYSIN   :      157                                          Cond parameter tests
                                                                results of compile step
XXLKED    EXEC PGM=IEWL,PARM='LIST,XREF,LET',COND=(5,LT,COB)           00001200
XXSYSLIN  DD   DSNAME=&LOADSET,DISP=(OLD,DELETE)                       00001300
XX        DD   DDNAME=SYSIN                                            00001400
XXSYSLMOD DD   DSNAME=&&GOSET(GO),DISP=(NEW,PASS),UNIT=3330,           00001500
XX             SPACE=(1024,(&SLMOD1,&SLMOD2,1))                        00001600
IEF653I SUBSTITUTION JCL - SPACE=(1024,(50,20,1))
XXSYSLIB  DD   DSNAME=&ADDLIB,DISP=SHR                                 00001700
IEF653I SUBSTITUTION JCL - DSNAME=SYS1.ADDLIB,DISP=SHR
XX        DD   DSNAME=SYS1.COBLIB,DISP=SHR                             00001800
XXSYSUT1  DD   UNIT=(3330,SEP=(SYSLIN,SYSLMOD)),                       00001900
XX             SPACE=(1024,(&SLUT1,&SLUT2))                            00002000
IEF653I SUBSTITUTION JCL - SPACE=(1024,(50,20))
XXSYSPRINT DD  SYSOUT=A,DCB=BLKSIZE=1936                               00002100
IEF236I ALLOC. FOR DANBB142 LKED
IEF237I 268    ALLOCATED TO SYSLIN
IEF237I 268    ALLOCATED TO SYSLMOD
IEF237I 251    ALLOCATED TO SYSLIB
IEF237I 251    ALLOCATED TO
IEF237I 269    ALLOCATED TO SYSUT1          End of linkage editor step
IEF237I 77E    ALLOCATED TO SYSPRINT
IEF142I - STEP WAS EXECUTED - COND CODE 0000
IEF285I    SYS76273.T113030.RV001.DANBB142.LOADSET     DELETED
IEF285I    VOL SER NOS= SCR001.
```

FIGURE 18.3 *System Output for COBUCLG Procedure*

```
IEF285I    SYS76273.T113030.RV001.DANBB142.GOSET          PASSED
IEF285I    VOL SER NOS= SCR001.
IEF285I    SYS1.ADDLIB                                     KEPT
IEF285I    VOL SER NOS= SYS002.
IEF285I    SYS1.COBLIB                                     KEPT
IEF285I    VOL SER NOS= SYS002.
IEF285I    SYS76273.T113030.RV001.DANBB142.R0002653        DELETED
IEF285I    VOL SER NOS= SCR002.
IEF285I    SYS76273.T113030.RV001.DANBB142.ASPOA002        DELETED
IEF285I    VOL SER NOS= ASP77E.

**  START - STEP=LKED       JOB=DANBB142    DATE= 9/29/76   CLOCK=11.31.18   PGM=IEWL
**  END   -                                 DATE= 9/29/76   CLOCK=11.31.47   CPU=    0.15 SEC;  CC=     0  **
**  EXCPS - DISK=    116,   CTC=     11,    TAPE=     0,    TOTAL=    127;   REGION USED=  128K OF  130K  **

        DDNAME     EXCP COUNT    PCI COUNT
        LINK/SVC:      10           15
        SYSLIN  :      10
        SYSLMOD :      15
        SYSLIB  :      81
           "    :       0
        SYSUT1  :       0      ── Step name – GO
        SYSPRINT:      11         (Beginning of execute step)
```

```
XXGO         EXEC PGM=*.LKED.SYSLMOD,COND=((5,LT,COB),(5,LT,LKED))        00002200
XXSTEPLIB  DD  DSNAME=SYS1.COBLIB,DISP=SHR                                00002300
XX         DD  DSNAME=&STEPLIB,DISP=SHR                                   00002400
IEF653I SUBSTITUTION JCL - DSNAME=SYS1.ADDLIB,DISP=SHR
XXSYSUT5   DD  DSN=*.COB.SYSUT5,DISP=(OLD,DELETE)                         00002500
XXSYSDBOUT DD  SYSOUT=A,DCB=BLKSIZE=1936                                  00002600
XXDISPLAY  DD  SYSOUT=A,DCB=(RECFM=FA,LRECL=121,BLKSIZE=121,BUFNO=1)      00002700
XXDELETE   DD  DSN=&&GOSET,DISP=(OLD,DELETE,DELETE)                       00002800
//GO.SYSUDUMP DD SYSOUT=A
//GO.PRINT DD SYSOUT=A
//GO.SYSIN DD *
//
IEF236I ALLOC. FOR DANBB142 GO
IEF237I 268    ALLOCATED TO PGM=*.DD
IEF237I 251    ALLOCATED TO STEPLIB
IEF237I 251    ALLOCATED TO
IEF237I 269    ALLOCATED TO SYSUT5
IEF237I 778    ALLOCATED TO SYSDBOUT
IEF237I 779    ALLOCATED TO DISPLAY
IEF237I 268    ALLOCATED TO DELETE
IEF237I 77B    ALLOCATED TO SYSUDUMP        ── Completion code for GO step
IEF237I 77C    ALLOCATED TO PRINT              indicates ABEND
IEF237I 77D    ALLOCATED TO SYSIN
COMPLETION CODE - SYSTEM=0C7  USER=0000
IEF285I    SYS76273.T113030.RV001.DANBB142.GOSET          PASSED
IEF285I    VOL SER NOS= SCR001.
IEF285I    SYS1.COBLIB                                     KEPT
IEF285I    VOL SER NOS= SYS002.
IEF285I    SYS1.ADDLIB                                     KEPT
IEF285I    VOL SER NOS= SYS002.
IEF285I    SYS76273.T113030.RV001.DANBB142.R0002652        DELETED
IEF285I    VOL SER NOS= SCR002.
IEF285I    SYS76273.T113030.RV001.DANBB142.ASPOA003        DELETED
IEF285I    VOL SER NOS= ASP778.
IEF285I    SYS76273.T113030.RV001.DANBB142.GOSET           DELETED
IEF285I    VOL SER NOS= SCR001.
IEF285I    SYS76273.T113030.RV001.DANBB142.ASPOA005        DELETED
IEF285I    VOL SER NOS= ASP77B.
IEF285I    SYS76273.T113030.RV001.DANBB142.ASPOA006        DELETED
IEF285I    VOL SER NOS= ASP77C.
IEF285I    SYS76273.T113030.RV001.DANBB142.ASPI0002        DELETED
IEF285I    VOL SER NOS= 026948.

**  START - STEP=GO         JOB=DANBB142    DATE= 9/29/76   CLOCK=11.31.47   PGM=PGM=*.DD
**  END   -                                 DATE= 9/29/76   CLOCK=11.31.55   CPU=    0.24 SEC;  CC= SOC7  **
**  EXCPS - DISK=      8,   CTC=     77,    TAPE=     0,    TOTAL=     85;   REGION USED=   22K OF  130K  **

        DDNAME     EXCP COUNT    PCI COUNT
        LINK/SVC:       2
        PGM=*.DD:       3            1
        STEPLIB :       3            1
           "    :       0
        SYSUT5  :       0
        SYSDBOUT:       9
        DISPLAY :       0
        DELETE  :       0
        SYSUDUMP:      61
        PRINT   :       3
        SYSIN   :       4
**  START - JOB=DANBB142    DATE= 9/29/76   CLOCK=11.30.40
**  END   -                 DATE= 9/29/76   CLOCK=11.31.55   ACCOUNTING TIME= 16.06 SECONDS;  MAX REGION USED= 128K  **
```

FIGURE 18.3 *(continued)*

JOB STATEMENT

Format: // jobname JOB (Acct information),programmer-name,
         //   keyword parameters
         Note: Continuation on a second card may be required.

Useful key words: CLASS
                   REGION
                   MSGLEVEL
                   TIME

Example: //SST001 JOB (123456,DP),'R.GRAUER',MSGLEVEL=(,0),
          //   TIME=(1,30)

The JOB statement may contain some or all of the following information: job name, accounting information, programmer-name, indication of whether or not control statements and allocation messages are to be printed, priority, and region size.

It has two positional parameters: accounting information and programmer name. In addition several of the key-word parameters have subparameters that are positional in nature.

The job name must begin with an alphabetic (A to Z) or national (#, @, $) character and may be up to eight alphanumeric characters in length.

If accounting information is supplied, it must be coded prior to any other parameters. It can consist of only an account number or other additional parameters required by the installation's accounting system. If more than one accounting parameter is supplied, all such parameters are enclosed in parentheses. If there is only one parameter, parentheses are omitted. In the preceeding example, two accounting parameters appear. The precise meaning of 123456 and DP are unique to the installation's accounting system and do not concern us here.

The programmer name, R. GRAUER, is a positional parameter that follows the accounting information. (Note, however, that in Figure 18.2 both positional parameters, i.e., accounting information and programmer-name, were omitted.)

Key-word parameters are explained:

REGION = NNNK   NNN specifies the amount of main storage (in units of 1024 bytes; i.e., 1K = 1024 bytes) that is to be allocated to the entire job.

MSGLEVEL = (S,M)   S = 0 if only job statement is to be printed.
                        1 if input job control and all catalogued procedure statements are to be printed.
                        2 if only input JCL is to be printed.
                    M = 0 if no allocation messages are to be printed.
                        1 if all allocation messages are to be printed.
                    Note that S and M are positional subparameters. Omission of S requires a comma, as shown in Figure 18.2.

TIME = (MM,SS)   MM = CPU time in minutes.
                  SS = CPU time in seconds.
                  These parameters need not be in parentheses if only minutes are specified. They are both positional subparameters.

CLASS = X   Where X indicates the class of a job. The meaning of each class is determined by the individual installation.

EXEC STATEMENT

Format: //stepname EXEC operands comments
Useful key words: PARM
                   COND
                   REGION
                   TIME
Example: //STEP1 EXEC COBUCLG,PARM.COB='PMAP,DMAP'   CREATES MAPS

The EXEC statement is used to execute either a single program or a procedure. If a program is to be executed, the key word PGM must be specified, e.g., // EXEC PGM=IKFCBL00. If a procedure is to be executed, the key word PROC can either be specified or omitted. Both of these statements are valid:

```
//    EXEC PROC=COBUCLG
//    EXEC COBUCLG
```

The step name is optional in the EXEC statement. If used, it must begin in column 3 immediately following the //; if omitted, a space is required in column 3. Accordingly, both of these statements are valid:

```
//STEP1 EXEC COBUCLG        (stepname—STEP1)
//     EXEC COBUCLG         (stepname not supplied)
```

The PARM parameter requests options for a job step and overrides any defaults that were established at system generation. The key word PARM is followed by a period and the step name for which the options are to apply. PARM.COB='PMAP, DMAP' supplies procedure and data division maps for the step name COB (the compile step). Remember, the procedure COBUCLG consists of three separate steps: compile, link-edit, and execute, with step names COB, LKED, and GO, respectively. Other compiler options are shown in Table 18.1.

The COND (condition) parameter avoids unnecessary usage of computer time by suppressing execution of specified job steps. Essentially, it ties execution of the present job step to the results of a previous step. Consider its use in the procedure COBUCLG shown in Figure 18.3:

```
//LKED EXEC PGM=IEWL,PARM='LIST,XREF,LET',COND=(5,LT,COB)
```

The precise format of the COND parameter is

```
COND=(code,operator,stepname)
```

TABLE 18.1 Compilation Parameters

SOURCE	Prints the source listing (suppressed by NOSOURCE).
CLIST	Produces a condensed listing of the procedure division map; only the first machine language statement of every COBOL statement is shown (suppressed by NOCLIST—cannot be used simultaneously with PMAP).
DMAP	Produces a data division map (suppressed by NODMAP).
PMAP	Produces a procedure division map (suppressed by NOPMAP—cannot be used simultaneously with CLIST).
LIB	Indicates that a COPY statement appears in the COBOL program (NOLIB indicates the COPY statements are not present and also provides more efficient compilation).
VERB	Prints procedure and verb names on the procedure division map (suppressed by NOVERB).
LOAD	Stores object program on direct-access device for input to the linkage editor or loader programs (suppressed by NOLOAD).
DECK	Punches object deck (suppressed by NODECK).
SEQ	Checks incoming COBOL statements for proper sequence in columns 1 to 6 (suppressed by NOSEQ).
LINECNT=nn	Specifies the number of lines to be printed on each page of output listing (60 is default).
FLAGW	Prints all diagnostic messages.
FLAG	Prints C-, E-, and D-level diagnostics; suppresses W-level diagnostics.
SUPMAP	Suppresses the PMAP option if an E-level diagnostic was present (suppressed by NOSUPMAP).
QUOTE	Specifies that quotation marks (") will enclose nonnumeric literals.
APOST	Specifies the apostrophe (') will enclose nonnumeric literals.
XREF	Generates a cross-reference listing (suppressed by NOXREF).
STATE	Prints the COBOL statement number being executed at the time of an ABEND.
FLOW=n	Prints the statement number of the last n procedure headers that were entered prior to the ABEND.
SYMDMP	Requests a formated dump in the event of an ABEND and allows symbolic debugging statements to be used.

Permissible operators are

LT	less than
LE	less than or equal
EQ	equal
NE	not equal
GT	greater than
GE	greater than or equal

The operator specifies the comparison to be made between the specified code in the COND parameter and the system return code. *The code in the COND parameter is compared to the system return code for the designated step. If the relationship is true, the step is bypassed; if the relationship is false, the step is executed.* Assume, for example, a return code of 8 after the compile step (i.e., a C-level diagnostic). The comparison is (5, LT, 8), which is true, and hence the step LKED would be bypassed. If however a warning were the most severe error, the comparison would become (5, LT, 4) which is *false,* hence the LKED step would be *executed.*

The REGION and TIME parameters are used in the EXEC statement in much the same way as in the JOB statement. The REGION parameter specifies the amount of memory to be allocated to a particular job step, e.g.,

```
//STEP1 EXEC PGM=PROGA,REGION=128K
```

The TIME parameter specifies the maximum amount of CPU time (minutes, seconds) for a job step:

```
//STEP1 EXEC PGM=PROGA,TIME=(1,30)
```

Both REGION and TIME are key-word parameters and can appear in the same EXEC statement in any order.

DD STATEMENT

```
Format:   //DDname DD operands
Example:  //GO.SYSIN DD *
          //GO.PRINT DD SYSOUT=A
```

The data definition (DD) statement appears more often than any other. Every data set requires ✱ its own DD statement, either as part of a proc or in the programmer-supplied job stream. The DD statement may contain both key-word and positional parameters.

Recall that the procedure COBUCLG consists of three separate steps: compile, link-edit, and execute. The DD statements of the execute (GO) step are tied to the COBOL SELECT statement. Consider

```
COBOL:
        SELECT PRINT-FILE ASSIGN TO UT-S-PRINT.
        SELECT CARD-FILE ASSIGN TO UT-S-SYSIN.
JCL:
        //GO.PRINT DD SYSOUT=A
        //GO.SYSIN DD *
```

The COBOL SELECT statement links a programmer-defined file name to a DD name; ✱ the DD statement provides information as to the location and disposition of that file. *The last entry in the SELECT statement must match the DD name; thus the appearance of PRINT and SYSIN in both SELECT and DD statements.* In the COBOL program, PRINT-FILE is tied to the system device PRINT. The corresponding DD statement causes PRINT to be assigned to a printer via SYSOUT=A. CARD-FILE is linked to SYSIN in the COBOL SELECT statement. The * in the matching DD statement means that the data set for SYSIN follows in the job stream; i.e., it is a card file.

SYSIN and PRINT are commonly used DD names for the card reader and printer, respectively. However, the programmer may supply any other suitable names as long as consistency is maintained. The DD name can be up to eight characters in length, the first of which must be alphabetic. Thus the following pair is perfectly acceptable:

```
COBOL:
          SELECT CARD-FILE ASSIGN TO UT-S-INCARDS.
JCL:
          //GO.INCARDS DD *
```

More than one printer and/or card reader can be conceptually specified via multiple pairs of DD and SELECT statements. Suppose that we are processing a series of card transactions, several of which are in error. The erroneous transactions are randomly scattered throughout the input deck, but the requirements of the problem call for separate reports for the valid and invalid transactions. This is easily accomplished by creating two print files:

```
COBOL:
          SELECT VALID-FILE ASSIGN TO UT-S-PRINT.
          SELECT ERROR-FILE ASSIGN TO UT-S-ERROR.
JCL:
          //GO.PRINT DD SYSOUT=A
          //GO.ERROR DD SYSOUT=A
```

In the COBOL program, valid transactions are output to the file VALID-FILE. Invalid transactions are written to ERROR-FILE. The two DD statements specify that both PRINT and ERROR are assigned to a printer, and the reports will list separately.

Additional DD Statements

Two other DD statements are frequently associated with COBOL jobs:

```
//COB.SYSLIB DD DSN=USERLIB,DISP=SHR
//GO.SYSUDUMP DD SYSOUT=A
```

SYSUDUMP specifies a memory dump in the event of an ABEND and causes the dump to appear on a class A output device (i.e., a printer). A DD statement for SYSLIB is required when the COBOL source program contains a COPY statement. (See examples in Chapter 8.) This statement specifies the name of the data set, e.g., USERLIB. (The LIB option must also be specified as a compilation parameter; see Table 18.1.)

We have covered the basic JCL needed for COBOL compilation and execution using only card input and printer output. Extension to tape and disk requires additional parameters for the DD statement. Table 18.2 summarizes these parameters, which are discussed further in the subsequent sections.

PROCESSING TAPE FILES

The concept of label processing was discussed in Chapter 17. Standard tape labels consist of volume, header, and trailer labels. The volume label appears at the beginning of each reel and contains information to verify that the correct tape has been mounted. Header labels appear before each file on a volume; trailer labels appear after the file. These labels contain almost identical information to identify the data set, creation date, expiration date, and much more. In addition, the trailer label contains a block count field, which contains the number of physical records recorded for the file. Label-processing routines ensure that the proper volume is mounted. They create new

TABLE 18.2 A Summary of Common DD Parameters

*	Indicates that a card file immediately follows in the job stream.
SYSOUT	Indicates a unit record (printer or punch) output device. SYSOUT=A and SYSOUT=B typically denote the printer (stock paper) and punch, respectively. Special forms are indicated by different letters established at the installation.
DSNAME or DSN	Indicates the name by which a data set is identified to the system.
UNIT	Specifies the device used by a data set.
VOL=SER	Specifies the volume serial number of a data set; causes a mount message to be printed if the volume is not already available.
DISP	Indicates whether the file already exists and its disposition in the event of a successful completion or abnormal termination of the job step.
SPACE	Requests a space allocation for a new file on a direct-access device.
DCB	Specifies characteristics of a file such as record length, blocking factor, fixed- or variable-length records, etc. This parameter can supply information not contained in the COBOL FD and hence provide a higher degree of flexibility.
LABEL	Specifies the type of labels used (if any), the retention period for a new file, and the location of an existing file on a tape containing several files.

labels for output data sets and can prevent accidental overwriting of vital data sets. Installations also have the opportunity to develop their own label (user labels) and label-processing routines.

Information required for tape processing is supplied on a DD statement with additional parameters as shown:

```
//GO.ddname   DD   DISP=(current status,normal disposition,cond disposition),
//     VOL=SER=nnnnnn,DSN=dsname,
```

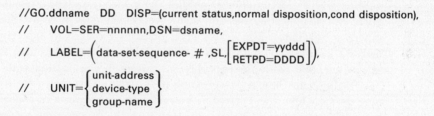

```
//     UNIT={ unit-address / device-type / group-name }
```

DISP (DISPosition) Parameter

The DISP parameter indicates the status of the data set at the start and conclusion of processing. It has three positional subparameters, with possible values as shown:

$$DISP = \left(\begin{bmatrix} NEW \\ OLD \\ SHR \\ MOD \end{bmatrix}, \begin{bmatrix} DELETE \\ KEEP \\ PASS \\ CATLG \\ UNCATLG \end{bmatrix}, \begin{bmatrix} DELETE \\ KEEP \\ CATLG \\ UNCATLG \end{bmatrix} \right)$$

The first parameter indicates the status of a data set at the start of the job step. NEW specifies the data set is to be created, whereas OLD means it already exists. SHR means the data set already exists and may be used simultaneously (shared) with other jobs. (Use of SHR is restricted to disk files.) MOD states the data set is to be added to (modified) and causes the read/write mechanism to be positioned after the last record in the data set.

The second positional parameter specifies the disposition at the normal conclusion of the job step. KEEP means the data set is to be retained. It causes the tape to be rewound and unloaded and a message to be sent to the operator directing him to retain the tape. PASS causes the data set to be passed for use by a subsequent job step. (The final disposition of a passed data set should be indicated in the last DD statement referring to that data set.) It causes the tape to be rewound but not unloaded. DELETE states the data set is no longer needed and allows it to be scratched. CATLG causes the data set to be retained and establishes an entry in the system catalog pointing to the data set. UNCATLG also causes the data set to be retained but removes the entry in the catalog. *Omission of the second positional parameter causes new data sets to be deleted and existing (old) data sets to be retained.*

The third subparameter specifies disposition if the job terminates abnormally. If this parameter is omitted, disposition defaults to that specified for normal processing. Some examples:

1. DISP = (NEW,KEEP,DELETE)
   Explanation: Creates a new data set, keeps it if job step successfully executes, deletes it if the step ABENDs.
2. DISP = (SHR,KEEP)
   Explanation: Allows an existing data set to be used simultaneously by other jobs; retains it under all circumstances. (SHR is restricted to disk files.)
3. DISP = OLD
   Explanation: Specifies an existing data set to be retained under both normal and abnormal termination. Note parentheses are not required since only the first positional parameter was specified.
4. DISP = (NEW,CATLG,DELETE)
   Explanation: Creates a new data set, catalogs it if job step executes successfully, deletes it if step ABENDs.

UNIT Parameter

The UNIT parameter indicates the physical device on which the data set is to be processed. It is specified in one of three ways: unit address, device type, or group name. Specification of the unit address UNIT=185 explicitly specifies the device, i.e., tape drive 185. This is not a particularly good way of indicating the unit since the system must wait for the particular tape drive even if others are available. The device type indicates the class of tape drive, e.g., UNIT=2400, which calls for a series 2400 tape drive to be used. The system determines which 2400 units are available, selects one, and issues the appropriate message in conjunction with the VOL parameter. UNIT= TAPE illustrates how a group name is specified. This instructs the system to use any available tape device. Often this corresponds exactly to specification of a device type, as in the case where only 2400 series drives are present. However, the group name can provide greater flexibility if all sequential devices (tape and disk) are combined under SYSSQ and the request is for UNIT=SYSSQ. Of course, such specification is not always feasible.

VOL (Volume) Parameter

The VOL parameter specifies the tape volume that contains the data set. VOL=SER=123456 causes a message to be printed directing the operator to mount tape 123456. (The physical device is determined by the UNIT parameter.) In addition, when standard labels are used, the VOL parameter causes IOCS to verify that 123456 is the volume serial number present in the volume label of the mounted tape. When an output data set is created on tape, the VOL parameter is typically omitted. In that instance the system will tell the operator to mount a scratch tape (i.e., a tape with nothing of value on it). After the job is completed, the volume serial number of the scratch tape is noted for future reference. It should be obvious that the VOL parameter is required for input data sets that are not cataloged, or else the system would not be able to locate the specified files.

LABEL Parameter

The LABEL parameter uses two positional subparameters to specify the type of label processing and the location of a data set on a volume. The first entry specifies the relative position of a data set on the reel. The second parameter indicates if labels are used and the type of label processing, e.g., SL—standard labels, NL—no labels, etc. Retention period is specified by keyword parameters in one of two ways. Either an explicit number of days is indicated with the key word RETPD, or an explicit expiration date is specified via EXPDT. RETPD=1000 retains a file for 1000 days. EXPDT=99365 retains a file until the last day of 1999.

DSN (DSNAME or Data Set Name) Parameter

The DSN parameter specifies the actual name of the data set. It may be up to eight characters, the first of which is alphabetic (qualified names that may be longer than eight characters are discussed in conjunction with Figure 18.5). The parameter is required if the data set is to be cataloged or passed to another job step. Its name is independent of all other names used in the program.

The information on tape processing is summarized via Figure 18.4, which contains the JCL for the sequential update of Chapter 15. Information for the COBOL files OLD-MASTER and NEW-MASTER is provided in the DD statements for OLDTAPE and NEWTAPE, respectively. Both files use standard labels. The OLD-MASTER file is the third data set on volume number 001234 (LABEL and VOL parameters). The NEW-MASTER file will be retained for 365 days after the job completes execution, or else it will be deleted (see LABEL and DISP parameters). Note that the VOL parameter is omitted for the output data set, denoting a scratch tape. A dump is printed in the event of an ABEND via the DD statement for SYSUDUMP.

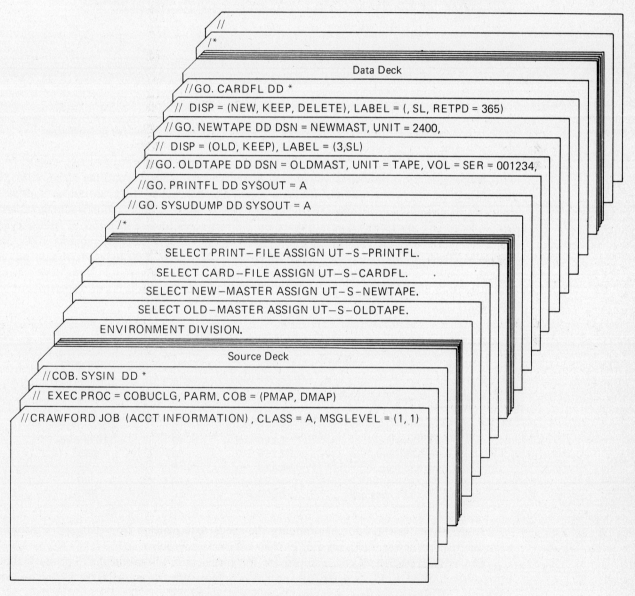

FIGURE 18.4 *OS Job Stream for Tape Processing*

PROCESSING FILES ON DIRECT-ACCESS DEVICES

A major difference in the organization of direct-access volumes is that, unlike tape, disk packs are not organized sequentially. The volume label of a direct-access device always appears on cylinder 0, track 0 and contains information similar to that in a tape volume label. In addition, it contains a pointer to the VTOC (volume table of contents), which is a separate data set, contained somewhere on the disk. The VTOC contains information about every data set on the volume, and it is through the VTOC that the system is able to locate data sets specified by the DSN parameter. The VTOC contains information analogous to the header and trailer labels of tape, i.e., creation date, expiration date, etc.

The OS JCL we present for disk processing is essentially the same as that for tape processing with one exception. Newly created direct-access data sets require a SPACE parameter in the DD statement to indicate the size of the file. In addition, we shall introduce the DCB parameter in this discussion; however, most of what we say about the DCB is applicable to the other data sets as well (i.e., tape, card, print, and punch). We shall discuss qualification in the DSNAME parameter and also changes in the UNIT parameter to cover direct-access devices.

SPACE Parameter

The SPACE parameter is required when creating data sets on direct-access devices. Its symbolic format is

$$SPACE = \left(\left\{ \begin{array}{l} TRK \\ CYL \\ blocklength \end{array} \right\} ,(\text{primary-quantity,secondary-quantity}),[RLSE],[CONTIG] \right)$$

Subparameters, other than those shown, are also available but beyond the scope of this discussion. The SPACE parameter indicates how much space is required for an output data set. It is not used for an input data set since the file already exists, and such information would be superfluous.

The SPACE parameter requests space on a direct-access device in terms of tracks, cylinders, or blocks. SPACE=(TRK,400) requests 400 tracks, SPACE=(CYL,100) requests 100 cylinders, and SPACE=(1000,3000) specifies space for 3000 blocks, each 1000 bytes. It should be obvious that the number of tracks or cylinders required for a given data set varies with the device. However, the number of blocks is a function of the file itself and is device independent. Capacities of various IBM direct-access devices are shown in Table 18.3.

TABLE 18.3 IBM Direct-Access Capacities

Device	Track capacity	Tracks per cylinder	Number of cylinders
2311 disk	3,625	10	200
2314 disk	7,294	20	200
3330 disk	13,030	19	404 or 808
3340 disk	8,368	12	348 or 696
3350 disk	19,254	30	555
2301 drum	20,483	8	25
2302 drum	4,892	10	80
2321 data cell	2,000	20	980

Table 18.3 is essential for determining the space requirements of a data set. Obviously, the same file requires fewer tracks on a 3330 than a 2311 (see Problem 2).

The SPACE parameter can also provide for a secondary allocation if the primary allocation is insufficient. SPACE=(TRK,(100,20)) specifies a primary allocation of 100 tracks and a secondary amount of 20 tracks. In this example, OS will add an additional 20 tracks to the data set if the primary allocation is insufficient. It will do this up to 15 times (total = 300 tracks), at which time the job step terminates if space is still inadequate.

Two additional subparameters, RLSE and CONTIG, are frequently specified. RLSE returns any unused portion of the primary or secondary allocation, a highly desirable practice. The CONTIG subparameter requires that the primary allocation be contiguous. A contiguous allocation generally speeds up subsequent I/O, since the access delay (seek time) is reduced. However, the programmer must be sure that sufficient contiguous space is available or else execution will be delayed and perhaps terminated.

UNIT Parameter

The UNIT parameter serves the same purpose with direct-access devices as with tape. Reference may be by unit address, device type, or group name. Device types for disks include 2311, 2314, 3330, 3340, and 3350. Other direct-access device types are drums (2301, 2302, and 2305) and the 2321 data cell. Group names are installation dependent, but UNIT=DISK or UNIT=SYSDA is used almost universally to specify a disk device.

The information on sequential disk processing is summarized in Figure 18.5. Very little, except for the SPACE parameter, is different from the job stream for tape processing in Figure 18.4. The EXEC statement invokes the procedure COBUCLG with procedure and data division maps and a cross-reference listing (Table 18.1). A dump is specified in the event of an ABEND via the DD statement for SYSUDUMP. Note the correspondence between the four COBOL SELECT statements and the JCL DD statements.

The DD statements for the two disk files do contain some new material. A SPACE parameter is provided for the COBOL file NEW-MASTER. The primary allocation is 50 tracks, which must be contiguous. Any unused amount will be returned to the system due to the RLSE subparameter. The SPACE parameter is omitted for the COBOL file OLD-MASTER since that file already exists (DISP=SHR.) Note also that only the DSN and DISP parameters are specified for this file as the data set is cataloged; i.e., the system remembers information such as UNIT and VOLUME. The newly created data set, MASTER.FEB01, will be deleted if the job ABENDs; otherwise, it will be retained until the last day of 1980.

The DSN parameter in the DD statements illustrates qualification. Qualification is used because a given installation may contain hundreds or even thousands of data sets, each of which must have a unique name. When the DSN parameter was first introduced, we stated it was limited to 8 characters. Qualification helps to ensure uniqueness and also provides more meaningful names. A qualified data set name consists of two or more levels, separated by a period, in much the same way the hyphen is used in ordinary COBOL data names. The entire qualified data name cannot exceed 44 characters, and the individual levels (i.e., entries between the periods) cannot exceed 8 characters. MASTER.FEB01 and MASTER.JAN01 are examples of qualified data set names.

Generation Data Groups

The job stream in Figure 18.5 poses one problem for subsequent updates: the DD statements have to be changed each time the master file is updated. Consider, for example, a monthly cycle. On February 1, the old master file, i.e., DSN=MASTER.JAN01, is used with the transactions accumulated during January to produce a new master, DSN=MASTER.FEB01. However, when the job is rerun on March 1, the old master (i.e., the data set specified in the GO.OLDDISK DD statement) is now DSN=MASTER.FEB01, whereas the new master (i.e., the data set for the GO.NEWDISK DD statement) would be MASTER.MAR01. If this explanation is confusing here, it becomes almost unworkable in a production environment. The problem is solved through the use of generation data groups that permit several generations (e.g., months) of the same data set name to exist.

A *generation data group* is a collection of data sets that is chronologically related. Each successive data set in the group reflects the same file as its predecessor, but with *newer* information. All data sets in a group have the identical data set name. The distinction between group members is made through a generation number. The current data set has a generation number of zero, e.g.,

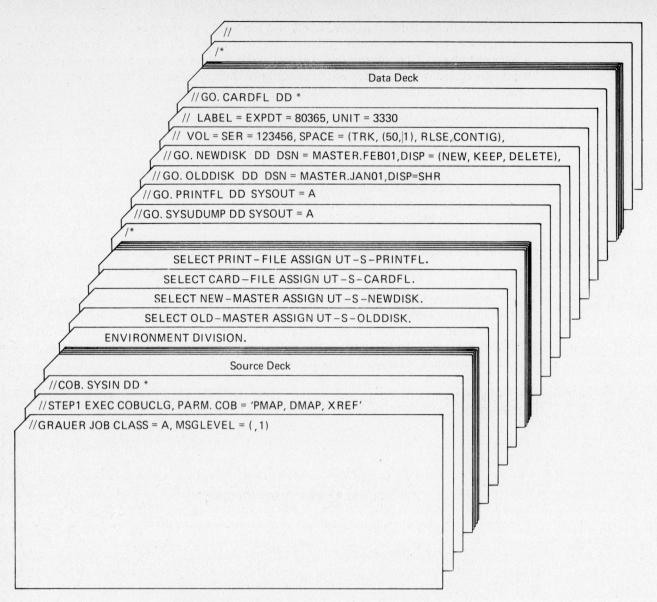

```
//
/*
                        Data Deck
//GO.CARDFL DD *
//  LABEL = EXPDT = 80365, UNIT = 3330
//  VOL = SER = 123456, SPACE = (TRK, (50,|1), RLSE,CONTIG),
//GO.NEWDISK DD DSN = MASTER.FEB01,DISP = (NEW, KEEP, DELETE),
//GO.OLDDISK DD DSN = MASTER.JAN01,DISP=SHR
//GO.PRINTFL DD SYSOUT = A
//GO.SYSUDUMP DD SYSOUT = A
/*
          SELECT PRINT-FILE ASSIGN UT-S-PRINTFL.
          SELECT CARD-FILE ASSIGN UT-S-CARDFL.
          SELECT NEW-MASTER ASSIGN UT-S-NEWDISK.
          SELECT OLD-MASTER ASSIGN UT-S-OLDDISK.
       ENVIRONMENT DIVISION.
                       Source Deck
//COB. SYSIN DD *
//STEP1 EXEC COBUCLG, PARM. COB = 'PMAP, DMAP, XREF'
//GRAUER JOB CLASS = A, MSGLEVEL = (,1)
```

FIGURE 18.5 *OS Job Stream for Sequential Disk Processing*

MASTER.FILE(0). Its immediate predecessor is referenced as MASTER.FILE(−1); its immediate successor as MASTER.FILE(+1).

Only two changes are required in Figure 18.5 to utilize generation data groups. The DSN parameters in the DD statements for OLDDISK and NEWDISK are changed to MASTER(0) and MASTER(+1), respectively.

The advantage of generation data groups is that all data sets have the same name, and, consequently, production job streams can remain unchanged. The system automatically adds and deletes successive generations. Generation data groups are used like any other data set, except for the appearance of the generation group in the DSN parameter. They can have either sequential or direct organization and reside on any device appropriate to their organization.

DCB Parameter

Every file in a COBOL program requires its own DCB macro to be completed before execution can take place. The DCB macro contains information about file characteristics such as record length, block size, record format, and file organization. The information may come from a combination of three sources: (1) the COBOL FD, (2) the DCB parameter on the DD statement, or (3) the data set header label. Further, there is a specified hierarchy for extracting information and building the DCB. The information in the COBOL FD has first priority, followed by the DCB parameter on the DD statement, and finally information on the header label. Consider the following code:

```
COBOL:
    SELECT TAPE-FILE ASSIGN TO UT-S-TAPEFILE.

FD TAPE-FILE
    LABEL RECORDS ARE STANDARD
    BLOCK CONTAINS 0 RECORDS
    RECORD CONTAINS 0 CHARACTERS
    DATA RECORD IS TAPE-INFORMATION.

JCL:
    //GO.TAPEFILE DD DISP=(OLD,KEEP),UNIT=2400,VOL=SER=000123,
    //   LABEL=(3,SL),DCB=(LRECL=100,BLKSIZE=500,RECFM=FB)
```

The COBOL FD implies that TAPE-FILE has standard labels. It specifies block and record size of zero characters each, which means this information is provided through appropriate key-word subparameters in the DCB key-word parameter. Record length is 100 bytes (LRECL = 100) and block size is 500 bytes (BLKSIZE = 500). The DCB parameter is also required for ISAM files as will be explained in conjunction with Figure 18.6.

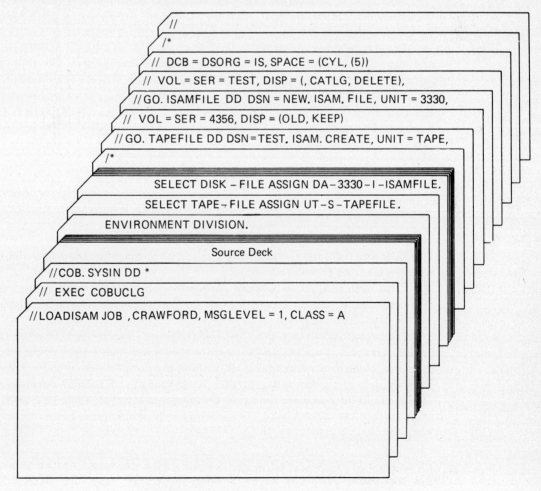

FIGURE 18.6 *OS Job Stream to Load an ISAM File*

What is to be gained by using the DCB over the COBOL FD? The answer, in a word, is flexibility. Often the same COBOL program may be used to process different files. If record length and block size are not specified in the COBOL FD, the only necessary modification would be in the execution time JCL, but the program need not be recompiled. The DCB parameter can be specified for any file type, i.e., tape, card, etc. It is optional in all cases except for ISAM files, which require the entry DCB=DSORG=IS (data set organization = indexed sequential). Figure 18.6 contains the JCL to load an ISAM file from tape. All statements have already been discussed in relation to Figures 18.4 and 18.5.

USING THE COBOL SORT

Chapter 10 contained several examples of the COBOL SORT verb that requires its own JCL. Consider the following:

```
SELECT SORT-FILE ASSIGN TO UT-S-SORTOUT.
        .
        .
        .

SORT SORT-FILE
    INPUT PROCEDURE 010-SORT-INPUT
    OUTPUT PROCEDURE 020-SORT-OUTPUT
    ASCENDING KEY IS EMPLOYEE-NAME.
```

Additional JCL must be provided in the job stream to accommodate the sort work areas, indicate where the sort program itself may be found, and provide a place for the messages created by the sort program. An example of a typical job stream is shown in Figure 18.7.

The sort program typically uses three work areas, SORTWK01, SORTWK02 and SORTWK03, and the space assigned to these work files is usually contiguous. Note that there need be no DD statement corresponding to the SELECT statement for SORT-FILE. A SORTLIB DD statement may be required to specify the location of modules called by the sort program. The disposition of this data set is SHR. No other parameters are specified, since SYS1.SORTLIB is presumed to be a cataloged data set. Finally, a DD statement is provided for SYSOUT to accommodate the messages produced by the SORT program.

SUBPROGRAMS

Chapter 8 illustrated the use of a subprogram, which is a complete COBOL program in its own right. Both the main and subprogram must be compiled and link-edited prior to execution. Figure 18.8 illustrates one way of accomplishing this.

Note well that in the job stream of Figure 18.8 the main program appears *before* the subprogram. Observe, also, the procedure associated with the main program is COBUC rather than COBUCLG. Hence the main program is compiled *prior* to the subprogram being compiled. A single load module is then created and executed only after both programs have compiled individually. The DD statements for the main program *follow the source statements of the subprogram*.

Note the presence of two SYSLIB statements in Figure 18.8. These are required whenever a COPY statement is used in a COBOL program. Recall that a COPY statement will bring a series of COBOL statements into a program without the programmer actually coding them. The system, however, has to be told where to find them; hence the SYSLIB statements. In Figure 18.8 the statements to be copied are found on the cataloged data set, COBOL.COPY.LIB. DISP=SHR is specified to allow other jobs to access this data set simultaneously.

SUMMARY

The discussion of OS JCL revolved about three basic statements: JOB, EXEC, and DD, with emphasis on the latter. The key-word and positional parameters, which were discussed, are listed:

JOB:

CLASS	Assigns a class to a job.
REGION	Assigns an amount of memory for the job (MVT only).
MSGLEVEL	Controls system output.
TIME	Assigns a maximum time allocation to a job.

EXEC:

PARM	Controls job step parameters.
COND	Prevents unnecessary job steps from execution.
REGION	Assigns an amount of memory for a job step (MVT only).
TIME	Assigns a maximum time for a job step.

DD:

*	Indicates the file follows immediately in the job stream.
SYSOUT	Directs an output data set to a printer or punch.
DSN	Specifies the data set name.
UNIT	Specifies the unit to process the data set.
DCB	Supplements the COBOL FD.
DISP	Specifies disposition of data sets.
SPACE	Assigns space for an output data set on a direct access device.
VOLUME	Directs the operator to mount a specified volume; also used in label checking.
LABEL	Specifies type of label processing, location of a data set on a volume (tape only), and retention period.

As often as not, a COBOL program fails in execution due to JCL-associated errors. Such mistakes are particularly irksome to the COBOL programmer who may incorrectly feel that JCL is not his province. We have tried to make it clear that working knowledge of JCL is very definitely in the realm of programmer responsibility and, further, that such knowledge is not difficult to achieve. As a pedagogic aid, we offer the following list of *errors to avoid:*

1. Improper format for EXEC statement: The syntactical rules for this statement are simple: // in columns 1 and 2 and a blank in column 3 if the job step is unnamed. If the step is named, then the step name begins in column 3 and is followed by a blank and then the word EXEC. Valid and invalid statements are shown:

```
Valid:    //  EXEC COBUCLG
Valid:    //STEP1 EXEC PGM=PROGA

Invalid:  //EXEC COBUCLG
Invalid:  //  STEP1 EXEC PGM=PROGA
```

2. Improper format for JOB statement: The job name begins in column 3, followed by a blank and the word JOB. (Other information is installation dependent and follows JOB.) Examples are shown:

```
Valid:    //JONES JOB
Invalid:  //  JONES JOB
```

3. Invalid continuation: The card to be continued (i.e., the first card) must end on a comma. Continued cards begin with // in columns 1 and 2 and a space in 3 and then continue anywhere in columns 4 to 16.

4. Misspelled procedure name: Procedure names are chosen for uniqueness, not necessarily mnemonic significance. Copy the name correctly and completely.

5. Misspelled key-word parameters: Misspellings, either through keypunch or programmer

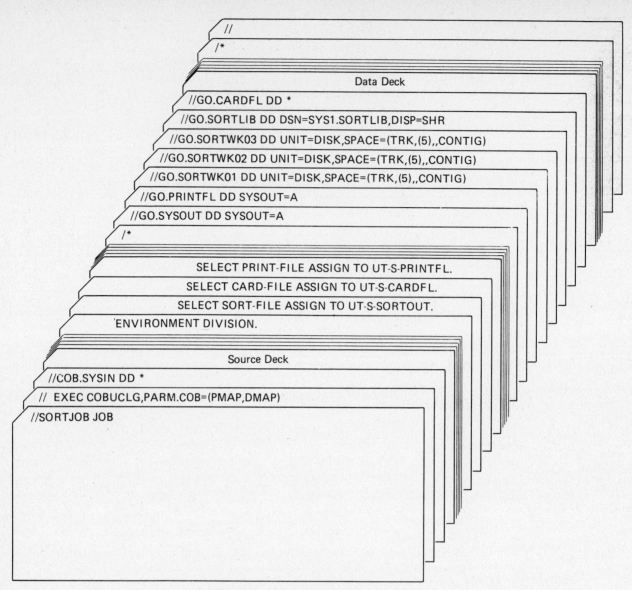

```
//
/*
                            Data Deck
//GO.CARDFL DD *
//GO.SORTLIB DD DSN=SYS1.SORTLIB,DISP=SHR
//GO.SORTWK03 DD UNIT=DISK,SPACE=(TRK,(5),,CONTIG)
//GO.SORTWK02 DD UNIT=DISK,SPACE=(TRK,(5),,CONTIG)
//GO.SORTWK01 DD UNIT=DISK,SPACE=(TRK,(5),,CONTIG)
//GO.PRINTFL DD SYSOUT=A
//GO.SYSOUT DD SYSOUT=A
/*
        SELECT PRINT-FILE ASSIGN TO UT-S-PRINTFL.
        SELECT CARD-FILE ASSIGN TO UT-S-CARDFL.
        SELECT SORT-FILE ASSIGN TO UT-S-SORTOUT.
     ENVIRONMENT DIVISION.
                            Source Deck
//COB.SYSIN DD *
// EXEC COBUCLG,PARM.COB=(PMAP,DMAP)
//SORTJOB JOB
```

FIGURE 18.7 *Use of the COBOL SORT Verb*

error, are far too common. BLKSIZE, LRECL, DSORG, LABEL, CATLG, SHR, and MSGLEVEL are *correct* spellings of frequently abused parameters.

6. Omission of // at end of job stream: While not technically an error, it can have serious consequences. Omission of the null (//) statement means that subsequent cards can be taken as part of your job stream. Thus, if the job after yours contains a JOB card JCL error, your job may "flush" through no fault of your own.

7. Omission of a positional parameter or associated comma: Positional parameters derive their meaning from a specified order. If omitted, their absence must be indicated by a comma.

8. Incorrect order of JCL statements: Occurs frequently when using a proc. In COBUCLG, for example, the COB step precedes the GO step. Thus all DD statements for the former (e.g., //COB.SYSIN DD *) must precede those of the latter (e.g., //GO.SYSIN DD *).

9. Omission of a DD statement: Every file, in every job step, requires a DD statement. Make sure you have them all.

10. Incorrect or omitted DSN for an input file: The purpose of the DSN parameter in the

SECTION V: FILE PROCESSING

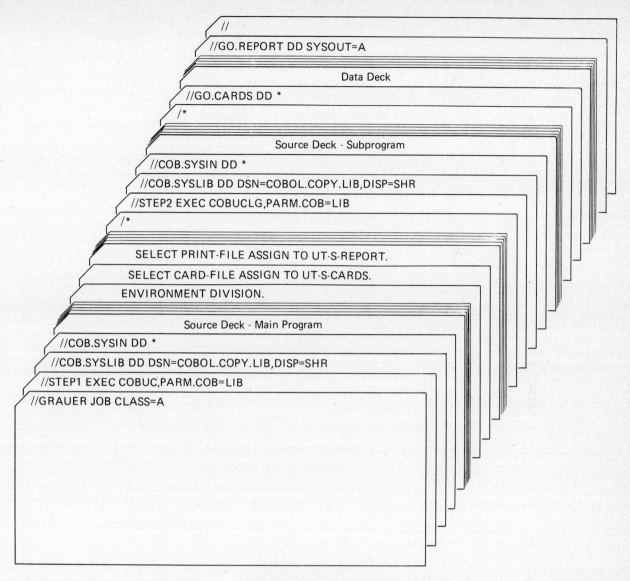

FIGURE 18.8 *Subprograms*

DD statement is to identify a data set. If this parameter is left out or misspelled, the system will not be able to locate the proper file on which to operate.

11. Incorrect or omitted VOL=SER parameter: This parameter causes a message to be printed informing the operator of the proper volume. Obviously, incorrect specification makes it difficult for the operator to comply with the request.

REVIEW EXERCISES

TRUE   FALSE

☐   ☐   **1.** A given DD statement may contain either positional or key-word parameters but not both.

☐   ☐   **2.** Every job stream must contain one and only one /* statement.

☐   ☐   **3.** A procedure may contain more than one EXEC statement.

☐   ☐   **4.** The DD and EXEC statements must have a blank in column 3.

☐   ☐   **5.** It is possible to continue any JCL statement to a second card.

□ □ **6.** Comments are not permitted on any JCL statement.

□ □ **7.** Accounting information is required on the JOB statement.

□ □ **8.** If the programmer-name parameter is omitted on the JOB statement, a comma is required to show its absence.

□ □ **9.** JCL for the MVT and MVS operating systems are significantly different.

□ □ **10.** The /* statement is the last statement in a job stream.

□ □ **11.** The omission of a positional parameter *always* requires a comma.

□ □ **12.** There are no positional parameters or subparameters on the JOB statement.

□ □ **13.** The EXEC statement does not require a step name.

□ □ **14.** The procedure COBUCLG will *always* attempt to execute the compiled program.

□ □ **15.** The same DD name may appear in two different steps of a procedure.

□ □ **16.** The MOUNT parameter *always* causes a message to be printed, directing the operator to mount a specific volume.

□ □ **17.** The VOL parameter is optional.

□ □ **18.** The SPACE parameter is required for input data sets.

□ □ **19.** The DISP parameter has three positional subparameters.

□ □ **20.** The SPACE parameter must specify required space in terms of tracks.

□ □ **21.** VOL=SER= is required if UNIT is specified.

□ □ **22.** The secondary space allocation in the SPACE parameter is attempted only once.

□ □ **23.** An * on a DD statement indicates a card file.

□ □ **24.** DD statements precede the EXEC card.

□ □ **25.** Certain parameters may appear on either the JOB or EXEC statement.

□ □ **26.** The DCB parameter overrides information in the COBOL FD.

□ □ **27.** The UNIT parameter is not required for a print file.

□ □ **28.** If the normal disposition of an existing data set is not specified, the data set is deleted at the end of the job step.

□ □ **29.** A data set name may consist of more than eight characters if it is qualified.

□ □ **30.** The DCB parameter is not permitted for a card file.

□ □ **31.** DSN=MASTER.FILE(0) is an invalid data set specification.

□ □ **32.** DSN=MASTER.FILE(+1) refers to the current version of the data set MASTER.FILE.

□ □ **33.** Generation data groups can only be used for direct-access files.

□ □ **34.** The same COBOL SELECT statement can be used for a sequential file if it is stored on tape or disk.

□ □ **35.** If an existing data set is cataloged, then DSN and DISP are the only required DD parameters.

□ □ **36.** If the COPY statement is used in a COBOL program, a SYSLIB statement is required in the JCL.

□ □ **37.** In a job stream containing both a main and a subprogram, the subprogram comes first.

□ □ **38.** The EXEC statements for a main and subprogram will typically be the same.

□ □ **39.** The DD statements for the main program will precede the EXEC statement for the subprogram.

40. Given the DD specification

```
//GO.TAPEFILE DD DISP=(OLD,KEEP),LABEL=(2,SL),
//  DSN=TESTFILE,VOL=SER=123456,UNIT=2400
```

answer true or false:

□ □ (a) TAPEFILE is the entry on the COBOL SELECT statement.

□ □ (b) TESTFILE is the first file on the tape.

□ □ (c) The operator will be directed to mount the tape with an external label "TESTFILE".

☐ ☐ (d) The tape will be scratched if the job ABENDs.
☐ ☐ (e) The tape will be mounted on any available tape drive.

41. Given the DD specifications

```
//GO.NEWFILE DD DISP=(NEW,KEEP),SPACE=(CYL,20),
//  DSN=OUTPUT,UNIT=DISK,LABEL=EXPDT=99365,
//  VOL=SER=123456
```

answer true or false:
☐ ☐ (a) OUTPUT is the entry in the COBOL SELECT statement.
☐ ☐ (b) The file will be retained indefinitely if the job executes successfully.
☐ ☐ (c) The file will be deleted if the job ABENDs.
☐ ☐ (d) The job will terminate if more than 20 cylinders are required.
☐ ☐ (e) The file will be stored in contiguous cylinders.
☐ ☐ (f) Any available disk device may be used.
☐ ☐ (g) A message to mount volume number 123456 will definitely be issued.

PROBLEMS

1. Complete the table; indicate whether the job step is executed or bypassed:

Code in COND parameter	Operation	System return code from last step	Executed or bypassed
5	LT	4	
9	GT	8	
5	LT	(C-Level diagnostic)	
5	LT	(W-Level diagnostic)	
12	EQ	(E-Level diagnostic)	
12	NE	12	

2. Complete the SPACE parameters for an output data set of 3300 blocks. Each block is 1000 bytes in length. (Assume that 3, 6, and 11 are the number of blocks per track for the 2311, 2314, and 3330, respectively.) In each case provide a secondary allocation equal to 10% of the primary allocation:
   (a) //GO.OUTDISK   DD   UNIT=2311,SPACE=(TRK,(   ))
   (b) //GO.OUTDISK   DD   UNIT=2311,SPACE=(CYL,(   ))
   (c) //GO.OUTDISK   DD   UNIT=2314,SPACE=(TRK,(   ))
   (d) //GO.OUTDISK   DD   UNIT=2314,SPACE=(CYL,(   ))
   (e) //GO.OUTDISK   DD   UNIT=3330,SPACE=(1000,(   ))

3. Show OS JCL necessary to compile, link-edit, and execute a COBOL program. The program reads a deck of cards and produces a tape. Your JCL must accommodate all the following:

   1. Produce procedure and data division maps and a dump in the event of an ABEND.
   2. Store the data set as the second file on tape.
   3. Retain the newly created tape file for 100 days if the job executes successfully; if the job ABENDs, scratch the tape.
   4. Use any available tape drive.
   5. Provide a DCB parameter for the tape file to show a logical record of 80 bytes and a blocking factor of 10.
   6. Store the newly created data set on tape volume 001234 as NEW.TAPE.
   7. Show a corresponding COBOL SELECT for every DD statement.

4. Repeat Problem 3, except that the newly created data set is to appear as a sequential file on a 3330 device. (Assume 10 cylinders for the file.)

5. Repeat Problem 3, except that the newly created data set is to appear as an ISAM file on a 3330 device. (Assume 30 tracks for the file.)

6. Analyze the JOB statements on page 352 for syntactical errors. Some statements may be correct as written, whereas others may contain more than one mistake.

(a)   //   FIRST JOB (ACCTNO,PROJNO),SMITH, CLASS=A

(b)   //SECOND JOB (ACCTNO,PROJNO),SMITH,MSGLEVEL=1,1

(c)   //THIRD JOB ,SMITH,MSGLEVEL=(1,1)
        //   TIME=(1,30),CLASS=A

(d)   //FOURTH$ JOB (ACCTNO,PROJNO),'SMITH − X0345',
        //   TIME=30,CLASS=A,REGION=120

(e)   //FIFTH$$$$ JOB ACCTNO,SMITH,CLASS=A,
        //REGION=120K,MSGLEVEL=(1,1)

(f)   //SIXTH JOB **

(g)   //SEVENTH JOB SMITH,(ACCTNO,PROJNO)

(h)   //EIGHTH ACCTNO,SMITH,TIME=2 CLASS=F

(i)   //NINTH JOB (ACCTNO,PROJNO)

(j)   //   JOB (ACCTNO,PROJNO),SMITH − X0345,
        //CLASS=F,TIME=3,MSGLEVEL=1

7. Analyze the EXEC statements for syntactical and or logical errors. Some statements may be correct as written, whereas others may contain more than one mistake. (Assume IEBGENER is a program name and COBUCLG a procedure name.)

(a)   //   EXEC PGM=IEBGENER

(b)   //EXEC PGM=IEBGENER

(c)   //STEPONE EXEC PGM=IEBGENER TIME=3

(d)   //STEPSEVEN EXEC PGM=IEBGENER

(e)   //STEP7 EXEC IEBGENER

(f)   //   EXEC PGM=IEBGENER ** CREATE MASTER FILE

(g)   //   STEP1 EXEC PGM=COBUCLG

(h)   //STEP1 EXEC PROC=COBUCLG,PARM.COB='PMAP,DMAP'

(i)   //STEP1 EXEC COBUCLG PARM.COB='PMAP,DMAP', REGION=120K,

(j)   //STEP1 EXEC IEBGENER,TIME(30),REGION=120
        //   COND=(4,LT,STEP2)

(k)   //   EXECUTE PGM=IEBGENER,
        //   TIME=(1,30),
        //   REGION=64K,

(l)   //LAST EXEC COBUCLG,PARM.COB=(PMAP,DMAP)
        //   TIME=(3,30)
        //   REGION=256

8. Analyze the DD statements for syntactical and/or logic errors. Some statements may be correct as written, whereas others may contain more than one mistake.

(a)   //FILE 1 DD DSN=FIRST,DISP=NEW,KEEP,VOL=SER=USR001,
        //   SPACE=(TRK,(1,1),UNIT=SYSDA

(b)   //STEP1FILE1 DD DSN=FIRST.FILE,DISP=(NEW,PASS)
        //   SPACE=(CYL,(10,1)),UNIT=TAPE

(c)   //FILE2 DD* A CARD FILE

(d)   //   FILE2 DD SYSOUT=A ** A PRINT FILE

(e)   //STEP3.FILE2 DD DSN=ABCDE,DISP=(NEW,KEEP),UNIT=DISK,
        //   DCB=BLKSIZE=80,LRECL=40,RECFM=FB

(f)   //FILE4 DSN=A.B.C.D,DISP=OLD,KEEP,DELETE,LABEL=(,SL),
        //   VOL=SER=USR003,UNIT=TAPE

(g)   //GO.SYSIN DD DSN=NEWERFILE,DISP=(NEW,KEEP),
        //UNIT=TAPE,DCB=(BLKSIZE=1000,LRECL=100)

(h)   //OUTPUT DD DCB=(BLOCKSIZE=1000,LREC=100),UNIT=3330,
        //   SPACE=(1000,(100,10)),DISP=OLD

(i)   //MARION DD DSN=A.B.C.D.E.F.G.H.I.J.K,
        //   DISP=SHR
        //   SPACE=(CYL,(10,2),,CONTIG),
        //   UNIT=DISK,

(j) //SYSOUT DD SYSOUT=A

(k) //PRINTER DD *

(l) //FILEEIGHT DD DSN=&&TEMP,DISP=(NEW,KEEP),
     //   UNIT=DISK,SPACE=(CYL,(3,1),CONTIG),
     //   DCB=(LRECL=50,RECFM=FB,BLKSIZE=540)

(m) //FILE9 DD DSN=MYTEMP.FILE,DISP=(OLD),
     //   SPACE=(CYL,3), VOL=SER=123456,UNIT=SYSDA

APPENDIXES

Appendix A

REPORT WRITER

OVERVIEW

Report Writer is one of the most powerful, yet least used, facilities in COBOL. It is always interesting to hear reasons from practitioners on why it is avoided. The following responses are typical:

1. I never learned it.
2. I tried to use it, but the documentation was impossible to understand.
3. I used it once and it didn't work.
4. My program "blew out" in Report Writer and I couldn't debug it.

The authors believe that the heart of the problem is in the documentation or lack thereof. The vendor's reference manual is often devoid of clear examples. Moreover, it is not designed to teach the subject, but rather to answer "nitty-gritty" questions from users already familiar with the material. To compound the education problem, many academic curricula consider Report Writer as an extra and omit coverage entirely or discuss it only briefly. In any event, the excuses listed can be traced, directly or indirectly, to poor documentation and/or lack of academic coverage.

The purpose of this appendix is to provide the reader with an appreciation for the capabilities of Report Writer and an introduction to its use. Report Writer is a convenient technique for many types of report formatting and almost indispensable for programs using multilevel control breaks.

The objective of Report Writer is to assume tedious tasks of programming from the programmer. These include page headings, proper spacing, and, most important, calculating totals and subtotals involving control breaks. The programmer describes in detail the physical appearance of a report in the data division and invokes the facility in the procedure division. To understand how this is accomplished, we must first define *control break* and *report group*.

VOCABULARY

A *control break* is a change in a designated field. For example, if an incoming file is sorted by employee location and location is the control field, a control break occurs every time location changes. If the file is sorted by location and department within location, it is possible to designate two control fields, department and location.

Let us assume a given file has been sorted on location and department within location. Hence

357

all employees in department 100 in the Atlanta office precede the Atlanta employees in department 200, who precede those in department 300, etc. Next come the employees in department 100 in Boston, followed by department 200 in Boston, etc. A single control break occurs as we change departments within the same location, e.g., from department 100 in Atlanta to department 200 in Atlanta. A double control break, on location and department, arises when we go from department 300 in Atlanta to department 100 in Boston.

Our second definition has to do with the way Report Writer generates output. The facility classifies every line appearing in any report as belonging to one of seven kinds of *report groups*. It is not necessary that a given report contain all seven report groups, and, further, any of the seven report groups can consist of one or more lines, i.e., a group of lines. The seven categories are

1. *Report heading:* one or more lines appearing only once at the beginning (initiation) of a report.
2. *Report footing:* one or more lines appearing only once at the conclusion (termination) of a report.
3. *Page heading:* one or more lines appearing at the beginning of each page after the report heading.
4. *Page footing:* one or more lines appearing at the end of each page.
5. *Control heading:* one or more lines appearing prior to each control break, i.e., when the contents of a designated field change.
6. *Control footing:* one or more lines appearing after each control break.
7. *Detail:* one line (or lines) for each record in the file.

AN EXAMPLE: A DOUBLE CONTROL BREAK PROGRAM

To better understand these terms and Report Writer in general, we develop a complete COBOL program with objectives similar to the control break program of Chapter 11. The purpose there was to illustrate the technique of stepwise refinement for a program requiring two control breaks. The purpose here is to demonstrate the ease with which Report Writer can produce similar results. Specifications are as follows.

Continental University consists of several colleges; each college has four levels of students: freshmen, sophomores, juniors, and seniors. A punched card, showing the number of students in a given major, year, and college has been prepared. These cards have been sorted by college (primary sort) and year (secondary sort). The problem is to

1. Sum all the major totals in the same year to provide enrollment totals for each year.
2. Sum the four year totals in a college to provide a college total.
3. Sum all the college totals to provide a single university total.

The specifications call for two control breaks, on year and college. A running total will be maintained for all majors in a given year. When a new year is encountered, the previous year's total is printed, and then the year total is reinitialized to zero. When a new college is reached, there is a double break (on year and college). Both totals are printed and then zeroed out, and processing continues. The university total is printed after the end of file has been reached. Test data for this problem were shown in Figure 11.3.

Figure A.1 shows three pages from a report produced by the COBOL program developed later in the appendix to conform to these specifications. Note, in particular, the presence of a page heading, control heading on a college change, and control footings on both year and college changes.

DATA DIVISION REQUIREMENTS

The use of Report Writer is best explained through Figure A.2, the COBOL program that produced the output of Figure A.1. At first, its data division may appear unduly long and complex. In reality, it is no longer than that of any meaningful COBOL program, with or without Report Writer.

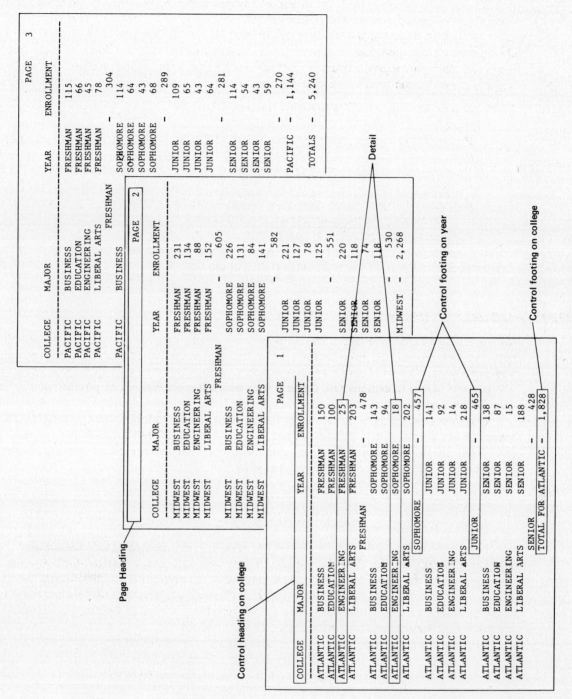

FIGURE A.1 *Output Produced by Report Writer*

Use "Objective statement" or method will take points off.

```
00001          IDENTIFICATION DIVISION.
00002          PROGRAM-ID.
00003              TOTALS.
00004          AUTHOR.
00005              EDWARD RAMSEY.
00006          ENVIRONMENT DIVISION.
00007          CONFIGURATION SECTION.
00008          SOURCE-COMPUTER. IBM-370.
00009          OBJECT-COMPUTER. IBM-370.
00010          INPUT-OUTPUT SECTION.
00011          FILE-CONTROL.
00012              SELECT STUDENT-FILE     ASSIGN TO UT-S-SYSIN.
00013              SELECT PRINT-FILE       ASSIGN TO UT-S-SYSOUT.
00014          DATA DIVISION.
00015          FILE SECTION.
00016          FD  STUDENT-FILE
00017              LABEL RECORDS ARE OMITTED
00018              BLOCK CONTAINS 0 RECORDS
00019              RECORD CONTAINS 80 CHARACTERS
00020              DATA RECORD IS CARD-REC.                     No 01 entry for this file
00021          01  CARD-REC                    PIC X(80).
00022          FD  PRINT-FILE
00023              REPORT IS CONTROL-BREAK                      Identifies report name in subsequent RD
00024              LABEL RECORDS ARE OMITTED
00025              BLOCK CONTAINS 0 RECORDS
00026              RECORD CONTAINS 133 CHARACTERS.
00027          WORKING-STORAGE SECTION.
00028          01  WS-BEGINS-HERE              PIC X(16)
00029                          VALUE ' WS BEGINS HERE'.
00030          01  WS-END-OF-FILE-SW           PIC XXX     VALUE SPACE.
00031              88  WS-END-OF-FILE                     VALUE 'YES'.
00032          01  CD-CARD-IN.
00033              05  CD-YEAR                 PIC X(9).
00034              05  FILLER                  PIC X(11).
00035              05  CD-COLLEGE-NAME         PIC X(10).
00036              05  CD-MAJOR-NAME           PIC X(19).
00037              05  CD-MAJOR-TOTAL          PIC S9(6).
00038              05  FILLER                  PIC X(25).
00039          01  WS-ENDS-HERE                PIC X(12)
00040                          VALUE 'WS ENDS HERE'.
00041          REPORT SECTION.                 Beginning of Report Section
00042          RD  CONTROL-BREAK
00043              CONTROLS ARE FINAL CD-COLLEGE-NAME CD-YEAR
00044              PAGE LIMIT 50 LINES
00045              HEADING 1                   Establishes control breaks
00046              FIRST DETAIL 5
00047              LAST DETAIL 45
00048              FOOTING 48.
00049          01  TYPE IS PAGE HEADING.       Indicates absolute line number
00050              05  LINE NUMBER 1.
00051                  10  COLUMN NUMBER 50    PIC X(4)
00052                          VALUE 'PAGE'.
00053                  10  COLUMN NUMBER 55    PIC ZZZ9
00054                          SOURCE PAGE-COUNTER.
00055          01  TYPE IS CONTROL HEADING CD-COLLEGE-NAME.
00056              05  LINE NUMBER 5.
00057                  10  COLUMN NUMBER 1     PIC X(17)
00058                          VALUE 'COLLEGE      MAJOR'.
00059                  10  COLUMN NUMBER 34    PIC X(20)
00060                          VALUE 'YEAR     ENROLLMENT'.
00061              05  LINE NUMBER 6.
00062                  10  COLUMN NUMBER 1     PIC X(60)
00063                          VALUE ALL '-'.
00064          01  DETAIL-LINE  TYPE IS DETAIL.      Detail report group is referenced in
00065              05  LINE NUMBER PLUS 1.            subsequent GENERATE statement
00066                  10  COLUMN NUMBER 1     PIC X(10)
00067                          SOURCE CD-COLLEGE-NAME.
00068                  10  COLUMN NUMBER 13    PIC X(19)
00069                          SOURCE CD-MAJOR-NAME.
00070                  10  COLUMN NUMBER 34    PIC X(9)
00071                          SOURCE CD-YEAR.
00072                  10  COLUMN NUMBER 43    PIC ZZZ,ZZ9
00073                          SOURCE CD-MAJOR-TOTAL.
00074          01  TYPE IS CONTROL FOOTING CD-YEAR.      Relative line number
00075              05  LINE NUMBER PLUS 2.
```

FIGURE A.2 *Report Writer Program*

```
00076              10   COLUMN NUMBER 24      PIC X(10)
00077                       VALUE 'TOTAL FOR '.
00078              10   COLUMN NUMBER 34      PIC X(9)
00079                       SOURCE CD-YEAR.
00080              10   COLUMN NUMBER 43      PIC XX
00081                       VALUE '- '.
00082              10   MAJOR-TOTAL
00083                       COLUMN NUMBER 45      PIC ZZZ,ZZ9
00084                       SUM CD-MAJOR-TOTAL.
00085   01   TYPE IS CONTROL FOOTING CD-COLLEGE-NAME.
00086        05   LINE NUMBER PLUS 2.
00087              10   COLUMN NUMBER 24      PIC X(10)
00088                       VALUE 'TOTAL FOR '.
00089              10   COLUMN NUMBER 34      PIC X(9)
00090                       SOURCE CD-COLLEGE-NAME.
00091              10   COLUMN NUMBER 43      PIC XX
00092                       VALUE '- '.
00093              10   COLLEGE-TOTAL
00094                       COLUMN NUMBER 45      PIC ZZZ,ZZ9
00095                       SUM MAJOR-TOTAL.
00096   01   TYPE IS CONTROL FOOTING FINAL.
00097        05   LINE NUMBER IS PLUS 5.
00098              10   COLUMN NUMBER 24      PIC X(21)
00099                       VALUE 'UNIVERSITY TOTALS  - '.
00100              10   COLUMN NUMBER 45      PIC ZZZ,ZZ9
00101                       SUM COLLEGE-TOTAL.
00102   PROCEDURE DIVISION.
00103   10-CREATE-REPORTS.
00104        OPEN INPUT STUDENT-FILE
00105             OUTPUT PRINT-FILE.
00106        INITIATE CONTROL-BREAK.                    ←── INITIATE statement
00107        READ STUDENT-FILE INTO CD-CARD-IN
00108             AT END MOVE 'YES' TO WS-END-OF-FILE-SW.
00109        PERFORM 20-PROCESS-ALL-TRANSACTIONS
00110             UNTIL WS-END-OF-FILE.
00111        TERMINATE CONTROL-BREAK.                   ←── TERMINATE statement
00112        CLOSE STUDENT-FILE
00113              PRINT-FILE.
00114        STOP RUN.
00115   20-PROCESS-ALL-TRANSACTIONS.
00116        GENERATE DETAIL-LINE.                      ──── GENERATE statement refers to
00117        READ STUDENT-FILE INTO CD-CARD-IN               DETAIL-LINE report group
00118             AT END MOVE 'YES' TO WS-END-OF-FILE-SW.
```

Control footing appears whenever there is a break on CD-COLLEGE-NAME

FIGURE A.2 *(continued)*

A report is written to a file defined in a SELECT statement. The FD for this file contains an additional entry, REPORT IS (line 23 in Figure A.2), which specifies the name of the report. Note that there are no 01 entries for this FD since the description of the file is handled in the report section. (Multiple reports can be written to the same output file, but that is not covered here.) The entry in the REPORT IS clause has a corresponding RD (report description) in the report section (lines 23 and 42) of the data division. The RD describes the structure and organization of the report and has the form:

RD   report-name

[WITH CODE mnemonic-name]

$$\left[\begin{Bmatrix} \underline{CONTROL} \ IS \\ \underline{CONTROLS} \ ARE \end{Bmatrix} \begin{Bmatrix} [\underline{FINAL}] \end{Bmatrix} identifier\text{-}1 \ [identifier\text{-}2] \ . \ . \ . \right]$$

$$\left[\underline{PAGE} \begin{bmatrix} LIMITS \ IS \\ LIMITS \ ARE \end{bmatrix} integer\text{-}1 \begin{Bmatrix} \underline{LINE} \\ \underline{LINES} \end{Bmatrix} \right.$$

[HEADING   integer-2]
[FIRST DETAIL integer-3]
[LAST DETAIL   integer-4]
[FOOTING   integer-5]   ].

The CODE clause of the RD specifies an identifying character placed at the beginning of each report line and has meaning only when multiple reports are written.

The CONTROL clause (line 43 in Figure A.2) identifies the control breaks. These are FINAL, CD-COLLEGE-NAME, and CD-YEAR. Subsequent specification of control headings and/or control footings will cause information to print before and/or after control breaks in these fields. Specification of CONTROL IS FINAL causes a control break at the end of the report. Note well that the identifier(s) in the CONTROL clause, i.e., CD-COLLEGE-NAME and CD-YEAR, appear in each incoming record.

The remaining clauses of the RD physically describe the pages of the report. One can specify the maximum number of lines per page (PAGE LIMIT), the first line on which anything may be printed (HEADING), the first line for a detail, control heading, or footing (FIRST DETAIL), the last line for a control heading or detail (LAST DETAIL), and the last line for a footing (FOOTING).

The RD is followed by several 01 entries to describe report groups within that report (just as an FD is followed by 01 entries to describe records within a file). Recall that there are seven types of report groups, and that a given report need not contain all seven, but could contain multiple entries for the same type of report group. Figure A.2, for example, does not contain either a page or report footing, but does contain three control footings (lines 74, 85, and 96).

A report group is described in an 01 entry and its associated subentries. The programmer specifies the physical and logical characteristics of the report group by including information on the following:

Function   Accomplished through the TYPE clause specified at the 01 level. This indicates the nature of the report group, i.e., control heading, control footing, etc.

Vertical spacing   Accomplished through the LINE clause. It can be specified as absolute, e.g., begin on line 5, or relative, e.g., begin two lines past the last entry.

Horizontal spacing Specified through the COLUMN clause.

Contents   Determines how the value of a report entry is obtained and is specified in one of three ways. The VALUE clause specifies a constant, i.e., a literal. The SOURCE clauses identifies a data name outside the report section whose current value is moved to the report entry. The SUM clause specifies that the entry is to be obtained by adding the specified field in detail records.

The COBOL syntax for specifying 01 and/or other subentries has four possible formats, as shown in Figure A.3. The most unusual aspect of all four formats is that the data name is *optional*. Hence, when reading a report section for the first time, it may be somewhat startling to find level numbers followed immediately by clauses other than data names. For example, there are six 01 entries in the report section of Figure A.2, but only one includes a data name, DETAIL-LINE (line 64), and that is because of a requirement in a subsequent procedure division statement (GENERATE in line 116). Our distinct preference is to omit data names in the report section where possible.

We now turn our attention to describing in detail some of the entries in Figure A.3. The TYPE clause is required for an 01 entry and cannot be used at any other level. It specifies the type of report group and has the general form

$$\text{TYPE IS} \begin{cases} \begin{cases} \text{REPORT HEADING} \\ \text{RH} \end{cases} \\ \begin{cases} \text{PAGE HEADING} \\ \text{PH} \end{cases} \\ \begin{cases} \text{CONTROL HEADING} \\ \text{CH} \end{cases} \begin{cases} \text{FINAL} \\ \text{identifier-n} \end{cases} \\ \begin{cases} \text{DETAIL} \\ \text{DE} \end{cases} \\ \begin{cases} \text{CONTROL FOOTING} \\ \text{CF} \end{cases} \begin{cases} \text{identifier-n} \\ \text{FINAL} \end{cases} \\ \begin{cases} \text{PAGE FOOTING} \\ \text{PF} \end{cases} \\ \begin{cases} \text{REPORT FOOTING} \\ \text{RF} \end{cases} \end{cases}$$

General format 2 in Figure A.3 describes a group entry, e.g., a single report line, which has several elementary items, i.e., fields, under it. Consider, for example, the control heading for CD-COLLEGE-NAME (lines 55 to 63). This report group, consisting of two lines, will print every time there is a control break on CD-COLLEGE-NAME. (Note that CD-COLLEGE-NAME was previously specified as a control field of the RD in line 43.) The first line will appear on line 5 of the page. This in turn is a group entry, as per general format 2, consisting of two fields beginning in columns 1 and 34, respectively. The second group item specifies line 6 and in turn has one elementary item, i.e., a field beginning in column number 1.

General format 3 in Figure A.3 describes an elementary item, as evidenced by the mandatory PICTURE clause. It specifies both a beginning column (COLUMN) for the field and also how the value of the field is determined, i.e., either through SOURCE, VALUE, or SUM.

Specification of SOURCE, e.g., SOURCE IS CD-COLLEGE-NAME (in line 67), says that the current value of the identifier CD-COLLEGE-NAME is to be moved to the output field. Specification of VALUE, e.g., VALUE 'TOTAL FOR' (in line 77), causes a literal to be moved to the output field. Finally, specification of SUM, e.g., SUM CD-MAJOR-TOTAL (line 84), causes report writer to total the field CD-MAJOR-TOTAL for each incoming record and print its value at the appropriate time. The sum is automatically reset to zero each time a break on CD-YEAR is encountered. (The RESET clause, which does not appear in Figure A.2, makes it possible to reset a total to zero at times other than the control break.) In this way, various totals and subtotals can be computed throughout a report.

PROCEDURE DIVISION REQUIREMENTS

The procedure division of Figure A.2 is remarkably short and contains three new verbs, INITIATE, GENERATE, and TERMINATE, all uniquely associated with report writer.

INITIATE is used to begin processing a given report. Execution of this statement initializes counters, totals, etc. Its syntax is simply

INITIATE report-name-1 [report-name-2] . . .

Note that the report name CONTROL-BREAK of the INITIATE statement in line 106 appears in the REPORT clause of the FD for PRINT-FILE (line 23). It appears again in the RD entry of the report section (line 42) in the data division.

The GENERATE statement (line 116) causes report writer to automatically produce any of the seven report groups where and when they are needed. It has the general syntax

GENERATE $\begin{Bmatrix} \text{report-name} \\ \text{data-name} \end{Bmatrix}$

Two types of reporting are possible: *summary reporting,* in which only heading and footing groups are produced, and *detail reporting,* in which the detail report group named in the GENERATE statement is produced each time the statement is executed.

The GENERATE statement in Figure A.2 calls for detail reporting by specifying the data name of a report group, i.e., DETAIL-LINE. (Note the latter was designated as a DETAIL report group in line 64.)

The TERMINATE statement (line 111) completes report processing after the end of file has been reached, as if a control break at the highest level occurred. All footing groups up to the highest level are produced, all counters are reset, and report processing is ended. The statement has the syntax

TERMINATE report-name-1 [report-name-2] . . .

General Format 1—level-01 Group Entry

```
01      [data-name]
        TYPE Clause
        [LINE clause]
        [NEXT GROUP clause]
        [USAGE clause].
```

General Format 2—Group Entry

```
level-number [data-name]
        [LINE clause]
        [USAGE clause].
```

General Format 3—Elementary Entry

```
level-number [data-name]

        [COLUMN NUMBER IS integer]
        [GROUP INDICATE]
        [LINE Clause]
```

$$\left\{ \begin{array}{l} \underline{SOURCE} \text{ IS identifier} \\ \underline{SUM} \text{ identifier-1 [identifier-2] . . . } [\underline{UPON} \text{ data-name-2}] \\ \quad [\underline{RESET} \text{ ON } \left\{ \begin{array}{l} \text{FINAL} \\ \text{identifier-3} \end{array} \right\} \ ] \\ \underline{VALUE} \text{ IS literal} \end{array} \right\}$$

```
        PICTURE Clause
        [USAGE Clause]
        [BLANK WHEN ZERO Clause]
        [JUSTIFIED Clause].
```

General Format 4—level-01 Elementary Entry

```
01      [data-name]
        TYPE Clause
        [LINE Clause]
        [NEXT GROUP Clause]
        [COLUMN Clause]
        [GROUP INDICATE Clause]
```

$$\left\{ \begin{array}{l} \text{SOURCE Clause} \\ \text{SUM Clause} \\ \text{VALUE Clause} \end{array} \right\}$$

```
        PICTURE Clause
        [USAGE Clause]
        [BLANK WHEN ZERO Clause]
        [JUSTIFIED Clause].
```

FIGURE A.3   *COBOL Syntax of Report Groups*

SUMMARY

A COBOL program was presented illustrating the use of report writer. This powerful, but often neglected, COBOL feature is well suited to "straightforward" reports, i.e., those with few or no exceptions. The reader should compare the easy logic of the program in Figure A.2 to the complex requirements of the control break program in Chapter 11. *Report writer is ideal for handling multilevel control breaks.*

In essence, report writer produces a report by describing its physical characteristics in the data division, rather than by specifying detailed instructions in the procedure division. This philosophy simplifies the involved logic in computing subtotals and rolling them forward. Moreover, because the report section is divided into distinct report groups, which specify control headings, footings, etc., it is easy to add (or remove) additional control breaks.[1]

REVIEW EXERCISES

TRUE   FALSE

☐   ☐   **1.** If report writer is used, the COBOL program must contain at least one of all seven report groups.

☐   ☐   **2.** Report writer requires that control headings and control footings occur in pairs.

☐   ☐   **3.** A report group is limited to a single print line.

☐   ☐   **4.** Input to report writer need not be sorted.

☐   ☐   **5.** A given COBOL program cannot contain both the SORT and report writer features.

☐   ☐   **6.** The procedure division of a program containing report writer is typically quite short.

☐   ☐   **7.** INITIATE, PROPAGATE, and TERMINATE are all associated with report writer.

☐   ☐   **8.** Report writer automatically sorts the incoming file if necessary.

☐   ☐   **9.** A COBOL program that calls a subprogram cannot use report writer.

☐   ☐   **10.** The report writer entries LINE NUMBER 2 and LINE NUMBER PLUS 2 are equivalent.

☐   ☐   **11.** Data names are frequently omitted (following the level number) when using report writer.

☐   ☐   **12.** It is possible for an FD not to have any 01 entries defined under it.

[1] The reader is referred to R. Grauer and M. Crawford, *The COBOL Environment,* Appendix C, Prentice-Hall, Inc., 1979, for additional examples, and to R. Grauer, *A COBOL Book of Practice and Reference* (Englewood Cliffs, N.J.: Prentice-Hall, Inc., 1981), for debugging examples.

Appendix B

COBOL RESERVED WORDS

ACCEPT	BOOLEAN	CONNECT
ACCESS	BOTTOM	*CONSOLE
*ACTUAL	BY	CONTAINS
ADD		CONVERSION
ADDRESS	CALL	CONVERTING
ADVANCING	*CANCEL	CONTROL
AFTER	CBL	CONTROLS
ALPHABET	CD	COPY
ALL	CF	*CORE-INDEX
ALPHABETIC	CH	CORR
ALPHANUMERIC	*CHANGED	CORRESPONDING
ALPHANUMERIC-EDITED	CHARACTER	COUNT
ALSO	CHARACTERS	*CSP
ALTER	CLOCK-UNITS	CURRENCY
ALTERNATE	CLOSE	*CURRENT-DATE
AND	COBOL	*CYL-INDEX
ANY	CODE	*CYL-OVERFLOW
*APPLY	CODE-SET	*C01
ARE	COLUMN	*C02
AREA	*COM-REG	*C03
AREAS	COMMA	*C04
ASCENDING	COMP	*C05
ASSIGN	*COMP-1	*C06
AT	*COMP-2	*C07
AUTHOR	*COMP-3	*C08
	*COMP-4	*C09
*BASIS	COMPUTATIONAL	*C10
BEFORE	*COMPUTATIONAL-1	*C11
*BEGINNING	*COMPUTATIONAL-2	*C12
BIT	*COMPUTATIONAL-3	
BITS	*COMPUTATIONAL-4	DATA
BLANK	COMPUTE	*DATE
BLOCK	CONFIGURATION	DATE-COMPILED

Note: This set of reserved words is based on the ANS 74 standard and CODASYL *Journal of Development* (January 1976). IBM extensions are identified with an asterisk.

DATE-WRITTEN	ENTER	INPUT-OUTPUT
*DAY	*ENTRY	*INSERT
DAY-OF-WEEK	ENVIRONMENT	INSPECT
DB-CONFLICT	EOP	INSTALLATION
DB-EXCEPTION	EQUAL	INTO
DB-KEY	EQUALS	INVALID
DB-PRIVATE-KEY	ERASE	IS
DB-REALM-NAME	ERROR	
DB-RECORD-NAME	ESI	JUST
DB-SET-NAME	EVERY	JUSTIFIED
DB-STATUS	EXCEEDS	
DE	EXCEPTION	KEEP
*DEBUG	EXCLUSIVE	KEY
DEBUG-CONTENTS	*EXHIBIT	
DEBUG-ITEM	EXIT	LABEL
DEBUG-LENGTH	EXTEND	*LABEL-RETURN
DEBUG-LINE	*EXTENDED-SEARCH	LAST
DEBUG-NAME		LEADING
DEBUG-NUMERIC-	FD	*LEAVE
CONTENTS	FILE	LEFT
DEBUG-SIZE	FILE-CONTROL	LENGTH
DEBUG-START	FILES	LESS
DEBUG-SUB	FILLER	LIMIT
DEBUG-SUB-ITEM	FINAL	LIMITS
DEBUG-SUB-N	FIND	LINAGE
DEBUG-SUB-NUM	FINISH	LINAGE-COUNTER
DEBUG-SUB-1	FIRST	LINE
DEBUG-SUB-2	FOOTING	LINE-COUNTER
DEBUG-SUB-3	FOR	LINES
DEBUGGING	FREE	LINKAGE
DECIMAL-POINT	FROM	LOCALLY
DECLARATIVES		LOCK
DELETE	GENERATE	LOW-VALUE
DELIMITED	GET	LOW-VALUES
DELIMITER	GIVING	
DEPENDING	GO	*MASTER-INDEX
DEPTH	*GOBACK	MEMBER
DESCENDING	GREATER	MEMBERS
DESTINATION	GROUP	MEMBERSHIP
DETAIL		MEMORY
DISABLE	HEADING	MERGE
*DISP	HIGH-VALUE	MESSAGE
DISPLAY	HIGH-VALUES	MODE
*DISPLAY-ST		MODIFY
DIVIDE	I-O	MODULES
DIVISION	I-O-CONTROL	*MORE-LABELS
DOWN	*ID	MOVE
DUPLICATE	IDENTIFICATION	MULTIPLE
DUPLICATES	IF	MULTIPLY
DYNAMIC	IN	
	INCLUDING	*NAMED
EGI	INDEX	NATIVE
*EJECT	INDEX-N	NEGATIVE
ELSE	INDEXED	NEXT
EMI	INDICATE	NO
ENABLE	INITIAL	*NOMINAL
END	INITIALIZE	NON-NULL
END-OF-PAGE	INITIATE	NOT
*ENDING	INPUT	*NSTD-REELS

NULL	REALM	*SKIP1
NUMBER	REALMS	*SKIP2
NUMERIC	REALM-NAME	*SKIP3
NUMERIC-EDITED	*RECEIVE	SORT
	RECORD	*SORT-CORE-SIZE
OBJECT-COMPUTER	RECORD-NAME	*SORT-FILE-SIZE
OCCURS	*RECORD-OVERFLOW	*SORT-MERGE
OF	RECORDS	*SORT-MESSAGE
OFF	REDEFINES	*SORT-MODE-SIZE
OMITTED	REEL	SORT-OPTION
ON	REFERENCE-MODIFIER	*SORT-RETURN
ONLY	REFERENCES	SOURCE
OPEN	RELATIVE	SOURCE-COMPUTER
OPTIONAL	RELEASE	SPACE
OR	*RELOAD	SPACES
ORDER	REMAINDER	SPECIAL-NAMES
ORGANIZATION	REMONITOR	STANDARD
OTHER	REMOVAL	STANDARD-1
*OTHERWISE	RENAMES	STANDARD-2
OUTPUT	*REORG-CRITERIA	START
OVERFLOW	REPLACING	STATUS
OWNER	REPORT	STOP
	REPORTING	STORE
PADDING	REPORTS	STRING
PAGE	*REREAD	SUB-QUEUE-1
PAGE-COUNTER	RERUN	SUB-QUEUE-2
*PASSWORD	RESERVE	SUB-QUEUE-3
PERFORM	RESET	SUB-SCHEMA
PERMANENT	RETAINING	SUBTRACT
PF	RETRIEVAL	SUM
PH	RETURN	SUPPRESS
PIC	*RETURN-CODE	SUSPEND
PICTURE	REVERSED	SYMBOLIC
PLUS	REWIND	SYNC
POINTER	REWRITE	SYNCHRONIZED
POSITION	RF	*SYSIN
*POSITIONING	RH	*SYSIPT
POSITIVE	RIGHT	*SYSLST
*PRINT-SWITCH	ROUNDED	*SYSOUT
PRINTING	RUN	*SYSPCH
PRIOR		*SYSPUNCH
PRIVACY	SAME	*S01
PROCEDURE	SD	*S02
PROCEDURES	SEARCH	*S03
PROCEED	SECTION	*S04
PROCESS	SECURITY	*S05
*PROGRAM	SEGMENT	
PROGRAM-ID	SEGMENT-LIMIT	TABLE
PROTECTED	SELECT	TALLY
PURGE	SELECTIVE	TALLYING
	SEND	TAPE
QUEUE	SENTENCE	TENANT
QUOTE	SEPARATE	TERMINAL
QUOTES	SEQUENCE	TERMINATE
	SEQUENTIAL	TEXT
RANDOM	*SERVICE	THAN
RD	SET	*THEN
READ	SIGN	THROUGH
*READY	SIZE	THRU

TIME	UNSTRING	VALUE
*TIME-OF-DAY	UNTIL	VALUES
TIMES	UP	VARYING
TO	UPDATE	
TOP	UPON	WHEN
*TOTALED	*UPSI-0	*WHEN-COMPILED
*TOTALING	*UPSI-1	WITH
*TRACE	*UPSI-2	WITHIN
*TRACK	*UPSI-3	WORDS
*TRACK-AREA	*UPSI-4	WORKING-STORAGE
*TRACK-LIMIT	*UPSI-5	WRITE
*TRACKS	*UPSI-6	*WRITE-ONLY
TRAILING	*UPSI-7	*WRITE-VERIFY
*TRANSFORM	USAGE	
TYPE	USAGE-MODE	ZERO
	USE	ZEROES
UNEQUAL	USING	ZEROS
UNIT		

Appendix C

IBM OS/VS COBOL REFERENCE FORMAT SUMMARY

IBM Reference Data

Operating System

IBM OS/VS COBOL

IBM OS/VS COBOL
Reference Format Summary

The general format of a COBOL source program is illustrated in these format summaries.

The first section. COBOL Program Structure, gives a general outline of the order in which COBOL Divisions. Sections. and Paragraphs must be written.

The following sections give detailed format summaries for each Division of a COBOL program and for the COBOL Special Features.

> IBM extensions to American National Standard COBOL. X3.23-1974, are shown within boxes.

All of these formats are more fully documented in the text of this publication IBM VS COBOL for OS/VS. GC26-3857-1.

COBOL Program Structure

IDENTIFICATION DIVISION.
[ID DIVISION.]

PROGRAM-ID. program-name.

[AUTHOR. [comment-entry] ...]
[INSTALLATION. [comment-entry] ...]
[DATE-WRITTEN. [comment-entry] ...]
[DATE-COMPILED. [comment-entry] ...]
[SECURITY. [comment-entry] ...]

ENVIRONMENT DIVISION.
CONFIGURATION SECTION.
[CONFIGURATION SECTION.]

SOURCE-COMPUTER. entry
OBJECT-COMPUTER. entry

[SPECIAL-NAMES. entry]
[[SPECIAL-NAMES. entry]]

[INPUT-OUTPUT SECTION.
FILE-CONTROL. entry
[I-O-CONTROL. entry]]

DATA DIVISION.

[FILE SECTION.
[file-description entry
[record-description entry] ...] ...]

[WORKING-STORAGE SECTION.

[data item description entry]
[record-description entry] ...]

[LINKAGE SECTION.

[data item description entry]
[record-description entry] ...]

[COMMUNICATION SECTION.

[communication description entry
[record-description entry] ...] ...]

[REPORT SECTION.
[report description entry
[report-group description entry] ...] ...]

Procedure Division – Format 1

PROCEDURE DIVISION [USING identifier-1 [identifier-2]...].

[DECLARATIVES.

{section-name SECTION [priority-number]. USE Sentence.

```
[paragraph-name. [sentence] ... ] ... } ...
END DECLARATIVES.]                            .
{section-name SECTION [priority-number].
[paragraph-name. [sentence] ... ] ... } ...
```

Procedure Division   Format 2

```
PROCEDURE DIVISION [USING identifier-1 [identifier-2]...].

{ paragraph-name. [sentence] ... } ...
```

Identification Division Formats

```
\ IDENTIFICATION DIVISION. /
/ ID DIVISION.            \

PROGRAM-ID. program-name.

[AUTHOR. [comment-entry] ... ]
[INSTALLATION. [comment-entry] ... ]
[DATE-WRITTEN. [comment-entry] ... ]
[DATE-COMPILED. [comment-entry] ... ]
[SECURITY. [comment-entry] ... ]
```

Environment Division Formats

Configuration Section

```
ENVIRONMENT DIVISION.

\ [CONFIGURATION SECTION. /
/ [CONFIGURATION SECTION.] \

SOURCE-COMPUTER. computer-name [WITH DEBUGGING MODE]

OBJECT-COMPUTER. computer-name
                        ⎧ WORDS      ⎫
     [MEMORY SIZE integer⎨ CHARACTERS ⎬  ]
                        ⎩ MODULES     ⎭
        [PROGRAM COLLATING SEQUENCE IS alphabet-name]
        [SEGMENT-LIMIT IS priority-number].
[SPECIAL-NAMES.
     [function-name-1 IS mnemonic-name] ...
     [function-name-2 [IS mnemonic-name]

  ⎧ ON STATUS IS condition-name-1]      ⎫
  ⎪    [OFF STATUS IS condition-name-2] ⎪ ] ...
  ⎨ OFF STATUS IS condition-name-2      ⎬
  ⎩    [ON STATUS IS condition-name-1]  ⎭

     [alphabet-name IS
     ⎧                                      ⎫
     ⎪ STANDARD-1                           ⎪
     ⎪ NATIVE                               ⎪
     ⎪          ⎡ ⎧THROUGH⎫            ⎤    ⎪
     ⎪ literal-1 ⎢ ⎨THRU   ⎬  literal-2 ⎥    ⎪
     ⎨          ⎢ ⎩       ⎭            ⎥    ⎬ ]...
     ⎪          ⎢ ALSO literal-3       ⎥    ⎪
     ⎪          ⎣   [ALSO literal-4] ...⎦    ⎪
     ⎪          ⎡ ⎧THROUGH⎫            ⎤    ⎪
     ⎪ [literal-5⎢ ⎨THRU   ⎬  literal-6 ⎥ ]..⎪
     ⎪          ⎢ ⎩       ⎭            ⎥    ⎪
     ⎩          ⎢ ALSO literal-7       ⎥    ⎭
                ⎣   [ALSO literal-8] ..⎦
     [CURRENCY SIGN IS literal-9]
    \ [DECIMAL-POINT IS COMMA].]        /
    / [DECIMAL-POINT IS COMMA].]]       \
```

Input-Output Section

Note: The key word FILE-CONTROL appears only once, at the beginning of the paragraph before the first File-Control entry.

FILE-CONTROL Paragraph   Sequential Files

```
FILE-CONTROL.
     SELECT [OPTIONAL] file-name
     ASSIGN TO assignment-name-1 [assignment-name-2] ...
                        ⎡ AREA  ⎤
     [RESERVE integer   ⎢       ⎥  ]
                        ⎣ AREAS ⎦
     [ORGANIZATION IS SEQUENTIAL]
     [ACCESS MODE IS SEQUENTIAL]
     [PASSWORD IS data-name-1]

     [FILE STATUS IS data-name-2].
```

FILE-CONTROL Entry   Indexed Files

```
FILE-CONTROL.
     SELECT file-name
     ASSIGN TO assignment-name-1 [assignment-name-2] ...
                        ⎡ AREA  ⎤
     [RESERVE integer   ⎢       ⎥  ]
                        ⎣ AREAS ⎦
     ORGANIZATION IS INDEXED
                       ⎧ SEQUENTIAL ⎫
     [ACCESS MODE IS   ⎨ RANDOM     ⎬  ]
                       ⎩ DYNAMIC    ⎭
     RECORD KEY IS data-name-3
          [PASSWORD IS data-name-1]
     [ALTERNATE RECORD KEY IS data-name-4
          [PASSWORD IS data-name-5]
        [WITH DUPLICATES] ] ...
     [FILE STATUS IS data-name-2].
```

FILE-CONTROL Entry – Relative Files

```
FILE-CONTROL.
     SELECT file-name
     ASSIGN TO assignment-name-1 [assignment-name-2] ...
                        ⎡ AREA  ⎤
     [RESERVE integer   ⎢       ⎥  ]
                        ⎣ AREAS ⎦
     ORGANIZATION IS RELATIVE
     [ACCESS MODE IS
     ⎧ SEQUENTIAL [RELATIVE KEY IS data-name-6]        ⎫
     ⎨ RANDOM                                          ⎬ ]
     ⎩ DYNAMIC     RELATIVE KEY IS data-name-7         ⎭
     [PASSWORD IS data-name-1]

     [FILE STATUS IS data-name-2].
```

Note: The key word I-O-CONTROL appears only once, at the beginning of the paragraph before the first I-O-Control entry.

I-O-CONTROL Paragraph – Physical Sequential Files

```
I-O-CONTROL.
     [RERUN ON assignment-name
              ⎧ integer-1 RECORDS ⎫
     EVERY    ⎨          ⎧ REEL ⎫ ⎬ OF file-name-1] ...
              ⎩ [END OF] ⎨ UNIT ⎭ ⎭
```

```
           ┌RECORD    ┐
    [SAME   │SORT      │ AREA
           └SORT-MERGE┘

       FOR file-name-2 {file-name-3} ... ] ...

    [MULTIPLE FILE TAPE CONTAINS

       file-name-4 [POSITION integer-2]

       [file-name-5 [POSITION integer-3]] ... ] ... .
```

I-O-CONTROL Paragraph – VSAM Files

```
I-O-CONTROL.

    [RERUN ON assignment-name

           EVERY integer-1 RECORDS OF file-name-1] ...

           ┌RECORD    ┐
    [SAME   │SORT      │ AREA
           └SORT-MERGE┘

           FOR file-name-2 {file-name-3} ...] ... .
```

Data Division Formats

File Section Formats

Format 1 – Physical Sequential Files

```
FILE SECTION.

FD  file-name
                                                      ┌CHARACTERS┐
    [BLOCK CONTAINS [integer-1 TO] integer-2          │          │]
                                                      └RECORDS   ┘

    [RECORD CONTAINS [integer-3 TO] integer-4 CHARACTERS]

          ┌RECORD IS   ┐  ┌STANDARD┐
    LABEL │RECORDS ARE │  │OMITTED │
          └            ┘  └        ┘

                                      ┌data-name-1┐
    [VALUE OF system-name-1 IS        │literal-1  │
                                      └           ┘

                                ┌data-name-2┐
        [system-name-2 IS       │literal-2  │  ] ... ]
                                └           ┘

          ┌RECORD IS  ┐
    [DATA │RECORDS ARE│ data-name-3 [data-name-4] ... ]
          └           ┘

               ┌data-name-5┐
    [LINAGE IS │integer-5  │ LINES
               └           ┘

                              ┌data-name-6┐
        [WITH FOOTING AT      │integer-6  │ ]
                              └           ┘

                       ┌data-name-7┐
        [LINES AT TOP  │integer-7  │ ]
                       └           ┘

                          ┌data-name-8┐
        [LINES AT BOTTOM  │integer-8  │ ]
                          └           ┘

   ┌─────────────────────────────────────────────────────┐
   │ ┌REPORT IS   ┐                                       │
   [ │REPORTS ARE │  report-name-1 [report-name-2] ... ]  │
   │ └            ┘                                       │
   └─────────────────────────────────────────────────────┘

[CODE-SET IS alphabet-name].
```

Format 2 – VSAM Files (Sequential, Indexed, Relative)

```
FILE SECTION.

FD  file-name
                                                   ┌CHARACTERS┐
    [BLOCK CONTAINS [integer-1 TO] integer-2       │          │]
                                                   └RECORDS   ┘

    [RECORD CONTAINS [integer-3 TO] integer-4 CHARACTERS]

          ┌RECORD IS  ┐  ┌STANDARD┐
    LABEL │RECORDS ARE│  │OMITTED │
          └           ┘  └        ┘

                                   ┌data-name-1┐
    [VALUE OF system name-1 IS     │literal-1  │
                                   └           ┘
```

```
                                  ┌data-name-2┐
        [system-name-2 IS         │literal-2  │  ] ... ]
                                  └           ┘

          ┌RECORD IS  ┐
    [DATA │RECORDS ARE│ data-name-3 [data-name-4] ... ].
          └           ┘

        ┌data-name   ┐
01-49   │FILLER Clause│
        └            ┘

        [REDEFINES Clause]
        [BLANK WHEN ZERO Clause]
        [JUSTIFIED Clause]
        [OCCURS Clause]
        [PICTURE Clause]
        [SIGN Clause]
        [SYNCHRONIZED Clause]
        [USAGE Clause].

[88     condition-name VALUE Clause.]

[66     RENAMES Clause.]
```

Note: Details of the above data description clauses are given in the following WORKING-STORAGE SECTION formats.

Working-Storage Section Formats

```
WORKING-STORAGE SECTION.

┌77   ┐  ┌data-name-1┐
│01-49│  │FILLER     │
└     ┘  └           ┘

    [REDEFINES data-name-2]
    [BLANK WHEN ZERO]
     ┌JUSTIFIED┐
    [│JUST     │ RIGHT]
     └         ┘
    [OCCURS Clause -- See Table Handling formats]
     ┌PICTURE┐
    [│PIC    │ IS character-string]
     └       ┘

                  ┌LEADING ┐
    [[SIGN IS]    │TRAILING│   [SEPARATE CHARACTER]]
                  └        ┘

     ┌SYNCHRONIZED┐  ┌LEFT ┐
    [│SYNC        │  │RIGHT│ ]
     └            ┘  └     ┘

                  ┌DISPLAY         ┐
                  │INDEX           │
                  │COMPUTATIONAL   │
                  │COMP            │
    [[USAGE IS]   │COMPUTATIONAL-3 │ ]
                  │COMP-3          │
                  │COMPUTATIONAL-4 │
                  │COMP-4          │
                  └                ┘

    [VALUE IS literal].

                         ┌VALUE IS   ┐
[88  condition-name      │VALUES ARE │
                         └           ┘

                ┌THROUGH┐
    literal-1 [ │THRU   │ literal-2]
                └       ┘

                      ┌THROUGH┐
        [literal-3 [  │THRU   │ literal-4] ] ...].
                      └       ┘

[66 data-name-1 RENAMES data-name-2

     ┌THROUGH┐
   [ │THRU   │ data-name-3].]
     └       ┘
```

Note: Valid clauses in the LINKAGE SECTION are given with the formats for the Subprogram Linkage feature. Valid clauses in the COMMUNICATION SECTION are given with the formats for the Communication Feature.

Valid formats for the REPORT SECTION are given with the formats for the Report Writer Feature.

Procedure Division Formats

Conditional Expressions

Class Condition

identifier is [NOT] $\begin{Bmatrix} \text{NUMERIC} \\ \text{ALPHABETIC} \end{Bmatrix}$

Condition – Name Condition

condition-name

Relation Condition

operand-1 IS [NOT] $\begin{Bmatrix} \underline{\text{GREATER}}\ \text{THAN} \\ > \\ \underline{\text{LESS}}\ \text{THAN} \\ < \\ \underline{\text{EQUAL}}\ \text{TO} \\ = \end{Bmatrix}$ operand-2

Note: Operand-1 and operand-2 may each be an identifier, a literal, or an arithmetic expression. There must be at least one reference to an identifier.

Sign Condition

operand IS [NOT] $\begin{Bmatrix} \underline{\text{POSITIVE}} \\ \underline{\text{NEGATIVE}} \\ \underline{\text{ZERO}} \end{Bmatrix}$

Note: Operand must be a numeric identifier or an arithmetic expression.

Switch – Status Condition

condition-name

Negated Simple Condition

NOT simple-condition

Combined Condition

condition $\begin{Bmatrix} \underline{\text{AND}} \\ \underline{\text{OR}} \end{Bmatrix}$ condition ...

Abbreviated Combined Relation Condition

relation-condition $\{ \begin{Bmatrix} \underline{\text{AND}} \\ \underline{\text{OR}} \end{Bmatrix}$ [NOT]

[relational-operator] object } ...

Procedure Division Header

PROCEDURE DIVISION [USING identifier-1 [identifier-2] ...].

ACCEPT Statement (for Data Transfer)

ACCEPT identifier [FROM $\begin{Bmatrix} \text{mnemonic-name} \\ \boxed{\text{function-name}} \end{Bmatrix}$]

ACCEPT Statement (for System Information Transfer)

ACCEPT identifier FROM $\begin{Bmatrix} \underline{\text{DATE}} \\ \underline{\text{DAY}} \\ \underline{\text{TIME}} \end{Bmatrix}$

ADD Statement – Format 1

ADD $\begin{Bmatrix} \text{identifier-1} \\ \text{literal-1} \end{Bmatrix}$ $\begin{bmatrix} \text{identifier-2} \\ \text{literal-2} \end{bmatrix}$ ...

TO identifier-m [ROUNDED]
    [identifier-n [ROUNDED]]...

[ON SIZE ERROR imperative-statement]

ADD Statement – Format 2

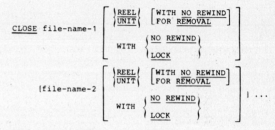

ADD $\begin{Bmatrix} \text{identifier-1} \\ \text{literal-1} \end{Bmatrix}$ $\begin{Bmatrix} \text{identifier-2} \\ \text{literal-2} \end{Bmatrix}$ $\begin{bmatrix} \text{identifier-3} \\ \text{literal-3} \end{bmatrix}$ ...

GIVING identifier-m [ROUNDED]
    [identifier-n [ROUNDED]] ...

[ON SIZE ERROR imperative-statement]

ADD Statement – Format 3

ADD $\begin{Bmatrix} \underline{\text{CORRESPONDING}} \\ \underline{\text{CORR}} \end{Bmatrix}$

identifier-1 TO identifier-2 [ROUNDED]
[ON SIZE ERROR imperative-statement]

ALTER Statement

ALTER procedure-name-1
        TO [PROCEED TO] procedure-name-2
[procedure-name-3
        TO [PROCEED TO] procedure-name-4] ...

CLOSE Statement   Physical Sequential Files

CLOSE file-name-1 $\begin{bmatrix} \begin{Bmatrix} \underline{\text{REEL}} \\ \underline{\text{UNIT}} \end{Bmatrix} \begin{bmatrix} \text{WITH NO}\ \underline{\text{REWIND}} \\ \text{FOR}\ \underline{\text{REMOVAL}} \end{bmatrix} \\ \text{WITH}\ \begin{Bmatrix} \text{NO}\ \underline{\text{REWIND}} \\ \underline{\text{LOCK}} \end{Bmatrix} \end{bmatrix}$

[file-name-2 $\begin{bmatrix} \begin{Bmatrix} \underline{\text{REEL}} \\ \underline{\text{UNIT}} \end{Bmatrix} \begin{bmatrix} \text{WITH NO}\ \underline{\text{REWIND}} \\ \text{FOR}\ \underline{\text{REMOVAL}} \end{bmatrix} \\ \text{WITH}\ \begin{Bmatrix} \text{NO}\ \underline{\text{REWIND}} \\ \underline{\text{LOCK}} \end{Bmatrix} \end{bmatrix}$] ...

CLOSE Statement   VSAM Files

CLOSE file-name-1   [WITH LOCK]
    [file-name-2   [WITH LOCK]] ...

COMPUTE Statement

COMPUTE identifier-1 [ROUNDED]
    [identifier-2 [ROUNDED]]...
    = arithmetic-expression
    [ON SIZE ERROR imperative-statement]

DECLARATIVES Procedures

PROCEDURE DIVISION [USING identifier-1 [identifier-2] ...].
DECLARATIVES.
{section-name SECTION [priority-number]. USE sentence.
[paragraph-name. [sentence.] ...] ...} ...}
END DECLARATIVES.

DELETE Statement

DELETE file-name RECORD
    [INVALID KEY imperative-statement]

DISPLAY Statement

DISPLAY $\begin{Bmatrix} \text{identifier-1} \\ \text{literal-1} \end{Bmatrix}$ $\begin{bmatrix} \text{identifier-2} \\ \text{literal-2} \end{bmatrix}$ ...

[UPON $\begin{Bmatrix} \text{mnemonic-name} \\ \boxed{\text{function-name}} \end{Bmatrix}$]

DIVIDE Statement   Format 1

DIVIDE $\begin{Bmatrix} \text{identifier-1} \\ \text{literal-1} \end{Bmatrix}$

INTO   identifier-2 [ROUNDED]
    [identifier-3 [ROUNDED]]...
[ON SIZE ERROR imperative-statement]

APPENDIX C: IBM OS/VS COBOL   **373**

DIVIDE Statement   Format 2

$$\underline{\text{DIVIDE}} \quad \begin{Bmatrix} \text{identifier-1} \\ \text{literal-1} \end{Bmatrix} \begin{Bmatrix} \underline{\text{INTO}} \\ \underline{\text{BY}} \end{Bmatrix} \begin{Bmatrix} \text{identifier-2} \\ \text{literal-2} \end{Bmatrix}$$

$$\underline{\text{GIVING}} \quad \text{identifier-3 [\underline{ROUNDED}]}$$

$$\text{[identifier-4 [\underline{ROUNDED}]] ...}$$

$$\text{[ON \underline{SIZE} \underline{ERROR} imperative-statement]}$$

DIVIDE Statement – Format 3

$$\underline{\text{DIVIDE}} \quad \begin{Bmatrix} \text{identifier-1} \\ \text{literal-1} \end{Bmatrix} \begin{Bmatrix} \underline{\text{INTO}} \\ \underline{\text{BY}} \end{Bmatrix} \begin{Bmatrix} \text{identifier-2} \\ \text{literal-2} \end{Bmatrix}$$

$$\underline{\text{GIVING}} \text{ identifier-3 [\underline{ROUNDED}]}$$

$$\text{[\underline{REMAINDER} identifier-4]}$$

$$\text{[ON \underline{SIZE} \underline{ERROR} imperative-statement]}$$

ENTER Statement

    $\underline{\text{ENTER}}$ language-name [routine-name].

EXIT Statement

paragraph-name. $\underline{\text{EXIT}}$ [$\underline{\text{PROGRAM}}$].

Note: The paragraph-name is not part of the EXIT statement format; however, it is always required preceding an EXIT statement.

GO TO Statement – Unconditional

    $\underline{\text{GO}}$ TO procedure-name-1

GO TO Statement – Conditional

    $\underline{\text{GO}}$ TO procedure-name-1 [procedure-name-2] ...
        procedure-name-n $\underline{\text{DEPENDING}}$ ON identifier

GO TO Statement – Altered

    $\underline{\text{GO}}$ TO.

IF Statement

$$\underline{\text{IF}} \text{ condition} \begin{Bmatrix} \text{statement-1} \\ \underline{\text{NEXT}} \ \underline{\text{SENTENCE}} \end{Bmatrix} \begin{Bmatrix} \underline{\text{ELSE}} \text{ statement-2} \\ \underline{\text{ELSE}} \ \underline{\text{NEXT}} \ \underline{\text{SENTENCE}} \end{Bmatrix}$$

Note: ELSE NEXT SENTENCE may be omitted if it immediately precedes the period for the conditional statement.

INSPECT Statement

    $\underline{\text{INSPECT}}$ identifier-1

    [$\underline{\text{TALLYING}}$ {identifier-2

$$\underline{\text{FOR}} \begin{Bmatrix} \underline{\text{ALL}} \\ \underline{\text{LEADING}} \\ \underline{\text{CHARACTERS}} \end{Bmatrix} \begin{Bmatrix} \text{identifier-3} \\ \text{literal-1} \end{Bmatrix}$$

$$\left[\begin{Bmatrix} \underline{\text{BEFORE}} \\ \underline{\text{AFTER}} \end{Bmatrix} \underline{\text{INITIAL}} \begin{Bmatrix} \text{identifier-4} \\ \text{literal-2} \end{Bmatrix} \right] \} ... \} ...]$$

    [$\underline{\text{REPLACING}}$

$$\begin{Bmatrix} \underline{\text{CHARACTERS}} \ \underline{\text{BY}} \begin{Bmatrix} \text{identifier-6} \\ \text{literal-4} \end{Bmatrix} \\ \left[\begin{Bmatrix} \underline{\text{BEFORE}} \\ \underline{\text{AFTER}} \end{Bmatrix} \underline{\text{INITIAL}} \begin{Bmatrix} \text{identifier-7} \\ \text{literal-5} \end{Bmatrix} \right] \\ \begin{Bmatrix} \underline{\text{ALL}} \\ \underline{\text{LEADING}} \\ \underline{\text{FIRST}} \end{Bmatrix} \{ \begin{Bmatrix} \text{identifier-5} \\ \text{literal-3} \end{Bmatrix} \underline{\text{BY}} \begin{Bmatrix} \text{identifier-6} \\ \text{literal-4} \end{Bmatrix} \\ \left[\begin{Bmatrix} \underline{\text{BEFORE}} \\ \underline{\text{AFTER}} \end{Bmatrix} \underline{\text{INITIAL}} \begin{Bmatrix} \text{identifier-7} \\ \text{literal-5} \end{Bmatrix} \right] \} ... \} ...$$

Note: Either the TALLYING option or the REPLACING option must be specified; both may be specified.

MOVE Statement   Format 1

$$\underline{\text{MOVE}} \begin{Bmatrix} \text{identifier-1} \\ \text{literal} \end{Bmatrix} \underline{\text{TO}} \text{ identifier-2 [identifier-3] ...}$$

MULTIPLY Statement   Format 1

$$\underline{\text{MOVE}} \begin{Bmatrix} \underline{\text{CORRESPONDING}} \\ \underline{\text{CORR}} \end{Bmatrix} \text{identifier-1 } \underline{\text{TO}} \text{ identifier-2}$$

MULTIPLY Statement – Format 1

$$\underline{\text{MULTIPLY}} \begin{Bmatrix} \text{identifier-1} \\ \text{literal-1} \end{Bmatrix} \underline{\text{BY}} \text{ identifier-2}$$

$$\text{[\underline{ROUNDED}]}$$

$$\text{[identifier-3 [\underline{ROUNDED}]] ...}$$

$$\text{[ON \underline{SIZE} \underline{ERROR} imperative-statement]}$$

MULTIPLY Statement – Format 2

$$\underline{\text{MULTIPLY}} \begin{Bmatrix} \text{identifier-1} \\ \text{literal-1} \end{Bmatrix} \underline{\text{BY}} \begin{Bmatrix} \text{identifier-2} \\ \text{literal-2} \end{Bmatrix}$$

$$\underline{\text{GIVING}} \text{ identifier-3 [\underline{ROUNDED}]}$$

$$\text{[identifier-4 [\underline{ROUNDED}]] ...}$$

$$\text{[ON \underline{SIZE} \underline{ERROR} imperative-statement]}$$

OPEN Statement – Sequential Files

$$\underline{\text{OPEN}} \begin{Bmatrix} \underline{\text{INPUT}} \text{ file-name-1} \begin{bmatrix} \underline{\text{REVERSED}} \\ \text{WITH NO \underline{REWIND}} \end{bmatrix} \\ \text{[file-name-2} \begin{bmatrix} \underline{\text{REVERSED}} \\ \text{WITH NO \underline{REWIND}} \end{bmatrix} \text{] ...} \\ \underline{\text{OUTPUT}} \text{ file-name-3 [WITH NO \underline{REWIND}]} \\ \text{[file-name-4 [WITH NO \underline{REWIND}]] ...} \\ \underline{\text{I-O}} \text{ file-name-5 [file-name-6] ...} \\ \underline{\text{EXTEND}} \text{ file-name-7 [file-name-8] ...} \end{Bmatrix} ...$$

OPEN Statement – Indexed Files

$$\underline{\text{OPEN}} \begin{Bmatrix} \underline{\text{INPUT}} \text{ file-name-1 [file-name-2] ...} \\ \underline{\text{OUTPUT}} \text{ file-name-3 [file-name-4] ...} \\ \underline{\text{I-O}} \text{ file-name-5 [file-name-6] ...} \\ \boxed{\underline{\text{EXTEND}} \text{ file-name-7 [file-name-8] ...}} \end{Bmatrix}$$

OPEN Statement - Relative Files

$$\underline{\text{OPEN}} \begin{Bmatrix} \underline{\text{INPUT}} \text{ file-name-1 [file-name-2] ...} \\ \underline{\text{OUTPUT}} \text{ file-name-3 [file-name-4] ...} \\ \underline{\text{I-O}} \text{ file-name-5 [file-name-6] ...} \end{Bmatrix} ...$$

PERFORM Statement   Basic PERFORM

$$\underline{\text{PERFORM}} \text{ procedure-name-1 } \left[\begin{Bmatrix} \underline{\text{THROUGH}} \\ \underline{\text{THRU}} \end{Bmatrix} \text{procedure-name-2} \right]$$

PERFORM Statement   TIMES Option

$$\underline{\text{PERFORM}} \text{ procedure-name-1 } \left[\begin{Bmatrix} \underline{\text{THROUGH}} \\ \underline{\text{THRU}} \end{Bmatrix} \text{procedure-name-2} \right]$$

$$\begin{Bmatrix} \text{identifier-1} \\ \text{integer-1} \end{Bmatrix} \underline{\text{TIMES}}$$

PERFORM Statement   Conditional PERFORM

PERFORM procedure-name-1 [$\left\{ \begin{array}{l} \underline{THROUGH} \\ \underline{THRU} \end{array} \right\}$ procedure-name-2]

UNTIL condition-1

PERFORM Statement – VARYING Option

PERFORM procedure-name-1 [$\left\{ \begin{array}{l} \underline{THROUGH} \\ \underline{THRU} \end{array} \right\}$ procedure-name-2]

$\underline{VARYING}$ $\left\{ \begin{array}{l} \text{index-name-1} \\ \text{identifier-1} \end{array} \right\}$ $\underline{FROM}$ $\left\{ \begin{array}{l} \text{index-name-2} \\ \text{literal-2} \\ \text{identifier-2} \end{array} \right\}$

$\underline{BY}$ $\left\{ \begin{array}{l} \text{literal-3} \\ \text{identifier-3} \end{array} \right\}$ $\underline{UNTIL}$ condition-1

[$\underline{AFTER}$ $\left\{ \begin{array}{l} \text{index-name-4} \\ \text{identifier-4} \end{array} \right\}$ $\underline{FROM}$ $\left\{ \begin{array}{l} \text{index-name-5} \\ \text{literal-5} \\ \text{identifier-5} \end{array} \right\}$

$\underline{BY}$ $\left\{ \begin{array}{l} \text{literal-6} \\ \text{identifier-6} \end{array} \right\}$ $\underline{UNTIL}$ condition-2

[$\underline{AFTER}$ $\left\{ \begin{array}{l} \text{index-name-7} \\ \text{identifier-7} \end{array} \right\}$ $\underline{FROM}$ $\left\{ \begin{array}{l} \text{index-name-8} \\ \text{literal-8} \\ \text{identifier-8} \end{array} \right\}$

$\underline{BY}$ $\left\{ \begin{array}{l} \text{literal-9} \\ \text{identifier-9} \end{array} \right\}$ $\underline{UNTIL}$ condition-3]]

READ Statement – Sequential Retrieval

$\underline{READ}$ file-name [$\underline{NEXT}$] RECORD [$\underline{INTO}$ identifier]
[AT $\underline{END}$ imperative-statment]

READ Statement – Random Retrieval

$\underline{READ}$ file-name RECORD [$\underline{INTO}$ identifier]
[$\underline{KEY}$ IS data-name]
[$\underline{INVALID}$ KEY imperative-statemnt]

REWRITE Statement

$\underline{REWRITE}$ record-name [$\underline{FROM}$ identifier]
[$\underline{INVALID}$ KEY imperative-statement]

START Statement

$\underline{START}$ file-name [$\underline{KEY}$ IS $\left\{ \begin{array}{l} \underline{EQUAL}\ TO \\ \underline{=} \\ \underline{GREATER}\ THAN \\ \underline{>} \\ \underline{NOT\ LESS}\ THAN \\ \underline{NOT} < \end{array} \right\}$ data-name]

[$\underline{INVALID}$ KEY imperative-statement]

STOP Statement

$\underline{STOP}$ $\left\{ \begin{array}{l} \underline{RUN} \\ \text{literal} \end{array} \right\}$

STRING Statement

$\underline{STRING}$ $\left\{ \begin{array}{l} \text{identifier-1} \\ \text{literal-1} \end{array} \right\}$ $\left[\begin{array}{l} \text{identifier-2} \\ \text{literal-2} \end{array} \right]$ ...

$\underline{DELIMITED}$ BY $\left\{ \begin{array}{l} \text{identifier-3} \\ \text{literal-3} \\ \underline{SIZE} \end{array} \right\}$

[$\left\{ \begin{array}{l} \text{identifier-4} \\ \text{literal-4} \end{array} \right\}$ $\left[\begin{array}{l} \text{identifier-5} \\ \text{literal-5} \end{array} \right]$ ...

$\underline{DELIMITED}$ BY $\left\{ \begin{array}{l} \text{identifier-6} \\ \text{literal-6} \\ \underline{SIZE} \end{array} \right\}$] ...

$\underline{INTO}$ identifier-7
[WITH $\underline{POINTER}$ identifier-8]
[ON $\underline{OVERFLOW}$ imperative-statment]

SUBTRACT Statement – Format 1

$\underline{SUBTRACT}$ $\left\{ \begin{array}{l} \text{identifier-1} \\ \text{literal-1} \end{array} \right\}$ $\left[\begin{array}{l} \text{identifier-2} \\ \text{literal-2} \end{array} \right]$ ...

$\underline{FROM}$ identifier-m [$\underline{ROUNDED}$]
[identifier-n [$\underline{ROUNDED}$]] ...
[ON $\underline{SIZE}$ ERROR imperative-statement]

SUBTRACT Statement   Format 2

$\underline{SUBTRACT}$ $\left\{ \begin{array}{l} \text{identifier-1} \\ \text{literal-1} \end{array} \right\}$ $\left[\begin{array}{l} \text{identifier-2} \\ \text{literal-2} \end{array} \right]$ ...

$\underline{FROM}$ $\left\{ \begin{array}{l} \text{identifier-m} \\ \text{literal-m} \end{array} \right\}$

$\underline{GIVING}$ identifier-n [$\underline{ROUNDED}$]
[identifier-o [$\underline{ROUNDED}$]] ...
[ON $\underline{SIZE}$ ERROR imperative-statement]

SUBTRACT Statement – Format 3

$\underline{SUBTRACT}$ $\left\{ \begin{array}{l} \underline{CORRESPONDING} \\ \underline{CORR} \end{array} \right\}$

identifier-1 $\underline{FROM}$ identifier-2 [$\underline{ROUNDED}$]
[ON $\underline{SIZE}$ ERROR imperative-statement]

TRANSFORM Statement

```
TRANSFORM identifier-3 CHARACTERS
   FROM  { figurative-constant-1
           nonnumeric-literal-1
           identifier-1           }
   TO    { figurative-constant-2
           nonnumeric-literal-2
           identifier-2           }
```

UNSTRING Statement

$\underline{UNSTRING}$ identifier-1

[$\underline{DELIMITED}$ BY [$\underline{ALL}$] $\left\{ \begin{array}{l} \text{identifier-2} \\ \text{literal-1} \end{array} \right\}$

[$\underline{OR}$ [$\underline{ALL}$] $\left\{ \begin{array}{l} \text{identifier-3} \\ \text{literal-2} \end{array} \right\}$] ...]

$\underline{INTO}$ identifier-4
   [$\underline{DELIMITER}$ IN identifier-5]
   [$\underline{COUNT}$ IN identifier-6]
   [identifier-7
   [$\underline{DELIMITER}$ IN identifier-8]
   [$\underline{COUNT}$ IN identifier-9]] ...
[WITH $\underline{POINTER}$ identifier-10]
[$\underline{TALLYING}$ IN identifier-11]
[ON $\underline{OVERFLOW}$ imperative-statement]

USE Sentence – EXCEPTION/ERROR Procedures

section-name $\underline{SECTION}$ [priority-number].

$\underline{USE}$ $\underline{AFTER}$ STANDARD $\left\{ \begin{array}{l} \underline{EXCEPTION} \\ \underline{ERROR} \end{array} \right\}$ $\underline{PROCEDURE}$

ON $\left\{ \begin{array}{l} \text{file-name-1 [file-name-2] ...} \\ \underline{INPUT} \\ \underline{OUTPUT} \\ \underline{I-O} \\ \underline{EXTEND} \end{array} \right\}$

WRITE Statement – Physical Sequential Files

```
    WRITE record-name [FROM identifier]

    [ ⎧ BEFORE ⎫ ADVANCING ⎧ identifier-2 ⎫ [ LINE  ] ⎫
      ⎩ AFTER  ⎭           ⎨ integer      ⎬ [ LINES ] ⎬
                           ⎨ mnemonic-name⎬           ⎭
                           ⎩ PAGE         ⎭

    [AT ⎧ END-OF-PAGE ⎫ imperative-statement]
        ⎩ EOP         ⎭
```

WRITE Statement   VSAM Sequential Files

```
    WRITE record-name [FROM identifier]
```

WRITE Statement   VSAM Indexed and Relative Files

```
    WRITE record-name [FROM identifier]
        [INVALID KEY imperative-statement]
```

Data Reference Formats

Qualification

Data Item References

```
    ⎧ data-name-1    ⎫ [ ⎧ OF ⎫ data-name-2 ] ...
    ⎩ condition-name ⎭     ⎩ IN ⎭
```

Procedure Name References

```
    paragraph-name [ ⎧ OF ⎫ section-name]
                     ⎩ IN ⎭
```

COPY Library References

```
    text-name [ ⎧ OF ⎫ library-name]
                ⎩ IN ⎭
```

Subscripting

```
    ⎧ data-name-1    ⎫ [ ⎧ OF ⎫ data-name-2] ...
    ⎩ condition-name ⎭     ⎩ IN ⎭

        (subscript [subscript [subscript]])
```

Indexing

```
    ⎧ data-name-1    ⎫ [ ⎧ OF ⎫ data-name-2] ...
    ⎩ condition-name ⎭     ⎩ IN ⎭

    ( ⎧ index-name-1 [ ⎧ ± ⎫ literal-2] ⎫
      ⎩ literal-1                       ⎭
                       .
     [ ⎧ index-name-2 [ ⎧ ± ⎫ literal-4] ⎫
       ⎩ literal-3                        ⎭
      [ ⎧ index-name-3 [ ⎧ ± ⎫ literal-6] ⎫ ] ])
        ⎩ literal-5                        ⎭
```

Table Handling Formats

Table Handling Data Division

OCCURS Clause – Fixed Length Tables

```
    OCCURS integer-2 TIMES

    [ ⎧ ASCENDING  ⎫ KEY IS data-name-2 [data-name-3]...].
      ⎩ DESCENDING ⎭

    [INDEXED BY index-name-1 [index-name-2]...]
```

OCCURS Clause – Variable Length Tables

```
    OCCURS integer-1 TO integer-2 TIMES
```

```
        DEPENDING ON data-name-1

    [ ⎧ ASCENDING  ⎫ KEY IS data-name-2 [data-name-3]...]...
      ⎩ DESCENDING ⎭

    [INDEXED BY index-name-1 [index-name-2]... ]
```

USAGE IS INDEX Clause

```
    [USAGE IS] INDEX
```

Table Handling Procedure Division

Format 1 – Serial Search

```
    SEARCH identifier-1 [VARYING ⎧ identifier-2 ⎫ ]
                                 ⎩ index-name-1 ⎭

    [AT END imperative-statement-1]

    WHEN condition-1 ⎧ imperative-statement-2 ⎫
                     ⎩ NEXT SENTENCE          ⎭

    [WHEN condition-2 ⎧ imperative-statement-3 ⎫ ] ...
                      ⎩ NEXT SENTENCE          ⎭
```

Format 2   Binary Search

```
    SEARCH ALL identifier-1
    [AT END imperative-statement-1]

    WHEN ⎧ relation-condition-1 ⎫
         ⎩ condition-name-1     ⎭

    [AND ⎧ relation-condition-2 ⎫ ] ...
         ⎩ condition-name-2     ⎭

    ⎡ imperative-statement-2 ⎤
    ⎣ NEXT SENTENCE          ⎦
```

Note: In Format 2, each relation-condition must be an
EQUAL TO (=) condition with an ASCENDING/DESCENDING KEY
data item for this table element as the subject.

SET Statement   Direct Indexing

```
    SET ⎧ index-name-1 [index-name-2] ... ⎫ TO ⎧ index-name-3 ⎫
        ⎩ identifier-1 [identifier-2] ...⎭      ⎨ identifier-3 ⎬
                                                ⎩ literal-1    ⎭
```

SET Statement – Relative Indexing

```
    SET index-name-4 [index-name-5] ...

    ⎧ UP   BY ⎫ ⎧ identifier-4 ⎫
    ⎩ DOWN BY ⎭ ⎩ literal-2    ⎭
```

Sort Merge Formats

Sort/Merge Environment Division

FILE-CONTROL Entry

```
    SELECT file-name
    ASSIGN TO assignment-name-1 [assignment-name-2] ... .
```

I-O-CONTROL Entry

```
    [RERUN ON assignment-name]

    [SAME ⎧ RECORD     ⎫ AREA
          ⎨ SORT       ⎬
          ⎩ SORT-MERGE ⎭

    FOR file-name-1 [file-name-2] ... ].
```

SD Entry

```
SD  file-name
    [RECORD CONTAINS [integer-1 TO] integer-2 CHARACTERS]


    [DATA  ⎧ RECORD IS   ⎫
           ⎨             ⎬  data-name-1 [data-name-2] ... ].
           ⎩ RECORDS ARE ⎭
```

Sort/Merge Procedure Division Formats

MERGE Statement

```
    MERGE file-name-1

        ON  ⎧ ASCENDING  ⎫
            ⎨            ⎬  KEY data-name-1 [data-name-2]...
            ⎩ DESCENDING ⎭

       [ON  ⎧ ASCENDING  ⎫
            ⎨            ⎬  KEY data-name-3 [data-name-4]...]...
            ⎩ DESCENDING ⎭

    [COLLATING SEQUENCE IS alphabet-name]
    USING file-name-2 file-name-3 [file-name-4]...

    ⎧ GIVING file-name-5                                      ⎫
    ⎪ OUTPUT PROCEDURE                                        ⎪
    ⎨                           ⎧ THROUGH ⎫                   ⎬
    ⎪    IS section-name-1 [    ⎨         ⎬  section-name-2]  ⎪
    ⎩                           ⎩ THRU    ⎭                   ⎭
```

RELEASE Statement (SORT Feature only)

```
    RELEASE record-name [FROM identifier]
```

RETURN Statement

```
    RETURN file-name RECORD [INTO identifier]
        AT END imperative-statement
```

SORT Statement

```
    SORT file-name-1

        ON  ⎧ ASCENDING  ⎫
            ⎨            ⎬  KEY data-name-1 [data-name-2]...
            ⎩ DESCENDING ⎭

       [ON  ⎧ ASCENDING  ⎫
            ⎨            ⎬  KEY data-name-3 [data-name-4]...]..
            ⎩ DESCENDING ⎭


    [COLLATING SEQUENCE IS alphabet-name]
    ⎧ USING file-name-2 [file-name-3]...                      ⎫
    ⎪ INPUT PROCEDURE                                         ⎪
    ⎪                           ⎧ THROUGH ⎫                   ⎪
    ⎨    IS section-name-1 [    ⎨         ⎬  section-name-2]  ⎬
    ⎪                           ⎩ THRU    ⎭                   ⎪
    ⎪ GIVING file-name-4                                      ⎪
    ⎪ OUTPUT PROCEDURE                                        ⎪
    ⎪                           ⎧ THROUGH ⎫                   ⎪
    ⎩    IS section-name-3 [    ⎨         ⎬  section-name-4]  ⎭
                                ⎩ THRU    ⎭
```

Report Writer Formats

Report Writer Environment Division

```
SPECIAL-NAMES.
    [function-name-1 IS mnemonic-name] ...
```

Report Writer Data Division

File Section – FD Entry

```
FD  file-name

    ⎧ REPORT IS   ⎫
    ⎨             ⎬  report-name-1 [report-name-2] ...
    ⎩ REPORTS ARE ⎭

    [RECORD CONTAINS [integer-1 TO] integer-2 CHARACTERS]
    [BLOCK CONTAINS Clause]
    LABEL RECORDS Clause
    [DATA RECORDS Clause]
    [VALUE OF Clause] .
```

Report Section – RD Entry

```
RD  report-name

    [WITH CODE mnemonic-name]

    ⎡ ⎧ CONTROL IS   ⎫⎧ FINAL   ⎫                              ⎤
    ⎢ ⎨              ⎬⎨         ⎬ identifier-1 [identifier-2]...⎬
    ⎣ ⎩ CONTROLS ARE ⎭⎩ [FINAL] ⎭                              ⎦

    [PAGE ⎡ LIMIT IS   ⎤  integer-1  ⎧ LINE  ⎫
          ⎣ LIMITS ARE ⎦             ⎨       ⎬
                                     ⎩ LINES ⎭

        [HEADING      integer-2]
        [FIRST DETAIL integer-3]
        [LAST DETAIL  integer-4]
        [FOOTING      integer-5] ].
```

Report Group Description Entry – Format 1

```
01 [data-name]

                  ⎧ ⎧ REPORT HEADING ⎫                       ⎫
                  ⎪ ⎨ RH            ⎬                        ⎪
                  ⎪ ⎩                ⎭                        ⎪
                  ⎪ ⎧ PAGE HEADING ⎫                         ⎪
                  ⎪ ⎨ PH           ⎬                          ⎪
                  ⎪ ⎩              ⎭                          ⎪
                  ⎪ ⎧ CONTROL HEADING ⎫⎧ FINAL        ⎫       ⎪
                  ⎪ ⎨ CH              ⎬⎨ identifier-n ⎬        ⎪
        TYPE IS   ⎨ ⎧ DETAIL ⎫        ⎩              ⎭        ⎬
                  ⎪ ⎨ DE     ⎬                                ⎪
                  ⎪ ⎩        ⎭                                ⎪
                  ⎪ ⎧ CONTROL FOOTING ⎫⎧ identifier-n ⎫       ⎪
                  ⎪ ⎨ CF              ⎬⎨ FINAL        ⎬        ⎪
                  ⎪ ⎧ PAGE FOOTING ⎫  ⎩              ⎭        ⎪
                  ⎪ ⎨ PF           ⎬                          ⎪
                  ⎪ ⎩              ⎭                          ⎪
                  ⎪ ⎧ REPORT FOOTING ⎫                        ⎪
                  ⎩ ⎨ RF             ⎬                        ⎭

                       ⎧ integer-1        ⎫
        [LINE NUMBER IS⎨ PLUS integer-2   ⎬ ]
                       ⎩ NEXT PAGE        ⎭

                       ⎧ integer-1        ⎫
        [NEXT GROUP IS ⎨ PLUS integer-2   ⎬ ]
                       ⎩ NEXT PAGE        ⎭

        [USAGE Clause].
```

Report Group Description Entry – Format 2

```
    level-number [data-name]
        [LINE Clause]
        [USAGE Clause].
```

Report Group Description Entry – Format 3

```
level-number [data-name]

   [COLUMN NUMBER IS integer]

   [GROUP INDICATE]

   [LINE Clause]

   ⎧ SOURCE IS identifier                                      ⎫
   ⎪ SUM identifier-1 [identifier-2] ... [UPON data-name-2]    ⎪
   ⎨                       ⎧ FINAL       ⎫                     ⎬
   ⎪         [RESET ON     ⎨ identifier-3 ⎬  ]                 ⎪
   ⎪                       ⎩             ⎭                     ⎪
   ⎩ VALUE IS literal                                          ⎭

    PICTURE Clause

   [USAGE Clause]

   [BLANK WHEN ZERO Clause]

   [JUSTIFIED Clause].
```

Report Group Description Entry – Format 4

```
01 [data-name]

    TYPE Clause

   [LINE Clause]

   [NEXT GROUP Clause]

   [COLUMN Clause]

   [GROUP INDICATE Clause]

       ⎧ SOURCE Clause ⎫
       ⎨ SUM Clause    ⎬
       ⎩ VALUE Clause  ⎭

    PICTURE Clause

   [USAGE Clause]

   [BLANK WHEN ZERO Clause]

   [JUSTIFIED Clause].
```

Report Writer Procedure Division

GENERATE Statement

```
              ⎧ data-name   ⎫
   GENERATE   ⎨ report-name ⎬
              ⎩             ⎭
```

INITIATE Statement

```
   INITIATE report-name-1 [report-name-2] ...
```

PRINT-SWITCH Statement

```
   MOVE 1 TO PRINT-SWITCH
```

TERMINATE Statement

```
   TERMINATE report-name-1 [report-name-2] ...
```

USE BEFORE REPORTING Sentence

```
   USE BEFORE REPORTING data-name
```

Segmentation Formats

SEGMENT-LIMIT Clause   Environment Division

```
   SEGMENT-LIMIT IS priority-number
```

Priority-numbers   Procedure Division

```
section-name SECTION [priority-number].
```

Source Program Library Formats

COPY Statement

```
                         ⎧ OF ⎫
   COPY text-name [      ⎨ IN ⎬  library-name]

        [SUPPRESS]

                    ⎧ ==pseudo-text-1== ⎫
        [REPLACING  ⎨ identifier-1      ⎬
                    ⎪ literal-1         ⎪
                    ⎩ word-1            ⎭

                    ⎧ ==pseudo-text-2== ⎫
               BY   ⎨ identifier-2      ⎬   ... ].
                    ⎪ literal-2         ⎪
                    ⎩ word-2            ⎭
```

Extended Source Program Library Formats (IBM Extension)

BASIS Statement

```
[sequence-number] BASIS basis-name
```

INSERT/DELETE Statements

```
                     ⎧ INSERT ⎫
[sequence-number]    ⎨ DELETE ⎬  sequence-number-field
                     ⎩        ⎭
```

Subprogram Linkage Formats

LINKAGE SECTION – Data Division

```
LINKAGE SECTION.

   ⎧ 77    ⎫   data-name
   ⎨ 01-49 ⎬   FILLER Clause
   ⎩       ⎭

    [REDEFINES Clause]
    [BLANK WHEN ZERO Clause]
    [JUSTIFIED Clause]
    [OCCURS Clause]
    [PICTURE Clause]
    [SIGN Clause]
    [SYNCHRONIZED Clause]
    [USAGE Clause].
[88 condition-name VALUE Clause.]
[66 RENAMES Clause.]] ...
```

Subprogram Linkage   Procedure Division

CALL Statement   Static Linkage

```
   CALL literal-1 [USING identifier-1 [identifier-2] ...]
```

CALL Statement   Dynamic Linkage

```
          ⎧ literal-2    ⎫
   CALL   ⎨ identifier-3 ⎬
          ⎩              ⎭

   [USING identifier-1 [identifier-2] ... ]
   [ON OVERFLOW imperative-statement]
```

CANCEL Statement

```
            ⎧ literal-1    ⎫   ⎡ literal-2    ⎤
   CANCEL   ⎨ identifier-1 ⎬   ⎢ identifier-2 ⎥  ...
            ⎩              ⎭   ⎣              ⎦
```

ENTRY Statement

```
   ENTRY literal [USING identifier-1 [identifier-2] ...]
```

EXIT PROGRAM Statement

```
paragraph-name. EXIT PROGRAM.
```

Note: The paragraph-name is not part of the EXIT statement format; however, it is always required preceding an EXIT statement.

GOBACK Statement

GOBACK.

Procedure Division Header – Called Program

PROCEDURE DIVISION [USING identifier-1 [identifier-2]...].

STOP RUN Statement

STOP RUN.

Communication Feature Formats

Communication Feature Data Division

Input CD Entry   Option 1

```
CD  cd-name FOR [INITIAL] INPUT
    [SYMBOLIC QUEUE IS        data-name-1]
    [SYMBOLIC SUB-QUEUE-1 IS data-name-2]
    [SYMBOLIC SUB-QUEUE-2 IS data-name-3]
    [SYMBOLIC SUB-QUEUE-3 IS data-name-4]
    [MESSAGE DATE IS         data-name-5]
    [MESSAGE TIME IS         data-name-6]
    [SYMBOLIC SOURCE IS      data-name-7]
    [TEXT LENGTH IS          data-name-8]
    [END KEY IS              data-name-9]
    [STATUS KEY IS           data-name-10]
    [MESSAGE COUNT IS        data-name-11].
```

Input CD Entry – Option 2

```
CD  cd-name FOR [INITIAL] INPUT
    [data-name-1 data-name-2 ... data-name-11].
```

Output CD Entry

```
CD  cd-name FOR OUTPUT
    [DESTINATION COUNT IS    data-name-1]
    [TEXT LENGTH IS          data-name-2]
    [STATUS KEY IS           data-name-3]
    [DESTINATION TABLE OCCURS integer-2 TIMES
       [INDEXED BY index-name-1 [index-name-2] ... ] ]
    [ERROR KEY IS            data-name-4]
    [SYMBOLIC DESTINATION IS data-name-5].
```

Communication Feature Procedure Division

ACCEPT MESSAGE COUNT Statement

ACCEPT cd-name MESSAGE COUNT

DISABLE Statement

$$
\text{DISABLE} \left\{ \begin{array}{l} \text{INPUT [TERMINAL]} \\ \text{OUTPUT} \end{array} \right\} \text{cd-name}
$$

$$
\text{WITH KEY} \left\{ \begin{array}{l} \text{identifier} \\ \text{literal} \end{array} \right\}
$$

ENABLE Statement

$$
\text{ENABLE} \left\{ \begin{array}{l} \text{INPUT [TERMINAL]} \\ \text{OUTPUT} \end{array} \right\} \text{cd-name}
$$

$$
\text{WITH KEY} \left\{ \begin{array}{l} \text{identifier} \\ \text{literal} \end{array} \right\}
$$

RECEIVE Statement

$$
\text{RECEIVE cd-name} \left\{ \begin{array}{l} \text{MESSAGE} \\ \text{SEGMENT} \end{array} \right\} \text{INTO identifier}
$$

[NO DATA imperative-statement]

SEND Statement Format 1

SEND cd-name FROM identifier-1

SEND Statement   Format 2

$$
\text{SEND cd-name [FROM identifier-1] WITH} \left\{ \begin{array}{l} \text{identifier-2} \\ \text{ESI} \\ \text{EMI} \\ \text{EGI} \end{array} \right\}
$$

$$
\left[\left\{ \begin{array}{l} \text{BEFORE} \\ \text{AFTER} \end{array} \right\} \text{ADVANCING} \left\{ \begin{array}{l} \left\{ \begin{array}{l} \text{identifier-3} \\ \text{integer} \end{array} \right\} \left[\begin{array}{l} \text{LINE} \\ \text{LINES} \end{array} \right] \\ \left\{ \begin{array}{l} \text{mnemonic-name} \\ \text{PAGE} \end{array} \right\} \end{array} \right\} \right]
$$

Debugging Feature Formats

Debugging Feature Environment Division

SOURCE-COMPUTER Paragraph

```
SOURCE-COMPUTER. computer-name
               [WITH DEBUGGING MODE].
```

Debugging Feature Procedure Division

USE FOR DEBUGGING Sentence

```
section-name SECTION [priority-number].
    USE FOR DEBUGGING
```

$$
\text{ON} \left\{ \begin{array}{l} \text{cd-name-1} \\ \text{[ALL REFERENCES OF] identifier-1} \\ \text{file-name-1} \\ \text{procedure-name-1} \\ \text{ALL PROCEDURES} \end{array} \right\}
$$

$$
\left[\begin{array}{l} \text{cd-name-2} \\ \text{[ALL REFERENCES OF] identifier-2} \\ \text{file-name-2} \\ \text{procedure-name-2} \\ \text{ALL PROCEDURES} \end{array} \right] \text{ ... .}
$$

Appendix D

ASSEMBLER FORMATS

MACHINE INSTRUCTIONS

NAME	MNEMONIC	OP CODE	FORMAT	OPERANDS
Add (c)	AR	1A	RR	R1,R2
Add (c)	A	5A	RX	R1,D2(X2,B2)
Add Decimal (c) (Packed)	AP	FA	SS	D1(L1,B1),D2(L2,B2)
Add Halfword (c)	AH	4A	RX	R1,D2(X2,B2)
Add Logical (c)	ALR	1E	RR	R1,R2
Add Logical (c)	AL	5E	RX	R1,D2(X2,B2)
AND (c)	NR	14	RR	R1,R2
AND (c)	N	54	RX	R1,D2(X2,B2)
AND (c)	NI	94	SI	D1(B1),I2
AND (c)	NC	D4	SS	D1(L,B1),D2(B2)
Branch and Link	BALR	05	RR	R1,R2
Branch and Link	BAL	45	RX	R1,D2(X2,B2)
Branch on Condition	BCR	07	RR	M1,R2
Branch on Condition	BC	47	RX	M1,D2(X2,B2)
Branch on Count	BCTR	06	RR	R1,R2
Branch on Count	BCT	46	RX	R1,D2(X2,B2)
Branch on Index High	BXH	86	RS	R1,R3,D2(B2)
Branch on Index Low or Equal	BXLE	87	RS	R1,R3,D2(B2)
Clear I/O (c,p)	CLRIO	9D01	S	D2(B2)
Compare (c)	CR	19	RR	R1,R2
Compare (c)	C	59	RX	R1,D2(X2,B2)
Compare and Swap (c)	CS	BA	RS	R1,R3,D2(B2)
Compare Decimal (c)	CP	F9	SS	D1(L1,B1),D2(L2,B2)
Compare Double and Swap (c)	CDS	BB	RS	R1,R3,D2(B2)
Compare Halfword (c)	CH	49	RX	R1,D2(X2,B2)
Compare Logical (c)	CLR	15	RR	R1,R2
Compare Logical (c)	CL	55	RX	R1,D2(X2,B2)
Compare Logical (c)	CLC	D5	SS	D1(L,B1),D2(B2)
Compare Logical (c)	CLI	95	SI	D1(B1),I2
Compare Logical Characters under Mask (c)	CLM	BD	RS	R1,M3,D2(B2)
Compare Logical Long (c)	CLCL	0F	RR	R1,R2
Convert to Binary	CVB	4F	RX	R1,D2(X2,B2)
Convert to Decimal	CVD	4E	RX	R1,D2(X2,B2)
Diagnose (p)		83		Model-dependent
Divide	DR	1D	RR	R1,R2
Divide	D	5D	RX	R1,D2(X2,B2)
Divide Decimal	DP	FD	SS	D1(L1,B1),D2(L2,B2)
Edit (c)	ED	DE	SS	D1(L,B1),D2(B2)
Edit and Mark (c)	EDMK	DF	SS	D1(L,B1),D2(B2)
Exclusive OR (c)	XR	17	RR	R1,R2
Exclusive OR (c)	X	57	RX	R1,D2(X2,B2)
Exclusive OR (c)	XI	97	SI	D1(B1),I2
Exclusive OR (c)	XC	D7	SS	D1(L,B1),D2(B2)
Execute	EX	44	RX	R1,D2(X2,B2)
Halt I/O (c,p)	HIO	9E00	S	D2(B2)
Halt Device (c,p)	HDV	9E01	S	D2(B2)
Insert Character	IC	43	RX	R1,D2(X2,B2)
Insert Characters under Mask (c)	ICM	BF	RS	R1,M3,D2(B2)

MACHINE INSTRUCTIONS (Contd)

NAME	MNEMONIC	OP CODE	FORMAT	OPERANDS
OR (c)	O	56	RX	R1,D2(X2,B2)
OR (c)	OI	96	SI	D1(B1),I2
OR (c)	OC	D6	SS	D1(L,B1),D2(B2)
Pack	PACK	F2	SS	D1(L1,B1),D2(L2,B2)
Purge TLB (p)	PTLB	B20D	S	
Read Direct (p)	RDD	85	SI	D1(B1),I2
Reset Reference Bit (c,p)	RRB	B213	S	D2(B2)
Set Clock (c,p)	SCK	B204	S	D2(B2)
Set Clock Comparator (p)	SCKC	B206	S	D2(B2)
Set CPU Timer (p)	SPT	B208	S	D2(B2)
Set Prefix (p)	SPX	B210	S	D2(B2)
Set Program Mask (n)	SPM	04	RR	R1
Set PSW Key from Address (p)	SPKA	B20A	S	D2(B2)
Set Storage Key (p)	SSK	08	RR	R1,R2
Set System Mask (p)	SSM	80	S	D2(B2)
Shift and Round Decimal (c)	SRP	F0	SS	D1(L1,B1),D2(B2),I3
Shift Left Double (c)	SLDA	8F	RS	R1,D2(B2)
Shift Left Double Logical	SLDL	8D	RS	R1,D2(B2)
Shift Left Single (c)	SLA	8B	RS	R1,D2(B2)
Shift Left Single Logical	SLL	89	RS	R1,D2(B2)
Shift Right Double (c)	SRDA	8E	RS	R1,D2(B2)
Shift Right Double Logical	SRDL	8C	RS	R1,D2(B2)
Shift Right Single (c)	SRA	8A	RS	R1,D2(B2)
Shift Right Single Logical	SRL	88	RS	R1,D2(B2)
Signal Processor (c,p)	SIGP	AE	RS	R1,R3,D2(B2)
Start I/O (c,p)	SIO	9C00	S	D2(B2)
Start I/O Fast Release (c,p)	SIOF	9C01	S	D2(B2)
Store	ST	50	RX	R1,D2(X2,B2)
Store Channel ID (c,p)	STIDC	B203	S	D2(B2)
Store Character	STC	42	RX	R1,D2(X2,B2)
Store Characters under Mask	STCM	BE	RS	R1,M3,D2(B2)
Store Clock (c)	STCK	B205	S	D2(B2)
Store Clock Comparator (p)	STCKC	B207	S	D2(B2)
Store Control (p)	STCTL	B6	RS	R1,R3,D2(B2)
Store CPU Address (p)	STAP	B212	S	D2(B2)
Store CPU ID (p)	STIDP	B202	S	D2(B2)
Store CPU Timer (p)	STPT	B209	S	D2(B2)
Store Halfword	STH	40	RX	R1,D2(X2,B2)
Store Multiple	STM	90	RS	R1,R3,D2(B2)
Store Prefix (p)	STPX	B211	S	D2(B2)
Store Then AND System Mask (p)	STNSM	AC	SI	D1(B1),I2
Store Then OR System Mask (p)	STOSM	AD	SI	D1(B1),I2
Subtract (c)	SR	1B	RR	R1,R2
Subtract (c)	S	5B	RX	R1,D2(X2,B2)
Subtract Decimal (c)	SP	FB	SS	D1(L1,B1),D2(L2,B2)
Subtract Halfword (c)	SH	4B	RX	R1,D2(X2,B2)
Subtract Logical (c)	SLR	1F	RR	R1,R2
Subtract Logical (c)	SL	5F	RX	R1,D2(X2,B2)

NAME	MNEMONIC	OP CODE	FORMAT	OPERANDS
Insert PSW Key (p)	IPK	B20B	S	
Insert Storage Key (p)	ISK	09	RR	R1,R2
Load	LR	18	RR	R1,R2
Load	L	58	RX	R1,D2(X2,B2)
Load Address	LA	41	RX	R1,D2(X2,B2)
Load and Test (c)	LTR	12	RR	R1,R2
Load Complement (c)	LCR	13	RR	R1,R2
Load Control (p)	LCTL	B7	RS	R1,R3,D2(B2)
Load Halfword	LH	48	RX	R1,D2(X2,B2)
Load Multiple	LM	98	RS	R1,R3,D2(B2)
Load Negative (c)	LNR	11	RR	R1,R2
Load Positive (c)	LPR	10	RR	R1,R2
Load PSW (n,p)	LPSW	82	S	D2(B2)
Load Real Address (c,p)	LRA	B1	RX	R1,D2(X2,B2)
Monitor Call	MC	AF	SI	D1(B1),I2
Move	MVI	92	SI	D1(B1),I2
Move	MVC	D2	SS	D1(L,B1),D2(B2)
Move Long (c)	MVCL	0E	RR	R1,R2
Move Numerics	MVN	D1	SS	D1(L,B1),D2(B2)
Move with Offset	MVO	F1	SS	D1(L1,B1),D2(L2,B2)
Move Zones	MVZ	D3	SS	D1(L,B1),D2(B2)
Multiply	MR	1C	RR	R1,R2
Multiply	M	5C	RX	R1,D2(X2,B2)
Multiply Decimal	MP	FC	SS	D1(L1,B1),D2(L2,B2)
Multiply Halfword	MH	4C	RX	R1,D2(X2,B2)
OR (c)	OR	16	RR	R1,R2

NAME	MNEMONIC	OP CODE	FORMAT	OPERANDS
Supervisor Call	SVC	0A	RR	I
Test and Set (c)	TS	93	S	D2(B2)
Test Channel (c,p)	TCH	9F00	S	D2(B2)
Test I/O (c,p)	TIO	9D00	S	D2(B2)
Test under Mask (c)	TM	91	SI	D1(B1),I2
Translate	TR	DC	SS	D1(L,B1),D2(B2)
Translate and Test (c)	TRT	DD	SS	D1(L,B1),D2(B2)
Unpack	UNPK	F3	SS	D1(L1,B1),D2(L2,B2)
Write Direct (p)	WRD	84	SI	D1(B1),I2
Zero and Add Decimal (c)	ZAP	F8	SS	D1(L1,B1),D2(L2,B2)

Floating-Point Instructions

NAME	MNEMONIC	OP CODE	FORMAT	OPERANDS
Add Normalized, Extended (c,x)	AXR	36	RR	R1,R2
Add Normalized, Long (c)	ADR	2A	RR	R1,R2
Add Normalized, Long (c)	AD	6A	RX	R1,D2(X2,B2)
Add Normalized, Short (c)	AER	3A	RR	R1,R2
Add Normalized, Short (c)	AE	7A	RX	R1,D2(X2,B2)
Add Unnormalized, Long (c)	AWR	2E	RR	R1,R2
Add Unnormalized, Long (c)	AW	6E	RX	R1,D2(X2,B2)
Add Unnormalized, Short (c)	AUR	3E	RR	R1,R2
Add Unnormalized, Short (c)	AU	7E	RX	R1,D2(X2,B2)

c. Condition code is set.   p. Privileged instruction.
n. New condition code is loaded.   x. Extended precision floating-point.

Floating-Point Instructions (Contd)   ④

NAME	MNEMONIC	OP CODE	FORMAT	OPERANDS
Compare, Long (c)	CDR	29	RR	R1,R2
Compare, Long (c)	CD	69	RX	R1,D2(X2,B2)
Compare, Short (c)	CER	39	RR	R1,R2
Compare, Short (c)	CE	79	RX	R1,D2(X2,B2)
Divide, Long	DDR	2D	RR	R1,R2
Divide, Long	DD	6D	RX	R1,D2(X2,B2)
Divide, Short	DER	3D	RR	R1,R2
Divide, Short	DE	7D	RX	R1,D2(X2,B2)
Halve, Long	HDR	24	RR	R1,R2
Halve, Short	HER	34	RR	R1,R2
Load and Test, Long (c)	LTDR	22	RR	R1,R2
Load and Test, Short (c)	LTER	32	RR	R1,R2
Load Complement, Long (c)	LCDR	23	RR	R1,R2
Load Complement, Short (c)	LCER	33	RR	R1,R2
Load, Long	LDR	28	RR	R1,R2
Load, Long	LD	68	RX	R1,D2(X2,B2)
Load Negative, Long (c)	LNDR	21	RR	R1,R2
Load Negative, Short (c)	LNER	31	RR	R1,R2
Load Positive, Long (c)	LPDR	20	RR	R1,R2
Load Positive, Short (c)	LPER	30	RR	R1,R2
Load Rounded, Extended to Long (x)	LRDR	25	RR	R1,R2
Load Rounded, Long to Short (x)	LRER	35	RR	R1,R2
Load, Short	LER	38	RR	R1,R2
Load, Short	LE	78	RX	R1,D2(X2,B2)
Multiply, Extended (x)	MXR	26	RR	R1,R2
Multiply, Long	MDR	2C	RR	R1,R2
Multiply, Long	MD	6C	RX	R1,D2(X2,B2)
Multiply, Long/Extended (x)	MXDR	27	RR	R1,R2
Multiply, Long/Extended (x)	MXD	67	RX	R1,D2(X2,B2)
Multiply, Short	MER	3C	RR	R1,R2
Multiply, Short	ME	7C	RX	R1,D2(X2,B2)
Store, Long	STD	60	RX	R1,D2(X2,B2)
Store, Short	STE	70	RX	R1,D2(X2,B2)
Subtract Normalized, Extended (c,x)	SXR	37	RR	R1,R2
Subtract Normalized, Long (c)	SDR	2B	RR	R1,R2
Subtract Normalized, Long (c)	SD	6B	RX	R1,D2(X2,B2)
Subtract Normalized, Short (c)	SER	3B	RR	R1,R2
Subtract Normalized, Short (c)	SE	7B	RX	R1,D2(X2,B2)
Subtract Unnormalized, Long (c)	SWR	2F	RR	R1,R2
Subtract Unnormalized, Long (c)	SW	6F	RX	R1,D2(X2,B2)
Subtract Unnormalized, Short (c)	SUR	3F	RR	R1,R2
Subtract Unnormalized, Short (c)	SU	7F	RX	R1,D2(X2,B2)

EXTENDED MNEMONIC INSTRUCTIONS†

Use	Extended Code* (RX or RR)	Meaning	Machine Instr.* (RX or RR)
General	B or BR	Unconditional Branch	BC or BCR 15,
	NOP or NOPR	No Operation	BC or BCR 0,
After	BH or *BHR*	Branch on A High	BC or BCR 2,
Compare	BL or *BLR*	Branch on A Low	BC or BCR 4,
Instructions	BE or *BER*	Branch on A Equal B	BC or BCR 8,
(A:B)	BNH or *BNHR*	Branch on A Not High	BC or BCR 13,
	BNL or *BNLR*	Branch on A Not Low	BC or BCR 11,
	BNE or *BNER*	Branch on A Not Equal B	BC or BCR 7,

After	BO or *BOR*	Branch on Overflow	BC or BCR 1,
Arithmetic	BP or *BPR*	Branch on Plus	BC or BCR 2,
Instructions	BM or *BMR*	Branch on Minus	BC or BCR 4,
	BNP or *BNPR*	Branch on Not Plus	BC or BCR 13,
	BNM or *BNMR*	Branch on Not Minus	BC or BCR 11,
	BNZ or *BNZR*	Branch on Not Zero	BC or BCR 7,
	BZ or *BZR*	Branch on Zero	BC or BCR 8,
After Test	BO or *BOR*	Branch if Ones	BC or BCR 1,
under Mask	BM or *BMR*	Branch if Mixed	BC or BCR 4,
Instruction	BZ or *BZR*	Branch if Zeros	BC or BCR 8,
	BNO or *BNOR*	Branch if Not Ones	BC or BCR 14,

*Second operand not shown; in all cases it is
D2(X2,B2) for RX format or R2 for RR format.

†For OS/VS and DOS/VS;
source: GC33-4010.

EDIT AND EDMK PATTERN CHARACTERS (in hex)

20—digit selector	40—blank	5C—asterisk
21—start of significance	4B—period	6B—comma
22—field separator	5B—dollar sign	C3D9—CR

INDEX

A:
  in PICTURE, 23
ABEND, 238, 242
Abnormal termination (see ABEND)
ACCEPT, 119, 120
Access arm, 294–95
ACCESS IS DYNAMIC, 308
ACCESS IS RANDOM, 303, 305
ACCESS IS SEQUENTIAL, 277–78, 303
Action list, 83
ADD, 36, 37, 73
Add (fullword), 259
Add packed, 244, 249, 258
AFTER ADVANCING, 41
AH, 264
Alphabetic class test, 107, 108
Alphabetic data, 23, 54
Alphanumeric data, 23, 54
ALTERNATE RECORD KEY, 307, 308
ALU, 5
A margin, 24
American National Standards Institute, 9
AND, 110, 111
AP (see Add packed)
APOST, 336
Arithmetic and logical unit, 5
Arithmetic expression, 40
Arithmetic symbols, 22, 73
ASCENDING KEY:
  in OCCURS clause, 160, 162, 167
  in SORT statement, 184, 186
ASCII, 109, 184
ASSGN, 315–17
ASSIGN, 53
Assumed decimal point (see Implied decimal
    point)
Asterisk:
  in arithmetic expression, 40
  in column 7, 24

  in JCL, 331
  in PICTURE, 135
AT END:
  in READ, 41
  in RETURN, 184, 187
  in SEARCH, 164
AUTHOR, 52, 53
AUTO FEED Key, 24

B:
  in Picture, 115, 134, 139
Backup, 283
BAL, 255–70
Base/displacement addressing, 233, 244
Base locator, 242, 261
Base register, 234
Batching transactions, 282
BEFORE ADVANCING, 41
Binary arithmetic:
    addition, 227
    decimal conversion, 226
    hex conversion, 229
Binary representation of data, 232
Binary search, 159–61, 167, 200
Bit, 230
Blank line, 95, 100
BL cell (see Base locator)
BLKSIZE, 345
BLOCK CONTAINS, 279
Blocking factor, 273–77
B margin, 24
Bottom-up development, 203, 204
bpi, 274
Braces, 35, 36
Brackets, 35, 36
Buffer, 278
BY (see DIVIDE, MULTIPLY)
Byte, 229–31, 233

CALL, 146–48
Called program (see Subprogram)
Calling program, 147
Carriage control (see AFTER ADVANCING)
Case structure, 201–2
CATAL, 314
Catalogued data set, 339, 340, 343
CATLG, 339
Central processing unit, 5
Channel, 278, 315
CHARACTERS, 115, 116
Checkpoint, 278
Check protection, 135
CLASS, 335
Class test (see IF)
C level diagnostic, 72
CLIST, 336
CLOSE, 42, 280–81
COBOL notation, 35, 36
COBUCLG, 332–34
Coding form, 23–26
Coding standards (see Standards)
Collating sequence, 108, 109, 184
COLUMN, 360, 362
Comma (see Punctuation symbols, Editing
    data)
  avoidance, 95
Comments:
  in COBOL, 24, 95
  in JCL, 312, 320, 335
COMP (see COMPUTATIONAL)
Compilation error, 71–76
Compilation parameters:
  DOS, 313–14
  OS, 336
Compiler, 6
Completion code, 240
Compound test (see IF)
COMPUTATIONAL, 144, 233

COMPUTATIONAL-3, 233
COMPUTE, 39–41, 121, 124
COND, 336–37
Conditional diagnostic (*see* C level diagnostic)
Condition name (*see* IF)
CONFIGURATION SECTION, 53
Console typewriter, 119
CONTIG, 342–43
Continuation:
  of COBOL statement, 24
  of OS JCL statement, 330, 331
CONTROL, 360, 362
Control break, 203–8, 357
Control footing, 358
Control heading, 358
Control unit:
  of CPU, 5
  of I/O device, 315–16
C01, 122, 125
COPY, 137–39, 147, 165, 336, 346
Core dump (*see* Dump)
Core-image library (*see* Library)
CORRESPONDING, 118
CPU, 5
CR:
  in PICTURE, 136
Crawford, M., 138, 230, 242, 270, 301
Cross-reference listing (*see* Compilation parameters)
Currency symbol (*see* Editing data)
CURRENT-DATE, 125
CVB, 256, 265
CVD, 257, 265
CYL, 342
Cylinder, 294–98, 342
Cylinder index, 299
Cylinder overflow area, 299

Data base, 307
Data cell, 293
DATA DIVISION, 12, 53–59, 134–57
Data division map (*see* DMAP)
Data exception, 198, 240
Data-movement instructions:
  in BAL (*see* MVC)
  in COBOL (*see* MOVE)
Data-name:
  prefixing, 93
  rules for forming, 20–22
DATA RECORD IS, 56
DATA RECORDS ARE, 137–39
Data-set, 330
Data-set-name (*see* DSN)
Data validation, 125
DATE, 119, 120, 123
DATE-COMPILED, 52–53
DATE-WRITTEN, 52–53
DAY, 119, 120
DB:
  in PICTURE, 136
DCB, 339, 344–45
DD statement, 337–46
Debugging, 71–91, 196–97, 238–52

Decimal alignment, 266–68
DECLARATIVES, 307
DELETE, 306
Density, 273–77
DEPENDING ON (*see* OCCURS DEPENDING ON)
DESCENDING KEY:
  in OCCURS clause, 162
  in SORT statement, 184, 186
Desk checking, 82
Detail report group, 358–61
Device address, 315–17
Device independence, 298
Dijkstra, E., 202
Direct access storage facility, 294
Direct access to table entries, 161–62, 168
Disaster diagnostic (*see* D level diagnostic)
Disk drive, 293–95
Disk Operating System (*see* JCL)
Disk pack, 293–95
DISP, 339–40
Displacement:
  base/displacement address, 234
  relationship to index, 158
DISPLAY:
  COBOL statement, 118, 119, 210
  in USAGE clause, 233
DIVIDE, 39
DLBL, 321–25
D level diagnostic, 72
DMAP, 73, 242–43, 259, 261, 336
Documentation, 20
Dollar sign (*see* Editing data)
DOS debugging, 251
DOS job control language (*see* JCL)
Double spacing (*see* AFTER ADVANCING)
Double-word, 232
Drum, 293
DSN (*see* DSNAME)
DSNAME, 339, 341
Dump, 238–40, 246, 248
DUP Key, 24
Duplicate data-names, 116–18
DUPLICATES, 307

EBCDIC, 109, 184, 230
Editing data, 57–59, 61, 63, 134–36, 141
Efficiency:
  algorithm, 200
  machine, 163, 268–69
EJECT, 95
Elementary item, 54
E level diagnostic, 72
ELSE, 45, 46
End-of-file test, 9–11
Entry point address (*see* EPA)
ENVIRONMENT DIVISION, 12, 53, 61, 277–78
EPA, 242, 243, 246–48, 250
Error detection (*see* Structured walkthrough)
Error diagnostic (*see* E level diagnostic)
Error processing, 198–99

ERRS, 314
EXAMINE, 116
EXEC statement:
  DOS, 314
  OS, 335–37
Execution error, 71, 76, 79–82
EXIT, 114, 198, 201
EXIT PROGRAM, 147–48, 151
EXPDT, 340
Expiration date (*see* EXPDT)
Exponentiation, 40
EXTEND, 280
EXTENT, 321–26
External label, 318

FCOBOL, 314
FD, 55, 61, 63, 277–79, 345
FEED Key, 24
Figurative constant, 43, 57
File, 53
FILE-CONTROL, 53, 277
File maintenance, 281–89
File-name, 20–22
File protect ring, 283
FILE SECTION, 55, 56
FILE STATUS (*see* STATUS)
FILLER, 55
FINAL, 362, 363
FIRST, 115
Fixed length records, 281
FLAG, 336
Floating dollar sign, 58, 59
Floating minus sign, 136
Floating plus sign, 136
Floating point, 230
FLOW, 249, 250, 336
Flowchart, 9–11, 62
  lack of use, 206
Format (*see* Instruction formats)
Forward GO TO, 191, 201
FROM (*see* SUBTRACT, WRITE)
Full-word (*see* Word)
Functional modules, 208–10

Generality in a program, 199–200
GENERATE, 360, 363
General-purpose register, 233
Generation datagroup, 320, 343
Generic assignment, 316
GIVING:
  with arithmetic verbs, 36–39
  with SORT verb, 184, 188–92
GO TO, 97, 202
  in a 'structured' program, 114, 191
  versus PERFORM, 99
GO TO DEPENDING, 201–2
Grauer, R., 71, 126, 138, 153, 168, 230, 242, 270, 290, 301
Group item, 54
Group move, 44

Half-word, 232
Header label (*see* Label)
Heading line, 125
Heading routine (*see* Page heading routine)
Hexadecimal, 243
  addition, 229
  binary conversion, 229
  decimal conversion, 238
Hierarchy:
  between data items, 54
  of arithmetic operations, 40, 41
  of logical operations, 111
Hierarchy chart, 208–9, 283, 284
Higher-level language, 5–8
HIGH-VALUES, 210, 303, 306
Hollerith code, 4, 5
Hollerith, Herman, 3
Housekeeping, 9, 11, 12
Hyphen:
  in data-name, 21
  as continuation, 208

IBG (*see* Interrecord gap)
IDENTIFICATION DIVISION, 12, 52, 53,
  61
IF, 35, 36
  class test, 107, 108, 198
  compound test, 110, 111
  condition names, 109, 110, 122, 136, 197
  implied, 111, 112
  nested, 98, 112, 113, 123, 147, 212
  relational test, 35, 36, 108, 109
  sign test, 109
  with period, 45, 46
IGN, 318
Ignoring assignments, 317–18
Implementor-name, 280
Implied condition (*see* IF)
Implied decimal point, 57
IN, 117, 118
Indentation (*see* Standards)
  of nested IF, 112
INDEXED BY, 162
Indexed sequential (*see* ISAM)
Indexing, 158–59
Initial program load (*see* IPL)
Initial read, 11, 82, 99
INITIATE, 361, 363
INPUT-OUTPUT SECTION, 53
INPUT PROCEDURE, 184–87, 191–92
Input validation (*see* Data validation)
INSPECT, 115, 116
INSTALLATION, 52, 53
Installation standards (*see* Standards)
Instruction explosion, 8, 242
Instruction formats:
  BAL, 234–36, 244
  COBOL, 35, 36
Instruction set (*see* Instruction formats)
Interblock gap (*see* Interrecord gap)
Internal Label (*see* Label)
Internal sort, 182
Interrecord gap, 273–77

INVALID KEY (*see* READ, WRITE)
Invalid subscript, 199
I-O CONTROL, 278
IPL, 311
IRG (*see* Interrecord gap)
ISAM:
  COBOL implementation, 302–6
  concepts, 299–301
  DOS JCL, 324–25
  OS JCL, 345–46
Iteration structure, 96, 99

JCL:
  DOS, 28, 29, 311–28
  OS, 28, 329–53
JOB statement:
  DOS, 313
  OS, 335
Job step, 332
Job stream, 28

KEEP, 339
Keypunch, 23–26
Key-word parameters, 330, 331

LABEL, 339, 340
Label, 277
  header, 318, 338
  trailer, 318, 338
  volume, 318, 338
Label processing, 318–22
LABEL RECORDS, 56, 72, 277, 280
Language translator, 311
LBLTYP, 319, 326
Leading blank, 115
Level number, 23, 54, 55, 93
LIB, 336
Library:
  core image, 312, 314
  procedure, 312
  relocatable, 312
  source statement, 312
Linear search (*see* Sequential search)
Line counter (*see* Page heading routine)
LINE NUMBER, 360, 361
LINES (*see* AFTER ADVANCING)
LINK, 314
Linkage-editor, 28, 29, 330
LINKAGE SECTION, 146–48, 151
Link-edit map, 251
LISTX, 314
Literal, 22
Literal pool, 261
LNKEDT, 314
Load instruction (BAL), 257
Load module, 330
Logical operator (*see* AND, OR)
Logical record, 274–77
Logic error (*see* Execution error)

Lower-level language, 6
LOW-VALUES, 303–306
LPR, 266
LRECL, 345

Machine language, 5–8
Magnetic tape, 273–77
Maintenance (*see* File maintenance)
Major key, 182
MFT (*see* OS/MFT)
Microsecond, 5
Minor key, 182
Minus sign:
  in arithmetic expression, 40
  in PICTURE, 135, 136
Mnemonic name (*see* SPECIAL-NAMES)
Mnemonic names, 119
MOD, 280, 339
MOVE, 42–44, 58, 59
MOVE CORRESPONDING, 118
MSGLEVEL, 331, 335
Multifile volume, 277, 318
Multilevel table (*see* Table)
MULTIPLE FILE, 278
Multiple record formats, 137
MULTIPLY, 38
Multivolume file, 277, 318
MVC, 235–36
MVS, 250, 329, 332
MVT (*see* OS/MVT)

Nanosecond, 5
Negative data (*see* Signed number)
Nested IF (*see* IF)
NEXT SENTENCE, 112
NEW, 339
Nine-track tape, 273
NOMINAL KEY, 303–5
Non-numeric literal, 22
Nonsequential processing, 282
Non-unique data names, 73, 83
NO REWIND, 280
NOT, 111
NSD, 319
Number systems, 225–29
Numeric class test, 107, 108, 198
Numeric literal, 22

OBJECT-COMPUTER, 53
OCCURS, 142, 143, 162
OCCURS DEPENDING ON, 162, 279
Octal, 229
OF, 117, 118
OLD, 339
OPEN, 42, 280–81
Operating system, 24
  DOS (*see* JCL)
  OS (*see* JCL)

Operator precedence rule:
  in COMPUTE statement, 40, 41
  in logical expression, 111
OPTION, 313, 320
OPTIONAL, 277
Optional reserved word, 35
Options:
  DOS, 313–14
  OS, 336
OR, 110, 111
Or immediate, 266
ORGANIZATION, 277–78, 304
OS job-control language (see JCL)
OS/MFT, 329
OS/MVT, 329
OS/VS COBOL, 307
OUTPUT PROCEDURE, 184–87, 191–92
Overflow area (see ISAM concepts)
Overlap, 278, 315

PACK, 247, 256
Packed representation, 231
PAGE, 41
Page footing, 358
Page heading, 358
Page heading routine, 125
Paragraph-name, 20–22
Parentheses:
  in COMPUTE statement, 40
  in logical expression, 111
Parity bit, 229, 273
PARM, 336
PASS, 339
PAUSE, 318, 320
PERFORM, 44, 45
  sections, 113, 114
  THRU, 114, 198
  UNTIL, 99, 114, 115, 153
  VARYING, 143, 148, 170–73
Period, 45
Permanent assignments, 315–17
PGM, 336
Physical record, 274–77
PICTURE clause, 54, 94
Plus sign:
  in arithmetic expression, 40
  in PICTURE, 135, 136
PMAP, 242–45, 261–63, 336
Positional parameters, 330, 331, 335
POWER, 312
Prefixing:
  of data name, 93, 100
  of paragraph name, 94
Primary key, 182
Prime area, 300
Priming read (see Initial read)
Print layout form, 5, 6, 60
PROC, 337
Procedure, 332–34
PROCEDURE DIVISION, 12, 35–51, 107–33
Procedure division map (see PMAP)

Program debugging and testing (see also Top down testing)
  during compilation, 71–78
  during execution, 76, 79–82, 238–52
PROGRAM-ID, 52, 53
Program identification, 24
Programmer logical unit (see Symbolic unit)
Programming standards (see Standards)
Programming style, 92–105, 196–222
Program status word (see PSW)
Program stub, 210, 212
Pseudocode, 8, 62, 204–6, 208, 283, 284, 304
PSW, 242, 243, 246–48
Punctuation symbols, 22

Qualification, 73, 117, 118
Quotation mark, 22
QUOTE, 336

Random processing (see Nonsequential processing)
Range check, 198
RD, 360–61
READ:
  AT END, 41
  INTO, 120, 197
  INVALID KEY, 303, 304
Read/write head, 293, 295
RECORD CONTAINS, 56, 72, 84, 197, 279
RECORD KEY, 303–5
REDEFINES, 118, 144
REGION, 335
Register (see General-purpose register)
Register assignment, 242–43, 261, 262
REG Key, 24
Relational operator, 22
Relational test (see IF)
Relative file, 298
Relative location, 242
Relative track, 323
REL Key, 24
RELEASE, 184, 187, 191
Relocatable, 234
Relocatable library (see Library)
REMAINDER, 39
RENAMES, 118
REPLACING:
  in COPY, 138
  in INSPECT, 115, 116
Report:
  footing, 358
  group, 357–65
  heading, 358
  Section, 360, 361
Report Writer, 206
RERUN, 278
RESERVE ALTERNATE AREAS, 278
Reserved word, 20, 35, 84, 366–69
Restart, 278
RETPD, 340
RETURN, 184, 187, 191

REVERSED, 280
REWRITE, 303, 306
RLSE, 343
Rotational delay, 298
ROUNDED, 121, 124
RPG, 311

S:
  in PICTURE, 135, 265
SAME AREA, 278
Scratch tape, 340, 341
Scrubbing data, 198, 283
SD, 184, 185
SEARCH, 159, 163
SEARCH ALL, 160–61, 163
Secondary key, 182
Section, 113, 191
SECURITY, 52, 53
SELECT, 3, 5, 53, 55, 336
  for indexed files, 307
  for sequential files, 277–78
Selection structure, 96
Semicolon, 22
SEQ, 330
Sequence structure, 196
Sequencing paragraph names, 94
Sequential processing, 282
Sequential search, 159
Sequential update, 282
Service program, 312
SET, 159, 160, 162–63, 168
Seven-track tape, 273
SHR, 339
Sign:
  of a binary number, 232
  of a packed number, 231
Signed number, 135, 136, 139
Sign test (see IF)
SIZE ERROR, 121, 124
SKIP, 95
/* card, 315
/& card, 315
// card, 348
SORT, 184–92, 346
Sorting, 182–95
Sort key, 182
SOURCE, 361, 362
SOURCE-COMPUTER, 53
Source-statement library (see Library)
Space, 23
SPACE:
  in DD statement, 339, 342–43
  in MOVE statement, 43
  in VALUE clause, 57
Spacing (see Print layout form)
SPECIAL-NAMES, 119, 121, 122, 125, 184, 280
Spooling, 312
Standard labels (see Label)
Standards, 92–95
START, 73, 309
Start/stop time, 276–77
STATE, 249, 250, 336

STATUS, 278, 307–8
Stepwise refinement, 204, 205
STOP RUN, 46
Storage dump (see Dump)
Storage printout (see Dump)
Store instruction, 258
Structured English, 8
Structured programming, 95–99, 202
Structured walkthrough, 82–83
Subprogram, 146–53
    JCL requirements, 346, 349
Subscript, 144
    versus index, 158–59
SUBTRACT, 37, 38
SUM, 361–62
Supervisor, 311
SVS, 329
SYM, 314
Symbolic address, 315
Symbolic unit, 317, 323
SYMDUMP, 336, 343
SYSLIB, 336
Systems generation, 317
SYSUDUMP, 336

Table, 158–81
    initialization, 145, 165
    lookup, 145, 146
    one dimension, 141–46
    processing, 143
    three dimension, 171–77
    two dimension, 164–65, 167–71
TALLY, 116
TALLYING, 116
Tape (see Magnetic tape)
Tape drive, 273–74
Temporary assignment, 315
TERMINATE, 361, 363
Testing (see Program debugging and testing)
Three-level table (see Table)

THRU:
    in PERFORM, 114
    in VALUE, 136
TIME:
    COBOL parameter, 119, 120
    JCL parameter, 331, 335
TIMES (see OCCURS)
TLBL, 319–21
Top down development, 203–16
Top down testing, 210–16
Track, 294–97, 342
Track index, 299
Trailer label (see Label)
Transfer rate, 276–77
TRK, 342
Two-level table (see Table)
Twos complement, 232–33, 266
TYPE, 363

UNCATLG, 339
UNIT, 339, 340
Unmatched transaction, 284, 304
UNPK, 256
Unsigned, 266
UNTIL (see PERFORM)
USAGE, 118, 144, 163, 200, 233, 245
USING:
    with subprogram, 146–53
    with SORT verb, 184, 188–92
Utility sort, 182

V:
    in PICTURE, 57
VALUE, 57
VALUE OF, 280
VALUES ARE, 136
Variable-length field, 231
Variable-length records, 162, 279, 281
VARYING (see PERFORM)

VERB, 336
VOL, 339, 340
Volume label (see Label)
Volume Table of Contents (see VTOC)
VSAM, 301, 302, 304, 306–9
VS1, 329
VS2, 329
VTOC, 342

Walkthrough (see Structured walkthrough)
WHEN, 164
W level diagnostic, 72
Word, 232
WORKING-STORAGE SECTION, 56, 61, 63, 64
WRITE, 41
    FROM, 120, 121, 197
    INVALID KEY, 305

X:
    in PICTURE, 23
XREF, 314, 336

Yourdon, E., 95

Z:
    in PICTURE, 134
ZAP, 265
ZERO:
    in MOVE statement, 43
    in PICTURE, 134
    in VALUE clause, 57
Zero suppression, 139
Zone bits, 230
Zone punch, 141

ex. Display 'FLD1', FLD1.